Library of
Davidson College

A THEORY OF SOCIAL ACTION

SYNTHESE LIBRARY

STUDIES IN EPISTEMOLOGY, LOGIC, METHODOLOGY, AND PHILOSOPHY OF SCIENCE

Managing Editor:

JAAKKO HINTIKKA, *Florida State University, Tallahassee*

Editors:

DONALD DAVIDSON, *University of California, Berkeley*
GABRIËL NUCHELMANS, *University of Leyden*
WESLEY C. SALMON, *University of Pittsburgh*

VOLUME 171

RAIMO TUOMELA

Department of Philosophy, University of Helsinki

A THEORY
OF SOCIAL ACTION

D. REIDEL PUBLISHING COMPANY

A MEMBER OF THE KLUWER  ACADEMIC PUBLISHERS GROUP

DORDRECHT / BOSTON / LANCASTER

Library of Congress Cataloging in Publication Data

Tuomela, Raimo.
   A theory of social action.

   (Synthese library; v. 171)
   Bibliography: p.
   Includes indexes.
   1. Social action.   I. Title. II. Series.
HM51.T777   1984   361.2   84-6863
ISBN 90-277-1703-6

Published by D. Reidel Publishing Company,
P.O. Box 17, 3300 AA Dordrecht, Holland.

Sold and distributed in the U.S.A. and Canada
by Kluwer Academic Publishers,
190 Old Derby Street, Hingham, MA 02043, U.S.A.

In all other countries, sold and distributed
by Kluwer Academic Publishers Group,
P.O. Box 322, 3300 AH Dordrecht, Holland.

All Rights Reserved.
© 1984 by D. Reidel Publishing Company.
No part of the material protected by this copyright notice may be reproduced or
utilized in any form or by any means, electronic or mechanical,
including photocopying, recording or by any information storage and
retrieval system, without written permission from the copyright owner.

Printed in The Netherlands.

TABLE OF CONTENTS

Preface   ix

Chapter 1:
PHILOSOPHY AND THE THEORY OF SOCIAL ACTION   1
I   Scientific Realism and the Social Sciences   1
II Theorizing about Social Action   10

Chapter 2:
INDIVIDUALISM AND CONCEPT FORMATION IN THE SOCIAL SCIENCES   17
I   'Holistic Social Concepts   17
II   Conceptual Individualism   25
III We-Intentions and Social Motivation   31

Chapter 3:
THEORIES OF ACTION   55
I   Views of Human Action   55
II   Mental Cause Theory   58
III Agency Theory   64
IV   Hermeneutic Theory   66
V   Arguments for and against Causal Theories of Action   71

Chapter 4:
THE PURPOSIVE-CAUSAL THEORY OF HUMAN ACTION   79
I   The Fundamental Elements of the Purposive-Causal
     Theory of Action   79
II   The Structure of Single-Agent Action   94

Chapter 5:
THE STRUCTURE OF SOCIAL ACTION   111
I   The General Nature of Social Action   111
II   Simple Social Actions   118
III Complex Social Actions   134
IV   The Acting of Social Collectives   144
V   Group Interests Revisited   150

Chapter 6:
ACTION GENERATION   159
I   Action Generation and the By-Relation   159
II   Action Generation and the Theory of Automata   170
III Social Actions, Grammars, and Social Conduct Plans   188

Chapter 7:
PRACTICAL INFERENCE AND SOCIAL ACTION — 197
- I   Loop Beliefs and Practical Inference — 197
- II Mutual Beliefs — 205
- III The Replicative Justification of Social Beliefs — 212
- IV Social Action and Practical Inference — 216
- V   Mixed Interest Games and Practical Inference — 221
- VI Social Rules and the Scope of Social Action — 229

Chapter 8:
NORMS, RULES, AND SOCIAL STRUCTURES — 236
- I   Social Norms — 236
- II Social Rules — 246
- III Similarity and Roles — 253
- IV Social Structures — 262

Chapter 9:
SOCIAL INTERACTION AND CONTROL — 269
- I   Acting in Social Relation — 269
- II Overt Social Interaction — 278
- III Covert Social Interaction — 284

Chapter 10:
A PRAGMATIC THEORY OF EXPLANATION — 312
- I   Explaining as Communicative Action — 312
- II Emphasis — 329
- III Understanding and Presuppositions — 333
-     Appendix — 338

Chapter 11:
PROXIMATE EXPLANATION OF SOCIAL ACTION — 345
- I   Explanation and Social Action — 345
- II Teleological Explanation — 357
- III Purposive-Causal Explanation — 365
- IV Reason-Explanation — 368
- V   Explaining the Style of Action — 378
- VI Understanding Action — 384

Chapter 12:
DYNAMIC EXPLANATION OF SOCIAL ACTION — 388
- I   Explanation and Other-Regarding Utilities — 388
- II Expected Utilities, Motives, and the Explanation of Social Action — 400
- III The Nature of Dynamic Action Explanations — 416

Chapter 13:
 FUNCTIONAL AND INVISIBLE HAND EXPLANATION OF SOCIAL ACTION 430
   I   Action-Functions and Functional Explanations 430
   II Invisible Hand Explanations of Social Action 448

Chapter 14:
 EXPLANATORY INDIVIDUALISM AND EXPLANATION OF SOCIAL LAWS 455
   I   Explanatory Individualism 455
   II Explanation of Social Laws 461

Notes   476
Bibliography   500
Name index   511
Subject Index   516
Index of Symbols, Definitions, and Theses   530

PREFACE

It is somewhat surprising to find out how little serious theorizing there is in philosophy (and in social psychology as well as sociology) on the nature of social actions or joint actions in the sense of actions performed together by several agents. Actions performed by single agents have been extensively discussed both in philosophy and in psychology. There is, accordingly, a booming field called action theory in philosophy but it has so far strongly concentrated on actions performed by single agents only. We of course should not forget game theory, a discipline that systematically studies the strategic interaction between several rational agents. Yet this important theory, besides being restricted to strongly rational acting, fails to study properly several central problems related to the conceptual nature of social action. Thus, it does not adequately clarify and classify the various types of joint action (except perhaps from the point of view of the agents' utilities).

This book presents a systematic theory of social action. Because of its reliance on so-called purposive causation and generation it is called the purposive-causal theory. This work also discusses several problems related to the topic of social action, for instance that of how to create from this perspective the most central concepts needed by social psychology and sociology. While quite a lot of ground is covered in the book, many important questions have been left unanswered and many others unasked as well. Some of the problems studied could perhaps have been discussed at greater length and depth and in a less idealized setting. But some lack (and shortness) of argumentation is perhaps compensated for by the highly systematic nature of the theory presented in this book. The central parts of the theory hang closely together and this gives systematic support to its parts.

To the reader who wants to find out quickly my main ideas and theses about social action I suggest he take a look at Chapters 5 and 6, perhaps complemented by Chapters 3 and 4 for some preliminaries. The book divides naturally into two parts. The first part, consisting of Chapters 1-9, creates the main systematic theory and the second part, Chapters 10-14, deals with relevant problems of explanation.

As to the syntactic conventions used in the book, first, symbols are generally used autonomously whenever this is not expected to cause confusion. Secondly, the single quote operation is used to form names of expressions, as usual. Numbered formulas and statements are referred to only by their numbers when they occur in the same chapter (e.g., (**18**)); otherwise they may be referred to by the number of the chapter and the formula number (e.g., by (**9.18**) when formula (**18**) of Chapter 9 is meant). Depending on chapter and context, special definitions and theses have been either numbered or given abbreviated names (e.g., (**WI**)).

I would especially like to thank Professors Robert Audi and Ingmar Pörn each of whom read drafts of several of the chapters and made important comments. I am also indebted to Professors Lawrence Davis, George Berger, Andreas Kemmerling, and David Copp, Dr Matti Sintonen as well as Martti Kuokkanen and Kaarlo Miller for stimulating criticisms and remarks concerning some topics dealt with in the book. I am indebted to Professor Michael McKinsey for checking the English of most of this work. My thanks are also due to Auli Kaipainen who patiently and skillfully typed and retyped my drafts.

A grant from the Academy of Finland for the latter half of 1981 helped me very much in the final work on the first draft of the manuscript.

With appropriate permission, I have in this book used some passages of the following papers of mine:

'Action Generation', in Niiniluoto, I. and Saarinen, E. (eds.), **Intensional Logic: Theory and Applications**, Acta Philosophica Fennica, vol. **35**, pp. 282-301

'Explaining Explaining', **Erkenntnis 15** (1980), 211-243

'Individualism and Concept Formation in the Social Sciences', in Agassi, J. and Cohen, R.S. (eds.), **Scientific Philosophy Today**, Reidel, 1981, pp. 425-438.

'Social Action-Functions', **Philosophy of the Social Sciences**, forthcoming

'Explanation of Action', in Flöistad, G. (ed.), (1982), **Contemporary Philosophy**, vol. 3, pp. 15-43.

Helsinki, May 1984

Raimo Tuomela

CHAPTER 1

PHILOSOPHY AND THE THEORY OF SOCIAL ACTION

I. SCIENTIFIC REALISM AND THE SOCIAL SCIENCES

1. Most of our actions are social in the wide sense that they conceptually presuppose the existence of other agents and various social institutions. Of actions that are social in this sense, some are performed by single agents while the rest are either performed jointly by several agents or performed by collectives of agents. Here I understand that an action's being performed jointly by several agents, and its being performed by a collective of agents, are not the same thing. Actions that are performed jointly by several agents we shall call multi-agent actions and also social actions proper. Multi-agent actions are of course social in the above wide sense. Examples of such multi-agent actions would be two or more agents' (jointly, rather than separately) carrying a table upstairs, playing tennis, toasting, or, at the other extreme, performing a political revolution.

It is the main purpose of this book to investigate the conceptual nature and the structure of multi-agent actions as well as the explanation of such actions. A great part of this study will, accordingly, be concerned with the conceptual nature of social interaction. To that extent at least, this book is about the philosophical foundations of social psychology, for social psychology is often defined just as the study of the interaction between people. The present chapter will serve to lay bare some of our underlying philosophical ideas as well as to give a brief preview of what the book contains.

To start with our philosophical views and commitments, some central general assumptions will be made. The first underlying assumption is that of (a specific kind of) **scientific realism**. The second assumption, which actually is part and parcel of our brand of scientific realism, is the importance of having a **descriptive-prescriptive** dichotomy of discourse and of, so to speak, centrally applying both sides of the dichotomy to the study of persons and their interaction. The third fundamental assumption we shall make is that men cannot be adequately studied as social beings and in a social setting unless they are treated as interacting **agents,** and this entails the adoption of the so-called framework of agency and cultural products. In this book these broad assumptions cannot be properly defended; however, we shall briefly discuss them below.

The brand of scientific realism accepted by us might be called causal internal realism. The internality means the essential relativity of our thinking to some conceptual framework or other, much as Kant argued. Yet no conceptual framework is a priori privileged and irreplaceable: there are no conceptual "givens" nor is there concept free cognitive commerce with the world. In addition to this Kantian-like internality aspect or dimension there is a **naturalistic** (and causal) dimension built into our scientific realism. It is, roughly speaking, concerned with the idea that the extra-mental entities, postulated by realism to exist, causally interact with human beings in a complex fashion making, e.g., evolution and learning possible.[1]

The descriptive-prescriptive dimension is concerned with dividing concepts and discourse into descriptive and prescriptive and denying the complete reducibility of the latter to the former. Let us begin by considering the descriptive side. Here we impose the famous scientific realist motto: **scientia mensura**. That is, in the dimension of describing (and explaining) the world science is the ultimate measure of what there is. Science will thus tell us of what exists that it exists and of what does not exist that it does not. More specifically, it is the best explaining, ideal scientific theory which in each field will specify the ontology, viz. what there is. Ontology thus becomes an epistemic category within causal internal realism, as it is based upon the best explanation.

It is a central presupposition of this book that the conceptual framework of agency should be employed in a study of people in a social setting. This framework is essentially just our common sense framework which conceives of human beings as thinking, sensing, willing and acting **persons** (agents) with moral commitments and responsibilities. More broadly, this framework includes such cultural products as norms, roles, institutions, values, work, art, science and so on. Accordingly, it also includes the conceptual tools for dealing with the economic and political features (or systems) of societies in addition to their cultural aspects (or systems).

The conceptual framework of agency is a part of the broadly conceived and idealized common sense framework of objects and properties (trees, animals, houses, sizes, smells, etc.) that Sellars (1963) has called the **manifest image** of the world. This is the framework in terms of which we, in our western culture, learn to conceive the world, including of course ourselves, our fellow beings, and various social relations. (See Tuomela

(1977), Chapter 1 for the **idealized** nature of the concept of the manifest image.)

The central topic of this book is (the conceptual framework of) social, viz. multi-agent actions and whatever can be constructed out of them. We shall approach this topic in terms of the framework of agency, as indicated. We are going to develop a certain technical conceptual framework which can be regarded as a kind of refinement of a part of the framework of agency. It should be emphasized that we shall operate primarily in the **order of conceiving,** so to speak, and thus mainly study and develop social action concepts. But we do not yet completely avoid making ontological claims. For instance, we shall be making claims not only about the existence of certain types of social actions and of some generational relations holding between them but also about the existence of certain mental states and episodes and about their causal relations to behavior. Such claims, which are claims in the **order of being,** are to be regarded as putative and relative to the framework of agency.

2. Our scientific realism says that science is the measure of what there is. Thus, to use Sellars' (1963) terminology, the ultimate **scientific image** (the one determined by the ideal, best-explaining theory) will determine what there "really" is. This (ideal) scientific image will most likely differ considerably from our present manifest image even in the social realm. If this is so, then the manifest image and the framework of agency, to the extent that they purport to deal with what there is, give us a false ontology. This may be understood on analogy with the way we as scientific realists say that, strictly speaking, there are no tables, viz. tables as perceptual, tactile, etc. common sense objects. The only tables that exist are the tables of the scientific image, viz. certain swarms of subatomic particles as specified by the best-explaining microphysical theory. In other words, although the common sense tables can be said to exist relative to (or as conceived within) the manifest image and the microphysically conceived tables to exist relative to the scientific image, our scientific realism advises us that only the latter "really" exist.

In the same vein, we may claim that although agents, social actions, groups, institutions, and so on, exist relative to the framework of agency, yet these do not "really" exist. So, to put it paradoxically and misleadingly, we shall in this book be studying what does not exist. What is more, there seems to be a double paradox involved. For we shall (at least tentatively) assume that a kind of ontological individualism is true and that, accordingly, there are no holistic social entities (such as groups, institutions and their properties). In other words, while agents, social actions, and other individualistic entities can be taken to exist relative to the framework of agency (even if they do not "really" exist), holistic social entities do not exist even relative to that framework.

The paradox, however, is only an apparent one. Our first reason for saying this is that our study is **mainly** concerned with the order of conceiving rather than with the order of being (and still less with the specific details of the order of being). Thus our concepts of agent, social action, group, and so on are **functional** (and "dot-quoted", to use Sellars' terminology). This means that they are specified in terms of their roles in our theories and in the uses to which we put our theories. Problems of ontology, viz. the specific ontic nature of the bearers of roles and functions, are, in the "last analysis", left for science to determine.

Our first response to the seeming paradox is not, however, quite satisfactory. This is because we cannot avoid dealing with ontic problems. For, as said earlier, we cannot help making some putative ontological assumptions of a general nature about, e.g., the existence of certain mental states and episodes. Furthermore, although I shall not argue for it here, no wedge can ultimately be driven between philosophy and science. Finally, (proper) social scientists would anyhow have to face the paradox of studying what does not exist, given that our scientific realism is tenable, and we cannot, as it were, leave our social scientists in such trouble. So, facing the paradox again, we may now simply retort that there is nothing wrong with working with a putative ontology which can be assumed to turn out false. For this is exactly what **any** scientist is doing. In no field of science have we, presumably, yet reached anything approximating the ultimate best-explaining theory, however it is characterized.

As to the case of social science, it must be added that the ideal best explaining theory must yet respect, in a certain sense, what we **now** say about agents, social actions, groups, etc., within the framework of agency. Features to be so respected are, or can be argued to be, various sensuous qualities, concepts relating to intentionality and, various prescriptive concepts related to personhood and responsibility. It would take us too far to enter a discussion of these matters here (however, cf. Sellars (1963) on the intimately connected issue of joining the framework of agency to the scientific image).

Let me here point out one thing concerning the possibility of a social science. It is compatible with what we have said above that there are lawful propensities, tendencies, episodes and processes in social science. Yet, to the extent that the framework of agency fails to give a correct ontology, the laws in question may fail to be more than approximate. The correct laws would be couched in a **successor** framework of the framework of agency. Such a successor framework would have to resemble our present framework of agency concerning, for instance, the respects mentioned above. Let me emphasize that all this does not exclude that there be approximately true generalizations, and laws and theories, in a weaker sense, couched in the framework of agency as we now have it.

There is a notion of social "reality" which is different from that discussed above in speaking of existence and "real" existence. In that sense a social event or pattern can be said to be socially real only if people have appropriate **mutual beliefs** concerning it. In other words, unless people somehow realize or recognize, etc., this event or pattern it fails to have the intersubjectivity needed to affect their social actions and, generally, the operating of the social community. We shall in this book strongly emphasize the role of mutual beliefs in "defining social reality".

3. So far we have said very little about the prescriptive side of the descriptive-prescriptive dichotomy of discourse. This dichotomy really amounts to the Kantian distinction between theoretical and practical discourse. We will assume that prescriptive (e.g., normative) discourse is necessary for theorizing about agents, social actions and patterns. This is hardly disputed today. We will also assume that prescriptive discourse is conceptually (even if not causally) irreducible to descriptive (naturalistic) discourse. This assumption will not be directly defended in this book, but there are plenty of forceful arguments available in the literature. (One line of argument, pertinent to the themes of this book, is related to the token-reflexive character of prescriptive discourse; see e.g., Sellars (1963), pp. 39-40.)

Prescriptive discourse can be regarded as having no ontological import (even if it may have "evidential" connections with descriptive discourse). Thus, for instance, there are no prescriptive properties (nor objects) in the world. This should make it understandable that we can at the same time endorse both the realist **scientia mensura** -thesis and emphasize the importance of prescriptive discourse. Science can then be taken to describe and explain the naturalistic aspects of the world. The rest belongs to the prescriptive dimension and goes beyond the descriptive powers of science.

As to the social case, the framework of agency and cultural

products contains both descriptive and prescriptive discourse. How is it that prescriptive discourse is so essential if it goes beyond science? To answer this question it is first proper to emphasize in more general terms that indeed prescriptive discourse is central for social science. As we shall see, this is because most social concepts are normative concepts, with the upshot that, conceptually, the social realm can be said to be through and through normative. For instance, it will be seen later in this book that social action done with reference to a rule (an "ought" or "may" rule) is very typical and central. Social rules are also essentially involved in agents' practical reasonings leading to social action and thus they are connected to the notion of acting for a reason.

Social rules and norms are central not only for social action concepts but also for a conceptual reconstruction of society. As will be seen, especially in Chapter 8, the concepts of role, group, institution, organization, community, and society are essentially prescriptive concepts. For instance, a social role could be defined roughly in terms of the following idea. The role concerns a certain social position, we assume, and it specifies that a holder of that position **ought to do** something X_1, given conditions C_1, X_2, given C_2, and so on.

The above remarks serve to illustrate the importance of the prescriptive dimension for social science and the philosophy of social science. Yet it does not make it clear in what sense exactly a social scientist and a social philosopher is committed to using prescriptive discourse. Let us now consider that. We start by asking how empirical social science can cope with the prescriptive dimension if it goes "beyond science" (i.e., if prescriptive discourse cannot be completely analyzed away in naturalistic terms).

One answer or retort, to begin with, is that empirical research in social science simply does not study prescriptive **concepts.** It may study conformative actions, actions violating norms, role behavior, and a plethora of other, as we may say, **normative** (or prescriptive) social phenomena and patterns, even if there are, ontologically speaking, no normative objects or properties in the world, at least in the ultimate account. Their descriptions can yet be regarded as **naturalized,** viz. as consisting of natural-normative statements. For example, the statistics of criminal norm violation are (or can be regarded as) natural-normative descriptions. No normative notions are strictly speaking **used** (but at most mentioned) in such descriptions. Natural-normative descriptions belong to the descriptive dimension, and they are the proper concern of science. It is then roughly in this sense that there can be an empirical (and factual) social science accounting for normative discourse. In saying this I will not exclude the possibility of using any appropriate descriptive concepts, e.g., completely new technical and theoretical ones, in social research as long as they respect the normative nature, naturalistically conceived, of social phenomena.

We may also consider an analogue to the above distinction between normative and natural-normative discourse from the point of view of conceptual study. Both theoretical social science and the philosophy of social science are concerned with the analysis of social concepts. But if our earlier claims about the normative nature of social concepts is right we seem to need normative discourse for such analysis and cannot get away with natural-normative descriptions. Is that so?

Recalling our example of a normative analysis of social rules, we will make a central distinction. We theoretically distinguish between the **prescriptive** and the **descriptive** occurrences of items of (what we have called) prescriptive discourse. Consider thus the statement 'You ought to do X, given C'. The prescriptive occurrence of this ought-statement issues a command, order, obligation or something of the kind, depending on the context, and it is not true or false in a descriptive sense. Contrary to this, we may treat the above sentence descriptively as giving information about an ought-rule (command, order, etc.) which is in force or "exists" in a given community. Taken in this sense the ought-statement can typically be paraphrased in terms of locutions like 'In community S there exists a norm to the effect that one ought to do X, given C' or something similar, depending on the further circumstances of the case. Such paraphrases are clearly true or false in the descriptive sense, and so is, derivatively, the corresponding original descriptively interpreted ought-statement. A similar descriptive-prescriptive distinction can be made concerning the use of such allegedly value-laden terms as 'welfare', 'equilibrium', 'explanation', etc., and it can be argued that a social scientist **qua** social scientist only commits himself to descriptive uses or descriptive aspects of the uses of prescriptive (and axiological) talk.[2)]

The point I am concerned with here is that a social theorist and a social philosopher theoretically, and in principle, need only commit himself to descriptively interpreted prescriptive statements while it can be emphasized that in actual practice value talk and fact talk may yet be strongly interwoven. I shall not argue for this point further but refer the reader to inspect the relevant analyses of normative social concepts given in this book (see, especially, Chapter 8). But given this, there is still the problem of what the descriptive use of prescriptive discourse commits one to. First, it obviously commits one to certain linguistic forms related to prescriptive statements. If we accept a standard view of the matter, this entails commitment to, e.g., the ought-operator (cf. Chapter 2). Secondly, as to the concepts of ought, may, and so on, there are various ways of analyzing them. What is relevant here is of course how ought- and may-statements figure in descriptively interpreted prescriptive talk, and here our analysis of norms, to be given in Chapter 8, is pertinent. Our characterization there partially analyzes descriptively used norm statements in terms of practical reasoning and mutual beliefs. (Yet our analysis does not completely reduce away ought- and may-talk.)

Now we have covered both empirical and conceptual research employing prescriptive discourse and found out in what senses they need to employ prescriptive concepts. We saw in effect that normative discourse is employed in a rather innocuous sense which, for instance, poses no serious threat at least to the objectivity of social science. (This is so even if social explanations are strongly dependent on presuppositions; cf. Chapter 10.)

Perhaps it should be emphasized that we do see a difference between social science and natural science which relates to the fact that normative concepts are in a sense needed for the description of the relevant subject matter in the former but not in the latter. This point is related to the platitude that people but not, say, stones or atoms, use prescriptive talk. Due to this, we claim, social theorists are committed to certain kind of descriptive use of prescriptive talk. Put slightly differently, social theorists need to use natural-normative descriptions while such discourse is not needed in physical sciences.

Considering this matter briefly, let us ask: How does the study of, say, the spin of electrons or the charm of quarks differ from the study of, say, norm-violating action or of status crystallization? The respective concepts of spin and of norm-violation can be studied by philosophers and scientists. Actual spins and actual norm-violating actions (and status crystallization) can be empirically investigated in similar fashion, it may seem. But can they? The problem is complex. One point that might be thought relevant is that in the physical case there are physical properties **in rerum natura** whereas in the social case there are, correspondingly, no normative properties. But this is a bad response, for one might of course be a nominalist with respect to physical properties (or, alternatively, one might perhaps try to be realist about normative properties, viz. assume their existence).

To repeat myself, the only central difference I can see is that there are no physical phenomena and patterns that are natural-normative in the same sense that, as we argued earlier, social phenomena and patterns are natural-normative. In the physical case no normative concepts are **applicable,** contrary to the social case. This applicability again is in a central respect due to **us**: we regard normative concepts as applicable in one case but not in the other. One may also argue that human beings are goal-directed, self-controlling and communicative beings in a way that no physical beings, and for that matter, no "lower" biological beings are, and that the applicability of normative discourse is **in part** also due to such features independent of us (see Sellars (1974), pp. 120-127 on the relevance of "pattern governed" behavior for this, also cf. Tuomela (1977), pp. 58-60 on related remarks). It suffices for the purposes of this book to emphasize the former aspect. Indeed the notion of we-intention and its connection with norms, to be discussed in Chapter 2, will clarify this aspect.

Our final remark on the prescriptive dimension here is that while we shall frequently and centrally employ prescriptive concepts in this book, we shall avoid committing ourselves to any **specific** ethical position. Our theory of social action is thus to be regarded as conceptually prior to specific theories of ethics and social philosophy. Conversely, specific normative theories can possibly be thought to presuppose a theory of social action, for instance ours.

To conclude this general discussion of our basic underlying philosophical assumptions, we shall indicate some specific contexts in this book where our scientific realism most clearly shows up. One point of course is that we leave specific ontological questions to be solved by science. This reflects the feature of scientific realism that there are no a priori privileged conceptual systems. A related fact is that so-called theoretical concepts in science have a genuine, first-order existential status. Since there are no types of concepts that are taken to be privileged in the way that observational concepts are taken by empiricists, any good theoretical concepts can **in principle** (though not necessarily "in practice") be used in direct, evidential reporting and in direct commerce with reality. This holds true of theoretical concepts in social science as well, with the proviso that what such concepts refer to, or deal with, are individualistic (non-holistic) entities (episodes, configurations, etc.); see our account in Chapter 2.

Our so-called postulational method of construing social concepts in Chapter 2 is clearly a realist one. Specifically, our construction of mental concepts (e.g., wanting, willing, believing, etc.) and of action concepts is causal or, better, causal-functional (cf. Chapters 4 and 5). Actions are behaviors suitably caused by certain mental antecedents. In fact it is **purposive causation** that is involved here (cf. Chapters 4, 5, and 6 below). Action-explanations, to be discussed in Chapters 10-12, are basically **causal** explanations and **nomological**, too. The role of causality and of laws here is one typical of scientific realism. Finally, our reinterpretative explanation of social laws, to be discussed in Chapter 14, relies heavily on the realist idea that there are no a priori privileged conceptual systems.

Our brand of scientific realism in principle views society in individualistic rather than holistic terms. Accordingly, it resists the complete reification and objectivation of holistic social entities and structures, and it emphasizes their dependence on social practices, individualistically construed. Yet all this is compatible with the acknowledgement of social entities and structures as quasi-objective, often stable configurations and patterns which can largely be studied in their own right, so to speak. In fact, I am willing to go so far as to recommend such a holistic approach for **present** day practice in social science. In other words, a holistic, realist practical methodology of theory formation in social science can be conceived and even recommended without this contradicting an **ultimate** individualistic scientific realism as sketched above.

II. THEORIZING ABOUT SOCIAL ACTION

1. The main task of this work is to create a certain philosophical theory of social (viz. multi-agent) action, to be called the **purposive-causal theory**, and to apply this theory and some accompanying theoretical ideas and results to create a comprehensive framework of social concepts. What is a philosophical theory of action? It is not easy to answer this question briefly, for in a sense this whole book can be regarded as an answer or at least a response to that question. But we may, anyhow, say roughly this. A philosophical theory of (social) action is one which, first, studies the various types of social action and elucidates them in philosophically illuminating ways (without restriction to a mere analysis of the meaning of action talk). It also makes some general assumptions relating various mental states (or episodes) to action and various environmental factors. It may also connect actions with their various social consequences in some general fashion. A philosophical theory of action differs from factual action theories (e.g., psychological

and sociological theories of action) in part in focusing on somewhat different issues (due to contingent facts about the development of philosophy, not due to conceptual necessity). But mainly the difference concerns only **specificity**. A philosophical theory operates on a general level and formulates very broad factual theses about, e.g., the nature of action while factual theories of action make specific relevant empirical claims.

It is perhaps worth emphasizing here that even though our theory of social action will be individualistic (or semi-individualistic) it will nevertheless make use of ideas often regarded as collectivistic or holistic. Thus we shall strongly rely on the notion of **we-pro-attitude** (especially we-intention and we-willing), reflecting the notion of a group, and on the notion of **mutual belief** (and knowledge), including mutual skills. Our reconstructions of these **prima facie** holistic notions will be individualistic, however.

In developing our purposive-causal theory of action we shall put much effort into creating a rather precise "structuralist" account of social action, an account that systematizes various social action concepts partly by reliance on action generation. In that connection naturally some philosophical assumptions are (and must be) made. These assumptions related especially to the mental antecedents of action (such as we-intentions) and to the purposive causation and generation of action. Not surprisingly, our purposive-causal theory emphasizes both the teleological (or, specifically, purposive) and causal aspects of acting. In particular, it answers the question about the (immediate) initiation of social action by reference to the acting agents' connected willings, viz. we-willings, and the purposive-causal generation of actions by such we-willings. (See our discussion in Chapter 3 of various earlier answers given to the problem of the initiation of action.)

As to our conceptual method, so to speak, we shall be mostly, but not solely, concerned with ideal examples and clear-cut paradigms. Thus the emphasis will more often than not be on rational agents as opposed to e.g., irrational, pathological, and mistake-making agents. We shall also concentrate on full blown intentional action rather than on nonintentional and unintentional action. Thus our approach conceptually goes from "top to bottom", as it were. In other words, human agents are to be studied, evaluated, and criticized from the point of view of the rational agent. The relevant rationality assumptions can and will gradually be relaxed to enable us to get closer to the bottom, viz. man as a naturalistic being with rather imperfect rationality. Some social psychologists seem to have thought that one might conceptually proceed from bottom to top, without accepting the conceptual framework of agency to begin with. I think that this view is clearly wrong and hope that my book will help to show that it is.

By a social action we will in this book broadly mean a joint action performed by several agents who suitably relate their individual actions to the others' actions in pursuing some joint goal or in following some common rules, practices or the like. By a single-agent action we mean roughly a performance, viz. something, usually a change, an agent brings about so that this something has an epistemically public character. A singular action is viewed as a process-like sequence of events: (1) an antecedent mental event (willing in the case of intentional action), (2) a bodily movement, and (3) a result event, viz. a change in the world. Sometimes acts are distinguished from actions. We have chosen not to make such a distinction but use the generic term 'action' to cover both acts and actions in that sense.

Social actions in our sense will include such diverse multi-agent actions as greeting, telephone conversation, playing tennis, carrying jointly a heavy object, asking questions and answering, getting married, and so on. We may ask of such actions whether they are performed intentionally, for an intrinsic end (e.g., singing a song) or extrinsic one (e.g., performing one's detested duty), and so on. (The so-called symbolic and semi-symbolic responses to challenges discussed by e.g., von Wright (1980) are interesting examples of actions performed for extrinsic ends; see Chapter 11.)

One of our central claims will be that all social, viz. joint many-agent, actions will involve some relevant **we-attitudes** (viz. we-intentions and mutual beliefs plus the we-pro-attitudes underlying them). In other words, we claim that the "sociality" or "social relatedness" central to people's acting together in a central sense comes from or even consists in their relevant we-attitudes. This is the point of view from which we approach such problems as the typology of multi-person actions, social practical reasoning, social control, and most importantly communicative action. Communication in its fullest and most interesting sense may be taken to involve so-called reflexive intentions and a Gricean mechanism. We shall discuss communicative action later (in Chapter 10) and show how our theory based on we-attitudes can be extended to handle them. In this sense, the concept of a we-attitude is in our action theory prior to communication. (Strictly speaking, it is social practice in general and especially non-actional notions such as "intending-out-loud" that are conceptually fundamental for us; cf. Chapter 2.) In any case, our action theory is a clear alternative to, e.g., Habermas' (1981) theory, and other similar ones, based on communication.[3] Communicative actions in more rudimentary senses of the word include conformative actions as well as what we shall call rule-referring actions (see Chapter 7).

Communication is obviously very central in giving an account of how people actually arrive at their we-attitudes and in explaining their actions. It is not, however, central for our philosophical purposes at hand to create anything like a general theory of interpersonal communication, for an account of communicative action will suffice, and that account relies on the conceptually more fundamental we-attitudes. Other problems of communication (such as its role in the genesis of we-attitudes) are left for social psychologists.

2. After the above introduction to some of the problems and ideas of this book, we will conclude by a concise preview of the main contents of the chapters of the book.

Chapter 2 outlines a program of individualistic concept formation, called Conceptual Individualism, which conceptually construes holistic social concepts out of individualistic social (and other) concepts, especially action concepts. The chapter also contains arguments for the necessity of employing concepts of other-regarding attitudes ("we-attitudes", especially "we-intentions") in a theory of social action. We-intendings are other-regarding intendings in a mode reflecting the concept of group ("us") on the level of an individual and they are different from mere self-regarding I-intendings. Various types of social motivation possibly underlying we-intentions are also briefly discussed in this chapter.

Given the general background provided by Chapters 1 and 2, Chapter 3 begins the discussion of action theory. It is a critical survey of the main current types of philosophical action theory. An attempt is made to characterize concisely these action theories not only in the single-agent case but, for the first time, also in the multi-agent case. Arguments for and against various action theories, especially causal ones, are presented and evaluated. The main extant action theories are criticized and thus the way is cleared for a new kind of theory.

Chapter 4 outlines the so-called purposive-causal theory of single-agent action developed in Tuomela (1977) and sketches how it may be extended to the multi-agent case, the main topic of this book. It is also argued that the purposive-causal theory can answer the criticisms that have so far been made of causal theories.

In Chapter 5 our structural-generational theory of social action concepts is developed in detail on the basis of the background developed in the earlier chapters. It gives a precise account of both simple and complex multi-agent actions. This central chapter presents several classifications and characterizations of social action, both intentional and non-intentional ones. In the case of intentional social actions (e.g., basic actions and actions which the agents have the power to do), the concept of a we-willing that derives from a we-intending, as well as the concept of purposive-causal generation, both play a central role. Olson's (1965) well known account of self-interested behavior is also critically commented on in this chapter.

Chapter 6 investigates various concepts of action generation which Chapter 5 in part relies on. It gives a general automata-theoretic account of (both so-called factual and conceptual) generation, an account that applies to both single-agent and multi-agent actions. The chapter also gives further classifications of social actions and discusses the formal structures of some social activities, such as ceremonies, argued to be representable by means of suitable formal grammars. As to the clarification of the notion of joint action (or acting together) Chapters 5 and 6 are the most central ones in the book.

In Chapter 7 the nature of **social** practical inference is the central topic. Such reasoning is what takes place when the acting agents suitably relate their reasonings; typically this goes via so-called social loop-beliefs. The chapter gives a semi-technical account of an important type of social practical reasoning, a type of reasoning that can be used to justify a great variety of social actions, in part by reference to the agents' relevant mutual beliefs. It is also argued that game-theoretic reasoning can be fruitfully analyzed from the point of view of the type of social practical reasoning that is elaborated here. Chapter 7 also contains further classifications of various types of social action.

In Chapter 8 the system of action concepts created in the preceding chapters is used as an underlying basis for an investigation of some social structures. The chapter starts with an analysis of social norms. Then, relying on it, the concept of social role is characterized, and it is argued that considerations of similarity can fruitfully be applied in this context. An exact characterization of the notion of social group is also given and some other structural concepts, such as those of an organization and a community, are briefly considered. It is argued that part of the "social reality" of such social constructs is due to certain relevant mutual beliefs the people in a society have concerning them.

Chapter 9 is an investigation of various types of social

interaction that can be construed on the basis of the account given in Chapters 5, 6, 7, and 8. Especially important is the account of various types of covert social control. To deal with them in exact detail a linear mathematical model is created. It is claimed that the forms of control thus isolated are to some degree present in all social interaction.

Chapter 10 presents a pragmatic and nomological theory of explanation starting from a question-theoretic basis. Basically, explanations are viewed as communicative actions producing answers to suitable explanatory questions. Our account emphasizes the importance of making explicit various underlying explanatory presuppositions and interests. Chapter 10 also serves to illustrate the illocutionary act of explaining as a two-person communicative social action of querying and answering.

Chapter 11 applies the general theory of Chapter 10 to the case of explaining intentional social (multi-agent) action. Various types of explanation are investigated and, as a result, detailed accounts of so-called intentional-teleological explanation, purposive-causal explanation and reason-explanation are presented. The interrelations between these types of explanation, which all employ proximate socio-mental explanatory factors and so-called act-relational concepts, are investigated.

Chapter 12 discusses what we call dynamic explanations of social action. These are motive-explanations in terms of more distant underlying socio-mental factors. This account is presented partly within a utility-theoretic framework, utilities representing want-intensities. It is argued, among other things, that in a suitably qualified and restricted sense, both individual and collective agents can be regarded as maximizing their expected gains or utilities when acting intentionally. It is important that the utilities here be construed as other-regarding ones.

The functional explanation of (intentional and non-intentional) social actions is the central topic of Chapter 13. A new account of functions, viz. action-functions, is presented and applied to functional explanation. Also the so-called invisible-hand explanations of social actions are analyzed from the point of view of the purposive-causal theory.

Chapter 14 argues for explanatory individualism and presents an account of the ("corrective") explanation of (holistic) social laws and theories in terms of (individualistic) social-psychological theories in which the latter in a sense correct the former. This account concentrates on the case of reinterpretative explanation where the social theory or law to be explained can be regarded as conceptually incommensurable with the social-psychological explanans, and it gives a technical account

of this in terms of some powerful new logical tools and results
from general logic. The analysis is applied to both functional
and invisible-hand explanations with laws as explananda.

CHAPTER 2

INDIVIDUALISM AND CONCEPT FORMATION IN THE SOCIAL SCIENCES

I. HOLISTIC SOCIAL CONCEPTS

1.   The main concern of this book is to develop and present a theory of multi-agent action. Given that we succeed in that and in creating a system of social action concepts, we may ask how other social concepts, such as the concepts of group, institution, and organization, relate to our system of social action concepts. To this question our answer is that from the conceptual point of view, or "in the conceptual order", all social concepts can in a sense be built out of social action concepts. This, if acceptable, bestows much extra importance to the enterprise of this book. As our general programme for the construction of social concepts (especially holistic ones) does not depend on the details of our theory of social action to be developed and as it is useful to have these broader perspectives in mind before going into the technical details of this theory of social action, we shall below sketch our view of how to build social concepts individualistically out of social action concepts (including we-intentions and mutual beliefs). The second aim of the present chapter is to elucidate individualistically the notion of **we-intention**. This concept is going to play a central role in our theory of social action quite irrespective of how our general programme of concept formation in the social sciences fares.

Our programme is basically functionalist: concepts are to be characterized in terms of their functions or roles in the theories where they are introduced and employed. Our view is individualistic in the sense that we accept a principle of **conceptual individualism** which entails a **partial** reduction of holistic social concepts to individualistic ones. The account to be given below is somewhat sketchy and general - detailed functionalist analyses of single social concepts will not be presented in this context.

My starting point is Sellars' functionalist programme of concept formation in psychology (see, e.g., Sellars (1956) and (1968)), which I have in Tuomela (1977) explicated and elaborated to some extent. In that approach the idea is to **conceptually** (i.e., in the order of conceiving) introduce "inner" mental concepts, such as the concepts of want, intention, belief, and perception, on the basis of concepts that concern "public social practice", concepts such as those of overt intelligent (especially verbal) behavior, and dispositions so to behave. Yet, even if mental concepts **conceptually** depend on social practice, **ontologically** (i.e., in the order of being) mental states and episodes (i.e., what the mental concepts stand for) are prior to overt behavior items. Thus, indeed, they may cause behavior, and hence mental concepts may play a central role in the (causal) explanations of behavior. In fact, the main motivation for introducing such inner mental concepts is just their **explanatory import**. (It is not paradoxical to say that "in principle" we could conceptually get along rather well by just having a "Rylean" language of overt actions and the like without any Cartesian remnants such as inner mental acts.)

Sellars' account of concept formation in psychology is stated by him in terms of a myth. Suppose we had Rylean ancestors, to use Sellars' terminology, who employed a somewhat limited behavioristic language in their communication. The descriptive predicates of the language concern only public properties of public objects located in space and enduring through time. This language permits the standard logical operations, and it also allows for subjunctive conditionals. The only way of Rylean ancestors could speak of anything resembling our notion of thinking was in terms of overt verbal episodes, most centrally "thinking-out-loud". Similarly, e.g., perceiving could only be approached through "perceiving-out-loud", and so on. No inner episodes, conceptual nor non-conceptual, are admitted by this Rylean language.

On the other hand, it should be noticed that **action**-talk (e.g., about speech acts) is permitted. That is, the language does not consider behavior only as movements, responses, and so on. Also theoretical and practical reasoning (and at least the rudiments of prescriptive discourse) are possible in our Rylean community.

Given this Rylean language, Sellars' claim now is that if we add to it the resources of (1) **semantical** and (2) **theoretical** (i.e., concerning unobservable inner episodes) discourse, that suffices to enable the language users to come to acquire the concept of mental episode (event, state, process) as we **now** have it.

Semantical (or metalinguistic) discourse will enable the members of the Rylean community to characterize overt verbal episodes in semantical terms and thus to give these episodes characteristics (e.g., "aboutness") analogous to the intentional characteristics we now give to mental episodes. Thus, it becomes possible to characterize an agent's verbal utterance, e.g., 'The earth is flat' as a **saying** (thinking-out-loud) that the earth is flat (roughly because 'The earth is flat' -utterance construed as a linguistic statement **means** that the earth is flat). Let us call Rylean discourse cum semantical discourse pre-Jonesian discourse. The addition of a theoretical discourse about inner episodes then gives a new kind of entities, which share the central (intentional) aboutness aspect with verbal episodes but which still are distinct from the latter. The resulting discourse will be called Jonesian.

This introduction of inner mental episodes in the mythical community is due to a genius, Jones by name. According to our philosophical myth he develops the hypothesis (or theory) that people's propensities to think-out-loud change during periods of silence as they would have changed if they had, during the interval, been engaged in a steady stream of thinkings-out-loud of various kinds. This is because they are the subjects of imperceptible episodic periods which (a) are analogous to thinkings-out-loud; (b) culminate, in candid speech, in thinkings-out-loud of the kind to which they are specifically analogous; (c) are correlated with the verbal propensities which, when actualized, are actualized in such thinkings-out-loud; (d) occur not only when one is silent but in candid speech, as the initial stage of a process which comes 'into the open', so to speak, as overt speech (or as sub-vocal speech), but which can occur without this culmination, and does so when we acquire the ability to keep our thoughts to ourselves. (Cf. Sellars (1968), p. 159.) Jones then goes on to teach his fellow members to use mental language (according to his hypothesis) not only in the third person case but also in the first person case. (The use of this full blown Jonesian language naturally presupposes appropriate mutual semantical and pragmatic beliefs to be had by the speakers.) In all, we may say then that the Jones myth is the answer to the problem of inner mental episodes once we give up the notion of a self-authenticating non-verbal episode of Cartesianism and the strain against inner episodes in Ryle and Wittgenstein.

According to this so-called analogy theory of thinking (i.e., of representational mental episodes) inner mental concepts derive primarily from concepts of overt intelligent (especially verbal) behavior and thus from public, culturally laden facts. I have elsewhere (in Tuomela (1977), Chapter 4) discussed from this perspective a reconstruction of the meaning-specifying psychological theory introduced by Jones in the above myth.[1] This reconstruction relies on the following principle of **Conceptual Functionalism** for a behaving system (e.g., organism, agent) to which psychological predicates apply:

(CF) Consider a meaning-specifying theory $T(\lambda \cup \mu)$, which has $\lambda \cup \mu$ as its set of extralogical predicates and which adequately describes a system S. The predicates in μ represent inner events, states, etc. of S and are theoretical with respect to the predicates in λ, which represent overt aspects of S. Then the meanings of all predicates in μ are assumed to functionally depend entirely upon their usage with the predicates in λ within $T(\lambda \cup \mu)$.

The principle (CF) amounts to saying that the meanings of the inner predicates in μ are to be specified functionally by means of the causal (and other) relations holding between inputs and inner states (and episodes), inner states and outputs as well as between the internal states (and episodes) themselves. The functional dependences between the μ-predicates and the λ-predicates are assumed to explicate just those relations in detail. (Furthermore, epistemic criteria such as incorrigible reportability may in addition have to be used if we want to distinguish between mental and physical theoretical predicates.) Notice, that in (CF) 'overt aspects' is to be understood broadly enough so as to cover not only behavior (action) but also various environmental factors such as inputs, stimuli, and suitable preconditions of behaving. The members of μ may be taken to be theoretical and those of λ observational (e.g., in the sense of Tuomela (1973)).

The thesis (CF) corresponds to a principle of "semantic empiricism" that, e.g., Rozeboom (1963) had advocated. In Tuomela (1973) I argue against the adoption of this principle in the case of physical theories. However, (CF) seems, by and large, appropriate for psychological theories (and for social theories in general). I say 'by and large' because my claim strictly speaking applies only to the situation described in the Jones myth. When applied to our psychological concepts - as we have them now - (CF) may seem a little strict. However, that is presumably due to the existence of **epistemic** variance and slack (problems related to the use of the μ-predicates in epistemically imperfect cases), I would argue. Purified from such epistemic problems the semantic situation seems correctly reconstructible by the principle (CF).

It should be emphasized here that, although (CF) can be logically specified in a number of ways it is far from being merely a reductionist view (such as logical behaviorism), when taken as a semantical doctrine (see Tuomela (1977), Chapter 4 on this). Furthermore, it should be emphasized that (CF) is not an ontological thesis and that, in fact, inner events and states of S may usually be regarded as ontologically autonomous, even if conceptually they are not.

Relying on (**CF**) it is possible to introduce conceptually the central mental concepts that an action theory (and, especially, our purposive-causal theory) employs. Thus, one can introduce wants, beliefs and intentions in terms of suitable uses of (**CF**). To take a simplified example, to intend that p entails, roughly, being in a dispositional state (with the structure p has) such that this state, given suitable internal and external circumstances, will cause whatever bodily behavior is required for the satisfaction of p (see Tuomela (1977) and Chapter 4 below for details). This functionalist account gives us, respectively, the basic affective, doxastic and conative concepts that are required for our purposive-causal theory of action. We shall not in this book analyze these notions much although we are going to employ them centrally in the coming chapters.

What interests us here more than the conceptual nature of mental concepts is how to conceptually introduce **social** concepts. This involves modifying the above Jones-myth in some respects. Let us see how.

2. We spoke above about the Rylean language employed by the mythical community. Let us now refine our description in one respect and assume that the extralogical predicates of this language may contain not only individualistic (psychological and social) predicates but also **holistic** social predicates as long as these holistic predicates are not clearly explanatory predicates introduced by some social theory. It would seem that, e.g., 'group' and 'school' are examples of such "observational" (and non-explanatory) holistic concepts. (Whether there indeed are such "observational" holistic social concepts depends on one's theoretical-observational dichotomy. The exact nature of this dichotomy is not so important for our present concerns.)

Let λ be the set of extralogical predicates of our antecedently understood Rylean language (or, better, pre-Jonesian language, as the presence of semantical, metalinguistic talk may be assumed). Let λ_i now be the subset of λ that consists of predicates which express properties (and states, etc.) of individuals (persons) and relations between individuals and which do not conceptually presuppose holistic social notions in the way that, e.g., 'cashing a cheque' presupposes the concept of bank, etc.[2] In fact, λ_i may be taken to consist of predicates expressing individualistically conceived social actions (and capacities for social action) in a sense to be clarified in detail in Chapter

5. Let $\lambda_h = \lambda - \lambda_i$ be the set of non-explanatory social predicates applying to, or at least conceptually presupposing, collectives of individuals or properties of such collectives (or relations between them).

Next we introduce our explanatory predicates. We first let μ_p be the set of inner mental predicates introduced by Jones' theory, call it $T_p(\lambda \cup \mu_p)$. This theory may be taken to comprise all the mutually consistent common sense psychological truths and approximate truths which we (presently) possess and which are constitutive of the predicates in μ_p. (We shall below consider what this constitutiveness means.) Secondly, we introduce a set μ_s which is the set of such holistic (and possibly other) explanatory predicates as a best-explaining social theory requires. (This talk about a best-explaining social theory is a piece of science fiction, but we cannot here try to clarify the notion.) Now we let $T_s(\lambda \cup \mu_s)$ be the conjunction of postulates which are constitutive of the predicates in μ_s and call the language of T_s simply $L(\lambda \cup \mu_s)$.

Whether or not T_s coincides with the just mentioned best-explaining social theory does not matter. Presumably, it does not, for the following reason. Our theory T_s, which is a counterpart to the Jonesian theory T_p in the psychological case, is meant to be **conceptually** adequate (viz. adequate in the order of conceiving) in a sense to be explicated. But even if it were conceptually adequate it need not yet be causally (and explanatorily) adequate (viz. adequate in the order of being). For T_s lacks the explanatory mental concepts of μ_p, and surely they are needed in the best-explaining social theory if there is any truth at all in explanatory methodological individualism.

To be a little more concrete let us consider some examples of holistic social concepts (members of μ_s and λ_h). Some familiar holistic predicates are: 'institution', 'organization', 'group', 'state', 'government', 'church', 'battallion', 'working class', 'free market', 'role', 'stratification', 'cohesion', 'status crystallization'. Of these predicates presumably at least those appearing towards the end of the list would seem to qualify as members of μ_s. But, as said, what matters is not which of the above and other predicates belong to λ_h and which to μ_s but rather which are members of $\lambda_h \cup \mu_s$ (call this set n_s) and which of λ_i. For our idea, to be soon discussed, is to construe the meanings of the predicates in n_s on the basis of those in λ_i, given the postulate conjunction T_s (= $T_s(\lambda \cup \mu_s)$ $T_s(\lambda_i \cup n_s)$).

It is often claimed that holistic social concepts are, o may be, **normative** (or at least prescriptive, viz., concerne with ought- and may-rules). Consider, for instance, the concep of role. It is definable in terms of norms, in terms of what the role bearer **ought to do** or **may do** in various circumstances (see, e.g., Chapter 8 below for this kind of treatment of roles). It is also easy to see that, e.g., organizations and institutions embody norms in analogous ways. As this matter is a familiar and an acknowledged one I shall not here further discuss it or argue for it in detail. Let me just put the matter in general terms and say that the social realm is through and through normative; yet, as we saw in Chapter 1, only the so-called **descriptive** (as contrasted with prescriptive) use of normative discourse is needed here.

The point I am concerned to make here is that it may be argued, and has been argued by Sellars, that the concept of norm cannot be expressed in the impoverished, individualistic pre-Jonesian language and thus in terms of the vocabulary λ_i even if we allow the logic of this language to contain normative operators (e.g., **'Ought'**, **'Shall'**). This is in part because many norms, e.g. all moral ones, are intersubjective and impartial and because these features cannot be accounted for in individualistic terms. More specifically, we shall tentatively accept an analysis of ought- and may-rules in terms of **we-intentions** (cf. (8.1) below). But the social concept of we-intention may fail to be strictly reducible to individualistic concepts (cf. Sellars (1963), pp. 202-205 and below). Even if this claim concerning irreducibility were correct (we shall oppose this claim below and include we-intentions in μ_p), the most that is needed in the ultimate analysis of holistic social concepts in addition to the concepts of $\lambda_i \cup \mu_p$ or of λ_i is an irreducible concept of we-intention, given that (**CF**) holds ultimately with the basis λ_i, also cf. Chapter 8.

There are also holistic concepts which are less explicitly normative than those mentioned above. Thus, it might seem that, e.g., group cohesion is not a normative concept. Much of the discussion concerned with methodological individualism has been concerned with concepts like it. It is not completely implausible to suggest that properties of systems of objects, such as social psychological groups, be reducible to properties of their constituents (individual agents in our example) and relations between them. Consider thus the following seemingly ontological and individualistic reduction principle:

(R) If an object is a system of objects, then the object's having a property must consist in its constituents having certain properties or relations.

We may perhaps agree that this strict reductionist principle indeed holds in the case of some systems. Yet I think it cannot a priori be required to be true of, e.g., social psychological groups. In any case, much hangs on the term 'consists'. What if, speaking of a social psychological group and its cohesion, the analysandum is a normative concept whereas the analysans is non-normative? The concept of group and hence the analysandum (e.g., a group's being cohesive) may be regarded as implicitly involving the concept of norm, while the analysans may seem to be non-normative. And even if normative properties were non-existent, (**R**) might seem problematic. But here we shall not go deep into problems of ontology and we leave (**R**) as it stands without committing ourselves to it. (Thus we allow that social systems may have emergent properties in the relevant sense.)

There is, however, a general ontological principle whose validity can be defended largely on a priori grounds. This principle has been called the Principle of Expression (**PE**) in the context of ontologically grounding psychological phenomena on physical ones (see, e.g., Tuomela (1977), p. 249). In the present context this principle says that all holistic social entities are individualistically embodied. More specifically it says that (a) every holistic social entity has some individualistic properties (or satisfies some individualistic predicates in λ_i (or, alternatively, $\lambda_i \cup \mu_p$)) and (b) there cannot be two entities that are alike in all individualistic respects but differ in some holistic social respect. Formally we may render this as follows:

(**PE**) (a) $(\forall x)(\forall P \in n_s)(P(x) \supset (EQ \in \lambda_i)Q(x))$
(b) $(\forall x)(\forall y)(\forall Q \in \lambda_i)((Q(x) \equiv Q(y)) \supset (\forall P \in n_s)(P(x) \equiv P(y)).$[3]

According to (a) of (**PE**) actual nations, organizations, etc. must be individualistically embodied. This clause excludes disembodied "group minds", for instance, as it should. Clause (b) in turn excludes such ontological emergence as is not individualistically characterizable. Note that (**PE**) does not require that differences concerning a certain predicate $P \in n_s$ be accounted for in terms of differences concerning the same predicate(s) in λ_i. Thus (**PE**) clearly falls short of defining n_s-predicates in terms of λ_i-predicates.

Notice, too, that (**PE**) does not as such account for normative features. However, to the extent that normative aspects are factually grounded and involve an entity's satisfying predicates from $\lambda_i \cup n_s$, (**PE**) deals with them, too. I shall not here try to argue for (**PE**) except by asserting that I simply cannot make any (ontic) sense of holistic entities if (**PE**) is not acceptable. I am inclined to accept ontological individualism in a sense involving (**PE**). (Were ontology our central concern (**R**) and (**PE**) would certainly need to be properly discussed.)

II. CONCEPTUAL INDIVIDUALISM

1. What is often called the doctrine of methodological individualism (as opposed to methodological holism) involves three ingredients which should be distinguished from each other. The first ingredient is **ontology**: What is the ontological nature of social objects and properties (cf. our (**R**) and (**PE**))? The second is **meaning** (semantics): How are social concepts, such as those in η_s, to be semantically understood? The third ingredient is **explanation**: How are social phenomena and regularities best explained? Do individualistic theories together with suitable correspondence principles suffice to explain (and thus reduce) holistic theories? **Prima facie**, these questions can be answered independently. Yet it is arguable, according to our causal internal realism, that the ideal and ultimate best-explaining theory will be involved in answering the ontological and semantical questions, too. Thus, if this theory is an individualistic one, we will also get an individualistic ontology and semantics, so to speak. This would make ontology and semantics dependent on epistemology. (It is not necessary to argue for this position here; but see Rosenberg (1980a).)

I will below be almost exclusively concerned with the second problem and advocate what I call the doctrine (or thesis) of **Conceptual Individualism** (cf. its analogue Conceptual Functionalism discussed above). To state this thesis, we employ the constitutive theory $T_s(\lambda_i \cup \eta_s)$ and rely on our above discussion of it:

(**CI**) The meanings of the social predicates in η_s depend entirely upon their usage with the predicates in λ_i, assumed antecedently understood, within the meaning-specifying theory $T_s(\lambda_i \cup \eta_s)$.

(**CI**) requires several comments. First, we note that this principle does **not** entail that the predicates of η_s be **explicitly** (or in any other strict sense) definable in terms of those in λ_i within T_s. (**CI**) only entails that any predicate in η_s gets whatever (inferential) meaning it has from the predicates in λ_i on the basis of the constitutive theory T_s. Thus (**CI**) is **not** reductionistic in a strong sense, but it only, as we may say, functionally and partially determines the meanings of the η_s-predicates in terms of the λ_i-predicates within T_s. While dependence relations in (**CI**) perhaps typically are functional ones, it is not necessary for our purposes to strictly require that (cf. (**CF**)).

(**CI**) allows for "open" social predicates and for multiply denoting predicates. Multiple denotation means the following. Suppose that T_s is a theory formalized in first-order predicate logic. Then, considering a predicate $P \in \eta_s$, if for some fixed interpretations of the predicates in $\lambda_i \cup (\eta_s \sim \{P\})$ it is possible to model-theoretically satisfy T_s by means of two or more interpretations (viz. two or more sets of ordered sequences of individuals or - if you are a strong intensionalist - two or more non-extensional properties), then P is said to multiply denote these interpretations.

It should be noted that as such (**CI**) says nothing about ontology; it does not even claim that the predicates in $\lambda_i \cup \eta_s$ are referring ones. As to the logical form of T_s in general, let me here just say that it can presumably be taken to be formalized in first-order logic or some second-order extension of first-order logic with the addition of some (sentential) intensional operators, e.g., **'Ought'**, **'Shall'**. Suitable metalinguistic discourse is of course assumed available. (As to the logical features of (**CI**), see my detailed discussion of its exact counterpart (**CF**) of Section I for the psychological case in Tuomela (1977), pp. 76-88.)

Let it be emphasized that I am presently operating on the assumption that (**CF**) holds in the psychological case and that the predicates in μ_p are conceptually foundable on the predicates in λ_i. Thus while I basically claim that the predicates in η_s are to be conceptually founded on the predicates in $\lambda_i \cup \mu_p$, they can also be said to be founded on those in λ_i, in view of (**CF**) and the transitivity of our notion of conceptual founding. (It may be objected that if (1) the **prima facie** conceptual fundamentum of η_s is $\lambda_i \cup \mu_p$ rather than λ_i - which I grant in view of the central role of the concept of we-intention (see (**WI**) below) - then, since (2) the relevant predicates in μ_p, such as 'we-intention' and 'belief', cannot be characterized without the whole set λ, and thus λ_h, my account moves in a circle. But I do not accept premise (2) in this argument, for, first, the holistic predicates in λ_h appear only opaquely in the contents of the intentions and beliefs, and thus no commitment to a holistic social concept follows without strong further assumptions (e.g., a person's intention to go to a bank does not as such entail that he has the holistic social concept of bank or banking system). What is more, I believe that such relevant intentions and beliefs can be conceptually founded, even if not strictly defined, on more rudimentary intentions and beliefs with individualistic contents by reference to rudimentary social concepts along the lines sketched below and in Section III of Chapter 8.)

We have been requiring all along that T_s be a theory constitutive of the predicates in η_s. (Note that the λ_i-predicates are assumed antecedently understood in (**CI**).) By our notion of constitutiveness the following is meant. The meanings of the extralogical predicates in a branch of science are determined, ideally, by the whole best-explaining theory in which the predicates occur (and in actual practice by an approximation of such best-explaining theory). (Cf. the meaning thesis (**M**) defended in Tuomela (1973), pp. 122-123.) This is the constitutive theory as meant in this chapter. But on pain of making the theory true a priori there must, it seems, be a way of separating the **meaning-giving** or analytic component from its **factual** or synthetic component (see Tuomela (1973) for discussion). I shall not here go into details except for pointing out a few things. First, I would like to emphasize that creating an analytic-synthetic distinction is - for me - ultimately a pragmatic affair depending on how the best-explaining linguistic theory available construes it. Secondly, it is the analytic component that matters here, and what the factual component is, is not so central. Also note that practically any postulate set introduced as constitutive for the meanings of some scientific predicates will turn out to have some factual content.

There is also another, and perhaps better, way of specifying the meanings of scientific predicates. It goes in terms of the **inferential** network in which these predicates occur. We may, at least for this purpose, think of scientific laws and theories as rules of inference licensing singular inferences. Corresponding to, say, the law 'Copper expands when heated', such a singular inference would, or might, have this form: From 'a is a piece of copper which is heated' one may infer 'a will expand'. Thus, e.g., 'copper' would get its meaning from all the inferential contexts (or some specified subset of them) resembling the mentioned one in which it is used. As, however, the inferential approach can at least in "standard" cases such as first-order logic and many of its extensions be translated back to the postulational approach I will not here discuss it further (cf. Tuomela (1976a), (1977), Chapter 5).

On many occasions it is appropriate to emphasize that (**CI**) is a principle for construing (or, if you like, **re**construing) holistic social concepts. Under this view, we start with some holistic social theories or, let us idealize, with either the explanatorily complete or, more realistically, with the conceptually constitutive social theory, say S. Then we suitably

correlate the concepts of S with their individualistically construed counterpart concepts in n_s and **translate** S into the language $L(\lambda_i \cup n_s)$. The translation of S may be taken to be, by the definition of $T_s(\lambda_i \cup n_s)$, the maximal subtheory of $T_s(\lambda_i \cup n_s)$ couched solely in the vocabulary n_s. Let us call this subtheory $\tau(S)(n_s)$, τ being the translation function. Thus, under this interpretation, the predicates in n_s are just our explicates and counterparts of the original social predicates. Accordingly, $\tau(S)$ is not only a translation of S into our individualistic conceptual framework but, in a sense, it **is** S viewed from the point of view of our framework. (We shall later in Chapter 14 rely on this philosophical interpretation of (**CI**) when discussing the individualistic explanation of social patterns and structures.)

We have above proceeded without giving specific arguments for the acceptability of (**CI**). Are there any and does it need any? As indicated in the previous paragraph (**CI**) should perhaps best be understood as a principle for constructing social concepts rather than as a principle underlying the meaning analysis of social concepts in our ordinary parlance. (**CI**) may then be backed by the general individualistic metaphysics accompanying our scientific realism (see Chapter 1). Thus, the argument for (**CI**) that we get from this is that concept formation in social science should go together with the underlying metaphysics, especially ontology, and should conform to one's tendency to think individualistically of ontological matters, especially causation, so that causation due to holistic entities is regarded as merely derivative (cf. Chapter 14).

2. Now some further remarks elucidating the philosophical content of (**CI**) are due. First, we may connect (**CI**) to Sellars' Jones-myth and tell a new story. We suppose the existence of an individualistic Rylean community speaking only the language of the λ_i-predicates. Then we enrich this restricted individualistic Rylean discourse by adding semantical discourse (and thus metalinguistic categories) to it. In fact we now also get (the logical aspects) of **prescriptive** discourse, if we assume (as we have) the presence of (individualistic) practical reasoning in our original community. For, it may be argued, practical thinking may have deontic conclusions - for instance, conclusions specifying what an agent should or ought to do. So we need ought- and may-rules from the beginning, and metalinguistic talk specifies the meaning of such prescriptive talk and enables the agents of our individualistic community to formulate oughts at least for themselves. (The concept of social norm involves still more - see Chapter 8.)

Given individualistic Rylean discourse as well as semantical and prescriptive discourse we still have to add theoretical discourse for new types of entities and properties. After that we may accept (**CI**) and introduce the predicates in η_s by specifying the functional connections these predicates have to the λ_i-predicates. For instance, if the concept of norm were available, we could semantically explicate the concept of church (let 'church'$\in \eta_s$) by specifying the oughts concerning priests, church members, and so on and, perhaps, further by functionally characterizing this concept as what explains various religious activities of people. Similarly, e.g., 'cohesion' may be partially and functionally characterized as what accounts for or, at least involves, the group-members' likings of each other (and suitable other attitudes) and, e.g., their contact frequencies. Group cohesion may also be functionally characterized as what "keeps the group together" (or something like that).

In total, we get a constitutive social story corresponding to the Jones-myth in the psychological case, a story that functionalistically accounts for concept formation in the social sciences. As an extra bonus we get a strengthening of the Jones-myth: If the social story is acceptable, then in view of (**CI**) Jones may start with the individualistic Rylean predicate set λ_i (to which at least the concept of we-intending or, rather, we-intending-out-loud, must be added) rather than having to employ the full Rylean set λ.

What our programme for concept formation in the social sciences amounts to can be summarized by means of some abbreviatory formulas in the following way. We assume that our task is to formulate for the social sciences a scientific language or discourse which gives an adequate conceptual foundation, as it were, for all theorizing. Let us call the fullest such language Socialese. Then what we have above said entails this abbreviatory slogan, using 'd.' for 'discourse':

(S1) Socialese = individualistic Rylean d. + semantical d. + prescriptive d. + holistic Rylean d. + psychological theoretical d. + social theoretical d.

A conceptually adequate but (perhaps) causally inadequate conceptual framework is given by

(S2) Socialese* = individualistic Rylean d. + semantical d. + prescriptive d. + holistic Rylean d. + social theoretical d.

We may now also put our basic problem here as follows: What are the conceptual fundaments of Socialese and Socialese*? To this question our (**S1**) and (**S2**) give their respective answers by listing the various conceptual components needed. We may also say, equivalently, that given (a) individualistic Rylean discourse, (b) semantical discourse, (c) (descriptively used) prescriptive discourse and (d) the conceptual resources for theoretical discourse on the whole (without regard to its substantive nature) then (i) the use of the principle (**CI**) (given that it is acceptable, of course) gives us Socialese* and (ii) the use of (**CI**) plus the use of its analogue (**CF**) for the psychological case give us Socialese. (See Chapter 8 for how to individualistically construe some central predicates, such as 'role', 'group', 'institution', of Socialese.)

It is worth noting in the present context that when employing Socialese there is the attractive possibility of defining the predicates of η_s **explicitly** in terms of the predicates in $\lambda_i \cup \mu_p$ even if such definitions are not possible in terms of only λ_i. I take it for granted that the predicates in μ_p cannot be explicitly defined in terms of the predicates in λ_i (this follows from the failure of strict logical behaviorism). Accordingly, there is no hope of explicitly defining the predicates of η_s in terms of the predicates in λ_i no matter how individualistic one wants to be, for surely individualistic accounts of holistic social concepts must refer to such mental features as wants, intentions, perceptions, beliefs and so on, viz., mental features expressed by μ_p-predicates.

In this chapter I have not presented nor will present strong philosophical arguments for or against the ultimate explicit definability of η_s-predicates generally in terms of predicates in $\lambda_i \cup \mu_p$ as I do not think there are such. There are yet several methodological arguments that could be brought up here in favor of the "present day" openness (viz. non-definability) of theoretical predicates in general and also of the η_s-predicates occurring in social theories. (For a detailed discussion of these arguments, relying on various methodological gains accruing from the use of open explanatory predicates, see Tuomela (1973), especially Chapter VI.) We shall, however, below consider, and oppose, Sellars' argument for the conclusion that the notion of we-intention (taken here to be represented by a predicate in η_s) cannot be explicitly defined by means of I-intentions and suitable personal beliefs and thus by means of predicates in $\lambda_i \cup \mu_p$.

III. WE-INTENTIONS AND SOCIAL MOTIVATION

1. Let us next consider the problem of what prescriptive discourse really amounts to. (The other components of Socialese should be clear enough.) As a great many social concepts presuppose the concept of norm (cf. Chapter 8), the question becomes how much content is conceptually needed in the concept of prescriptive (and normative) discourse. For instance, if strict naturalism were acceptable, then we would not need irreducible prescriptive discourse at all. But if we do need some kind of irreducible oughts and mays, how rich a conceptual framework does that require? We shall below briefly consider this problem from a certain angle, viz. from the point of view of practical reasoning.

Sellars (1963), (1968) has attempted to give a fairly naturalistic analysis of norms in terms of intentions and practical thinking. As I find his analysis an interesting starting point, let me briefly skecth some of its main features. Let us here tentatively accept that practical reasoning gives a good basis for an analysis of (moral and other) norms. Now it is an acknowledged feature of moral norms that they are **intersubjective**: The same norm should in principle be applicable to different agents. Let us now, following Sellars, assume that practical reasoning is intimately connected with norms in the sense of entailing conclusions as to what one shall do and thus conclusions which are expressions of intentions to do something. If this, perhaps with some additional qualifications excluding non-normative uses of 'shall', is taken to be what connects practical reasoning with norms, then the problem of intersubjectivity arises. A person A can intend (to bring about) that, say, B do X and a person C can intend that B not do X. But both of these intentions are egocentric and the problem is to make them genuinely contradictory. In terms of expressions of intention we have 'Shall$_A$(B will do X)' and 'Shall$_C$(B will not do X)' where 'Shall$_i$(p)' expresses agent i's intending that p. These expressions do not formally contradict each other. Sellars (1963), pp. 196-205, emphasizes this problem and introduces the concept of **we-intention** to handle it. Given this account, both A and B can be taken to intend in the we-mode (expressed in Sellars' analysis by locutions of the form 'We shall do X') rather than in a personal mode, and a real comparison between we-intentions can be made in the sense required by intersubjectivity.

Sellars (1963) also offers other, broader arguments for the need of we-intentions. One is that we-intending involves a special form of consciousness ("we-consciousness", yet utterly different from Durkheimian "group-mind") which is the internalization of the concept of group. A third argument in effect reconstructable from Sellars (1974), pp. 41-42, is the familiar point that in the context of failure to act on the welfare of one's community (as opposed to one's personal happiness) the notion of **akrasia** involves a **conflict** between we-intention and "I-intention" (personal intention) and that therefore we need a concept of we-intention which is irreducible to I-intentions.

A fourth, and very general argument by Sellars (1963), p. 205, is that having the notion of we-intention, with 'we' referring to the class of rational human beings, indeed amounts to having moral discourse and hence, more broadly, normative discourse (recall here our problem about the content of normative and prescriptive discourse). To comment on this, let us point out some distinctions Sellars makes. First, in a group there are **we-intentions**, viz. intendings in the mode 'We shall do - ', or briefly 'Shall$_w$ - '. Secondly, there are **shared intentions** in a group (community). Thirdly, we have the presence of **moral discourse** within a group. Sellars suggests that we-intentions and moral discourse go together - to the extent that they are two aspects of one and the same phenomenon, at least when the group in question is the community of all rational beings. But shared intentions are not necessary for we-intentions or moral discourse. If Sellars is right, the achievement of shared intentions by a group is a task set by intending in the we-mode, it is not an antecedent condition of such we-intendings. Below, in Chapter 5, when speaking of actually occurring social actions, we shall, however, assume that all the relevant we-intendings **are** present.

Given Sellars' account and a proper understanding of 'we' as the class of rational human beings, we may also say, loosely, that what one ought to do pragmatically conceived amounts to what we will insist upon and what one may do to what we will allow. This broad argument has the expected technical counterpart in Sellars' system so that we-intentions come in an appropriate sense to co-vary necessarily with oughts.[4]) Connecting we-intentions with moral discourse in this strict Sellarsian sense makes we-intentions impartial (or generalizable) in something like the Kantian sense.

There is a weakness in Sellars' conceptual system in that he characterizes we-intendings in terms of moral discourse and moral discourse in terms of we-intendings, thus moving in a circle. It seems to me that there is no good philosophical solution to this problem. A partial break out of the circle may be obtained by giving suitable naturalistic-evolutionary "underpinnings" for the concept of we-intending. It may proceed along similar lines as Sellars' naturalist account of attitudes (cf.

Sellars (1974), pp. 93-117 and 122-127 and Tuomela (1977), pp. 58-64).

A fifth argument for the postulation of we-intentions which may be considered here is that to have a notion of a rational agent acting for reasons we need a "non-vacuous I", a notion of self which contrasts with and is not characterizable without the concept of we-ness (cf. Sellars (1968), pp. 223-226, and Rosenberg (1980a)). "I" in this sense is concerned with 'one of us' and thus with what it is to be a member of **our** community. The need for this kind of non-vacuous "I" can also be seen from the plausibility of certain types of practical inference. Thus if we as a group (viz. jointly) do something, and I perform my part of this joint action, then we may want to make the concept pair "I"-"we" satisfy the following simple and idealized schema which is supposed to represent my practical reasoning, where (i) is meant to be an expression of a we-intention by me and (ii) to be an expression of a belief of mine:

(**W1**)   (i)   We will do X.
       (ii)   I am one of us.
       (iii) I will do X.

In (**W1**) we may also use, without loss of its soundness, the following more generally applicable conclusion:

       (iii') I will do whatever I regard as necessary for me to do for our doing X.

For instance, if we will (jointly) sing then I will sing. There is no essential difference between (iii) and (iii') as long as the (presystematically conceived, individualistically Rylean) social action X consists of all the members' doing the same action X. Here X at least typically represents a joint action, something we will do "as a group". In some cases, e.g., when the two of us will move a heavy piano or sing a duet, I cannot perhaps properly say I will do it. Then I may use (iii') or X_i, if that is the action I believe (iii') amounts to, or I may accept (iii) with the reading 'I will do (my part of) X'. Given (**W1**), I do what I do at least in part **because** we will do X and I am one of us. Note that schema (**W1**) is idealized as it omits reference to circumstances and to the (possible) conditions of the intentions, but that is not so central here (but see schema (**WI**) below).

Not only does the we-concept figure in simple reasonings of the above kind but also in more complex ones. Thus we may consider the following practical inference schema, containing intention and belief expressions, to represent my reasoning. Here my being one of us serves as a partial, other-regarding reason for my doing one or more other actions, such as Y below, less directly connected to our jointly doing X:

(W2)   (i)   We will do X.
       (ii)   A is one of us.
       (iii) I intend (to bring about) that A will do whatever I regard as necessary for him to do for our doing X.
       (iv) I will do whatever I regard as necessary to bring about that A does whatever I regard as necessary for him to do in order for us to do X.
       (v)   My doing Y (e.g., teaching A to do something) is such a thing.
       (vi) I will do Y.

I shall not here elaborate the schemas (W1) and (W2). Their role in the present context is to indicate that one may regard the concept of we-intention as a functionally introduced notion, which inference schemas such as (W1) and (W2) partially characterize. We may even bring this closer to our postulational method of concept formation and our (CI). For we may translate these schemas into postulates. Consider thus the simpler (W1). Corresponding to it we may, for instance, describe an agent's reasoning directly in terms of (i)-(iii) of (W1) or we may (not completely unproblematically) employ an indirect (and simplified) third-person translation such as the following:

(P)   (A)(G)(X) (If an agent A we-intends, or "group G-intends", to do X and thinks he is one of us, viz. a member of group G, then he intends to do whatever he regards as necessary for our (the group G's) doing X.)

Whether or not our above discussion has fully conceived the reader of the necessity of at least some kind of we-discourse (at least we-intention), we shall take that need to be established (for further arguments see Chapter 5). What remains is to lay out the possibilities that we have for an exact characterization of the concept of we-intention.

First, we may follow Sellars and regard the concept of we-intention as an individualistically irreducible primitive concept which, furthermore, conceptually serves to give us normative discourse. If we opt for this alternative, then in our (S1) and (S2) of Section II we may substitute for 'normative discourse' the phrase 'we-discourse' (meaning we-intention talk primarily). But we must also at the same time say, in so far as the notion of we-attitude does not belong to λ_i or even $\lambda_i \cup \mu_p$, that λ_i (together with (**CI**) and (**CF**)) does not create a sufficient descriptive (or factual) basis for social science.

Secondly, we may accept the concept of we-intention as a primitive concept and accept a Sellarsian analysis of normative discourse in terms of it but introduce we-intentions only functionally in terms of (**CI**). Then, contrary to the first alternative and to Sellars' view, λ_i and (**CI**) serve as a sufficient descriptive (or factual) basis for Socialese and Socialese*.

Thirdly, we may disregard Sellars' arguments (cf. especially the fourth and fifth) against the reducibility of we-intentions and change the preceding alternatives by claiming that the concept of we-intention is **explicitly definable** essentially in terms of I-intentions and I-beliefs (viz. in terms of predicates in $\lambda_i \cup \mu_p$). Let us thus consider a presystematically conceived, individualistically Rylean social action X (e.g., moving a table, playing soccer, conserving energy) which can be performed (jointly) by all the members of a collective (e.g., a group) performing it. Without elaborating fine points, the definition can be given as follows for simple intentions, for i=1,...,m:

(**WI**) A member A_i of a collective G **we-intends** to do X if and only if
 (i) A_i intends to do X (or his part of X), given that (he believes that) every (full-fledged and adequately informed) member of G or at least that a sufficient number of them, as required for the performance of X, will (or at least probably will) do X (or his part of X).
 (ii) A_i believes that every (full-fledged and adequately informed) member of G or at least that a sufficient number of them, as required for the performance of X, will (or at least probably will) do X (or his part of X).
 (iii) there is a mutual belief in G to the effect that (i) and (ii).

A central point about (**WI**) is that the social character of A_i's intending of clause (i) is expressed by making it conditional on the other agents' actions. He will not and cannot alone embark on doing a possibly complex social action X (or even his part or component, or the like, of X), we may say. The weakened alternative condition in (i) and (ii) claims that it is motivationally sufficient for A_i to intend to do his part of X if he believes that sufficiently many will do (or probably will do) their parts (cf. A_i's belief that four members out of five will carry a piano where he regards four carriers as sufficient).[5] In the case of small groups beliefs of this kind would presumably be **de re** while in the case of large groups (cf. mass action) they can be **de dicto**.

Another central idea contained in (**WI**) is one of intention-justification. For it can be shown to "logically" follow from (i)-(iii) that A_i intends to do (his part of) X unconditionally and (in part) **because** he believes that everyone in G, i.e., each of us or at least a sufficient number of us, will (or probably will) do (his part of) X. (The exact nature of this justification is made clear by our Figure 7.2 of Chapter 7, essentially putting '(his part of) X' for 'X_1' and 'Y_1' in that schema, with 'A_1 intends to do (his part of) X' as its conclusion. We refer the interested reader to that context.) The notion of mutual belief in clause (iii) serves to make we-intentions intersubjective in a strong sense going much beyond (ii). This concept of mutual belief will be defined in Chapter 7. Without discussing more details here let me just emphasize that the definiens of (**WI**) not only entails that A_i intends to do (his part of) X (and that this is mutually believed) but also that he intends to do (his part of) X at least partly **because** he believes that everyone in G at least probably will do (his part of) X; and the definiens of (**WI**) can accordingly be taken to satisfy the schema (**W1**) when distributively interpreted and when using the conclusion 'I will do (my part) of X' and 'we' referring to the members of G. Note that a complex we-intention, e.g., a we-intention to do X by doing Y, can be defined analogously (although one must carefully specify what Y can be).

(**WI**) is assumed to concern a we-intention to perform a social action X. As we shall see later (especially in Chapter 5), a social action type X can, relative to a context, technically be analyzed as a conjunction $X_1 \& ... \& X_m$, where X_i represents agent A_i's "part" of the social action X. (How X comes to be identical with $X_1 \& ... \& X_m$ may in some cases be due to the constitutive meaning postulates, or the like, of the language $L(\lambda_i \cup n_s)$ or it may be due to, e.g., highly contextual features. Analogous remarks apply to the problem of how A_i will be assigned just X_i.) The definiens of (**WI**) entails that each member of G intends to do either X or his part of X. If, for instance, X is playing tennis or conserving energy then the X_is coincide and we may use the same verbal phrase, e.g., 'conserving energy' in our example, both for X and its parts, the X_is. In this sense each member of G may be said to both we-intend and I-intend to do X. If, on the other hand, X is, say, an irreducible multi-agent action (such as getting married) so that each agent A_i is assigned a component action X_i, perhaps even so that $X_i \neq X_j$ for some j, then it seems more problematic to say that an agent intends to do X, as no agent A_i alone can do X (cf. our discussion of intentions in Chapter 4). Therefore (WI) allows the possibility that A_i intends to do his part of X rather than X itself, the part-whole relation here being exactly that which our generational account in Chapters 5 and 6 characterizes. Note that it is not required yet that A_i be required to know a more specific description or name of his part of X, although he must have a correct belief concerning what that part is. (As to the notion of collective used in (WI) we assume that a suitable individualistic analysis of it can be given; see our remarks in Section IV of Chapter 8.)

Given (WI), other requirements on we-intentions may possibly be imposed. Indeed, we shall below normally take inferences such as elucidated by the schema (W2) to be satisfied by any we-intention. Note, however, that the definiens of (WI) may occasionally be regarded as satisfied even if (W2) is not. To take a specific example, consider the ten kilometer track race in the Moscow Olympics. The definiens of (WI) may be regarded as true for every participant runner, assuming their I-intention is to run the distance successfully (or, perhaps, to win). Yet (W2) fails to be true in the case of many runners' we-intentions (but is true for the Ethiopian team, if it is taken as G). (As claimed, when suitably interpreted (W1) may be regarded as satisfied whenever the definiens of (WI) is.)

I am inclined to accept either the second or the third of the above alternatives as viable and have settled for the third one (and normally require (W1) and (W2) to hold of the definiens of (WI), too). It does not matter much for the purposes of this book which of these alternatives is chosen provided that in the second alternative we require the definiens of the we-intention in the third alternative to hold true of it.

Why is it justified to accept a reductionist analysis such as the second or the third of the above alternatives? Let us reconsider Sellars' arguments for the introduction of we-intentions. The first point about intersubjectivity poses no problem as we may technically continue to use we-intentions even if we would be able to give an explicit definition for them. Thus no logical problem of intersubjectivity arises. Furthermore, no philosophical problem of intersubjectivity need arise either, as the notion of mutual belief in the definiens accounts for intersubjectivity (cf. Chapter 7). Sellars' second argument concerning the internalization of the concept of group also seems to be accounted for by the requirement of mutual belief, for the mutual belief in question just involves the concept of group (or collective).

Sellars' third argument concerning **akrasia** can be handled, too. For whether or not we-intentions are individualistically definable we may here speak of two modes of intending (applicable to an individual): (i) self-regarding intending (viz., **mere** I-intending or personal intending as normally understood, not required to satisfy, e.g., schema (**W2**) and (ii) other-regarding intending (viz. intending satisfying, e.g., schema (**W2**) and opposed to mere selfish intending). This distinction between self-regarding and other-regarding intentions is vague, perhaps, but I will assume there are genuine other-regarding intentions as distinguished from self-regarding ones. (Consider, for instance, a person's other-regarding intention to save another, unknown person's life at the risk of his own life; also see Subsection 4 below.) The distinction in question can be used to handle the akrasia in question just as well as Sellars' distinction between we-intentions and I-intentions. In other words, we only need to employ suitable other-regarding intentions (and may even call them we-intentions) and do this quite independently of whether an individualistic definition of them can be given. This answer also covers the fifth argument about the need for a concept of "non-vacuous I".

Sellars' fourth argument connects we-intentions with moral discourse. I cannot see that it crucially matters here whether we use an irreducible we-intention concept or a concept defined individualistically in terms of I-intendings and mutual belief. But Sellars' point that we-intentions do not presuppose shared intentions may seem to contradict our reductionistic analyses (viz. the second and third alternatives). If so, Sellars' fourth argument is incompatible with our proposed individualistic analyses.

But in fact our reductionistic analysis does not entail shared intentions in the sense opposed by Sellars. For what we have said in our analysis only entails that if a person M in G we-intends to do X then he also I-intends to do X or his part of X. Two things must be emphasized here. First, M's we-intending does not entail that any other member of G I-intends, for the mutual belief in our definiens need not be true. Secondly, we have not in our reductionistic analysis claimed that a group's (viz. our) we-intending to do X entails that its every member we-intends to do X. But that is what Sellars basically opposes in his fourth argument. We do basically accept Sellars' view, even if we later in the context of certain central types of social action, perhaps in a somewhat idealized manner, do require shared we-intendings. There we assume that the group has properly internalized its task, and that entails that every member comes to we-intend to do X. As to the connection of our analysis with normative discourse, we shall not assume that it has to be made in Sellarsian way (cf. Note 4), and, especially, we will keep our notion of we-intending neutral with respect to any specific ethical position (cf. Subsection 4 below). In general, with the above qualifications, our reductionistic analysis of we-intentions can be taken to come close to complying also with Sellars' fourth argument.[6]

We may now sum up what we are going to require of the concept of we-intention used in this book. First, it is individualistically characterizable in the sense of the third discussed alternative (viz. the one satisfying (**WI**)). In addition, it is normally (but not invariably) in a broad sense an other-regarding intention, satisfying the schemas (**W1**) and (**W2**); see our comments in Subsection 4, too. While we-intentions in our sense may be assumed to be easily connectable with moral discourse they are yet to be regarded as noncommittal and neutral with respect to any particular ethical doctrine. Accordingly, we shall not even require we-intentions to be impartial in the ethical sense.

2. Our notion of we-intention may still be profitably illustrated and elucidated by reference to two related problem areas. First, we may ask whether it in any interesting sense resembles the notion of social welfare function as discussed within the rationalistic framework of modern welfare economics. Secondly, we may ask what kind of social motives (wants, desires) may generate or lead to or be presupposed by we-intentions. We shall consider both of these problem areas. This subsection is devoted to a digression into welfare economics.

The first interesting connection to be made is to the attempt to build a social welfare function from individual utility functions. Let us thus assume that we are dealing with a collective consisting of m agents $A_1,...,A_m$. We have above discussed the possibility of ascribing to such agents both personal attitudes (e.g., I-intentions and I-beliefs) and we-attitudes (e.g., we-intentions and we-beliefs). We have also noted that the relation between I-intentions and we-intentions is problematic as we-intentions may be supposed to be based (in part) on other-regarding attitudes in a broad sense while I-intentions (personal intentions) may well be, and often are, purely self-regarding. In the context of welfare economics we will speak of personal preferences and desires (rather than I-intentions), and they will be assumed to be (primarily) self-regarding.

While I-intention and we-intention are (logically) qualitative concepts, viz. concepts on a nominal scale in measurement-theoretic terminology, we may also discuss their comparative (ordinal) and metric counterparts. In doing this we in fact enter welfare economics. There one of the central problems is how to create a social utility function (viz. ordinal or metric we-want) out of (respectively, ordinal or metric) individual utility functions (viz. personal wants). Disregarding the difference between wants and intentions, we are basically dealing with the same conceptual problem on three levels or scales (nominal, ordinal, and interval) of measurement. We shall now briefly sketch a Bayesian way of handling the problem. It is the account by Harsanyi (1977), (1979).

We start by considering our agents' preferences over situations (or issues). The following two postulates, employing the terminology of utility theory, are then imposed. (1) The (non-strict) preferences ($\geq_i$) of agent A_i, $i=1,...,m$, establish a complete preordering over the space of all possible situations, viz. points in an m-dimensional Euclidean space (Postulate of complete preordering). (2) Suppose that some sequence $s_1, s_2,...,$ of situations converges to a given situation s_0, and that another sequence $r_1, r_2,...,$ of situations converges to r_0, with $s_k \geq_i r_k$ for $k=1,2,...$. Then, $s_0 \geq_i r_0$ (Postulate of continuity). It is known from utility theory that (1) and (2) entail this for cases under certainty: If an individual's preferences satisfy the two basic utility postulates then this behavior will be equivalent to maximizing a well-defined (ordinal or metric) utility function, say u_i.

To characterize rational behavior under risk and uncertainty, we need two further rationality postulates. To avoid the introduction of unnecessary conceptual machinery I shall state these postulates only informally, relying on the reader's familiarity with the concept of **prospect** or **lottery**. Briefly speaking, a prospect L is a set-up specifying that a "prize" (situation) s_k is obtained if a certain event e_k occurs, where $k=1,...,n$ and the events e_k are mutually exclusive. Only the occurrence probabilities (p_k) of these events are available in the case of risky prospects. We postulate: (3) A rational individual will be indifferent between two risky prospects yielding him the same prizes with the same probabilities, even if the two prospects use quite different physical processes to generate these probabilities (Postulate of probabilistic equivalence). (4) Other things being equal, a rational individual will not prefer a prospect yielding less desirable prizes over a prospect yielding more desirable prizes (Sure-thing postulate).

Postulates (1)-(4) may be called **Bayesian rationality postulates**. When considering ideal rational agents, they seem plausible (however, at least (3) and (4) are problematic, cf. Tversky (1975), Sen (1977)). (We shall later criticize the idealized nature of these principles.) They entail the so-called expected utility maximization theorem. That is, given (1)-(4), we have the result that there exists a metric utility function

(EU) $\quad u_i(L) = \sum_{k=1}^{n} p_k u_i(s_k)$,

where L is a lottery, s_k a situation, and p_k the probability of event e_k, k=1,...,n, and this is the quantity that the agent A_i will maximize by his actions. If L is a risky lottery then p_k is usually regarded as an objective probability; if L again is an uncertain prospect then p_k may be regarded as a subjective probability. The expected-utility property (EU) is characteristic of the so-called von Neumann-Morgenstern utilities.

The metric utility u_i (which is defined on an interval scale) may now be called agent A_i's personal utility function and the preferences it is based on his personal or I-preferences. These preferences are different from moral preferences, it may be argued, and these are the preferences that welfare theory is concerned with. For moral preferences, contrary to personal ones, are impersonal and impartial in that they embody some kind of generalizability and intersubjectivity idea (cf. Harsanyi (1977)). Roughly, a person's moral preferences and preference judgments should not depend on his idiosyncratic personal features nor on his social position. Given this, the problem arises how to characterize a person's moral (or social welfare) utility function.

Harsanyi's (1977), (1979) solution is as follows. Consider an agent A_j who is an actual or potential member of our collective of agents. Let us assume, for simplicity, that A_j is one of the m actual members of the collective. Harsanyi now proposes the following postulates:

(A) The personal preferences of all the m agents satisfy the four Bayesian postulates (1)-(4) (Postulate of individual rationality).

(B) The moral preferences of agent A_j satisfy the four Bayesian rationality postulates (Postulate of rationality of moral preferences).

(C) Suppose that at least one of the m agents personally prefers a social situation s over another social situation r, and that none of the other agents prefer r over s. Then, agent A_j will morally prefer s over r (Pareto optimality postulate).

Postulates (A) and (B) are rather obvious, (C) may seem less so. But let us here accept all these principles at least for the sake of our argument. The interesting thing about them is that they imply the linearity of the social welfare function as will be seen below (cf., e.g., Harsanyi (1979), p. 294).

Speaking in exact terms, (A), (B), and (C) entail that the social welfare (or moral) utility function of an agent A_j must be a real-valued function over all social situations s, and it must have the mathematical form

(SW) $\quad w_j(s) = \sum_{i=1}^{m} \alpha_{ij} u_i(s)$, with $\alpha_{ij} > 0$ for $i=1,\ldots,m$.

(SW) does not depend on the possibility of interpersonal utility comparisons. But, on the other hand, if interpersonal utility comparisons are allowed the following postulate can be employed to express this:

(D) If all agents' utility functions $u_1,\ldots,u_m$ are expressed in equal utility units, as judged by agent A_j on the basis of interpersonal utility comparisons, then the social welfare function w_j of agent A_j must assign the same weight to all these utility functions.

Postulate (D) entails that $\alpha_{1j} = \ldots = \alpha_{nj}$, for all $j=1,\ldots,m$. By making these constants equal $1/m$ (by rescaling) we have

(SW*) $\quad w_j(s) = 1/m \sum_{i=1}^{m} u_i(s)$.

What (SW*) says is that the social welfare utility w_j is simply the **arithmetic mean** taken over all the m agents' personal utilities. Obviously $w_1(s) = w_2(s) = \ldots = w_m(s)$. Thus we have explicitly defined social welfare utilities in terms of personal utilities.

There is also another way of arriving at (SW*). Suppose that the agents A_j have to make their moral judgments without knowing their own social position, so that each agent has an equal probability of being anyone (or, a it were, of being put into anyone's shoes); cf. Rawls' (1971) notion of "the veil of ignorance". But, an agent's choice over alternative social situations would be a choice among m alternative risky lotteries, all the probabilities being 1/m. Then (**EU**) gives (**SW***).

After this presentation of Harsanyi's account we are ready to ask whether the social utility function w (= w_1 = ... = w_m) can indeed be regarded as some kind of metric counterpart of the agents' we-intentions or, more broadly, we-wants in the context of social welfare. w indeed shares some features with intentions. For instance, it is (even) analytically true that rational moral agents satisfying (**A**)-(**D**) act so as to maximize their expected w-values. In this sense w-utilities are stronger than wants and resemble intentions. But I shall not here try to investigate in detail how close w-utilities come to intentions and what additional requirements the (maximal expected) w-utilities must satisfy to become completely analogous to we-intentions (but cf. Chapter 12).

Let us again consider Sellars' arguments for the introduction of we-intentions. His first argument concerns the intersubjective nature of such we-intentions. The counterpart to this in the metric case is interpersonal utility comparison. w_i-utilities become intersubjective simply by postulation, viz. by imposing requirement (**D**). Sellars' second argument compares we-intentions to we-consciousness, a special form of consciousness concerned with the internalization of the concept of the group. To the extent that this is a clear idea at all, I think w-utilities closely resemble we-intentions on this point, as (**SW**) and (**SW***) make them depend on the community or group $\{A_1,...,A_m\}$.

Sellars' third point is concerned with the conflict between we-intentions and I-intentions in cases of **akrasia**. This conflict is essentially the same as that between w-utilities and u-utilities, viz. moral and personal utilities. The fourth argument for we-intentions proposed by Sellars has to do with the conceptual connection between (Sellarsian) we-intentions and normative discourse (cf. Note 4). This is a central point in Sellars' ethics (but recall that our notion of we-intention does not require quite this much). But even here there is a close correspondence. For, given the postulates (**A**)-(**D**), acting morally entails maximizing expected w-utility. In other words, when acting morally (viz. on w-utilities) agents ought to maximize expected w-utilities. To be sure, this is a tautology relative to (**A**)-(**D**), for w-utilities indeed are just by definition those utilities an agent maximizes when acting on a moral norm. But at least formally the situation is quite parallel to the Sellarsian case.

As to the fourth point, Sellars does not require that there be shared group-intentions whenever there are we-intentions: "Yet the actual existence of shared universal intentions is no more an antecedent condition of participating in moral discourse than actual agreement on matters of fact is an antecedent condition of participating in factual discourse. In each case the forms of discourse set this agreement as a **task**" (Sellars (1963), p. 205). But here we can see a parallel in that full rationality (in the above Bayesian sense) can be regarded as a similar "task" for agents. To the extent agents fall short of full rationality shared w-utilities need not exist.

Sellars' fifth point is that the full notion of rational agent requires we-intentions. As in the case of the third point w-utilities tautologically satisfy this requirement if we define a rational agent in part by reference to the postulates (**A**)-(**D**).

In all, we have argued for a far reaching parallel between both Sellarsian (and also our individualistic we-intentions, especially when they satisfy (**W2**)) and Bayesian w-utilities in the context of social welfare. How is it possible, then, that w-utilities are explicitly definable in terms of personal utilities while Sellarsian we-intentions are not? One answer to this is that it is important to remember that (**SW***) follows only from the strong postulates (**A**)-(**D**). Thus while indeed the concept of w-utility (moral utility) is explicitly definable by means of the concept of personal utility it is so only relative to (**A**)-(**D**) and relative to the personal utilities of all the members of a community. Perhaps Sellars would still think that this is not enough. Thus he might want to claim that some additional features are needed to distinguish between we-intentions (or moral utilities) and I-intentions (or personal utilities). But then it is up to him to provide for some new arguments to that effect. What he has given us so far does not get him where he wants. But in any case, the parallel between explicitly defined w-utilities and our above individualistic notion of we-intention defined (or, when imposing (**W2**), partially defined) by (**WI**) is strong.

The above digression into welfare economics may be taken to show at least that our principle (**CI**) seems adequate as far as we-concepts are concerned. Indeed, the above considerations suggest even that we-concepts can be constructed out of I-concepts by means of explicit definitions, especially in the case of fully rational decision making and action. We have above considered only the concept of we-intention, which is one of our key concepts and also probably the most problematic we-concept. Notice that there seem to be no serious problems in giving explicit definitions for we-beliefs in terms of I-beliefs. We-beliefs are just I-beliefs together with the mutual belief concerning everybody else's I-believing, analogously with our schema (**WI**) for defining we-intentions.

3. When sketching a method for constructing cardinal utilities out of preferences in the previous subsection we pointed out that several idealizations were involved. Let us now briefly consider them, for this will turn out to be useful for our developments below.

For decision making under certainty we first used the Postulate of complete preordering, involving the connectedness and transitivity of an agent's preferences. But as is well known from psychological literature, not all preferences can be meaningfully compared and connected. It is also known that an agent's preferences are not always transitive. We may have transitivity only given a certain stable and coherent background of relevant wants and beliefs (cf. Davidson (1974) on this). Secondly, we used the Postulate of continuity. This postulate deals with infinitesimally small changes in preferences and with limit preferences. It is clearly quite possible that people's preferences are not orderly in this highly idealized sense.

The third and fourth postulates, viz. the probabilistic equivalence postulate and the sure-thing postulate, may also be regarded as idealized. Whether or not they hold true depends on what is assumed as the background. They are not unqualifiedly true of ordinary human beings. Without arguing in a detailed way against these postulates here let me just say the following. The idealizing and rationalizing background assumptions needed in the case of all (or most) of the mentioned four postulates involve the assumption that the agents have suitable wants and beliefs which, furthermore, do not change in the situation in question. The agents must also be assumed to have a perfect (or nearly perfect) memory; they must be free from emotional disturbances; they must not be too tired; they must be able to make up their minds in cases where changes may be infinitesimally small, and so on and so forth.

On the whole, then, preferences can be represented by metric utilities only by assuming the presence of certain stable wants and beliefs, and this seems to make the procedure conceptually circular if utilities are regarded as quantified wants or something closely related (see Chapter 12). Given that the above postulates concerning preferences are highly rationalistic, then the expected utility theorem (**EU**) may well also fail to hold in those real life cases where the underlying rationalistic postulates fail to hold. This fact of the non-occurrence of maximization behavior accords with common sense, too. Wants and beliefs may be regarded as conceptually connected to action and even to the "best" action, but that connection turns out to be a rather complex one when spelled out in detail. (See our discussion in Chapter 12 below and, e.g., the "want theory" in Tuomela (1977), pp. 75-80, for this complexity.) The connection specified by ordinary utility theory accordingly is too idealized and too simple-minded from a psychological point of view.

What I am driving at is not really the abandonment of the notion of metric utility - for it is useful idealization.[7] Rather I am hinting at the possibility of defining such utilities in a less rationalistic and idealized way as want intensities (or strengths or wants). I shall not here make any attempt to really carry this out. But I will assume that it can be done and done **without** straightforward analytic entailment of the maximization of personal (or other) utilities (see Chapter 12 for a further discussion). Thus below we shall think of utilities as **strengths of wants** and accept that a stronger want tends to yield action to a greater extent than a weaker want does, ceteris paribus. Yet I will assume that no simple-minded utility maximization principle need by analytically true. Only the kind of maximization idea which involves intention formation can be taken to be straightforwardly connected with action (cf. our (SA_i) of Chapter 7 and see Chapter 12, too). This view is based on the assumption that it is analytically true that if an agent intends to do something X then, ceteris paribus, he (in a general sense) wants to do X, and this want is the maximal or strongest of his wants at that moment (see Chapter 4, esp. Note 3, and Section III of Chapter 12 on intentions).

Given the above view of utilities we can construct a kind of motivational basis of we-intentions in terms of the underlying utilities. Our starting point is the fact that our above connection of we-intentions with the social welfare situation is one-sided in two central respects. First, we-intentions can of course exist in many other contexts which are quite unrelated to the social welfare case. Secondly, in our above connection of we-intentions with w-utilities some interesting aspects were accordingly left out. In particular, that connection does not sufficiently emphasize the difference between utilities which **depend on what others do and on what they get as their payoffs from what they do,** and utilities which do not so depend on the social context. Thus while w-utilities indeed take into account other agents' utilities they do not really concern the strategic and interactive dependencies of utilities on other agents' actions.

Let us thus broaden the scope of our discussion and discuss we-intentions in terms of the underlying social utilities quite generally. I will below employ a set-up similar to those used by some social scientists. My basic framework below is, accordingly, related to that employed by MacCrimmon and Messick (1976) and by Griesinger and Livingston (1973), although these authors' discussion does not specifically concern we-intentions.

To simplify our presentation, we consider a case where only two interacting agents are present. They have the same mutual beliefs about the situation and especially about the joint utilities. Let me thus assume that such joint utilities or payoffs have somehow been defined - and defined without committing the agents to simple maximization of their own personal utilities. More will be said about the interpretation of utilities later but this will suffice here.

Considering the two-person case with the two agents A and B we then assume that their personal utility functions u^A and u^B are given. For convenience, we make the assumption that the utility values range over a continuum of real numbers $-\infty \leq u^A, u^B \leq \infty$. We will now be interested in how the joint utilities or social utilities related to the individual (or personal) utilities. Let us call the social utility function u^{AB} in the case of the two agents A and B. Accepting our individualistic definition of we-intentions and accepting that we-intentions are related to underlying we-wants (or we-pro-attitudes) as u^{AB} represents them, it is plausible to think that u^{AB} be definable in terms of u^A and u^B (perhaps relative to suitable underlying mutual beliefs which we abstract from here).

Let us accordingly assume that there is some function f such that $u^{AB} = f(u^A, u^B)$. Here u^{AB} may be regarded as a kind of motivational background for the formation of a (metric) we-intention. We shall later ask whether there are social utility functions which cannot stand as such motivational background. Our present main problem is, however, what can be said of the function f and, especially, how it relates the agents' A and B utilities and motivations concerning each other.

Let us start by considering the simple suggestion that the function f is a **linear** function. In general f does not seem to be linear but in some local contexts, at least, it can be reasonably well approximated by a linear function (see Section I of Chapter 12). Furthermore, even if the linearity assumption is an idealization, it is conceptually illuminating to operate as if it were true. Accordingly, we propose that for some constants a and b

(1) $u^{AB} = au^A + bu^B$.

While it seems that (1) is not an analytic truth about social utilities but an empirically testable hypothesis (which also has been tested), it nevertheless interestingly displays some analytic features of our conceptual system. For it can be related to some intuitively basic human motives. To be more specific, it can be shown to relate to the general motives of **self-interest, self-sacrifice, altruism, aggression** (or harm), **cooperation,** and **competition.**[8] More specifically, these basic social motives can be given an interesting **partial** analysis in terms of (**1**). As a result we get specific social utility functions which motivate social action termed competitive, cooperative, aggressive, and so on.

To go to the details, we shall deal only with pure cases of the above motives. Let us first look at the matter graphically. We consider a two-dimensional Euclidean space and consider some arbitrarily selected reference point, say P, representing the utility $\langle u^A(X), u^B(Y) \rangle$ that A gets for doing something X and B for doing Y. Now we assume that the horizontal axis represents A's utilities and the vertical axis B's utilities. Consider now P and the action motivation or tendency of the social collective consisting of the agents A and B to choose some other (joint) action. In this situation we can classify the options, in terms of our linear model, as is shown in Figure 2.1. If, for instance, A and B move from P up to some point in the upper section between the vertical self-interest line and the equality line, with $u_A = u_B$, that may be due to several motives. First, A

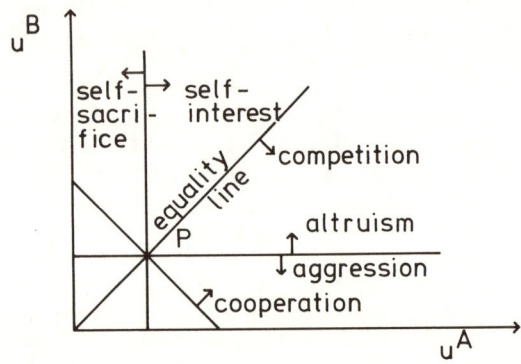

Fig. 2.1.

and B may both be acting out of self-interest: both act so as to thereby increase their individual utilities. They may also, or alternatively, be acting on a cooperative motive and trying to maximize the sum of their individual payoffs. Or they may be acting competitively, with B having the lead, where competition means trying to increase the difference between one's own and another's payoff. I have indicated the mentioned motives in Fig.

2.1 from A's point of view. B's motives could of course be written out symmetrically. As to the unexplained motives, self-sacrifice entails trying to decrease one's own payoff and aggression (harm doing) entails trying to decrease the other's payoff.

These motives can be illustrated in terms of our linear model (1) by giving the parameters a and b the special values -1, 0, and 1. We get 9 logically possible combinations, out of which the empty case with a=0, b=0 is excluded below:

(2) (i)   A's self-interest (B's altruism):
          $u^{AB} = u^A$ (a=1, b=0)
    (ii) A's self-sacrifice (B's aggression):
          $u^{AB} = -u^A$ (a=-1, b=0)
    (iii) A's altruism (B's self-interest):
          $u^{AB} = u^B$ (a=0, b=1)
    (iv) A's aggression (B's self-sacrifice):
          $u^{AB} = -u^B$ (a=0, b=-1)
    (v)   cooperation:
          $u^{AB} = u^A + u^B$ (a=1, b=1)
    (vi) competition (A's point of view):
          $u^{AB} = u^A - u^B$ (a=1, b=-1)
    (vii) competition (B's point of view):
          $u^{AB} = u^B - u^A$ (a=-1, b=1)
    (viii) destruction (mutual aggression):
          $u^{AB} = -u^A - u^B$ (a=-1, b=-1).

Let us start my comments by emphasizing that the concepts of (2) are illustrated in terms of "pure" cases. Thus pure self-interest, for instance, entails one's trying to get everything ("the whole cake") for oneself: $u^{AB} = u^A$ in the case of A. In less pure cases there will be a mixture of motives out of which one (in our example self-interest) will dominate. (2) cannot be regarded as a conceptually adequate definition of self-interest nor of the other motive concepts elucidated. It only gives an idealized **extensional** characterization of them. But that will do for our present purposes.

As (2) is based on the linear model (1) the motives of A and B are interlocked in a complementary way. Thus A cannot be fully self-interested unless B is fully altruistic in the social group or collective formed by A and B. Similarly, self-sacrifice and aggression are interlocked and complementary. In the less pure cases we have linear mixtures of motives. For instance, the mixture $3/4 u^A + 1/4 u^B$ may result from A's relatively strong self-interest and B's less strong self-interest. (In the case of dividing a given social utility we assume that a+b=1.) But it may equally well be a result of the operation of other motives, e.g., A's and B's weighed cooperation. In general, a given social utility value can come about in a number of different ways, viz. due to the operation of different motives. This illustrates the extensional character of (2). Essentially the same phenomenon can be seen from Figure 2.1. Consider an arbitrary point $<u_0^A, u_0^B>$ in A's and B's utility space. Given (1), a continuum of widely varying social utility values corresponds to any such point where we let the parameters a and b vary continuously through their value spaces. Conversely, corresponding to any value u_0^{AB} there is a continuum of pairs $<u_0^A, u_0^B>$ into which u_0^{AB} can be decomposed, given (1).

Let us take still a further close look at our Figure 2.1. We can see that the horizontal line going through the point P is the boundary for A's altruism and aggression while the vertical line through P is the boundary for A's self-sacrifice and self-interest. For B the interpretations are reversed, of course. These two lines determine the extensional interpretations of self-interest, altruism, aggression, and self-sacrifice and hence of (i)-(iv) and (viii) of (2). The line with slope +1 through P, viz. the equality line, is the boundary for competition. On the left side of it, $u^B - u^A$ is positive (cf. (2)(vii)) and on the right side $u^A - u^B$ is positive (cf. (2)(vi)). The line with slope -1 through P is the boundary for cooperation. It is of interest to note that Harsanyi's w-utilities essentially correspond to such lines of cooperation. This can be seen by considering the quantity $1/2(u_A + u_B)$ in the present case. Our (2)(v) divided by the factor 2 amounts to just that.

The mentioned lines partition A's and B's utility space into eight sectors around P in Figure 2.1. All the points in a given sector may be regarded as motivationally equivalent in the sense that if any of the points in a sector is preferred or dispreferred to P then any other point in that sector is, respectively, preferred or dispreferred to P.

The interlocked motives in (2) could of course be defined less coarsely than above and their relationships might be taken to be **non-linear** in the general case. That does not take away the conceptual interest of our present idealized characterization, however, for some related interlocking of these motives will have to obtain between these motives merely on conceptual grounds.

While I will not here discuss in depth other social utility functions besides (1) let me yet mention two well known non-linear functions. Consider thus

(3) $\quad u^{AB} = c \cdot u^A / u^B$ and

(4) $u^{AB} = d \cdot u^A \cdot u^B$,

where c and d are suitable parameters. While (1) is concerned with sums and differences of the individual utilities (3) is concerned with their rations and (4) with their products. (3) may be termed the criterion of **proportionate competition**: try to increase the ratio of A's (= your) payoff to B's (= the other's) payoff. (4) again may be called the criterion of **proportionate cooperation**: try to increase the product of both agents' payoffs.

Note that maximizing (2)(vii) involves maximizing the total size of the cake to be distributed, so to speak, without regard to the sizes of the agents' shares. (4) again is concerned with both the size of the cake and with how it is sliced.

What if the agent's motives vary depending on where their utilities are located in the utility space? Till now we have assumed that the motives are constant through the utility space, and that may seem rather unrealistic. (One reason for the change of utilities is the well known phenomenon of cognitive dissonance.) Let me here mention two conditional motives that have been widely discussed in social philosophy. Let us consider the equality line in our Figure 2.1. Now if A (B) is competitive when above (below) the line but anticompetitive when below (above) the line we are dealing with **egalitarianism**. In general, egalitarianism as a social motive says: try to make your payoff and the other's payoff more equal, viz. minimize $u^A - u^B$.

Another conditional motive that has proved to be important in discussing fairness and justice is the **maximin** criterion: try to make the worse off agent better off. Thus when you are ahead of the other you should be altruistic, but when you are behind you become self-interested. We can say that maximin is composed of self-interest and altruism. Egalitarianism again is composed of competition and anticompetition. Thus there is a clear difference in their underlying basis.

The above considerations can be generalized in various ways. In addition to allowing non-linear social utility functions and to employing simple conditional motives of the above kind we may also consider other modes of combining social motives. Thus our primary motives discussed in the linear case may be combined, e.g., **conjunctively, disjunctively,** or **hierarchically**. Furthermore, such combinations may be conditionalized in various ways. (See the relevant remarks in MacCrimmon and Messick (1976).)

The above motive concepts may also be extended to the general m-person case with m>2. Let me just note here that such extensions are not unambiguous in all cases. Thus, for instance, in the case of altruism a person can be maximally altruistic toward a certain agent (or agents) and unaltruistic toward the others or he can be to some degree altruistic toward all the other agents. An eye must be kept on this and other analogous distinctions in the general m-person case.

4. Let us now return to we-intentions and consider their relationships to social utilities. For simplicity, we concentrate on the two-person case with the agents A and B. Suppose thus that the collective consisting of A and B we-intends to do something X. Let us think, furthermore, that we are dealing with full blown we-intending which entails that both A and B must individually we-intend to do X. Next we assume that both A's and B's we-intendings to do X can be analyzed in terms of their I-intendings to do their parts of X, given that the other does, and their justifying beliefs that the other one intends to do his part of X (recall (**WI**)). Let us now accept that an agent's intending to do his part of X conceptually entails at least that (1) he believes he is capable (or capable to some significant degree) of doing his part of X and that (2) he in some sense wants to do his part of X and, indeed, wants on balance to do his part of X (see Chapters 4 and 12 for further remarks on intending).

Now consider the utility space of Figure 2.1. We may think that it represents the agents' wants (or wants on balance) underlying their intentions. More exactly, the utilities u_A and u_B represent the intensities or strengths of these wants. The question now becomes whether A's and B's we-intending to do something is compatible with all combinations of values of u_A and u_B or whether one or more sectors around P in Figure 2.1 will be excluded on conceptual grounds.

I can see no conceptual barriers preventing A and B from arriving at any point, say $<u_0^A, u_0^B>$ in the utility space of Figure 2.1. Given this, it is **conceptually** possible that both A and B are capable of jointly doing X and of mutually believing so. They also both (in a broad sense) want to do their parts of X and, by implication, X. The strength of the dyad's want is, however, not properly represented by $<u_0^A, u_0^B>$. If the social action X consists of or is generated by A's performing X_1 and B's performing X_2 then u_0^A may be regarded as A's utility from doing X_1 and u_0^B as B's utility from doing X_2. The dyad's utility from A's and B's performing the social action X should not be regarded as the ordered couple $<u_0^A, u_0^B>$ but rather as the social utility u^{AB} where $u^{AB}=f(u^A, u^B)$ for some function f. This social utility u^{AB} (but not $<u_0^A, u_0^B>$) takes into account the interaction between A's and B's action (or, rather, what is believed by A and B of it), we may claim. Thus we should take the group's (dyad's) we-intention to do X to be motivationally based on u^{AB}, in the first place.

We are now led to investigate the social utility functions f. Are there any conceptually impossible ones, relative to the agents' we-intention to do X? In order to be able to answer this question conclusively it might seem that we should know what it is for a group's we-intention to be based on (or generated by) a social utility u^{AB}. But in fact it is not necessary to say more than that if a collective we-intends to do X then this intention must rely for its motivational content on a social utility and, usually, some relevant beliefs concerning the attainment of that utility. This reliance relation is a kind of presupposition: the intention presupposes some social utility (cf. Section III of Chapter 12). But any (consistent) social utility function will do from a purely conceptual point of view, I argue, for none of the conceptually necessary features of intending that we mentioned earlier are violated by this liberality.

It can similarly be said that our individualistically understood notion of we-intention (in the sense of (**WI**)) is a purely "**formal**" notion in the sense of not requiring any specific type of **intrinsic** want-basis. Thus any social motive in (2) will do as its intrinsic basis. For instance, it is even conceptually possible that the members of a collective form a we-intention to harm each other (cf. (2)(viii)). (Compare the present claim, too, with our earlier claim in Section III about the neutrality of the concept of we-intention with respect to any specific ethical position.)

Not only is the concept of we-intention formal (content-independent) but so is in fact our notion of social utility. The utility space of Figure 2.1 was in effect built by assuming that the degree of self-interest (or, at least, personal utility involving self-interest) grows with growing utility value, ceteris paribus. But you may now ask what happens in the case of genuine masochists, for instance. For them low utility values in the sense of the scale of genuine personal interest are in fact high. The answer is that naturally we can, accordingly, build a masochism scale as well, if wanted, and locate all the other social motives on that scale. Figure 2.1 can in fact be built on any **intrinsic** interest, and in this sense it is formal, viz. independent of intrinsic interest. What is central about it is the **pattern of relations** between the various social motives.

It is of course possible to classify we-intentions in the sense of (**WI**) with respect to the social motives they rely on. Thus we may speak of non-aggressive we-intentions which, in terms of (2), cannot be based on aggression. This notion excludes (ii), (iv), and (viii). A still stronger notion of non-aggressive we-intention is obtained by, in addition, excluding competition (vi) and (vii)). This stronger notion, which might be dubbed **proper** we-intention, is based only on one or more of the motives of self-interest, altruism, and cooperation (and, generalizing, on their various combinations), and it can be taken to satisfy our earlier schema (**W2**) (and (**W1**), of course). In the terminology of game theory, we would here exclude zero-sum games - which are based on aggression - and in mixed motive games we would not allow we-intentions to be formed with respect to strategy alternatives that are competitively related (however that exactly is characterized).

We may also make a distinction between the types of motivation in a collective or a group and say that a group is motivationally homogeneous if all its members act on the same type of social motive, e.g., competition, cooperation, duty, etc. On the other hand it is said to be non-homogeneous if its members act on different social motives, perhaps on complementary ones (e.g., self-interest versus altruism; compare (i)-(iv) of (2)).

Various other, and more refined, classifications of social motives and of we-intentions based on them can well be made, but we shall not in the present work really need those further notions, and we can conclude our present investigation here.

CHAPTER 3

THEORIES OF ACTION

I. VIEWS OF HUMAN ACTION

It is a commonplace that human actions can be viewed in a variety of different and even incompatible ways. It is not surprising, therefore, that competing theories of action exist in all fields where the subject of study is human action. In this book our focus will be on **philosophical** accounts of action and especially of social action (viz. multi-agent) action. There are also **factual** theories of action, for instance in psychology and social psychology. For instance, the so-called theories of motivation are such factual theories of action. We shall be less concerned with them in this work. Finally, there are what might be called **normative** theories of action. Here I have in mind not only traditional ethical theories but also and especially (factually interpreted) decision theory and game theory. Although we shall discuss game theory in this work we shall do it not so much because this theory is a normative theory of action as because it serves to clarify the structure of strategically interconnected multi-agent actions. Thus, while game theory is not a philosophical theory of action, our theory to be developed will have important connections with this theory because both theories are concerned with the **structural** aspects of multi-agent actions and with strategic interdependencies between such actions.[1)]

When reviewing the literature on the philosophical accounts of action a surprising fact emerges. It is that all systematic philosophical theories of action are - at least to my knowledge - really theories of **single**-agent action, at least as they have been formulated (Pörn's (1977) account may be regarded as an exception). In this respect, then, the present work can be regarded as the first systematic **philosophical** theory of social, viz. multi-agent, action.

To set the stage, it seems useful and appropriate to start by surveying the major extant philosophical theories of action. In this connection we shall make an attempt to extend these theories to the field of multi-agent actions as well. (I should perhaps apologize in advance to representatives of rival action theories for possibly extending their theories in ways which they do not find acceptable.)

Although I shall not specifically argue for it here, it is plausible to take philosophical and factual (psychological and social) theories of action to deal with roughly the same subject matter - human action and its determination - and to differ from each other mainly in their **specificity**. Philosophical accounts thus, so to speak, operate on a more general level than, say, psychological and social psychological theories of motivation. Yet there is no clear line of demarcation, as it were, to be drawn between the philosophical and the factual accounts. Thus, in my view it is quite wrong to draw a sharp line between conceptual (or philosophical) and empirical (or, better, factual) problems and to say that philosophical theorizing can only deal with the former while the concern of psychological and social psychological theorizing is merely the latter. Rather, we should consider factual theories of motivation to rely conceptually on a certain underlying, general philosophical conception of human action and of its determination and/or interpretation.

Below I shall make an attempt to classify and summarize some central philosophical theories of human action, differentiated primarily on the basis of how they characterize intentional action. All of these basic views have had "a great past" in the history of philosophy. They are also quite prominent in current discussion. From a systematic point of view I will group them into the following three classes: (1) mental cause theory, (2) agency theory, and (3) hermeneutic theory. Below I will interpret these classes broadly so that they will in fact come to cover practically all the prominent philosophical theories of action. (The so-called performative account developed by Austin and others will, however, be left out of our consideration. It is not particularly "alive and well" today, in my view; see, e.g., Shaffer (1968) for devastating criticism.)

Before discussing the central claims of our three types of action theories let me roughly indicate in terms of a preview concerned with the single-agent case what thoughts and thinkers each of them comprises. The mental cause theory analyzes intentional action as bodily movements caused by certain kinds of mental events or states (e.g., wants or volitions). Examples of this account are the views of Davidson (1963), (1973), (1974), Fodor (1968), (1975), Goldman (1970), Alston (1967), (1974), Danto (1973), and Sellars (1968), (1973). Under a broad interpretation of this type of theory also the "nomological" view of Brandt and Kim (1963), Churchland (1970), and Audi (1973) as well as even my so-called purposive-causal theory (Tuomela (1977)) may be listed here.

The majority of psychological (and social psychological)

motivation theories can be regarded as exemplifying the claims of the mental cause theory. Although I cannot in this chapter make an attempt to classify the major theories of motivation with respect to our classification scheme, a few examples will nevertheless illustrate the matter. Thus, of those theorists who are willing to conceptualize behavior intentionalistically as actions (as opposed to, e.g., merely spatiotemporally specified chunks of behavior or "colorless movements"), we may regard, for instance, Freud, Lewin, and Tolman as relying on the mental cause theory. Even such behaviorists and neo-behaviorists as Dollard and Miller, Bandura, and Osgood may be fitted in here, it seems. (For relevant discussions see especially Alston (1974) and also Turner (1971), Sherwood (1969.), Madsen (1961), (1974) and Tuomela (1977).) Also modern information processing psychology can be regarded as compatible with the mental cause theory (see Fodor (1975) and Tuomela (1977)). The same can also be said of the Marxist view of action, it seems. As to sociologists, e.g., Parsons' (1951) account of actions seems also to fit in here, although it is not easy to decide whether he would accept mental causes in the narrow event-sense or only advocate something like the nomological view mentioned above.

According to the agency theory, the cause of the behavior involved in the action (the behavioral component of the action) is simply the agent himself (and in this context no further cause is or, perhaps, can be asked for). R. Taylor (1966) and Chisholm (1966), (1970), (1976) are the foremost modern philosophical representatives of this old view. As to psychology and social psychology, it seems that at least the theory of Heider (1958) and the so-called attribution theory can be regarded as representing agency theory.

What I have above called the hermeneutic theory could also equally well be called the **non-causal** theory or the **Wittgensteinian** theory. According to it, intentional actions are not - and perhaps (logically) cannot be - caused by any mental events or states. Rather, the essential thing about an action is that it somehow consists in or involves some bodily movements by which the agent **intends** or **means** or **aims at** something and/or that the movement, accordingly, is something which is to be conceived in the context of some "meanings", rules, norms or social practices. Action-explanations are explanations in terms of (the agents') reasons, and reason-explanations are **sui generis** (and thus not reducible to, e.g., causal ones).

Of the theories of action prominent during the last few years, von Wright's (1971) important theory very clearly represents this group. The views of Melden (1963), Malcolm (1968), Stoutland (1975), (1976a), (1976b), and Abelson (1976) are also clear representatives. Other recent examples are Dray (1957) and Martin (1977).

C. Taylor's important goal theory (1964), (1970a), (1970b) may perhaps also be included fruitfully in our somewhat heterogeneous category of hermeneutic action theory, broadly conceived. According to the goal theory, what makes a movement an action is that the movement is to be characterized and explained by citing a goal rather than some antecedent (Humean) cause.

So far - and I have not investigated this much - I have not found a clear-cut example of a major psychological motivation theory which could adequately be called hermeneutic in the above sense. To be sure, e.g., Allport's, Maslow's, and Moore's "humanistic" theories are sometimes called hermeneutic (see Madsen (1974)). But it seems that these theories involve dynamic (causal) features excluding them from our class of hermeneutic theories.

Below when discussing the (philosophical) hermeneutic theory we shall mostly rely on von Wright's theory as it is most fully developed among the mentioned accounts. When drawing philosophical conclusions on the basis of it, one must note that, of course, not all of these conclusions need without further qualification apply to all the other mentioned examples of hermeneutic theory.

II. MENTAL CAUSE THEORY

Let us now go on to a somewhat more detailed presentation and evaluation of our three basic types of action theory. First we introduce some technical concepts. We say that the **result** of my (singular) action of opening the window is the (singular) event of the window's becoming open. In more general terms, the result of an action is an end event (or state) of that action such that this action (logically) cannot take place unless that terminating event occurs (cf. von Wright (1971), p. 67). Events and states which actions generate but do not logically presuppose are called **consequences**. Thus, if in opening the window I (inadvertently) let in a Mosquito, the event of the mosquito's coming in is called a consequence of my action in question. As we shall think of actions as **achievements** with certain public aspects, any action will have a logically built-in result. It will also have plenty of consequences. (The result-consequence distinction is far from unproblematic, though; cf. Stoutland (1975), Tuomela (1977). In effect, every action theory can be taken to give its own technical characterization of these two notions.)

For a person to perform an action there must of course be a logical opportunity for him to do it. Thus he cannot open a window if it is already open. A result cannot be produced if it (or a result event of that specific type) is already there. Consider thus an action type connected with a result type R. We can distinguish between the following four possibilities concerning the world at the occasion of acting:

(a) R obtains (or occurs) and continues to obtain unless the agent interferes;
(b) R obtains but will cease to obtain unless the agent interferes;
(c) R does not obtain but will change and begin to obtain unless the agent interferes;
(d) R does not obtain and continues in this way unless the agent interferes.

In case (a) the agent's interference would be to bring about R's ceasing to obtain. In case (b) the agent would by his interference sustain R (make it continue to obtain; cf. holding a book), whereas in (c) he would sustain the non-obtaining of R. Finally, in case (d) the agent properly brings about an event of the type R. We shall below restrict our formulations to cases of kind (d), viz. ones involving properly the bringing about of an event (or state) of a certain kind. But this restriction is for reasons of convenience rather than for reasons in principle.

Next we make a distinction between the **intrinsic** and the **extrinsic aim** (purpose, intention, end) of the action. Suppose I unreflectively pass the salt to my dinner companion just out of politeness, without any (further) motive or aim. Then there is no extrinsic aim in the action, but there is yet an intrinsic aim in the action, namely my bringing it about (by my action in question) that the salt reach my dinner companion (the result of the action), and this is just the **telos** of my action of passing the salt. Here, 'intrinsic aim' denotes the teleology in terms of which actions can be explained. There is an intrinsic aim in every intentional action; the terminating event for the aim is just the result of the action. There is not, however, an extrinsic aim in every intentional singular action, but only in those actions whose explanation requires a reference to the intention with which the agent acted.

Now we are ready to give a summary reconstruction of how "standard" mental cause theory analyzes an **intentional** action. More specifically, the following analysis, which uses our above terminology, states what it is for a presystematically understood singular action u, with a singular result event r, to be an intentional action of some kind, say X. Davidson (1963), (1974), Goldman (1970), and Alston (1967), (1974), for instance, accordingly take as their point of departure the following core idea (also cf. Stoutland (1975)):

(MC) An agent performed an **intentional action** u if and only if
(1) the result r of u occurred because of the agent's behavior (bodily movements) involved in the action u;
(2) there was some end the agent wanted to realize and which he believed his behavior (of the type believed by him b exemplified) would (tend to) bring about or at least be conducive to; and
(3) this want and belief together caused the behavior in u to occur.

The so-called basic actions require a small modification of this scheme, but we shall not discuss them here. Nor shall we discuss how well the fine points in (MC) reconstruct the various mental cause theorists' writings. In any case, on (MC) the explanation of action in a sense goes together with the explanation of the behavior in the action (as clause (3) speaks of the causation of the **behavior** in the action). To say that an agent is on a certain occasion opening a window (viz. performing X) is to say that his behavior (in the action) on this occasion is caused by his wanting **some** end (action type) to which he believes his behavior (of the type b exemplifies in his opinion) is (suitably) conducive. This attribution of action may perhaps be taken to give an explanation of the behavior but it does not in any case give an explanation of the action. But we can make it an explanation of action by specifying the agent's want. For instance, if we learn that the agent wanted to let in some fresh air we get an explanation of his action. If we indeed accept that the statement of the agent's opening the window intentionally serves to explain the agent's "mere" bodily behavior in the action, we can then say that explanations of action are, on (MC), only more detailed explanations of (mere) behavior; and since explanations of behavior are causal, so are explanations of action.

Note that clause (3) faces the problem that it seems to exclude the possibility of indeterminism right at the start. To help the mental cause theorist here one might suggest that (3) be interpreted broadly enough to cover indeterministic (e.g., probabilistic) causation. Or one might, alternatively, claim that (MC) is concerned with our common sense conceptual framework only, or in the first place, and that determinism in the sense of (3) could then to some extent tolerate indeterminism **in**

rerum natura.

On (**MC**), (a) the internal teleology of actions is analyzed in terms of causality, since the mental cause theorist construes the intrinsic aim or **telos** in the action as the content of the agent's causally active want, viz. his aim to bring about the result. (It is assumed that this want is always somehow present - perhaps due to causal want-transferral from the want in clause (2) of (**MC**) or because the end wanted in clause (2) may be only a more general "conceptualization" of an action with the result exemplified by r.) Furthermore, (b) the external teleology of actions - and thus their teleological explanation - is analyzed causally. But (a) and (b) are too strong, it may be argued. First, (a) in effect reduces the concept of intentionality to the concept of causality, and that is rather much to accept (see, e.g., Stoutland (1976a), (1976b) for arguments against this). Secondly, if only mere event-causation is meant (b) is affected by the existence of so-called wayward causal chains, which also (and this is more important) serve to provide a **direct** counterexample to (**MC**).

What are wayward causal chains? An example of such a chain is provided by the following example modifying somewhat one due to Chisholm (1966): (i) a certain man wants to kill his uncle (cf. the want in clause (2)); (ii) he believes that if he drives over his uncle he will kill him (cf. the belief in clause (2)); and (iii) this desire and this belief agitate him so severely that he accidentally drives over and kills a pedestrian who, unknown to the nephew, is none other than the uncle (cf. clauses (1) and (3)). Our agent did not **intentionally** drive over his uncle, even if conditions (1), (2), and (3) of (**MC**) can be regarded as satisfied. (There are plenty of other examples of wayward causal chains if this one does not seem convincing enough - e.g., due to the vagueness of the phrase 'behavior of the type believed by him b exemplified' of clause (2).) Analogously, because of the possibility of wayward causal chains a teleological explanation given for an intentional action in the manner sketched in the previous paragraph is not satisfactory unless the causation (both in clauses (1) and (3)) takes place "in the right way" or "in a certain characteristic way" (cf. Goldman (1970), p. 57).

The problem of wayward causal chains, especially, seems to me fatal for (**MC**) (as in fact some proponents of (**MC**) have conceded), and it is at least an enigma for its more refined versions (such as Goldman's (1970), formulated by means of the notions of action plan and action-generation). We shall in the next chapter see how (**MC**) can be replaced by a better account in terms of suitable mental causation involving conation.

To end our present account of the mental cause theory for single agents we may note an interesting feature of the psychological theories of motivation that rely on the mental cause theory. It is that they do not, after all, account for how the bodily behavior in the action comes about. Rather they only try to say something about the determination of action tendencies, "locomotions", intentions, or the like. As emphasized by Alston (1974) and Tuomela (1977), giving a full account of the bodily and other overt aspects of actions is a very complicated task which, furthermore, may be taken to lie beyond the scope of psychology (as ordinarily conceived). Yet giving such an account seems possible in principle, and this is what the causal theory of action is concerned with.

What about the multi-agent case? Instead of one single agent we now are dealing with a finite number of agents, say, $A_1,...,A_m$. They jointly perform an intentional action u of type X, say. For instance, two agents' A_1 and A_2 carrying a table or toasting would serve as examples (for more examples, see Chapter 5). Each agent performs his part (e.g., lifting his glass appropriately in the case of toasting) of the total social action. We may then say that each A_i performs his own subaction u_i and that all the u_is finally generate or make up the full action token u. Other examples of social actions are two agents' greeting each other, carrying on a conversation, and so on. An important class of social actions, already mentioned in Chapter 1, is the class of "responses" to challenges such as questions or orders (cf. your asking me to pass the salt and my responding to this request by doing it). We shall later in this book (in Chapters 5 and 6) present a detailed account of the structure of social actions and of the generational mechanisms involved. Then we shall also see that when speaking of intentional action tokens and of their generation we have to rely on the notion of action type. Thus, in the present case, u is a social action of type X such that X can be regarded as a kind of context-relative conjunction $X_1\&...\&X_m$, and each subtoken u_i tokens X_i. But for the present purposes we can get along without directly speaking of action types at all.

What is involved in the agents' $A_1,...,A_m$ intentionally jointly producing u according to the mental cause theory? In answering this question we go into so far unexplored territory. I will now suggest the simplest possible extension of the mental cause theory I can think of. In doing so, I will for the present only be concerned with a **strict** or **full blown** sense of intentionality which presupposes that **every** agent A_i, i=1,...,m, does his subaction u_i intentionally when u is intentionally (jointly) performed by this collective of agents.[2]

Let us thus consider the following extension of (**MC**) to the social case:

(**MCS**) The agents $A_1,...,A_m$ (jointly) performed an **intentional social action** u if and only if
  (1) the result r of u occurred because of the result events r_i, $i=1,...,m$ (involved in the u_is);
  (2) there was some (joint) end the agents A_i wanted to realize and which they believed their respective behaviors (of types believed by them respectively their b_is exemplified) would (tend to) bring about or at least be conducive to;
  (3) these wants and beliefs, respectively, caused, in a certain characteristic way, the agents' behaviors and, intermediately, the results r_i of the u_is to occur; and
  (4) each agent A_i performed his subaction u_i intentionally.

Let us now briefly go through the clauses of (**MCS**). (1) is the exact counterpart of the first clause of (**MC**). As in (**MC**) also here the 'because' is often (but not always; cf. conventional actions) a causal notion. (1) will be clarified in detail in Chapter 6 and I shall not here discuss it further. Clause (2) - in analogy with its counterpart in (**MC**) - postulates some joint end action which the agents wanted and it may be taken to require implicitly mutual awareness of this joint end (cf. our (**WI**) of Chapter 2). This end action need not of course be an end having as its result an event of the same type that r tokens. Clause (3) assumes that the wants (concerning a joint end) and the beliefs of clause (2) together causally bring about the u_is. We use the - here unanalyzed - phrase 'in a certain characteristic way' to indicate that this causal process must be a "normal" one, blocking wayward causal chains (cf. Goldman (1970), p. 61). It is arguable that clause (4) is redundant, for one might be warranted in assuming that this causal process takes place in a way which satisfies clauses (1), (2), and (3) of (**MC**) with u_i and r_i substituted for u and r in the case of each A_i, $i=1,...,m$. On our intended or standard interpretations of clauses (1), (2), and (3) of (**MCS**) this indeed holds, the behaviors producing r via the r_is and the wants in clause (2) of (**MC**) coinciding with the wants spoken about in (2) and (3) of (**MCS**). But we do not need here to make this assumption, however plausible, and we will retain clause (4). (For more discussion on some of the key concepts, such as "jointness", of (**MCS**) see Chapters 5 and 6.)

III. AGENCY THEORY

R. Taylor (1966) and Chisholm (1966), (1970), (1976) have been the most prominent advocates of the agency theory during the recent years. If we overlook some fine points, we can put its basic idea as follows (cf. Chisholm (1970), (1976)). To say an agent intentionally did u is to say that he caused some event to occur with the intention of making the result r of u or, rather the event type (he believes) r tokens or instantiates occur, and the event he caused did make r occur. Thus we propose:

(A) An agent performed an **intentional action** u if and only if
  (1) the result r of u occurred because of his behavior in u;
  (2) the agent aimed at performing (or intended to perform) an action with a result of the type r instantiates; and
  (3) his behavior in u was caused by the agent himself in aiming at performing an action with a result of the type r instantiates.

To say, then, that an agent intentionally opened a window is to say that the window opened because of his (bodily) behavior, that he aimed at performing an action with that result and that his behavior was caused by something he himself caused in aiming at opening the window. (The latter causation is meant by Chisholm to be agent causation, not to be analyzed in terms of event causation. But does not the phrase 'in aiming at' just invoke event causation?)

Because of the existence of intentional actions not **specifically** aimed at, clause (2) must be understood broadly enough to cover this. We shall not here discuss this problem nor shall we consider the exact content of (3) (see, e.g., Thalberg (1976)).[3]

The essential feature of the agency theory is, of course, its use of the notion of agent causality in addition to ordinary event causality. While the proximate cause of the behavior in the action is (presumably) some neural event, this neural event is (ultimately) caused by the agent himself in aiming at the end. Agent causality is an essentially teleological notion, accordingly, for it operates exactly in the agent's aiming at an end. The intrinsic aim in the action is just that specified by clause (2).

The agency theory takes the intrinsic aim in the action to explain the behavior involved in the action. Accordingly, the

agent's bodily behavior in his opening the window is explained
by saying that it was behavior aiming at (or by which the agent
aimed at) his opening of the window and therefore this behavior
was caused by the agent in aiming at opening the window. To
attribute an action to an agent is, then, to explain his behavior but not yet to explain his action. When we attribute an
action to the agent we imply that he is aiming at bringing about
a result. When we ask for an explanation, viz. a why-explana-
tion, of his action we in effect ask why he is aiming at performing an action with that result. The typical answer to this
last question within the agency theory is given by specifying
some further, extrinsic aim or end for the sake of which (or in
order to achieve which) the agent performed the action at hand.
In other words, typically a teleological explanation involving
some relevant further goal is taken to explain the action.

Furthermore, the agency theorist argues that such a teleological explanation is not reducible to a causal explanation.
Thus, in the agency theory both the intrinsic aim of the action
and the extrinsic aim of the action are seen to involve essentially the teleology of agent causality.

The most basic difficulty related to the agency theory is
perhaps the murkiness of the notion of (irreducible) agent
causality itself (cf. Goldman (1970), Thalberg (1976)). It is
simply hard to make clear sense of the idea of an agent's causing some neural events (and, a fortiori, his behavior) to happen
in aiming at a certain result. (It seems to me that examples of
internal causal wayward chains might be invented as counterexamples also to (A), but I shall not press this point here.)
If, however, the notion of agent causality can be made good
sense of, the agency theory may seem attractive and viable,
since it otherwise handles questions like intentional acting and
responsibility satisfactorily.

Let us finally consider the social case from the point of
view of agency theory. We can proceed analogously with the
"socialization" of (MC). Let me thus propose the following
extensions of (A) to the multi-agent case:

(AS) The agents $A_1,...,A_m$ (jointly) performed an **intentional
social action** u if and only if
(1) the result r of u occurred because of the result
events r_i, i=1,...,m (involved in the u_is);
(2) the agents A_i (jointly) aimed at performing (or
intended to perform) an action with a result of the
type r instantiates;

(3) their behaviors were, respectively, caused by the agents themselves in aiming at performing an action with a result of the type r instantiates; and

(4) each agent A_i performed his subaction u_i intentionally.

Given our comments on (**MCS**), clauses (1), (2), and (4) of (**AS**) should be clear enough. As to clause (3), I shall assume here (for the sake of simplicity) that the agency theorist is able to analyze his notion of an agent's causing-in-aiming-at so that wayward causal chains are blocked. We cannot without further assumptions take (1), (2), and (3) to entail that each A_i, i=1,...,m, performed his subaction u_i intentionally, viz. that (1)-(3) of (**A**) are satisfied with u_i and r_i replacing u and r in it. (**AS**) cannot, at least plausibly, be interpreted so strongly that it entails that each A_i aimed at performing an action with a result of the type instantiated by r_i. For that presupposes that each A_i's somehow aiming at bringing about the result r exemplifies will entail his aiming at bringing about the result r_i exemplifies, and it is far from clear that the notion of agent causation can account for that (cf. the definition of aiming in Note 3 and cf. (**WI**) of Chapter 2 as exemplifying, and perhaps explicating, **joint** aiming). Because of this clause (4) is needed in (**AS**) to get hold of a full blown intentional social action. (Of course, it may be claimed that even (1)-(3) suffice to define an interesting weaker notion of intentional action but I shall not discuss that here.)

IV. HERMENEUTIC THEORY

As we said earlier, the hermeneutic theory encompasses a great variety of views. One common denominator to them is the claim that Humean event causality plays no role in the analysis of intentional action. Another common feature is the emphasis on the conceptualization and, especially, **understanding** of behavior. It is often claimed, accordingly, that to understand an item of behavior is to read off from it (in a certain cultural context) the agent's relevant wants, intentions, beliefs, and so on, and to thereby come to understand and classify behavior **as** a certain kind of action. Then, by specifying a suitable further reason of the agent for the action (or at least for his thinking he should do so), one explains (gives further understanding of) it.

To get a better insight into this kind of hermeneutic theory we shall now consider in some detail von Wright's (1971) theory, which has been quite prominent recently. For simplicity, in our presentation of this theory we shall concentrate on von Wright (1971), although his later works contain some relatively substantial modifications and relaxations of his original theory (see, e.g., his (1974), (1976), (1980)).

The perhaps most central concept in von Wright's action theory is that of the agent's **aiming by his (bodily) behavior at bringing about a certain result.** (We may also speak of the agent's **intending** or **meaning** by his behavior a certain end.) I take it that von Wright would be willing to claim that this central concept is not reducible to a statement about the agent's aiming at the end cum some other statements relating that aim to the behavior in question. This notion thus irreducibly involves the locution 'by his behavior', and it figures in von Wright's (1971) analysis of intentional action as follows:

(H) An agent performed an **intentional action** u if and only if
   (1) the result r of u occurred because of the agent's behavior in u, and
   (2) the agent by his behavior aimed at bringing about a result of the type r instantiates.

(Von Wright in fact relaxes condition (1) for basic actions, but we shall not here discuss that special case; see, however, the criticism in Tuomela (1977), Chapter 10.)

Thus, on (H), an agent intentionally opens the window if and only if (a) the opening of the window is brought about or caused by the agent's behavior and (b) the agent by that bodily behavior aimed at opening the window.

In von Wright's theory, to speak of the intrinsic aim in the action is to speak of the intentionality of the agent's behavior in the sense of clause (2), viz. the agent's intending or meaning something by his behavior. There are two things to be emphasized here. First, the intrinsic aim in the action here has both an object and a "vehicle", namely the behavior. It is by his behavior that the agent intends an action. Secondly, the intentionality of behavior in no way derives from the causal antecedents, or the like, of the behavior. Intentionality rather is "in" the behavior, and behavior is normally "seen" as action. Intentional behavior resembles the use of language. An agent's aiming at something by his behavior is to be regarded as closely analogous with a speaker's meaning something by an utterance. Thus both behavior and sentences (and other linguistic items) get their meaning and are understood in essentially the same context- and culture-dependent way. (As indicated above in the analogous case of the agency theory, 'aiming at' must be construed widely enough so that it does not require the agent to have specifically the intention to do X, u being of the type X.)

In von Wright's theory (as far as (H) is concerned) the bodily behavior in the action is strictly speaking left unexplained - contrary to the mental cause theory and the agency theory. To be sure, von Wright accepts that the agent's bodily behavior involved in his opening the window may be causally explained. It is only that this explanation is in no central and intimate way connected to (H) nor to the (teleological) explanation of agent's action of opening the window.

In von Wright's (1971) theory actions, as distinguished from non-intentionalistically understood behavior, are to be explained intentionalistically in teleological terms. A teleological explanation, giving the extrinsic motivation of the action, refers to some end action of the agent and to some belief that a means is seen by the agent as conducive towards that end. (Such teleological explanations do not depend on any objective nomic relationships between means and ends.) Not just any teleological explanation in that sense will do, however. An acceptable teleological explanation of action must be **"logically conclusive"** (in the sense of the explanans in a broad sense logically entailing the explanandum) in von Wright's view (see (1971), p. 100). The class of such conclusive teleological explanations is claimed by him to coincide with the class of explanations given in terms of **practical syllogisms**. (For related theses see, e.g., Nordenfelt (1974) and Martin (1977).)

The basic form of a (descriptive) practical syllogism is as follows (cf. (1971), p. 96):

(**PS**)   The agent intends to bring about p.
           The agent considers that he cannot bring about p unless he performs an action (of the kind) X.
           Therefore, the agent sets himself to perform X.

(Here 'p' of course refers to an end-result the agent aims at bringing about.) As it stands (**PS**) need not yet be regarded as logically conclusive. But given certain qualifications related to so-called normal conditions and time-considerations it can be so regarded (cf. (1971), p. 107), even if von Wright's notion of logical conclusiveness could be clearer. (Note that no law-statement occurs in the premises of (**PS**).) When we use (**PS**) for the purposes of explanation in the explanandum action u (of the kind X) has of course occurred and the conclusion of (**PS**) speaks about A's doing an action of the kind X rather than his only setting himself to do it. The premises of (**PS**) can then be said to state the agent's **reason** for his doing u. It is, furthermore, a consequence of von Wright's theory that an agent performed u intentionally if and only if there is a practical syllogism which in the sense indicated by our (**PS**) backs it. (The last mentioned analysans could in fact redundantly be added as a third condition to (**H**) to back its second condition, so to speak. For (2) of (**H**) must be understood to rely on this kind of justification in terms of a practical syllogism.)

As said, on von Wright's view, to explain an action means to give it an "acceptable" (viz. logically conclusive) teleological explanation, which is claimed to be equivalent to constructing a practical syllogism (with true premises) for the action-statement in question. The first premise of (**PS**) gives a further **intended** end of the agent and the second premise tells us what he considers necessary for this end. Note that the use of, e.g., 'wants' (or some other "looser" attitude term) in the first premise of (**PS**) does not suffice to make (**PS**) logically conclusive. In the second premise we need to claim that X be considered **necessary** for the end. If it were only regarded (by the agent) as sufficient or conducive (**PS**) would lose its logically binding character. That von Wright's requirement of logical conclusiveness concerning teleological explanation is too strict has been argued, e.g., by Kim (1976) and Tuomela (1977). For this reason alone one has to regard the following statement by von Wright (1971) as at best misleading and strongly exaggerated: "It is a tenet of the present work that the practical syllogism provides the sciences of man with something long missing from their methodology: an explanation model in its own right which is a definite alternative to the subsumption-theoretic covering law model" (p. 27). It is only fair to say, however, that von Wright has later modified his views to some extent, but we shall not here discuss these changes (see von Wright (1974), (1976), (1980)).

Other non-causal or hermeneutic theories have not in general formulated their views with quite the strictness of von Wright. Still their basic views are closely related, as is to be expected. To take an example, Abelson (1976), following the ideas of Peters (1957), Dray (1957), and Melden (1963), presents a non-causal account in which intentional (and, broader, voluntary) actions are said to be explainable in two ways. First, we may give a so-called reason-terminating explanation by indicating that the action is one that the agent could be expected to perform under the circumstances (e.g., "because he enjoys doing it", "because it is his habit to do so", "because Jones asked him to do it"). This type can be called reason-terminating because it indicates that no (further) reason can be asked for. The action is not in need of justification or excuse. Secondly, we may explain a voluntary action by giving a means-end purposive explanation of it. The most common form of such an explanation is the familiar 'A did u in order to get p'. This kind of explanation is reason-giving explanation. Abelson argues that, e.g., explanations by reference to an emotion or a desire belong here for they are connected to reasons and justification. Thus he also rightly broadens the scope of teleological action-explanations as compared with von Wright's above account. However, Abelson says very little in detail about what it is that makes, e.g., reason-explanations work. The suggestion seems to be that they make the action expectable. But how do they do it if no dynamic (e.g., causal) principle is referred to?

In general, on a hermeneutic theory of action we just give the attitudinal or other motivational conditions in terms of which we derive the understanding of the agent's behavior as the action which was somehow reasonable or appropriate for the agent to do on the occasion. The behavior is seen in this way, first, as an action, and, secondly, in a broader psychological and perhaps socio-psychological and social context, often an explicitly normative and evaluative one. However, and this may be regarded as a strong criticism, a non-causal theory does not attempt to account for how the behavior item in question really came about, it does not attempt to give anything like sufficient causal (or other determining) conditions for it and it does not specify exactly what initiates action and makes the actors move. (To say, e.g., in the manner of Abelson that an action could be expected is yet far from giving factual determinants for that action type to be exemplified.)

The extension of schema (**H**) to the social case is rather obvious in view of our (**AS**). We thus get:

(**HS**) The agents $A_1,...,A_m$ (jointly) performed an **intentional social action** u if and only if
  (1) the result r of u occurred because of the result events r_i, $i=1,...,m$ (involved in the u_is);
  (2) the agents A_i (jointly) aimed at bringing about, by their behaviors, a result of the type r instantiates; and
  (3) each agent A_i performed his subaction u_i intentionally.

Clauses (1)-(3) do not really require further explication in view of our earlier discussion. (The need for (3) of (**HS**) can be argued for quite similarly as the need for (4) of (**AS**); also cf. our notion of we-intending as an explicate of joint aiming.) Let me finally point out that while (**HS**) summarizes a non-causal theory of action still in typical cases the phrase 'because' in (1) of both (**H**) and (**HS**) expresses a causal connection.

V. ARGUMENTS FOR AND AGAINST CAUSAL THEORIES OF ACTION

When sketching the main views of human action we did not really undertake a systematic criticism and evaluation of them even if some critical points were made. As we are in this book developing and defending a causal theory of social action it is of interest to see whether existing criticisms of causal theories have any bite against current theories such as our purposive-causal theory. As far as I know, no direct criticisms specifically against causal accounts of social action have been made. This is probably due to the simple fact that no such systematic causal theory has existed so far. However, it is of interest to review briefly both the criticisms against and the arguments for single-agent causal theories. For, since our purposive-causal account, to be presented later, builds social actions out of the participating agents' actions, this account obviously cannot be regarded as tenable, unless the purposive-causal theory of social action can handle criticisms directed against the special case with one acting agent only. Our plan is as follows. First, we shall discuss arguments for the need of the notion of event causality (and thus arguments against non-causal theorists) in accounts of action and action-explanation. Secondly, we shall present and comment on some criticisms that have been directed against the causal theory.

Perhaps due to the earlier criticisms against causal theories in the literature (by Ryle (1949), Melden (1963), and others), causal theorists, at least in the 1960s, tended to concentrate on arguing that the connection between the relevant mental states (events, episodes) and actions can be causal, instead of arguing that it **must** be so (cf. Davidson (1963)). I shall now briefly present some arguments which can be regarded as giving either direct or indirect evidence for the actual presence of a causal connection between (suitable) pro-attitudes and the relevant actions.

(1) The causal theorist may accept a **functionalist** account of the nature of mental phenomena, an account which **conceptually** introduces mental states and events on the basis of "social practice" as something causing behavior (including actions) in suitable circumstances. (For instance, Sellars (1968), (1973), Aune (1977), and Tuomela (1977) - also see Chapter 2 above - have adopted this approach.) Thus, on this account, to intend that something p entails, roughly, being in a dispositional

state with the structure p such that this state, given suitable internal and external circumstances, will cause the bodily behavior needed (in the agent's view) for the satisfaction of the intention. (Note that the above functionalist account is not open to the traditional criticisms directed against volition theories (cf. Ryle (1949), Melden (1963), R. Taylor (1966)).

On a functionalist account mental events (e.g., wantings, willings) actualizing mental dispositions may act as efficient event causes of behavior, while there is at the same time a conceptual ("logical") connection between the concepts representing such dispositions (e.g., intentions), on the one hand, and, on the other hand, both the generic action which ultimately satisfies the intention, and the generic means-actions which are related to the intention via a practical syllogism (cf. our later discussion of the so-called logical connection argument). In Tuomela (1977) much effort is devoted to developing this kind of conceptual functionalism which, so to speak, conceptually builds causality into our mental concepts (cf. (**CF**) of Chapter 2). If this functionalism is acceptable, we have a strong argument for the causal theory of action. It should also be mentioned in this connection in support of functionalism that **causal idioms** are often used when speaking of the coming about of actions. To take an example, consider a man who intended to shoot someone and who in fact happened to shoot him. This shooting was intentional, in the typical case, only if the man's intending brought about or caused his shooting. (Of course, here the question may be raised whether a non-causalist could somehow legitimately use this kind of causal talk but without an ontic commitment to causes.)

(2) By altering what a person intends, wants or believes, or by getting him to have new intentions, wants or beliefs, one is often able to control and manipulate his actions. In other words, changes in some suitable mental states and events may be systematically corresponded by changes in some relevant actions. This may be taken to indicate causal connection (without entailing that the person is not acting freely). Note that the underlying metaphysical model of causation here is that a change in a substance produces another change in the same substance.

(3) Concerning one and the same action, we may construct two different practical syllogisms with true premises and the same true action description as the conclusion, while only one of these practical syllogisms is explanatory (see Tuomela (1977), Ch. 8). Barring overdetermination, this difference is indicated by the fact that only in the case of the explanatory one do we

have a true counterfactual statement of the form: "Had the agent not intended so and so and believed so and so he would not, ceteris paribus, have performed the action". The truth of this counterfactual statement may be regarded as evidence for the presence of a causal connection between the mental episode satisfying the premises and the action satisfying the conclusion in these circumstances.

(4) A related argument is this (cf. Davidson (1963)). We may make a distinction between the (mere) **rationalization** and the **explanation** of an action. One may rationalize a person's doing an action by citing a reason that one has even if one did not act **on** or **because of** that reason. However, one cannot explain an action by citing a reason unless the agent acted because of it. Next, the obvious claim is made that this explanatory **because-of**-relation indicates the presence of a causal connection. (Cf. Wilson (1980) for a good critical assessment of the present line of argumentation.)

(5) One may argue that both practical and theoretical inference requires that the inferring person must have **internalized** some principles of inference (such as modus ponens) before he is able to infer properly. Tuomela (1977), Chapter 8, argues that this supports the view that in practical inference a causal process takes place.

(6) As mentioned earlier, the causal theories of action in a sense account for the **possibility** of action. That is, they account for the bodily behavior involved in the action in the special sense of giving a causal account of the action non-functionally and non-intentionally described (cf. Tuomela (1977), Chapter 8). The hermeneutic theory fails to satisfy this requirement and does not even accept it as its task.

(7) A central criterion of adequacy for (at least deductive) scientific explanation is that the explanans should give reasons for expecting the explanandum to be true. An explanatory pattern which fits this requirement is the cause-effect relationship. It accounts for the explanandum episode's coming about, and it gives a good reason to think that an explanandum episode is to be expected whenever the explanans is true.

It has been argued by Gean (1965), Hempel (1965), Stegmüller (1969), Brandt and Kim (1963), Tuomela (1977) and others that what is required of scientific explanation in general must also typically be required of action-explanations, at least of those answering why-questions. Hermeneutic action theorists, on the contrary, do not seem willing to consider the discussed requirement central or else they dismiss it outright (cf. von Wright (1971), Dray (1957), (1963), and his reasonable-in-the-light-of-pattern, Stoutland (1976a), Abelson (1976)). This suggests that different views of explanation itself are also at stake here.

Let us emphasize here that, undeniably, there are explanatory questions that do not necessarily require an account of the explanandum event's coming about. This is the case when we, for instance, ask what an agent is doing. Being told that he is X-ing (e.g., signing a contract) we have **classification** of his behavior and hence an answer to the what-question. Note also that asking a why-question always presupposes some classification of the behavior event in question and that presenting and answering a what-question does not exclude asking a why-question.

At least considered jointly the above arguments for the central presence of a causal connection between active mental attitudes and action seem strong. To be sure, some of the arguments have been so recently presented that non-causal theorists have not yet taken the time to try to refute them. As to the topic of social action, it is clear that if the above arguments are taken to support the causal theory of single-agent action they equally well support multi-agent causal theory (cf. (**MCS**)).

There are some relevant difficulties for a causal theorist that must now be considered, starting with the single-agent case.

(a) First there is the disposition-argument presented by Ryle (1949) and others. According to this argument the mental factors (wants, intentions, beliefs, etc.) appealed to in action-explanations are not events (but dispositions or states) and therefore cannot be causes. As, e.g., Davidson (1963) and Gean (1965) have pointed out, first, states and dispositions (or rather the bases of dispositions) can be regarded as causal factors (cf. brittleness as a causal factor of a window's breaking). Secondly, we may also have **event** causes here as, e.g., onslaughts and "activations" and flights of dispositions (wants, for instance) are events (see Davidson (1963) and cf. (**MC**)). Sellars (1966), (1968), (1973) regards volitions and Tuomela (1977) willings as **episodic** entities introduced according to functionalism, which qualifies them as potential causes of actions and makes their existence in principle a broadly contingent scientific matter.

(b) One of the most discussed arguments against the mental cause theory is the so-called logical connection argument. According to it, roughly, reason-explanations cannot be causal because there is a logical connection between wants (intentions) and beliefs and the action to be explained (see, e.g., Melden (1963), C. Taylor (1964), R. Taylor (1966), von Wright (1971), Abelson (1976)). Causal theorists have either claimed that there is no such logical connection (see, e.g., Davidson (1963)), or that the existence of a logical (conceptual connection of a suitable kind is compatible with the existence of a causal connection (see Sellars (1973), Gean (1975), Tuomela (1977)).

I think that Gean's (1975) recent treatment of the matter is quite illuminating. He argues convincingly that a causal connection between suitable mental events or episodes and the relevant action is compatible with a **de dicto** necessary connection between the mental factors and the action in question. It is only a **de re** necessity linking wanting and acting that might present a trouble for a causal theorist. In a relevant simplified but crucial example a **de re** necessity could be formulated as follows in a semiformal notation:

(Ex)(Ey) (x = an event of John's wanting to do X cum believing so and so in circumstances C, and y = an event of John's doing X and necessarily (Ez)x=z $\supset$ (Ew)y=w).

This schematic statement expressing a **de re** necessity is quite strong and few theorists would be willing to accept it (whatever 'necessarily' exactly is taken to mean). Note, furthermore, even in this **de re** statement y and x are still non-identical and distinct events.

(c) The mental cause theory in its "standard" form requires that the pro-attitudes play a double role in both accounting for intentionality and causing behavior. (Note, the purposive-causal theory denies this, see Tuomela (1977) and Chapter 4 below.) This double role is a source of difficulties, one of the toughest of which is that due to wayward causal chains (see the discussion above and in, e.g., Chisholm (1966), R. Taylor (1966), Goldman (1970), Davidson (1973), Stoutland (1976a), Woodfield (1976), and Tuomela (1977)).

Mental cause theorists and their critics have discussed various types of wayward causal chains but the basic difficulty in all of them seems to be how to characterize causation taking place in a "right" or in a "characteristic" way (cf. Section II above). Davidson (1973) takes the problem to be insurmountable, Goldman (1970), in my view question-beggingly, makes it a scientific one. Woodfield proposes, essentially, that we require that the desire-belief pair initiates and sustains a desire to do X (the means-action), which, after joining forces with a belief that the time is ripe, gives rise to an internal state that **controls** the performance of X (Woodfield (1976)). In Tuomela (1977) I propose that, basically, it is **purposive** causation (in distinction to mere causation), and hence acting **on** the operative conduct plan, that is missing in wayward causal chains.

In the case of purposive causation (to be discussed below in Chapters 4-6) it is the agent's self-referential intending (willing) to do by his bodily behavior whatever is thought by him necessary for satisfying the purpose in question that plays a central role, and it accounts for the elements of control because the willing cannot be satisfied unless the causation takes place as intended. This conative notion is accordingly central for solving the problem: in the case of wayward causal chains the problematic item of behavior (or behavior cum result) must be something by which the agent intended to satisfy the purpose (cf. Tuomela (1977), p. 256 ff., and Audi (1982b), pp. 300-301, for relevant discussion). This notion of willing is necessarily act-related and it cannot be reduced away by using simpler notions, while it yet is naturalistic enough. Wilson (1980) has recently argued persuasively for the need of so-called act-relational intentions in this type of context, and our notion of willing is just such a notion.[4]

Stoutland (1976a) argues that the hermeneutic theory, viz. (**H**), is capable of a handling wayward causal chains on the basis of the act-relational notion of the agent's intending a result by his behavior. But it seems to me that Chisholm's example (Section II) works also against (**H**), for a man may intend to kill his uncle by driving over him and so kill him (because of his agitated state) without intentionally killing his uncle. I would like to claim that this is because of missing purposive causation. As to (**A**), possibly its act-relational notion of intending will not help by itself unless the agent is required to "purposively cause" his behavior (whatever such purposive agent-causation means).

(d) Stoutland (1976a) claims that the analysans of (**MC**) does not give a **necessary** condition for intentional acting, either. He argues that, given (**MC**), the agent will act on a pro-attitude only if the attitude is the causally strongest one at the time of acting. But, he claims, an agent may well act on an attitude which is not causally strongest at the time. I find Stoutland's last claim badly supported but for lack of space I will not here discuss this matter further. Note that, in any case, the hermeneutic theory certainly claims that the conjunction of (1), (2), and (3) of (**MC**) is not a necessary condition for intentional acting.

(e) The final central problem related to the mental cause theory is related to the existence and role of psychological laws. In general, mental cause theorists have committed themselves to some kind of regularity or backing law account of causality. For instance, Davidson (1967), Danto (1973), and Tuomela (1977) explicitly require the existence (but not the knowledge of) of backing laws in their analyses of singular causation. This is the first reason for the importance of laws. The second reason is that, in general, mental cause theorists accept some kind of nomological model of explanation, such as Hempel's (1965) (cf. Davidson (1963), Gean (1965), Goldman (1970), Danto (1973), Tuomela (1977)). Thus, at least standard mental cause theorists characterize intentional actions by reference, among other things, to the existence of causal laws, and in explaining them they may even require the specification of the laws (see Tuomela (1977), Ch. 9 for a somewhat different account).

There are two ways in which laws may be involved in the analysis of causality and in explanation. First, one may require that there be relevant psychological laws relating attitudes to action. One may either require the laws to be couched in exactly the same vocabulary as the pro-attitudes and actions or one may allow redescriptions in different (usually more "general") psychological terminology. Let us speak of the **covering law** theory in both of these cases. Secondly, one may think that only physical types (universals) account for causality and that hence only physical laws may back singular causal claims. This view is held by Davidson (1967), (1970). We call it the **oblique** theory.

In the literature one can find many claims against the conceptual possibility of psychological laws. They are usually related to one or more of the mentioned claims against causal theories, to the freedom of the will and/or of action, or to the holistic and "open" nature of the mental (see, e.g., Dray (1957), R. Taylor (1966), von Wright (1971), Davidson (1970)). We shall not here discuss these arguments, which typically share one common fault: they assume that one can find sound a priori arguments against the possibility of nomological "reason-psychology" (see, e.g., Gean (1965), Churchland (1970), Pears (1975), Beckermann (1977), and Tuomela (1977)) for a rebuttal of some a priori arguments against psychological laws. Let me here only retort that surely there are in psychology lawlike propensity patterns such as a once-burnt child avoids (or tends to avoid) the fire. The trouble is not with the existence of nomological psychological patterns and processes but with their "openness" and with the difficulty of formulating relatively non-idealized closure conditions for open psychological systems (see Chapter 12 below).

Stoutland (1976b) presents forceful criticisms against Davidson's action theory, which accepts the oblique view of causation in conjunction with a denial of the possibility of psychological laws. Consider the claims that (1) an agent's attitudes are reasons for his acting and that (2) they cause his behavior. In Davidson's theory (1) and (2) have no determinate and lawful connection. In particular, (2) cannot be true **because** (for the reason that) (1) is, which connection would surely be desirable. Other difficulties follow as well, but even the mentioned one is grave enough for Davidson. (Note: if one accepts the possibility of psychological laws one need not get into trouble here.)

This ends our discussion concerning the difficulties the **standard** version (**MC**) of the mental cause theory faces. I think that the above arguments, especially (c) and (e), have shown it (as well as all "tougher" causal accounts) to be in difficulty.

Let us finally consider whether, and to what extent, the arguments (a)-(e) against causal theories bear on the multi-agent mental cause theory, viz. (**MCS**). As in the single-agent case, obviously the "double role" argument affects (**MCS**) equally well as (**MC**), and (e) affects (**MCS**) to the extent that it accepts a Davidsonian type of view of social psychological laws. As I think that (c) in itself is a grave enough difficulty I will not further consider (**MCS**).

As to the comparative tenability and adequacy of the types of action theory considered in this chapter, we may summarize the upshot of our discussion as follows. The mental cause theory, at least its versions (**MC**) and (**MCS**), has been argued to be in grave trouble. As to the agency theory, we recall that the basic difficulty associated with the agent cause theory seems to be the **philosophical** obscurity of the notion of agent causality itself. Furthermore, this theory seems to be affected by the problem of wayward causal chains - as is also the hermeneutic theory. The most basic difficulty associated with the hermeneutic theory is that it lacks a dynamic (e.g., causal) principle accounting the factual possibility of intentional behaving. Accordingly, the door stands wide open for the construction of a better theory, and our candidate is the purposive-causal theory.

CHAPTER 4

THE PURPOSIVE-CAUSAL THEORY OF HUMAN ACTION

I. THE FUNDAMENTAL ELEMENTS OF THE PURPOSIVE-CAUSAL THEORY OF ACTION

1. In Chapter 3 we discussed three important types of philosophical action theory, viz. the mental cause theory, the hermeneutic theory, and the agency theory. We concluded that all of them have serious defects. Thus, to recall one grave difficulty in the case of each, the mental cause theory is subject to the difficulties due to wayward causal chains, for instance. The agency theory is troubled with the inherent obscurity of its central notion of agent causality. The main criticism against the hermeneutic theory is connected to the fact that it, so to speak, lacks the dynamic element which would account for the action coming about.

We shall not discuss further the above action theories. Instead we shall below sketch (and summarize) a new type of causal action theory which avoids the criticisms against other causal theories discussed in the previous chapter and which, furthermore, gives a unifying account of all human activities. This new theory is the **purposive-causal** theory developed for single-agent actions in Tuomela (1977). It may at first sight be regarded as a rather special "intentionalistic" and "conative" version of the mental cause theory. Yet it is in important ways (e.g., due to its act-relational concept of willing) different from the standard mental cause theory (cf. Davidson, e.g. (1963)). It avoids the mentioned criticisms against that theory but retains many of its attractive features.

One of the main aims of this book is to extend the single-agent purposive-causal theory to the social case, viz. to the multi-agent case. The multi-agent purposive-causal theory accordingly comes to rely on some central features of the single-agent theory. We shall devote the present chapter mainly to the presentation of those features. (Also some general issues related to social actions will be taken up, however.) We hope that our presentation will make this book self-containing to the extent that readers not familiar with Tuomela (1977) will be able to follow the technical treatment in the chapters to come (especially in Chapter 5). Let it be noted here, however, that we will not in this chapter present our treatment of single-agent action generation - for a summary of it we refer the reader to Chapter 6, Section I.

To begin our discussion, by an action (be it a single-agent or a multi-agent one) we mean roughly a **performance**, viz. something, usually a change, an agent brings (or some agents bring) about so that this something has a "public", viz. epistemically public, character.

When giving an adequate systematic account of the notion of action one has to refer both to the antecedents and the consequences of the behavior involved in an action. The antecedents will be activated propositional attitudes like wanting (the evaluative or "affective" component), believing (the doxastic component), and intending (the conative component). As will be seen, the notion of intentional action is intimately linked to intending. As to consequences, only behaviors with certain achievement or **result** aspects will classify as actions. Intentional actions can be regarded as a kind of 'responses' to tasks and challenges so that the correctness of the actions as task solutions can be publicly assessed in terms of result events.

Ontologically viewed a singular action is hypothesized, to be a complex event brought about by an agent (or several agents, in the case of a social action). It is complex in the sense of being process-like: a singular action consists of a sequence of events. (We are technically going to call actions events although in many cases it would be more according to ordinary usage to call them processes.) In any case, it should be emphasized that we don't think the ontological aspects can at least fully be settled a priori, especially in view of the assumption that actions involve hypothesized covert elements (such as willings, volitions, and other motivational factors) in addition to overt components.

Let us now briefly consider the antecedents of action (for a comprehensive account see Tuomela (1977), Chapters 3-6). According to my view intendings, believings and other related propositional attitudes may be **functionally** characterized as realistically conceived dispositional states with a certain propositional structure (cf. (**8.5**) on dispositions). Conceptually (or semantically) these states are introduced in terms of intelligent linguistic and non-linguistic behavior, i.e., actions and other intelligent behavior, as described in Chapter 2 above. We can then say that they are introduced by reference to social conventions and social 'practice', as such behavior is conceptualized in terms of a social and public conceptual framework (cf. (**CF**) and (**CI**) of Chapter 2).

This introduction of mental states (and non-dispositional

episodes as well) as "theoretical" or "theoretico-reportive" entities is functional and hence indirect, and it is given causal-theoretically in terms of the "input-output" behavior of the person, especially in terms of these inner states **causing** his relevant behavior in various circumstances. Thus, to intend that p entails being in a dispositional state with the structure p (or with the structure p has) such that this state, given suitable internal and external circumstances, will cause the bodily behavior believed by the agent to be needed for the satisfaction of p, viz. the content of the intention. In a finer analysis we also need here an epistemic criterion of "mentality", accounting for the agent's privileged epistemic access to his mental states.

Put briefly, this kind of conceptual functionalism semantically introduces propositional attitudes as states with a certain causal power. It is essential that these states are realistically construed. One can then, for instance, conjoin with this some version of materialism and claim that these states are material states which future neurophysiology will tell us more about.

A related, essential matter is that these dispositional states can be mentally "manifested" and actualized, viz. singular mental events or episodes actualize them. This actualization need not be conscious, and in the "final" scientific analysis these mental events will presumably be given a **non**-functional (categorical) description. Now some, though perhaps not all, of these actualizing inner singular events can be said to **activate** the disposition. This I take to mean that these disposition-activating actualizations **cause** behavior or at least that they occur in a suitable constellation of states and events causing behavior.

An agent's wants (including aversions) and beliefs are the most important proximate dispositional determinants of his actions (there are even conceptual connections between these elements, as indicated). From time to time these wants (cum the relevant beliefs) become activated due to environmental factors and "self-stimulation". Then we, typically, say that the agent forms intentions to act on these wants (cum beliefs) and thus commits himself to action. In other words, we may say that the wants generate intentions (i.e., states of intending). This little studied type of generation is presumably causal, but still we do not **a priori** rule out, e.g., indeterministic non-causal generation (cf. Chapter 12 below).

A want (in our **broad** sense) is either **intrinsic** (when something is wanted for its own sake) or **extrinsic** (related to a duty, an obligation, challenge, etc., often ultimately serving some intrinsic want). As our extrinsic wants may seem problematic, let us say a little more about them. When, e.g., a duty is, by way of abbreviation, said to be, or to be related to, a person's extrinsic want what is meant is, roughly, the person's being disposed to think he ought to act on a duty and to so act. Thus, if a person extrinsically wants to visit his sick aunt this entails that he is disposed to think that he ought to visit his aunt and to act on that thought. (Here the ought in question may be called the person's duty.) While acting on a duty can be called acting on an ought-belief it still seems that there must be a conative aspect involved (expressing, striving, determination, resolution or something related). That conative aspect is typically an intending. At least there can not be volitional acting on mere belief without conation, it seems (cf. Chapter 11, Section IV, below). But there need not be an intrinsic, self-regarding desire or want present then. Thus we reject what has been called psychological hedonism.

Intentions (intendings) are partly characterized in terms of wants (wantings), i.e. extrinsic wants (e.g., duties) and intrinsic wants (e.g., primary desires). Intendings (as purely conative) are not reducible to wantings but they may be taken to entail the presence of wantings, indeed wantings on balance. We may say, in any case, that both intrinsic desires (and other "affective" internal determinants), together with appropriate beliefs (doxastic determinants) may, and do, suitably construed, generate intentions. A conceptual feature of intentions as opposed to wants is that if a person intends to do something X then it must be the case that he believes he can do X (or can learn to do X), at least with some non-negligible degree of probability (see Tuomela (1977), Chapter 6 and below Chapter 12, Section III).[1])

Intendings may generate other, usually more specific intendings. For instance, the practical syllogism represents one such intention transferral mechanism (cf. von Wright (1971); Kim (1976), and for arguments concerning its causal character Tuomela (1977), Chapter 8).

Let us consider an agent who has formed an intention to illuminate the room. His deliberation leads him - through intention transferral - to form an **intention to flip the switch**. When the time for flipping the switch arrives, this intention results in his causally effective **willing** (or "inner" **trying** as I have called it) by his bodily behavior to flip the switch then and, in fact, to flip the switch as intended (or willed). Accordingly, willing is in a sense **"self-involving"** (see Tuomela (1977), esp. p. 151). Summarizing briefly, the mental event of willing, viz. an effective intending to do something **now** (or **then**, when speaking in past tense), an event participating in the activation of the agent's "conduct plan", may be characterized functionally (partly) in terms of what it causes. Thus a willing to raise one's arm is a singular occurrent event which, the world suitably cooperating, causes, in the intended (willed) way or by way of carrying out the willing, the bodily events (behaviors) believed by the agent to be required for the satisfaction of the intention. Here it causes the arm's going up, which constitutes the overt embodiment of the arm raising action. Note that a willing may or may not be preceded by a deliberation, deciding or an intending or something analogous.

A willing is act-relational in that it irreducibly involves reference to bodily action in a **de re** sense (cf. Chapter 3, Note 4 and below). Thus the agent in our examples wills to raise his arm by his bodily behavior or greet by raising his arm. (This act-relationality of willing is a feature strongly suggested also by the empirical research of **non-verbal** communication - see, e.g., Birdwhistell (1970), Swensen (1973).) Considering the agent's flipping the switch **ex post actu** we may say that the agent willed of his bodily action that it bring about, in the intended way involving appropriate force and direction, the switch-flipping event: the willing is not properly realized or satisfied unless the terminating event occurs in the intended fashion via the agent's bodily behavior (cf. the technical notion of satisfaction$_2$ of Tuomela (1977), Chapter 9 designed to capture this). This **de re** act-relationality of willing together with its feedback-sensitive act-controlling character (explicable in terms of purposive causation) serves to exclude wayward causal chains, e.g., between the bodily behavior and the end result (recall Section II of Chapter 3 and cf. Chapters 6, p. 168 and 11, p. 366).

Note, too, that while willing is a representational event in the mentioned sense it yet, according to its above functional characterization, operates in the causal order by producing causally both the behavior involved in the bodily action its content refers to and, intermediately and partially, the result event of the whole action. If that result fails to occur we speak of the agent's mere trying to perform the action. We may also say he tried without success if even the bodily behavior in question fails to occur. The phrase 'trying' used for our willing event obviously derives from this context - we just add that that kind of inner trying is present in any intentional action, successful or not.

A willing then is an agent's intentional and executive mental act which directs and controls, via its act-relational character, his carrying out his plan of action. But yet it is not a purposive action caused by another willing. Thus it is not caused by, e.g., a willing to will, which may be regarded as, if anything, only willing. (Actually, to speak of willing to will does not make much more sense than to speak of willing to feel sorrow for someone.) Notice, too, that I have not required a willing to be a conscious event, even if the general requirements (referred to earlier) concerning the self-knowledge of mental entities of course apply to willings as well. A related matter a willing involves or entails is that the agent normally comes to be directly aware that he is doing by means of his bodily behavior what is required to satisfy the content of the willing.

According to the purposive-causal theory a human action (performance) can be regarded as a sequence of events involving as its conceptually necessary components (1) an event realizing a motivationally active propositional attitude, (2) a bodily behavior event, and (3) a public result event (or state). In the case of intentional action the propositional attitude in question is the agent's (performed or concurrent) intending. The inner mental event instantiating the intending is a willing in our above sense. To illustrate, an agent's action of opening the window is taken to consist of his willing, by his bodily behavior, to open the window, of his bodily movements involved in the action, and of the result event of the window becoming open. (For the notion of result and for remarks about the "logical opportunities" an action presupposes see Section 3.II.) I argue in Tuomela (1977) that my version of the functionalist account of the meaning and nature of mental events avoids the classical difficulties associated with volitional theories of action; see, e.g., Melden (1963), R. Taylor (1966).[2)]

We may represent a singular intentional action u by the causally (but not necessarily temporally) ordered "internally" connected sequence $<t,...,b,...,r>$, where t is a willing, b is a (maximal) bodily event, and r is a result (where possibly r=b; cf. arm raising). More exactly, t represents the agent's willing (or trying or causally effective intending) to do **now** by his bodily behavior whatever he regards as required for satisfying the purpose (the propositional content) involved in the intending that t instantiates. The description given of a willing in the previous sentence is our outsider's description. The agent need not, however, be taken to possess the concept of intending in order to be able to will even if our description may seem to suggest so. A description better suited here might be the following. Considering a willing to do X, we now characterize it more fully (but omitting, e.g., the self-referential aspect) by saying that the agent A wills to do, by his bodily behavior, anything which he believes is required for him to do X. This can be taken to have the following form: (∀Y)[A wills that (if he believes that it is required for him to do X that (Ey)(he will now perform y & y is a Y), then (Ez)(he will now perform z & z is a Y))]. Here Y ranges over types of bodily actions; otherwise my shorthand notation should be understandable. Note that A's performing Y is taken to amount to his performing a token of Y. Y occurs in **de re** position so that A need not have the concept of any action Y ranges over. The phrase 'required' should be taken to involve causal bringing about, at least partly. Note that, based on this formalization, we may also speak of such instantiations of it as 'A willed, by his bodily behavior b, to do X', where b is a singular item of behavior of some type Y, required in the definiens; and here A's will can in fact be taken to be about b in a **de re** sense. This **de re** character of willing may be taken into account when characterizing its conditions of satisfaction (see Tuomela (1977), pp. 265-267 for such an attempt).

In our technical treatment below the symbol 't' will sometimes stand for an episode activating a conduct plan (a plan for acting), and that episode is normally a complex willing-believing episode. We shall here take for granted the distinction between the agent's overt bodily behavior and his covert activities (e.g., mental episodes). A maximal bodily event b may be defined as the fusion or maximal sum (in the sense of the calculus of individuals) of all the bodily events caused by the willing t and participating in bringing about the result r. (Let me note here that when dealing with the concept of work, for instance, and more generally with actions employing tools (instruments, media) it is often appropriate to involve tools in b as a kind of extensions of body, for it is by means of tool-using behavior that an agent moulds the external world.)

In the case of an intentional action it is true to say that an agent must at least in some minimal sense be directly **aware** of it when performing it. Or, better, the agent must be aware to some degree of the basic action part of the full intentional action or at least of trying to perform that action. If, say, I am opening a window intentionally then I necessarily have some "non-observational knowledge" of my involved bodily actions. Furthermore, I am normally observationally aware of the window's becoming open. (See Davis (1979) on this; also cf. Chapter 9 of Tuomela (1977).)

The purposive-causal theory employs the technical notion of a **conduct plan** in a broad sense to represent an agent's plan for acting (see Chapter 7 of Tuomela (1977)). Roughly speaking, a conduct plan of a single agent is technically a generalization of the concept of a practical syllogism or, better, the premises of a practical syllogism. Thus, for instance, the conjunction of the premises of an ordinary practical syllogism is a conduct plan (or, strictly speaking, a conduct plan description).

It should be emphasized that our technical notion of a conduct plan does not necessarily involve planning or deliberation in the usual sense of these words. We can even tolerate unconscious conduct plans. Given such a wide notion of a conduct plan also **habitual** action can be accounted for in terms of it. Habitual action can be intentional or fail to be. What is interesting is that at least typically intentional habitual action is something not specifically intended at the moment of acting (even if originally habitual actions psycho-genetically arise from specifically intended actions). Habitual action can be said to be governed by **script**-based conduct plans, to use Schank's and Abelson's (1977) term (see below Chapter 11, Section VI, for a relevant discussion).

In the case of social action we have to do with social conduct plans which are special conjunctions of the participating agents' individual conduct plans. It is, however, central that in the case of **intentional** social action there be a common, although not necessarily consciously had goal of these agents which is referred to or, at least, is involved in each of the members of this conjunction (see Chapters 5.II, 6.III, 7.I, 9.II, 11, and 12 below on some details of social conduct plans).

Conduct plans are needed in two central places in the purposive-causal theory. First they are needed in the elucidation of the concept of intentional action. Secondly, as will be seen below especially in Chapters 11 and 12, they play a central role in our theory about the explanation of social action.

2. We can now summarize our purposive-causal theory in terms of a simple schema as we did in the case of the other theories of action in the previous chapter. We thus give the following general condition (which is in fact, a broad **nomic** statement) of the purposive-causal theory for a singular action $u = \langle t,...,b,...,r \rangle$ of type X being intentional, in analogy with (**MC**) of Chapter 3 and given the logical presuppositions of acting specified there:

(**PC**) An agent performed an **intentional action** u if and only if
(1) the agent's behavior (b) purposively generated r;
(2) there was a conduct plan, K, of the agent which involved an end which the agent effectively intended to realize then by his bodily behavior (of the type

believed by him b exemplified) and which he believed his behavior will (tend to) bring about or at least be conducive to; and
(3) this effective intending (as a willing, t) and this belief together purposively generated the behavior b in u.

(PC) is somewhat idealized as it stands and it must be taken **cum grano salis**, but it will do for our present purpose of putting philosophical action theories in a Procrustean bed. In clause (1) it is allowed that b generates r only probabilistically. Otherwise (1) differs from clauses (1) of (**MC**), (**A**), and (**H**) in its use of purposive rather than mere generation (see below). In (2) the notion of a conduct plan involving an intended end is used. This can be taken to mean simply that, according to K, the agent effectively intended to realize that end (which may but need not be an end of the kind r exemplifies). Note that (2) does not require the agent to have any intention (or willing) formed prior to action.

In clause (3) of (**PC**) the central so far unexplicated notion is that of the agent's effective intending purposively causing or generating his behavior (or, equivalently, the agent's acting purposively on his conduct plan). The contained relation of **purposive generation** guarantees that the purposive **direction** and **control** of action is adequately maintained in the course of the agent's acting. This notion receives different explicates in the case of different action types in my theory (see Chapter 10 of Tuomela (1977) and Chapter 6 below). In any case, it is always at least in part a **causal** notion, even if probabilistic generation is allowed in principle, too. In the case of simple bodily actions (e.g., arm raising) the involved functionally characterized non-Humean, feedback-sensitive notion of event-causation can simply be called **purposive causation** (or even final causation, without teleological ontic commitments). It is a "purposive-preserving" relation holding between the act-relational willing (trying) event t (cum the relevant belief) and the overt behavior (in this case b simpliciter), and this feature guards against wayward causal chains (see Tuomela (1977),Chapter 9,and below Chapters 6,p. 168 and 11, p. 366). Note that it would of course be a mistake to say that the willing caused the action.

Before going on let me comment on a critical point that may be made against teleological intention-related accounts such as (**PC**). It is that there are intentional actions that allegedly involve no end. Thus it may be claimed that an agent may intentionally hum a tune without **any** relevant intended end (in the sense of clause (2)) being there or he may intentionally jump for joy without any such end. My general answer to this criticism is that these cases are borderline cases which cannot be resolved by relying on one's presystematic intuitions but require the help of systematic theory.

How does (**PC**) deal with the above examples? I claim that, in so far as the example actions can be regarded as intentional performances at all, they must belong to an integrated action-complex which does involve an end in a relevant sense such that these actions are believed to be somehow conducive to this end even if they need not be related as means are to ends; cf. thus an agent's humming as a "part" of his action of walking home. We may also say that these actions, if intentional, must be effectively intended or aimed at or meant in a broad act-relational sense (in a broader sense than referred to in Note 3 in Chapter 3), even if the agent does not have to have an intention to do them. This also involves some degree of awareness of the action (or at least its basic action part) by the agent. Thus I claim that all intentional actions are weakly teleological in this sense. To the extent they fail to be that they also fail to be intentional (and sometimes performances as well). (It might indeed be plausible to substitute 'to the extent that' for 'if and only if' in (**PC**).)

I would like the critic of (**PC**) to concentrate on specific action tokens in his purported counterexamples, and then I think it would be seen that, e.g., humming may in some cases be clearly intentional and in some other cases fail to be intentional, and the distinction can be drawn as by (**PC**). Note that actions which fail to be intentional in the sense of (**PC**) include a broad spectrum of cases. Thus they include, e.g., (a) actions produced by uncontrolled anger, say, and "pattern-governed" actions, e.g., perceptual takings; (b) unintentional actions such as mistakes, e.g., confusing the light and the fan switch, and (c) such foreseen non-intentional actions as one's disturbing the nearby air molecules when raising his arm. In some cases humming and jumping for joy (and related expressive actions) might perhaps be taken to resemble the last type of non-intentional actions.

Let me also note that we may distinguish between (i) causal (or factual) intentionality and (ii) semantical intentionality (aboutness) in the case of actions. It is (i) we are concerned with in (**PC**). As to semantical intentionality, see our functionalist analogy-theory sketched in the beginning of Chapter 2.

How does our purposive-causal theory, viz. (**PC**), compare with the mental cause theory (**MC**) of Chapter 3 (p.60)? Because of the complex and a posteriori nature of the notion of conduct plan a strict comparison cannot be made. As a first approximation we can, however, say the following. Clauses (1) of (**MC**) and (**PC**) coincide. As to clause (2) of (**MC**), let us pretend that it represents the agent's conduct plan (this is a clear simplification). Then it seems to be a special case of clause (2) of (**PC**), given that the agent's wanting could be taken to play the conative role of intending there (viz. 'intends' can be substituted for 'wants'). But note that for an agent to act properly on a want that p entails his forming an **intention** to act so that he believes that p may become satisfied (cf. Stoutland (1976a), Tuomela (1977), Chapters 8 and 9). Furthermore, clauses (2) and (3) of (**PC**) involve the act-relational notion of willing (or effective intending) by one's bodily behavior to realize an end in contradistinction to the notion of wanting in clauses (2) and (3) of (**MC**), which is not act-relational (see Note 4 of Chapter 3 and cf. Wilson (1980)). Note, too, that in (**PC**) we deal with purposive causation (or generation) instead of mere causation.[3]

Recalling our discussion in Chapter 3 we may say that in the purposive-causal theory the intrinsic aim of the action belongs to the agent's causally active willing to do by his bodily behavior whatever is required in his opinion to satisfy the intention (purpose, viz. extrinsic aim) in question. Thus the intrinsic aim covers at least what 'whatever' here picks out. If the purpose concerns just doing X - as is usual - then also it belongs to the intrinsic aim of the action. Our account of the role of the intrinsic aim of the action does not reduce it to the role of causality as Davidson's theory does. In fact, our view resembles both the account given by the agency theory (cf. (**A**) in Chapter 3) and also von Wright's theory (cf. (**H**)). But it must be emphasized, that (**PC**) is a "broadly factual" nomic statement about the world rather than merely a piece of conceptual analysis. In this respect it differs from (**A**), (**H**) and some interpretations of (**MC**).

How does the purposive-causal theory account for the explanation of action? First, as to the explanation of the "mere" behavior in the action there is no other central difference as compared with the standard Davidsonian (**MC**) than the use of the conative notion of intending instead of the non-conative notion of wanting.

As to the explanation of action there are two essential sources of difference. The first is simply that the purposive-causal theory employs purposive causation instead of mere or "ordinary" causation. The second is that in the purposive-causal theory an (intentional) action is ontically regarded as a singular sequence $u = \langle t,...,b,...,r \rangle$, whereas standard mental cause theory does not include the relevant want (and belief), viz. its counterpart of our t, as any kind of component in the action.

Let us note here that as the information that t purposively caused b has already been used when classifying the agent's behavior as an intentional action one cannot, on pain of circularity, explain (the occurrence of) u merely by stating that t purposively caused b. Yet u can be explained by referring to the agent's operative conduct plan at the moment of acting, for that conduct plan typically gives a fuller characterization of t and embeds it in the constellation of the agent's (other) conative and doxastic attitudes, perhaps emotions and feelings, and so on.

In the purposive-causal theory explanations of actions are given by reference to the agent's operative conduct plan. This makes these explanations teleological, for a conduct plan typically mentions the agent's (further) goal (or goals), or at least it indicates that the agent is inclined to behave in a certain direction or mentions some related broadly teleological matter. Since conduct plans also, one way or other, involve the agent's relevant intending(s), we may here speak about **intentional-teleological** explanations of action. (In Tuomela (1977) a question-theoretic approach to explanation is presented and some theses concerning intentional-teleological explanations of intentional actions are defended. As to their formal-logical nature such explanations are nomological arguments of a certain exactly specified sort (see Chapter 9 and 12 of that book and Chapters 10-12 below). Roughly, if determinism is true they are so-called ε-arguments (which are deductive) and if indeterminism is true they are so-called ρ-arguments (which are inductive). I will not here discuss my more specific philosophical theses, but see Chapter 11 below for a defense of closely related theses in the case of social action.)

I have above been making a plea for a **dynamic** account of mental states and episodes and of action, suitable as a basis for scientific psychology. The 'forces' I have been speaking about are of course the causal powers - 'active' and 'passive' - of the agent as exercised in, e.g., want-intention generation, intention transferral, and, most centrally, in his conative willings, which in a sense purposively cause his body to move in the way required for the purpose expressed in his intentions to become satisfied. In our causal, dynamic account of action it is then assumed that intentional actions are a causal outcome of the interplay between **"affective"** attitudes (intrinsic and extrinsic wants in the first place), **doxastic** attitudes (especially beliefs, including the so-called normative beliefs) as well as **conative** episodes, viz. willings (or effective intendings). What ultimately moves an agent to act (intentionally) and what initiates his acting is his willing, we may say, and this is our quick answer to Brand's (1979a) "fundamental question of action theory", viz. to "What initiates action?".

3. What I have sketched above and discussed in detail in Tuomela (1977) will also, mutatis mutandis, apply to social actions, for social actions are actions suitably put together from the actions of single agents (cf. carrying jointly a heavy object). A joint social token u, of some type X, thus is for us both **conceptually**, viz. in the order of conceiving, and **ontically**, viz. in the order of being, in a sense reducible (or partially reducible) to the participating individuals' actions, say u_i, $i=1,...,m$, such that $u_i = <t_i,...,b_i,...,r_i>$ is a component token of type X_i. As to the conceptual dimension, it suffices here to refer to our thesis of Conceptual Individualism of Chapter 2. The ontic dimension will be given, as it were, a technical elucidation in the next chapter.

We shall now go on to state a general schema for the purposive-causal theory in the social case. This concise schema generalizes (**PC**) in analogy with the way (**MCS**) was taken to respectively generalize (**MC**) in Chapter 3.

We propose the following characterization for what it is for a social action token (cf. (5.5) for this notion) to be intentional:

(PCS) The agents $A_1,...,A_m$ (jointly) performed an **intentional social action** u if and only if
(1) the results r_i, $i=1,...,m$, of the agents' component action tokens u_i together purposively generated r;
(2) there were conduct plans, say $K_1,...,K_m$, of $A_1,...,A_m$, respectively, which involved an end action the agents effectively we-intended to realize then by their bodily behaviors (of the types they took the b_is to exemplify) such that they believed their respective behaviors will (tend to) bring it about or at least be conducive to it;
(3) the agents' effective we-intendings (as we-willings) and the beliefs referred to in clause (2) together purposively generated their behaviors in the u_is, and intermediately, the results r_i; and
(4) each agent A_i performed his subaction u_i intentionally.

As to clause (1), we shall clarify in Chapters 5 and 6 in what sense the behaviors of all the agents are (or must be) involved. (1) is meant to allow overdetermination. In clause (2) the notion of we-intending is employed. As Chapters 2 and 5 contain discussions of it we shall not here comment on it except for pointing out that it is a notion of a we-intention, as expressed by, e.g., 'We will do X', or actually a we-willing, which each member A_i, $i=1,...,m$, of the group accepts (and has internalized) in the case of full blown intentional social action. Yet this does not entail that the agents have formulated a we-intention to do X prior to action. We shall not either discuss clause (3) here for Chapters 5, 6, 7, and 11 are concerned with that issue. Clauses (1)-(3) may be argued to entail that subactions u_i are intentional. For, first, (3) of (**PCS**) can be taken to entail (1) of (**PC**). As (2) of (**PCS**) guarantees the presence of a we-intention in every K_i, $i=1,...,m$, then, using our (**WI**) of Chapter 2, that we-intention gives us the required I-intention in (2) of (**PC**). Next, given schema (**W1**) of Chapter 2, the causation in clause (3) of (**PCS**) takes place via the agents' I-intentions, and the truth of (3) of (**PC**) follows. But in order not to have to assume even this much of we-intentions in this general context we employ a separate clause to make sure that the u_is are intentional.

In general, we may say that most of this book can be regarded as an elucidation and elaboration of the purposive-causal theory of social action which (**PCS**) somewhat oversimply presents as a kind of summary prolegomenon.

4. Let us end our presentation of the general features of the purposive-causal theory by considering briefly whether it is able to handle the criticisms (a)-(e) of Section V of Chapter 3 directed against causal theories of action. (To save space we shall not here reproduce these criticisms but refer the reader to pp. 74-78.) Let us first consider our single-agent theory summarized by (**PC**). As to the disposition argument (a) and the logical connection argument (b), our discussion (and references) in Chapter 3 should suffice to save the purposive-causal theory from them.

How about the "double role" argument (c) which seems fatal to the mental cause theory? As we have seen, (c) does not affect the purposive-causal theory, for it simply does not make the double role assumption. As to the problem of wayward causal chains, the notion of purposive causation, involving act-relational intending and willing, is supposed to take care of that problem (see Tuomela (1977), pp. 255-258 and Chapter 11 below). Concerning the argument (d) (concerned with the strength of wants), it does not affect (**PC**), which speaks of intentions rather than wants (cf. Tuomela (1977), Chapter 6). As to the backing law argument (e), which seems fatal to Davidson's theory, the purposive-causal theory does not accept Davidson's view of psychological laws.

How about the multi-agent purposive-causal theory, then? Let us go through the arguments (a)-(e) one by one. As can be seen from (**PCS**), there are two (but not really more) central features to keep an eye on when judging (**PCS**) as compared with (**PC**). The first is that the causal mental factor is an effective we-intention (assumed to be shared by each A_i, $i=1,\ldots,m$). The second feature is that the u_is (causally or conceptually) generate or make up the full social action token u.

Let us start by asking whether the critical arguments affect we-intention-causation. We-intentions are representational states of agents equally well as ordinary I-intentions are, and we-willings are episodes equally well as I-willings are (see Chapters 2 and 5). The fact that 'we' refers to a group of agents does not seem to diminish the possibility of we-intendings having causal force. Clearly, then, argument (a) works no better in the case of we-intentions than in the case of I-intentions. Argument (b) would now presumably amount to saying that the logical connection between a we-intention and a social action (e.g., X and its components X_i) precludes the causation of the component actions of types X_i, where $i=1,\ldots,m$ and $X=X_1 \& \ldots \& X_m$. But this argument does not work, for we can obviously show in parallel with Gean's argument for single-agent case (discussed in Section V of Chapter 3) at least that no **de re** necessity needs to be or is involved. (To show this, we would use we-intendings instead of wantings in Gean's formula and X_i for X.)

Argument (c) can only cause trouble for the purposive-causal theory of social action if it cannot handle **social** wayward causal chains. What are such chains? Think of the different causal chains that lead from we-intendings to action in the case of each A_i, $i=1,\ldots,m$. Suppose some or all of these causal chains are wayward and yet serve to generate the result r of u. Here we have a social wayward causal chain (see Chapter 11, Section III, for a concrete example). Now the notion of purposive causation (or generation, more generally), involving act-relational and self-involving willing, can be supposed to handle this. It will be seen in Chapter 6 that, at least from a structural point of view, there is really no difference between the single-agent and the multi-agent cases as to purposive generation. Thus, given the basic adequacy of the discussion of the single-agent case in Tuomela (1977), Chapter 9, nothing more need really be said to block wayward causal chains also in the social case. This serves to answer argument (c) against (**PCS**).

As to argument (d), it does not seem to add anything to the

social case as compared with the single-agent case. Finally we consider (e) and the possibility of social psychological laws. I think it is up to the critics to formulate arguments which would amount to saying that there cannot be at least tendency (or propensity) laws governing the acting (doing X) of m agents, granting (cf. our remarks in Chapter 3) that there can be laws governing the single agents' actions (each A_i's, $i=1,...,m$, doing X_i). In other words, we need an argument against the possibility of "composition laws". I do not know of any such arguments (cf. our discussion in Chapter 12 below), and I doubt that there can exist any a priori arguments to that effect.

Does the assumption that the u_is must generate u have any relevant connection with the arguments (a)-(e)? I do not think so. The only possible connection I can think of is to (e) in that the mentioned requirement would seem to make social psychological laws more complicated. But that is far from saying that the relevant laws cannot be there.

The present section has served to set the philosophical stage for a detailed and rigorous development of the purposive-causal theory of social action, to be begun in Chapter 5. As that treatment will rely and build on some technical concepts of the single-agent purposive-causal theory we shall devote a section to the presentation of these **fundamenta**.

II. THE STRUCTURE OF SINGLE-AGENT ACTION

1. The framework of action concepts created in Tuomela (1977) emphasizes the structural features of single-agent actions and accounts for complex actions in part by reference to some simpler components of action which causally (factually) and/or "conceptually" **generate** them. To present the basic features of that conceptual framework and to begin to lay ground for our detailed structural account of social action concepts (to be presented in Chapter 5) we need a few central distinctions.

Our first distinction is a most simple one. It distinguishes between **single-agent** and **multi-agent** action concepts. Thus, when the acting agents are $A_1,...,A_m$ we are dealing with the multi-agent case if and only if m>1.

Secondly, we distinguish between **simple** action types, denoted by an atomic letter such as X, and **compound** action types, denoted by conjunctions, such as $X_1\&...\&X_m$, of simple action types. There are no other compound action types than conjunctions. Thus, in particular, there are no disjunctive action types or negative ones.[4] (Of course, in our language we may use negative and disjunctive action descriptions; cf. 'John opened the window or put the fan on'; 'John did not open the window'.)

Our general claim now is that compound actions can be **generationally** put together from simple actions, in a sense to be clarified.

A third distinction we need is that between (mere) **bodily** action types versus action types intrinsically (viz. in terms of their results) concerned also with **extrabodily** objects or events or states. An example of the latter would be John's opening the window. This action has as its **result** the window's becoming open, and this result is an event external to John's body. An obvious example of a bodily action type is raising one's arm.

A fourth distinction is between **epistemic** (or, if you prefer, **doxastic**) and **non-epistemic** action concepts. Epistemic ones take into account the acting agent's (or agents') relevant knowledge or beliefs about, e.g., the success conditions of his action, whereas non-epistemic concepts do not. Our notions of basic action, as formulated below, are epistemic while our notions of bodily action and compound action are non-epistemic. Let us still note here that in the case of social actions the epistemic aspect will involve all the acting agents, and it will amount to their having certain relevant mutual, intersubjective beliefs.

We shall start the construction of our conceptual framework of social action concepts on the basis of a fifth dichotomy, viz. that between **basic** and **non-basic** actions. Action theories commonly divide actions into basic and non-basic ones. What are the reasons for making this distinction? While several reasons have been offered, one central reason comes from considering so-called collateral actions: the agent turns on the light **by** flipping the switch. Most actions seem to be performed by performing some more "basic" actions and they can in this sense be said to have been **generated** by the latter. As not all actions can be generated ones, on pain of regression, there must be basic or non-generated ones, the argument goes. (For technical reasons we will present our account of action generation only in Chapter 6. Readers totally unfamiliar with the concept of action generation, e.g., in the sense of Goldman (1970), may profit from reading Section I of Chapter 6 at this point.)

I will below accept the core of the above argument and thus its conclusion that basic actions must be non-generated ones, but I strongly emphasize the **relativity** of the basic versus non-basic distinction. Double relativity is in fact involved as the dichotomy depends both on the conceptual framework (and social practices) of the social community we are dealing with and also on the factual skills the agents in that community happen to possess (at a given time). Another requirement often imposed on basic actions is that they in some central sense be (merely)

bodily actions. A third important feature basic actions are thought to have is that they are something an agent has the power (or ability or skill) to do intentionally in standard (or normal) circumstances. They belong to his **action repertoire**, we may say.

We shall now go on to discuss a notion of basic action which in a reconstructive sense takes into account all the above three features. Our emphasis is on the third aspect. A basic action (in the single-agent case) is one that an agent fully **can** perform or has the full or complete **power** or **ability** to perform intentionally in normal circumstances. We may say that if he willed to do it then he would normally succeed. Here the 'if-then' connective expresses a subjunctive conditional. (As to the required normal conditions, see Tuomela (1977), p. 293 and Chapter 7 below.) We shall later in this chapter discuss the adequacy of the above analysis of power in terms of subjunctive conditionals but below we shall take it for granted.

It is also central to our notion of a basic action type that it be a minimal "power-unit" in the sense that no basic action token is generated by a still more "primitive" (basic) action. Thus we hypothesize not only that singular actions are or can be generationally connected but also that for a certain agent at a given time there are basic actions in his repertoire which are not generated by any other of his actions involving overt bodily movement ('movement' understood broadly to cover even "relative" or "near" standstill as in an agent's action of holding a book).

These basic actions in question represent the agent's (primitive) skills. The agent can do them "just like that". They do not require any further beliefs and knowledge to be acquired on the part of the agent or any "recipe" to be learned by him. To be sure, such basic actions may involve a lot of implicit knowledge. Performing a somersault, to take an example, may be one agent's basic skill but not another one's. The knowhow information involved here may perhaps in part be put in the explicit form of a recipe when teaching the skill; yet the essential thing is that once one has learned it no recipes are needed. No further analysis into the components is needed either, for the agent does his somersault holistically, without in any sense having to compose it from further behavior atoms. It has become a routine performance for him, one that does not require any special attention by him. (Cf. the "subroutines" that are built into robots by scientists in the field of artificial intelligence.) Note that what the basic skills of an agent are at a given moment is of course relative to his "gifts" and to what he has learned.

Our notion of basic action, to be formulated below, does not, however, cover all the basic skills of an agent. It is only concerned with bodily actions. This is for technical reasons only, so to speak. For we are interested in creating the notion of all that an agent can do (perform) from the notion of his basic actions and suitable notions of action generation. Thus, while our ordinary conceptual framework is not committed to the existence of basic actions in our sense, we argue that nevertheless postulating basic actions helps considerably to clarify the conceptual structure of action concepts and that it also can be hypothesized to be ontically adequate (viz. relative to the "manifest image" of common sense objects and properties, including the framework of agency).

We shall later formulate notions concerned with an action's belonging to an agent's **action repertoire** (see (8) and (9)). These notions correspond perhaps better to the "traditional" or "received" idea of a basic action as it, strictly taken, comprises only the first and the third of the above aspects of a basic action, viz. it is concerned with extrabodily and non-generated actions in an agent's (or in some agents') power.

2. I have in Tuomela (1977) formulated a notion of epistemic basic action type for single agents along the above lines. I will below reproduce for it my two definitions or reconstructive analyses, which, respectively, cover **simple** and **compound** basic actions (for a single agent A at a time T). Some clarifications follow after the definitions or analyses, which are as follows (cf. Tuomela (1977), p. 292 and pp. 301-302). Let X be a simple (viz. non-compound) action property or type. Then we define:

(1) X is a **basic action type** for A at T if and only if for any singular event u exemplifying X at T it is true that:
 (a) If u had the internal structure $<t,b>$ and if A were in normal conditions with respect to X at T and if he truly believed that he is, then the causal conditionals $'D(t) \mathrel{\triangleright\mkern-5mu\rightarrow} D'(b)'$ and $'{\sim}D(t) \mathrel{\triangleright\mkern-5mu\rightarrow} {\sim}D'(b)'$ would be true in that situation. Here D describes t as A's willing (by his bodily behavior) to exemplify X and D' expresses that b is a maximal simple overt bodily component event of u and that b is the result event of u (as an X);
 (b) there is no statement D" which satisfies clause (a) as a substitute of D' and which is such that conditional $'D''(u) \circledast_2 D'(u)'$ is true in this situation by virtue of the semantic principles internalized by A.

(2) X is a **compound basic action type** for A at T if and only if
   (a) X is the conjunction of some basic action types $X_1, X_2, \ldots, X_m$ for A at T; and
   (b) it is physically and psychologically possible for A to be in normal conditions at time T with respect to each of $X_1, X_2, \ldots, X_m$;
   (c) for any exemplification u of X it is true that if u had the internal structure $\langle t, \ldots, b \rangle$ and if A were in normal conditions with respect to $X_1, X_2, \ldots, X_m$ at T and if he truly believed that he is, then the following causal conditionals would be true in this situation for $i = 1, 2, \ldots, m$:
   (i) $D_i(t_i) \Rightarrow D'_i(b_i)$
   (ii) $\sim D_i(t_i) \Rightarrow \sim D'_i(b_i)$
   (iii) $D''(t) \Rightarrow D_i(t_i)$.

Here t is described by D'' as A's willing (by his bodily behavior) to do X; each t_i, for $i = 1, 2, \ldots, m$, is described by D_i as A's willing (by his bodily behavior) to do X_i; and D'_i expresses that b_i is a maximal simple overt bodily component event of the respective event $u_i = \langle t_i, \ldots, b_i \rangle$ tokening X_i in this situation; $b = b_1 + \ldots + b_m$ ('+' means sum in the sense of the calculus of individuals). In addition, b is assumed to be the result event of u (as an X).[5]

Above, A represents the agent and T a point of time (or a set or interval of points, if you like). Action tokens such as u are assumed to be ordered singular events or episodes with some components or parts. (Note: even if we write, e.g., $u = \langle t, b, r \rangle$ the brackets are not analyzable in terms of sets but just serve to mark a singular entity with some parts.) In the case of basic action, as defined above, r coincides with or belongs to b. The symbol $\Rightarrow$ denotes a singular "purposive" causal conditional defined exactly in Tuomela (1977), p. 253, and below by (**6.10**)). Briefly and somewhat roughly put, '$D(t) \Rightarrow D'(b)$' is true just in case t is a purposive cause of b, viz. t-as-described-by-D is a cause of b-as-described-by-D' and the causation takes place according to and because of the agent's underlying operative conduct plan. The episode t here is just the agent's willing, viz. his effective episodic intending (to now do X). More generally, $\Rightarrow$ can be defined in terms of any feasible notion of a causal conditional (our suggestion is the conditional $\Rightarrow$ of Tuomela (1976a)) which is then required to suitably respect the agent's conduct plan (see (**6.10**)).

The symbol $\otimes_{\overrightarrow{2}}$ represents a singular conditional for purposive conceptual action generation (see Tuomela (1977), p. 255 and (**6.10**) below). Roughly put, 'D'(u) $\otimes_{\overrightarrow{2}}$ D(u)' is true just in case u-as-described-by-D' conceptually generates u-as-described-by-D (or u-under-D' conceptually generates u-under-D) and, in addition, the conceptual generation, as described, is in accordance with the semantic principles of the acting agent's operative conduct plan. As we admit redescriptions of action tokens (cf. our locutions like 'u as an X') result events may change due to redescription. Note that the locution 'as an X' in (a) reflects this intensional aspect of results. In all, clause (b) is relative to the agent's conceptual system, and this is reflected in its reference to the semantic principles internalized by A.

As shown in Tuomela (1977), Chapter 12, and below in Chapter 6 our $\looparrowright$ as well as all the generational concepts can be liberalized so as to include probabilistic generation. I am inclined to think, however, that in the case of our core system of action concepts created in this and the next chapter (and ending up with (**7**) and (**8**) below as well as (**5.7**) and (**5.9**)) that liberalization is not really needed, for relative to the right normal condition assumptions our common sense framework of action concepts (that we are here refining and reconstruing) is non-probabilistic or strict, although I cannot defend myself better than referring to everyday parlance and the deterministic world view it seems to rely on (cf. our discussion of the by-relation in Chapter 6 and see Goldman (1970), Chapter 2, for relevant points). Finally note that the mereological sum '+' used in clause (c) is defined as usual. Thus, the sum of two singular events x and y becomes: $x+y =_{df} (\imath z)(w)((w \circ z) \leftrightarrow (w \circ x \vee w \circ y))$, where '∘' represents the primitive notion of overlapping.

After a clarification of the technicalities of (1) a few more philosophical comments on it may be made. First, we notice that the subjunctive conditional analyzing ability and power, referred to earlier, is taken to be captured by the conditionals 'D(t) $\looparrowright$ D'(b)' and '∼D(t) $\looparrowright$ ∼D'(b)', assumed to express causal purposive conditionals translatable, roughly, by 'If A willed he would succeed in bringing about b, as intended ' and 'If A would not will he would not succeed in bringing about b as intended'. As b here also represents the result episode of the action in question we indeed have explicated 'If A willed, he would (normally) succeed', our starting formula, given the satisfaction of the normal conditions clause in (a). Thus we can see that our account deals with an agent's basic powers and abilities. Notice also that our account is both causal and teleological (or purposive) just because of the central role of the purposive-causal conditional $\looparrowright$.

The conditional $\looparrowright$ refers to an operative conduct plan of A that is postulated to underlie A's acting. Whatever implicit knowledge (and principles of inference) A relies on may be taken to be embedded in it. (Another possibility would be to embed such background knowledge in his long-term memory.) But, as is seen, our (1)(a) does not (explicitly) require A to have any specific beliefs or items of knowledge, only the general belief that the appropriate normal conditions obtain. But there is more to be said concerning the epistemic situation and our claim that (1) expresses an epistemic action concept. For we may now recall the claim that A is here acting on his conduct plan (which may be very rudimentary, perhaps without reference to any specific beliefs). This, in any case, entails that A is **aware** of what he is doing, at least that he is, by his present bodily behavior, doing an X in each situation (1) nonvacuously deals with. (In Tuomela (1977), pp. 262-266, this awareness was explicated technically in terms of an epistemic notion of satisfaction, defined in terms of so-called wh-beliefs.) As clause (b) of (1) is concerned with principles **internalized** by A this clause, too, is epistemic, for at least implicit knowledge of those principles must be involved.

Our basic actions will include such action types as raising one's arm, moving one's finger, the bodily action involved in tying one's shoe laces, and so on, in the case of typical agents. For instance, flexing one's muscles for raising one's arm, tying one's shoe laces and signalling for a left turn will be excluded. Note that the case of signalling for a left turn becomes excluded due to clause (b) (rather than (a)) of (1), since its instances are generated by simpler actions such as lifting (appropriately) one's left arm, and so on, as the case may be. Also note that this in no way means conceptually reducing away the concept of signalling from our conceptual system.

Even if our (1) is narrow in that it excludes actions with "extrabodily" or "agent-external" results it is still rather wide in another respect. This is because it does not account for variation in, for instance, the degree of effort, skill, and attention involved. Nor does it say anything about the manner (or style) with which a basic action is performed. In fact, as will be seen, this objection applies to many of our other action concepts as well. Let me just say here that the mentioned factors are important in many contexts. While (1) only qualitatively takes into account skill, as seen, and attention (in terms of awareness) it does not account for their degree. (1) does not account for the notions of effort and manner (but see Chapter 11 for manner). My suggestion now is that (1) should be taken to define a broad "supernotion" of basic action. Interesting subclasses of basic actions may then be obtained by adding further clauses, which specify requirements about manner, degrees of effort, skill and attention, and, if desired, about the agent's specific reasons for performing the basic action in question. We shall not here investigate these special extra qualifications (which may naturally be extended to our other action concepts as well).

Our definition (2) in a sense just amounts to putting together, in a coordinated and co-realizable way, m basic actions of an agent. The coordination is in part due to the "comprehensive" willing t to do the compound action X (cf. clause (c)) and the co-realization is mainly due to clause (b). The notions of physical and psychological possibility in (b) are not very central below, and we shall not here discuss them further. In (2) the compound action property X is assumed to have been analyzed into the longest, often situation-dependent conjunction of simple action properties: $X = X_1 \& ... \& X_m$.[6] A very simple example of a compound basic action might be an agent's (simultaneously) raising his arm and shaking his head.

As seen, our technical notion of basic action is that of a **non-generated bodily** action that the agent has the (full) **power** to do. So far it agrees with what philosophers commonly think of basic actions. However, it differs from the common conceptions in that a basic action token does not comprise any agent-external result. Thus, if we denote an intentional action tokening (exemplifying, instantiating, realizing) an ordinary simple action type (e.g., opening the window) by $u=<t,...,b,...,r>$ = $<t,b,r>$ where t is a willing, b is a maximal overt bodily behavior component (the fusion of all behavior components caused by t), r is a result event. Now, in the case of our technical notion of a basic action all intentional tokens have the form $<t,b>$ (thus r=b or, perhaps, r is a part of b, r<b, in the sense of the calculus of individuals). As said, the notion of an action belonging to an agent's action repertoire defined in Tuomela (1977), pp. 297-298 and by (8) below corresponds better to the "received" concept of a basic action for single agents.

3. One of the claims of the purposive-causal theory is that all that an agent can do ("can" in an epistemically rich sense) is in a sense conceptually constructable from his (simple and compound) basic actions by means of action generation. We have just above defined the building blocks of this enterprise. A related claim of our theory is that the structures of all non-

epistemic actions can be conceptually constructed out of bodily actions by means of action generation. We shall now give our definitions of the relevant building blocks for this case.

In Tuomela (1977), pp. 308-309, non-epistemic single-agent bodily actions are defined parallel to the case of basic actions as follows:

(3) X is a simple **bodily action type** for A at T if and only if every exemplification u of X at T which is an action token$_1$ of A is of the form u=<v,...,b> such that b is the result event of u (as an X).

(4) X is a **compound bodily action type** for A at T if and only if
(a) X is the conjunction of some simple bodily action types $X_1, X_2, ..., X_m$ ($m \geq 1$) for A at T; and
(b) it is at least conceptually possible that $X_1, X_2, ..., X_m$ are jointly tokened$_1$ by A at T.

These definitions employ the broad notion of an action token$_1$ of Tuomela (1977). We shall soon elucidate it. Let us just say here that in a bodily action token$_1$ u=<v,...,b> (e.g., arm raising) the mental event v is supposed to instantiate a propositional attitude and cause b, the maximal overt bodily component event of u (e.g., the arm going up). A bodily action token$_1$ does not have any agent-external result component built into it. It goes without saying that any such action token nevertheless has plenty of agent-external consequences and it has them as a matter of contingent fact.

It is easily seen on the basis of our (1) and (2) that every basic action type (for A at T) is a bodily action type (for A at T) and that every compound basic action type (for A at T) is a compound bodily action type (for A at T). Examples of bodily action types which are not basic action types for all agents would be performing a somersault and wiggling one's ears.

Definitions (3) and (4) rely on the notion of an action token$_1$. This is a very central notion in the purposive-causal theory for it is supposed to give a partial naturalistic characterization of a very broad class of actions. Let us now present our causalist definition of a single-agent action token$_1$ (see the discussion in Tuomela (1977), pp. 305-306):

(5) Singular event u=<v,...,b_1,...,b_m,...,r_1,...,r_m,r> is an **action token$_1$** by A if and only if
(a) v is a singular mental event (or episode) activating a propositional (or representational) attitude of A;

v is a direct or indirect cause (i.e., causally contributing event) of the events $b_1,\ldots,b_m$ and an indirect cause or an indirect factual generator (via the events $b_1,\ldots,b_m$) of the events $r_1,\ldots,r_m,r$;
(b) each b_i, $i=1,2,\ldots,m$, is a bodily event which does not cause any other bodily events in u;
(c) each r_i, $i=1,2,\ldots,m$, is a public result event (possibly identical with some b_i), and r is the result event of the total event u.

The notion of a single-agent action token$_1$ is supposed to give us a broad action concept which does not in a strong and vicious sense rely on the concept of action type (not at least on a systematically defined one). The singular event v realizes a propositional or, more broadly (to cover "prelinguistic" agents), representational attitude. For instance, a perceptual belief might qualify. Yet it is arguable that v might **always** in part be regarded also as a **conation** (e.g., a "volition"), thus making u **directed**. If so, it should presumably also involve some pro-attitude (broadly understood) of A. (But we need not yet take a firm stand on this last issue and do not technically require the attitude in (a) to be a pro-attitude.) We could perhaps also say that clause (a) deals with a very rudimentary conduct plan of A, but we have chosen not to use this stretched way of talking.

Note that, e.g., various non-intentional actions (e.g., my mispronouncing your name or your hitting me because of your uncontrolled anger) as well as Sellarsian "pattern-governed" behaviors such as "inferrings-out-loud" and "perceptual takings-out-loud" are action tokens$_1$ in the broad sense of our definition (see Tuomela (1977), pp. 306-308 for a discussion). The propositional (or representational) content of the event v need not be that which the result r instantiates or makes true. Note also that in (3) and (4) we are dealing with action tokens$_1$ where the behaviors b serve as result-events.

At this point we are ready to discuss action types which properly account for agent-external results and which may be arbitrarily complex. We start by giving the definition of a compound action type for a single agent. In Tuomela (1977), pp. 315-316, it was argued that this concept (jointly with the notion of bodily action type) in fact is strong enough to conceptually cover any complex action such as felling a tree, drinking a cup of coffee, giving a lecture, and so on.

I will below assume that a suitable generational account of compound non-epistemic single agent actions is available (cf. Chapter 6). Such a generational account conceptually builds compound actions out of simple actions by means of a mechanism of action generation and normally in a sense accounts for the factual genesis of the complex action. I will now without further ado reproduce in slightly rephrased version the definition of compound single agent actions developed in Tuomela (1977), p. 310:

(6)   X is a **compound action type** for A at T if and only if
     (a) X is the conjunction of some simple types $X_1,...,X_m$ ($m \geq 1$) at least one of which is not a bodily action type for A at T;
     (b) it is at least conceptually possible that
        (i) each X_i, $i=1,...,m$, has exemplifications by A which are action tokens$_1$ and that
        (ii) the conjunction $X_1 \& ... \& X_m$ is exemplifiable by A at T;
     (c) (i) each action token$_1$ $u = <v,...,b,...,r>$ of X is (directly or indirectly) generated by some action tokens$_1$ (occurring at T) of the action types X_i, $i=1,...,m$, which are conjuncts of X;
        (ii) for each conjunct X_i such that X_i is not itself a simple bodily action type nor does X_i occur as a conjunct in any compound bodily action type consisting of conjuncts of X, it is true that every action token$_1$ of X_i is (directly or indirectly) generated by simple or composite bodily action tokens$_1$ (occurring at T) of A.

In (c) v is assumed to be describable as an initiating event as required in clause (a) of the definition of an action token$_1$; b = $b_1+b_2+...+b_m$; and r is the (possibly composite) full result event of X. Note that in clause (c)(i) the action tokens generating u must be exemplifications of different action types X_i.

In (6) much depends on the exact content of the notion of action generation. The following principle of Tuomela (1977), p. 314, anyway seems appropriate in the single-agent case:

(**PG**) $IG(u_1+...+u_m, u)$ if and only if $IG(r_1+...+r_m, r)$.

In (**PG**) we use the same notation as above. 'IG' means (direct or indirect) event-event generation; some r_is may coincide with the respective bodily movements b_i. We shall discuss action generation in Chapter 6 and there we will in fact generalize (**PG**) to a m+1-place relation of generation. The idea remains the same, however. Factual action token generation thus is claimed to amount to the corresponding result-event generation. How, viz.

through which vs and bs, the results are obtained is thus considered irrelevant. This indicates that our above definitions are relatively "theory-independent". It would be easy to formulate their counterparts for rivalling action theories such as the hermeneutic theory.

No more complex action types than those defined by (6) are needed. We can thus go on and define:

(7) X is a **complex action type** (an arbitrary action type) for A at T if and only if X is either (1) a simple or compound bodily action type for A at T or (2) a compound action type for A at T.

Thus, we can claim that all single-agent actions are complex actions in this sense independently of their other special characteristics (such as their being "parallel", "hierarchical", "sequential", etc.). Much of course depends here on the notions of generation employed in our definitions. Our new automata theoretic account, to be presented in Chapter 6 below, should help to clarify them much beyond the elucidation given in Tuomela (1977), Chapters 9 and 10.

4. Let us now return to epistemic action concepts. We shall define the notion of the **action repertoire** of an agent or, equivalently, his **power to do** something intentionally. What does it mean to say that an agent A has the power to do something X, where X is an action type? To this question our blunt answer, discussed earlier, is: If A willed to do X (and had the appropriate active beliefs), then he would succeed in doing it (intentionally), given normal conditions. Let us elaborate on this pre-systematic dispositional account.

I have in Tuomela (1977), pp. 297-298, presented the following analysis of an epistemic notion of power, elucidating the above conception, for simple (non-compound) action properties:

(8) A has the **power** to do X (or X belongs to A's **action repertoire**) at T if and only if either
(a) X is a basic action type for A at T, or
(b) for any singular event u exemplifying the property X it is true that if u had the internal structure $\langle t,\ldots,b,\ldots,r \rangle$ and if A were in normal conditions with respect to X at T and if he truly believed that, then the statement 't purposively generated r' (viz. $IG^*(t,r)$) would be true of u in that situation. Here t is described as A's willing (by his bodily behavior) to exemplify X, and b cum r is

described in A's operative conduct plan K (underlying IG*(t,r)) as a maximal overt component event of u (as an X), and r is the result event of u (as an X).

The above definition elucidates a rather strong epistemic notion of power. It employs the notion of purposive generation (IG*), having the force of a conditional, to be defined exactly in the Chapter 6 (see (**6.9**) and Tuomela (1977), p. 255). Here it suffices to say that it means generation according to the agent's conduct plan. Note that it follows from our account of willing, first, that A is (to some degree) aware of his attempt to do X and, secondly, that if an agent can intentionally do something, and thus can will its doing, it is also possible for him to will not to do it (see Tuomela (1977), Chapter 6). If A wills (effectively intends) not to do X then he would intentionally omit doing X. To the extent that this idea of intentional failure to do X characterizes the notion of power to do X it has already been built into our account.

Let me now comment on some relevant philosophical issues connected with (8). First, note that we work here with the conditional 'If A willed to do X then he would have succeeded in doing it intentionally'. Instead, Moore used choosing and Goldman wanting in the antecedent. But such other antecedents as choosing, deciding, wanting, etc., while broad in one respect are still to strict in a crucial sense. For, first, mere wanting to do X does not guarantee that X will be done **intentionally**, which we take to be required by the notion of the power to do X in our analysandum. Choosing again does give us intentional action, but one could certainly have the power to do X without ever choosing (or, for that matter, desiring) to do it. The above conditional would then sometimes be false with 'choosing' in its antecedent. For instance, Tom, who has a slight speech defect, could have the ability to pronounce a certain word directly but every time he chooses to pronounce that word he gets very nervous and, as a result, mispronounces the word. Yet he is able to intentionally pronounce the word correctly under normal circumstances, we may consistently imagine. Thus we may think that the use of 'choosing' in the antecedent may simply always make the conditional false in some, admittedly contrived examples. (Technically, in our (8)(b) t would then presumably have to be a choosing event and the whole clause would become false.)

As to our (8), it must be noticed that our notion of willing (to do X) amounts to effective intending (now to do X) and that our notion of intending entails that the agent be able to

learn to do X, if he does not already have the ability to do X (see Note 1). Thus our analysis implicitly connects power with ability to learn. The latter notion is a conceptual relative of the former, yet our analysis is not made directly circular by this fact.

Davis (1979) presents an example which may be regarded as creating a difficulty for our analysis, which analyzes power (partly) in epistemic terms:

> "Now imagine an apparently poor marksman who consistently hits a spot to the left of the spot he aims at. Using [the conditional analysis 'At t, if A had tried to do an X, he would have done an X (thereby)'] we would conclude that he lacks the ability to hit the bull's-eye, since 'At t, if he had tried to hit the bull's-eye, he would have done so (thereby)' is false. But it seems he does have the ability to hit the bull's-eye: all he needs to do is aim for - try to hit - a spot to the **right** of the bull's-eye!" (Davis (1979), pp. 45-46).

But, as Davis admits, we may respond by distinguishing between an epistemic and a non-epistemic sense of power. Davis' example does not falsify the analysis given by (8) which is concerned with epistemic power only. Thus the falsity of the analysans of our (8) is compatible with A's having the non-epistemic power to do X. But Davis now argues that "the marksman may have the ability to hit the bull's-eye, though through ignorance (not inability) he keeps missing" (Davis (1979), p. 46). He thus comes to regard the non-epistemic sense of power as primary. Thus he suggests that the original analysis he is discussing should be amended to: There is an act-type Y such that at t, if A had willed to do a Y, he would have done an X (thereby). (In our example Y would of course be hitting a spot to the right of the bull's-eye.) Epistemic power would then be analyzed on the basis of this new formula.

What should we say here from the point of view of our analysis? First, Davis' example does not have a bite against epistemic power, as noticed. Secondly, I claim that **any** notion of ability or power must be connected to successful **intentional** action tokens. If a person can never under normal (or at least favorable) circumstances intentionally perform something X, he cannot be said to have the ability to do X (cf. Davis' above example). But Davis' analysis does not make this required connection to successful intentional acting. What is more, were we to employ the analogue of our (8) for an analysis of non-epistemic power - and to continue speaking in this analogue about willings in **our** sense - we would not need to speak of action types other than X. This is because we might now take A's willing by his bodily behavior to exemplify X to contain his moving his body in the right way. But this amounts in our example, roughly, to aiming and shooting to the right of the bull's-eye. So even an analysis of non-epistemic power does not have to refer to action types other than X.

I shall not here further elucidate (8) nor defend it. Let me here only add that if you think the requirement of strict or deterministic generation in (8) is too strong we can instead require probabilistic generation only. Thus in the original presystematic formulation we would use the phrase 'would probably succeed' instead of 'would succeed'.

How about compound action properties (types)? For them I have in Tuomela (1977), p. 317, presented the following elucidation, meant to generalize (8):

(9) A has the **power** to do X (or X belongs to the **action repertoire** of A) at T if and only if
    (a) X is the conjunction of some simple action properties $X_1,...,X_m$ (m>1) for A at T;
    (b) it is physically and psychologically possible for A to be in normal conditions at T with respect to each of $X_1, X_2,..., X_m$;
    (c) (i) each action token $u=<v,...,b,...,r>$ of X is (directly or indirectly) generated by some action tokens$_1$ of the action types X_i, i=1,...,m, occurring as conjuncts in X, such that when u is intentional, purposive generation is required;
        (ii) for each conjunct X_i such that X_i is not itself a simple basic action type nor does X_i occur as a conjunct in any compound basic action type consisting of conjuncts of X, it is true that each action token$_1$ of X_i is (directly or indirectly) generated by some intentional (simple or composite) basic action tokens$_1$ by A. In the case of intentional action tokens$_1$ (occurring at T) of X_i purposive generation is required.

In clause (c) v is assumed to be describable as an initiating event, as required in clause (1) of the definition of action token$_1$; $b=b_1+...+b_m$; and r is the (possibly composite) result event of X. As is seen, (9) in a sense reduces what A has the power to do to his basic actions. In the case of intentional action tokens u of type X A's willing to do X again, analogously with (8), purposively generates the result r of u, but now via the subtokens u_i (of X_i, respectively). It suffices for our present purpose to say that an action token u performed by an agent A was intentional just in case there was a conduct plan of A such that A purposively brought about u because of this conduct plan (for details see Tuomela (1977), pp. 320-325; also cf. our above (**PC**)).

The notion of power analyzed by (9) is not the only interesting notion of power. For instance, we may speak of an agent's power with respect to some issue, his control over another person's behavior, interests, or psychological states. Goldman (1972) has analyzed these notions in an informative way. With some modifications his account could be translated into our framework. According to him the central idea in the concept of power is getting what one wants (notwithstanding the possible resistance or opposition of others). Furthermore, one has to get what one wants somehow due to one's acting. Thus Goldman ends up giving an account which can be roughly stated as follows: An agent A has power with respect to an issue E (connected to an outcome e) just in case a) if A wanted e it would occur (due to his actions) and b) if A wanted not-e it would occur (due to his actions). Within our framework we would speak of willing (or effective intending) instead of wanting and we would suitably rephrase clause b) as we do not accept negative events. We shall not here, however, go into more details (but see our discussion in Chapter 9 below).

One thing to be noted here about our notion of power is connected to the fact that, as the conditional 'If A willed to do X, he would succeed (given normal conditions)' indicates, it is a disposition concept. As is well known, dispositions can be construed either instrumentalistically or realistically. In the realistic construal conditionals of the above sort are backed by a categorical **basis** property. This basis property (or state) is one **in virtue of which** the conditional holds. Although we have above kept our formulations neutral with respect to the problem of the existence of a basis for a disposition, we in fact favor the realist construal. (In Tuomela (1977), Chapter 5, a realist construal of dispositions is given and applied specifically to the dispositional notion of wanting. As intendings in our analysis in a sense are wantings playing a special role, it is easy to see that that account applies to the present case, mutatis mutandis.)

This concludes our summary exposition of the basic elements of the purposive-causal theory of single-agent action. As said earlier, our account of action generation is to be found in Chapter 6. A technical account of the intentionality of actions is summarized in Section III of Chapter 5. The explanation of both single-agent and multi-agent actions will be discussed in the final chapters of the book, especially in Chapters 11 and 12.

CHAPTER 5

THE STRUCTURE OF SOCIAL ACTION

I. THE GENERAL NATURE OF SOCIAL ACTION

1.   Given the presentation of the purposive-causal theory of single-agent action in the previous chapter we are now ready for the case of social actions, viz. multi-agent actions. In this chapter we shall be concerned with the conceptual nature, and, especially, the structural aspects of multi-agent actions. Accordingly, we are going to create a conceptual framework of action concepts which relies on the structural (and generational) relationships holding between various (e.g., simple and compound) multi-agent actions. More broadly, it is our view that in acting, agents are exercising their causal powers. Accordingly, our account amounts to creating a causal philosophical theory which we shall call the **purposive-causal** theory of social action. Some of its basic features were sketched in Chapter 4 and summarized there by the schema (**PCS**). As already emphasized, this theory relies heavily on causally active **we-attitudes** of which we-intentions and mutual beliefs stand out. In the present chapter we will be more concerned with a detailed development of various action concepts than with a philosophical defense of our purposive-causal theory. We regard our discussion in Chapters 2, 3, and 4 as giving a (partial) defense and justification for our present developments.

In the way of a preliminary sketch, by a social action we shall here, as before, broadly and roughly mean an action performed by several agents who suitably relate their individual actions to the others' actions in pursuing some joint goal or in following some common rules, practices, or the like. Consider thus two or more agents' doing something X, say carrying a table or writing a book (linguistically, e.g., 'Tom and John wrote a book'). We will below be interested in the interpretation under which they **jointly** (rather than each of them separately) did X. Or consider the still better example sentence 'All the king's men surrounded the castle'. Here the organized action of surrounding the castle is an irreducible joint or multi-agent action.

Social actions in our sense will include such diverse multi-agent actions as carrying jointly a heavy table, riding a tandem-bicycle, playing tennis, playing jointly Bach's concerto for two violins, getting married, greeting, asking questions and answering, conversing, quarrelling, and, given our later analysis in this chapter, also the actions involved in a group's solving a problem, a bank staff's performing its daily routines, a community's electing a leader, a nation's declaring war, and so on and so forth (also cf. our discussion of communicative actions in Chapter 10). What we shall attempt to do below is to look for some basic types of social action such that the clarification of the (overt) structure of such types of action together with the postulation of some generational mechanism will show that they can be used as a basis for constructing all types of actions, and thus for constructing all the possible action structures that can be named and conceptually employed in any society.

Social actions may of course be classified and grouped in a number of informative ways. There are some pertinent criteria of classification giving important ingredients of social action that are worth mentioning here. One is whether, or to what extent, the full result event of the social action in question comes about or is generated **causally** rather than **conventionally** (broadly understood). For instance, two agents' carrying jointly a heavy table is causally brought about by their component actions of carrying the table (whatever those component actions are in each particular case). Technically speaking, the results, say r_1 and r_2, of the component actions causally generated the full result, say r, of the social action of carrying jointly the table. Here causal generation is all that matters. But consider next two agents' toasting by appropriately lifting their glasses. Here the full result of the social action, viz. a toasting getting performed (r), is conventionally generated by the individual glass liftings (r_1 and r_2), the results of the agents' component actions. Here we may assume that r is only a mereological sum of r_1 and r_2 and that the conventional generation amounts to a redescription (according to the toasting-convention) of r_1+r_2 as r. In many social actions (such as communicative actions, e.g. asking questions - answering) both causal (or factual) and conventional (or "conceptual", as we will say) generation plays a role. Our above examples can in fact all be classified from the generational point of view that we shall develop in detail later in this chapter and especially in Chapter 6. We shall also discuss the matter from a mereological point of view.

Another, quite different criterion of classification is whether the original agents themselves, as it were, carry out the whole social action or whether at some point they employ some **representatives** or "proxies". For instance, when a nation declares a war or negotiates a treaty it is (or its members are) represented by, say, the cabinet or perhaps the prime minister only; or when a worker's union negotiates a wage increase it takes place by means of some representatives only. In the case of proxying, accordingly, action generation takes place with respect to actions by different agents, as we will show in Chapter 6.

Our treatment below will emphasize the above features even if the technical details will be cashed out only in the next chapter in the context of our automata-theoretic treatment of action generation. There are many other central criteria and features that can be used for classifying social actions. We shall consider some of these criteria below in Chapter 6, after having completed our conceptual framework of social action concepts and action generation (see Section III of Chapter 6). Chapter 7 will involve a detailed discussion and classification of types of social action in terms of social practical inference, and in Chapter 9 we will investigate and classify social actions from the point of view of social interaction, with special emphasis on the various types of (covert) social control.

2. Before starting our technical developments a few general underlying features of social actions may still be noted. We will in this chapter concentrate on actions that several agents perform **jointly** or together (as opposed to separately or alone). We shall use the phrase 'jointly' in a broad sense, partly as a technical term. There are in any case some facts about this sense that can be taken to follow from the way we ascribe actions to people in a social setting.

Let us consider a finite number, m, of agents, say $A_1, A_2, \ldots, A_m$, who have performed jointly a social action X (e.g., played together Sibelius' **Finlandia**). Then the following is obviously a true principle:

(a) $A_1, A_2, \ldots, A_m$ jointly performed X if and only if $A_2, A_3, \ldots, A_m, A_1$ (or the agents permuted in any other way) jointly performed X.

If A_1 and A_2 jointly carried a table then, accordingly, A_2 and A_1 jointly carried it. How about cases where A_1, say, does X with the help of A_2? Whether or not (a) will then be true depends on how helping is understood. If the helper A_2 does a part of X then he is a joint actor, we say, and (a) holds true. But if A_2 does not properly take part in doing X he is not a joint actor and (a) becomes inapplicable. Consider, respectively, my carrying a parcel jointly with my small daughter who is helping me carry it, versus her helping me in writing this book by staying out of my sight and hearing.

If $A_1,...,A_m$ jointly performed a social action X then it seems obvious that each of these agents must relevantly act in this situation. Let us thus consider:

(b)   If $A_1,...,A_m$ jointly performed X, then $(EX_1)...(EX_m)$ (A_1 performed X_1 & ... & A_m performed X_m).

We shall regard (b) as a valid framework principle. It entails that there are no idle agents, so to speak. Thus if it is found out that an agent, say A_m, did not do anything when $A_1,...,A_m$ performed X, e.g., carried a table, we cannot say that $A_1,...,A_m$ jointly performed X but only that $A_1,...,A_{m-1}$ (assuming that they all acted) jointly performed X. Since in (b), $A_1,...,A_m$ can perform $X_1,...,X_m$ separately (say, each separately write a book), the converse of (b) is obviously not true of joint action.

(b) can in fact be considerably strengthened, for we shall argue below that the actions $X_1,...,X_m$ in a sense generate or make up the full social action X; and much of our work in this chapter and in the next chapter will be devoted to studying this. As in Chapter 4, we shall here write $X=X_1\&...\&X_m$, taking the identity to be context relative. It is hard to formulate the general idea involved except by using just the notion of identity or saying something related such as that X consists of the X_is (together with the various relations between them). However, since tokens of X are taken to be generated appropriate tokens of the X_is I will below use that phrase "make up" to cover all this. Thus we have

(c)   If $A_1,...,A_m$ jointly performed X, then $(EX_1)...(EX_m)$ (A_1 performed X_1 & ... & A_m performed X_m & $X_1,...,X_m$ make up X).

The X_is will here be called parts or components of X. (We may, in fact, allow that each X_i be a complex action, and thus tokens of X_i may consist of several subtokens. We may even allow that A_i performs more than one token of X_i, although we shall normally assume there is one such token only.) Accordingly, (b) and (c) entail that every agent A_i performs his part, X_i, of X. (Note than when **collectives**, e.g., institutions, act there may in a sense be idle agents, but that is a different matter; see Subsection II.4.) The converse of (c) an be regarded as true under a suitably broad interpretation, we shall in effect argue below (see (5) and (C1) in Section II).

If $A_1,\ldots,A_m$ jointly performed X, then we may ask if the agents in any or all subsets or supersets of $\{A_1,\ldots,A_m\}$ did so or even could have done so. Since this is a rather interesting problem let us consider it at some length. As above, when we write $X=X_1\&\ldots\&X_m$ we mean that relative to the circumstances at hand the above identity is a conceptual truth. The circumstances obtaining at a certain time can here be construed as merely specifying the number of participating agents. Thus, given m participating agents it is a conceptual truth (cf. (b)) that X amounts to (is identical with) the type-conjunction $X_1\&\ldots\&X_m$, where X_i, $i=1,\ldots,m$, specifies A_is, possibly complex, component action type. (Since, however, an agent may be required to repeat one and the same action in a certain social action it is not always very perspicuous to take the circumstances in the above impoverished sense.) It has been noted in the literature that at least some (if not all) social action predicates are "multi-grade" as to the number of their argument places; they take **variably** many, as opposed to a fixed number of, arguments (cf. Massey (1976), and Brooks (1981)). Thus, e.g., carrying a table and toasting can be performed by a varying number of agents, depending on the context, and so 'carrying a table' and 'toasting' are multigrade predicates.

Indeed, it has been claimed that there is no fixed upper limit to the number of agents that can participate in such social actions (see Brooks (1981)). However, e.g., playing jointly a game of chess or singing a duet seems, and even for conceptual reasons, to allow properly for no more than two agents. Of course, a person may be helped by another person when performing his part of a social action, say, but that would be non-standard and would not properly conceptually introduce a new **agent** to participate in that social action (even if a new human body would become involved).

It is, furthermore, relatively obvious that certain actions such as playing a game of chess cannot be properly performed by less than a certain number (here two) of agents, as conflicting intentions are involved (cf. the intention to beat the other player in chess). Thus, a social action may have a lower limit as to the number of its agents, and there are "minimal" actions in this sense, even on conceptual grounds. Hence there seem to be social actions which are, on conceptual grounds, necessarily m-agent actions, for some m, in the sense of m being both the lower and upper limit.

Finally note that, on the other hand, there are actions such as conserving energy which have no upper limit and no lower limit (unless we emphasize **jointly** conserving energy, which involves the participation of at least two agents). Mob actions, such as rioting or fleeing in panic, also basically belong to this last mentioned category, except that of course a few persons do not yet make a mob.

While the above "numerical" considerations might deserve a fuller discussion we shall not here dwell longer on the matter. The issue is not very significant for our developments to come. Let us therefore conclude by summarizing our relevant conceptual truths and conjectures as follows:

(d) (i) There are actions with an upper bound (as to the number of participating agents);
(ii) there are actions with a lower bound;
(iii) there are, for some m, necessarily m-agent actions and thus actions with both an upper and a lower bound;
(iv) there are actions with no lower and no upper bound.

We may here recall our remarks on the external logical presuppositions of action from Section II of Chapter 3. We may also define the same four cases of actions with respect to them in the case of joint action. Thus we may speak of sustaining the obtaining of a result event or its non-obtaining and of bringing about its occurrence or non-occurrence depending on how the world is independently of our agents' joint acting. As before, our verbal formulations below will be concerned with the case where the result type R does not obtain and where it would not (or at least would not probably) come about unless the agents acted jointly. So we assume that there is logical room for joint acting in this sense, and this is completely parallel with the single-agent case.

However, the situation is somewhat different if we consider a participant agent. Recalling our discussion above of the numerical aspects of action we may first say that often a single agent's contribution is indeed needed for R to come about and that given the other participants' actions his "interference" in the world will bring about R. However, often a given single agent is not needed in this way. A heavy table can be jointly carried by four men or by five men, say. The fifth man can be said to genuinely take part in the joint action, however, even if the result of the action would have come about without him.

We can also view such dependencies more broadly. Let us consider a certain agent A_m in a collective consisting of the agents $A_1,...,A_m$. According to (d)(i), for some m, there are actions X such that $A_1,\ldots,A_{m-1}$ can (logically or conceptually) perform X jointly while $A_1,\ldots,A_{m-1},A_m$ cannot. According to (d)(ii), there is an action X such that, for some m, $A_1,\ldots,A_{m-1}$ cannot jointly perform X while $A_1,\ldots,A_{m-1},A_m$ can jointly perform X. Here is a clear sense in which $A_1,\ldots,A_{m-1}$ can be said to depend on A_m concerning X. Next, according to (d)(iii), there are actions such that, for some m, A_m is (numerically) indispensable as $A_1,\ldots,A_{m-1}$ cannot jointly perform X nor can $A_1,\ldots,A_{m-1}, A_m,A_{m+1}$, while $A_1,\ldots,A_m$ can. These cases suggest that a certain agent can play a central, indispensable role with respect to a joint action getting performed. He may be indispensable not only numerically but also in some other way, e.g., in social actions involving a strong task-specialization. Analogous remarks can be made concerning dyads, triads, etc., of agents among the agents of the collective in question, but as these points are rather obvious we shall not here go into them. Not only can the indispensability of an agent or group of agents concerning a social action be investigated but also a single agent's (or dyad's, triad's, etc.) dependencies relative to certain other agents (or coalitions and groups of agents) in the collective. (Some remarks on this will be made in Chapter 9; also cf. formula (9) below relating the agents' joint ability to do X to the agents' abilities to do their parts of X.)

Related to (d) and out above discussion we may further note that if $A_1,\ldots,A_m$ jointly perform X it may be the case that there are some social "subactions" involved. As we have seen, social actions are differentiated - there is some kind of division of activities and tasks. Accordingly, if some agents A_1, A_2, and A_3, say, jointly perform X then, for instance A_1 and A_2 may jointly perform Y, equalling $X_1\&X_2$, and analogously A_2 and A_3 jointly perform the action Z (= $X_2\&X_3$) while A_1 and A_3 do not jointly perform any social action having X_1 and X_3 as its parts (e.g., A_1, A_2, and A_3 jointly negotiate a pact with the party A_2 acting as a kind of participant middle man or arbitrator).

Let me end this preliminary treatment of joint action by emphasizing that a great richness of cases is involved. Thus, to mention some relevant factors, when performing a social action the participating agents may or may not be contiguous (temporally or spatially) and, accordingly, causally interacting in such a contiguous way. The agents may interact and influence each other in a number of different ways (much of this book being concerned with just that). When performing a joint action they may perform the same action or very different actions. What is involved in each case will depend, for instance, on the type of social action, on the social setting and circumstances, and on the division of activities (see Apostel (1978) for relevant points). Analogous remarks can and should also be made of the **intentional** elements (e.g., aims, purposes, intentions) involved in social actions. Even if we have not so much emphasized these factors above they will turn out to be very central for our treatment of not only intentional social action but also for our analysis of social action in broader senses. After the above preliminaries concerning non-intentional elements, we can in fact proceed directly to our detailed, systematic discussion of social action, and we will immediately face some intentional aspects of social acting.

II. SIMPLE SOCIAL ACTIONS

1. We shall now proceed to create, in structural terms, the central social action concepts our theory will need. Our treatment will be analogous to the single-agent case, discussed in Chapter 4. Accordingly, we will employ many of the notions defined there and create both "epistemic" (or "doxastic") and "non-epistemic" action concepts as well as the notion of a fully intentional social action. As in the single-agent case, we shall start with basic actions, the minimal "power-units". But before going to them some preliminary remarks and some general arguments are needed.

We shall sometimes below use the notation $\{A_1,...,A_m\}$ for the corresponding collective with the members $A_1,...,A_m$. It should be noted, however, that this notation in itself does not commit us to any specific ontological or conceptual view of the nature of social collectives (but cf. the Conceptual Individualism of Chapter 2). It should also be noted here that in speaking about the collective $\{A_1,...,A_m\}$ we do not make any prior social psychological assumptions about its nature except those to be discussed below. Thus, for instance, this collective is not a priori assumed to be a social group (or to be "organized"). While the primary area of application of our account is unorganized collectives it seems that at least our central concepts and results apply to "formally" organized collectives as well.

Even if $A_1,...,A_m$ are not antecedently assumed to be socially related, our social action concepts do require them to be. In the case of basic social actions (such as the agents' jointly waving their arms) it is, in the first place, the agents' relevant intentions and beliefs that create this social relatedness. In their case and generally in the case of actions the agents can jointly intentionally perform it seems necessary that they must share a **common intended goal**, normally (but not necessarily) the goal to perform the total action, say X. Indeed, they must share a relevant group-intention, normally one to do X, even if this intention need not be formed prior to action. But is this not an overly strong requirement? Indeed, why do any mental factors have to be involved? What is wrong with a non-intentional and non-psychological characterization of action, purified of any intentional features? Let us briefly consider the matter.

As we said in Chapter 1 we shall take it for granted in this book that the intentional framework of agency is needed for the characterization of human action. Non-intentional behaviorism - abandoning intentional mental factors - is simply wrong and has been shown to be so convincingly. How an agent views the world and what he desires and strives for are determinants of his action, and these elements cannot be given a purely non-intentional behavioristic characterization (but cf. Chapter 2 for a metalinguistic and "behavioristic" analysis of intentionality). So, we shall take it for granted that, e.g., wants, beliefs and intentions, etc., need to be referred to when speaking of intentional (and, especially, reasoned) action, irrespectively of how these mental factors are conceptually analyzed. We shall also take it as at least a plausible thesis that conations (viz. intentions) are motivationally and conceptually indispensable factors in an account of intentional human action (see Chapter 4). This can be strengthened to involve something like our (**PC**) of Chapter 4 and accordingly the presence of a goal (broadly understood) in any intentional single-agent action.

Assuming that something like this is defensible we may now ask why a **common** intended goal, or indeed a group intention, should be present in intentional joint action (and why our (**PCS**) of Chapter 4 is plausible). Let me first say that as our intuitions about social actions are not very sharp some amount of stipulation will have to be involved. But given this, what I want to claim is that at least a **full blown** epistemic notion of intentional basic social action (and in fact any intentional social action) should be taken to involve such a group-intention or we-intention on the part of every agent. (As to social relatedness in other cases of social action see, e.g., (5) below.) Let us now concentrate on such a full blown concept. Suppose thus some agents $A_1,...,A_k,...,A_m$ (perhaps repeatedly) jointly perform X, e.g., sing a song or play a game of cards, and do it intentionally. We cannot say they did it fully intentionally, viz. intentionally as a collective (at least if the collective was antecedently unorganized), if any of them lacked a certain relevant group-intention (usually one to do X) expressing the agents' common goal, even if each A_i would have performed his part intentionally. If, e.g., A_k would have performed his part of X intentionally but without sharing the other agents' common goal (e.g., reason for action) he would not have intentionally acted **jointly** with them, we may say. Because of this, the agents would not intentionally have acted as a group and so their social action would not have been fully intentional.

Consider next an example where agent A gave lethal poison to C and so did B. Both A and B gave an amount sufficient to kill C. A and B acted without knowing of each other's intention. Can we say that they jointly killed C? Obviously not - rather each killed C separately. Why is this so even if A and B in a sense both had, and acted on, the same intention to kill C by poisoning? Essentially because they lacked the mutual awareness of each other's intentions. But when we add this mutual awareness of each other's plans we arrive basically at our we-intentions in the sense of (**WI**) of Chapter 2 (apart from the fact that in (**WI**) I-intentions are conditional) and at the requirement of acting on such we-intentions. Thus, arguing on the basis that individual agents' intentional actions involve relevant intentions and that full blown intentional social actions involve intentionally performed single-agent actions we have come to the view that the social relatedness of intentional social actions in addition requires we-intentions, viz. mutually known or believed I-intentions (actually I-intentions conditional on the other agents' actions). The difference between acting separately and acting jointly in the case of fully intentionally performed social actions lies between acting on (possibly different) I-intentions and acting on a common we-intention (for weaker kinds of intentionality see the end of Section III).

We may also view the situation from the point of view of a collective's action. Why does not a mere shared intention (rather than a we-intention) to do X (or something else relevant) suffice? Suppose things go wrong when the collective starts exercising its power to do X. For instance, one of the agents may fail to do his component action. Then, ideally at least, the others will help, exert pressure, and do whatever they think is necessary in order for the collective to do X (cf. schema (**W2**) of Chapter 2). This again indicates that it must be believed by everyone in the collective that everyone else shares the relevant intention leading them to do X. To the extent that these beliefs are justifiable we may speak of the agents' mutual belief here. A mutual belief that everyone (in the collective) intends to do X ideally consists in everyone's believing that everyone intends to do X and everyone's believing that everyone believes that everyone intends to do X, and so on **ad infinitum**. The iteratability of 'everyone believes that' can be regarded as giving justification to the lower degree beliefs. (See Chapter 7 for a more detailed discussion of mutual beliefs, for a relaxation of the above characterization, and for the desirability of postulating them over and above not only 1st order but also 2nd order beliefs.)

Even more is involved here. For we may assume that this mutual belief concerns not only actual but also **potential** members of the collective. Thus every member may reason to the conclusion: were somebody a member of the collective then, in this situation, he at least should or ought to have the intention to do X. Indeed, that conclusion may at least ideally be required to be the content of a mutual belief held by the agents. This indicates the normatively binding character of group intentions and it also gives an argument for their presence in intentional social actions.

Given our above discussion, I will require the (direct or indirect) presence of a **we-intention** (to do X, or something motivationally relevant in any case) in the context of any full blown intentional social action (cf. (10) below). By a we-intention we mean an intention in the we-mode satisfying the definition (**WI**) as well as, suitably interpreted, the schema (**W1**) and normally also the schema (**W2**) of Chapter 2, and indicated by the agents' other relevant dispositions. An intentional performance of a social action X does not in the general case require the presence of an intention to do the very action X, and hence we cannot always require that kind of direct presence of a we-intention either. Yet, as will be seen, a relevant we-intention, in fact a we-willing, must be indirectly involved (in the sense explicated by (10) below).

A we-intention to do X is expressible by means of 'We shall do X' and volitional uses of 'We will do X'. I will not below distinguish between these statements whenever the latter is used "volitionally" and "non-predictively". The term 'we' in them of course refers to the collective $\{A_1,...,A_m\}$. We may also say that one of the dispositions related to a we-intention is, accordingly, the disposition to intend-out-loud 'We shall do X' when asked of the agents what they will do.

I will assume below that, corresponding to schema (**W1**) of Chapter 2, each agent A_i in effect accepts, perhaps stated in his own idiolect, the following, somewhat idealized inference as sound for we-intentions:

(S)   (i)   We will do X.
      (ii) I am one of us (viz. the collective $\{A_1,...,A_m\}$).
      (iii) I will do whatever I regard as necessary for our doing X.

It may be assumed that (iii) (and hence (i)&(ii)) entails, in the present context, for A_i:

(iii') I will do X_i,

in view of the additional fact that we may take A_i to believe that it is necessary for him to do X_i in order for the collective to manage to do X jointly.

2. As to intentional basic (and other "epistemic") social actions, we assume that it is mutually believed by $A_1,...,A_m$ that in standard conditions each agent A_i accepts (S) whenever $A_1,...,A_m$ we-intend to perform X. Accordingly, we require that for each A_i, i=1,...,m, there is an effective intending t_i expressed by (iii') such that, given normal conditions, this intending has been purposively obtained by means of (S) from an effective we-intending, say t_{we}^i, expressed by (i) (cf. clause (iii) of (c) in our definition of a compound single-agent basic action (4.2)). (Note that neither t_{we}^i nor t_i need be formed prior to action.) Let us specifically denote the purposive-generative (thus "purposive-preserving") relation between t_i and t_{we}^i, defined relative to (S), by $S*(t_{we}^i, t_i)$. We may comment on our present requirement in broader terms by saying that, accordingly, each A_i must at least be able to represent himself as an acting member of the collective $A_1,...,A_m$ and thus to recognize the other agents.

Our definition of a basic social action will to a great extent parallel our definition (4.2) of a compound basic action in the single-agent case. In the social case the simple action property conjuncts are now performed by the different agents of the collective, each A_i, i=1,...,m, exemplifying X_i by u_i, where X_i represents A_i's part of the total action X. In addition to requiring each A_i to be able to represent himself (and his fellow-agents) as a member of "us" (viz. $A_1,...,A_m$), we will also assume that in the case of basic action each A_i is aware that $A_1,...,A_m$ are performing a social action X whenever they are performing it. Indeed, we will assume that $A_1,...,A_m$ mutually believe (in some suitably weak sense of 'believe') that they are then performing it. This in turn requires the mutual belief that each has his component action X_i to perform and that indeed the X_is are jointly performable. Thirdly, it is required that the agents be mutually aware of their ability to perform the social action in question (cf. (c) of (4.2)).

Thus I propose the following characterization, employing notions defined in Chapter 4:

(1) X is a **basic social action type** for $A_1,...,A_m$ at T if and only if
   (a) X is the conjunction of some basic action types $X_1,...,X_m$, respectively, for $A_1,...,A_m$ at T;
   (b) it is physically and psychologically possible for $A_1,...,A_m$, respectively, to be in normal conditions at time T with respect to $X_1,...,X_m$;
   (c) for any exemplification u of X it is true that if u had the internal structure $<t,...,b>$ and if $A_1,...,A_m$ were, respectively, in normal conditions with respect to $X_1,...,X_m$ at T and if they truly mutually believed so, then, for $i=1,...,m$, the following conditions would be satisfied in this situation:
   (i) $D_i(t_i) \twoheadrightarrow D_i'(b_i)$
   (ii) $\sim D_i(t_i) \twoheadrightarrow \sim D_i'(b_i)$
   (iii) $S^*(t_{we}^i, t_i)$,
   where each t_i is described by D_i as A_i's willing by his bodily behavior to do X_i (and, possibly, as the relevant believings); $t = t_{we}^1 + ... + t_{we}^m$, and t_{we}^i is describable as a we-willing (or effective we-intending) of A_i to do X. D_i' expresses that b_i is a maximal overt bodily component-event of $u_i = <t_i,...,b_i>$ which represents A_i's action token exemplifying X_i in this situation; b_i is the result event of u_i (as an X_i); $b = b_1 + ... + b_m$, and b is the result event of u (as an X); and $S^*(t_{we}^i, t_i)$ expresses that t_i has been purposively generated by t_{we}^i.
   (d) $A_1,...,A_m$ have a mutual belief to the effect that (a), (b), and (c) are true.

Several comments on (1) may be made here. Clause (a) should be clear enough as it stands. The normal conditions of (b) include at least that there is an external opportunity for action (e.g., one's arm must not be up if one is to raise his arm) and that the agents are not prevented from performing the action in question (cf. the discussion in Chapters 3 and 7).

In clause (c) the essential new aspect, as compared with clause (c) of (4.2), is the employment of the effective we-intentions or we-willings t_{we}^i as the counterparts of the intention t in (c) of (4.2). Note that the third clauses of (4.2) and (1) are not completely parallel as to their intention components. In (4.2) the intentional action tokens u of X standardly (but not necessarily) involve A's intention t to do X. But in (1) the corresponding role is played by the t_{we}^i's while the intention t in clause (c) of (1) is a mere technically constructed sum of the t_{we}^i's. This is of course because a group or collective is not a self-sufficient agent in itself, in our view. Group-intentions (or we-intentions, in our terminology) do exist, all right, but they don't exist independently of the members of the group. Group-intentions can only exist by being individually represented in group members, so to speak.

Completely analogously with what we said about the logical form of ordinary willings in Subsection I.1. of Chapter 4 we may now say that we-willings are act-relational and self-involving as well and that their form can be spelled out as follows. We start with A_i's we-willing to do X and claim that in the present context it can in its strongest form be stated more fully by saying that A_i wills to do in the intended way, by his bodily behavior, anything which he believes is required for us (viz. $A_1,...,A_m$) to do X jointly. The logical form of this can be taken to be basically: $(\forall Y)[A_i$ wills that (if he believes it is required for us to do X jointly that (Ey) (he will now perform y & y is a Y), then (Ez) (he will now perform z & z is a Y))]. As earlier, Y ranges over bodily actions, and it as well as y occur in **de re** positions as in the earlier single-agent case. It follows that, although A_i need not have the concept of any action Ŷ that Y ranges over, he wills of Ŷ that it is required in the specified sense. The requiredness above is at least partly causal and thus we-willing typically involves causal production. (The self-involving character of we-willing expressed by the phrase 'in the intended way' can be spelled out, e.g., in terms of the intensional notion of satisfaction of Tuomela (1977), pp. 265-267, relying on the agents' mutual wh-beliefs.)

The parallel between clauses (c) of (4.2) and (1) breaks down not only due to the use of we-intentions in the former but also because of the fact that in (4.2) we require each t_i to be purposively generated by t. In (1) again we require corresponding purposive generation of each t_i by the respective we-intention t_{we}^i. We shall not here make specific ontological assumptions concerning t_{we}^i and t_i. However, note that the possibility of explicitly defining we-intentions in terms of I-intentions (and mutual beliefs) does not in any case make t_{we}^i and t_i the same, since t_{we}^i and t_i are directed toward different actions. Note that clause (c) (and (1) as a whole) allows for intentional action tokens of X where $A_1,...,A_m$ do not have the (effective) we-intention to do X (although they must have a relevant we-intention, we argue). As claimed in Chapter 4, central action concepts seem non-probabilistic when considered relative to the right background. Thus we follow common sense here and below and use only strict generation even if we have available the more liberal probabilistic notions (see Chapter 6, Note 4).

Clause (d) of (1) also seems to lack its parallel in (4.2). But we noticed that in the case of a basic action, as defined by (4.1), an agent is aware of "what he is doing" and our previous discussion of that can be extended to (4.2) as well. The present problem is rather why we need a special clause to account for the epistemic nature of our notion of basic social action. Let us consider the matter.

Our clause (d) of (1) requires that $A_1,\ldots,A_m$ mutually believe something which in effect amounts to believing that (a), (b), and (c) are true. Now clause (d) has been phrased in this way because we cannot of course assume that the agents $A_1,\ldots,A_m$ are familiar with the technical notions, such as $\looparrowright$, of our action theory. We might perhaps directly require that the agents mutually believe that (a) and (b). But in the case of (c) a vaguer mutual belief may have to suffice. Thus, $A_1,\ldots,A_m$ must perhaps be assumed to believe that their common intention to do X and their subintentions to do their component actions will normally lead to a successful performance of X. But they do not have to be familiar with our specific formulation (c) of this. What I am thus saying here is that the phrase 'to the effect that' in (d) should be understood widely enough to cover different, and vaguer, formulations.

We may perhaps also say that (1) expresses a full blown basic social action concept, so to speak. We might think of substituting 'to the extent that' for 'if and only if' in (1) and in this way allow for vaguer formulations of both (a)-(c) and of the mutual belief condition. This remark is pertinent to all of our definitions below.

Let us return to the problem that while in the case of single-agent basic action there was no need to introduce explicitly a special requirement of awareness of action, in the social case there is, even if both in the single-agent and the social case such awareness is equally central. This is basically due to the fact that a group of agents cannot in the same way be aware of its social action as a single-agent is aware of his own action. A single-agent is a coherent epistemic unity in a way a group is not. The need for a mutual belief clause is still there even after we require in clause (c) the existence of we-intentions to do X, which, we recall from Chapter 2, entails mutual belief in everyone's intending to do (his part of) X. For the latter mutual belief does not yet cover the needed mutual awareness of the information in (i), (ii), and (iii). Furthermore, mutual belief in the holding of normal conditions in (c) is both necessary and clearly separate from a mutual belief in the agents' ability or power to do X (which is what the mutual belief that (c) amounts to). Mutual belief that (a), (b), and (c), presystematically, means mutual belief in the possibility of basic social action X, viz. in a basic social ability, we may say. The role of the mutual belief requirement is in part to create the "social reality" of that basic social action construct.

Let us, however, note that each time X is intentionally exemplified by $A_1,...,A_m$, each agent A_i is of course aware of his own action (recall our discussion of (4.1)), and due to the mutual belief in the holding of normal conditions and the other agents' sharing the we-intention to do X, A_i may also be taken to be aware of the other agents' intending to do their parts of X. To the extent that it is a mutual belief among the agents that they reason according to the schema (S), we may take the last point for granted (cf. our (**WI**)). But that would not yet give us mutual belief in (i) and (ii) of clause (c). But we may nevertheless get this on the basis of the conditional $\triangleright\!\!\!\rightarrow$. Let us see how.

In the social case that conditional is defined on the basis of the agents' social conduct plan. Now, a social conduct plan involves the relevant we-intention and it may also plausibly be taken to contain implicitly the schema (S) as an underlying rule of inference (cf. our discussion at the end of this chapter). The crucial point here is that corresponding to the discussed requirement of we-beliefs about the components of a basic action in the single-agent case (and the resulting technical notion of satisfaction) we must have an analogue, and it may be taken to be **mutual wh-belief**, viz. dynamically active **mutual** awareness of which or what, etc. entities satisfy the social conduct plan. Then we may plausibly assume also that mutual belief in the conditionals (i) and (ii) is entailed. I shall not here press this line of argument, since we already have the desired mutual belief on the basis of clause (d) of (1). But it is of interest to notice that by suitable, rather non-restrictive qualifications we can do without the assumption of mutual belief concerning (at least) clause (c), and thus (1) might be made more closely parallel to the single agent case, in spite of our earlier comments to the contrary.

At this point the objection may be raised that if we keep clause (d) of (1) intact and explicate, or perhaps think that we must explicate, awareness of (basic) social action as just indicated, we get a confused doubling of the mutual belief requirement. But that will not be the case. For, first, the contents of the mutual beliefs seem at least overtly different. (The matter, however, ultimately depends on the distribution properties of the mutual belief operation.) But the central point is that even if the contents of the differently obtained mutual beliefs could be taken to coincide, iteration of mutual belief does not really matter. This is because of the following property of the mutual belief operation. Mutual belief that p entails mutual belief in mutual belief that p, but not conversely. Yet mutual belief in mutual belief that p conjoined with the assumption that everyone in the collective believes that p is provably equivalent with mutual belief that p (see Chapter 7 for a discussion). The point which is relevant here is that we can certainly in our present case assume that everyone believes that p (where p may just be clause (c) of (1)· or its "in effect" equivalent form). So in the present case iteration of mutual belief would not matter anyhow.

As in the single agent case, it must be emphasized here that our definition (1) is rather broad in that it does not account for variation in **manner, skill, effort,** and **attention,** and so on. Here we again say that more detailed notions of basic social action may of course be construed on the basis of (1) by adding various requirements concerning the mentioned factors. While we shall not here move in that direction let us make one relevant comment. It is that in the social case we encounter the problem of allowed variation in the degrees of the above factors. Suppose that the performance of a social action, say building a house or singing a duet, requires a certain degree of skill. Now it may suffice that there are in the group both highly skilled agents and agents with just minimal skill. Suppose a group composed of only such minimally skilled agents could not perform the whole social action with the required skill. But could we now think that a group where most of the agents are minimally skilled and only some are highly skilled could yet perform the total social action very skillfully?

The general problem is that degrees of skill, effort, attention, etc. and variation in manner do not seem to be "summative". Compensation may occur in some cases where agents exemplifying a high degree of the factor (e.g., skill) compensate (and overcompensate) for the poor or minimal performance of others. Or conversely, one bad singer in a chorus may spoil the performance of the whole social action of singing. But I shall leave the matter here. My intention was to call attention to this problem area without entering a proper discussion.

Note finally that, like our concept of single-agent basic action, the present concept does not allow for agent-external results. As examples of possible basic social action in the above sense we may mention the **bodily actions** involved in shaking hands and kissing. A more interesting example would be the following. Suppose that A and B have agreed to greet C by waving their arms when they see C arriving in his boat. The resulting social action of A's and B's jointly waving their arms is a good candidate for satisfying our definiens of a basic social action.

In our definition (1) each agent A_i performs a simple basic action of his. If A_i is allowed to perform a compound basic action, we get in an obvious way the following broader concept as our generalization (cf. (4.2) especially concerning (i), (ii), and (iii) of clause (c)):

(2) X is a **compound basic social action type** for $A_1,\ldots,A_m$ at T if and only if
  (a) X is the conjunction of some compound basic action types $X_1,\ldots,X_m$, respectively, for $A_1,\ldots,A_m$ at T, where each $X_i = X_i^1 \& \ldots \& X_i^{k(i)}$, for some $k(i)$;
  (b) it is physically and psychologically possible for $A_1,\ldots,A_m$, respectively, to be in normal conditions at time T with respect to $X_1,\ldots,X_m$;
  (c) for any exemplification u of X it is true that if u had the internal structure $<t,\ldots,b>$ and if $A_1,\ldots,A_m$ were, respectively, in normal conditions with respect to $X_1,\ldots,X_m$ at T and if they truly mutually believed so, then the following conditions would be satisfied in this situation for each $i=1,\ldots,m$ and the corresponding $j=1,\ldots,k(i)$:
   (i) $D_i^j(t_i^j) \rhd D_i^j(b_i^j)$
   (ii) $\sim D_i^j(t_i^j) \rhd \sim D_i^j(b_i^j)$
   (iii) $D_i^u(t_i) \rhd D_i^j(t_i^j)$
   (iv) $S^*(t_{we}^i, t_i)$,
   where t_i is described by D_i^u as A_i's willing by his bodily behavior to do X_i; each t_i^j is described by D_i^j as A_i's willing by his bodily behavior to do X_i^j; and D_i^j expresses that b_i^j is a maximal simple overt bodily component-event of the respective event $u_i^j = <t_i^j,\ldots,b_i^j>$ tokening X_i^j in this situation; $b_i = b_i^1+\ldots+b_i^{k(i)}$; b_i is the result event of u_i (as an X_i); and t_{we}^i is describable as a we-willing (or effective we-intending) of A_i to do X. Furthermore, $t = t_{we}^1+\ldots+t_{we}^m$ and $b_1+\ldots+b_m$, where b is the composite result event of u (as an X); and $S^*(t_{we}^i, t_i)$ expresses that t_i has been purposively generated by t_{we}^i.
  (d) $A_1,\ldots,A_m$ have a mutual belief to the effect that (a), (b), and (c) are true.

Having commented rather extensively on (1) the present definition does not seem to need additional clarifications (given the clarity of (4.2)). However, note that the mutual belief that (a) differs from the mutual belief required in clause (d) of (1). It may also be noted here that our concept of compound basic social action does not involve agent-external results either. A notion of basic social action incorporating them may be formulated on the basis of our concept of the agents' power to do something, to be discussed below.

3. One of our general claims is that all that the agents of a collective can jointly or collectively do is conceptually constructable from these agents' basic social actions by reference to suitable generational processes (involving factual and conceptual generation). This 'can do' refers to an **epistemic** notion of power (or ability), and thus we may speak of the reduction of complex epistemic action concepts to basic action concepts. Next, we claim that the structure of all social actions can be explicated by reference to bodily social actions and what they factually generate. This thesis, then, is concerned with the conceptual reduction of complex **non-epistemic** social actions to bodily social actions.

We have already elucidated our first set of building blocks, viz. basic social actions. Now we shall briefly explicate the second set of them, viz. non-epistemic bodily social actions. This is easily done by generalizing the corresponding single-agent concepts, as defined by (4.3) and (4.4), to the social case.

We propose:

(3) X is a **simple bodily social action type** for $A_1,...,A_m$ at T if and only if
  (a) X is the conjunction of simple bodily action types $X_1,...,X_m$, one, respectively, for each $A_1,...,A_m$ at T;
  (b) it is at least conceptually possible that $X_1,...,X_m$ are jointly tokened$_1$ by $A_1,...,A_m$ at T.

(4) X is a **compound bodily social action type** for $A_1,...,A_m$ at T if and only if
  (a) X is the conjunction of compound bodily action types $X_1,...,X_m$, one, respectively, for each $A_1,...,A_m$ at T;
  (b) it is at least conceptually possible that $X_1,...,X_m$ are jointly tokened$_1$ by $A_1,...,A_m$ at T.

Both of these definitions rely on the (non-epistemic) concept of a social action token$_1$, which we shall soon characterize. But even without an exact characterization of the class of social action tokens$_1$ we may note the following. Given our (1) and (2) it is obvious that every basic social action type (for $A_1,...,A_m$ at T) is a simple bodily social action type (for $A_1,...,A_m$ at T) and every compound basic social action type (for $A_1,...,A_m$ at T) is a compound bodily social action type (for $A_1,...,A_m$ at T).

Let us now discuss social action tokens$_1$ and present a causalist analysis of them. As our characterization is analogous to our definition (4.5) of single-agent action tokens$_1$ we may immediately proceed to our definition:

(5) Singular event $u = <v,...,b,...,r>$ is a **social action token**$_1$ by $A_1,...,A_m$ if and only if
 (a) u contains as its parts the respective action tokens$_1$ $u_i = <v_i,...,b_i,...,r_i>$ produced by the agents A_i, $i=1,...,m$; in the general case $u_i = <v_i,..., b_i^1,...,b_i^{k(i)},...,r_i^1,...,r_i^{k(i)},r_i>$, where $b_i = b_i^1+...+b_i^{k(i)}$ and the r_i^js ($j=1,...,k(i)$) either generate r_i (r_i being a separate event) or else $r_i = r_i^1+...+r_i^{k(i)}$;
 (b) $v = v_{we}^1+...+v_{we}^m$, where v_{we}^i is an event describable as instantiating a propositional (or representational) social attitude (or we-attitude) of A_i, and in u each v_i, $i=1,...,m$, is an event describable as instantiating a propositional (or representational) attitude of A_i such that v_{we}^i (causally) generates b_i via v_i;
 (c) $b = b_1+...+b_m$, where each b_i is the maximal bodily component event of u_i, and the b_is generate the corresponding r_is with the exception that for some k, $k=1,...,m$, it may be true that $r_k=b_k$;
 (d) r is the (full) result event (or episode, more generally) of u; either $r = r_1+...+r_m$ or else the r_is, $i=1,...,m$, generate r (where $r \neq r_1+...+r_m$).

Our broadest, motivational notion of joint social action, defined by (5), is meant to cover not only all the technical notions of social action we have defined and will define in this chapter but also a large variety of social behaviors beyond that. As to the latter, for instance, a crowd's panic reaction to a common stimulus, say a fire, may be due to a social belief (cf. (b)) and then its panicky behavior will be a social action token$_1$ in our sense. In addition to panic behaviors our (5) seems to include crazes and hostile outbursts and, in general, mob actions that social scientists have called actions due to "generalized beliefs" which are social attitudes, indeed often mutual beliefs, in the sense of clause (b). We can say that such mob actions are rather uncoordinated yet rigid (nonplastic). They are social just because of the social beliefs from which they result; people without them would not act so. Naturally all the examples of single-agent action tokens$_1$ when generalized into multi-agent actions are also going to satisfy (5) (see Chapter 4).

I am willing to claim that there cannot be social acting on mere belief (such as "generalized belief" above). If this is accepted then, even when v_{we}^i explicitly is only described as a we-belief, clause (b) in fact entails the presence of a we-want (we-pro-attitude) or at least I-wants, possibly differing in content, in the case of each acting agent.

Various non-intentional and partly intentional social actions belong to the scope of (5) along with typical intentional ones. Thus partly intentional goal-directed actions fit in here. Thus a group may work towards achieving a certain goal without being aware of it or without all the members being aware of it (cf. the Manhattan project and the Red Orchestra). The we-attitude in clause (b) typically gives the goal (which may or may not known) to the acting agents. In cases of actions of organized groups and their members as exemplified by the Manhattan project, we may assume - although it is not necessary - that a functionalist analysis of the we-attitudes in question will suffice to characterize the group ("us"), even if all the agents need not have a conscious conception or be clearly aware of whom the group consists of nor of the content of the we-want, viz. the goal of producing the atom bomb - a belief in the **existence** of a group goal is enough. Assuming that the group or "we", rather, can be so delineated, it is not necessary to require full consciousness of the group and its organization and division of labor; cf. Section I of Chapter 13. Let me here also warn the reader not to confuse the action of a group with the joint action of some of its active members, for the acting group may contain many more members than those who actually jointly performed the action in question - see Section IV and especially analysis (16) below. In the case of the Manhattan project presumably the broadest group of agents (with the functionalistically characterized we-want to produce the bomb) consists of more agents than those which can be said to have jointly produced the bomb. The presence of the we-attitude - be it specific or only existential - is decisive here.

Cases of distorted (and even contradictory) communicative interaction, such as the so-called double-bind interactive pattern, belong or can belong to the scope of (5) because of some of the mutual beliefs involved (even if there may be much contradictory and confusing information present).

Also social behaviors corresponding to Sellarsian pattern-governed behaviors in the single-agent case belong here. It would seem that conforming perceptions (or "perceivings-out-loud") in Asch type experiments may count as examples of social pattern-governed behaviors. According to the Asch phenomenon some people in a group may influence the perception of, e.g., the length of objects, by some other agents in the group so as to make these perceptions grossly non-veridical. The joint action here might be the agents; (nonintentionally) producing a certain distribution of length judgments, for instance.

Let me comment further on the central but problematic notion of a **social** propositional attitude employed in clause (b), to be discussed in more depth in Chapter 7. In the case of intentional social actions we would have a situation where each v_{we}^i in v is describable as an event realizing a relevant effective we-intention (not necessarily a we-intention to do what r satisfies), and each v_i is derived from such a we-intention v_{we}^i (recall our schema (S)). Furthermore, v_{we}^i may in addition often be regarded as a complex event realizing a (social) loop-belief. This is plausible when v_i is construed broadly as an event satisfying a social conduct plan (and thus, for instance, the premises of a suitable practical inference; see Chapter 7). The loop-belief involved here will typically have the following content: A_i (for all i=1,...,m) believes (thinks, expects) that A_j (for all j=1,...,m with i≠j) believes that A_i should (or intends to or will) perform the action X_i. We shall later in Chapter 7 discuss such loop-beliefs in more detail, and see Chapter 12 for socially looped utilities (or wants).

More generally, we may say that each v_{we}^i would realize either a **we-pro-attitude** or a **we-expectation** (or both) of $A_1,...,A_m$, and then each v_i, i=1,...,m, realizes an I-attitude suitably derived from (or generated by) a corresponding we-attitude (cf., e.g., the purposive generative relation $S^*(t_{we}^i, t_i)$). It is primarily such we-attitudes, generalized analogically from the case of we-intentions, that we shall call **social** attitudes. But one should be careful here not to require that the members of the collective have a clear we-concept. The concept of a social attitude is an analogical, functionally construed concept and, in the general case, it involves the notion of we (or us) only in a vague, analogical sense. Therefore, the term 'social attitude' is preferable to 'we-attitude' in the most general context.

There are weaker notions of social action not even involving we-attitudes. Thus one may consider a social attitude (such as a social belief) to be one which in its propositional content contains essential reference to some other agents with respect to which the agent is acting (see (9.1) and (9.2)). However, this gives a notion too weak to be called joint social action. Thus if A walks on B's land and B walks on A's land we get a two-agent social action in this generalized sense (but not in the sense of (5)). But even this notion may exclude some multi-agent behavior. Consider, for instance, Max Weber's famous example of people in the street simultaneously opening their umbrellas when it starts to rain does not represent a social action even in the generalized sense. Not only do these people lack a relevant motivating we-attitude but they do not even act in relation to each other in the above sense. We shall below mostly restrict ourselves to full blown social actions involving we-attitudes; however in Chapters 7, 9 and 13 broader social actions are involved.

As to the notion of generation used in (5), we shall in Chapter 6 discuss in detail. We are here dealing solely with what will be called **factual** generation. At least clause (b) is concerned with **causal** generation (a subtype of factual generation). It is arguable that at least typically in (c), too, generation means causal generation. Below in Section IV (cf. (11)) we shall take up several cases, including ones where the full result event (episode) r equals the sum $r_1+...+r_m$ (rather than being a separate event), and our discussion there will serve as a motivation for what clauses (a) and (d) say about the generation of the r_is and r (see especially Section II of Chapter 6).

In those cases where the full result event r is distinct from the sum $r_1+...+r_m$ the action token u fails to equal the sum $u_1+...+u_m$ (cf. the phrase 'contains as its parts' in clause (5)(a)). My argument for this is the following. At least in the present type of cases we may plausibly accept "vectorial" addition for ordered events. Thus my proposal for adding action tokens (ordered events) is: $u_1+...+u_m = <v_1,...,b_1,...,r_1>+...+<v_m,...,b_m,...,r_m> =_{df} <(v_1+...+v_m),...,(b_1+...+b_m),...,(r_1+...+r_m)>$. Given this principle we can easily see that, given (5), $u = u_1+...+u_m$ only if $r = r_1+...+r_m$. Thus, as often $r \neq r_1+...+r_m$ also $u \neq u_1+...+u_m$. Note finally that we assume in (5) that the result events can here be viewed quasi-extensionally without reference to a specified action type and we do not here use the intensional-making locution 'as an X' familiar from some of our previous definitions.

III. COMPLEX SOCIAL ACTIONS

1. Note surprisingly, we shall also characterize complex social actions in analogy with the single-agent case. As before, the analogy is between the components (subactions) of a compound single-agent action (see (4.6)) and the components (subactions, performed by different agents) of a compound social action.

The generalization of definition (4.6) for the social case is rather obvious (cf. e.g., carrying out a conversation). We propose:

(6) Property X is a **compound social action type** for $A_1,\ldots,A_m$ at T if and only if
  (a) X is the conjunction of some compound action types $X_1,\ldots,X_m$ ($m \geq 1$), one, respectively, for each $A_1,\ldots,A_m$ at T;
  (b) it is at least conceptually possible that $X_1,\ldots,X_m$ are jointly tokened$_1$ by $A_1,\ldots,A_m$ at T;
  (c) each social action token$_1$ u = <v,...,b,...,r> of X is (directly or indirectly) generated by some action tokens$_1$ (occurring at T) of the action types X_i, i=1,...,m, which are conjuncts of X.

Note that we do not need in (6) the counterpart of clause (c)(ii) of (4.6), for the idea involved in it is already taken care of by the requirement that the X_is be compound action types for the respective agents A_i.

Our (6) employs the notion of action generation centrally. As we shall clarify that notion in the next chapter we will ask for the reader's patience to hold out until then. Note here, however, that the generation principle

(PG) $IG(u_1+\ldots+u_m)$ if and only if $IG(r_1+\ldots+r_m,r)$

discussed in Chapter 4 seems as appropriate in the multi-agent case as in the single-agent case and we shall adopt it, with the obvious reinterpretation of the symbols in it.

Let us illustrate the scope of our notion of a compound social action by the following game of "Pile of Four Stones". In this game two players, A_1 and A_2, take turns removing stones from a pile. The pile has four stones at the start, and each player in turn may remove one or two stones. Whoever gets the last stone wins. A_1 acts first. Consider now the tree-structure shown in Fig. 5.1 for this game.

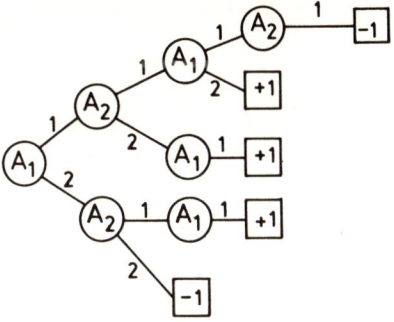

Fig. 5.1.

The game begins at the left and moves to the right. The numbers 1 and 2 on the branches mean the number of stones removed at that choice. The numbers +1 and -1 in the squares indicate the payoffs (the game is a zero-sum one, of course). The squares are, each of them, taken to instantiate the end result of the action of removing the pile. Let us now consider the topmost branch of the tree as an example of a token of the social action or removing the pile of stones (say X). A_1's subtoken consists of two components: his first removing one stone (u_1^1) and then removing another one after A_2 has removed his first stone (u_1^2). A_2's subtoken similarly has two components (u_2^1 and u_2^2) the latter of which brings about the final result event. A_1's component action type, say X_1, consists of two subaction types, the ones that u_1^1 and u_1^2 exemplify. The analogous remark can be made in the case of A_2 (whether or not we can make $X_1 = X_2$ here does not matter). In sequence $<u_1^1, u_2^1, u_1^2, u_2^2>$ we obviously have exemplified both a conceptual (rule-governed) and a factual connection. (The factual connection is of the causal precondition-type.) The present game can easily be generalized to the case of m (>2) agents and n (>4) stones or objects.

We can actually see that any token of a compound social action, when described "structurally' in the above generational fashion, can be represented by a branch of a suitable game-tree (in the technical sense in which the extensive form of a game is a tree). The converse of course does not hold, for a variety of reasons. The most central reason is that game-theoretic descriptions are completely abstract and thus do not as such contain a specification of any factual generational relations.

Other examples of compound social actions are not hard to

find. Let me here still mention a few types of social action (also see Chapter 6). Coordinative actions such as speaking in turn and driving on the right may be analyzed as social actions in our sense. In these rule-governed actions the point is that people try to do more or less the same thing with a minimum of interference from others, while such an interference will take place without coordination. (See our discussion of coordination in Chapter 7.) Next there are cooperative actions requiring each (or most) participants' cooperation. For instance, carrying a heavy table might require the cooperative acting of several agents. On a broader scale conserving energy or going on strike might be mentioned as examples. These latter two actions, furthermore, deal with achieving collective goods (or preventing collective evils). (Collective goods are goods that everyone enjoys if anyone does, such as higher wages or clear air, etc.) Let me finally mention collective social actions which rely on some division of labor, tasks, and activities in a community. For instance, rituals like wedding ceremonies belong here and so does a basketball team's activity.

Next we define what we mean by an arbitrary complex (non-epistemic) action type:

(7)   X is a **complex social action type** for $A_1,...,A_m$ at T if and only if
      (a) X is a simple or compound bodily social action type for $A_1,...,A_m$ at T, or
      (b) X is a compound social action type for $A_1,...,A_m$ at T.

Now we may formulate a stronger concept of a social action token (for a collective $\{A_1,...,A_m\}$ of agents):

(8)   u is a **social action token$_2$** if and only if
      (a) u is a social action token$_1$, and
      (b) u exemplifies a complex social action type.

On the basis of our developments we can now make two general conjectures the second of which follows from the first, given our account:

(C1) All that it is conceptually possible for any agents $A_1,...,A_m$ to jointly do (perform) intentionally is to perform a complex social action (i.e., to produce a social action token$_2$).

(C2) All that any agents $A_1,...,A_m$ ever directly do (perform), jointly or separately, is to move their bodies; the rest is up to "nature" (the environment, including the social environment).

Both of these theses must be taken **cum grano salis**, with a perhaps somewhat technical use of 'jointly' and with all the qualifications on generation to be presented later, especially in Chapter 6. But in any case (**C1**) gives our broadest (perhaps partly stipulative) characterization of joint action performable at will (see (**10**) for intentionality). However, note that, of course, there are lots of non-intentional action tokens$_2$. Also note that those action tokens$_1$ which are not action tokens$_2$ (e.g., social pattern governed behaviors) are not performable at will.

The joint performance in (**C1**) need not be cooperative and may be even competitive in its nature (cf. Chapters 2, Sect. III, 7, Sect. V, and 12, Sect. III). Thesis (**C2**) must be understood strictly in the sense of our definition of a compound action and of a compound social action. Direct doing here means the performance of bodily action. It must be emphasized that the doing (in the sense of performance) involved in (**C1**) is broader and involves agent-external results. Thus we are not here reducing the agents' doings (actions) to bodily actions.

Notice that all along we rely on socially fixed conceptualization (and verbalization) of action structures (i.e., conceptualizations fixed relative to a given social practice; cf. the set λ_i of individualistically acceptable predicates of Chapter 2). Only then can we account for the fact that the statement 'the rest is up to "nature"' refers only to **factual** action-generation (see Chapter 6). Let me also point out that our notion of factual generation should here be understood broadly enough to cover probabilistic (and other indeterministic) generation.

We shall not here attempt to give stronger arguments for (**C1**) and (**C2**) than those already incorporated in our above definitions (also cf. the treatment of complex single-agent actions in Chapter 4 above and in Chapter 10 of Tuomela (1977)). One further point worth making here is that the truth of (**C1**) and (**C2**) depends very little on the specific features of our purposive-causal theory of social action. It thus seems that our generational account of social actions could easily be modified to fit suitable rivalling accounts (e.g., those discussed in Chapter 3).[1)]

2. In Chapter 4 we discussed a couple of epistemic notions of ability or power, as we called them. We shall now generalize one of those, viz. (4.9), to the social case. Our characterization of "social" or "joint" power thus comes to rely on single-agent power (ability). Accordingly, we require A_i to have the power to do X_i, $i=1,...,m$, in a social action type $X=X_1 \& ... \& X_i \& ... \& X_m$. (Very often X_i will involve bringing it about that some other agent(s) do something, willingly or not; cf. Chapter 9.) Given this, there is no need to formulate a counterpart to clause (c)(ii). We shall need below the notion of purposive generation for the social case. Given (PG), the result r of a token u = <t,...,b,...,r> of X is required to be purposively generated by the r_is, $i=1,...,m$, or a suitable selection of them. As in the case of all of our epistemic social action concepts we employ a requirement of mutual belief.

We define for a complex social action X:

(9) $A_1,...,A_m$ have the **joint power** to do X (or X belongs to the **social action repertoire** of $A_1,...,A_m$) at T if and only if
    (a) X is the conjunction of some complex social action types $X_1,...,X_m$, one, respectively, for each $A_1,......,A_m$ at T such that A_i, $i=1,...,m$, has the power to do X_i at T;
    (b) each social action token$_1$ u = <v,...,b,...,r> of X is (directly or indirectly) generated by some tokens$_1$ (occurring at T) of the action types X_i, $i=1,...,m$, which are conjuncts of X, such that when u is intentional, purposive generation is required;
    (c) $A_1,...,A_m$ have a mutual belief to the effect that (a) and (b) are true.

The notion of power (or ability or competence) employed in clause (a) above is primarily meant to be that defined by (4.9). But in fact any viable account should do here (and partly because of that we did not in Chapter 4 really defend the details of (4.9)). A stronger notion of power can be obtained by requiring that no subset of $\{A_1,...,A_m\}$ suffices to give $A_1,...,A_m$ the joint power to do X, but this seems a very stringent notion. In (9) the notion of intentionality is employed. Intentionality in the case of social action presents problems going beyond those present in the single-agent case. We shall now briefly comment on this notion.

We suggested earlier in this chapter that a social action performed by $A_1,...,A_m$ is intentional only if the individual actions are intentional. But this is problematic. We have above in the definientia of our characterizations of social action concepts required that the collective $\{A_1,...,A_m\}$ is not a mere aggregate but is connected through some social attitudes (we-attitudes and we-beliefs). If the collective has (antecedently) some more organization, e.g., in terms of the power and control some agents have concerning some others it might perhaps be possible to falsify the above proposal. For instance, there could perhaps be cases where the leaders do something intentionally while (some of) the underdogs perform their actions nonintentionally or intentionally but under a "wrong" description, without explicit awareness of the leaders' group-intention (we-intention). In such cases we might still want to claim that the social action was intentionally performed by the collective. I am not, however, at all sure whether we should accept these examples as counterexamples against **full blown** intentionality (see Section IV below).

In order to characterize the full blown intentionality of social action we thus seem to need to have an account of the intentionality of single-agent action. Put briefly, an action token u performed by an agent A was intentional (in a "causal" and not only "semantical" sense) if and only if there was a conduct plan of A such that A purposively brought about u because of this conduct plan (see Tuomela (1977), pp. 320-325; also cf. (**PC**) of Chapter 4). In view of the above, I now propose for a social token u = <t,...,b,...,r> which may be assumed to exemplify a complex social action type (to match (**PCS**) of Chapter 4):

(10) Social action token$_2$ u jointly performed by $A_1,...,A_m$ was (fully) **intentional** if and only if there were (complete) conduct plans K_i, one, respectively, for each A_i, i=1,...,m, such that $A_1,...,A_m$ purposively brought about u because of the social conduct plan $K = K_1\&...\&K_m$, where each conduct plan K_i makes essential reference to a we-intention (not necessarily one performed prior to action) that $A_1,...,A_m$ shared.

As said in Chapter 4, the notion of a conduct plan (or, technically, a conduct plan description) is a generalization of the notion of a plan of action that the premises of a practical syllogism form. In addition it should be noted that the language of the conduct plan description may be taken to contain some suitable rules of practical inference which go beyond pure logic. A **social** conduct plan can be technically defined as the conjunction of the operative conduct plans of each single agent A_i in the collective with the proviso that a **social** attitude is referred to (or is involved) in an "essential" sense in each individual conduct plan. The essentiality in question is not only the essentiality of logic (viz. denial of the possibility of the existence of logically equivalent reformulation of the conduct plan making no reference to the we-intention) but a motivational essentiality (viz. having essential motivational impact on action). An example of a social conduct plan would be the conjunction of the premises of a social practical inference, such as an instantiation of the schema (SA_i), for $i=1,...,m$, to be discussed in Chapter 7; also see Chapters 6, pp. 191-196, and 9, Section III.

The notion of bringing about in (10) is a causal (or partly causal) one. It seems adequate here to say that $A_1,...,A_m$ purposively brought about u because of K (or, alternatively, when acting on K) just in case each A_i (intentionally) brought about u_i because of K_i and the r_is purposively generated the full result r. This is a strong enough analysis as long as the we-intention appears in each K_i as required in (10). An agent A_i's bringing about u_i because of K_i can be analyzed "generationally" (cf. Tuomela (1977), pp. 320-325). The essential idea is simply that the event t_{we}^i that is described as a we-intention, indeed we-willing, in K_i and that is also taken to technically satisfy some relevant beliefs (such as those in our schema (SA_i) of Chapter 7) is required to purposively generate r. (But it need not have as its content the end r realizes nor need it have been formed prior to action.)

Note that the requirement that each u_i be intentional entails (cf. (PC) of Chapter 4) that A_i has a relevant effective intention (relevancy being motivationally characterized in terms of the acting on -concept). However, this does not yet guarantee that the different A_is intentions be directed to the same end. The postulation of a we-intention guarantees that. Although this demand may seem strong I have not found clear enough counterexamples - perhaps due to the vagueness of our intuitions concerning intentional multi-agent actions (recall the discussion in Section II and see our later remarks on weaker notions of intentionality). While our notion of intentional social action may thus seem strong note that the we-intention required to be involved need not be an "altruistic" and "proper" one, and so it need not satisfy our schema (W2). Thus, e.g., some agents' jointly running a ten kilometer race might satisfy our (10) (cf. our related example on p. 37 in Chapter 2). Let me emphasize here that to be adequate, (10) and (11) must be read liberally (or modified) to include probabilistic generation, in the sense of "probably generates" to be discussed briefly in Chapter 6.

We have now basically completed the presentation of the

social action concepts needed for explicating what it is conceptually possible for $A_1,...,A_m$ to do and what they have the power to do (intentionally). We may accordingly formulate the following explications, where the presystematic 'doing' should again be understood in a performance sense (which excludes, e.g., snoring); cf. (C1) and (C2):

(C3) All that any agents $A_1,...,A_m$ (epistemically) can jointly intentionally do is to perform a social action belonging to their social action repertoire (as defined by (9)).

(C4) All that any agents $A_1,...,A_m$ (epistemically) can jointly intentionally do is generated by the most elementary social actions they can do, viz. by the basic actions of the members of the collective.

Thus, in all, we have come to explicate **joint social action** in several ways starting from the very broad class of actions in the sense of (5), strengthening it by (8) and (10) (also cf. (C1)) as well as (9) (also cf. (C3)); and recall the possibility of relying on we-intentions in the "proper" sense ((**WI**)&(**W1**)&(**W2**)) instead of using only (**WI**) in (9) and (10).

3. Let us now tackle social actions from a mereological point of view. In particular, we shall consider the relationship between the results of social actions and the results of their individual "component" actions in some clean-cut cases. As before, we let r stand for the result event of the total social action, say X. For simplicity, we shall consider only two-agent actions, and thus $X=X_1 \& X_2$ such that the results of X_1 and X_2 are denoted by the placeholder symbols r_1 and r_2, representing respectively the types R_1 and R_2, say. I shall assume that the results have been appropriately conceptualized for the cases at hand so that we need not below deal with conceptual generation (cf. (6.15)).

We shall now consider some conceptually central cases that our generational account covers. Let me list these cases as follows:

(11) (a) r equals the sum of r_1 and r_2 (viz. $r=r_1+r_2$);
(b) r contains the sum of r_1 and r_2 as its part (viz. $r>r_1+r_2$);
(c) r equals the product of r_1 and r_2 (viz. $r=r_1 \cdot r_2$);
(d) r contains the product of r_1 and r_2 as its part (viz. $r>r_1 \cdot r_2$);

(e) r equals or contains the (ordered) concatenation of r_1 and r_2 (viz. $r=r_1r_2$, or $r>r_1r_2$);
(f) r is independent of both r_1 and r_2 (viz. r/r_1 and r/r_2).

Here sum, product, part, and independence are defined in terms of the primitive notion '∘' of **overlapping** of the calculus of individuals in the usual fashion as follows (cf. Goodman (1966)):

(12) (i) $r_1+r_2 =_{df} (\imath z)(w)(w \circ z \equiv (w \circ r_1 \vee w \circ r_2))$;
      (ii) $r_1 \cdot r_2 =_{df} (\imath z)(w)(w \circ z \equiv (w \circ r_1 \& w \circ r_2))$;
      (iii) $r' < r =_{df} (z)(z \circ r' \supset z \circ r)$;
      (iv) $r/r' =_{df} \sim(Ew)(w \circ r \& w \circ r')$.

What kind of examples of (11) can one give? Let me briefly list a few examples. Case (a) contains, e.g., cases like toasting or singing in chorus (see the comments in Subsection II.4. of Chapter 6 and formula (6.17)). How about (b) where r usually is properly generated by, and in any case contains, the sum r_1+r_2? For instance, two group leaders' shaking hands (r_1+r_2) might bring about the full result r of their making some group members happy.

Cases of type (c) involving products are somewhat tricky. Consider the following game. Two agents are on the opposite sides of a board with three holes in it. Each has a stylus which he is supposed to insert in one of the holes. The agents are rewarded if they succeed in matching. We can assume that here the rewarded joint action has as its result just the product $r_1 \cdot r_2$. (Our notion of cascade generation to be defined by (6.18) covers this.)

It seems that some cases where r_1 and r_2 causally bring about a distinct total result r are nevertheless such that $r>r_1 \cdot r_2$ (cf. (6.18)). Consider a safety door in a bank. It has two locks such that clerk A is required to open one of them and clerk B the other one. The total result r of the door's opening now is not only jointly caused by r_1 and r_2 but contains $r_1 \cdot r_2$ as its part, for the total social action involves not only the door's opening but its opening due to A's and B's actions. Thus we can take this to be a case of (d).

Cases such as requesting (asking) and responding (answering) can be taken to exemplify (e), since we may assume that $r=r_1r_2$, where r_1 is the result of the action of requesting, r_2 that of responding, and r the result of the total social action of requesting and responding (also cf. Section I of Chapter 10).

More generally, the turn-taking pattern, much emphasized by social psychologists, fits in here, for sequences such as $r_1 r_2 r_1 r_2$ (= r) qualify as their results (see Section 6.III. for further examples). Here we are dealing with sequential individuals in the sense of the calculus of individuals and the theory of formal grammars. Recall that we have earlier used the notation $<e_1,\ldots,e_k>$ for sequential individuals (cf. u = $<v,\ldots,b,\ldots,r>$ for action tokens.

Finally we have case (f) where r is mereologically independent of r_1 and r_2. Typical cases of the causation of r by r_1 and r_2 seem to fit in here. For instance, two agents' jointly building a house, say, exemplifies or at least contains exemplifications of this pattern.

Social actions may also be classified as **disjunctive** or **conjunctive** according to the nature of the tasks involved (cf. Thibaut and Kelley (1959), pp. 162-164). We may call a social action disjunctive if it suffices that one of the participating agents brings about the total result of the action. Group problem solving can be mentioned as an example: the group has solved the problem as soon as one of its members has. A purely conjunctive social action would be one requiring an active contribution from every participating agent (cf. the agents' carrying a piano). Naturally, many complex real-life social actions may also involve both conjunctive and disjunctive component social actions.

To clarify the conceptual nature of disjunctive and conjunctive social actions it seems that we must explicitly speak of the **occurrence** of result events. Let thus $occ(r_i)$ stand for r_i's occurring. Then a disjunctive two-agent social action satisfies

(13) $occ(r) = occ(r_1) \lor occ(r_2)$,

while a conjunctive one satisfies

(14) $occ(r) = occ(r_1) \,\&\, occ(r_2)$.

Note especially that

$occ(r_1+r_2) \neq occ(r_1) \lor occ(r_2)$,

viz. the occurrence of a sum r_1+r_2 (as in the toasting example) is different from either r_1's occurring or r_2's occurring. Completely analogously

$occ(r_1 \cdot r_2) \neq occ(r_1) \,\&\, occ(r_2)$.

Cases with satisfying (14) are easy to come by while cases with $occ(r) = occ(r_1 \cdot r_2)$ are not. (Our stylus inserting example satisfies the latter condition, as we in effect claimed above.) Analogously, we may discuss, for instance, cases of conditional dependence where

(15) $\quad occ(r) = occ(r_1) \rightarrow occ(r_2)$,

and cases where the occurrence of the individual results combine in more complex ways, truth-functional or not.

IV. THE ACTING OF SOCIAL COLLECTIVES

1. A discussion of collectives and their intentional actions is now in order. Let us begin by noting that we have not required much of the collective $\{A_1,...,A_m\}$ relative to which we have defined action concepts above. One might want to be more specific and require that this collective be a social psychological group. This requirement may or may not add new information to the present account, depending on one's notion of group. Merton (1957) characterizes a group by this: (1) It consists of "a number of people who interact with one another in accord with established patterns" (p. 285); (2) "they have patterned expectations of forms of interaction which are morally binding on them and on other 'members', but not on those regarded as 'outside' the group" (p. 286); (3) the interacting people are regarded by others as belonging to the collective (p. 286). Our social action concepts in effect incorporate requirements (1) and (2); requirement (3) is not explicitly mentioned in any of our definientia. We shall in Chapter 8 discuss social groups (and other relevant concepts) in some detail and give a precise characterization of that notion.

Whatever may be the exact nature of the collective to which the agents $A_1,...,A_m$ belong, we may now briefly consider the problem of **collective** agents. We have above in our technical definitions always spoken about some agents $A_1,...,A_m$ as the agents of a social action. Thus, while these agents belong to, or at least represent, a collective, we have not, so to speak, officially recognized collectives as agents even if we may have occasionally used locutions outside our definitions that have this suggestion. What can be said of collectives as agents?

We first recall that, in accordance with our individualistic position sketched in Chapter 2, **conceptually** collective concepts, such as just collective agents, are constructable out of individualistic concepts, primarily social action concepts.

Analogously, collectives do not **ontically** amount to more than what such concepts represent, either. Yet we use locutions like 'Firm F produced the goods G', 'Nation N_1 attacked nation N_2', 'The board dismissed Jones', 'The team scored', and so on, attributing actions to collective agents.

I see no harm in attributing actions to collectives as long as it is recognized that collectives are entities clearly different from single human persons. Persons have (biological) bodies and perform bodily actions in contrast to collectives (but cf. robots which act, too). Persons have a full blown mental life while collectives do not. Thus, while I accept that collectives may in a sense have wants and beliefs and may act for a reason these mental notions make only rather crude behavioristic and dispositional sense in the case of collectives (but cf., e.g., robots, dogs, worms). We shall nevertheless below attribute actions, wants, and beliefs to groups. Groups can also be said to intend to act. I think all this is plausible as long as the somewhat metaphorical character of this usage is recognized and our Conceptual Individualism is kept in mind. (Note, too, that groups cannot be characterized fully extensionally in terms of their sets of members, for they can gain and lose members without change of identity.)

Actually I am willing to go somewhat further and maintain that a collective is not a self-sufficient agent (e.g., in the sense of performing basic bodily actions) and that the actions of collectives are "constituted" by actions of persons. Thus, more specifically, if a collective does something X then at least some of its members, say $A_1,...,A_k$ must, respectively, do, in the right circumstances, something $X_1,...,X_k$, generatively relevant to X. For instance, if a nation declares war against another nation, this may take place through suitable actions by the members of its government, parliament and by its president. Or consider a hockey team's scoring. Some player or, perhaps, players did the scoring. Let us say that it was the "operative" or "representative" members of the team (collective) who did it. The team's scoring was constituted by their actions. (Note that the statement about the team's scoring holds under different conceptions of how to define the membership of the team - cf. the players not presently on the ice.)

Let me thus propose the following general analysis of a collective's doing something X intentionally in a full blown sense relative to some relevant circumstances, to be commented on later:

(16) A **collective**, G, with the operative agents $A_1,...,A_m$, **performed an action X intentionally** in circumstances C

if and only if $A_1,\ldots,A_m$ jointly performed X intentionally (in the sense of (10)) in circumstances C.

The satisfaction of the right hand side of (16) entails that $A_1, \ldots, A_m$ performed some appropriate actions $X_1,\ldots,X_m$ such that these actions generated or probably generated (and thus "made up") X, generation understood in the technical sense $IG^*(u_1,\ldots, u_m,u)$ of Section 6.II such that the agents' conduct plans involved a relevant we-intention and where $u_1,\ldots,u_m,u$ tokened $X_1,\ldots,X_m,X$ respectively.

The above analysis makes a distinction between the **operative** (or representative) and the **non-operative** (or non-representative) agents of G. Consider a state's making a pact with another state. This takes place by, say, the cabinet ministers' agreeing to the pact and the prime minister's signing it. Most citizens of the state do nothing relevant here, we may assume; the cabinet represents them. I shall not here try to give an analysis of how the operative representatives of collectives are selected, for I think that it cannot be done without performing empirical studies of the power and information structures of various collectives. If we would like to remove the relativization to the named agents $A_1,\ldots,A_m$ we can do it by requiring, instead, on the definiens side that, for some m, **there exist m** such operative agents in G (or at least such operative **non-member**-agents **for** G).

What are the circumstances C that (16) relies on? It seems obvious that they must satisfy the right social and normative constraints. Thus if a prime minister signs a treaty proposal it does not qualify if it is unlawful. Similarly the members of the board of an institution cannot nominate somebody for a post, say, if it does not have the (formal) power to do it. What the acceptable circumstances are I cannot really clarify here, but I refer the reader to the recent, largely acceptable analysis by Copp (1979). Let me just say generally that the following two types of constraints are needed. First, C will satisfy all the constraints due to the constitutional rules, laws and by-laws or organized collectives. Secondly, C will satisfy constraints concerning the composition and dynamics of, or patterns of interpersonal relations within, given unorganized collectives.

Given the right C, I claim that (16) is acceptable for **full blown** intentional action, in part due to semantical stipulation. We shall in Section 6.II discuss Copp's (1979) analysis of what representation or proxying of actions amounts to generally. It will then be argued that (16) is compatible with his analysis, and we shall also clarify the technical "generational" issues that (16) involves. We need not go into such technical issues here, since our main concern below will be the intentionality of social acting.

Given (16), the problems related to the intentionality of a collective's action become directly connected to those related to the intentionality of joint multi-agent action. We may now ask whether the full blown intentionality of (16) is too strong. Cannot collectives act intentionally without all the operative agents acting intentionally? Or, which in view of (10) amounts to the same thing, need all the operative agents have the we-intention that serves to make their social action intentional?

I submit that the word 'intentional' can be used in weaker senses making an affirmative answer possible. My basic claim is, however, that the full blown notion of intentionality is the, admittedly idealized, core notion from which all the weaker notions of intentionality derive their significance. This full blown notion is a core notion because of the analogy between the collective and the single agent, viz. we wish to view the collective as if it were a single agent. Consider a single agent's action X (= X_1&...&X_m), e.g., his drinking a cup of coffee or reading an article. If X is intentional then it is purposively generated by his relevant willing-belief complex (cf. above and Chapter 4). This entails that the agent controls his action and is to some degree aware of it (or at least of the bodily actions involved in it). But to the degree that kind of control (and awareness) over the total action diminishes, the degree of intentionality also diminishes, ceteris paribus.

To see the analogy, consider the following collective action. Some people (perhaps unknown to each other) arrive at a public meeting at which a foreign guest with a hard-to-follow accent will speak. How do the listeners seat themselves? As it happens (we assume) they leave the first three rows completely vacant even if the talk would be easiest to follow from the seats in them. Instead they fill every chair from the fourth row on. Every auditor surely acted intentionally, whatever reason each one had for his choice of seat. We can yet argue that the collective did not act intentionally because the control and awareness afforded by a relevant we-intention was lacking. With such an effective we-intention (concerning rational seating), assumed to be shared by every auditor, the distribution of vacant and filled seats would certainly have been different. What I am trying to stress is that a we-intention, together with relevant beliefs, will make a collective an action-controlling unit comparable to a single agent and that such unity cannot be arrived at without a relevant we-intention on the part of all acting agents in the case of intentional social action. This idea naturally gives direct support to (16). My intuition and claim then is that such a group's action is (fully) intentional just in case all the members of the group act on the same relevant we-intention (cf. our (**PCS**) of Chapter 4 and (**10**)). Had some agents acted without the we-intention, the group's action, say X would not have been fully controlled and unitary and hence not fully intentional (cf. Section I and also our discussion of (**10**) above).

2. How about weaker notions of intentionality? Or can we speak of degrees of intentionality relative to the above strong notion of intentionality? Consider the following example. A group of passengers intentionally pushed a broken bus up the hill. Let us suppose that each member of the group intended (and therefore in some suitably broad sense wanted) to do his part of the pushing, given that at least some of the other agents do theirs. Yet they might not have known how many of them are required to get the bus moving, and even had they known it they might have doubted that a required number of them will push, and we may (but not undisputably) regard the definiens of our definition (**WI**) of we-intention as unfulfilled. But, we assume, everything turned out all right and they succeeded in pushing the bus up. This might perhaps be regarded as an intentional social action and thus a counterexample to my (**10**). Here I would like to say that my intuitions are not firm enough. Why not say then that the passengers' pushing the bus was intentional in a **weak** sense but not in our strongest, full-blown sense? I think that as our intuitions about group actions are not so strong no harm is done if we leave the matter at this kind of "classificatory level".

There are also several other factors that speak for adopting weaker senses of intentionality. Let me mention a couple of such aspects related to a multi-agent action X. One of the agents might intend to do something Y and fail to know or believe that Y=X, viz. he would intend X under a wrong description. Still a further, and weaker, possibility is that the agent intends to do something Z and knows (or correctly believes) that Z is a subgoal of the group. This subgoal-relation might involve the agent's believing that there is an action X such that were he to intend to do X he would in those circumstances be justified in intending to do Z (cf. the Manhattan project example in Section II). The agent's so intending to do Z might accordingly strongly limit the class of actions that the group can perform, and thus the member in question might well be acting "in the right direction" without being exactly aware of the specific action X the group intends to perform. In the above cases the group's action is to at least some extent intentional.

Let us now imagine that we can measure the degree of intentionality of each agent's action (with respect to his having the we-intention to do X or some other relevant shared we-intention; cf. (10)). We then go through all the **operative** agents A_i, $i=1,\ldots,m$, and compute the average of the degrees of intentionality relative to the whole group. Let d_i be a measure of how **close** an agent A_i comes to having the relevant we-intention. (I shall not here investigate how to define d_i; but cf. Section II of Chapter 8.) Then, for instance, the index $I(X) = \Sigma \frac{d_i}{m}$, with $0 \leq d_i \leq 1$, would be a natural candidate for measuring the **degree of intentionality** (in the full blown sense) of the group's performing X. The mathematical properties of the average I are simple and obvious. Note that a certain value of I can come about in widely varying ways. Thus, in a dyad both the combination $d_1=0,5$ and $d_2=0,5$ and the combination $d_1=1$ and $d_2=0$ yield $I=0,5$. Note that in a dyad with A_1 as its leader and only operative member the latter situation would give full intentionality.

We have above been relying on a distinction between the operative (or representative) and the non-operative agents of a collective. While I doubt that much of interest can be said of this distinction on purely conceptual grounds, let me nevertheless make one relevant remark. Let us distinguish, roughly, between collectives which are "egalitarian" (and usually unorganized) and those which are not, with respect to the issue at hand. By an egalitarian collective we mean one in which no agent, or clique of agents, has absolute or nearly absolute (economic, political, informational, etc.) control (power) over the other agents' (relevant) actions or the reasons or volition-belief complexes on which these agents act; see our later definition (9.31) and the relevant discussion in Chapter 9. (We may, in fact, assume more generally that in an egalitarian group there is no binding "decision rule" for arriving at group goals and intentions.) Thus, an egalitarian group in this sense is one without a leader (with enforceable power), and a non-egalitarian group is one with leadership (be it "formal" or "informal").

The remark I would like to make is that in the case of egalitarian groups we may plausibly take all the members of the group to be operative agents (and all of the latter to be members of the group). I take this to be almost like a conceptual truth, if not a semantical stipulation, concerning egalitarian groups of the defined kind. In the case of such groups we can drop references to operative agents in (16). In the case of non-egalitarian groups the corresponding relativization to operative agents is of course central, for the leader or the leading clique controls the group. The other members are more like helping hands.

How about the more realistic cases where there is not such a clearcut difference between operative and non-operative agents or topdogs and underdogs? How about cases where a decision rule, e.g. the simple majority rule, is used? (If the members really do abide by the decision that would presumably entail their forming a we-intention to do X, and our index I would get 1 as its value.) I will leave these problems open here. Yet I would like to claim that the above ideas can be further liberalized to fit such real life cases.

V. GROUP INTERESTS REVISITED

1. Given our discussion of we-intentions and, more generally, group interests in the previous chapters and the present chapter, it is now of interest to consider them in a somewhat different, dynamic setting. We shall consider an argument to the effect that acting on group interests is impossible when rational self-interested individuals are concerned. If this argument were sound quite generally, for all kinds of group interests, it would seem to have unpleasant implications for liberalistic social philosophy and ethics. It would also affect our theory of social action, which largely builds on the possibility of acting on other-regarding interests, irrespective of whether such interests are always ultimately based on something like pure self-interests or not. While we think that there are genuinely altruistic we-interests our theory of social action certainly must admit that at least on some occasions we-interests may be based on rational individuals' pure self-interests only (cf. our discussion in Chapter 2).

Olson (1965) argues that if individuals, in a group, act out of self-interest to achieve their individual goals, it does not follow that groups of individuals will further their group interests. Even more: "unless the number of individuals in a group is quite small, or unless there is coercion or some other special device to make individuals act in their common interest, **rational, self-interested individuals will not act to achieve their common or group interests**" (Olson (1965), p. 2). Olson goes on to say that this implies that "even if all of the individuals in a large group are rational and self-interested, and would gain if, as a group, they acted to achieve their common interest or objective, they will still not voluntarily act to achieve that common or group interest".

Olson's interesting argument is, in the first place, concerned with providing some collective (or common or public) good for a group of agents such that getting that collective good is supposed to be the group interest (or goal). A collective good is defined to be any good such that if any agent A_i in a group having $A_1,...,A_i,...,A_m$ as its members consumes it, it cannot feasibly be withheld from the others in that group. Examples of collective goods would be clean environments, secure surroundings, higher wages, etc. Olson's above thesis entails that it is rational to be a "free rider" (and thus not to, e.g., join, and pay the fees of one's professional organization).

In order to be able to evaluate Olson's thesis let us now concisely present his argument for it (see Olson (1965), pp. 22-24 for more details). Let T be the rate or level (of, e.g., security) at which the collective good (say wage or security) is obtained. Next we assume that C is the (marginal) cost of increasing T.[2] As usual, C is taken to be a U-shaped function of T. (This is a consequence of the "law of diminishing returns"; cf., e.g., Lipsey (1979), p. 217.) Next Olson lets S_g be the "size" of a group. S_g depends not only upon the number of individuals in the group but also on the value of a unit of the collective good to each individual in the group. Let now V_g be the total group gain: $V_g = S_g T$. Every agent A_i gets a fraction of the total gain. Let A_i's gain be V_i. Then his fraction is $F_i = V_i/V_g$; thus $V_i = F_i S_g T$. The advantage (A_i) that any agent A_i (prepared to pay alone for the total cost of the collective good at T) would get from obtaining any amount of the collective good is $V_i - C$, and this expression is positive whenever $V_i > C$.

Now, given the assumption of the U-shapedness of C as a function of T, the argument is simple. What a group does will depend on what the individuals in that group do, and what the individuals do depends on the relative advantages to them of alternative courses of action. Let us thus consider the individual gain or loss from buying different amount of the collective good. It is assumed that A_i (= $V_i - C$) changes with changes in T (viz., $dA_i/dT = dV_i/dT - dC/dT$). If F_i and S_g are assumed constant (which perhaps may be granted) we get for the maximum advantage (i.e., for $dA_i/dT = 0$) the expression $F_i S_g - dC/dT = 0$. Thus the optimal amount of a collective good for an agent to obtain, if he should obtain any, is found when the rate of gain to the group, multiplied by F_i, equals the rate of increase of the total cost of the collective good.

If we ask whether any collective good will be provided at all, the answer is this. At the optimum point for the individual acting independently, the collective or group good will be provided just in case $F_i > C/V_g$. For in that case $V_i > C$, viz. the gain to an individual from seeing that the collective good is provided will exceed the cost.

The situation can be illustrated in terms of the diagram shown in Fig. 5.2, where the axis represents amounts of money, e.g. dollars, and the rate of (relative) amount T of the collective good provided.

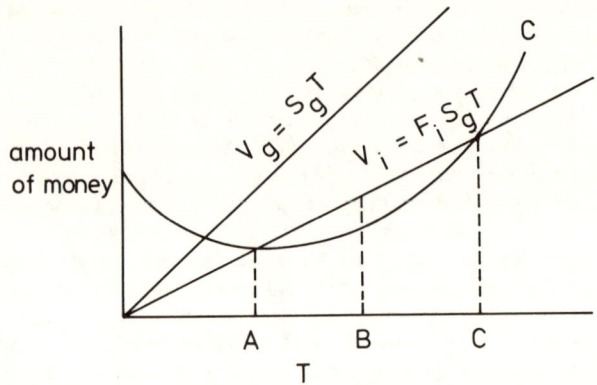

Fig. 5.2.

We immediately see from Figure 5.2 that some collective good will be provided by an individual A_i having to pay the total cost between points A and C. Point B gives the optimal point for this individual in the sense of maximizing.

The optimal (Pareto-preferred) provision of a collective good for the whole group is still another matter. For that the marginal cost of additional units of the collective good must be shared in exactly the same proportion as the additional benefits (cf. Olson (1965), p. 30). But it is quite plausible to think, as Olson does, that the larger the group, the farther it will fall short of providing an optimal amount of a collective good and even any amount of it at all. This is because of the very nature of the collective good: As soon as someone provides it for the group (by paying all the costs) it is freely available, at the provided level, for everyone in the group. Now, in small groups there are often members with a large quota F_i, whence the condition $V_i > C$ is easier to satisfy than in the case F_i is small. And consequently the members with a small quota will have a "free ride" and will thus exploit the mighty members of the group. But as the size of the group increases the shares (F_is) are likely to decrease, and the collective good will less likely be provided by anyone even at a suboptimal level for the group (for we have here a multi-person prisoner's dilemma situation; see below). And when some collective good is provided by a member he is more likely to stop buying it before an optimal level for the group is reached, since it is relatively quite expensive for him and since he may, in addition, sometimes get some amount of the collective good free from other members.

Thus the size of the group affects the provision of a collective good, viz. the attainment of a common goal. Because of the U-shape of the cost-curve, the level T will also affect the situation. Increasing T quickly decreases the possibility of obtaining any amount of collective good at all. After point C in Figure 5.2 no collective good will be provided by A_i if he acts on egoistic interests (viz. on keeping his advantage $A = V_i - C > 0$). With increasing T we soon come to a point where **no** member of the group is able to provide any amount of the collective good (when acting self-interestedly).

In his analysis Olson distinguishes between three types of groups according to their size. First, there are small groups where there is at least one member getting such a large fraction of the total benefit that he would be better off if he paid the entire cost himself, rather than go without the good. So there is some presumption that the collective good will be provided. Next we have groups in which, although no one gets such a large benefit from the collective good that he would have an interest in providing it even if he had to pay all of the cost, there is nevertheless an individual in the group who is so important that his contribution (or lack of it) to the group goal would have a noticeable effect on the costs or benefits of others in the group. In such groups it is sometimes possible that two or more individuals strategically communicate and interact (in terms of agreement, cooperation, and so on) in order to provide the collective good. But the communication, agreement and organization of activity have their costs, too. The larger the group is, the larger such additional costs become. Increasing group size then again entails not only suboptimal provision but lack of provision of the collective good.

Finally, we have those large groups in which no single individual's contribution makes a perceptible difference to the group as a whole, or to the cost or advantage of any single member of the group. In such groups a collective good will not be provided unless there is coercion or some outside inducement that will lead the members of the large group to act in their common interest. This is just the type of case (in fact a multi-person prisoner's dilemma) which Olson's argument is meant to apply to with its fullest force.[3] Notice, too, that Olson's emphasis here is not on self-interest but on rationality. People in large groups may act unselfishly to some degree as long as that unselfishness of individuals does not amount to their jointly (i.e., the whole group's) acting on the common interest. The emphasis here is rather on the imperceptibility of an individual's contribution and the lack of motivation (presumably) caused by it for rational behaving (cf. Olson (1965), pp. 64-65).

After the above presentation of Olson's argument we are ready to evaluate it and put it in a broader perspective. What does the argument really show? Is it that unless some special situation or device is involved, "rational, self-interested individuals will not act to achieve their common or group interests"? Let us first consider Olson's set-up. He deals with independent individuals trying to maximize their (self-interested) gains in attempting to achieve a common objective, viz. to provide an (optimal) amount of some collective good. Keeping to this frame, the following comments can be made. First, there is the problem of the epistemic nature of the argument. The U-shaped cost-curve must be regarded as an empirical law rather than a conceptual truth. What qualifications it needs to be true and, given such qualifications, what its scope will be, I cannot discuss here. But in any case it seems to contain an important germ of truth, and I expect that it is true in all cases that interest us in this context. In general, I think that Olson's argument (even with its simplifying assumptions) is acceptable for the dynamic situation with collective goods he is concerned with. Thus there are or at least seem to be important cases of social action where self-interested individuals, rational in a gain-maximizing sense, may act collectively and yet fail to achieve a collective good (which everyone would prefer to have), and where although some amount of collective good is being provided, it is below the optimum level (and everyone would prefer to increase it). But I consider his argument to indicate the need for the presence of we-intentions, or at least of other-regarding interests, and for acting on them in the situations at hand (cf. our discussion in Chapter 2). What is more, we will see that while Olson's general thesis seems to hold for social actions aiming at securing collective goods there are several other types of social actions to which it cannot - as a matter of conceptual impossibility - be extended, even in the case of purely self-interested individuals.

2. An extension of Olson's argument seems possible. For the cost-law could equally well be stated for utilities, so that it becomes a law of diminishing marginal utility. That is, we can make exactly similar observations as above when we substitute 'utility of amount of money' for 'amount of money' in our Figure 5.2.

Another extension of Olson's argument that may be considered is the following. While Olson considers a situation where the agents act independently and where each one must be prepared to pay the full cost C of the collective good, we may relax this. Thus, we may divide C in some suitable way. One obvious proposal is to divide it in direct proportion to the fractions F_i, i=1,...,m. Thus we would deal with costs C_i adding up to C, each member having to contribute in all situations in which the collective good, or some amount of it, is provided (cf. the collective good of quiet in a library). While this requires cooperation between members (and represents a clear departure from Olson's original set-up), conclusions follow that are rather similar to those in the original situation. Looking at the new situation in terms of our Figure 5.2, the C_i-curve now goes lower than the C-curve, its first intersection with the V_i-line comes earlier (on the T-axis) and its second intersection later than it does in the case of the C-curve. But qualitatively the situation is quite similar. Accordingly, increasing group size and/or increasing T-level make it more and more difficult to provide any amount (and still less an optimal amount) of the collective good.

While the change to sharing costs means a step towards interesting situations of social interaction it still falls far short of those cases of social action we are most concerned with in this book. Before taking up such cases, it is worth remarking that even Olson's original situation can be conceptualized as a case of the prisoner's dilemma (see Chapter 7 for a characterization of this type of game). The choice alternatives for any (sufficiently wealthy) member could be taken to be to cooperate or not to cooperate, when cooperation means paying the cost C (or, if using the liberalized schema, a fraction of C) and non-cooperation not-paying (but rather waiting for a free ride). If all of the members refuse to pay the situation would be harmful to all of them, but if someone pays and provides for (some amount of) the collective good, those who did not pay might benefit most. If we simplify the situation of Figure 5.2 by considering only a static situation (between points A and B on the T-axis), disregard the exact amounts of gained advantage, and, for the purpose of presentation, consider only a case with m=2, then even if the argument depends on the group size being sufficiently large and generally represents a multi-person prisoner's dilemma, we get a prisoner's dilemma of the sort illustrated in Figure 5.3.

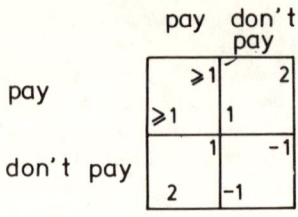

Fig. 5.3.

If you like, the one player might be the Individual who plays against the collective agent Society. Under this interpretation our assumption m=2 is unproblematic. I have chosen the utility values somewhat arbitrarily, but they comply with Figure 5.3 and do exemplify the prisoner's dilemma pattern. The first or cooperative cell (pay, pay) gives at least one utility unit to both participants. As not-paying dominates paying in Figure 5.3, the cooperative cell will be chosen only when the players somehow have come to agree to cooperate. Such cooperation can be due to a special norm (see Chapter 7 on prisoner's dilemma norms). In any case, a special "device" seems to be needed for ensuring cooperation here. This special device, such as an agreement or norm (or norm-governed role or social position), will affect the players' acting via their cooperative we-intentions to act so, we may assume.

Olson's general argument is concerned only with a special case of collective action involving a minimal or non-existing amount of interaction. In fact, the cases represented by his original set-up need **not** qualify as cases of intentional social action (in our technical sense) at all, for no we-intentions (concerning the provision of a collective good) need be involved in our required sense. But, we may ask, can an argument be constructed specifically for proper intentional social actions to show, paradoxically, that **no** social action (requiring freely acting on a common interest) is possible, at least in large groups? My general answer is no. There is clearly some ground for accepting Olson's thesis for social actions concerned with the provision of **collective** goods and for claiming that, in the case of them, rational, self-interested individuals form we-intentions only because of the existence of "special devices" and "inducements".[4] But in the case of social actions concerned with the provision of individual, **non-collective** goods no special devices are needed (cf. below).

Furthermore, it is compatible with Olson's argument to claim not only that social action involves acting on common interests but that social actions in this sense indeed are performed and **also** that **collective** goods get provided. This only shows that not all the premises in Olson's argument can be true. Thus the argument indirectly comes to indicate the need for we-intentions or we-interests (or at least other-regarding interests of a broader kind). And, indeed, as "everyone knows" and as social psychologists have been busy pointing out, people do act on common interests, e.g., they respect public property, pay taxes (and, e.g., choose the cooperative outcomes in prisoner's dilemma-cases, as has been experimentally verified).[5] Often acting on a we-intention involves acting on a (moral) norm (not a "special device"?) or out of duty and in such a case Olson's utilitarian considerations do not typically hold true. (Cf. also our claim in Chapter 2 that we-intentions are neutral as to utility basis.)

One feature about proper intentional social actions that Olson's set-up obscures is that they typically require the joint, coordinated acting of several, perhaps all, of the agents in a group (see Sections I and II above and Chapter 7). To take an example, consider a ballet group rehearsing a dance. If we represent this as a social action $X=X_1 \& ... \& X_m$, we in general have some interaction between the subactions $u_1,...,u_m$ (tokening $X_1,...,X_m$) producing the action u (tokening X). In this case at least we may assume that every u_i, $i=1,...$, is causally necessary for u. Now each u_i involves a (utility) cost to its performer and u involves a gain to be shared by the m agents. There are no free rides here, since no public good is involved and since everyone must participate in the costs.

It is, however, interesting to note that some aspects of Figure 5.2 apply here, too. First, every member A_i can evaluate his cost of performing X_i with respect to his share of the total gain (of performing X) to the group. His cost involves rehearsal costs (e.g., costs due to mental and physical exhaustion) and costs of actually performing X_i at a show, and so on. (Let us here ignore the organization built around all this and consider unorganized, informal groups only.) How the size of the group affects the gains here is an unsettled empirical issue, depending on the case. (Size does not always play a role here analogous to the case involving a collective good; even in large groups these individual contributions may be "perceptible" and non-negligible.) Secondly, we may take T to be the aesthetic quality of the action X. The costs involved in increasing that quality can plausibly be taken to follow a U-shaped curve. We may also assume that at some point on the T-axis the group will dissolve as the costs to the group for achieving that level would become too great as compared with the gains accrued.

The above example of the dancing group can plausibly be analyzed so that common interests, indeed altruistic we-intentions, are present and the agents act on them. Yet it would be possible to speak only about self-interests (or ultimately self-interest based we-interests) in this (and any similar) situation and to treat it strictly in terms of Figure 5.2. Anyhow, we may plausibly assume that the agents act on a common interest here, even if this common interest is not concerned with the provision of a collective, but instead a non-collective good. Consequently, we have here a type of social action where rational self-interested individuals may act to achieve their common or group interests. No "special device" is present here either. It follows that Olson's general thesis is false for this and, as could be equally easily shown, for many other ordinary types of cases of social action. His thesis may be true for situations involving collective goods, as seen above (even if this is an unsettled empirical issue; also cf. notes 2 and 3). Yet people act on common interests in many such situations, and this (given the truth of his thesis) shows that they are not rational (and selfish) in **his** sense. But he has neglected acting on we-intentions - whatever their motive basis is.

As emphasized, Olson's thesis is in any case not generally true for situations involving non-collective goods, and I think Olson does not really mean his thesis to apply to non-collective goods either. Thus in his general thesis that we started with, we must understand group interests to be restricted in this way, and this is certainly an important restriction.

CHAPTER 6

ACTION GENERATION

I. ACTION GENERATION AND THE BY-RELATION

1. Agents do not only do something **simpliciter** but they often do what they do **by** doing something else. Consider, for instance, the following statements: 'Lee killed John by shooting him', 'John ventilated the room by opening the window', 'Tom apologized by sending a bouquet of roses', and 'Bob signaled by extending his arm out the car window'. How are we to account for the 'by' of method in these statements?

We shall assume - what is widely accepted - that the above example statements can be regarded as action descriptions and that actions can be taken to be events (or episodes, if you like). Given this, it may seem plausible to take the logical form of an action statement such as

(1)   Lee killed John by shooting him

to be

(2)   (Ex)(Ey) (Killed (Lee, John, x)
      & Shot (Lee, John, y) & By (x,y)).

Here x and y range over events and 'By' stands for a kind of counterpart of the by-relation. I shall accept (2) as a sufficiently correct rendering of (1) but I will not here discuss the adequacy of this programme of formalization on the whole (see Tuomela (1977), Chapter 2).

The purpose of the present chapter is to clarify the by-relation which I will call a relation of **action generation.** Action generation is a technical concept employed by Goldman (1970) and many others, including myself, after him. We shall start by a critical summary of Goldman's account.

Goldman presents an elaborate account of action generation in his book. Although my theoretical approach is somewhat different from his, I basically agree with his analysis of the underlying situation - "the data". Goldman distinguishes four different categories of generation whereas I only speak of two, viz. (a) **factual** and (b) **conceptual** generation. Goldman's categories are causal generation, conventional generation, simple generation, and augmentation generation. The first three of these notions can be taken to explicate locutions of the form 'A does a **by** doing b', Goldman argues.

Consider now (1), which represents a typical case of causal generation: Lee's shooting at John causally generated Lee's killing John. In cases of causal generation the defining characteristic in Goldman's account is that there is a causal relation between Lee's shooting at John and the event of John's dying. Thus an action token a of agent A causally generates action token b of A only if (1) a causes a certain event e, and (2) b consists in A's causing e (Goldman (1970), p. 23). What I call factual nomic generation is slightly different from Goldman's causal generation. I analyze the above example as follows. We have there the two events of the shot being fired at John and John's dying. It is assumed that the first of these events is a cause of the second. (Goldman would say that, rather, Lee's action of shooting at John is a cause of John's dying). Thus, in my account the **result-events** of the two actions in question are in cause-effect relationship in the case of causal action generation. Other examples of causal generation, e.g., John's ventilating the room by opening the window, are analyzed similarly. In addition to causal relationships my notion of factual nomic generation also involves other, non-causal, nomic relationships.

According to Goldman, the action of A's extending his arm out the car window conventionally generates A's signaling for a turn. More generally, an action token a of agent A is said to generate **conventionally** an action token b of agent A only if the performance of a in circumstances C (possibly null), together with a rule R saying that a done in C counts as b, guarantees the performance of b (Goldman (1970), p. 26). (Goldman only gives this necessary condition.) In our example the circumstances C include the agent driving his car on the road, and so on. The rule R says that extending one's arm out the car window while driving on public road counts as signalling. Another example of conventional generation would be Tom's apologizing by sending a bouquet of roses, for sending roses conventionally counts as apologizing.

A's coming home after midnight may in suitable circumstances generate A's breaking his promise. Examples of this sort are for Goldman cases of **simple** generation. Goldman argues that while conventional generation might be schematized "a and R and C jointly entail b" simple generation can be schematized as "a and C jointly entail b". (See Gold-man (1970), pp. 26-28, and note the obscurity of "entailment".) I would like to claim, however, that even cases of simple generation in a sense involve general rules. In our example C includes the promise that A will be back by midnight. The rule R is a meaning postulate for promising to the effect that speech acts called promising involve their fulfillment. Thus I see no fundamental difference between conventional and simple generations of at least the above kind, though perhaps a detailed botanization of such rules R, e.g., in terms of their specific culture-dependence, might bring out some differences worth being emphasized.

Other examples of simple generation perhaps should be mentioned here, too, for this category is a broad one. Thus we consider the following generational claims (presumably acceptable by Goldman as belonging to this category):

(i)   A's jumping 2 meters simply generated A's outjumping B;
(ii) A's asserting that p (while disbelieving p) simply generated A's lying that p;
(iii) A's killing B simply generated A's revenging himself;
(iv) A's breaking a precious vase simply generated A's doing a bad thing.

In example (i) the generation involves a semantic rule relating outjumping and jumping. Examples (ii) and (iii) are concerned with A's mental states (belief and motive). From a semantic point of view they, respectively, deal with the concepts of lying and revenge and the respective semantic rules, we may think.

Example (iv) deals with an evaluation and is in this sense special. But (iv) may be taken to be true or acceptable in part because of cultural conventions (concerning what is good and bad) I think (iv) can be treated on a par with the other examples put in this category (even if Goldman does not mention examples of this sort).

Goldman's last type of generation is **augmentation**. It is represented by examples like this: A's extending his arm generated A's extending his arm out the window in those cases when A extends his arm out the window; A's saying "hello" (in certain circumstances) generated his saying "hello" loudly. Intuitively, augmentation generation is based on the fact that actions are always performed in some manner or other; and this extra information may be taken into account in redescribing the action. Furthermore, contrary to augmentation generation, in all the other species of generation a generated action is formed by making use of some additional fact not implicit in the generating action. In the case of augmentation generation the preposition 'by' is clearly inappropriate. But it also seems that no augmentation **generation** is needed as nothing is really generated but only a **redescription** takes place (cf. Baier (1971), p. 277 for a discussion).

We have seen that Goldman's conventional, simple, and augmentation generation concern a wide variety of generational relationships. However, they all deal only with semantic or normative or conventional redescription (or reconceptualization) of actions (cf. Chapters 7 and 8 on rules and norms cum the relevant mutual beliefs). They do not involve nomic factual producing (between action-results) in the sense that causal generation does. Thus even if, e.g., my jumping counts as out-jumping John only given certain circumstancial facts, this case is essentially different from Lee's trigger pulling causally generating his killing John.

I will accordingly below lump together conventional, simple and augmentation generation and call them cases of **conceptual** generation. Causal and other nomic generation again will be called **factual** generation. We will assume that, thus understood, factual and conceptual generation are mutually exclusive and jointly exhaustive.

Both the exclusiveness and the exhaustiveness assumption may be questioned, perhaps. The exclusiveness assumption is obviously connected to broader philosophical issues concerning what is conceptual and what is factual. We shall not here worry about that, especially since the exclusiveness assumption is not very central for our developments. On the other hand, the exhaustiveness assumption is central for us. Nothing we have said, nor anything that Goldman's (1970) rich treatment contains, amounts to a very conclusive proof of this. There are nevertheless some considerations that can be brought to bear on the issue here. Let us discuss them.

There are relationships between actions which have been claimed not to be generational in the sense discussed above. These are exemplified by (a) subsequent actions, (b) co-temporal (or, more generally, independent) actions, (c) at least some actions relating to each other in a part-whole relationship, and (d) actions by which certain agents represent some other agents. (Of these Goldman (1970) discussed subsequent and co-temporal actions as well as temporal parts of wholes.)

We may say in linguistic terms that an action token b of A is subsequent to action token a (of A) just in case it is correct to say that A did **a and then** did b (cf. Goldman (1970), p. 21). For instance, when having lunch I may first eat my salad and then my beef. The idea here is to try to capture temporally distinct and consequent but (conceptually and factually) independent action pairs. This linguistic criterion, in spite of its vagueness as a clue to ontological matters, tells us that our earlier discussed examples of generated actions are not in general subsequent to the actions that generate them (e.g., A did not flip the switch **and then** turn on the light). (Yet the account of action generation to be offered in this chapter will incorporate subsequent actions as separate component actions, even if the 'and then' relation will not as such turn out to be a species of generation.)

Subsequent actions are independent, we said. But there are also other types of conceptually (or semantically) and factually independent actions. Goldman (1970) considers co-temporal actions as another type of case. For instance, an agent may wiggle his ears **while also** writing a letter at the same time. Two co-temporal acts in this "while also" sense fail to be in any generational relationship to each other, and this can be checked against our earlier examples concerning action generation. Our complex actions of Chapters 4 and 5 include such co-temporal actions, for in many cases complex actions in part consist of such co-temporal actions. For instance, when levelling a nail I do the hammering with one hand while holding the nail with the other. The action of levelling a nail comes about due to actions of these two kinds. Another example would be an agent's shooting the basketball at the basket while jumping up. The co-temporal actions of jumping and shooting jointly generate the agent's scoring.

There are lots of other types of actions which are independent in the sense of not being in a generational relationship. For instance, if I build a house I must obviously do lots of things which are generationally independent in this sense but which are neither co-temporal nor subsequent to each other (e.g., I must lay the ground and put on the roof). These kinds of independent actions (which nevertheless contribute to the end result, e.g. the house becoming erected) are covered by our discussion of complex actions, of which building a house is just one example (recall our analyses in Chapter 4).

Next consider cases in which one of the actions is a temporal part of the other. By this we mean the following. Suppose that I want to play a certain melody. Then I may have to play the note c followed by a, followed by f, and so on. The whole melody consists of the playing of this sequence of notes, but it is not generated by any single element in this sequence. Yet I would like to claim, apparently contra Goldman, that my playing the notes in the right way constituted, and in this sense generated, my playing the melody. In this book we shall use the notion of generation in a broad sense allowing this kind of rather natural usage. Thus, in the case of social actions, viz. multi-agent actions, we will say that the agents' component actions generate the total social action. Thus, for instance, when two agents are singing a duet we say that this is generated by their individual component actions. Thus, understood as above, we do not exclude part-whole cases, nor do we exclude cases of representation (proxying). Thus we accept locutions like 'Tom's attorney's signing the document generated Tom's buying the house'.

Goldman does not really formally elaborate the notion of action generation (nor that of the by-relation), even if his analysis is quite illuminating philosophically. (But see my criticism in Tuomela (1977), pp. 162-163, of his technical notion of level-generation.) What we shall do below is to elucidate the formal or structural aspects of action generation. Our account will cover both actions (viz. task-performances) performed by a single agent and social actions, viz. actions jointly performed by several agents, in the sense of Chapter 4. Before going to that we shall comment further on the by-relation in general terms.

2. In addition to Goldman, many other authors have discussed the by-relation. Thus, for instance, Thomson (1977) discusses the 'by' of method in great technical detail, but she thinks that 'by' is merely a syncategorematic word. I disagree with this. As to the analysis of this notion in the context of statements such as (2), I think it can be given a **causal** account (where 'by' is nevertheless in a sense analyzed away). To be sure, it is true that Lee's shooting did not cause his killing John, as Thomson (1977), p. 19, argues. Yet, contrary to her claims, this does not destroy the possibilities of giving a causal account. For, as said earlier, we may take the causal connection in question to hold between the **results** of the action tokens rather than between the action tokens themselves. Thus, in our example, the result event (say r_1) of the action token (y) of shooting by Lee can be taken to be a bullet's being (suitably) fired from Lee's gun. We may then take r_1 - an event Lee made happen - to have causes the event of John's dying (r_2). We may also say here that y **causally generated** the action token (x) of the killing of John by Lee.[1])

Accordingly, I propose the following account of an action token x being a killing by shooting, where an action token is regarded as a sequence consisting of a volition v (not necessarily a willing), a behavior component b, and a result event r (as clarified in detail in Tuomela (1977) and in Chapter 4 above):

(3) x is a killing of B **by** shooting (performed) by A if and only if

(a) x is a killing of B by A and it is assumed that x is an action token$_1$ with the structure $<v,\ldots, b,\ldots,r_2>$, where r_2 = the dying of B;

(b) there is a shooting action token$_1$ y by A such that y has the structure $<v,\ldots,b,\ldots,r_1>$ (indirectly) causes r_2.

I am assuming above that $r_1 \neq$ B's dying. If, however, 'shooting' is used in the strong sense of shooting-to-death in which that does not hold, then of course r_1 does not cause r_2 but $r_1=r_2$ and x=y. Note that while (3) is not quite an explicit definition of the by-relation, yet if x and y satisfy (3) we have By(x,y). (Note that clause (a) speaks of the performance of an action **by** an agent. This 'by' is the relation of agency, and it is not to be confused with our analysandum.)

What are the killing and shooting action tokens (3) speaks about? They are tokens of **simple action types** of A (in the sense of Chapter 4) in which a causal relationship holds between the bodily movement and the result. Thus they are not in need of further analysis here. It seems that in (3) no explicit qualifications concerning times are needed as our analysis of causality takes care of that (see Tuomela (1977), p. 245).[2]

(3) is immediately generalizable to cover at least such "causal verbs" as 'break', 'move', and so on. It can in fact be generalized so as to hold true of all causal verbs expressing arbitrarily complex actions. If we, furthermore, substitute 'generated' for 'caused' in (3) we cover quite a lot of ground. Thus we arrive at the following formulation which employs the variables 'verbing$_1$', 'verbing$_2$', p and q (the two latter for the objects of the verbs):

(4) x is a verbing$_2$ p **by** verbing$_1$ q performed by A if and only if

(a) x is a verbing$_2$ p action token$_1$ by A and it is assumed that x has the structure $<v,\ldots,b,\ldots, r_2>$;

(b) there is a y such that y is a verbing$_1$ q action token$_1$ by A and such that y has the structure $<v,\ldots,b,\ldots,r_1>$ and that r_1 (indirectly) generates r_2.

(In (4), r_1 and r_2 are of course the results of verbing$_1$ q and verbing$_2$ p.) What is the scope of (4)? As said, it is meant to cover causal verbs like 'killing', 'moving', 'opening', etc. in which the results of their appropriate action tokens are suitably caused. Also verbs like 'kicking' fall under this **broadly** defined category of causal verbs (for a somewhat different view of causal verbs see Thomson (1977), p. 133). Note that in principle the generation in (4) may even be non-causal factual generation (if there ultimately is such).

How about conceptual generation? Consider Bob's greeting Tom by lifting his hat. Here the hat lifting expresses greeting. In our example of Tom's apologizing, his sending the roses expresses Tom's apologizing. (4) handles these cases (cf. (7) below with $e=r_1=r_2$ and D_1, D_2 corresponding to the above descriptions).

Using the technical terms that have been defined in Tuomela (1977) and that will be again defined below, we could say either that indirect generation in (4) means the notion of purposive generation $IG^*(r_1,r_2)$, analyzed with reference to a special conduct plan containing only meaning postulates, broadly understood; or indirect generation could be defined by requiring $IG(r_1,r_2)$ and by allowing suitable conceptual generation in the case of r_1 or r_2, viz. $R_2(r_1,D_1,D_2)$ or $R_2(r_2,D_1,D_2)$); see Tuomela (1977), pp. 252-255 and below (6)-(9).

As said earlier, the so-called augmentation generation fails to be expressible by means of the by-relation. It also seems that no notion of augmentation-generation is needed, since nothing is generated in Goldman's example cases; rather, only a **redescription** occurs in these cases. Now, given that this line of argument works, it seems that (4) gives us an adequate analysis of the by-relation in the case of all single-agent actions. (Otherwise we would have to exclude the use of augmentation generation in (4).) It should be emphasized, though, that what has been said above may not amount to a strong argument for (4) even if augmentation generation is excluded. In any case, (4) seems to handle the problematic examples meticulously discussed by Thomson (1977), but we shall not now go into these details.

I suggest that the following is an adequate generalization of (4) for the social (multi-agent) case with m agents $A_1,...,A_m$:

(5) x is a verbing$_2$ p **by** verbing$_1$ q jointly performed by $A_1,...,A_m$ if and only if
   (a) x is a verbing$_2$ p social action token$_1$ by A_1, ..., A_m and it is assumed that x has the structure $<v,...,b,...,r_2>$;
   (b) there is a y such that y is a verbing$_1$ q social action token$_1$ by $A_1,...,A_m$ and such that y has the structure $<v,...,b,...,r_1>$ and that r_1 (indirectly) generates r_2.

Note that when, e.g., $r_1 = r_1^1+...+r_1^m$ we must define our notion of generation to account for the fact that, so to speak, several generation chains may lead to r_2, viz. presumably each r_1^i can be taken to partially generate r_2 in those circumstances. We shall return to this below.

As an illustration of (5) we may consider the moving of a heavy table by carrying it as performed by Smith and Jones. I take this example to obviously satisfy the analysans of (5).

3. Below we shall discuss some mainly formal aspects of action generation by relating it to the theory of automata. Let us start by briefly recalling the technical distinctions and definitions for the single-agent case made in Tuomela (1977). There we distinguished between factual and conceptual event-generation as just specified above. Direct factual generation (R_1) is, roughly, our counterpart to Goldman's (1970) causal generation, while our conceptual generation (R_2) roughly covers Goldman's conventional, simple, and (if it is needed) augmentation generation. Based on R_1 and R_2, several other notions can be defined, such as (indirect) factual generation (IG). Furthermore, by requiring generation to take place according to the agent's operative conduct plan, we get several notions of purposive generation such as (indirect) purposive generation (IG*).

We present below (essentially) our earlier definitions for R_1, R_2, IG*. Note that causality (C) represents a special case of R_1 (viz. $C(e_1,e_2)$ entails $R_1(e_1,e_2)$ where e_1 and e_2 are singular events). The ε-relation relied on below refers to some formal conditions here interpretable as conditions for (nomic) subsumption (see Tuomela (1977), Chapter 9 and below Chapter 10, p. 340). This relation also serves to block some paradoxes that generational models of simpler kinds face. One such paradox, affecting Goldman's (1970) treatment, is that it can be proved in effect that in his model any action generates every other action (see Tuomela (1976a) on this). Below **M** has the structure of a Tarskian model. Our definitions then are as follows (cf. Tuomela (1977), pp. 252-255):

(6) '$R_1(e_1,e_2)$' is true (with respect to a situation **M**) if and only if (with respect to **M**) there are true descriptions D_1 of e_1 and D_2 of e_2 (e.g., $D_1 = e_1$ is an X-ing at t_1, $D_2 = e_2$ is a Y-ing at t_2) and a suitable factual theory L such that $\varepsilon(D_2,D_1\&L)$.

(7) '$R_2(e,D_1,D_2)$' is true (with respect to a situation **M**) if and only if (with respect to **M**) there is a suitable true meaning postulate (or conjunction of meaning postulates) of L such that $\varepsilon(D_2,D_1\&L)$, where D_1 and D_2 truly describe e.

(8) '$IG(e_1, e_n)$' is true (with respect to **M**) if and only if (with respect to **M**) $R_1(e_1,e_2) \& R_1(e_2,e_3) \& \ldots \& R_1(e_{n-1}, e_n)$ for some singular events $e_2,\ldots,e_{n-1}$.

(9) '$IG^*(t,r)$' is true for an action token $u = \langle t,\ldots, b,\ldots,r\rangle$ (with respect to **M**) if and only if
(a) '$IG(t,r)$' is true (with respect to **M**) such that t stands for e_1, b is the value of one of the variables $e_2,\ldots,e_{n-1}$, and r stands for e_n;
(b) there is a (complete) conduct plan description K satisfied by **M** such that in K t is truly described as A's willing to do by his bodily behavior what u ($= \langle t,\ldots,b,\ldots,r\rangle$ tokens according to K, and u_o (a sum of b and r) is truly described as a maximal overt part of an action which is (directly or indirectly) factually, and not merely conceptually, generated by some of A's actions in this behavior situation **M**; t, b, and r are assumed to belong to the domain of **M**.

The notion of (indirect) purposive generation needs two special remarks. First, while it is above defined for a willing event t and a result event r only, it can obviously be defined for **any** events that K is about, and we shall later rely on that and freely use locutions like $IG^*(u,u')$ where u and u' are action tokens. (The "aboutness" of K concerning b and r is a kind of act-relational **de re** aboutness, explicated in terms of wh-beliefs in Tuomela (1977), pp. 265-267.) Thus, for instance, purposive generation between different results can be made sense of. The second feature to be emphasized is that, contrary to IG, IG* may involve conceptual generation (viz. applications of R_2). This is needed in some cases, and recall that K contains meaning postulates in virtue of which R_2 may become applicable.

IG* is the central notion of purposive generation claimed in Tuomela (1977), pp. 255-259, to block wayward causal chains (cf. Chapter 3 above). Intuitively speaking, IG* technically explicates the notion of (intentionally) **acting on a conduct plan** (or performing an action because of a conduct plan), and this is claimed to explicate in part such notions as intentionally acting for a reason, following a rule, and, more generally, intentional teleological behavior (cf. our later discussion in Chapters 11 and 13). Wayward causal chains become blocked, since they always seem to involve some kind of deviation from one's operative conduct plan. If you like, purposive causation (and generation) can on the whole be regarded as the type of causation pertinent to the human sciences and also as a modern explicate of final causation (in the realm of human agency), without a finalist ontology.

So much for the single-agent case. How about the social case? Definitions (6), (7), and (8) of course do not require any changes, but (9) does. In the parallel social cases we are dealing with (intentional) action tokens u = <t,...,b,...r> where $t = t_{we}^1 + \ldots + t_{we}^m$ and $b = b_1 + \ldots + b_m$. r is the full result event which is either generated by the results r_i, i=1,...,m, of the involved individual action tokens u_i or $r = r_1 + \ldots + r_m$. What changes do we need in (9)? First, in clause (a) we give t and r the above "social" reading. Secondly, in (b) the (complete) conduct plan description K is to be regarded as a **social** one (see Chapter 5 for our characterization). As indicated, t is now described as a we-willing, and instead of a single agent A we now speak of $A_1,\ldots,A_m$. Viewed purely syntactically, the social case needs only the following linguistic changes. In (b) insert the word 'social' before 'conduct plan', change 'willing' into 'we-willing', use 'the agents' $A_1,\ldots,A_m$' instead of 'A' in two places, and change 'their' for 'his'. Let us call the resulting definition (9').

On the basis of the above notions of generation one can define several conditionals, such as ▷→ and ⊛→, employed in Chapters 4 and 5. To illustrate, we define these two conditionals and a new third one, viz. ▷→ for indirect purposive generation, and assuming D_1 and D_2 to, respectively, truly describe the events a and b:

(10) (i) 'D_1 ▷→ D_2' is true (with respect to a situation M) if and only if a is a cause of b in M and clause (b) of (9), in the single-agent case, or (9'), in the social case, is satisfied with a and b replacing t and r, respectively.

(ii) 'D_1 ▷→ D_2' is true (with respect to a situation M) if and only if IG*(a,b) in M.

(iii) 'D'⊛→D' is true (with respect to a situation M) if and only if R_2(a,D',D) in M, where D' and D are true descriptions of a and it is entailed by the agent's operative conduct plan that R_2(a,D',D).

It is obvious that conditionals can be analogously defined corresponding to all the generational relations to be defined later in this chapter.

Let us now consider our basic notion of factual generation. Definition (6) says that each singular factual generation claim can be backed by a **suitable** law or theory L, or, non-linguistically speaking, by a suitable nomic process (which L represents). (8) and (9) obviously also come to rely on the existence of such underlying nomic processes or connections. Now, of course, any talk about just the existence of such a process is bound to be rather vague. Unfortunately, it seems hard to do much better in the general case. However, one possibility that seems worth exploring is the use of automata theory in this connection. In fact, Pörn (1977) has built his account of single-agent action generation on this idea. We shall below apply automata theory to our conceptual system (which differs very much from that of Pörn) to treat action generation. (The system to be created below is meant to be relatively self-contained and it does not presuppose knowledge of the technical details of the above account of Tuomela (1977).)

II. ACTION GENERATION AND THE THEORY OF AUTOMATA

1. We start our automata-theoretic account by defining the notion of a finite automaton (following Salomaa (1973)). Let us thus call a non-empty set V of letters (elements) an alphabet. A word over an alphabet V is a finite string consisting of zero or more letters of V. Thus, e.g., 1, 0, 110, are words over the alphabet $V = \{0,1\}$. The set of all words over an alphabet V is denoted by W(V).

Now let I be an alphabet called the **input** alphabet and let O be an alphabet called the **output** alphabet. Furthermore, let S be a finite set of states (the internal states of an automaton). We define a certain notion of a (deterministic) finite automaton by:

(11) A system $M = <I,O,S,f,\phi>$ is a **deterministic generalized sequential automaton** if and only if
(a) I is an input alphabet;
(b) O is an output alphabet and W(O) the corresponding output set;
(c) S is a finite set of (internal) states;
(d) $f : S \times I \rightarrow S$ is called the transition function;
(e) $\phi : S \times I \rightarrow W(O)$ is called the output function.

We may interpret our finite automaton (or machine) M in several ways. For instance, if the letter e stands for a singular action (or, alternatively, a result of an action), then, if M is in state s at time t and receives the input e at t+1, it will at time t+1 be in state $f(s,e)$ and have the output $\phi(s,e)$ (or, alternatively, it will have that output at t+2).

A generalized sequential automaton is called a **Mealy automaton** (or machine) just in case the output words consist of only one letter each. We shall below only discuss Mealy machines, unless otherwise stated. Then we may as well use

(e*) $\phi : S \times I \to O$

instead of (e) in (11).

In some automata all transitions entering a given internal state have the same output. Here the output function can be defined as $\phi(s,e) = g(f(s,e))$ where $g:S \to O$. Such an automaton is called a **sequential Moore machine**. If, furthermore, the sets O and S coincide and g is the identity function, we get an **automaton without outputs**.

The transition function of a sequential automaton was above defined for the input alphabet, and so was the output function. They may both be recursively extended to cover the set of words over the alphabet as follows, letting λ be the empty word:

(a) $f(s,\lambda) = s$ for all $s \in S$
     $f(s,Ee) = f(f(s,E),e)$ for all $s \in S$, $E \in W(I)$, $e \in I$.
(b) $\phi(s,\lambda) = \lambda$ for all $s \in S$
     $\phi(s,eE) = \phi(s,e)\phi(f(s,e),E)$ for all $s \in S$, $e \in I$, $E \in W(I)$.

Combining the above sequential generalization with (11) thus gives us the possibility of having words both as inputs and as outputs. (See, e.g., Pörn (1977), p. 47 for a relevant illustration.) The result of this generalization of (11) will be called (11') below.

After these preliminaries we may go to action-generation. How can automata clarify it? The obvious suggestion is to begin by connecting the input with the agent's (or the agents', in the social case) generating action and the output with the generation action. If we accept the generational principle (**PG**) of Chapter 4, p.104, then it does not matter whether we take the inputs to be singular actions or results (in the technical sense) of singular actions. ((**PG**) says that an action token by an agent (or some agents) is generated by some other action tokens by him (or them) just in case the result of that token is jointly generated by the results of the latter tokens.) Thus, considering an input letter a, it could be taken to stand for an agent A's exemplifying an action type X; thus a would stand for an action token by A or the result of an action token by A. We shall below settle for (**PG**) and use results as inputs, writing r_a for the result of action token a.

What will the outputs be? Here it seems definitely better to use result events rather than generated actions, and so the automaton is going to tell us something about the generation of one real event by another one. Actually, we should say that, in the terminology of von Wright (1971), p. 67, what a result event r_a in the general case generates is a **consequence** event of a. But we shall here be interested only in cases where this consequence event has been conceptualized as the result event of some action, say b, by the agent(s).[3] (Such a conceptualization seems always possible, although it need not be "institutionalized" in a given social practice.) What we thus want to clarify in the first place is how factual generational claims of the kind $R_1(a,b)$ and $IG(a,b)$ can be clarified in terms of automata.

The obvious suggestion then is to think of the theory or law L in our (6) and (8) as somehow representing an automaton. But how? Let us work towards a solution. First we recall that the singular actions a and b are assumed to have actually occurred (thus $(Ex)(x=a)$ and $(Ey)(y=b)$). Looking at (6) we notice that it makes factual generation depend on conceptualization (viz. how the events are described). We want to account for this feature in our automata-theoretic account below. Let us thus assume that our automata operate with conceptualized ("structured") events and states. When we now use the symbols r_a and r_b we agree to mean the result events of a and b **suitably conceptualized** (and possibly reconceptualized vis-à-vis their original conceptualizations).

In our automata-theoretic interpretation of factual generation we take the internal states of the automaton to represent the agent-external conditions or circumstances that the generation requires. Consider here, for instance, my turning on the light by flipping the switch, which succeeds in standard conditions. Below only the existence of such conditions (viz., a suitable state) is postulated.

What our automata-theoretic explication will concern in the first place is obviously indirect generation $IG(a,b)$, of which $R_1(a,b)$ is a special case. (How to give an automata-theoretic condition for singling out R_1 as the special case representing **direct** generation need not bother us here or below.) Now it seems true to say this:

(12) $IG(a,b)$ only if $(EM)(Es \epsilon S_M)(r_b = \phi_M(s, r_a))$.

That is, action token a (indirectly) factually generates action token b only if there is a finite machine (automaton) M and a state s in the set S_M of its internal states such that fed in with s and r_a the output function ϕ_M gives r_b as its value.

Before we discuss whether (12) can be strengthened to give a sufficient condition for $IG(a,b)$ let us note one thing. The existential quantification over finite automata in (12) makes the analysis rather uninformative, at least as long as a and b are simple events. Just try to think of some constellation involving two simple events which is not a finite automaton! As to composite events, the claim (12) is not perhaps as empty, even if presently I have no good argument for its not being so. (We know that a finite machine cannot, e.g., multiply two arbitrarily large numbers. Could considerations of this sort be used here?)

Once you succeed in specifying the automaton in (12) you, however, have quite a lot of information. For the you know exactly **how** (by what mechanism) r_a generated r_b.

(12) cannot be strengthened to an equivalence, it seems. For one thing, almost anything finite can be seen as a finite automaton, as we just claimed. Such a conceptualization might be performed quite arbitrarily on purely formal grounds, without reference to the "real" connections between a and b, and in particular without reference to any operative **lawlike** connections holding between the event types that a and b token. A simple illustration may be obtained from the well known and well worn barometer case. The barometer's going down surely does not causally generate the coming about of a storm. The reader can verify for himself that by regarding the barometer changes as inputs and storming vs. non-storming as the outputs we get a finite automaton in the sense of (11).

So it seems that we have to require the generating automaton to somehow represent an operative lawlike real process (or processes). But the domains of laws cannot a priori be restricted to finite ones. Now we may formalize a finite automaton in a way that does not a priori make its input and output sets finite. But (a) in the case of all singular generational claims one seems to be able to find (in principle) an automaton with finite input and output sets (I do not have a strict proof of this to offer), and (b) there are requirements for operative lawlikeness other than the discussed condition.

Based on (a) and (b) I now suggest we require that the generating automaton be suitably subsumable under an operative law (or theory) or a "law of working". What this requirement amounts to is not quite easy to explicate exactly. I have two partial suggestions for carrying this out. The first says that for any singular "generational chains" (input-internal state-output "chains") that the machine M produces there is a backing argument such that the same operative backing law appears in all these cases. This backing law is said to represent ϕ (in the sense of "intralinguistic" representation), which means that it is a description of ϕ generalized over the arguments. We thus get the following ontologically demanding analysis for simple action tokens a and b:

(13) IG(a,b) if and only if
    (a) $(EM)[(Es \varepsilon S_M)(r_b = \phi_M(s, r_a))$, and
    (b) for all generational chains i that M produces there are true descriptions D_1^i of the input-event cum the internal state and D_2^i of the output-event (such that the generational chain i is made up of the input, internal state and the output) and there is an operative factual law (or theory) L, representing ϕ, such that $\varepsilon(D_2^i, D_1^i \& L)$].

My second suggestion seems simpler, but it in turn relies on the difficult notion of an automaton representing (in the sense of "language-world" representation) a law of nature, viz. the law "underlying" the functioning of the machine:

(14) IG(a,b) if and only if
    (a) $(EM)[(Es \varepsilon S_M)(r_b = \phi_M(s, r_a))$, and
    (b) (EM') (M' represents an operative law of nature "underlying" M and M' is an extension of M)].

The notion of extension in (14) that is needed for the representation of laws (not restricted a priori to finite domains) is not much easier to define than the notion of a law representing an automaton. One suggestion would be to say simply that M' is an extension of M just in case $I \subseteq I'$, $O \subseteq O'$, $S \subseteq S'$, and f and ϕ are obtained from f' and ϕ' as the appropriate restrictions (to I, O, and S), given that $M' = <I', O', S', f', \phi'>$ is a finite automaton and $M = <I, O, S, f, \phi>$ is one, too. But it is not at all clear that such an M' would suffice to capture the relevant "law of working", for we may need stronger automata for that. But if M' does suffice (a question, it seems, that cannot be answered on a priori grounds) then it will of course also be relatively easy to understand what could be meant by its representing the law of nature underlying the working of M.

    I shall not here try to make a definite choice between (13) and (14), even if I find (13) somewhat clearer. As to their substantial content, they seem to me to be interpretable so as to amount to the same thing. In any case, this will be assumed below.

2. We may now ask whether the generational relation IG adequately represents the factual by-relation (for the single-agent case) within our system, in the sense of explicating the factual aspects of the notion of generation that was used in our

earlier definition (4) of the by-relation. We have above discussed only simple (non-compound) actions, and thus only non-composite action tokens. As to them, our answer is affirmative. Concerning compound (single-agent and multi-agent) actions something additional must still be said.

Let us thus consider compound actions where, assuming (**PG**), some result event $r_1,...,r_m$ generates a result r. This full result may be a string $r^1...r^k$ or, e.g., a sum $r^1+...+r^k$, $k \leq m$. How do we apply automata-theoretic considerations to this case? Let us assume that we are dealing with a compound single agent or social action. There are (at least) two ways to handle the situation, which will now be taken up in turn.

Our earlier generalization (11') to cover words gives us the possibility of handling a sequence of actions, viz. the case of the generation of an output word (a sequence of simple results, rather) by an input word (a sequence of simple results). Thus we may think of the generating events $r_1,...,r_m$ as constituting a word $r_1...r_m$. In some cases the same also works for the output: $r=r^1...r^k$, $k \leq m$. But if, rather, $r=r^1+...+r^k$, then, as summation is commutative but (ordered) concatenation is not, the generation of any word with $r^1,...,r^k$ as its letters (no matter in which order) should be taken to amount to the generation of the composite r. Let us call this generation pattern the **A-model** (irrespective of whether the result r is a word or a letter in the above sense).

It seems to me that the above model of generation of events by composite concatenated events is appropriate exactly in those cases where there is a clear "natural" (e.g., causal) order between the (simple) events. For instance, consider an agent's flushing some nails by hammering them several times. Here the total process of hammering, which consists of several successive action tokens of hammering (yielding a string $r^1...r^k$), is causally ordered in this sense. (See Tuomela (1977), pp. 314-315 and Pörn (1977), pp. 47-48 for a discussion of this type of example.) Among social actions, for instance, the complex action of asking questions and answering seems to fit the present pattern. Asking a question precedes answering both timewise and, suitably qualified, it is also a causal precondition of the latter. In its most general form the A-model would formally be concerned with one word (string of letters) generating another word.

The other model of generation for composite events that I have in mind has two versions. The simpler version (call it the **B1-model**) simply takes the sum $r_1+...+r_m$ to be an event generating r exactly in the fashion of (13) or (14) (viz. by $r_1+...+r_m$ replacing r_a and r replacing r_b). This simple model will work whenever (i) there is no "natural" ordering between the simple events in question and (ii) only one lawful generational chain (i.e., only one automaton) is involved. I shall not here try to spell out these conditions in detail. As to the tenability of (ii), let me just say that at least in the case of many social actions several different lawful processes and thus **several automata** obviously seem to be involved. To see this, you may consider two or more agents playing tennis, dancing, or conversing. As to the single agent case, for instance, building a house or cooking a dinner may serve as examples. We shall discuss this more complex version (call it the **B2-model**) in detail below in the context of social actions. (See Subsection 4.) In sum then, when we write $IG(r_1,...,r_m,r)$, for $m+1$-place generation, one of the above explications is to be used, depending on the case, as indicated.

Let us recall that our IG, as defined, is a **deterministic** notion. A **probabilistic** generalization of it can be made in the immediate and obvious way by relying on a probabilistic rather than a deterministic machine in the definition (see Tuomela (1977), Chapter 12, esp. pp. 394-397).[4]) By **probable** generation we shall in this book normally mean generation with a probability greater than one half.

3. To finish our automata-theoretic discussion of generation in the single-agent case we shall briefly consider **conceptual** (or "normative" or "rule-referring") generation. We recall that IG* (purposive generation) is not definable without a notion of conceptual generation. Similarly, in our definition (4) of the by-relation we need conceptual generation (see our earlier remarks). Pörn (1977), pp. 52-54 has analyzed conceptual generation in terms of automata, and I shall follow some of his suggestions below.

Consider an agent A's opening a bank account as an example of a conventional action in which conceptual generation is involved. A signs a certain form at the presence of some authorized bank officials, who (perhaps) themselves also have to sign the form. A's signing the form in the present context may be said to conceptually generate his opening a bank account, provided it happened according to the norms defining bank account opening. We may now think of an automaton without outputs as follows. The action of A's signing his name (plus any other action of A possibly needed) will be the input. All the other circumstancial conditions needed here will constitute an internal state of the automaton. Finally, the next state as specified by the transition function f will represent the existence or establishment of a bank account of A. Accordingly, the transition function here plays the role of a "meaning postulate" or rule by virtue of which the bank account becomes established.

In order to accommodate this analysis with our (7) we may think of the internal states of the automaton as different descriptions of A's action in that context. Then we may give (7) the following automata-theoretic interpretation (cf. (13)):

(15) $R_2(a,D_1,D_2)$ if and only if
 (a) (EM)[(M is an automaton without outputs, D_2 is an internal state of M, $D_1 = D_1^1 \& D_1^2$ such that D_1^1 is an input of M and a description of a and D_1^2 is an internal state of M and a description of the designated contextual conditions, and $D_2 = f(D_1^2,D_1^1))$; and
 (b) for all generational chains i that M produces there are true descriptions D_1^i for the input and the designated contextual conditions and D_2^i for the next state (specified by f) and there is an applicable true (or assertable) meaning postulate L, representing f, such that $\varepsilon(D_2^i,D_1^i \& L)$].

Our (15) is modelled along (13). An analogous characterization corresponding to (14) could also be formulated, of course. Definition (15) can be taken to apply to arbitrary composite events and thus to the social case as well.

We should now be in the position to see that our definitions of IG and R_2 in principle suffice for all notions of action-generation, including purposive generation IG* (which, in view of (9), does not require separate discussion) and for the by-relation in the single-agent case. But we shall still clarify the multi-agent case somewhat better. This social case was claimed to deal with "multi-machine" generation (the B2-model), which also seems to be needed sometimes in the single-agent case (but which was left almost unclarified above).

4. In the case of social actions the agents $A_1,...,A_m$ severally perform some, possibly complex, actions. Jointly these actions generate the "full" (complex) social action (see our definitions (6), (7), and (9) in Chapter 5). We shall now try to say a little more of this notion of generation, which concerns the generation of (possibly) composite events by composite events. In the social case the above models A, B1, and B2 of composite event generation may be thought to have applications. We noticed that often the most complicated of them - the B2-pattern - may have to be resorted to. This pattern will now have to be clarified to some extent. To the extent we succeed, our above account of generation for the single-agent case becomes

applicable in the social case, too.

What is basically left to clarify in the social case is the generation of the full result r (or u) by the r_is (i=1,...,m), which are the respective result events of the single-agent action tokens u_i. Thus a clarification of $IG(r_1,...,r_m,r)$ (or of $IG(r_1+...+r_m,r)$ when we can use the sum of the r_is) seems to be what is needed here in the first place. In general, we must interpret the situation according to the B2-pattern: each r_i "partially" generates, or contributes to the generation of, r. Thus there will be, in principle, several different generational chains which in the appropriate circumstances jointly suffice for r. (I shall not here discuss the necessity and/or sufficiency of the generating event(s) for the generated one nor any relevant probabilistic counterparts; see Tuomela (1977), pp. 245-246 for remarks on this matter. Nor shall I try to investigate the exact formal criteria for when the more general m+1-place generation $IG(r_1,...,r_m,r)$ must be used instead of $IG(r_1+...+r_m,r)$.)

The obvious suggestion that we already have mentioned is that for each generational chain, and thus for each agent A_i, there will be a (finite) automaton which accounts for the generation. How are we to build up the total generation pattern out of these single generational chains? We might also ask the reverse question. Given the total generation pattern and assuming it to be representable by a finite automaton, how can we decompose this automaton in a way that the atoms or building blocks will be the single-agent automata? We shall below discuss primarily the first of these interconnected questions.

Let us assume, for notational simplicity, that we are dealing with two agents, A_1 and A_2, only, A_1 performs an action u_1 and A_2 another action u_2. The inputs r_1 and r_2 are now thought to jointly generate r, which is the result of the joint action u by A_1 and A_2. (Suppose, for instance, that A_1 and A_2 sing a duet or move a table to the next room by carrying it.) We associate with A_1 a machine M_1 and with A_2 a machine M_2. The question now becomes how we are to combine the machine generations in the general case to yield the right output. To this question I cannot presently give a firm and detailed answer. But let me still illustrate some possibilities and make some conjectures.

The machines might be thought to be combined either in **series** or **parallelly**. I shall below define these notions, following Arbib's (1968) presentation. As every finite machine is provably equivalent (with respect to the input-output behavior) to a sequential Moore machine (see our earlier definition), we can give our definitions for sequential Moore machines. Thus, as $\phi(s,e) = g(f(s,e))$, we will use the g-function below.

ACTION GENERATION

(16) The **series connection** of two automata $M_1 = \langle I_1, O_1, S_1, f_1, g_1 \rangle$ and $M_2 = \langle I_2, O_2, S_2, f_2, g_2 \rangle$ for which $O_1 = I_2$ is the automaton $M = \langle I_1, O_2, S_1 \times S_2, f, g \rangle$ where $f(\langle s_1, s_2 \rangle, e) = \langle f_1(s_1, e), f_2(s_2, g_1(s_1)) \rangle$ and $g(s_1, s_2) = g_2(s_2)$, for all $e \in I_1$, $s_1 \in S_1$, $s_2 \in S_2$.

(17) The **parallel connection** of two automata $M_1 = \langle I_1, O_1, S_1, f_1, g_1 \rangle$ and $M_2 = \langle I_2, O_2, S_2, f_2, g_2 \rangle$ is the automaton $M = \langle I_1 \times I_2, O_1 \times O_2, S_1 \times S_2, f, g \rangle$ where $f(\langle s_1, s_2 \rangle, \langle e_1, e_2 \rangle) = \langle f_1(s_1, e_1), f_2(s_2, e_2) \rangle$ and $g(s_1, s_2) = \langle g_1(s_1), g_2(s_2) \rangle$, for all $e_1 \in I_1$, $e_2 \in I_2$, $s_1 \in S_1$, and $s_2 \in S_2$.

It seems clear that a pattern of series connection can be discerned in many social actions. For instance, when A_1 requests A_2 to do something (e.g., to ventilate the room), A_1's request (or its result event) is the input to M_1 (and to M) and the output is something like the request-event's (be it an utterance or whatever) reaching A_2 cum, perhaps, A_2's initiating his response, e.g., opening the window, and this will also be the input to M_2. A_2's response, or, rather, its result or consequence (e.g., the room becoming ventilated) will be the output of M_2 (and also of M). (The total social action consisting in requesting and responding may perhaps be taken to have as its result the ordered sequence $r_1 r_2$ of the results of A_1's and A_2's actions rather than merely r_2; cf. (5.11), case (e).) A_1's persuading A_2 to do something would be another example analyzable along similar lines. More generally, causally chained action sequences (e.g., ones realizing nested power structures in organizations) can be fitted in here.

How about parallelly connected actions? This case may be regarded as covering at least situations where $r = r_1 + r_2$ (cf. (5.11), case (a)) and also cases where $r = r_1 \cdot r_2$ (cf. (5.11), (c)). For instance, some purely conventional rituals, such as A_1's and A_2's greeting each other (where, roughly, $r_1 = A_1$'s lifting his hat; $r_2 = A_2$'s lifting his hat and $r = r_1 + r_2$) fit this case; cf. the stylus inserting example of Section 5.II.3 as illustrating $r = r_1 \cdot r_2$.

When we allow for combined parallel and series composition of machines we get hold of the structure of quite complicated generation patterns. We shall now give a definition for a notion which hopefully accomplishes this. It is the notion of a cascade combination of automata. We define it for sequential Moore machines as follows (cf. Arbib (1968), p. 275):

(18) Given two machines $M_1 = \langle I_1, O_1, S_1, f_1, g_1 \rangle$ and $M_2 = \langle I_2, O_2, S_2, f_2, g_2 \rangle$, and a triple K comprising the maps $\eta: I \to I_1$, $Z: I \times O_1 \to O_2$, and $\gamma: O_1 \times O_2 \to O$ **the cascade of** M_1 **and** M_2 **with connection** K is defined to be the machine
$M_K = \langle I, O, S_2 \times S_1, f_K, g_K \rangle$
where $f_K(\langle s_2, s_1 \rangle, e) = \langle f_2(s_2, Z(e, g(s_1))), f_1(s_1, \eta(e)) \rangle$ and $g_K(s_2, s_1) = \gamma(g_1(s_1), g_2(s_2))$, for all $e \in I$, $s_1 \in S_1$, $s_2 \in S_2$.

The diagram shown in Fig. 6.1 illustrates this cascade:

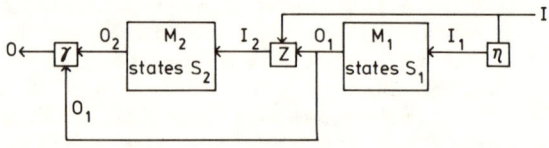

Fig. 6.1.

The notion of cascade combination is somewhat stronger than the notion of series-parallel composition, for so-called delay machines may be needed when going from cascades to series-parallel compositions (see Arbib (1968)).

From cascade composition we get series composition by making Z independent of I and $\gamma(O_2, O_1) = O_2$. To get parallel composition we take $I = I_1 \times I_2$ and set $Z(\langle e_1, e_2 \rangle, O_1) = e_2$, $\eta(e_1, e_2) = e_1$ and $\gamma(O_2, O_1) = \langle O_2, O_1 \rangle$. Note that as O is different from the product $O_1 \times O_2$ we can easily deal with cases where the total result of the social action is caused by the results of the individual actions and fails to equal their sum or product (cf. several agents' polluting slightly and spoiling thereby the water of a lake as an example of $r > r_1 + r_2$). (18) covers all the cases of our (**5.11**), but cf. especially (b), (d), and (f).

The notion of combination of machines that we now come to is that of **cascade formation** and, furthermore, the **repeated formation of cascades** (which includes symbol-by-symbol encodings and decodings). (See Arbib (1968) for discussion.) My conjecture now is that this notion of repeated cascade formation, with respect to some suitable cascade connection K, gives us an explication of action generation in the general case (and hence for the B2-pattern). In other words, I conjecture that this much may be needed, but not more, in the general case. Note that in Figure 6.1 there is no feedback loop from O to I, but we will omit considering such loops explicitly in the present context.

However, if needed the notion of repeated formation of cascades can be assumed to take care of them by making the input of, say, the k'th cascade a function of the output of the k-1'st cascade. Note that even without doing that we may anyway have several machines (and action tokens) corresponding to each agent and in this sense allow feedback loops coming back to the agents (cf. the greeting-example of Section III).

To confirm or disprove the above conjecture convincingly one would at least have to go through a great number of complex examples of social and single-agent actions (cf. an orchestra's playing Sibelius' first symphony, an army unit's saluting its commander, a bank staff's daily activities). This I will have to leave in part for future research and be satisfied here by the observation that at least the rich variety of examples discussed in this book seems to fit our analysis (see especially Subsection III.3 of Chapter 5 for a systematic overview).

A loose and vague argument in favor of the above conjecture can be obtained from the central Krohn-Rhodes decomposition theorem. One of its versions says that each finite state-automaton can be built as a cascade of two-state automata and so-called simple group automata. I do not want to claim that a single agent's contributions must be identified with the decomposing automata here, given that the total generation pattern corresponds to the automaton to be decomposed. Yet the fact that such decomposition (and recomposition, accordingly) is possible suggests that complex social actions can also be suitably decomposed, as we have been arguing, and that the single agent's contributions can be built from the decomposing automata. This means that I am advocating a kind of conceptual individualism in the sense of Chapter 2, for no holistic social terms are employed here. (I am, furthermore, inclined to accept a nominalistic interpretation of set theory and so there will be no real sets of inputs, outputs, etc.)

In this connection it may also be remarked that any finite automaton can be simulated by a network of logical and-and not-modules, provided that we allow loops of arbitrary complexity in the network (see Arbib (1968)). It seems to me that this decomposition is not intuitively what we have in the case of action generation. It is too atomistic on the one hand, and to allow arbitrary loop connections is too much, on the other hand.

Let me finally summarize our account of (indirect) generation in the case of composite events. I shall not give a complete explicit definition because it would be rather complicated. But the sketch to be offered should be helpful enough. For simplicity, I will model the definition on (14), which seems easier to generalize to the present context. We shall assume that cascades have been defined for the m machines representing our agents $A_1,...,A_m$ (even if we above did it only for m=2). (In some cases, such as in the greeting-example to be discussed in Section III we may need more than one machine for each agent; to incorporate this explicitly we might use the index m' and have m' machines.) We next assume that the input set I contains tokens for the result events of the agents' actions u_i. Thus I will contain strings of the type $r_1...r_m$. Let such a string be called E. We assume that the cascade functions, such as η and Z in the case m=2, will "direct" the input elements r_i in E to their respective machines. In the present case the function ϕ_M of (14) is replaced by the cascade output function $g_K(f_K(s_1,...,s_m,E))$ for some suitable states $s_1,...,s_m$ of the respective machines $M_1,...,M_m$. Let us finally make the (simplifying) assumption for the purposes of exposition that no repeated formation of cascades is needed. (The case of repeated cascades can be formulated on the basis of the definition below by allowing feedback loops coming back to the machines; it remains to show convincingly the need for such repeated cascade formation - but see our comment on (5.13)-(5.15) below.) We then get for the m+1-placed relation $IG(u_1,...,u_m,u)$, which it is more correct to use now for '$u_1,...,u_m$ generate u' than the summative notion $IG(u_1+...+u_m,u)$:

(19) $IG(u_1,...,u_m,u)$ if and only if
 (a) there exist finite automata $M_1,...,M_m$ and a cascade connection K such that there is a cascade of $M_1,...,M_m$ with connection K and such that there exist states $s_1,...,s_m$ of $M_1,...,M_m$, respectively, such that if E is the string $r_1...r_m$ (and the cascade functions appropriately "direct" the elements r_i, i=1,...,m), then $r = g_K(f_K(s_1,...,s_m,E))$, where r is the result event of u; and
 (b) for every i=1,...,m, there exists an automaton M_i' such that M_i' represents an operative law of nature, M_i' is an extension of M_i, and there is an analogously law-representing cascade of $M_1',...,$ and M_m' with a connection K' such that K' is an extension of K.

(Here K' may be supposed to be an extension of K in the ordinary set theoretic sense corresponding to how M_i' extends M_i.)
  (19) is meant to be a generalization not only of (14) but also of (13), for (13) and (14) are interpretable as equivalent. I have not tried to present a direct generalization of (13) as it would here become rather cumbersome. While (19) is a very general schema it is easy to see that its definiens may be false

in some cases - in those where no generation takes place. Thus, in the case of social actions requiring the cooperation of every agent, if some agents' actions block some others' actions we do not get generation. This involves that some of the outputs going into the γ-function in (18) fail to come into existence.

Note that (19) allows for cases of **overdetermination**. For instance, if we have $IG(u_1,...,u_m,y)$ where y is performed by an agent A_j, $j \neq 1,...,m$, then (19) does not bar y from being partially generated (or generatable) by some other tokens $u'_1,...,u'_m$ as well. If that is thought to be a problem (but I don't think it is) overdetermination must be blocked by, for instance, a special clause to that effect. A related point is that (19) does not deal only with social actions that are minimal in the sense of y not coming about with less than m operative agents. For as long as all the m agents do exert appropriate causal influence in the sense of (19) we have generation (even if, e.g., m-1 agents could have brought about y). (As to the probabilification of (19) see our earlier remarks; also see our discussion of the formula (**CON***) in the next subsection for a condition assumed satisfied by IG, viz. (c) of (**CON***).)

Our definition (15) takes care of conceptual generation also in the social case, when applied step by step. Thus we do not need an extra analogue of (19) for conceptual generation. Let me note here, for further reference, that when we later on speak of **purposive** generation in the case of social action we will technically be concerned with our analysis (9') with (19) used for the relation IG in clause (a) of (9'), and with (19) as explicating factual generation and (15) conceptual generation in clause (b) of (9'). Given all this, we have finished our technical investigation of the structure of event generation (but see below and Section III for examples and interpretations).[5] (It should be at least plausible on the basis of our discussion earlier in this section that all the cases discussed in Section III.3 of Chapter 5 also fit our generational account as summarized by (19). Note, however, that cases (5.13)-(5.15) seem to require combining cascades truth-functionally although every instantiation of each (5.13), (5.14), and (5.15) (etc.) will fit (19) and thus a single cascade.)

Let me finally note that one may profitably study various properties of the class of possible event chains leading to a given kind of result or consequence event, say R, of a social action from the participating individuals' actions. Thus R (or its elements, rather) may be generated economically or uneconomically, for instance, or the R-events may be generated skillfully (cf. Section II of Chapter 5). When again R fails to be realized one may study the reasons why. Thus one may be able to pinpoint some event that blocks the other agents' properly exercizing their powers and that as a result prevents R from being realized.

Our analysis in this section of action generation coupled with the mereological analysis of Section 5.II should have made it clear that we are dealing with a great variety of cases when discussing the generative patterns underlying the joint actions by several agents. While we hope to have created adequate tools for the study of any social actions from a generative point of view, much remains to be done at least as far as careful case study of complex cases is concerned.

5. Our formal results may be given different interpretations and they may be applied to various situations, of course. I shall below briefly consider the above generational relation IG (and IG*) and three different applications. Let us assume that we have, as above, $IG(u_1,...,u_m,u)$, where u_i tokens an action type X_i, $i=1,...,m$, and u tokens a social action type X. Then, in our earlier notation $X = X_1\&...\&X_m$ in the generative situation at hand.

First, our main interpretation above has been the one where the X_is represent component actions of the social action X. Thus the agents $A_1,...,A_m$ are supposed to do $X_1,...,X_m$, respectively, and that will generate their jointly or collectively doing X. In this situation, at least, it seems plausible to accept the generational principle (PG) according to which $IG(u_1,...,u_m,u)$ if and only if $IG(r_1,...,r_m,r)$.

Our second interpretation assumes that the agents $A_1,...,A_m$ do $X_1,...,X_m$, respectively, and that their actions jointly generate some **other** agents' performing an action, say Y. This may take place in two different ways. First, the agents' $A_1,...,A_m$ action tokens $u_1,...,u_m$ may be required to generate an action token u which tokens a social action type X by $A_1,...,A_m$. Then u is taken to generate an action token, say v, of Y by some (individual or even collective) agents, say $A_k,...,A_{k+p}$, not necessarily distinct from $A_1,...,A_m$. Given the generational principle (PG) this amounts to r_u's generating r_v, where r_u and r_v are the respective results of u and v. The second way $u_1,...,u_m$ may generate v is the more direct one where it is not required that $u_1,...,u_m$ first generate u but where they may directly generate v.

A simple illustration of our second interpretation is given by the so-called "proxy actions" or, as they also have been called, "secondary actions" (see Copp (1979) and below). A secondary action is one which is attributed to an individual or collective agent (or several agents) on the basis of actions of some other agents. A simple example would be an **agent A**'s buying stocks from a stock exchange by authorizing an agent B to do it for him. Another example, more pertinent to social acting, would be provided by a group of workers negotiating wage increases for themselves via their representatives. A third example would be a nation's (a collective agent) negotiating an agreement with another nation where both nations are represented by their prime ministers, say.

When translated into our framework we have in these examples again a situation where some agents $A_1,...,A_m$ perform a social action X by producing a token u, and u generates a token v of another social action type Y by some (possibly quite different) agents, say $A_k,...,A_{k+p}$. Next, the agents' $A_1,...,A_m$ performing X is suitably **redescribed** so that it accounts for the fact that it produces r_y. For instance, in our example the workers produced a token u (e.g., hired some lawyers) which generated a wanted result r_y, viz. wage increase. We redescribe the whole action and call it negotiating a wage increase. As seen, I do not want to make a sharp distinction between primary actions, viz. actions that an agent does without involving other agents' actions, and secondary actions (but cf. our (**CON***) below).

Notice that our second kind of interpretation for the generational relation is pertinent to the study of social influence, and we shall employ this interpretation in Chapter 9 in that context.

In our third interpretation $IG(u_1,...,u_m,u)$ is taken to say that the agents' $A_1,...,A_m$ performing $X_1,...,X_m$ (via producing their tokens $u_1,...,u_m$) generated a performance of X by the group (collective agent) G which group has just, or at least, $A_1,...,A_m$ as its members. Given this interpretation, we can use IG to explicate, say, a business firm's negotiating a deal, a parliament's ratifying a law proposal, or a nation's declaring war in terms of the members of the collective in question doing something appropriate where some members may be more actively engaged than the others. (Recall our earlier analysis (**5.16**).)

In the case of a collective's action overdetermination may be present: the vice prime minister acts for the prime minister if the latter is incapacitated, and so on. This means that there may be several alternative sets of operative agents. But overdetermination poses no problem for our analysis, it seems. For G's doing X does not as such depend on whether or not there are alternative ways of generating the result-event of X; but at least one way is required. Note that the relation of purposive generation IG* must be taken to have the right social and normative constraints, called C earlier in Chapter 5 and below, built into it, via the relevant inner states of the automata in question. How to do that is a problem which I briefly commented on in Section IV of Chapter 5 (see Copp's (1979) relevant and acceptable analysis).

Let me now connect the above account to Copp's (1979) analysis of what it is for some agents' actions to "constitute" and thus proxy another agent's (e.g., a collective's) action. His final analysis, below termed (**CON**), is as follows, where A_1 may be a single agent or a collective (cf. Copp (1979), p. 183):

(**CON**) For agents $A_1, A_2, ..., A_m$ and actions $X_1, X_2, ..., X_m$ A_1's doing X_1 was **constituted** by A_2's doing X_2, A_3's doing $X_3, ...,$ and A_m's doing X_m if and only if
(a) under the circumstances C, A_2's doing X_2, A_3's doing $X_3, ...$ and A_m's doing X_m was a sufficient condition of A_1's doing X_1, but
(b) neither the obtaining of C, nor the performing of $X_1, X_2, ..., X_m$ by agents $A_1, A_2, ..., A_m$ respectively was sufficient by itself for A_1's doing X_1, and
(c) if it had not been the case that (A_2 did X_2, or A_3 did $X_3, ...$ or A_m did X_m), it would not have been the case that A_1 did X_1, assuming there was no $A_{m+2}, ..., A_{m+r}$, and $X_{m+2}, ..., X_{m+r}$ such that either
(i) it was not the case that A_{m+2} did $X_{m+2}, ...$ and A_{m+r} did X_{m+r}, but this **would** have been the case had it not been the case that (A_2 did $X_2, ...$ or A_m did X_m), and, under the circumstances, A_{m+2}'s doing $X_{m+2}, ...$ and A_{m+r}'s doing X_{m+r} would have been sufficient for doing A_1's doing X_1, or
(ii) where $A_{m+i} \neq A_1$, for all $2 \leq i \leq r$, it was the case that A_{m+2} did $X_{m+2}, ...$ and A_{m+r} did X_{m+r}, and under the circumstances, this would have been a sufficient condition of A_1's doing X_1 even if it has not been the case that (A_2 did $X_2, ...$ or A_m did X_m), and
(d) $\{<A_2,X_2>,<A_3,X_3>,...,<A_m,X_m>\}$ is the union of sets $\phi_1, \phi_2, ..., \phi_m$, each ϕ_i ($1 \leq i \leq m$) of which is such that
(i) given $\phi_i = \{<A_j,X_j>,<A_{j+1},X_{j+1}>...<A_{j+p},X_{j+p}>\}$, A_j's doing $X_j, ...$ and A_{j+p}'s doing X_{j+p} was a sufficient condition of A_1's doing X_1, under the circumstances C, but

(ii) it is **not** the case that there is a proper subset of ϕ_i, $\{<A_k,X_k>, <A_{k+1},X_{k+1}>, \ldots, <A_{k+q},X_{k+q}>\}$, such that, under the circumstances C, A_k's doing $X_k,\ldots$ and A_{k+q}'s doing X_{k+q} was a sufficient condition of A_1's doing X_1.

But (**CON**) may seem somewhat too strict. Let me briefly indicate why. First, the sufficiency condition (a) may seem too strong. Suppose a group of passengers pushes a bus up a hill. We may say that the group's pushing the bus (X) was constituted by the passengers' actions (X_i). Yet it may be the case that their actions only probabilistically generated the group action in that situation (C); thus seemingly $p(X/C\&X_1\&\ldots\&X_m)<1$, contradicting sufficiency. However, this is not the case as the set C must be taken to be complex enough to include, e.g., the fact that the bus reaches the top of the hill (cf. Copp (1979), p. 180). Thus sufficiency obtains.

How about clause (c), which is concerned with cases of overdetermination? Copp's motivation for it seems to be that it helps avoid counterexamples of a certain kind. Suppose that we would not require necessity of the constitutive actions for the constituted action in anything like the sense of (c) and would try to get along with sufficiency in something like the senses (a) and (b). But then, for instance, my watching Jones do what he is doing would constitute Jones' tying his shoelaces in the circumstances where what Jones is doing is tying his shoelaces. Note that here we of course have no sufficient factual generation in our sense; yet there is conceptual sufficiency. To block this example and to block the employment of arbitrary conceptual generation to create counterexamples we need the necessity clause (c). Note that (c) does not contradict our earlier analysis. For (c) does not, for instance, block overdetermination. Rather it allows the constitution relation to hold between X_1 and $X_2,\ldots,X_m$ in spite of the fact that the constituted action X_1 was overdetermined. Thus (c) prevents overdetermination from blocking the constitutive relation, we may say. We shall, accordingly, assume that (c) holds true of our relations IG and R_2. (This is a property which perhaps cannot be read directly from our (19) (because of the unperspicuousness of our notion of law-representation) but which would be a formal consequence of it had it been formulated as a direct generalization of (13) rather than (14).)

The function of clause (d) is to allow that, e.g., all the relevant operative agents' actions serve to constitute A_1's action even if they would not strictly have been needed in that situation, while, on the other hand, no irrelevant actions are included. This idea is correct. Note that in our analysis a counterpart of (d)(ii) is not really needed because of our reliance on the ε-relation (cf. (13)) to exclude irrelevancies.

Given the above, I would like to propose tentatively that (a), (b), (c) and (d) (or only (d)(i) perhaps) could be accepted as severally necessary and jointly sufficient conditions for the analysandum in (**CON**), but with the qualification that sufficient and necessary conditions in it be analyzed as sufficient and necessary **generative** conditions and thus partly in terms of our IG and R_2 (and IG* in the case of intentional constituting). I take it that in clause (d)(ii) the required non-existence of the mentioned subsets may be a matter of nomic necessity but also, in some cases of irreducible multi-agent actions, a purely conceptual matter (cf. our remarks in Section I of Chapter 5). Here we then have a proposal, call it (**CON***), using our generative framework, for the "individualistic basis" of a collective's acting, when A_1 is a collective. If we now identify the operative agents $A_1,...,A_m$ referred to in our earlier analysis (5.16) of a collective G's acting with $A_1,...,A_m$ in (**CON***) my claim is that these analyses are equivalent. This is seen to be the case in part due to the fact that intentional acting in (**CON***) is to be interpreted in terms of (5.10). Given this, the analysans of (**CON***) obviously satisfies the analysans of (5.16). As to the converse entailment, recall that we required our (19) to satisfy clause (c) of (**CON***) (and (19) is used to explicate generation in (5.10)). I do not have a proof to show that the analysans of (19) satisfies (a), (b) and (d)(i) in circumstances C as the notion of the circumstances C is not very clear. But I think that until C has been made more precise we can regard the entailment in this direction as an acceptable conjecture and thus accept the claimed equivalence. Note that relativizations to the agents $A_1,...,A_m$ and to the actions $X_1,...,X_m$ can be removed by performing existential quantification over them in the analysans of (**CON***) and by letting the number index m become an existentially quantified variable as well.

Our (**CON***), amending Copp's definition (**CON**), can be used for defining the relation of proxying or representing. Thus if $A_1,...,A_m$ are ordinary agents we can say that A_1's doing X_1 was **proxied** by A_2's doing X_2, ... , A_m's doing X_m if and only if A_1's doing X_1 was constituted by the latters' actions.

III. SOCIAL ACTIONS, GRAMMARS, AND SOCIAL CONDUCT PLANS

1. In this and the previous chapter we have presented our basic conceptual system of social action concepts. As we have

repeatedly emphasized, our classification essentially relies on the notion of action generation. Action generation can be factual or conceptual, and we have interpreted it widely enough to cover the relation of proxying. One central aspect of action generation is that it is an **overt** notion in the sense of concerning only the directly and straightforwardly public aspects of action. Consequently, our system of action concepts is to a great extent overt too, even if we do centrally refer to the acting agents' conduct plans, willings, volitions, and beliefs, etc. These latter notions are **covert** (as contrasted with overt). Perhaps it would be correct to say, then, that our classification system is partly overt and partly covert, where the emphasis as to fine details is on the overt side.

There are many ways our system could be further qualified and enriched. Let me here mention a few characteristics that might be used to so complement it, even if we shall not here enter into a detailed discussion. (Some of the characteristics to be mentioned will be discussed in the later chapters.) Consider thus the following list of labels: **time, location, rigidity, skill, manner,** and **division of activities and tasks.** What kind of aspects (or variables) are these labels meant to refer to?

Considerations of **time** have to do with the duration of the social action and its components. The temporal order of the component actions also belongs here. Thus, e.g., the components may be simultaneous or sequential. Note that our notions of parallel versus serial order of Section II can normally be taken to coincide with this temporal distinction. Considerations related to location have to do with the spatial arrangement of the social action and thus with questions such as the following. How much space does it take? Are the components spatially connected or disconnected? What central spatial relations are there between the components and how do these components spatially related to their environment?

By the **rigidity**, or, rather, the degree of rigidity, of a social action I mean the extent to which it exemplifies a rigid or "formal" pattern. Thus a ritual like a traditional wedding ceremony is formal to a high degree, since it can be regarded as following a script that allows for little spontaneity. (We shall below in Subsection 2 consider rituals from the point of view of formal grammars; also see our remarks on script-based behavior in Section VI of Chapter 11.) Note that our above treatment of action generation is of course compatible with both highly rigid and highly spontaneous (non-formal) social actions.

The factor of **skill** required by a social action is a complex one. For instance, it is related to the degree of **precision** required by the social action. To take an extreme example of physical skill, consider a group of acrobats performing a social action (e.g., on the trapeze). The skill required or exemplified may of course also be mental (cf. group problem solving). We may distinguish between the (minimal) skill required by a social action and the (additional) degree of skill affecting the quality of the social action. Note that the more a social action requires a high degree of skill the smaller is its degree of **repeatability**, ceteris paribus.

We have in Chapter 5 briefly considered the **manner** aspect, and we shall later in Chapter 11 return to it. I shall therefore omit considering it here and go on to the **division of tasks and activities**. This is a broad topic, which we have already briefly commented on in Chapters 2 and 5. First we note that there are social actions, say X, whose components are completely **symmetric** (and exchangeable). Thus, e.g., the carrying of a symmetric object by two or more agents or their shaking hands or their collecting litter can be regarded as symmetric social actions. Thus if $X = X_1 \& ... \& X_m$ we have $X_i = X_j$ for all $i,j=1,...,m$ in the case of fully symmetric social actions. The degree of symmetry or exchangeability may perhaps be measured in terms of the degree of similarity of the components (e.g., in the sense explicated by either formula (10) or (11) in Chapter 8).

It should be clear that social actions with rather dissimilar component actions are very common. Very often simply the demands of the environment require such division of activities in order for a group to achieve its goals. Thus if a family travels by car, one parent must drive and the other one must take care of the children, say. The environment does not allow all to drive or all to be passengers. (A related question is whether there can be a distinction between active and passive participants in a group; cf. our discussion of proxying.) There is of course a great variety of patterns for dividing activities asymmetrically. Let me here take up some of these patterns, naturally without any claim to an exhaustive characterization. One type of division comes from situations of **coordination**. For instance, if our telephone connection is broken one of us (but not both) must call back while the other one waits (see Chapter 7 for an extensive discussion). Another type is that called **turn-taking** in social psychology (see Chapter 12 and, e.g., Duncan and Fiske (1977)). Thus, if we both want to talk we should take turns in order to create a conversation. Our next pattern is concerned with action **control**. Thus a military commander controls his men by his orders and this creates asymmetry between his actions and the order-obeying actions of his men. (See Chapter 9 for a discussion of various aspects of social control.) Yet another pattern worth mentioning is the asymmetry due to the relation of **proxying** or representation. If a company sells something, for instance, it does it via its representatives. Not all of the stockholders participate in such business activities.

While we have above been concerned mainly with overt characteristics of social actions let us now briefly turn to aspects that may be called covert. As above I will only mention some illustrative examples. Thus, we may distinguish between social actions depending on whether they are performed for **internal** or **external** reasons (see Chapter 11). Communicative actions such as **threat** and **persuasion** as well as **exchange** belong to this context. All these factors are interesting because they exemplify various patterns of **covert control**. (We shall discuss the basic elements of covert control in Chapter 9.)

Some general (covert) criteria of classification have been employed in game theory. Thus **cooperation, competition** and **conflict** can be explicated in terms of payoff matrices and can accordingly be used to characterize the resulting social actions. Let me finally mention two characteristics discussed in the previous chapter. First, the **degree of intentionality** of a social action is often of interest (cf. our discussion of invisible hand explanations in Chapter 13). Secondly, as we saw in Section V of Chapter 5, there are interesting differences between social actions having as their goal the provision of a **collective good** (or evil) and those correspondingly concerned with non-collective or individual goods (and evils).

2. We shall end this chapter by illustrating a social conduct plan and the formal aspects of a few kinds of social activities. Accordingly, we will be mainly dealing with the covert aspects of social actions in the sense of the previous subsection. First we want to recall the obvious fact that the conceptual machinery of social action concepts that we have developed can be applied when studying such various social concepts as power, influence, interaction, communication, role, organization, social group and system, social order, and so on (see Chapters 7, 8 and 9 below). As social actions occur in such diverse contexts, obviously also their explanations in terms of social conduct plans will have to make reference to these complex social concepts.

We shall briefly discuss the structural aspects of some **ceremonial** social actions, such as a wedding ceremony, (old-fashioned) dinner party, or, more prosaically, the meeting of two friends in the street. These actions are in part **rituals** in which several actions are performed in sequence in a certain manner (as the "liturgy" specifies). Ceremonial social actions of this rigid type are analyzable as complex social actions in our technical sense, and we could have discussed the "overt" formal aspects of them in Chapter 5. One reason for taking them up here is that we are now also interested in the social conduct plans that explain the overt social action sequences.

In discussing the social conduct plans relevant to ceremonial actions we shall not care about niceties concerning the logical forms of action descriptions in conduct plans (see Tuomela (1977), Chapter 2 and pp. 164-170 and pp. 260-268 for the single-agent case, obviously generalizable to this case). Rather we shall look upon ceremonial actions as having a certain **formal organization**, viz. the organization defined by a suitable formal grammar (for the close relationships between automata and grammars see the results in, e.g., Salomaa (1973)).

We may then view ceremonial social actions as follows. To use the terminology appropriate to formal grammars and automata (see Section II), we represent arbitrary one-agent singular action tokens$_2$ by the letters $a_1, a_2, \ldots$, treated here as ambiguous names and indexed appropriately. Assume as earlier that there are m agents and n "stages" or "occasions" and, correspondingly, (at most) n action types to be tokened and hence n singular actions by each agent. Some of these actions may be omitted, viz., some of the letters a_i below may be empty letters.

It now seems that the structural generation of at least some ceremonial actions can be viewed in terms of the n×m matrix shown in Fig. 6.2.

	1	2	...	m
1	a_1^1	a_2^1	...	a_m^1
2	a_1^2	a_2^2		a_m^2
.	.	.		.
.	.	.		.
.	.	.		.
n	a_1^n	a_2^n	...	a_m^n

Fig. 6.2.

In the matrix of Figure 6.2 the first row specifies what action (possibly a **complex** one) each single agent performs at the first stage, and similarly for all the other $i=2,\ldots,n$ stages. Whether our matrix representation is feasible depends on the following feature. We assume, idealizing somewhat, that we are dealing with purely conventional ceremonies in which no factual generation of actions and no factual "interaction" effects between their results occur. Then the full result of the whole social activity may sometimes be regarded as $r_1+\ldots+r_m$ or, in some cases, as just the sum of the end results of the individual contributions, viz. $r = r_1^n+\ldots+r_m^n$. In making this last point I assume that (a) if r has to be reconceptualized to become the result of the full social action, then this has been accomplished and that (b) the ordering of the stages has been made so that the r_i^ns ($i=1,\ldots,m$) indeed represent the "final" results of the individual contributions; otherwise some further tinkering with the indices will be needed.

Given the above, we can simply view our ceremonial action components as bound together merely by convention and do not have to speak of factual generation at all (and may ignore most of the heavy machinery developed for it in Section II). This is of course idealized, but I think it is useful idealization. We may now think of our matrix as follows. Given the initial word $P^1=a_1^1,a_2^1,\ldots,a_m^1$, it specifies how to sequentially rewrite it into the words $P^2,\ldots,P^n$. What we have here is a **rewriting system** $<V,F>$ in the sense of the theory of formal grammars (see Salomaa (1973), p. 6). Here V is the alphabet consisting of the letters a_i^j ($i=1,\ldots,m$; $j=1,\ldots,n$), and F is the set $\{<P^1,P^2>,<P^2,P^3>,\ldots,<P^{n-1},P^n>\}$. The elements of F are called **productions** or **rewriting rules**.

When our m agents perform a ceremonial activity we assume that they all have in some sense embedded the information in our above matrix into their conduct plans. (We shall not discuss the details of this here.) If our above formal construal is to be useful at all we must try to see whether some interesting formal generational properties may be found for the single-agent actions. Are there some informative, relatively "atomistic" production rules that a single agent can be said to follow? By this I mean to ask whether something more can be said over and above the triviality that $<V,F>$ is a rewriting system. The point is that $<V,F>$ is fully context-bound in the stated form. But could we perhaps find some interesting special cases in which a production rule relating two singular actions a_i^j and a_i^{j+1} would depend on less than the whole context of the words P^j and P^{j+1}? It seems that rigid ceremonial actions may provide examples when at most some small amount of context sensitivity is present. For such cases it seems that suitable Lindenmayer grammars are applicable (cf. Pörn (1977), pp. 59-61).

A Lindenmayer grammar is a word manipulating system which differs from an ordinary formal grammar in that in it all the letters of a word are rewritten in one step of the operation of the system (see Salomaa (1973), pp. 234-252). A Lindenmayer system therefore permits the simultaneous application of several single-letter productions. We shall here define only the simplest type of a Lindenmayer grammar, called an OL-system, in which there is no "interaction" or dependence between the individual letters (singular actions at a given stage). Basically, an OL-system corresponds to simultaneous context-free rewriting, in the terminology of formal grammars. The definition goes as follows (cf. Salomaa (1973), p. 235): An OL-system is an ordered triple OLS = $<V, P_0, F>$ where V is an alphabet, P_0 is a nonempty word over V (called the axiom or the initial word), and F is a finite set of ordered pairs $<a,P>$ with $a \in V$ and $P \in W(V)$. Furthermore, for each $a \in V$, there is at least one word $P \in W(V)$ such that $<a,P> \in F$. The elements $<a,P>$ of F are called productions and written $a \rightarrow P$.

We may define a production rule ($\Rightarrow$) for words as follows: $P \Rightarrow Q$ holds if and only if there is a $k \geq 1$, and words Q_k, $1 \leq k \leq n$, such that $P = a_1 \ldots a_n$, $Q = Q_1 \ldots Q_k$, and $a_k \rightarrow Q_k$ is in F for $k = 1, \ldots, n$. Accordingly, we can say that in each step of the operation of the grammar an entire word is transformed by as many applications of productions to the word as there are letters in the word. Each production may be applied to a word in respect of a letter occurring in it independently of what the neighboring letters are (viz., what the "neighboring" actions by other agents at that stage are).

As said, I believe that **ideally** some rigid social rituals are performed in a way approximately describable by means of an OL-grammar, where the order of productions suitably reflects the time order of actions. There are also Lindenmayer grammars in which the productions are taken to depend on one or both neighbors of the letter. Of course, there are lots of "non-rigid" social activities which are not describable even by such more complicated L-grammars.

In many cases it is useful to assume that a singular action of one agent "produces", or is "rewritten", as a singular action of another agent when applying a grammar. Suppose two friends A_1 and A_2 meet each other in the street, for example. A_1 says 'Hello' (a_1), and A_2, accepting A_1's "interpretation" of the situation and the same greeting-convention, answers 'Hello' (a_2). A_1 next says 'How are you?' (a_3). This action a_3 is followed by A_2's conventional answer 'Thanks I'm fine. What about you?' (a_4), to which A_1 also conventionally answers 'Thanks I'm fine, too' (a_5). Action a_5 is followed by A_2's saying 'I must be going now. Good-bye' (a_6). The whole meeting episode is ended by A_1's saying 'Good-bye' (a_7).

To describe this whole social episode with several turn takings by means of a formal grammar we may either use our earlier matrix method or, alternatively, simply claim that we have here an OL-system $<V,P_0,F>$, where $V=\{a_1,...,a_7\}$, $P_0=a_1$, $F=\{<a_i,a_{i+1}>\}_{i=1}^{6}$. Let us accept the latter way (and abstract here from the communicative aspects of the episode; cf. Chapter 10). (Note that since in our example P_0 is a one-letter word only, we are here dealing with a trivial OL-system.) Consider now the productions $a_i \to a_{i+1}$. The formal grammar does not give semantic truth conditions for '$\to$', but we have been assuming that here some social rule (norm) backs this production rule. Perhaps we may say that there are social ought-rules involved: a_1 (performed by A_1) ought to be followed by a_2 (performed by A_2), and so on.

We shall not here discuss these ought-statements nor their logic. What I am suggesting amounts formally to this, given that the agents and actions have already been suitably paired. We introduce an operator **'Ought'** to apply to the production statements '$a_i \to a_{i+1}$' or '$F(a_i)=a_{i+1}$' (for F is here a function if we agree to give a_7 a suitable value). Thus **'Ought** $(F(a_i)=a_{i+1})$' may be read, for example, 'a_{i+1} ought to be performed (next), given a_i', a reading which makes clear the conditional nature of this form. (In the more general case we would have norms of the type **'Ought** $(P \Rightarrow Q)$' and we should make the involved turn taking more explicit by suitable indices referring to the agents.) What we get is a **normative organization** $<V,P_0,F,\text{Ought}>$. We shall not here discuss it further except to note that, due to the way F has been defined, there seems to be no need for quantifiers here.

In the fully general case, which takes us beyond ordinary formal grammars, the alphabet V will not be finite. Then we must operate with different tools, and, for instance, the Davidsonian formalization of action statements (and hence employ quantifiers), with the addition of the **Ought**-operator applied to action statements, will do the work for us (cf. Tuomela (1977), Chapters 2, 6, and 9). We shall then also need — at least initially — to make a clear distinction between individual oughts and social oughts in terms of appropriate operators (cf. Chapter 2 and Sellars (1968)).

What do we have at the level of conduct plans? Recall that each acting agent A_i (i=1,...,m) is thought to act on his conduct plan involving a we-intention. The conjunction of the m individual conduct plans is the **social conduct plan** or, technically, social conduct plan description (cf. our characterization in Chapter 5).[6] If an agent acts on a norm (rule) then he must in some "internalized" sense know it or believe it. Thus, it would very often be the case that in situations of the kind treated above each agent A_i believes (or thinks) that, given a condition C, he ought to do X (cf. our schema (SA_i) and (PR_i) of Chapter 7). Given suitable further qualifications, this may generate A_i's intending to do X_i, given C (cf. our discussion in Chapter 7). The condition C may be A_i's own previous action, or it may be the other agents' actions X_j, or it may be a completed previous social action. Which of these it is depends on the type of action to be performed.

CHAPTER 7

PRACTICAL INFERENCE AND SOCIAL ACTION

I. LOOP BELIEFS AND PRACTICAL INFERENCE

1. The purpose of this chapter is to study the conceptual nature of social action conforming to (or violating) community rules. More broadly, we shall be discussing some relevant philosophical issues underlying the conceptual framework of social action concepts and other social concepts created in the previous chapters. We shall start with a discussion of social loop beliefs and social practical inference, and our results will then lead to a clarification of various types of rule-conforming and rule-referring social action, as well as to a discussion of some aspects of the philosophical foundations of game theory.

In this section we shall study what can be called **social practical inference**. Let us say vaguely that social practical inference is practical inference performed by a collective of agents such that this inference leads to a conclusion favoring the intentional performance of a social action by these agents. This conception of social practical inference entails that the agents perform individual practical inferences leading to their concluding that they should do their component actions (of the social action in question). What is interesting is that these individual practical inferences must be "socially" connected in order to do what is required of them. What such social connectedness amounts to in general we shall not really try to explicate. Instead we shall concentrate on socially interconnected practical inferences involving **social loop beliefs** and create some central (even if idealized) patterns of practical inference involving them. Such loop beliefs have been investigated by, e.g., Schelling (1960), Shwayder (1965), Grice (1957), (1969), Scheff (1967), Lewis (1969), Schiffer (1972), Bennett (1976), and Pörn (1977). Yet our main interest, the theory of social practical inference (employing, e.g., we-intentions and loop beliefs), has not been much discussed (but see Lewis (1969)).

One interesting route to the study of social loop beliefs and social practical inference goes via the rationalistic doctrine of game theory, especially the theory of nonzero-sum games (cf. our discussion of game theory below and in Chapter 9). We shall start with this approach and later try to remove some of the strictest game-theoretic restrictions.

Let us start by a consideration of simple two-agent situations requiring full cooperation in the sense of coordination. Suppose you and I are rowing a boat together. If we row in rhythm, the boat moves smoothly; otherwise it does not. We both want the boat to move smoothly, and it does not essentially matter at what rate we row. We have thus to choose a common rate at which to row. Another example is this. Suppose we are talking on the telephone, and the line is cut off every two minutes. We want to restore the connection immediately. This happens just in case one of us (but not both) calls back immediately. We must thus agree on who is the one to call back.

Cases like the above may be handled in terms of game theory as follows. We assume that you and I are the two players A_1 and A_2. We assume as before that talk about interpersonally comparable utilities (which may be taken to "value" the agents' goals and other wanted and/or anticipated action-consequences) and payoff matrices can be made sense of; see Chapter 2. Thus we assume that in examples of the above kind the agents **mutually share** a payoff matrix (say P), which could be as is shown in Figure 7.1.

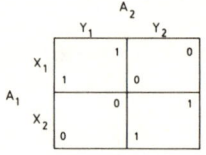

Fig. 7.1.

In the telephone conversation example, for instance, the actions X_1 and Y_2 would stand for calling back and the actions X_2 and Y_1 for waiting. The combinations $<X_1,Y_1>$ and $<X_2,Y_2>$ give a utility unit of 1 to both A_1 and A_2 while the other two combinations give only zero units to both. In this case $<X_1,Y_1>$ and $<X_2,Y_2>$ are equally good action-pairs (or, if you prefer, action-strategies). A convention or agreement to act coordinatively has to be established between A_2 and A_2 in this so-called **coordination** game. We require that the interests - viz. payoffs - of the players of a coordination game either fully or nearly coincide.

For finite n-person coordination games of the above sort we may define the following technical concepts (see, e.g., Lewis (1969), pp. 8, 14, for more details). We first say that an action combination (with independently performed actions) is an **equilibrium** just in case each agent likes it at least as well as any other combination he could have reached, given the others' choices. An equilibrium is a **proper equilibrium** if each agent likes it better than any other combination he could have reached, given the others' choices. Finally, we call an equilibrium a **coordination equilibrium** just in case no one would have been better off had **any** agent alone acted otherwise, either himself or someone else.

Let us next say that a proper coordination equilibrium is a coordination equilibrium which is proper, viz. a combination each agent prefers to any other in which some one agent, himself or another, would have acted otherwise. Now we may say that given a symmetric matrix with two proper coordination equilibria coinciding (or nearly-coinciding) in value we are confronted with a **coordination problem**. Thus the matrix P in Figure 7.1 represents a coordination problem. (Gilbert (1981) argues that the presence of two or more proper coordination equilibria in a game of coinciding or nearly-coinciding interests is in the general case neither necessary nor even sufficient for the existence of a coordination problem. Accepting that, the above qualified sufficient condition still seems plausible; and, in any case, giving an exact definition of a coordination problem is not central for our developments below.)

To solve a coordination problem the involved agents typically establish a **convention** (mutual agreement, norm, rule, or whatever you want to call it). Lewis (1969), for one presents such an analysis (cf. Gilbert (1981) for criticisms). It is not, however, necessary to discuss here the exact nature of convention (at least in Lewis' sense) partly because our concept of conformative social action is broader than at least Lewis' concept of a conventional action. Yet, as said, conventional actions in the sense of our above examples (deterministic coordination games) give us a good starting point.

Consider our above matrix P, which is symmetric with respect to the agents A_1 and A_2. Let us focus on A_1. We assume here that A_1 is rational in the sense that he intends to satisfy his preferences and, in our technical context, to maximize his operative (expected) utilities - be they egoistic or altruistic or whatever. Thus in the present chapter we will assume that our agents are rational in the sense that they intend to perform the actions which maximize their expected utilities. (This is an idealized assumption - see Chapters 2 and 12 for criticisms and for necessary qualifications to the maximization of expected utility assumption.) Maximization of expected utilities entails in our example that A_1 and A_2 intend to act so that one of the coordination equilibria will come about.

Suppose now that A_1 and A_2 have, one way or other, come to establish the convention to always choose the first alternative in our coordination game. Although we shall not attempt to analyze the concept of convention here we may in any case accept that in this situation it is a mutual belief of A_1 and A_2 that the first alternative will be chosen. This we take to imply that A_1 believes that A_2 believes that A_1 will do X_1 (or, at least, that A_1 intends to do X_1, but let us assume here that intentions are successfully carried out). Here we have a loop belief relating A_1 and A_2. But this loop belief does not yet alone give A_1 a decisive or even a good reason for doing X_1. What we still need is that A_1 believes that A_2 acts according to their convention, viz. that A_2 will do Y_1. We may also say here that this follows from the fact that A_1 believes that A_2 intends to act so as to maximize his expected (utilities expected relative to his beliefs) in this situation and from the underlying fact that A_1 believes that A_2 shares the convention with him. Thus, in order to maximize his own (expected) utilities A_1 will have to choose X_1. (The above remarks obviously hold true for A_2 as well, viz. if 'A_1' and 'A_2' switch places.)

Let us condense the above information into the following schema for our coordination game with the payoff matrix P and the players A_1 and A_2:

(SA_1) ($P1_1$) A_1 intends to (act so as to) maximize his (expected) utilities.
    ($P2_1$) A_1 believes that A_2 believes that A_1 will do X_1.
    ($P3_1$) A_1 believes that A_2 intends to act so as to maximize his (expected) utilities.
    (C_1) A_1 does X_1.

Can we regard the above schema as conceptually binding? At least when viewing it non-predictively or **ex post actu**, I think we can, given that we assume that normal conditions, including obvious rationality conditions, obtain (see below and Tuomela (1977), Chapter 7 on them). For, intuitively, (SA_1) comes to say just what A_1's maximization of his expected utilities here amounts to, viz. doing X_1. The logical conclusiveness of (SA_1) can be seen to hold on the basis of the following considerations.

That (SA_1) is logically binding depends essentially on the fact that A_1's and A_2's practical inferences in this situation are completely parallel. We may thus write out A_2's schema as follows:

(SA_2) ($P1_2$) A_2 intends to maximize his (expected) utilities.
($P2_2$) A_2 believes that A_1 believes that A_2 will do Y_1.
($P3_2$) A_2 believes that A_1 intends to act so as to maximize his (expected) utilities.
(C_2) A_2 does Y_1.

Now it is true to say that if A_1 has the intentions and the beliefs specified by (SA_1) and if in addition A_1 believes that A_2 has the intentions and beliefs specified by ($P1_2$)&($P2_2$)&($P3_2$), then, given the relevant rationality of A_1's beliefs, it follows logically in the coordination game specified by P that A_1 believes that A_2 will do Y_1.

Our above considerations show that if A_1 believes that A_2 reasons analogously with him then he will have reason to believe and, indeed, if rational he will come to believe that A_2 does Y_1. Since parallel remarks can be made of A_2, we may say that the relevant mutual knowledge (or belief) between A_1 and A_2 entails their beliefs that the other one will do his conforming action. Thus, for instance, under the assumption that A_1 believes that ($P1_2$)&($P2_2$)&($P3_2$), it is true that in addition to ($P3_1$) we have

($P3_1'$) A_1 believes that A_2 will do Y_1.

Now, together with the rationality assumptions and the assumptions built into the payoff matrix P, ($P3_1'$) entails

($P3_1''$) A_1 believes that unless he does X_1 he cannot maximize his (expected) utilities.

($P1_1$) and ($P3_1''$) can be taken to entail (C_1), given normal conditions. Thus, given ($P1_1$)&($P2_1$)&($P3_1$) and the assumption that A_1 believes that ($P1_2$)&($P2_2$)&($P3_2$), (C_1) cannot fail to hold true (under normal conditions). More generally, the mutual belief assumption and the conjunctions ($P1_1$)&($P2_1$)&($P3_1$) and ($P1_2$)&($P2_2$)&($P3_2$) entail that the agents A_1 and A_2 will do their conforming actions, given normal conditions. Note, furthermore, that the role of the loop beliefs ($P2_1$) and ($P2_2$) in the agents' reasoning is that they serve to single out or **indicate** a particular proper coordination equilibrium defining conforming actions.

Let us consider further the practical reasoning involved in our example. We have above relied on the notion of a normal condition. What are the required normal conditions for doing something X? Let me reproduce the list of them from Tuomela (1977), p. 177:

(i) A is able to do the (conforming) action X;
(ii) there is an opportunity in the particular situation at hand for A to perform this action (i.e., the specific "non-agentive" facts and circumstances of the situation allow him to perform X;
(iii) A is "locally" rational in the sense of not being seriously emotionally disturbed, suffering loss of memory, etc.;
(iv) A is not prevented by other agents from doing X.

I will not here discuss these conditions in more detail. One further important thing must be said, however. It is that the premises of a practical inference must be causally (or, rather, purposive-causally) connected with its conclusion. This may be regarded as a kind of normal condition clause, too; and it follows from the basic assumptions of the purposive-causal theory of action (see Chapters 4 and 5 above and Tuomela (1977), pp. 179, 184, 224, 277-280). A further relevant, and needed, assumption is that the notion of intending used above is a strong act-relational one (see Chapter 4) and that the notion of believing satisfies the rationality requirement mentioned above. Below we shall generally require that the normal conditions obtain and that it is also mutually believed by all the acting agents that they obtain in the case of every agent. It must be admitted that our normal conditions are strong, but if they do not hold there is no logical guarantee that the action comes about. (However, this matter is not important for our purposes, especially since we are primarily interested in the premises of the practical reasoning.)

Given the above discussion and our assumption of normal conditions we can now take the premises of (SA_1) and (SA_2) to give A_1 and A_2, respectively, decisive or overriding reasons to perform their conforming actions. The overridingness is primarily due to our use of not, e.g., wants but intentions in these schemas; an agent cannot knowingly have incompatible intentions, for conceptual reasons.

Even if the above schemas (SA_1) and (SA_2) can be regarded as being logically conclusive and as stating overriding reasons, given the further mentioned assumptions, it may be argued that they do not correctly represent the agents' practical inferences. This is so, the argument goes, because the conclusion of a practical inference cannot really be an action description (as (C_1) and (C_2) specify). The proper conclusion of a practical inference is a **statement** to the effect that an agent **should** or **ought to** do so-and-so. Let us thus consider

(C$_1^{\prime}$) A$_1$ ought to do X$_1$.

The premises (P1$_1$), (P2$_1$), and (P3$_1$) together with the mutual belief assumption may be taken to entail (C$_1^{\prime}$) without further normal condition assumption other than that A$_1$ can (is able to) do X$_1$. The ought here may be, e.g., a prudential, moral, legal or a "technical" (means-end) one, depending on the case. The ought is, furthermore, an **overriding** ought as contrasted with a **prima facie** ought. An overriding ought not only ranks highest in priority among the agent's **prima facie** oughts, but it also amounts to an intention in the following sense. I argue that the following is an analytic truth in the first-person case: If I believe that I ought overridingly to do X then, under normal conditions, I will do X. Here 'will' is to be taken in its **volitional** sense. In the third person case it seems that we may directly say that, given normal conditions, the statement 'A ought overridingly to do X' and 'A intends to do X' are non-accidentally equivalent in truth value (even if they are not synonymous). The reference to normal conditions has the primary function of excluding cases of **akrasia**, for weak-willed persons may believe they ought overridingly to do X yet not intend to do X.

When A$_1$ successfully carries out his overriding ought to do X$_1$ we of course get (C$_1$). (Our normal conditions (ii)-(iv) essentially account for that.) That the above connections indeed are as specified I shall not pause to argue for in detail here, as the matter is not central for our present purposes. (See Aune (1977), pp. 187-193 and Castaneda (1975), pp. 298-305, and Raz (1979), pp. 128-143, for somewhat similar views and for relevant discussion.[1])

2. Since the agents' positions in a coordination game are strategically symmetrical, we may immediately generalize our above considerations to the case of any finite number (say m) of agents with a fixed finite number (say k) of choice-alternatives X$_1$,...,X$_k$. (Let us denote X=X$_1$&...&X$_k$.) If we now lay bare all the assumptions needed for the logical conclusiveness of the practical inferences we get the following schema (abstracting from circumstantial relativizations) for any agent A$_i$, i=1,...,m, and for some X$_k^i$, where X$_k^i$ represents the conforming action type for agent A$_i$:[2]

(SA_i) ($P\alpha_i$) A_i believes that he is playing a (coordination) game with the payoff matrix P.
(P1$_i$) A_i intends to act so as to maximize his (expected) utilities (given in P).
(P2$_i$) A_i believes that, for all $j=1,\ldots,m, j \neq i$, A_j believes that A_i will do X_k^i.
(P3$_i$) A_i believes that, for all $j=1,\ldots,m, j \neq i$, A_j intends to act so as to maximize his (expected) utilities, as specified by P.
(Pβ_i) Normal conditions for doing X obtain, and A_i believes they obtain.
[(Pγ_i) It is mutually believed by $A_1,\ldots,A_m$, for all $j=1,\ldots,m$, that $((P\alpha_j)\&(P1_j)\&(P2_j)\&(P3_j)\&(P\beta_j)$, and that hence $(C_j))$.)]
(C$_i$) A_i does X_k^i.

As compared with the two-person case, we have above laid bare some premises only implicitly assumed earlier. In ($P\alpha_i$) we require that A_i **believes** that he is a participant in a (coordination) game with the payoff matrix P. This entails that A_i is familiar with the rules of the game in the technical sense that he is aware of (at least) the so-called normal form of the game (cf. Luce and Raiffa (1957), pp. 51-53). This again entails that A_i is aware of the other m-1 players, the pure strategies of the game, as well as of the payoffs associated with the various strategy combinations (or action combinations, in our applications). We shall later remove the restriction that the game must be a coordination game.

As the premises (P1$_i$), (P2$_i$), and (P3$_i$) are rather obvious generalizations from the two-agent case I shall not specifically comment on them here nor on the logical validity of (SA_i). (Pβ_i) assumes categorically that normal conditions for performing the complex activity X obtain. It also assumes that A_i believes so. Note that while the latter would, ceteris paribus, suffice for getting A_i to attempt to do X_k^i we still need the objective obtaining of normal conditions to guarantee the success of A_i's attempt.

The premise (Pγ_i) representing the mutual belief assumption is not, strictly speaking, needed for the logical validity of (SA_i). It is a kind of **underlying** assumption **justifying** the reasoning rather than a proper premise in the schema itself, and therefore it has been put in brackets. Note that it is symmetrical with respect to the agents. We shall comment further on the specific role of (Pγ_i) in the next section after defining mutual belief and discussing its conceptual importance.

Let me note here, for further reference, that, on the basis

of our earlier remarks, (SA_i) does not lose its soundness if instead of (C_i) we employ in it the conclusion

(C_i') A_i ought to do X_k^i.

Let it also be remarked, that, under favorable conditions, our schema can retrospectively be thought to give a singular intentional-teleological explanation of A_i's action; A_i did X_k^i because $P(\alpha_i)\&(P1_i)\&(P2_i)\&(P3_i)\&P(\beta_i)\&P(\gamma_i)$ (with verb tenses appropriately changed in the explanans). (See Chapter 11 below for such intentional-teleological action-explanations.) We shall primarily concentrate below on questions of justification rather than explanation of action. (These connected notions are logically independent on my view, viz. justification, in the weak sense of rationalization, neither entails nor is entailed by explanation; cf. Chapter 2.)

Notice that we have not required above that the agent's loop beliefs be **true**. Our account of social practical inference thus works even without such a correctness assumption, but it is nevertheless to be expected that at least in the case of **recurrent** social action, agents would soon cease to entertain and act on loop beliefs which are false, for they would most likely come to find out that they don't reach their intended equilibrium outcomes.

II. MUTUAL BELIEFS

1. Let us start by defining for the two-agent case what their mutual belief in each other's reasoning patterns, viz. (SA_1) and (SA_2), amounts to. We notice that what is required is that A_1 believes that A_2 reasons analogously with him, and vice versa. In ($P\gamma_i$) the phrase 'hence' is meant to reflect the assumption that the conclusion becomes true by means of reasoning from the premises and not in some other way. Let us then ask what A_1's and A_2's mutual belief in the arguments (SA_1) and (SA_2) amounts to. (Strictly speaking, we consider their mutual belief in these arguments minus the respective mutual belief premises ($P\gamma_1$) and ($P\gamma_2$).)

Generally speaking, we now want to have an analysis of what it is for A_1 and A_2 to mutually believe that p (where p = (SA_1) & (SA_2) in our special case). Mutual belief in the strong sense of intersubjective belief amounts to more than shared (firstdegree) belief, as we have in effect noticed. Following in part Lewis (1969) and Schiffer (1972), who analyze mutual knowledge rather than belief, I suggest that ideally mutual belief essentially amounts to iterable layers of loop beliefs. Thus I suggest that, ideally, A_1 and A_2 mutually believe that p if and only if (or to the extent that, if you prefer) A_1 believes that p, A_2 believes that p, A_1 believes that A_2 believes that p, A_2 believes that A_1 believes that p, A_1 believes that A_2 believes that A_1 believes that p, A_2 believes that A_1 believes that A_2 believes that p ... (and so on **ad infinitum**). This account entails that in the case of mutual belief each agent is assumed to have perpetually iteratable beliefs concerning p. Adding a new loop, viz. 'A_i believes that A_j believes that ...', $i,j=1,2$, $i \neq j$, gives additional rationalization (in the sense of reasons for believing). The beliefs in question may be taken as awareness (not necessarily conscious awareness), and they need not be assumed correct (or true) nor need they be psychologically realized when rationalization only is concerned. In the case with $p=(SA_1)\&(SA_2)$ we assume that belief in the whole conjunction of arguments entails belief in (or awareness of) the individual arguments, premises, and the conclusions.

The above account of mutual belief may be generalized (and strengthened). Let us consider a collective S of agents: $S = \{A_1,...,A_m\}$. We now define in an idealized sense what mutual belief in S, or among $A_1,...,A_m$, amounts to (cf. Chapter 5):

(**MB**)   It is **mutually believed** in S that p if and only if
   (1) everyone in S believes that p;
   (2) everyone in S believes that everyone in S believes that p;
   (3) everyone in S believes that everyone in S believes that everyone in S believes that p;
   and so on ad infinitum.

We notice that, when $S=\{A_1,A_2\}$, (**MB**) may appear somewhat stronger than our first definition of mutual belief, for (**MB**) involves iterated self-beliefs, viz. loops where the same agent is mentioned on two consecutive levels, because it clearly involves all the possible agent-permutations at all levels. Thus, for instance, 'A_1 believes that A_1 believes that A_2 believes that p' is a loop allowed by (**MB**) but not by our first definition. However, we may either employ a notion of belief which makes self-iteration vacuous or else exclude self-iteration by a "meaning postulate" so that, e.g., the above statement collapses to 'A_1 believes that A_2 believes that p'.

2.   Later on, when discussing norms, roles, groups, and various related social concepts we shall assume that **in part** their reality is determined by the agents' relevant mutual beliefs, typically arrived at on the basis of communication (in ways

social psychologists can be supposed to specify in detail). Thus, a norm or prescription, for instance, fails to be in force and to "exist" unless people have mutual beliefs (including "know-hows") about it (and in this sense recognize it). This does not amount to **esse est concipi**; but nevertheless, what is social and intersubjective about social reality is in part (but not completely) determined by mutual beliefs. Incidentally, it seems that on a broader scale the notions of **Zeitgeist** and, perhaps, in part "national spirit" can be explicated just in terms of suitable general mutual beliefs. No doubt also the concept of social practice should be explicable in terms of social action performed at least in part because of suitable mutual beliefs.

In social psychology and sociology the importance of something like mutual beliefs has long been recognized. Often theoreticians in these fields speak about **consensus** in this connection. The notion of consensus has been regarded as relevant to, for instance, the topics of public opinion, values, mass action, norms, roles, communication, socialization, and cohesion. Also fads, fashions, crazes, religious movements, and many other related phenomena have been analyzed partly in terms of shared beliefs, consensus, shared consensus, mutual belief or some similar notions. As pointed out by the sociologist Scheff (1967), such analyses have often gone wrong because they have treated consensus merely as agreement (shared belief). Thus, as Scheff argues, consensus as mere agreement does not properly account for "pluralistic ignorance" (where people agree but do not realize it) and "false consensus" (where people mistakenly think that they agree). Scheff proposes an analysis in terms of levels of agreement corresponding to our hierarchy of loop beliefs. As is easily seen, pluralistic ignorance and false consensus are second-level phenomena. The third level will have to be brought in when speaking about people's awareness of these phenomena. Here is one good argument for the necessity of requiring mutual belief rather than mere consensus (or dissent, for that matter). Other well known social psychological notions requiring more than shared belief are Mead's concept of "taking the role of the generalized other", Dewey's "interpenetration of perspectives", and Laing's metaperspectives (see, e.g., Scheff (1967)).

At this point it is proper to ask: Given that mere shared beliefs is not enough (as, e.g., the phenomena of pluralistic ignorance and false consciousness show), why is it necessary or even plausible to introduce a whole (potentially) infinite hierarchy of nested beliefs as (**MB**) requires? One possible answer to this question is that social practical inference can at least ideally be justified in terms of such a hierarchy of beliefs. This answer, which basically is due to Schelling (1960) and Lewis (1969), will be discussed below in the context of our Figure 7.2. Our second answer goes through a consideration of just such examples as pluralistic ignorance and false consciousness. Let us briefly take up this line of argumentation. It is helpful to introduce some formalization to do this.

Let us introduce a sentential operator B_E by:

(1) $B_E p =_{df}$ it is believed in S that p (= everyone in S believes that p).

We are claiming in (1) that 'it is believed that ...' is referentially equivalent to the phrase 'everyone believes that ...'. Thus if we assume a strict logical interpretation (**sensu diviso**) of the latter, then no exceptions are allowed to either general belief. Alternatively, we may treat both as stating a **stereotype.** Then they allow for exceptions. Such a stereotype might yet be rendered exceptionless, in the way of idealization, by speaking of **full-fledged** members of S only (thus: 'every full-fledged member of S ...'). Of course, one might also want to be more liberal than above and consider an operator such as **'most people in S believe that ...'.** Our present considerations below are not essentially affected by such a liberalization.

Given the operator B_E, we can define mutual belief, denote it by B_M, in the sense of the definiendum of (**MB**) in terms of iterations of B_E as follows:

(2) $B_M p =_{df} B_E p \& B_E B_E p \& B_E B_E B_E p \& \ldots$ (ad infinitum) $= \overset{\infty}{\underset{i=1}{\&}} B_E^i p$.

The index i in (2) of course refers to the number of iterations of B_E, and the infinite conjunction collects all the iterations. Given (2) (which is just a formal rendering of (**MB**)), we are in a better position to discuss alternative definitions of mutual belief. Let us see why we should do that.

One problem with iterated beliefs is their complexity. If we rely on Occam's razor we should be careful in introducing new "entities". Another problem with higher level beliefs is the question whether, and in what sense, people can actually have such beliefs. Let us consider first the necessity of an infinite hierarchy of beliefs in view of examples. Does pluralistic ignorance, for instance, require mutual belief in the above sense? It seems that it does not, for a weaker account allowing nonrational beliefs will suffice. And instead of positive belief we may, on higher levels, require only absence of disbelief. Let us thus introduce a new operator:

(3) $B_E^* p =_{df}$ it is not disbelieved in S that p (= none in S disbelieves that p).

Now consider the following alternative definition of mutual belief:

(4) $B_M p =_{df} B_E p \,\&\, \overset{\infty}{\underset{i=1}{\&}} B_E^{*i} B_E p$

In (4) we have positive belief on the first level and the absence of disbelief (viz. negation of belief in the falsity of argument). Now if pluralistic ignorance is taken to mean that people agree but don't realize it, I think absence of second-order disbelief accounts well for that failure of realization. If failure of realization continues on all higher levels we can clearly apply (4) here, but we can not plausibly analyze this in terms of positive second-order belief at all. Note that I have above used B in a very broad sense covering (possibly depending on level) belief, awareness and realization, and so on. In a finer analysis more distinctions would be needed here and the B's on different levels should be kept separate.

How about false consensus? There we lack first-order agreement, and we have $B_E(\sim p)$ (or, in some cases, $\sim B_E p$) on the first level. On the second level again we have $B_E B_E p$. (Note that if $B_E B_E p \vdash B_E p$ we get contradiction with at least $\sim B_E p$. Should we allow a contradiction or prevent the inference? I prefer the latter, but we are in any case dealing with belief and awareness in an unorthodox and not very rational sense here.) On higher levels the use of B_E^* rather than B_E seems plausible. However, people's realization of their false consensus requires B_E on the third level: $B_E(B_E(\sim p) \& B_E B_E p)$.

I shall not here discuss further examples but go on to make some general observations (cf. Lewis (1969), pp. 52-68 for a discussion of other relevant examples). First, our examples indicate that higher order beliefs and thoughts (in whatever varieties they come) are, or may be, needed for the analysis of social constructs. Our examples also indicate that it is not only positive higher-order belief (awareness, realization, understanding, etc.) that comes into question but lack of belief and disbelief as well. But this does not of course as such count against our notions of mutual belief, even (**MB**). While psychological simplicity may favor the use of (4) as a definition of mutual belief, we must note the following. Given an analysis of mutual belief which employs B_E up to a certain level (level 1 in (4)) and B_E^* from thereon, one may always start asking questions about people's realizing (or believing) so and so, where 'so and so' prefers, e.g., to the next level below. Such talk, in other words, starts with a statement p which already involves iterated beliefs, and we can use the old arguments (for the case where p was a simple descriptive statement without belief operators) to show the need for at least one higher level of beliefs. And so the game is seen to be relative to its starting point, and it may go on **ad infinitum**. Here we have an inductive argument (in the mathematical sense) for the open and infinitary character of the hierarchy of nested beliefs.

Can we plausibly think that people (except possibly spies!) can actually have higher-order beliefs than third or fourth order? To this we may say that only **potential** beliefs are at stake here. In this sense I only potentially, but not actually, believe that statements like '127×692=87884' are true prior to performing the actual computation. In a similar sense, the higher-order beliefs can be required to be had only potentially, upon reflection and, furthermore, only relative to lots of abilities and skills (which normal people may well lack). We can then speak of potential higher-order believing even in the case of people who are, e.g., totally unable to actually handle more than second-order beliefs in their reasoning. Such people can share mutual beliefs in the sense of (**MB**), even if only in some vague, idealized sense, not literally in the sense of actually psychologically having an infinite hierarchy of beliefs (any more than their bodies involve mass points, say). The extent to which people have (stable) **actual** higher-order beliefs can now be left as an open empirical question. (I am not aware of any social psychological theories explaining how people come to have higher-order beliefs. On the other hand, there are several rivalling partial accounts of how people arrive at consensus in the sense of shared first-order belief (cf. the balance or dissonance theory, Cohen's and Lee's theory of conformity, various accounts emphasizing communication, etc.).)

In fact we may go further than above and distinguish between potential beliefs of two kinds. First, there are potential or dispositional beliefs in the above sense of beliefs which become actualized given suitable releasing conditions. But we need not limit ourselves to only this kind of beliefs, for our (2) which requires an infinite hierarchy of (potential or actual) beliefs, may be interpreted in a still weaker sense. Thus it is even compatible with (2) to say that a person has only a **finite** number of (potential or actual) beliefs, viz. lower-level beliefs, and, in addition, is disposed (or disposed, if rational) to **come** appropriately **to acquire** the relevant higher-order beliefs on the basis of the general idea or principle underlying the formation of the hierarchy. In this sense, then, (2) is quite compatible with a finitary account of the human mind (cf. Audi (1982b) for a closely related finitary account of an infinity of non-nested beliefs).

As to which account of mutual belief to employ "officially" in this book, the idealized characterization (**MB**) (or (2)) can often be used, given the tenability of the above remarks mitigating its infinitary character. But, since the matter may be regarded as **context dependent** and since, except for our discussion of social practical reasoning, nothing much hangs on this, the weaker definition (4) - or some version in between (2) and (4) or even one requiring only a variable finite number (cf. (5)) - can also be used. The important matter, not properly paid attention to by social scientists, is that a notion of mutual belief going - as the case may require - one, two or even more layers beyond mere shared first-order belief is certainly needed for an analysis of social concepts. We need a full notion of intersubjective belief and that amounts just to mutual belief. Consequently, mutual beliefs play a central role in this book. Yet we by no means want to reduce social reality to mutual beliefs (or anything related) but emphasize the importance of objective causal relationships as well.

As a more technical comment on our above discussion let me formulate a liberal parameter-dependent schema of higher belief that might be called a schema of mutual belief-disbelief and that can be employed for a variety of purposes:

(5) $MBDp =_{df} (\pm)B_E(\pm)p \ \& \ \overset{n}{\underset{i=1}{\&}} (\pm)B_E^{r,i}(\pm)p.$

Here MBD is a new operator for mutual belief and disbelief. In schema (5) ($\pm$) in front of an expression means that $\pm$ is to be replaced by a negation sign or, when opting for the other alternative, by nothing at all. The new index r is a variable which is a function of i. Each value of i (i=1,...; possibly i$\to\infty$) introduces a sequence of operators which are determined by r to be either B_E or B_E^*. Thus, e.g., i=3 might give r = <B_E^*,B_E^*,B_E>, yielding the string $B_E^*B_E^*B_E$. Our earlier remarks on pluralistic ignorance and false consensus can be fitted into this schema and so can various new definitions of mutual belief over and above our (2) and (4); but we shall not here go into more details. (Most of the interesting consensus (and dissent) concepts discussed by, e.g., Scheff (1967) can be analyzed with the help of (5).)

Coming back to the premise $(P\gamma_i)$ of (SA_i) we may notice the following points. First, $(P\gamma_i)$ entails that A_i believes that the normal conditions obtain. But, for perspicuousness, we still prefer to keep this piece of information in $(P\beta_i)$. A more significant observation is the following. As can be checked from our definition of mutual belief (in the orthodox, rational sense) this holds: If it is a mutual belief among the agents A_i, i=1,...,m, that p, then it is a mutual belief among the agents A_i that each A_i believes that p. Even if the converse does not hold we still get the following result, relevant to (SA_i): If the agents A_i, i=1,...,m, mutually believe that each A_i believes that p and if each A_i believes that p then (and only then) the agents A_i mutually believe that p. Thus, for instance, $(P\gamma_i)$ and $(P\alpha_i)$, for i=1,...,m, entail that it is a mutual belief among the agents A_i that they are playing a (coordination) game with the payoff matrix P.[3)]

III. THE REPLICATIVE JUSTIFICATION OF SOCIAL BELIEFS

1. The structure of the justification of rational social beliefs $(P2_i)$ and $(P3_i)$ as well as the conclusion (C_i) in terms of mutual belief in my account is essentially the same as Lewis' (1969) justification by a replication schema. Lewis operates in terms of **conditional desires**. Formulated in terms of **conditional intentions** instead, the essentials of our approach come out as follows. First, concentrating on the two-agent case for simplicity, we note that in (SA_1) the premise $(P1_1)$ is analytically equivalent (given the matrix P) to

(P1┥) A_1 intends to do X_1, given that (A_1 believes that) A_2 will do Y_1, and A_1 intends to do X_2, given that (A_1 believes that) A_2 will do Y_2.

Then we recall that our assumptions (incorporated in (SA_1)) yield

(P3┥) A_1 believes that A_2 will do Y_1.

Now (P1┥) and (P3┥) entail that A_1 intends to do X_1. This assumes that the following detachment rule holds for conditional intentions; from 'A intends p, given q' and 'A believes that q' one may infer 'A intends p', given normal conditions (excluding, e.g., **akrasia**). I think this principle is sound. Given that normal conditions obtain, (P1┥) and (P3┥) can then be taken to entail (C_1). Our basic schema for conformative behavior has now been translated into talk about (carrying out) a relevant conditional intention, as specified by the argument '(C_1) because $(P1_1^*)\&(P3_1^*)$'; in fact we can and shall from hereon omit mention of the second, here idle, conditional intention in $(P1_1^*)$.

Social loop beliefs do not enter the basic practical reasoning involved here. Instead they come to play an essential role in the justification of the belief $(P3_1^*)$. For $(P3_1^*)$ is now justifiable (rationalizable) by means of the mutual belief assumption as follows. The mutual belief assumption entails the truth of

(i) A_1 believes that A_2 will do Y_1, given that (he (A_2) believes that) A_1 will do X_1;

and $(P2_1)$ gives us

(ii) A_1 believes that A_2 believes that A_1 will do X_1.

Now the conditional belief (i) together with the loop belief (ii) entails the statement $(P3_1^*)$, given the rational detachment rule that from 'A believes that p, given q' and 'A believes that q' one may derive 'A believes that p'. The reasoning herein may be perpetuated and so we may get a kind of justification of every loop belief involved (thus (ii) can be analogously justified, and so on). If we omit the premises dealing with detachment from intentions and beliefs and the normal condition assumptions guaranteeing the successful carrying out of intentions, we get the schema shown in Fig. 7.2. It is easily seen that the infinite schema expressed by Figure 7.2 has exactly the same structure as Lewis' replication schema (see Lewis (1969), pp. 31, 112). Furthermore, our new schema is independent of any game-theoretic assumptions. Now, comparing Figure 7.2 with our (SA_i) for the two-person case, we can say the following. Corresponding to every instantiation of (SA_i), which yields a sound social practical inference, we get a sound inference on the basis of Figure 7.2 (which is of course restricted to the coordination game case as it was just assumed to satisfy (SA_i)). We have just seen that the two lowest levels (above the conclusion) of Figure 7.2 are entailed by (SA_i) (in part due to the very construction of the figure). The higher levels are simply consequences of the justifications of the loop beliefs involved in the mutual belief, as discussed above.

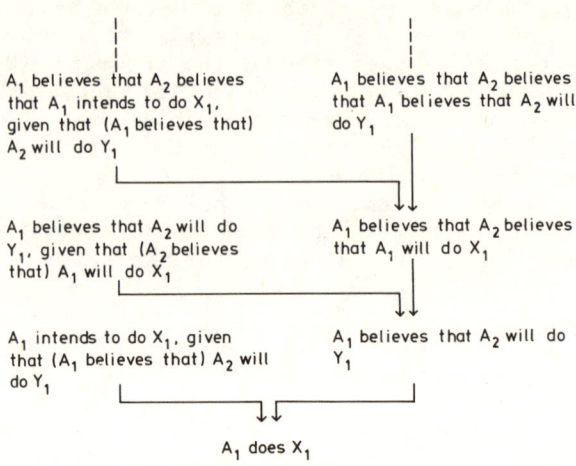

Fig. 7.2.

How about the converse entailment? Does every sound inference instantiating Figure 7.2 in the coordination game case yield a sound instantiation of (SA_i)? The answer is yes. A couple of noncontroversial qualifications are needed, however. First, applying the schema of Figure 7.2 in the coordination game case is assumed to entail the truth of ($P\alpha_1$). Secondly, we recall that (P1¼), the intention premise of Figure 7.2, can be regarded as analytically equivalent to ($P2_1$), given the information that A_1 believes he is playing a coordination game with the payoff matrix P. As to premise ($P2_1$), it has its identical counterpart in Figure 7.2. Premise ($P3_1$) is also entailed by Figure 7.2, given A_1's awareness of P. For it is, analogously with ($P1_1$) and (P1¼), seen to become analytically equivalent (under that information) to 'A_1 believes that [A_2 intends to do Y_1, given that (A_2 believes that) A_1 will do X_1 and A_2 intends to do Y_2, given that A_2 believes that A_1 will do X_2]. Now Figure 7.2 provides us with 'A_1 believes that A_2 believes that A_1 will do X_1'. The application of the detachment rule for conditional beliefs (referred to above) then gives us ($P3_1$).

How about the normal conditions clause ($P\beta_1$)? Figure 7.2 does not explicitly contain a counterpart of it. But I think we can safely assume that it is implicitly there whenever Figure 7.2 is considered to yield a sound inference. So let us make the qualifying assumption that it is there and that it amounts to ($P\beta_1$). (We should thus in fact have mentioned this earlier when discussing the entailment of the schema of Figure 7.2 by (SA_i).)

The "official" premises $(P\alpha_i)$, $(P1_1)$, $(P2_1)$, $(P3_1)$, and $(P\beta_1)$ have now been argued to follow from the schema of Figure 7.2. The mutual beliefs involved in Figure 7.2 and (SA_i) are the same, and are easily seen to be the same by considering the simplified argument with $(P1_1')$, $(P2_1)$, and $(P3_1')$ as its premises. We first notice that Figure 7.2 gives the reasoning process only in the case of A_1. Switching 'A_1' and 'A_2' as well as 'X_1' and 'Y_1' gives us the corresponding schema for A_2. Now the iterations of beliefs in these two schemas (or, better, instantiations) are seen to give us the total mutual belief which we take to be involved in our present simplified version of (SA_i) (and which could be written out as the obvious simplified analogue of $(P\gamma_i)$ of the complete (SA_i)). As above we may consider the mutual beliefs to concern implicitly also normal conditions as well as, in our present application, the information contained in $(P\alpha_1)$. Thus, in all, in view of our above discussion of the relation of the premises $(P1_1')$ and $(P3_1')$ to (SA_1), we can say that the same mutual beliefs are involved in (SA_1) and Figure 7.2, when the latter is applied to both A_1 and A_2.

Now we have seen that in the two-agent case, (SA_i) (together with the justification of the involved mutual belief) and the schema of Figure 7.2 can be applied to the coordination game case by means of non-controversial qualifications to yield the equivalent sound inferences. The generalization of our above discussion to the case of m agents is obvious and need not be further commented on. We shall later relax (SA_i) and allow it to cover many other types of games in addition to coordination games.

2. At this point we may recall our individualistic analysis of we-intentions that we gave in Chapter 2 in terms of the schema (**WI**) (also cf. Chapter 5). Let us start by considering a collective consisting of the members $A_1,...,A_m$. We claimed at the end of Chapter 5 that if such a collective is "egalitarian" then it we-intends to do something X if and only if every A_i we-intends to do X. But we emphasized that the we-intention in question is a full blown one and that in the case of "non-egalitarian" and organized groups this analysis seems too strong even for full blown we-intending.

Leaving this matter aside, we consider our notion of we-intention in the sense of (**WI**) (and, for simplicity, only take up its strict and unqualified version). An agent A_i is said to we-intend to do X if (i) A_i intends to do (his part of) X, given that (he believes that) everyone in the collective will do (his part of) X; (ii) A_i believes that everyone in the collective will do (his part of) X; and (iii) there is a mutual belief in the collective to the effect that (i) and (ii). The content and tenability of this analysis can be demonstrated both on the basis of our schema (SA_i) and our above Figure 7.2. As the latter is more perspicuous we shall concentrate on it. Since Figure 7.2 explicitly concerns only two agents, and since that restriction is easily removable, we may also concentrate on a collective with only two agents, A_1 and A_2. Now we make the following small and harmless changes in Figure 7.2. First, we use 'his part of X' for 'X_1' and for 'Y_1', to keep to our present terminology. Secondly, we weaken the conclusion of our schema and use 'A_1 intends to do (his part of) X' in its place.

Given our discussion in the present section we are warranted in saying in our present case that A_1 intends to do (his part of) X (in part) **because** (1) A_1 intends to do (his part of) X given that (A_1 believes that) A_2 will do (his part of) X and (2) A_1 believes that A_2 will do (his part of) X. That is, given a true (first-level) conclusion of our modified Figure 7.2 we can in part justify (if not explain) it by reference to the second-level premises (assumed true). A fuller justification is obtainable by going up to the higher levels of the schema, which, we recall, have been created by the mutual belief assumption. When commenting on (**WI**) in Chapter 2 we claimed that it entails the following (partial) justification of the agent's I-intention: the agent intends to do (his part of) X (in part) because he believes that everyone in the collective, viz. "each of us" or at least a sufficient number of the members, will do (his part of) X. We have just substantiated this claim in terms of our justificatory schema 7.2 in the case of two agents for the unqualified strict case. (The qualified case can be handled analogously.)

IV. SOCIAL ACTION AND PRACTICAL INFERENCE

1. We shall next, partly on the basis of our above discussion, present yet another schema of practical reasoning specifically for social actions. We consider a (complex) social action type X and assume, in view of our discussion in Chapter 4, that it can be rendered as a context-relative conjunction $X=X_1\&...\&X_m$. To each agent A_i, $i=1,...,m$, we here assign a component action X_i. Thus when we speak of A_i's doing his part of X we mean his doing X_i. How the component actions of X become distributed to the various participating agents may depend on a division of activities and tasks due to tradition, norms, etc. or it may be decided on the spot more or less randomly, all depending on the content of X and the practices of the social community we are

dealing with.

It will be assumed below that we may speak of a participating agent's intention to do X, which may be taken to entail, under normal conditions, that he will do whatever he regards as necessary (and factually possible) for $A_1,...,A_m$ to do X but not yet specifically that he will do his part X_i. As we do not take it for granted that A_i's intention to do X entails his intention to do X_i, we therefore need assumptions for both.

Our new schema is independent of any specific game-theoretic assumptions and it uses conditional intentions. This schema, call it (PR_i), can be formulated in essentially the same terminology as (SA_i). Instead of speaking of a conformative action X_k^i we now deal with an agent A_i's action X_i, i=1,...,m.

We propose the following schema (for the strict, non-probabilistic case):

(PR_i) ($P1_i$) A_i intends to do (his part of) X, given that (he believes that), for all j=1,...,m with j≠i, A_j will do (his part of) X.

($P2_i$) A_i believes that unless $A_1,...,A_m$, respectively, do $X_1,...,X_m$, they cannot jointly do X.

($P3_i$) A_i believes that, for all j=1,...,m with j≠i, A_j will do (his part of) X.

($P4_i$) A_i believes that, for all j=1,...,m with j≠i, A_j will do X_j (as his part of X).

($P5_i$) Normal conditions for doing X obtain, and A_i believes that they obtain.

[($P6_i$) It is mutually believed by $A_1,...,A_m$, for all j = 1,...,m, that ($P1_j$)&...&($P5_j$), and that hence (C_j)).]

(C_i) A_i does X_i.

Some clarifying comments are due here. First, we can see that the social reasoning involved in (PR_i) is essentially of the type exemplified by our Figure 7.2 (and hence (SA_i)), with the addition of intention specification. Basically the reasoning corresponds to the first row above the conclusion of Figure 7.2. The mutual belief assumption ($P6_i$) gives the upper rows and thus the social loop beliefs. (PR_i) does not speak of any loop beliefs in premises other than ($P6_i$). Thus it has no counterpart to ($P2_i$) of (SA_i). This is basically because the explicitly mentioned loop belief in (SA_i) served to indicate what the specific conforming action is. In (PR_i) the corresponding information is given by ($P2_i$).

In (PR_i), the first premise ($P1_i$) just states A_i's intention to do (his part of) X, given that the other agents do (their parts of) X. ($P2_i$) specifies what the agents' parts of X are. In ($P2_i$) we have now explicitly written out the phrase 'jointly', but it should be understood quite broadly. It is thus meant to cover all the structural-generational aspects involved in the instantiations of $X_1,...,X_m$ generating an instantiation of X. Thus it covers all the social action types in the sense of Chapter 5. For instance, we may have cases of conditional actions here, such as those involved in our example of a greeting "ritual" at the end of Chapter 6 (also see below). Each X_i may thus be a complex action whose components are performed conditionally on what some other agents have performed, and so on.

($P3_i$) and ($P4_i$) just state A_i's beliefs that the other agents will do (their parts of) X and respectively do X_j as their parts (cf. the premise 'A_1 believes that A_2 will do Y_1' in Figure 7.2). The normal conditions premise ($P5_i$) and the mutual belief premise ($P6_i$) do not require extra comments here.

On the basis of our earlier discussion it should be clear that (**PR_i**) represents a conceptually valid schema of social practical reasoning. We shall later in Chapter 11 comment further on this question and, in particular, we shall apply (**PR_i**) to the explanation of social action.

At this point we may make some comments on what might be called the dynamic aspects of social practical reasoning. To be sure, our previous treatment in terms of (**SA_i**), the schema of Figure 7.2, and (**PR_i**) involve some dynamic aspects. What I am after here is how to make those aspects more explicit. The problem is whether they can be highlighted in ways analogous to the discussion in Tuomela (1977), pp. 196-205, where some dynamic aspects of a single agent's practical reasoning were studied. There two situations were focused on. The first was concerned with repeated intention-transference (or, more generally, goal-specification) and it led to the technical notion of a PS-sequence (a certain sequence of intention-transferring practical syllogisms). The second case was concerned with the so-called **TOTE**-hierarchy (test-operate-test-exit hierarchy). This notion was discussed from the point of view of practical reasoning and specifically the problem was how to account for the role of perceptual feedback. It was suggested that the (major) belief premise (the analogue of ($P2_i$) of (**PR_i**)) of the practical syllogism could be taken to express such feedback loops.

In the case of social practical reasoning, where instead of one agent we are dealing with several interdependent agents, it seems possible to carry out analogous extensions. We shall not here, however, do this. Instead we shall discuss an example which serves to highlight some of the dynamical features related to a ceremony-like social action.

What we shall do is to consider the greeting example briefly discussed at the end of Chapter 6 (see pp.194-195). We may now call the full greeting exchange X. We let X_1 be agent A_1's and X_2 agent A_2's component action. X_1 consists of the four part actions X_1^1, X_1^2, X_1^3, and X_1^4, tokened, respectively by a_1, a_3, a_5, and a_7, to use the notation of Chapter 6. Correspondingly, X_2 consists of the three part actions X_2^1, X_2^2, and X_2^3, tokened by a_2, a_4, and a_6. Thus we may say that the whole greeting ceremony X can be written as follows:

$$X = X_1 \& X_2 = (X_1^1 \& X_1^2 \& X_1^3 \& X_1^4) \& (X_2^1 \& X_2^2 \& X_2^3).$$

We recall from Chapter 6 that the structure of the full social action X can be given by an OL-system. What matters here is simply that the a_i's, i=1,...,7, occur in a sequence such that a_i is a generational precondition for a_{i+1}, i=1,...,6. Now viewing the situation from the perspective of our (PR_i), we see that acting jointly here involved conditional action. Considering A_1, for instance, the performance of each X_1^{i+1} is conditional on the performance (by A_2) of X_2^i, i=0,1,2,3. (I have here, for technical reasons, introduced a new action X_2^0 for A_2. It simply means the empty action.) We may now construe practical reasonings to back and justify each of the interconnected action tokens $a_1,...,a_7$ and to in this sense complement our account of Chapter 6, an account which operates on the overt level of actions in the first place. Let us here do it for A_1 only. We get the following schema, corresponding to (PR_i):

($P1_1$) A_1 intends to do (his part of) X, given that (he believes that) A_2 will do (his part of) X.

($P2_1$) A_1 believes that unless he does X_1^{i+1} upon his believing that A_2 has done X_2^i, i=0,1,2,3 and unless A_2 does X_2^i upon believing that A_1 has done X_1^i, i=1,2,3, A_1 and A_2 cannot jointly do X.

($P3_1$) A_1 believes that A_2 will do (his part of) X.

($P4_1$) A_1 believes that A_2 has done X_2^i, i=0,1,2,3, as his part of X.

($P5_1$) Normal conditions for doing X obtain and A_1 believes that they obtain.

[($P6_1$) It is mutually believed by A_1 and A_2, for i=1,2, that (($P1_i$)&($P2_i$)&($P3_i$)&($P4_i$)&($P5_i$)), and that hence (C_i)).]

(C_1) A_1 does X_1^{i+1}, i=0,1,2,3.

From a technical point of view it should first be noted that, as compared with (PR_i), I have above changed the tense of ($P4_1$), but that is inessential. Also note that in the case of A_2 the range of i in ($P4_2$) is {1,2,3}.

For reasons of exposition I have above compressed four instantiations of (PR_1) into one schema. But what we essentially have above is a sequence <$PR_1^1, PR_1^2, PR_1^3, PR_1^4$> of reasonings with X^1, X^2, X^3, X^4, respectively, in their conclusions. This **PR-sequence**, as we may call it, backs and justifies the action token sequence <a_1, a_3, a_5, a_7>, where the action tokens just exemplify the respective conclusions. Now, comparing A_1's sequence with A_2's PR-sequence <PR_2^1, PR_2^2, PR_2^3> we can say the following. PR_1^1 partially generates (in a way involving a_1 but which I will not exactly specify) PR_2^1, PR_2^1 partially generates PR_1^2,..., and PR_2^2 partially generates PR_1^4. The generational relations between the action tokens $a_1,...,a_7$ can be explained in terms of the above dynamic interplay between A_1's and A_2's PR-sequences. Finally, we recall that in the conclusions of the above reasonings we might also have used oughts: 'A_1 ought to do X_1^{i+1}', and so on. These oughts are just relative oughts arising from the respective reasonings. Thus, when technically speaking of "normative organizations" (and in this case of a normative OL-system) as in Chapter 6, the oughts in question act like tags (and reminders) of the underlying justificatory (and, here, explanatory) reasonings. (Above we have analyzed greeting as a ritual-like social action rather than as a full blown communicative illocutionary action; cf. Chapter 10 on them.)

2. In social psychology conforming (and conformative) behavior have been the subject of a great deal of study. Whatever disagreement there is among social psychologists concerning the determinants of conforming behavior it is generally agreed that, to use holistic talk, a social group affects the behavior of its members. This influence appears in two ways. First, the social group offers its members a **"frame of reference"** - some indication of what to do in "unclear" cases. Such an unclear case could be just a situation in which there is a coordination problem in the sense discussed in this chapter. Secondly, there is a **group pressure** against deviation from what most group members believe everyone in the group should and will do in a given situation.

Our discussion in this chapter nicely elucidates the above features (at least in the case of situations of coordination - but also in other cases, as will be indicated below). If we think of our collective {$A_1,...,A_m$} of agents as forming a social group (cf. our discussion in Chapters 5 and 8 on the notion), then a look at our schemas (SA_i) and (PR_i) gives us what we want. First, these schemas partly serve to "define the situation" for the members of the group in setting up the basic action alternatives and beliefs of the agents. In particular, the social loop beliefs serve to indicate what each member is expected by the other members to do in the situation at hand. So here we have an elucidation of the frame of reference-aspect. Secondly, group pressure can be seen especially well from the **ante actu** application of our schemas, where the conclusion 'A_i does X_k' is replaced by 'A_i ought to do X_k'. The specific ought-rule in question is rationalized and justified in terms of the premises of the schema in question, and these premises involve the other members' behavior expectations (concerning A_i) in an essential sense. The effect of group pressure becomes still clearer when we recall that the agents are here performing an intentional social action in the sense of Chapter 5. (This assumption is explicit in (PR_i) and it is one we normally make in the case of (SA_i).) Intentional social actions, we recall, require we-intentions, and we-intentions normally satisfy schemas for "other-regarding" behavior such as (W2) in Chapter 2. (W2) may be concerned not only with other members' helping an agent to perform his part of the social action in question but also with reminding him and even demanding him to do it. This is a clear indication of the presence of group pressure.

V. MIXED INTEREST GAMES AND PRACTICAL INFERENCE

1. As we have so far only considered coordination games it is now proper to take a closer look at the practical inferences that underlie (or may underlie) some other types of games. It is our view that game theory should be a part of a general theory of social inference and action. Thus it should be possible to attach to every game-theoretic solution (in the technical sense) a rational social practical inference (in some cases perhaps a degenerate one only) which concludes in favor of the players acting so as to realize that solution, viz. to perform the actions resulting in the outcome or outcomes specified by the solution in question.

Games, in the sense of "classical" game theory (cf. Luce & Raiffa (1957)), can be divided into three groups:

(1) games where the players have strictly identical interests;
(2) games where the players have strictly opposite interests (so-called zero-sum games):

(3) games where the players have mixed interests, i.e., where their interests are partly similar and partly dissimilar.

Our coordination games, discussed earlier in this chapter, are just games of type (1), and we shall not now consider them further. As to zero-sum games, we can also dismiss them. This is because, as normally treated, they do not involve proper social practical inference at all. By proper social practical inference I here mean the essential use of premises about conditional intentions such as (P1↑) above, viz. conditional intentions making an agent's intention to act conditional on what another agent is expected to do. Zero-sum games are normally solved by reference to the maximin-principle: maximize your minimal expected gains over action-alternatives. In other words, a player chooses his action-alternative "come what may", viz. independently of what he thinks the other player is doing. This follows just from the fact that the players' interests (payoffs) are opposite; no useful purpose could be served by agreeing on some joint strategy, because the players have no common interests which they could promote by such agreements (cf. our discussion of social utilities in Chapter 2). Thus, in all, I take zero-sum games (and, more generally, class (2)) to correspond to only limiting, degenerate cases of **social** practical inference. There is not need to specifically discuss them further here.

Games with mixed interests (class (3)) form a rather comprehensive class. We shall here concentrate on a very intriguing and central type of game with mixed interests, viz. prisoner's dilemma-type games. In this type of game we may start with the following background story. We are dealing with two companion prisoners who are being interrogated separately. There are two alternative actions available to each of them: to confess the crime (= X_2 = Y_2) or not to confess it (= X_1 = Y_1). If both confess they both go to prison for five years. If both keep silent they are both sentenced to one year in prison. If only one confesses he is set free while the other one gets a term of ten years in prison.

Let us assume that the payoff matrix looks as shown in Figure 7.3 (my utility scaling is somewhat arbitrary):

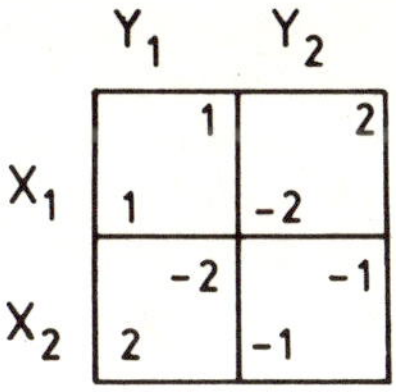

	Y_1	Y_2
X_1	1, 1	2, -2
X_2	-2, 2	-1, -1

Fig. 7.3.

Here $<X_2,Y_2>$ represents an equilibrium (in the game-theoretic sense) but it is rather unsatisfactory in terms of utilities. Both players would prefer the cooperative outcome $<X_1,Y_1>$ to it. But that outcome is inherently unstable for there is a temptation for both confessing and being let free. In general, in a prisoner's dilemma situation each player has a dominant strategy. If both players use the dominant strategy the result is a suboptimal or Pareto-inferior outcome, viz. both players get less than if both had instead used their dominated strategy.

It has been argued by many game-theoreticians that $<X_2,Y_2>$ is the only reasonable solution as long as no **binding** agreements between the players are possible to achieve, given that the players are rational in the game-theoretic sense of the prudentially safety-first minded pursuit of personal advantage. I will here accept this view while admitting that altruistic agents might well accept the cooperative solution.[4] Our present problem is how to conceptualize the present situation from the point of view of social practical inference.

Let us now try to apply our schema (SA_i) to the present situation. Obviously, in ($P\alpha_i$) we must now specify that P is a payoff matrix in a prisoner's dilemma game. But in other respects this premise is acceptable; and so is ($P1_i$), for both of our players are assumed to be (strongly) rational, and rationality in the game-theoretic sense can be taken to involve maximization of expected utilities. For instance, Bayesian rationality in the sense discussed in Chapter 3 indeed entails this premise (cf. Harsanyi (1977) and (1979); but also cf. Subsection III.3 of Chapter 2 as well as III.2 of Chapter 12). Similarly, premise ($P3_i$) can be regarded as acceptable.

But premise ($P2_i$) may seem problematic. What should we take a rational agent to believe about the other player's actions (or action-intentions)? Suppose A_1 believes that A_2 believes that A_1 will do X_2 (confess). Then, acting on this belief, it would seem that A_1 should think that A_2 then must choose Y_2 instead of Y_1

(to get -1 instead of -2). A_1's best reply to Y_2 both intuitively and in the game-theoretic sense is X_2. So A_1 should choose X_2. His further motive here may be the hope to gain the maximal payoff and/or his fear of being exploited by the other. In any case premise ($P2_i$) fits together with the conclusion (C_i), and in the case of A_1 we put $X_k=X_2$ and in the case of A_2 we have $X_k=Y_2$. ($P2_i$) also fits in with ($P\gamma_i$). In fact we just employed ($P\gamma_i$) when discussing how A_1 should reason on the basis of ($P2_1$). As the normal condition clause ($P\beta_i$) causes no further problems it seems that we can say that (**SA$_i$**) has been applied to the prisoner's dilemma game without any syntactic changes.

We may note here that X_k in (**SA$_i$**) must represent the equilibrium strategy for A_i, viz. X_2 in the case of A_1. For suppose on the contrary that ($P2_1$) would say that A_1 believes that A_2 believes that A_1 will do X_1. But this would be incompatible with premise ($P\gamma_2$) and thus, specifically, with A_2's believing that ($P1_1$), viz. that A_1 will maximize his expected utilities, given that A_1 forms his beliefs rationally according to game theory. Thus we should always use the equilibrium action both in ($P2_i$) and in (C_i), whenever games with equilibria in pure strategies are concerned.[5]

There are mixed motive games where an investigation of the players' underlying reasonings may help more than above. Let us change our Figure 7.3 slightly. Let the payoffs associated with the action pair <X_2,Y_1> now be <0,-2> and let those associated with <X_1,Y_2> be <-2,0>. The payoffs attached to <X_1,Y_1> and <X_2,Y_2> remain as in Figure 7.3. In the resulting game (called the assurance game) the action combinations <X_1,Y_1> and <X_2,Y_2> both give equilibrium points, but neither is a dominating or proper equilibrium point. Now A_1 stands to lose more by X_1 (if A_2 chooses Y_2) than by X_2 (if A_2 happens to choose Y_2). So playing on maximin A_1 should choose X_2. Analogously A_2 should choose Y_2, and the payoffs <-1,-1> would be obtained on maximin. But if it is a mutual belief among A_1 and A_2 (no matter whether this mutual belief is created through communication and explicit agreement or not) that A_1 will do X_1 and A_2 will do Y_1, then A_1 will reason that he ought to do X_1 and A_2 that he ought to do Y_1. Ordinary game theory, on the contrary, would give the maximin outcome <X_2,Y_2> as a solution if an assumption about the presence of communication and cooperation is not made.

We shall not here attempt to analyze in detail other examples of mixed interest games even if it would appear to be a fruitful area of research (but see Chapter 9, Section III and Chapter 12, Section I). In general much the same issues will come up as in our above treatment, even if there are problematic games having several rational solutions (of which none can be preferred).

Even if our (SA_i) (and the schema of Figure 7.2) may not always be very informative about the details of the agents' practical reasonings when applied to games other than coordination games, they nevertheless have the advantage of generality. With appropriate changes in premise ($P\alpha_i$) (as indicated above) schema (SA_i) indeed applies to a great variety of games. In view of the discussed equivalence between (SA_i) (with an appropriate formulation of ($P\alpha_i$)) together with the justification of the involved mutual belief and the schema of Figure 7.2 one can see, generally, that it applies to any situation with a finite number of agents and a finite number of action-alternatives in which the premises ($P1_i$), ($P2_i$), ($P3_i$), ($P\beta_i$), and ($P\gamma_i$) can be made sense of, viz. whenever clear conditional intentions and expectations - justifiable by loop beliefs - in the sense of Figure 7.2 are applicable to the collective $\{A_1,...,A_m\}$. This means, in a game-theoretic context, that in Figure 7.2 (and in the corresponding version of (SA_i)) we are dealing with the broad class of "n-person games" having a **proper** equilibrium (cf. Lewis (1969), p. 116). (Recall from game theory that according to Nash's result **every** "non-cooperative" finite classical game - in the sense defined in game theory - has an equilibrium, although not always one in pure strategies. Here 'non-cooperative' means, roughly, lack of "side-payments"; see Luce and Raiffa (1957), pp. 89, 106.) This proper equilibrium in question - which rational agents here are concerned with achieving - obviously need not be in a coordination game, and it may be a unique equilibrium in a game of mixed interests and even in a game of pure conflict. Lewis discussed the game of "calling off", which is a game of pure conflict and which is justifiable by Lewis' replication schema or actually his equivalent "rearranged replication schema" (see Lewis (1969), p. 117 and recall the equivalence between our schema of Figure 7.2 and Lewis' schemas).

2. It is possible to state a still more general connection between game theory and practical inference than the connection described above. We shall do this with respect to Harsanyi's version of game theory which gives a unique solution to every "classical" game, viz. every game which (1) is a game with complete information, (2) is either fully cooperative or fully non-cooperative, and which (3) is a game representable by its normal form (see, e.g., Harsanyi (1977), Chapter 5, for the technical terms).

Harsanyi's solutions are derived on the basis of two types of rationality postulates. First, we have the postulates of rational behavior in a narrower sense, stating (Bayesian) rationality criteria for the strategies to be used by the players. This group (call it **A**) consists of the Maximin postulate (**A1**), Best reply postulate (**A2**), Subjective best reply postulate (**A3**), Acceptance of higher payoffs postulate (**A4**), Equiprobability postulate (**A5**) (see Harsanyi (1977), pp. 116-117). (Of these (**A1**) and (**A4**) represent versions of the sure-thing principle and (**A2**) and (**A3**) of the expected utility maximization principle; cf. Chapter 2.) I will not here describe the contents of these postulates.

Secondly, and more interestingly, Harsanyi relies on a group (**B**) of three postulates of rational expectations stating rationality criteria for the expectations that rational players can entertain about each other's strategies. As there are interesting similarities between our above treatment (arrived at independently of knowledge of Harsanyi's work) and these postulates, we shall state them informally here (cf. Harsanyi (1977), pp. 117-118):

(**B1**)   Mutually expected-rationality postulate: In the same way that you will follow the present postulate (i.e., postulates (**A1**) through (**A5**) and (**B1**) through (**B3**)) if you are a rational player, you must expect and act on the expectation that **other** rational players will likewise follow these rationality postulates.

(**B2**)   Symmetric expectations postulate: You cannot choose your bargaining strategy on the expectation that a rational opponent will choose a **different** bargaining strategy from your own and, in particular, that he will choose a bargaining strategy **more concessive** than you would choose in the same situation.

(**B3**)   Expected-independence-of-irrelevant-variables postulate: You cannot expect a rational opponent to make his bargaining strategy dependent on variables whose relevance for bargaining behavior cannot be established on the basis of the present rationality postulates.

The essential content in (**B2**) and (**B3**), as Harsanyi understands them, is given by the so-called **Zeuthen principle**. This principle, which is formally entailed by the postulates (**A1**)-(**A5**) and (**B1**)-(**B3**), amounts to saying that at any given stage of bargaining between two rational players the next concession must always come from the party less willing to risk a conflict, where each party's willingness to risk a conflict is measured by the highest probability of conflict that he would be prepared to face rather than accept the terms proposed by the other party.

Of Harsanyi's postulates of rational expectations (B1) clearly is a (partial) counterpart to ($P\gamma_i$) of our (SA_i). It is interesting to notice that postulates (A1)-(A5) (based on payoff-dominance relations) and (B1) suffice to determine a unique solution for every game with strictly identical interests and every game with strictly opposite interests. (B2) and (B3) are needed only for games with mixed interests. We recall that our (SA_i) is somewhat uninformative just in the case of games with mixed interests. This indicates that it might be possible to add to (SA_i) a further premise amounting to the conjunction of (B2) and (B3) or to Zeuthen's principle. This would account in detail for how the discussed entailment of (P3$''_i$) by (P3$'_i$), the rationality assumptions, and the payoff matrix P indeed comes about. However, we shall not follow this proposal, but operate somewhat differently.

We generalize (SA_i) by reference to the fact that Harsanyi's postulates (A1)-(A5) and (B1)-(B3) determine a unique game-theoretic solution to every classical game (cf. Harsanyi (1975), (1977)). We also write out explicitly the counterpart to (P3$''_i$), and we modify the first premise of (SA_i) to explicitly concern the rules of the game (with the payoff matrix) P they are playing. (The general rules covering any classical game are to be found, e.g., in Luce and Raiffa (1957), pp. 44-50.) We get:

(GSA_i) (P1$_i$) A_i believes that he is playing a game with the payoff matrix P.
(P2$_i$) (a) A_i intends to act rationally,
(b) A_i has a belief to the effect that unless he acts on the postulates (A1)-(A5) and (B1)-(B3) he cannot in general act rationally.
(P3$_i$) A_i believes that unless he does X_i he cannot act on the postulates (A1)-(A5) and (B1)-(B3).
(P4$_i$) Normal conditions for doing X obtain, and A_i believes that they obtain.
[(P5$_i$) It is mutually believed by $A_1,...,A_m$ that, for all $j=1,...,m$, ((P1$_j$)&(P2$_j$)&(P3$_j$)&(P4$_j$), and that hence (C_i)).]
(C_i) A_i does X_i.

In (P2$_i$) of (GSA_i) we have two general clauses which jointly entail clause (P2$_i$) of (SA_i) (but not vice versa). It is quite obvious that (GSA_i) is logically valid.

It may be emphasized that (GSA_i) still is not very perspicuous, since it does not formalize the concrete reasoning process by which A_i arrives at (C_i). In particular, it does not specify what it is for A_i to have a belief to the effect that he must act on (A1)-(A5) and (B1)-(B3) in order to be rational. (Obviously we do not need to require that, e.g., he be familiar with Harsanyi's theory!)

Let me also point out that premise ($P2_i$) of (GSA_i) is a strong rationality principle which may fail to hold true of many agents. (Furthermore, in some cases (A1)-(A5) and (B1)-(B3), as technically explicated by Harsanyi, lead to solutions that are not very intuitive; see the example in Harsanyi (1977), pp. 136-138, 287 and judge for yourself.)

(GSA_i) covers all classical games, as said, but it does not yet cover, e.g., "ethical" games or arbitration games (cf. Harsanyi (1977) on the notions). Neither does it cover incomplete games nor games involving explicitly threat or other comparable psychological mechanisms. A detailed study of social practical reasoning related to such nonclassical games must be left to another occasion (except for a few remarks on incomplete games in the next section).

There are various ways of weakening our schemas (SA_i) and (GSA_i). The weakenings that I primarily have in mind are **probabilistic**. Thus, at least the following possibilities arise. First, we may allow probabilistic games (defined in terms of chance moves, cf. Luce and Raiffa (1957), pp. 40-44). Then outcomes will not be achieved with probability of degree one but with some lesser degree. Thus also **expected** utilities must be employed in appropriate places (e.g., ($P1_i$) and ($P3_i$) of (SA_i)). The next "probabilification" concerns the beliefs of A_i. Instead of strict beliefs we might go over to probabilistic degrees of belief in the relevant premises (in, e.g., ($P2_i$), ($P3_i$), and, to iterated ones in ($P\gamma_i$) of (SA_i)). Or, if we want to stick to qualitative beliefs we might weaken locutions like 'A believes that p' to 'A does not disbelieve p'. We may, furthermore, want to relax the quantifier 'all' in these premises to 'most' or something else appropriate (cf. our earlier remarks in the context of mutual belief).

These changes have the important consequence that (SA_i) and (GSA_i) lose their logical conclusiveness. Instead of providing **deductive** justification for acting it then only gives **nondeductive** (or inductive) justification.

A certain weakening of (SA_i) and (GSA_i) relates to the agents' epistemic situation. As we know, all classical games are games with **complete** information (not to be confused with the different technical concept of **perfect** information). We say that a game is a game with complete information if the players have full information of the extensive form of the game (cf. Luce and

Raiffa (1957), Chapter 3). Thus, in particular, they must have full knowledge of the other players' action possibilities and utility functions. In the case of our schema we could analogously characterize incomplete information but with reference to beliefs rather than knowledge.

The requirement of complete knowledge is rather strong in view of real life situations. For many such social situations, to the extent that they yield to game-theoretic analysis at all, are situations where the players lack knowledge of each other's action-options and utilities. But even the parallel requirement of having definite, all or none (mutual) beliefs may seem strong in the case of (SA_i) and (GSA_i). We should relax this requirement. In the next section, we shall consider one possible way to proceed in this direction.

VI. SOCIAL RULES AND THE SCOPE OF SOCIAL ACTION

1. Now we are in a position to take a closer look at the scope of the class of social actions as well as at the notion of social rule. We recall that our notion of complex social action type was claimed to exhaust all social actions. That notion, however, depends on the notion of social action token$_1$ which in turn depends on the notion of social propositional attitude and thus on the notion of we-attitude.

There is a broad notion of social belief which we only briefly mentioned in Chapter 5 but which is relevant to the question about the scope of the class of social actions. In this very broad sense an attitude, and the corresponding action, is social simply if it **makes (essential) reference to some other agent**. Although there is some reason to think that this notion is too broad for our purposes we shall later give a technical account of the notion, in order to get our broadest class of social actions. (We refer the reader to (2) and (9) of Chapter 9.) The class of all singular social action tokens satisfying the above reference requirement will be called S_1 below, while the class of social action tokens$_1$ defined by (5.5) will be called S_1^*. S_1^{**} will be the class of social action tokens$_2$ (recall that $S_1^{**} \subset S_1^* \subset S_1$). Our discussion in this section amounts to a clarification of the notion of **intentional** social action token$_1$ involving a social loop belief. Let us call the class of such intentional social action tokens$_1$ S_2. S_2 is defined to be the class of intentional social action tokens$_1$ rationalizable by means of (SA_i). If we relax our basic schema (SA_i) to (SA_i^*) by using 'wants' (in a broad sense) instead of 'intends' in its premise (P1) (and make (SA_i) lose its logically binding character), we get hold of a broader class of social action tokens$_1$.

We may thus speak of volitional conformative social action tokens$_1$ and denote by S_2^* the class of such volitional conformative social action tokens$_1$, instantiating a complex social action type. Obviously S_2 is a proper subclass of S_2^*.

Next we consider the class of actions justifiable by Lewis' replication schema or actually his equivalent "rearranged replication schema" (see Lewis (1969), p. 117). As we saw above, this class and our class S_2 coincide, except possibly for one thing. Namely, Lewis speaks of desires only (cf. our S_2^*) but nevertheless he seems to treat them as intentions in our sense. (I shall assume below that his desires play the role of our intentions.) Let us note here that the class of **conventional** actions defined by Lewis (1969), p. 78, is a subclass of the class of actions satisfying the rearranged replication schema. Hence Lewis' class of conventional actions forms a proper subclass of S_2.

We need still another class of social actions if we want to get hold of the class of actions justifiable by reference to (social) **rules**. Let me first explain why this is an interesting goal for us. It is so simply because social behavior is often taken to be just rule-following (in a broad sense including rule-violating) behavior, at least in the sense that it is justified and (often) explained by reference to social rules: an agent's reason for acting is often just that he intends to obey a social rule ("I do X because that's the rule"). Now the question arises of what counts as a social rule in this context. Following Shwayder one might want to accept that rules are at bottom (suitable) systems of mutual expectations (see Shwayder (1965), pp. 252-259). (Even so-called private rules involve this aspect in Shwayder's account.) Translated into our approach, the system of expectations in question may be taken to be defined by the schema of Figure 7.2 or, equivalently for a broad class of situations, by our (SA_i) (together with the justification of the involved mutual belief). Each rule - in Shwayder's sense - can be summarized (somewhat inadequately) by this: Every agent expects every other agent to do so and so (to conform) in this situation. In view of the conclusion (C_i) of (SA_i) we may also say as follows: Each agent ought to conform in this situation (relative to the premises of (SA_i)). This suggests that - contra Shwayder - we might rather want to characterize a social rule as an ought-statement of the mentioned kind, provided that this statement is justifiable by (SA_i) (or by the replication schema of Figure 7.2). However, the difference is essentially verbal only.

Shwayder's definition of a rule as a system of mutual expectations tending to produce regular behavior seems intolerably broad. This is because Shwayder's systems of expectations incorporate only a part of the schema of our Figure 7.2 (or, if you prefer, of Lewis' replication schema). For an effective criticism against the width of Shwayder's notion we refer the reader to Lewis' treatment (see Lewis (1969), pp. 115-118). What is basically wrong with Shwayder's account is that he leaves out of his mutual expectation system the information that agent A_1 intends to conform to A_2's expectations **because of** the way A_1 expects A_2 to act on his expectations.

Even if we restrict ourselves to rules justifiable by means of our replication schema of Figure 7.2 we get a rather broad notion of social rule (cf. Lewis (1969), pp. 117-118). Yet it seems an interesting candidate for defining an important class of rule-obeying social actions (viz., our S_2). However, it may be argued that S_2 does not succeed in capturing the class of **norm**-obeying social actions. We shall in Chapter 8 discuss the concept of **social norm** - as distinct from a **social rule** in the above sense, but for our present purposes the above remarks will suffice.

2.   We started this section by considering two broad classes of social action, S_1 and S_2. Now, after our discussion of the concept of social rule, some additional classes of social action can be discerned. One type of social action arises from considering the violation of social norms and rules in general. The concept of violating (or deviating from) a norm (rule) of course conceptually derives from the concept of obeying a norm (rule). Obeying a rule and violating it equally make reference to that rule - to the extent that the possibility of violating a rule is sometimes even considered to be a defining feature of a rule.

Let us start by considering coordination situations. For example, Figure 7.1 shows us that if one (but not both, in this case) violates, zero utility units will be the payoff for both players. We can say that as long as the players are rational Bayesian maximizers of expected individual utilities this can never happen in normal conditions, at least given the possibility of communication. This is due to the inbuilt sanction mechanism of coordination games that we have been emphasizing. It follows that if violation of a coordination norm, e.g., a convention, can take place it must be due to the players' acting on some other utilities than their personal ones or to their somehow misperceiving the whole coordination situation. There are several ways that reasoned, intentional rule-violating behavior can come about even if we ignore such factors as the exact **type** of the violating action, say X_r, as well as the **manner** with which it is performed.

I will here consider only one (but central) way that an

agent A_i may come to misrepresent the coordination situation. It is concerned with his construing the payoff matrix differently from the other agents. Accordingly, in (SA_i) we now require that A_i's utilities are given so that their maximization entails performing an action X_r^i, which will be different from X_k^i in the case of non-conforming action (and only then). The non-conforming agent A_i is now required to believe that all the other agents share the matrix P and also that his own matrix is P', a matrix preferring non-conforming acting to conforming. The conclusion of (SA_i) now becomes: A_i does X_r^i, and (SA_i) can be regarded as giving A_i an overriding reason to do X_r^i.

In terms of our Figure 7.2 and our coordination game example we now also get a change in agent A_1's conditional intentions. His conforming intentions are changed into non-conforming ones by substituting X_2 for X_1 to give: A_1 intends to do X_2, given that (A_1 believes that) A_2 will do Y_1. No other changes in Figure 7.2 are needed except, of course, that the conclusion now is that A_1 does X_2 (which will equal X_r^1). Note that A_2 continues to believe that A_1 will conform (do X_1). It is, alternatively, possible to make the assumption that A_2 indeed comes to believe that A_1 is a non-conformist; but we shall not here discuss this particular case more deeply (but cf. next paragraph). This situation would obviously take us beyond the scope of coordination games not only in a **subjective** sense (as above) but in an **objective** (or at least intersubjective) sense.

Interesting cases of intersubjectively known violations may occur in prisoner's dilemma type games of mixed interests. (The case of intersubjective norm violation at the end of the last paragraph may well have a prisoner's dilemma structure.) Suppose now that there is a norm which prescribes the cooperative outcome to be chosen (see Chapter 8 on such norms). Then cases of violation by one but not both players would be advantageous, as we have seen. But in the case of fully rational players both will violate if one does. That is, the norm is fully binding or nobody will obey it. As soon as one player violates the other player will follow and the equilibrium $<X_2,Y_2>$ will result, as we have noticed.

But in actual life things are not as in the King's Realm of fully rational players. Consider for instance taxation in a modern society. This can be considered to be a prisoner's dilemma type situation. If all (or almost all) people pay their income taxes according to law we arrive at the cooperative outcome. If all (or most) evade paying their taxes a situation resembling the equilibrium outcome is reached where the state would have to strongly cut its expenses and lower general welfare. (This situation would normally also lead to strong measures for establishing heavy sanctions for violating the norm.) If only a few succeed in evading tax payment they gain most, while the others presumably would have to pay their share. (Cf. our discussion in Chapter 5 concerning public goods.)

In any case, while real life is much more complicated than those simple game theoretic situations we have been considering, it is undeniably very illuminating to use the conceptual tools and classifications of game theory to illustrate such phenomena as norm violation. It would be an interesting task to discuss also other types of mixed motive games from the point of view of norm-violation, but we shall leave that for another occasion.

While we have not displayed the exact inferential nor the game-theoretic structure of all cases of reasoned rule-obeying and rule-violating action, we have nevertheless investigated violation of coordination norms and suggested a change to (SA_i) to cover this, and we have in effect noted that prisoner's dilemma situations do not give rise to changes in (SA_i). We recall that (SA_i) applies (by suitable rephrasing of its premise $(P\alpha_i)$) to any non-cooperative classical games with a proper equilibrium. Given this as our basis we denote by (SA_i') the suggested modification of (SA_i) in the case of violation of coordination norms. Now we define a class S_3 of social actions by reference to (SA_i') rather than (SA_i), but otherwise like S_2. S_2 obviously is a subclass of S_3. We may also form a class S_3^* from S_3 just as S_2^* earlier in Subsection 1 was formed from S_2; now we only use the corresponding schema $(SA_i'^*)$.

We note here without detailed argument that the just defined class S_3 becomes a proper subclass of Shwayder's class of (intentional) **conformative** actions (see Shwayder (1965), pp. 257-259). This follows directly from the discussion in Lewis (1969), pp. 107-118, and our earlier claim that S_2 equals Lewis' class of actions definable in terms of the (rearranged) replication schema. Let us call this latter class S_{RE} and Shwayder's mentioned class S_S. Let us further call Lewis' class of conventional actions S_C (see Lewis (1969), p. 78); and call the class of actions due to a rule S_{RU}. Then we may summarize our above results and conjectures about the scope of various classes of social actions as follows (using '⊂' for proper subclass):

(SSA) (a) $S_C \subset S_{RE} = S_2 \subset S_3 \subset S_3^* \subset S_{RU} \subset S_i'^* \subset S_i^* \subset S_1$
(b) $S_2 \subset S_2^* \subset S_3^*$
(c) $S_3 \subset S_S$.

The class S_{RU} of actions due to a rule consists of all social action tokens₁ obeying or violating a rule. In our treatment this means actions justifiable by reference to a process of practical reasoning making an essential reference to a rule under some description of that rule, e.g., as (SA_i) does. Briefly and roughly put, actions in S_{RU} can be described in terms of reasons such as 'A_i does X_i because that's the rule and A_i wants to obey to it' or 'A_i does X_r because X_r violates a rule that A_i wants to violate'. We in effect noted that S_3^* is a proper subclass of S_{RU}, since the latter covers all those game-theoretic cases that (SA_i^*) doesn't cover. These cases are primarily cases of (complete or incomplete) games with mixed interests without a proper equilibrium. Under what further assumptions (SA_i^*) could be extended to cover such cases we shall not here consider, although we shall below make some remarks on incomplete games. Notice here also that S_{RU} of course covers cases falling beyond classical game theory, including incomplete games.[6]

When discussing the violation of norms by reference to (SA_i) we introduced an element of incomplete information - conforming players were assumed to incorrectly think that all players shared the payoff matrix P. A more general treatment of norm-violation, and of (subjectively) incomplete information in general, could be obtained along the following lines in the case of (SA_i). We assume that all the players share a (subjective) probability distribution over the set P of all the utility matrices thought possible in that situation. P will contain all the relevant conforming and non-conforming utility matrices, for instance. Let us consider a simple example with two agents A_1 and A_2. Both of them could share a subjective probability distribution with the information that A_1 is a conformer type agent with some probability p and a non-conformer type agent with probability 1-p. The corresponding probabilities in the case of A_2 are also mutually known. Each player knows in his own case whether he is a conformer or a non-conformer.

Given this basic information each player can compute the conditional probabilities of conforming action pairs (<X_2,Y_1> and <X_2,Y_2>) and of non-conforming ones (<X_1,Y_2> and <X_2,Y_1>) on the four conditions that both players are either conformers or non-conformers or that A_1 is a conformer but A_2 is not or vice versa. As a consequence we can compute the expected utilities for the actions X_1, X_2, Y_1, and Y_2. The result is a probabilistic schema of inference which accounts for the agents' conforming and non-conforming in terms of inductive reasons (cf. Section I of Chapter 12).

Harsanyi (1967-68) has analyzed incomplete games much along the above lines. What he succeeds in doing technically amounts to this. He starts with a game G with (objective) **incomplete** information. This incompleteness may concern the players' knowledge of the physical outcome function of the game, the other players' utility functions, or the strategy spaces (action possibilities). Technically, this can all be reduced to incomplete knowledge about the other players' utilities. Now, Harsanyi's solution consists in construing for G an equivalent (in a Bayesian sense) game G* which is a game with complete information. The incomplete information that the players had in G about the basic parameters of the game is represented in the new game G* as **imperfect** information about a certain chance move at the beginning of the game, viz. the one which determines the types of the players. As game G* is a game with complete (but imperfect information) it can be analyzed with the usual methods of classical game theory.

There are also other types of weakening of (SA_i) which make the practical inferences it represents non-deductive. I shall not here discuss them. It is in any case important to keep in mind that our original (SA_i) and its (non-probabilistic) variants represents **ideal types** against which the various weakenings are judged. This also gives a partial justification for our not discussing the weakened versions in detail here.

CHAPTER 8

NORMS, ROLES, AND SOCIAL STRUCTURES

I. SOCIAL NORMS

1. In this chapter we shall extend our conceptual system of social concepts ultimately to cover concepts representing social structures. Our analysis will strongly rely on the concept of social norm and on the notion of role definable on the basis of it. Thus we shall begin by a conceptual clarification of social norms. We shall analyze norms partly on the basis of the notion of social practical reasoning investigated in Chapter 7. When speaking of social rules and norms we shall be exclusively concerned with impersonal community rules and leave such personal rules as commands and requests out of our discussion. We shall ignore directives for use ("technical" rules).

Given this, we may in a somewhat preliminary way suggest that a social norm (existing in a given community) is a mutually known (or believed) prescriptive rule (ought-rule or may-rule) for action such that there is pressure towards obeying the rule and such that, as a consequence, it is obeyed in general (or at least in most normal cases). This characterization is very general, to be sure. Yet it emphasizes some features usually connected with norms and leaves out a number of aspects often proposed as definitory of norms. The above characterization brings out the features of **prescriptiveness, pressure,** and **uniformity of relevant conforming action.** That norms are something prescriptive implies that they obligate or at least impose tasks or standards on agents. I will return to this feature as well as to the behavioral conformity to norms below (cf. also our discussion in Chapter 7 related to the schema (SA_i)). There are both ought-to-do (and may-do) norms and ought-to-be (and may-be) norms. We shall below concentrate on the former.

The feature of pressure involves many aspects. First, there may be (internal and external) pressure coming from the agents of the community reasoning according to (SA_i) or some other relevant pattern. The essential thing here is the agents' mutual expectations of action. These expectations create pressure, for instance, in the sense that disobedience might entail the other agents' becoming dissatisfied as they fail to attain their goals (cf. coordination games). As a consequence, they may come to apply (external) sanctions (e.g., threats of physical or economic punishment) and thus external pressure towards the nonconformer. (Here the other agents may reason, for instance, according to inference schemas such as our (**W2**) of Chapter 2, and act accordingly. The resulting actions may function as sanctions against norm-violators.)

But viewed from another perspective, internal pressure also involves the agents' ability to act for the **reason** "that's the rule" or, specifically, e.g., "I want to achieve goal G and rule R is a means for that".

The above characterization does not, at least explicitly, contain the requirement that a norm, whether it is legal, moral, religious, or something else (e.g., recreational), be **functional** for the ends of the community (cf. Chapter 13 on functions). While most norms perhaps are, there are more or less clearly dysfunctional ones too (think of unofficial norms governing alcohol consumption, for instance). Another feature my characterization ignores is **norm-authorities** (and norm-senders). Many social norms do not involve such authorities unless merely one's peers or co-agents are meant (cf. moral norms such as "You ought to be polite").

A modern classic on norms is the account by Hart (1961). At one point he is concerned with distinguishing rules or norms of **obligation** from social rules in general. He claims that, for instance, social rules of etiquette and of correct speech are not rules of obligation. Thus, e.g., 'One may not say "you was"' is not a rule of obligation according to Hart. What, then are the features distinguishing norms of obligation from other social rules? Hart gives the following three criteria (Hart (1961), pp. 84-85):

(a) "Rules are conceived and spoken of as imposing obligations when the general demand for conformity is insistent and the social pressure brought to bear upon those who deviate or threaten to deviate is great."
(b) "The rules supported by this serious pressure are thought important because they are believed to be necessary to the maintenance of social life or some highly prized feature of it."
(c) "[T]he conduct required by these rules may, while benefiting others, conflict with what the person who has the duty may wish to do."

As to these criteria, I think that the idea of pressure, perhaps introduced as in (a), is indeed necessary and central. I also think (c) is necessary and relatively unproblematic. But, as argued above in bypassing (b) - which makes rules functional or at least requires them to be so thought of (note the ambiguity of (b) on this point) - cannot be regarded as a necessary condition of norms in general. What is more, I think that conditions (a), (b), and (c) when strictly taken are not jointly sufficient either (nor, of course, are (a) and (c), then). Without pausing to argue for this explicitly here I refer the reader to our characterization (1) below.

2. Ullmann-Margalit (1976) discusses a variety of norms in her interesting and illuminating book. Her starting point is game theory. She distinguishes between three different types of norms on the basis of different game-theoretic situations: (1) coordination norms; (2) PD (prisoner's dilemma) norms; and (3) norms of partiality. Of these, coordination norms are just the norms related to the conclusions such as our (C↑) of the schema (SA_i) of practical inferences connected to coordination games (see Chapter 7, p. 203). We shall not here discuss them further. PD norms of course relate to prisoner's dilemma type games (cf. Ullmann-Margalit (1976), pp. 22-25). Finally, norms of partiality relate to certain (rather vaguely defined) games with mixed interests involving a kind of dominance structure.

To explain what PD norms are, let us consider a payoff matrix for a prisoner's dilemma game such as that of Figure 7.3. The content of the PD norm for that matrix is that the players ought to play cooperatively, viz. choose the outcome $<X_1,Y_1>$. This norm is to be made effective by whatever sanctions are needed.

A norm of partiality also selects a certain cell of a payoff matrix in a game of mixed interests to be chosen. Consider, for instance, the following payoff matrix:

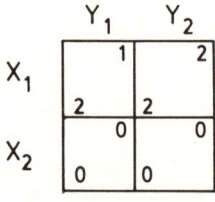

Fig. 8.1.

For historical or other reasons $<X_1,Y_1>$ might be the cell protected by a norm of partiality. Note that $<X_1,Y_2>$ game-theoretically dominates $<X_1,Y_1>$ and that, furthermore, the first party A_1 would loose nothing in absolute terms (but only relative to A_2) if A_2 were allowed to switch from Y_1 to Y_2.

Ullmann-Margalit discusses the above three types of norms also by reference to Hart's three conditions claimed to define norms of obligation (Ullmann-Margalit (1976), p. 13). She points out that PD norms in general meet the three conditions. I think this is correct except that condition (b) may fail (but recall the phrase 'in general'). Norms of partiality satisfy (a) and (c) but satisfy (b) at best only partially. I find this acceptable, but I shall not here further discuss these norms, which somewhat resemble PD norms, and I refer the reader to Ullmann-Margalit's book. (PD norms will be commented on below.)

Ullmann-Margalit claims that coordination norms do not all classify as norms of obligation in Hart's sense. Although she does not clarify, I suspect she thinks like Hart that condition (a) may fail. I am also willing to claim that coordination norms (e.g., norms of correct speech) may fail to be norms of obligation. Yet it seems that they may be taken to satisfy condition (a), if they can - as I think they can - be justified in terms of our schema (SA_i) or something related. That they need not be norms of obligation is possible due to the social context in which the system of mutual expectations, characterizing coordination norms, operates (cf. various informal conventions of, e.g., dressing which, in spite of satisfying (a), are intuitively far from obligating). But it is not necessary to argue for this here, as our concept of social norm will include typical coordination norms.

There are interesting differences between coordination norms and PD norms due to the differences in the underlying game-theoretic situations. Thus we recall that in a coordination problem there are at least two equilibrium points, while in the paradigmatic prisoner's dilemma there is one (but cf. Harsanyi (1977), pp. 278-280, for examples with several equilibria). In the case of the latter, contrary to the former ones, we do not have a **coordination** equilibrium, for when the equilibrium in the prisoner's dilemma has been reached each player wishes the other one had acted differently. Next, the equilibrium of a prisoner's dilemma game is both individually and socially (i.e., collectively) relatively undesirable while in a coordination game the coordination equilibria are both individually and jointly satisfactory. Furthermore, the cooperative outcome in a prisoner's dilemma game is socially desirable (but less so individually) and it is unstable (in the sense of not being an equilibrium).

As a consequence, mere agreement (on a particular coordination equilibrium) is sufficient for solving a coordination game, for clearly no agent has any motive not to conform. But if we want to secure the jointly satisfactory, cooperative outcome in a prisoner's dilemma game a **binding** agreement - an enforceable and enforced PD norm - is needed. (And the presence of such a binding agreement, if it is really strictly binding, entails changing the game, for some action options become closed and, in general, the whole payoff matrix changes; cf. Chapter 12.) Furthermore, while conformity to a coordination norm serves equally both best individual and best collective interests, conformity to a PD norm serves only best collective interests but not best (but only second best) individual interests. Thus a PD norm lacks the self-enforcing character that a coordination norm has. (Analogous comments can often be made when comparing norms of impartiality with coordination norms; cf. Ullmann-Margalit (1976), Chapter IV.)

3. Our above excursion into the problems connected to social norms has not been much more than a vague sketch of how we view social norms. To recapitulate some of the main ideas, (ought-to-do) norms are, for us, prescriptions for acting in a certain way in given circumstances such that these prescriptions are justifiable by means of certain patterns of practical inference, which at least in the case of coordination problems give the agents reasons to act and also create some pressure against deviation. As a result at least some substantial degree of conformity to the norms will come about. We also noticed that the underlying game-theoretic situation, which specifies the agents' action powers, is very relevant. Thus, for instance, in prisoner's dilemma situations social practical inference alone cannot create pressure against deviation from the cooperative solution, but external sanctions are typically needed to create binding agreements (and to, as a consequence, change the game). Accordingly, the practical inferences related to them are different and so are the types of norms (coordination and PD norms as well as norms of partiality) generated by these different game-theoretic situations.

Putting the matter as above we have come to stress the relevant practical reasonings (and the mutual expectations) more than in the beginning, where we especially emphasized the feature of pressure. In the case of coordination problems this is perhaps all right, because in their case pressure is taken care of by the relevant practical reasonings. For in a sense only internal pressure (pressure related to how agents **think** about the situation at hand) counts, and is needed, in those situations. External sanctions (e.g., penalties) may of course be present and be relevant, but their relevancy consists in their explaining (in part) why the agents think as they do (e.g., think that they ought to act so and so). Thus we may here account for pressure in terms of the agents' practical reasonings. Furthermore, in the case of coordination problems, practical reasonings are also central in that they account for the relevant uniformities of conforming behavior. It is important that the agents behaviorally **obey** the norm and do not merely uniformly act in accordance with it. The point is that rule-obeying action is action with reason. The reason cannot be just any reason but it must be the overriding reason given by the premises of a relevant practical inference schema involving social loop beliefs in something like the manner of our schema (SA_i). (Whatever **further** reasons agents generally have for conforming to the norm is a matter social psychologists can be supposed to tell us.)

Could we now follow the theorists defining social rules (and norms) simply as mutual expectation systems (such as characterized by our (SA_i)) justifying people's actions? My answer is no. I have already earlier expressed some reservations about this even in the case of coordination problems. Here it must be emphasized that mere mutual expectation is not enough in the case of, e.g., prisoner's dilemma type situations, as we have repeatedly emphasized. Some external sanctions or, in general, external pressure seems to be called for in those cases. Let me here still take up some further problems.

First, if norms were **only** mutual expectation systems then it seems to follow that the concept of norm has been naturalistically reduced away to expectations. Whether or not this is the case depends, however, on how one analyzes expectations and whether or not the agents are indeed supposed to draw conclusions to the effect that they **ought to** do so and so. While I strongly object to conceptually analyzing away the "normative dimension" I have nothing against a suitable kind of non-reductive naturalism (cf. Chapters 1 and 2). Thus my present remark is directed only against some crude naturalistic analyses of norms as expectations.

There is, however, a somewhat related criticism that seems more serious. If norms are strictly identified with mutual expectation systems it is difficult to see how such systems can account for features like the **fairness, justness** and **correctness** of norms. If, e.g., correctness goes beyond what (all or most) people de facto think then a mutual expectation theorist seems to be in trouble. (Cf. examples of correct speech and legally correct action in which cases people frequently have incorrect beliefs.) It may seem that experts must then be appealed to in order to determine what is correct. As a consequence one would be drifting towards some kind of "ideal observer" account. The problem then becomes whether the idealizing conditions can be given without the use of normative concepts (and without reliance on the concept of social norm). If it can, then a modified and qualified mutual expectation account might still be made work (at least as a partial account), otherwise not.

4. Let me now go on **in medias res** to state a proposal for an ought-to-do rule qualifying as a (motivating) social norm (N) in a community (S). The norm could, e.g., have the simple form 'Everybody ought to do X when in C'. My proposal, based essentially on the above discussion, is this:

(1) Rule N is a **social norm** in S if and only if
  (a) the members of S, when in situation C (and believing so) are disposed to reason in ways justifiable by the schema (SA_i) or a similar schema that they ought to do X in C;
  (b) most (or at least many) members of S do X in C and some of them at least sometimes do X because of their so reasoning that they ought to do X in C;
  (c) there is in S some (socially accepted) pressure, typically due to sanctions, against deviating from doing X in C; and
  (d) the members of S have a mutual belief to the effect that (a), (b), and (c).

Clause (a) is supposed to guarantee that rule N not only (potentially) figures in the agents' practical thinking, when in C, but also that rule N is justifiable in terms of social practical reasoning. One problem is what justification exactly means here, I shall not try to explicate it more than to say that, when (SA_i) is employed, it must contain the idea that the members of S under favorable conditions indeed do reason according to this schema, viz. the premises are true and the conclusions follow in the strong sense of the agents' actually inferring them. Favorable conditions include, often counterfactually, that the agents are intelligent, educated, and reflective to some sufficient degree. What the releasing conditions for the disposition to reason according to (SA_i) are over and above this I shall not here try to spell out. In any case, our (a) does not assert that the favorable conditions obtain, whereas (b) can be taken to assert this for those members of S that the quantifier 'some' covers.

We recall that (SA_i) (or, if you like, our schema of Figure 7.2) in principle covers at least all game-theoretic situations with a proper equilibrium, and thus it can be connected to coordination norms, PD norms, and norms of partiality, for instance. In other situations some suitable analogue of (SA_i), such as (PR_i), may be employed. As a limiting "real-life" case I would, in fact, like to admit rather defective reasonings (as compared with (SA_i)), as long as they lead to the right conclusion, viz. that the agent ought to do X in C.

Clause (a) also in part accounts for the pressure towards doing X and against deviating from doing it. This is of course due to the agents' (potentially) reasoning (according to (SA_i)) that they ought to do X and their mutually believing that all the other agents are disposed to reason similarly. As we saw earlier, this creates the needed pressure in the case of coordination problems whose solutions are self-rewarding and self-enforcing. But in many other cases, such as in prisoner's dilemma type situations, external sanctions (or, more generally, pressure) are needed, and clause (c) is supposed to take care of that. What such sanctions can and will be, from where they "come", how they are backed, and how they create the required pressure seems to depend on the case and, in any case, I will not here consider the problem (cf. Ullmann-Margalit (1976) and our remarks in Chapter 12). Because of clause (c), social practices such as eating baked pork at Christmas become excluded (for they are not appropriately sanctioned) but the case of customs such as greeting by shaking hands seems to be different.

Clause (b) accounts for the supposed fact that any social norm is generally followed and, at least in some cases, obeyed in terms of reasoned action. (See, e.g., Sellars (1968) and Raz (1979) and our earlier remarks on overriding oughts for rule-governed behavior.) Clause (b) has two components, as it were. First, it says that most (or at least many) people in S indeed behave in accordance with the norm. This is the regularity or uniformity aspect of the norm. Secondly, there is the requirement that at least some agents on some occasions C obey the norm in the strong sense of having reasoned (in terms of (SA_i) or its analogue) that they ought to do X in C. This "normative" component is central to the "existence" of the norm. If nobody obeyed N it would not count as a norm even if all people somehow accidentally happened to do X when in C. Norm-governed behavior is essentially behavior with a reason which contains or entails the idea that the agent should or ought to act in accordance with what the rule says.

Ideally, we would like to think, everybody would act in accordance with the norm and, indeed, obey it (when the norm is in force). I have employed 'most' (or 'many') and 'some' for the regularity and normative aspects, respectively, in (b). Which such "statistical" requirements it is reasonable to accept is not very central here. Indeed, I suggest that the phrase 'if and only if' in (1) could be relaxed to 'to the extent that'. Then, the strength of the statistical requirements we use in clause (b) is proportional to the extent that rule N is in force in S and (1) allows for norms obeyed by only a small proportion of the members of S.

Let me here emphasize that 'because' in (b) signifies that when agents obey (in the strong sense) the norm their actual practical reasonings in question in favor of doing X may be taken to **explain** their doing X. To avoid the problem of wayward causal chains in those cases 'because' may be taken to be explicable in terms of purposive generation (**IG***).

I shall not here make additional comments on clause (c). This leaves us with the mutual belief requirements as expressed by clause (d). Why do we need it? In answer to this I would like to recall what was said earlier in Chapter 7 about the social reality of social constructs. The reality of norms consists in part of intentional rule-obeying actions, reasonings leading to such rule-obeying actions, and sanctions fortifying, as it were, these two factors. But in part it also consists of the members of S having a mutual belief to the effect that the mentioned three factors are there. This is what clause (d) is meant to capture.

We recall from Chapter 7 that schema (SA_i) contains a certain mutual belief requirement, viz. that contained in its premise ($P\gamma_i$). But mutual belief in clause (a) of (1) is different from ($P\gamma_i$), for (a) does not yet guarantee that the agents in fact do reason according to (SA_i). Thus, we need the requirement of mutual belief concerning clause (a). There seems to be nothing specifically problematic about requiring mutual belief concerning clauses (b) and (c), so I will not comment on that here.

Let us point out here that (d) does not directly require that the members of S mutually believe that (a), (b), and (c). Rather they are required only in a vaguer sense to mutually believe approximately what (a), (b), and (c) amount to saying, under some suitable paraphrase. Given (d), the members of S need not be able to formulate their belief in our philosopher-analyst's language and terminology at all. (d) can be satisfied, for instance, by the members of S having a mutual belief that N is a social norm, where that belief amounts in our technical talk to a belief that N is a norm as far as its non-epistemic aspects (as we have elucidated them by our (a), (b), and (c)) are concerned (cf. our discussion in Chapter 5).

The above wide interpretation of clause (d) should suffice to dismiss the criticism in the present context at least. Notice still the following general underlying systematic feature here. We have in this book divided social concepts into **non-epistemic** and **epistemic** ones. In the case of such social concepts as norms, roles, groups, and so on, the division is simple. For it is the mutual belief requirement which acts, as it were, as an epistemic operator making the difference. Thus, above, clauses (a)-(c) might be taken to define a non-epistemic notion of social norm while adding clause (d) transforms that notion into an epistemic one.

Note that (a) and (d) of (1) go some way towards saying that the members of S we-intend to do X, a requirement which, e.g., Sellars (1968) puts on **moral** social norms (cf. our remarks in III.2. of Chapter 7 related to (SA_i)). Yet (a) at best entails that the members of S are disposed to we-intend to do X (given that the 'ought' is an overriding one).

There are few further remarks related to (1) that may be made here. First, we have so far said nothing about social actions in the present connection. But nevertheless we are concerned with them here in the context of norms, at least in typical cases. We recall from Chapter 7 that schema (SA_i) was originally designed to account for coordination situations. In such situations we are dealing with coordinative social actions where people are doing more or less the same thing. Thus X_k means a conforming action in the coordination situation at hand and the total social action is made up of each agent's doing his X_k^i. In prisoner's dilemma type cases X_k^i normally (when no binding agreement exists) means the equilibrium action. It may also mean a cooperative action, but then we must have a binding agreement and it is arguable that we then have changed the whole game to become or at least resemble a coordination game, to the extent that we get a game in the game-theoretic sense at all. (See Ullmann-Margalit (1976), pp. 31-37, for relevant discussion; also see Chapter 12 below.)

Collective actions where each agent has a prefixed different action to perform also fit in with (1). The X_k^is will just be the appropriate different component actions. In general, when dealing with (1) we are at least typically dealing with social actions in our technical sense of (at least) class S_1 as defined in Chapter 7. At least to the extent we are dealing with (SA_i), either a we-intention or a social attitude is involved in the required sense. In those cases it is plausible to claim that social actions in our technical sense are present. But since (1) allows **analogues** of (SA_i) to be employed as well, the problem is whether we can strictly exclude the possibility that social behavior not qualifying technically as a social action (even in the sense of class S_1) might be involved. What to say about this of course depends on what the notion of an analogue of (SA_i) amounts to, but it is hard to believe that such an analogue would not at least involve the notion of making reference to another person's action. Thus it seems quite plausible that social actions at least in the sense of class S_1 must be present here.

Another problem is what to say about norms concerning "negative" actions (e.g., omissions). As there are no negative actions in the strict sense - and thus no ought-to-do rules for them - we go about this as follows. We take our analysandum to be the rule 'One ought not to do X in C' or, equivalently, 'It is not the case that one may do X in C'. We would technically deal with this situation by requiring the following. The agents should be disposed to reason that they ought not do X in C (cf. clause (a) of (1)). Next, it is required that most members of S do not in fact do X in C, and that at least some omit doing X in C because of their so reasoning (cf. clause (b) of (1)). Thirdly, corresponding to clause (c) of (1), we would require that there be sanctions against doing X in C.

Finally, how does (1) stand up to the problem of accounting for fairness and correctness? It bypasses the problem altogether, and it can do so because it is a **nonreductive** account of normhood. According to (1) N may be a social norm even if it is wildly unfair (or incorrect), for example. Given proper pressure (sanctions) an unfair norm may well get established. (1) simply does not address itself to the problem (as it does not identify norms with anything non-normative). On the other hand, (1) can be conjoined with an account of correctness, for instance, by relating the practical reasonings of clauses (a) and (b) directly to (altruistic) we-intentions (cf. our discussion in Chapter 2).

II. SOCIAL ROLES

1. Proceeding to an investigation of the concept of role, we shall conceptually base it on the concept of social norm. We shall also claim that the concept of role involves considerations of similarity and that hence all the social concepts built from roles do also. Later we shall sketch a system of interlocked social concepts that indicates the importance of the concept of role. In creating this conceptual system we will start with the concept of norm and build roles from them (or, rather, their "factual counterparts"). Given the concept of role we can define positions as collections of roles. Collections of interrelated positions again define a certain structural concept of group. Organizations can then be defined as collections of interrelated groups. Finally, societies can be regarded as collections of interrelated organizations and groups. In the case

of the notions to be built up from norms, it is central that the members of the community in question mutually believe that the factors or components in our analysantia "are there". This is because mutual belief in our view partially explicates the "social reality" of the entities to be defined; recall our discussion in Chapter 7 of this point.

We considered above the concept of a social norm, especially ought-rules of the kind 'Every member of the collective S ought to do X, given that circumstances C obtain'.

At this point it is appropriate to make a remark on the logical structure of norms. One may distinguish between three components of a norm: its (1) restriction, (2) condition, and (3) prescription (cf. Stenius (1972)). Our example above is concerned with every member of S. The restriction of the norm then is to the members of S. Of course, the restriction might concern only a subclass of S as well. Thus depending on the case, it might concern, e.g., all retired members of S, or divorced or red-haired members, and so on. It might also be concerned with a single position holder, say the president in a society or the father in a family.

We may now write a simple social norm either as

(2) $(\forall A \in F) \text{Ought-to-do}_A(X/C)$ or
(3) $(\forall A \in F) \text{May-do}_A(X/C)$,

where F denotes the restriction class or "role-category" in social psychologists' terminology, viz. the class of members ("social types") or positions of S which the norm prescription concerns. As before, C gives the condition (of application) of the norm. The prescription of (2) is that A ought to do X and that of (3) that he may do X, where X is an action (or at least a doing by A, e.g., resting). The action X is often, or even typically, directed toward another agents (or positions), since interaction between agents, of course, is a central element in the social realm. Often norms are connected by "reciprocal" norms (cf. the social psychological phenomena of taking turns and our examples in Chapter 6). Agent A (say, a teacher) thus often does something related to some other agents (his pupils) and these other agents (pupils) again may be prescribed to act suitably towards the first agent. Thus, concerning two interacting agents A and B (say husband and wife), the reciprocality may, if needed, be written out symbolically. Thus when A's action X is directed towards B we may write X(B) and, conversely, Y(A) for B's action.

We have, above, mentioned and discussed only simple or single-track norms. Multi-track norms are taken to have prescriptions (either ought- or may-prescriptions, possibly combined) concerned with an agent's doing X_1 in C_1, X_2 in C_2,..., and so on. We shall not here discuss multi-track norms. Nor shall we discuss deontic logic (viz. the formal properties of norm-statements) here, for our purposes do not require it.

Let us now go to our construal of structural social concepts relying on norms (cf. our conceptual individualism of Chapter 2). Our starting point is, on the one hand, the notion of a motivational social norm (existing social norm) as characterized by (1). On the other hand, we start by considering an agent (or agents) of a certain kind (or a member of a certain class) acting in a suitable social environment. The kinds of agents correspond to the restriction classes F discussed above. Such classes, called role-categories, may be somehow naturally given classes (e.g., race, sex, region of inhabitance, etc.) which are used in S to classify people and mutually believed by the members of S so to be used, or they may be defined "socially" or "normatively" by, say, law or religion (e.g., a retired person, school teacher) and mutually believed by the members of S to be used to classify people according to those definitions. Next we consider an agent of type F (viz. a member of F) in his social setting understood here only in a "proto-sense". That is, for the purposes of our systematic treatment, we assume only that this agent belongs to a collective capable of social acting in our technical sense of Chapter 5. Thus this collective can be regarded as a social group in a minimal sense, as pointed out in Chapter 5, but nothing stronger is initially assumed.

Let us thus consider a collective, S, consisting of the agents $A_1,...,A_i,...,A_m$. Assume A_i is of type F. Next we assume that our collective recurrently performs some actions which are (typically) functional for it. Now it may be a matter of fact that corresponding to such (functional) actions some norms regulating them exist in this collective. Thus, for instance, A_i may reason that he ought to do X in C; and, indeed, this may be a norm in this collective S. By this we mean that (1) is applicable here with a certain modification. The modification is that the clauses (a), (b), and (c) of (1) should be taken to concern only members of S that are of kind F. Thus clause (a) of (1) is modified by employing 'the members of kind F in S' instead of 'the members of S' and (b) by using, correspondingly 'most members of F in S' instead of 'most members of S'. The pressure spoken about in clause (c) must now be taken to be directed towards the members of F, of course.

We get for a rule N of the form 'Every member of F in S ought to do X in C':

(1')   Rule N is a **social norm** in S if and only if
   (a) the members of S of kind F, when being in situation C (and believing so), are disposed to reason in ways justifiable by the schema (SA_i) or a similar schema that they ought to do X in C;
   (b) most (or at least many) members of F in S do X in C and at least some of them because of their so reasoning that they ought to do X in C;
   (c) there is some pressure (typically due to sanctions) in S against the members of F deviating from doing X in C; and
   (d) the members of S have a mutual belief to the effect that (a), (b), and (c).

Now, let us, for simplicity, take A_i to be the only agent of kind F in S. We are then dealing with a norm applying only to A_i in this special case. There may be several such norms applying to A_i only, or to A_i and some others as well. We may, accordingly, define the **role** of A_i in S to be the set (or conjunction) of norms (in the modified sense (1')) applying to A_i in S. Thus, informally speaking, the role of A_i is just the oughts and mays concerning A's acting in S.

More precisely, we here define role as an epistemic concept, viz. as a concept incorporating the mutual belief requirement. This is done on the basis of our definition (1') of a norm and the concept of a norm-conjunction. While we shall not here really technically formulate our definition of norm-conjunctions, it is easy enough to see how that could be done. Given (ought or may) norms $N_1,...,N_p$ in the sense of (1'), we analyze the conjunction $N_1\&...\&N_p$ essentially as the conjunction of the respective clauses (a), (b), and (c) in the analyses of the individual norms N_i, i=1,...,p, and add a mutual belief requirement (corresponding to, and generalizing, (d) of (1')).

Now we define roles simply by:

(4) R is a **social role** for A_i, **qua** a member of the restriction class F, in S if and only if
R is the conjunction of the ought-to-do and may-do norms applying to the restriction class F in S.

As noticed, the analysans of (4) contains a built-in mutual belief requirement, characterizing in part the intersubjective recognizability of roles. (Of course, we might define a nonepistemic notion of role by simply omitting the mutual belief requirement.)

In social psychological literature one finds different uses

of 'role'. Some authors speak of role standards where we speak of roles, whereas their roles are the actions (or behaviors, to use their jargon) that the norms in question concern. Sometimes roles are not connected even to norms when roles are defined as "those behaviors characteristic of one or more persons in a context" (Biddle (1979), p. 58). Even if our norms need not be prescribed in any sense and even if they may characterize divisions of activities quite generally, Biddle's characterization is nevertheless definitely broader than our (4). A further, and common, characterization of roles goes in terms of expectations. Thus, a class of actions by A_i, as a member of F, would then be called a social role just in case it is mutually believed in S that members of F in S regularly perform those actions (Bach and Harnish (1979), p. 279). Or, in the manner of Secord and Backman (1974), p. 405, one may define social roles by reference both to a role category (our restriction class F) and its associated expectations without a performance requirement.

When social scientists speak of roles as behavior expectations (or anticipations) it is not always clear whether they mean **normative** expectations (viz. what people should or ought to do) or **factual** expectations (viz. what people in fact generally do). This distinction is, of course, central. Notice that roles in our sense (4) concern both normative and factual expectations, as reflected, respectively, in the mutual belief concerning both clause (a) and clause (b) of (1'). Accordingly, what is especially interesting about our (1') (and (4), by implication) is that A_i has a disposition to reason that he ought to do X in C (cf. clause (a) of (1')). If he has properly **internalized** the norm he will typically act on it, thus making (b) of (1') true of himself and also making the actual employment of the sanctions of clause (c) unnecessary. Now, corresponding to the disposition discussed in clause (a) of (1') there may exist a factual basis (in A_i). If we accept a realistic account of dispositions (as in Chapter 4 above), then indeed there will be such a factual basis. This basis becomes activated when A_i indeed reasons (and comes to accept) that he ought to do X in C. We may now say that corresponding to each norm applying to A_i there is, on the realistic account, such a basis which we may call the **factual basis** of the norm N in A_i. Note that if A_i indeed does X in C we have a further factual feature corresponding to the norm.

2. In view of our further analysis, let us now briefly discuss the notion of disposition. I have elsewhere, e.g., in Tuomela (1977), Chapter 5, defended a realistic account of dispositions. This account can be, somewhat roughly, summarized as follows. We

represent 'A_i has the disposition D' by '$D(A_i)$' and try to clarify this time-relativized "single-track" predicate in terms of the following account:

(5) $D(A_i)$ if and only if
$(\exists K)(\exists C) \, [(K(A_i) \,\&\, C(A_i) \,\&\, (A)(K(A) \,\&\, C(A) \supset (G(A) \supset H(A)))$ is a true causal law such that it, together with some singular statements $K(A_j)$, $C(A_j)$, and $G(A_j)$, causally-deductively explains any true singular statement of the kind $H(A_j)$, i.e. the causal law backs the singular **causal** conditionals of the form $K(A_j) \,\&\, C(A_j) \,\&\, G(A_j) \mathrel{\vartriangleright\!\!\!\rightarrow} H(A_j)$ for all j).]

There are many comments to be made concerning this second-order definition or analysis. Let us first go through the notation. Of the predicates 'K' stands for a basis property ('basis' broadly understood), 'C' stands for the "normal" circumstances required to hold before a dispositional ascription applies. 'G' and 'H' stand for a relevant overt "stimulus" and "response". (For instance, 'G' could be 'put in water' and 'H', correspondingly, 'dissolves' in an analysis of the solubility of, say, sugar, the crystallic structure of which would be K.) All these predicates may be relativized to time, if needed.

The basic idea in our analysis is to analyze a disposition by reference to a basis and to a "basis law" which **explains** the object's H-ing by reference to its being G-ed, assuming the presence of a basis and the obtaining of normal conditions. In particular, the law does its explanatory work on any occasion (5) is concerned with. As before, the deductive explanation in question is technically analyzed in terms of the DE-model of Tuomela (1973) (cf. the appendix of Chapter 10 below and Tuomela (1976) for the conditional $\mathrel{\vartriangleright\!\!\!\rightarrow}$).

I will not here clarify nor defend this realistic account in more detail. For our present purposes the important and central thing about it is that statements about dispositions are in effect equivalent to statements about the existence of a basis (K) and suitable circumstances and about the existence of an explanatory law explaining the relevant overt manifest behavior (e.g., that when in C, A_i does X). For our present purposes we can simplify (5) and assume, to avoid second-order quantification, that D in fact means a disposition with basis K. (We so to speak assume, for simplicity, that K has been specified.)

Let us now look at our (1') and at the statement that an agent of kind F has a certain role, say R, in S. For simplicity, let us assume that R consists of one norm only. Now it becomes apparent that as to its factual content R coincides with a certain disposition, say D, as characterized by (a) of (1') and further characterized by (b), (c), and (d) of (1'). In the case of A_i we can then say:

$R(A_i)$ if and only if $D(A_i)$, given that K has been specified.

In fact, we may regard A_i as a variable (and let i vary). Thus we may universally quantify over the agents A_i, and we may consider statements like $(\forall A \in F)R(A)$ quantifying over the agents (or position- or role-holders) in F. As we will below be interested in role holders rather than concrete agents we shall consider only the latter type of statements. Thus we shall deal with dispositional statements of the type $(\forall A \in F)D(A)$. In view of (5) we get in our above new analysans of $R(A_i)$ only general (non-singular) statements, and this will well suit our technical treatment below.

Let us now go on to discuss the similarity (and analogy) of roles. Why do we need such considerations? While my main answer will be given later, let us here consider an illustration. As we know, every individual in a society belongs to numerous different groups. Yet he may have the **same** or a **similar** or **analogous** role in several of these groups. Thus, e.g., a father may have a disciplinarian's role towards his children at home and as a teacher at school he also has the role of a disciplinarian towards his pupils, and so on. Or consider two different agents A_1 and A_2. Both may have the role of a provider in their families, viz. the same role which yet may be carried out in quite different ways.

The point of our two examples is that the concept of role seems to be a **functional** notion rather than a categorical one. Roles should then be related to action-functions in the sense that the norms defining roles should be concerned with action-functions (in the sense of Chapter 13 below). Thus the action type X of (1') should be regarded as an action function in our sense. Our examples also indicate that considerations of sameness of function may be difficult to avoid. That is, in cases like the disciplinarian's and the provider's role sameness of function must be defined on the basis of comparing relevant counterpart functions in different groups (or organizations), but such sameness in the sense of identity seldom obtains. But the role concepts of a disciplinarian or a provider do not in fact presuppose sameness. **Similarity** (or analogy) is enough even on conceptual grounds. Thus, for example, a person can have the role of a disciplinarian in two or more groups even if his role norm-obeying actions are not only descriptively different but are different (but similar) functionally as well. What degree of similarity will suffice, then, for two or more "intra-group-roles" in different groups to be connected with one single inter-group role (such as the disciplinarian's role)? I am inclined to think that this is a strongly pragmatic problem which cannot ultimately be solved a priori, viz. without considering people's (especially sociologists') actual use of role-talk. Yet it may be helpful to bring in detailed considerations of similarity. Thus, before continuing our substantive discussion I shall summarize my previous technical account in Tuomela (1980) of similarity and analogy in terms of conceptual **distance**. It will then be shown that that account brings clarification and elucidation to our present problem.

III. SIMILARITY AND ROLES

1. Consider claims such as that there is similarity or analogy between, for instance, light and sound, thinking and speaking or, say, the father-child and teacher-pupil disciplinarian roles. When in cases like these we say that two things, systems, events, processes, universals, or what have you, are analogous (or similar) we ordinarily mean that there are some **central** (or **important** or even **essential**) properties with respect to which these "entities" are similar. (The notion of centrality is ultimately a pragmatic one.)

Typically, we can say that if two entities x and y are (positively) analogous and if x has the central properties expressed by the predicates $O_1,...,O_k$ then y has some **counterpart** properties expressed by $P_1,...,P_k$ such that O_i and P_i are identical or similar, for i=1,...,k. Here $\lambda_1 = \{O_1,...,O_k\}$ and $\lambda_2 = \{P_1,...,P_k\}$ are counterpart sets. The counterpart relation in part explicates the comparability (of λ_1 and λ_2), which any talk about analogy presupposes. (The restrictions, made here, that λ_1 and λ_2 have equal cardinality and that the counterpart relation be a one-to-one function are relaxed later in the section in terms of the notion of linkage.)

Our first task in evaluating claims about analogy is to characterize the similarity between two counterpart predicates O_i (in λ_1) and P_i (in λ_2). Technically, we ask how to define a distance measure $\delta(O_i,P_i)$ that measures the dissimilarity of O_i and P_i. One feasible way of doing this depends on the **second-order** (or, if needed, higher order) predicates which the O_is and P_is share or fail to share. Let $F = \{F_1,...,F_m\}$ be a (pragmatically determined) finite set of second-order predicates, taken as the basis of comparison. Let $F(O_i)$ stand for the set of second-order predicates in F applying to O_i. ($F(P_i)$ is of course defined similarly.) Then we may use the symmetric difference $F(O_i) \triangle F(P_i)$ to characterize the distance δ between O_i and P_i. More exactly, we define:

(6) $\delta(O_i, P_i) = $ **wcard** $(F(O_i) \triangle F(P_i))$.

Here **'wcard'** means 'weighted cardinality'. The weighted cardinality of the symmetric difference set is obtained by associating with its each element a weight such that the weights sum up to 1. The weighting is done on the basis of the importance of that element for the comparison of the distance between O_i and P_i. Our measure δ varies between 0 and 1. It is maximal if O_i and P_i do not share any properties in F and minimal when they share all of them.

The measure (6) is crude in that it does not account for the following case. Suppose $F_j(O_i)$ and $\sim F_j(P_i)$. Yet it may be that P_i is "very close" to possessing F_j. We might now want to resort to third-order properties to explicate and account for this closeness. In the general case we get a hierarchy of levels, which, however, must stop at some level on pain of infinite regression. Above I have assumed it to stop (for some reason or other) at the second level.

How about the similarity or distance, say d, between the set λ_1 and λ_2? Presumably it may be regarded as some kind of weighted average distance obtained on the basis of the $\delta(O_i, P_i)$s. My suggestion is accordingly the simple one:

(7) $d(\lambda_1, \lambda_2) = \sum_{i=1}^{k} w_i \, \delta(O_i, P_i)$.

Instead of using λ_i, i=1,2, in (7) we could also have used the conjunction of the predicates in λ_i. The weights w_i in (7) are assumed to sum up to 1, whence $0 \leq d(\lambda_1, \lambda_2) \leq 1$.

The right hand side of our (7) may also be used for measuring the distance (d') between two individuals, e.g., objects or systems, say e_1 and e_2:

(8) $d'(e_1, e_2) = \sum_{i=1}^{k} w_i \, \delta(O_i, P_i)$.

In (8) it is understood that e_1 has $O_1, \ldots, O_k$ and e_2 has $P_1, \ldots, P_k$ and that the distance is thus defined relative to the predicate sets λ_1 and λ_2.

In the case of metric predicates, (6) and (7) may be replaced by more exact and informative accounts. Although I cannot go here into details, let me indicate the basic idea of the account given in Tuomela (1980c). There it is assumed that the extensions of any two counterpart predicates O_i and P_i (having the same arity) can suitably be compared in each possible situation (or "world"). More specifically, we measure the maximum and minimum distances of the extensions of O_i and P_i in each possible situation in which O_i and P_i can meaningfully be used. The weighted average of these maxima and minima give the distances of O_i and P_i in each situation. The full, "situation-independent" distance between O_i and P_i is then obtained as a suitably weighted average over the set of all possible situations. Our account can be related to the results of mathematical psychologists in defining the distance and similarity between stimuli (and the like).

On the basis of (7) and (8) we may now define what we mean by the degree of **prima facie** analogy (or similarity) between λ_1 and λ_2 (say a) as well as between e_1 and e_2 (say a') respectively:

(9) $\quad a(\lambda_1, \lambda_2) = 1 - d(\lambda_1, \lambda_2)$

(10) $\quad a'(e_1, e_2) = 1 - d'(e_1, e_2)$.

Our (9) and (10) are about the simplest explicates of the inverse relationship between analogy and distance.

Concentrating on the analogy between two sets of predicates, it must be emphasized that the **full** analogy between them must also take into account the postulates (and other statements) constitutive of the predicates in them. (This is especially pertinent in the case of role-predicates for, as we claimed, they are intimately connected with underlying law-statements.) Accordingly, it seems that full predicate-analogy and full theory-analogy (which we have not discussed so far) amount to much the same thing, for obviously theories cannot be compared as to their similarity without comparing their (primitive) predicates. So what we ultimately have to clarify is the analogy between two conceptual systems (sets of predicates together with the statements constitutive of them), and what our technical treatment gives us is a recursive characterization of the similarity (or analogy) between global entities like conceptual systems in terms of considerations of similarity between (atomic) predicates.

To see what exactly the **full** analogy between λ_1 and λ_2, constituting the sets of primitive predicate sets of two respective languages L_1 and L_2, involves, we first note that one of our basic assumptions above has been that a one-to-one counterpart relation (together with the associated δ) for the languages L_1 and L_2 can be found. If we think of the Ct-predicates (or Carnapian Q-predicates) that can be formed, respectively, on the basis of λ_1 and λ_2, we have in effect mapped them (and the "cells" associated with them, in the monadic case) to each other in a one-to-one fashion.

Given this, one thing we still need to do on our way to defining full analogy in addition to using (9) is to measure the distance between the meaning postulates characterizing L_1 and L_2. The same goes for other postulates, be they metaphysical or empirical, that are constitutive of L_1 and L_2 (and expressible in them). Let us call the conjunctions of all such postulates that we wish to take into account in our similarity comparison, T_1 and T_2, respectively. (T_1 and T_2 are assumed to have been rendered into their distributive normal forms.) And let CS_1 and CS_2 be constituted by L_1 and L_2 plus T_1 and T_2. Then I suggest that the full analogy (a^*) between λ_1 and λ_2, or, what amounts to the same thing, the analogy between the two conceptual systems CS_1 and CS_2 be defined by:

(11) $\quad a^*(CS_1, CS_2) = \eta a(\lambda_1, \lambda_2) + (1-\eta) a(T_1, T_2)$.

The definiens here may also be taken to define the full analogy between T_1 and T_2 and between two proper scientific theories, say T_1' and T_2', "included" in T_1 and T_2, respectively. In (11), $0 \leq \eta \leq 1$ is a weight for the respective contribution of the analogy of λ_1 and λ_2 (defined by (9)) and of the similarity or analogy of T_1 and T_2. How is $a(T_1, T_2)$ to be defined? As we have a one-to-one mapping between the Ct-predicates CS_1 and CS_2 we may translate T_2 into CS_1 in terms of the Ct-predicates of L_1 that T_2 specifies to be exemplified and those it specifies not to be exemplified. Let us call this translation T_2^*. Then we define

(12) $\quad a(T_1, T_2) = 1 - d(T_1, T_2^*)$.

Here the distance $d(T_1, T_2)$ can be defined by formula (10) of Tuomela (1978) in the monadic case and by formulae (21) and (22) of the same paper in the polyadic case, where T_1 and T_2 are theories formalizable within full first-order predicate logic.

Now we have at our disposal an account of the analogy between two (first-order) conceptual systems (treated "linguistically" in terms of logical forms) which are in one-to-one correspondence. Our account also applies to the analogy of two entities e_1 and e_2 which have been conceptualized within their respective conceptual systems and which are understood to satisfy the conjunctions of the predicates in λ_1 and λ_2, respectively. As to a treatment of the case where λ_1 and λ_2 do not have equal cardinality, we shall now sketch briefly what to do.

Our final task thus is to remove the restriction that λ_1 and λ_2 have equal cardinality, so that an arity-preserving correspondence relation between them can be defined. The correspondence relation we are looking for is a kind of translation relation defined for two conceptual systems with $\lambda_1 = \{O_1,...,O_k\}$ and $\lambda_2 = \{P_1,...,P_m\}$ as their extralogical predicate sets. As we have been claiming, analogy judgments relating λ_1 and λ_2 presuppose some such presystematic correspondence relation. We shall not here inquire how the existence of such a relation can be philosophically justified in general (but see our remarks in the next section for the case of scientific reduction).

Formally, we formulate a counterpart definition $C \subseteq \lambda_1 \times \lambda_2$ by listing the counterparts: $C = \{<O_1,P_1>,...,<O_k,P_m>\}$, for a suitable indexing of the predicates. We assume that if $<O_i,P_j> \in C$ then the arities of O_i and P_j match. As we now may have $k \neq m$, we are dealing with the general comparison situation. The presystematically given C need not cover all the analogically related predicates. This is so because we must allow that analogical inference may predictively give us more such pairs. Thus we need a broader translation relation for the two conceptual systems CS_1 and CS_2 at hand. We shall here thus assume that C is given for CS_1 and CS_2 and define:

(13) A relation K is an **analogy-linkage** for the system $<CS_1,CS_2,C>$ if and only if
  (a) K is a linkage from λ_2 to λ_1 in the sense that the domain of K is λ_2, its range is λ_1, and card(K) $\leq$ card(K') for all relations K' with the same domain and the same range;
  (b) $C \subseteq K$.

The notion of linkage is due to Tichý (1976). We note that a linkage K maps the larger of the sets λ_1 and λ_2 onto the smaller one, and card(K) = max{**card**(λ_1),**card**(λ_2)}.

Next we need the notion of a **breadth** ($\beta(K)$) of a linkage K:

(14) $\beta(K) = 1/\textbf{card}(K) \sum_{<O_i,P_j> \in K} \delta(O_i,P_j).$

Now we may define the distance between the predicate sets λ_1 and λ_2 by:

(15) $d(\lambda_1, \lambda_2) = \min_K \beta(K).$

One may wonder from where K "comes". My brief answer is that ultimately and ideally it is determined by how people use the language L_1 and L_2 (and, thus, the predicates in λ_1 and λ_2). There is no way to a priori determine K. In any case, empirical investigation may show us that a certain color predicate, say O*, in L_1 is connected to both 'red' and 'orange' in L_2 (fragment of English). Then both <O*,red> and <O*,orange> will belong to K.

Can we now apply our basic formula (11) for full analogy? No, we only have its first component so far. (I am assuming, of course, that $a(\lambda_1, \lambda_2)$ and all other technical notions now make use of (15), wherever needed.) We still have to clarify how $a(T_1, T_2)$ is to be defined. As it relies on (12), what we are after is how to get T_2^* from T_2.

There may be many good ways of solving this difficult problem. Let me sketch one here and another one later on in Chapter 14. First, let us agree that we name our predicate sets so that λ_2 is at least as potent as λ_1. Let us furthermore assume that λ_1 and λ_2 only contain predicates which are primitive (unanalyzable) with respect to L_1 and L_2, respectively. (If the predicate sets and the analogy-linkage we originally started with do not satisfy this, it seems we may perhaps achieve this by suitable redefinitions of these sets and the linkage.) Let me now illustrate my idea in terms of the monadic case, where we can think of the conceptual frameworks in terms of a classification system of cells, marked exemplified, empty or with a question mark (see Niiniluoto and Tuomela (1973)). Then we have two systems of cells, say S_1 and S_2. S_2 may be considered to be a richer classification system than S_1 if **card**(λ_2) > **card**(λ_1). (Recall that adding a new monadic predicate to the language splits every old cell into two, and so forth.) But we may now impoverish S_2 by finding a subsystem S_2^* of it which has equally many cells as S_1. Then instead of using the original analogy-linkage K connecting S_2 and S_1 we now define a **one-to-one** analogy-linkage K* to connect S_2^* and S_1. Then we may use our original account (12) defined for the one-to-one case.

But how do we reduce S_2 to S_2^*? This we may technically do by means of the reduction operator (r) defined and discussed in Hintikka and Tuomela (1970) and Tuomela (1973). This operator, defined essentially on the basis of Craig's elimination theorem for distributive normal forms, reduces a (first-order) statement s of L_2 in the vocabulary λ_2 into a statement r(s) in a sublanguage L_2^* (of L_2) with $\lambda_2^* \subset \lambda_2$ such that K* links λ_2^* with λ_1 in a one-to-one fashion. This gives us a technical solution (for first-order theories) to our problem, given that impoverishing S to S* can be considered tolerable (or even inessential) for similarity comparison. But if the extra content of S over and above that of S* is considered central, more general methods of translation are needed. We shall discuss them in Chapter 14.

2. Let us now return to the comparison of roles. How do we apply our account of similarity and analogy to this problem? I propose we do it in terms of the **factual bases** of roles. Thus, consider a role R_1 in a social group (or subgroup) G_1 and another role R_2 in group (or subgroup) G_2. We have earlier defined the notion of a role in a collective S. This collective can here be regarded as a group of a certain kind. The notion of group involved is a structural one, obtained as follows. Consider all the roles of each agent A_i, $i=1,...,m$, in S. This totality is, in view of our definition, a conjunction of norms. We take the conjunction of all such conjunctions, with varying i, and identify the **structure** of the group S with this conjunction. Then, for our present purposes, we can say that the group itself consists of the agents $A_1,...,A_m$ together with that bunch of norms. (We shall below define a social group more exactly but the core will be as stated.)

The problem we now face is how to account for inter-group roles (such as the disciplinarian's role). This problem is solved if we can account for how the above roles R_1 and R_2 serve to generate a "superrole" or inter-group role R such that R applied to G_i yields R_i, $i=1,2$. As indicated, my proposal is to operate in terms of the factual contents D_i of R_i, $i=1,2$, and to claim that R is created on the basis of the similarity between D_1 and D_2. Or, actually, as specified in Section II, we will operate with the factual bases or contents corresponding to all the roleholders in the case of R_1 and R_2. Technically this amounts to dealing with the analysantia of the respective instances of (1') quantified over the members of F. This again amounts to comparing two theories, say T_1 and T_2. My suggestion for comparing the roles R_1 (in G_1) and R_2 (in G_2) now comes to saying that it should be based on the application of (11) to this case. This equals the employment of

(11') $a^*(R_1,R_2) = a^*(T_1,T_2) = \eta a(\lambda_1,\lambda_2) + (1-\eta)a(T_1,T_2)$,

where a* stands for full and a for partial analogy. The set **F** used for comparing the distance between λ_1 and λ_2 can in this case be taken to concern second-order predicates concerned with the **functions** of the predicates in λ_1 and λ_2. The predicates in

λ_1 and λ_2 are, as earlier, the predicates of T_1 and T_2 and, especially, λ_1 and λ_2 contain the predicates representing the action-functions that the role-norms are concerned with. We may in fact construe the predicates in λ_1 and λ_2 so that each predicate corresponds to a single (simple) norm. This is achieved, for instance, if λ_1 and λ_2 are taken to consist just of the disposition predicates corresponding to the norms in question. Then in the simplest case we would have $\lambda_1 = \{D_1\}$ and $\lambda_2 = \{D_2\}$. As just seen above, our technical apparatus also allows for cases where λ_1 and λ_2 both contain several disposition predicates and where λ_1 and λ_2 may differ as to their cardinalities.

How do we now create the (or a) intergroup norm R on the basis of R_1 and R_2? I suggest that we get such a concept only when $a^*(R_1,R_2) > \delta$, where δ is a number close to 1. How close should δ be to 1? I take this to be an issue to depend on the "pragmatics" of the situation at hand. Whether or not the above condition of analogy (or similarity) between R_1 and R_2 is sufficient (and not only necessary) for the characterization depends on how well (and how completely) the second-order predicate set F takes into account the functional similarities between R_1 and R_2. To the extent it does we may define, for every i:

(16) $R(A_i)$ if and only if $R_1(A_i)$ & $R_2(A_i)$ & $a^*(R_1,R_2) > \delta$.

This characterization is easily seen to account for cases such as an agent A_i's being a disciplinarian both in G_1 and in G_2. How about the provider's role where **different** agents are claimed to have the same role? To cover this type of cases we change our previous interpretation a little and take A_i to refer to the concrete agent A_i in the group G_j, j=1,2, or, if A_i does not belong to G_j, to his counterpart role-holder in G_j. This is a possible maneuver because we are assuming here that λ_1 and λ_2 are connected by a counterpart relation which, furthermore, connects the roles of G_1 and G_2 in an one-to-one fashion (even when the roles themselves are multi-track ones). More generally, inter-group roles are definable in the manner of (16) as long as R_1 and R_2 are connected by a counterpart relation with each other but so that neither is connected with any other roles in the other group. (Thus G_1 and G_2 need not necessarily have the same number of roles and role-holders.)

There is still a more general suggestion available for defining and measuring inter-group roles. Consider thus k (≥ 2) different groups with the counterpart roles $R_1,...,R_k$. We may now consider a candidate role R and consider its (full) similarity with each of the roles in the class $\mathbf{R}=\{R_1,...,R_k\}$. Then take the average similarity of R with respect to those roles; let R be a variable and define the inter-group role to be the one maximizing that average distance. Technically, we consider

(17) $\quad a^*(R,R) = 1/k \sum_{i=1}^{k} A^*(R,R_i)$

and select the value of R maximizing (17) as the inter-group role.

The above considerations of analogy and similarity can also be used to characterize the similarity between two groups (or subgroups, cliques, etc. if you like) G_1 and G_2 (cf. definition (11) and our remarks for applying it to characterize the similarity between two entities e_1 and e_2). Since groups are presently characterized in terms of agent collectives suitably obeying role norms, we can here utilize the notion of role sets as follows. Let the agents $A_1,\ldots,A_m$ be all the agents occupying roles in G_1 and let $B_1,\ldots,B_k$ be the corresponding agents in the case of G_2. We may either assume that each agent has only one role or, if that seems wildly implausible, we may operate in terms of role-holders. Choosing the latter possibility here, we then let $p(\geq m)$ be the number of role-holders in G_1 and $r(\geq k)$ in G_2. As our groups are essentially bunches of roles we may now directly employ our earlier technical developments in the case of the similarity or analogy between two predicate sets λ_1 and λ_2 with unequal cardinality. The application is quite straightforward, since we may take λ_1 to be the set of roles R_i, $i=1,\ldots,p$, of G_1 and λ_2 the set of roles R_j, $j=1,\ldots,r$, of G_2. Given this we can directly employ definition (13) of analogy-linkage to the present case. In definition (14) of the breadth of a linkage we now of course use the sum $\sum_{<R_i,R_j>\in K} (1-a^*(R_i,R_j))$

K being the linkage, and get

(18) $\quad \beta(K) = 1/\mathbf{card}(K) \sum_{<R_i,R_j>\in K} (1-a^*(R_i,R_j))$.

Then we may define the degree of full similarity or analogy between the groups G_1 and G_2 to be

(19) $\quad a^*(G_1,G_2) = \min_K \beta(K)$.

The essential technical difference between our previous development and the present one is that while (14) employs the measure δ of predicate distance we now use a measure of full role distance characterized in terms of full role analogy or similarity. This means that we now have already built in the information contained in (11) (for this was done by (11')). Thus (19) gives us what we are after, viz. full group similarity.

IV. SOCIAL STRUCTURES

1. As indicated in the beginning of this chapter we may envision the following conceptual framework of structural social concepts or "social structures", if you like. We first start with our system of **social action** concepts as created in Chapter 5 above. Next we characterize social norms (cf. Section I of the present chapter). **Social norms** are in a sense prescriptions concerning social actions, and corresponding to these internalized norms there are dispositions (or powers) to perform social actions in a norm-obeying way. **Social roles** are defined in terms of social norms (of an appropriate kind), as discussed in the preceding subsection. Because of this roles can also be discussed in terms of the underlying factual dispositions to act, and this proved to be important in our treatment of the concepts of similarity of roles and groups.

Groups can be defined in terms of roles, and this was done in a preliminary way above. But the reader has to be reminded that in social psychology groups have been characterized in a variety of ways and our above line of thought is only one of many suggested so far (recall our preliminary remarks in Chapter 5). Thus, Zander and Cartwright (1968), after surveying several attempts to define the notion of a social group, conclude (p. 48):

> "It seems likely, then, that when a set of people constitutes a group, one or more of the following statements will characterize them: (a) they engage in frequent interaction; (b) they define themselves as members; (c) they are defined by others as belonging to the group; (d) they share norms concerning matters of common interest; (e) they participate in a system of interlocking roles; (f) they identify with one another as a result of having set up the same model-object or ideals in their super-ego; (g) they find the group to be rewarding; (h) they pursue promotively interdependent goals; (i) they have a collective perception of their unity; (j) they tend to act in a unitary manner toward the environment."

We shall not here attempt to clarify in detail these features of groups nor their relative importance (but see our discussion below).

To start our discussion, it seems helpful to make a distinction at least between **face-to-face groups**, **crowds**, and (proper) **social groups**. In social psychology so-called **face-to-face** interaction has been regarded as central. Our social action concepts, of course, allow for many broader types of interaction as well, as will be clarified in detail in Chapter 9. To be sure, it has not become quite clear to me what social psychologists mean by face-to-face interaction. (Would a telephone conversation qualify, for instance?) In any case, there seems to be an intuitively important distinction between two kinds of (direct) interaction situations, viz. situations allowing spatial and/or temporal contiguity as well as some degree of control of the others' behavior - and the resulting causal feedback processes - and situations which do not allow this. The former type of situations partly characterize what might be termed face-to-face situations **sensu lato** (cf. also our discussion and formulas (12) and (13) in Chapter 9). The persons involved in face-to-face interaction may belong to the same social group (normatively characterized) or organization, but they need not. Quite casual encounters between unacquainted and unrelated persons may suffice for their forming a face-to-face interaction group, provided they share at least some relevant mutual beliefs or expectations concerning each other's actions in that situation.

Crowds are formed out of aggregates of people which initially have no clear common goal directing their behavior as a group (cf. people in a street or passangers in a train). But a suitable common stimulus may emerge which creates such a common goal (e.g., an explosion) and makes the aggregate a crowd. Thus, Landis defines a crowd as a "temporary collection of people in close physical contact reacting together to a common stimulus" (Landis (1971), p. 211). As Bach and Harnish (1979), p. 280, emphasize, it must be added that the members of a crowd be mutually aware of the common stimulus.

We shall not here attempt to give an exact analysis of face-to-face groups nor of crowds. Instead we shall consider full blown social groups in some more detail. In Chapter 5 we noticed that whenever a collective $G = \{A_1,...,A_m\}$ performs social actions there is some patterned interaction between the agents in question and also a relevant we-intention is involved. These two aspects, as analyzed in Chapters 2, 5, and below in 9, in part cover (a), (b), (h), (i), (j), and perhaps indirectly (c) and (g) in the above characterization by Cartwright and Zander. We shall now attempt to give an analysis of the concept of social group which also takes into account the relevant normative aspects, such as (d) and (e) in Cartwright's and

Zander's characterization, as well as our above discussion of similarity.

We shall require of a social group that its members share at least one we-interest (a we-want or we-proattitude) such that they, because of sharing this we-interest, tend to form we-intentions to perform specific social actions (and interact) so as to promote this (more general) we-interest. In a full blown social group much of this action typically has been institutionalized and become norm-governed. Thus, there are roles (and a division of tasks and activities) for the agents in the group, and the roles (ultimately) serve the common we-interests of the group. Norms defining roles need not be the only norms operative in the group.

Let us now consider the following definition of a social group in the full sense:

(20) The agents $A_1,...,A_m$ form a **social group** if and only if
   (1) there is a we-interest I that the agents $A_1,...,A_m$ share such that, because of sharing I, $A_1,...,A_m$ tend to form we-intentions to perform such social actions (and interactions) as promote the satisfaction of I and to carry out these social actions;
   (2) there are norms in the collective $\{A_1,...,A_m\}$ at least some of which define roles for A_i, $i=1,...,m$, such that the actions governed by these norms belong to the class of actions of clause (1) assumed to promote the satisfaction of I;
   (3) there is a mutual belief among $A_1,...,A_m$ to the effect that (1) and (2).

In (20) we-interests and we-intentions are to be understood in the sense of Chapter 2, social actions in our technical sense (7) of Chapter 5, and interaction in the broad sense (2) to be defined in Chapter 9. Norms and roles are defined, respectively, by (1') and (4) of the present chapter. Note that the mutual awareness related to we-intentions (see Chapters 2, p. 35, and 7, p. 206) and to norms, see (1') above, does not suffice to guarantee mutual awareness of the special we-intentions or of the special norms spoken about in (20). Thus its clause (3) is needed.

Is (20) an adequate characterization of a social group or, rather, of some agents' forming or constituting a social group? First we recall that (20) at least in part respects the criteria of Cartwright and Zander quoted above (except the psychoanalytic criterion (f)). To the extent that this is the case our definition does more than, for instance, Cartwright and Zander think is possible, for according to them "these various definitions simply identify different kinds of groups" (Cartwright and Zander (1968), p. 46). These authors then settle for the following platitude: "a group is a collection of individuals who have relations to one another that make them interdependent to some significant degree" (Cartwright and Zander (1968), p. 46). This latter characterization is intolerably broad and includes both face-to-face groups, crowds, and, e.g., football fans and the class of fat people, all disqualified by our (20), and it also fails to account for the normative aspects of groups.

Why we claim that (20) is adequate is, then, that it (explicitly or implicitly) accounts for several, in fact all of the central, important desiderata for full blown social groups (such as families, cliques, clubs) and that it plausibly excludes aggregates, which have less permanence and far fewer social aspects in common (cf. crowds and, e.g., the class of fat people).

Two technical remarks concerning (20) are still due. First, our construal of "superroles" on the basis of similarity considerations in terms of (16) and (17) is highly relevant here. For, as already indicated, when a superrole R is so constructed from some roles $R_1, R_2, \ldots$, the latter may be roles characteristic of some **sub**groups (or **sub**systems) of the full blown social group we are now dealing with. Thus R would be a role our (20) speaks about.

Secondly, there is the question what to do with group-identity through time when members change. Our (20) bypasses this problem but let me indicate what my line of thought here would be. We have treated the symbols $A_1, \ldots, A_m$ in (20), logically speaking, as constants. But we could also regard them as variables. This would in fact amount to speaking about positions or role-holders rather than about concrete agents. In this latter case we might construct a definition of a group by requiring there to **exist** m agents satisfying the analysans of (20). Furthermore, m might be a variable with some suitable lower and upper bounds. Discussion of group-identity could be carried out within this broadened frame, e.g., by considering how many (and what kind of) concrete agents can change membership without the group losing its identity. I shall not here enter that discussion.

Let me here answer a potential criticism. Our official definition (**WI**) of we-intentions is relative to a collective, but not necessarily a group. Yet the question arises whether the notion of collective can be analyzed without presupposing the notion of we-intention - for note that our notion of group as defined by (20) does rely on the concept of we-intention. My general answer is that some suitably overtly interacting agents can already form a collective, and this specification, compatible with our (**CI**) of Chapter 2, does not rely on the concept of we-intention - or any other we-concept. For instance, (a), (b), (c), (g), and (i) in Cartwright's and Zander's above list might be explicable in the required way. Thus no vitiating circle needs to be involved here.

2. Given our conceptual machinery of norms ((1) and (1')), roles ((**4**), (**16**), and (**17**)) as well groups ((**20**)), we can build most of the central analytical concepts needed for the study of society. While such a project clearly falls outside the scope of this book let me just briefly sketch how the broader (and ambiguously used) notion or organization, community, and society may be arrived at.

Technically, organizations might be characterized simply as suitable emergent systems of interrelated groups, if groups are defined in terms of role-holders (positions and social types) rather than concrete agents. But nevertheless there is much more to be said. First, in an organization such as a business company or a school, the members are differentiated by their positions to which specific duties and responsibilities, and procedures for acting, are attached. The roles are suitably interconnected, often on an intergroup level (when we take social groups to be parts of an organization). The various positions are distinguished in terms of factors such as direction of power (authority) and of communication, and so on. There are also specific conventions for recognizing the above mentioned features.

Communities may be characterized as systems of interconnected organizations and groups. Finally, societies are complexes of communities, organizations, and groups. While we shall not here present any details it is important to realize that the purposive-causal theory of social action created in this book gives the central tools for building up the basic social concepts. (See Bates and Harvey (1975) for an attempt to proceed along the lines of the above sketch, yet without the help of an account of social action.)

On the level of agents, too, we may create some broader concepts. Thus we may, not surprisingly, define the (total) **position** of an agent in a group to be his set of roles together with the normative action-expectations directed towards him, in a sense, by the roles of other agents in that group. The expectations in question are those which appear in the justifications of (personal) social norms, such as those referred to in the premises of our schemas (**SA_i**) and (**PR_i**) of Chapter 7. For our present purposes we may speak of these expectations in terms of locutions like 'A_i believes (or expects) that A_j will (or should or ought to) do X_j', and so on. We shall not here further characterize these expectations except for recalling that in the last premise of both (SA_i) and (PR_i) the agent A_i's belief that A_j will or should do X_j is exactly such an expectation.

We may also consider the set (or conjunction) of expectations directed towards an agent in a group. With some reservations, this collection might be called the ("subjective") **status** of A_i in that group.

Finally, we may define concepts analogous to group-position and group-status in the case of organizations and societies, as well. On the basis of our above considerations it is clear how to do it. The central thing to note here is that, if our claims have been true, such inter-group (and inter-organization) concepts will involve considerations of similarity or analogy (cf. (16)). This is a further reason for our having discussed similarity and analogy to such a great extent in this chapter.

Let us finally return to our basic argument for introducing the concept of similarity (or analogy) to our conceptual framework of social concepts. This argument, which we have not so far clearly spelled out, is that similarity-considerations are due to the basic similarity of the main functions and goals of various social units and systems. We said in the beginning of this chapter that social norms defining roles at least typically concern action-functions. We then assumed, in defining inter-group roles (etc.), that different groups have functions (and goals and ends) which are somehow basically similar. The same goes for organizations and societies. Furthermore those ends and functions are intimately connected with the basic individual goals and functions.

I shall not try to produce a satisfactory account of such basic social ends and functions - that is the job of a sociologist. Let me just remind that they will involve various biologically based ends (e.g., food, sex, shelter), psychologically based ones (e.g., security, love), social (relatedness, respect, etc.), religious, cultural, and other ends (cf. Maslow's (1970) similar list). Whatever the list best fitting a functional account of society will look like, it should be clear that our above account relies on some kind of social functionalism. This functionalism need not be regarded as an a priori true set of assumptions but rather as a broad scientific hypothesis or theory. Yet, whatever its epistemic nature is taken to be, my claim is that the conceptual framework of social concepts can best be elucidated and made precise by relying on the assumption of the centrally functional nature of social units and systems.

Over and above being functional, our agreement is also to a

high degree naturalist, due to our realist interpretation of the dispositions (tendencies) underlying social structures. Accordingly, the factual bases of social roles and positions (etc.) may be regarded as objective and as relatively enduring mostly. This makes possible a systems-theoretic and naturalistic study of society, however with the qualification that it is grounded in actions and tendencies to act. Social structures may be reproduced and transformed by social actions through affecting the relevant action tendencies underlying social positions. On the other hand social actions in a way factually and **prima facie** conceptually presuppose social structures as they take place in a social setting involving institutions, relations of production and exchange, and so on, even if such social structures in the last analysis can be conceptually built out of (relatively) individualistic notions, as indicated above.

CHAPTER 9

SOCIAL INTERACTION AND CONTROL

I. ACTING IN SOCIAL RELATION

1.   Social interaction is obviously a very broad topic which can be approached from several directions. I shall below distinguish between two logically independent yet closely related "dimensions" and concentrate on them. First, we have the behavioral or **overt** point of view: that an agent's (observable) actions are somehow related causally or generationally is taken as the basis of a characterization of interaction. Secondly, we have the **covert** or, perhaps better, explanatory (or, more widely, justificary) dimension. Here we characterize interaction in terms of the agents' interdependent attitudes, such as intersubjective utilities (wants) and loop beliefs, which serve as their reasons for acting and which, accordingly, must be referred to in the (best) explanation (viz. social psychological explanation) of their actions. In Chapter 7 we characterized some aspects of this second dimension of social interaction and below we will discuss both of these dimensions starting with the first, or overt, dimension.
   Before starting, a remark is due. We shall below define **non-epistemic** notions of social relationship. Corresponding **epistemic** notions are obtained by adding to the definientia below a clause to the effect that the agents involved, viz. A and B in our definitions, mutually believe that the other clauses of the definition in question are true. (Recall our discussion in Chapter 7 concerning the importance of the mutual belief requirement for "defining social reality".)
   We shall start by defining a very general notion of social action, viz. of what it is for an agent A to act **in relation to** another agent B. Before starting the definition we consider two examples. Suppose A kicks B. Then we say that A acts in relation to B. If A and B are singing a duet then A's action of singing his part of the duet is related to A's and B's joint action and hence to B's action. If A performs an action token u of type X and B another one v of type Y and if X&Y is a social action type (in the sense of (5.7)) that u and v jointly token then we say that A and B are co-agents with respect to each other's action tokens. Clause (a) of (1) below handles the case of co-agency.

269

If A writes with B's pen then A's action is in relation to B. Clause (b) below takes care of this type of dependence. We thus define (cf. Pörn (1977), p. 74):

(1) An action token u of type X by A is an action **in relation to** B if and only if
(a) B is either a co-agent of A with respect to u; or
(b) non-vacuous reference to B is necessarily made in the description of the result of u when u is described as an X.

Let us consider kicking (=X) to clarify (1). Assume we have an action token u = <v,...,b,...,r> of A's kicking B, where r is described by the nominalization 'B's getting kicked by A'. Here we have a necessary and non-vacuous (successful) reference to B, we can say. (We may allow that some other description or name of B than 'B' be used, e.g., 'C's brother' if B is C's brother.) The description of u as an X can be taken to be '(Ex) Kicked (A,B,x)', from which the mentioned description of r in a sense "derives". (I shall not here try to explore the general linguistic mechanism underlying this "derivation".)

Our (1) can in a sense be generalized to encompass cases such as the following. A offers some food to C who eats it. Unbeknownst to A, the food had been poisoned, and as a consequence C dies. Thus we may say that A (nonintentionally) killed C by offering that portion of food to him. Thus also A makes C's wife a widow. This last mentioned action by A was generated by his first action of offering food to C, and the generated action contains conceptual reference to B when described as A's making B a widow. Let us try to define this tricky notion as follows;

(2) An action token u of type X by A **makes reference** to B if and only if
(a) u is an action in relation to B, or
(b) there is an action type Y and an action token$_2$ u' of type Y by A such that
(i) u generated u'; and
(ii) u' is an action token in relation to B.

We understand the notion of generation here in the sense (6.13) (or (6.19)) and (6.15) (or, if you like, as its **probabilistic** counterpart defined for probabilistic automata). We may say that in (2) the indirect reference made to B is **through** Y. If (2) is to be non-empty we need a restricted, preferably finite, list of the action types Y over which we quantify and, as above, an account of what it is necessarily to make a reference to something in an action-description. I must bypass these difficult problems in the present context. It may be remarked here that analogues of (1) and (2) for action **types** X (rather than for the tokens of X) can be formulated by requiring that (1) and (2), respectively, be satisfied for **all**, or at least all **standard**, tokens of X.

It can be seen that (2) captures a broader class of actions than (1). Thus, if we call the class of action tokens satisfying (2) K_2 and that corresponding to (1) K_1, then $K_1 \subset K_2$.

Next we consider stricter types of interaction having to do with A's somehow affecting or influencing B's acting. An example would be this. Suppose A persuades B to vote in a certain way. Then A can be said to affect, indeed control, B by his act of persuading. We shall indeed finally arrive at cases of control like this (see (5) and (6) below) but we start with weaker notions of affecting. Let thus first consider the following notion of (weak) affecting:

(3) Agent A **weakly affects** B if and only if there is an action type X such that for every action token u of type X by A it is true that
(a) non-vacuous reference to B is necessarily made in the description of the result of u when u is described as an X.
(b) in the non-vacuous reference made to B when describing u as an X specifically an **action** by B is referred to.

Note that the affecting in (3) is not necessarily concerned with A's making B do something but is much weaker. For instance, even A's telling a story about B's performing an action Y would qualify as an X satisfying (3). Also note that the affecting need not be intentional.

It might be claimed that (3), on the other hand, defines a rather strong notion of affecting in the sense that it concerns action types (rather than tokens) and requires that clauses (a) and (b) be satisfied for **every** token of X. This criticism might be answered by relaxing that requirement to hold only for **standard intentional** tokens of X, for instance. But it is not at all clear that the criticism is valid in the first place.

Related to (3) we may also define a much weaker notion of affecting for action tokens. It relativizes affecting to a single token u ("A weakly affects B by his action token u of type X") and requires (a) and (b) to be satisfied in the case of u but not necessarily for every token of type X. This characterization would be the precise analogue for (1) and (2) in the present case. But I prefer to continue with (3) as we now are primarily speaking about relations between their action tokens. (We shall accordingly say that A affects B whenever he produces an action token u satisfying the analysans of (3).)

If, instead of using the notion of acting in relation in (3), we use the notion of an action token making reference we get a still broader notion of affecting (cf. A's indirectly and weakly affecting B by doing something which leads somebody else to tell a story about B's performing Y):

(4) Agent A **indirectly and weakly affects** B if and only if there is an action type Y and there is an action type X such that for every action token u of type X by A there is an action token$_2$ u' of type Y by A such that
(a) u generates u';
(b) u' is an action token in relation to B; and
(c) in the non-vacuous reference made to B when describing the token u' as an Y specifically an **action** by B is referred to.

Let us call the class of action tokens by A satisfying (the definiens of) (3) K_3 and that corresponding to (4) K_4. Obviously $K_3 \subset K_4$, and thus $K_3 \subset K_4 \subset K_1 \subset K_2$. Note that what we said about the weakening of (3) applies, mutatis mutandis, to (4). Also note that (4) could be weakened by dropping the requirement that the tokens u' be of the same type Y, and an analoguous remark applies to (2) above and (IP), (5), (5'), and (6) below, too.

2. Next we define some stronger notions of influence in terms of an agent's power to do something. Here I will rely on the notion of direct intentional power defined by formulas (4.8) and (4.9) (as well as (5.9), in the multi-agent case) earlier. Partly in terms of it we can define a notion of indirect power of an agent A to do something X (not necessarily intentionally):

(IP) Agent A has the **indirect power to do** X if and only if there is a (possibly complex) action type Y such that
(a) A has the (direct) power to do Y intentionally (in the sense of (4.9)); and
(b) for each action token u of X by A there is an action token v of Y by A such that IG(v,u).

In (4) and in (IP) we may say that it is through Y that A affects B or has indirect power, respectively. Clause (b) may seem strong because of its requirement concerning all tokens of X; for some purposes 'most' instead of 'each' might be preferable. Note that A may do X without having the power to do X. Note, too, that if A has the direct power to do intentionally something then he also has the power to refrain from doing it. (This remark does not apply to indirect power as this notion does not involve A's doing v intentionally.) Note that we may say that A did u **by** doing v in the case of (**IP**). This also comes out from definition (**6.4**) of the by-locution by describing X as verbing$_2$ and Y as verbing$_1$ and by assuming that v and u only differ with respect to their result episodes.

It is to be noted here that, to emphasize A's influence over B taking place through A's actions, we have not specifically spoken about B's actions (except for mentioning them in (3) and (4)). We have also noticed that the notions of A's affecting B defined by (3) and (4) are rather weak in that it is not required in them that A's action token u' in a strong sense determines an action token performed by B to come about. Let us now define a concept of control (or power) in which we do require that A's action token u' determines an action token by B:

(5) Agent A has **control over** agent B if and only if there is an action type Z and another action type X such that
(a) A has the indirect power to do X; and
(b) for every action token u of type X in which A exercises his indirect power to do X there is an action token z of type Z performed by B such that u determines z.

We first notice about (5) that it is concerned with an **action** type of B. We could also define an analogous control notion also for B's **mental states** such as intentions, desires, interests, beliefs, and so on (cf. (6) below). Also B's **environment**, central for his well-being, can be controlled (cf. Cartwright and Zander (1968), pp. 219-222). Presently, we are merely interested in behavior control or control over a person's actions rather than, say, his wellbeing or his mental life. Secondly, we notice that clause (b) speaks of action **determination**. Usually **causal** determination is involved here. We shall not further explicate it here except by saying that it will have to involve a suitable causal chain from the result event of the token u by A (or a suitable complex of events involving that result event) to the result event of the token z by B. That such a determination takes place of course presupposes that "normal conditions" obtain viz., that nothing obviously bizarre and outlandish occurs (cf. our remarks in Chapter 7).

For reasons which are usually epistemic (lack of knowledge) rather than conceptual or ontic, behavioral scientists typically speak of **probabilistic** determination only. Probabilistic determination may involve A's making B's action probable, or probable to some degree.

Let us try to make this idea of A's having the power of probabilistically affecting B's action more precise by the following modification of (5):

(5') Agent A has **probabilistic control** over agent B if and only if there is an action type Z and another action type X such that
(a) A has the (indirect) power to do X; and
(b) X is probabilistically causally relevant to Z in the sense that A's exemplifying X by his action makes B's exemplifying Z by his action more probable than it is without A's action.

In (5') (b) probabilistic causal relevance might be partly analyzed in the technical terms of probabilistic relevance, i.e. $p(Z/X)>p(Z)$, and some suitable screening off requirement (see Tuomela (1977), Chapter 11 for various possibilities).

For our present purposes it is not essential that (5') (b) be analyzed in detail. Let me, however, make a distinction between two components of action control (cf. Section III). Let us consider as our example the payoff matrix 7.3, objectively interpreted. Here A_1 has both **absolute** and **conditional** probabilistic control over A_2 due to his possibility to switch from X_1 to X_2 and back. A_1's action may here in a sense be regarded as an environmental condition for A_2's acting. (Note the A_1 has the power to do X_1 and the power to do X_2 and (5') can be applied twice to this situation with X_1 and X_2 replacing X). As to A_1's absolute power, he controls A_2's payoffs with the amount of three units, viz. the difference between -2 and 1 (in the case of Y_1) and that between -1 and 2 (in the case of Y_2). The exact probabilistic amount of action control cannot, however, be computed unless A_2's (subjective) choice probabilities are known, too. A_1 also has conditional probabilistic control over A_2 here. By this is meant the amount of A_1's effect on A_2's acting which is conditional to A_2's choice of his action. This is a true interaction effect. Now we are speaking about (jointly determined) cells rather than rows in Figure 7.3. Here A_1's effect on A_2's outcomes is contingent on what A_2 does; they jointly affect A_2's outcomes and his probabilities of doing Y_1 and Y_2.

(5) (any more than (5')) does not use the somewhat vague and problematic notion of making a non-vacuous reference to B's action. We may, however, ask whether (5) entails that A indirectly and weakly affects B with respect to some action type

(cf. (4)). The essential question then is whether B's action z can somehow be seen to be involved when describing u. If u can be described through its consequence z, it seems that an affirmative answer can be given. For u can be characterized functionally as what brought about z, which is an action token of type Z by B. Let us say that we then have described u as an F. Next suppose that the functional type F is identical with some intrinsic (non-functional) type G. The we are dealing with a token of G, call it u', of which we know that IP(u,u'). Thus, given that such a G can be found (which we shall plainly assume), u makes indirect reference to B (through G) in the sense of (2). It is also immediately seen that A indirectly and weakly affects B (with respect to action type G) in the sense of (4). But we do not get indirect weak affecting in this sense with respect to action type Z, of course. Anyhow, technically our (5) is a special case of (4) (given the existence of G, which we assume), and thus control entails indirect weak affecting.

We may say that the **influence** A has in relation to B is defined by specifying what A **can** (and **cannot**) do in relation to B, and our notion of control therefore can be used to elucidate A's influence over B. Note that (5) may be formulated alternatively by speaking of A's control over B **with respect to** Z, where Z now is a specific action type replacing the notationally same variable Z in the original (5). Let thus $Z_1,\ldots,Z_m$ be such action type constants qualified to replace the variable Z in (5). Then we may define the range or scope of this influence by:

(SI) The **range of** the **influence** A has with respect to B is the width of the set $\{Z_1,\ldots,Z_m\}$ of action types such that A has control over B with respect to Z_i for i=1,... ...,m.

Next we define a more specific notion of control that employs "an intentional channel". Let us consider an example to clarify this. Suppose B's wife hides B's shoes and thereby prevents him from going to the nearby pub. This represents control by A over B which obtains without intentional channel. But now consider the situation where A persuades B not to go to the pub (by, for instance, making B believe he cannot afford it financially or for reasons related to his health). We may assume that A's persuasion causes (or generates) B's intention to stay home (or to do something else than going to the pub).

Using the automata-theoretic explication (**6.13**) for indirect generation with the interpretation that an action token u by A generates and thus **determines** (cf. (5)(b)) an action token z by B we now require that the internal state (represented by the variable s) of the automaton M postulated to exist in (**6.13**) be a relevant state of intending by B. Thus we get for control with intentional channel the following:

(6) Agent A has **intentional control** over agent B if and only if there is an action type Z such that
(a) A has control over B; and
(b) in the relation of determination (**IG**) of (5)(b) the state (represented by) s which is required by (**6.13**) to exist is describable as B's intending (possibly conditional on something) to do Z.

Given (6) we may say that A may actually make B to Z if he in addition takes care that B carries out his intention (in (b)). This means seeing to it that the intention is or becomes non-conditional and that the necessary normal conditions (e.g., that B is not physically prevented) obtain. We shall not here try to specify exactly what is required for A's successfully exercising his control over B. Note, however, that its exercise need not necessarily be intentional on A's part - to guarantee that we would have to use purposive generation **IG*** instead of **IG** in the definiens. Also note that (6) is compatible with B's coming to have the intention to do X in a variety of ways. Thus we may have a case of activating an existing intention or commitment and a case of inducing a new intention or commitment (cf. Pörn (1977), pp. 70-73, for relevant discussion). Notice that (6) may of course be weakened to a probabilistic notion by requiring only probabilistic control over B in its clause (a). As in the case of (5'), such a probabilistic notion would better correspond to the practice of social scientists than the use of deterministic determination.

At this point it must be emphasized that what we have said in Chapter 4 and in this chapter about the concept of social control (a power notion) is in many respects incomplete. Indeed, it has not been our purpose at all to cover all (or most) the central notions or aspects of social power. Rather we have taken up some isolated, but central aspects of social power which serve our other purposes. Let us, however, here briefly mention some other views of social power.

Dahl (1957), analyzing an agent A's power to affect another agent B's behavior, distinguishes the following ingredients in the power relation:
(a) the **base** of power, i.e., the various informational (e.g., expert knowledge) and non-informational (e.g., wealth, prestige, skill) resources available to A for influencing B's behavior;
(b) the **means** of power, i.e., the specific actions (e.g.,

threats) by which A can exercise his power;
(c) the **scope** of power, i.e., the set of actions that A can get B to perform;
(d)   the **amount** of power, i.e., the net increase in the probability of B's performing some action X which is due to A's exercising his power to make B do X; and what we will call
(e)   the **extension** of A's power, i.e., the set of individuals over whom A has power.

As to Dahl's components of power, in fact our analysis can be seen either to account directly for them or at least to be easily extendable to cover them. As to (a), part of it is accounted for by our above (**IP**) and (5) together with what we said earlier in Chapter 4 about the (inner) basis properties of dispositions, such as action powers, and about the informational base of power (cf. our definitions (4.8) and (4.9)). That does not cover the agent-external non-informational resources of power, however. But I would rather count the latter type of base-resources as belonging either to the circumstances of acting or to a social theory explaining powers and thus not in any case to what is intimately connected with the concept of social power.

As to the means of power ((b)), our (5) existentially quantifies over such means-actions X. It is easy to see what the totality of these means-actions is (even if their concrete epistemic identification of course may be problematic). Our (**SI**) states rather exactly our counterpart to Dahl's concept of the scope of power ((c)). The probabilistic amount of power, corresponding to (d), was defined above. We shall not here further discuss Dahl's (e) which is a concept applying as such to our framework.

Harsanyi (1962) has extended Dahl's components of power to cover considerations of (opportunity) **cost** (also cf. Goldman (1972)):
(f)   the opportunity costs to A of attempting to influence B's actions;
(g)   the opportunity costs to B of refusing to do what A wants him to do.

Harsanyi (1962) considers the following example to show clearly the need of the element of cost:

"For instance, suppose that an army commander becomes a prisoner of enemy troops, who try to force him at gun point to give a radio order to his army units to withdraw from a certain area. He may very well have the power to give a contrary order, both in the sense of having physical ability to do so and in the sense of there being a very good chance of his order being actually obeyed by his army units - but he can use this power only at the cost of his life. Though the scope, the amount, and the extension of his power over his soldiers would still be very great, it would clearly be very misleading to call him a powerful individual in the same sense as before his capture." (Harsanyi (1962), pp. 165-166.)

But I refuse to accept this argument. Surely the commander in capture, still has his full power, even if it would be very costly to exercise it. That is, I maintain that we should not include the element of cost in the very concept of power, even if it is a highly important (factual) feature of the situations where power is exercised. Power and cost are separate concepts although they clearly are factually connected through the costs of power-exercise situations. I am willing to say that in the above example the commanders power to exercise his power has been seriously reduced. Yet I think that (f) and (g) are not intimately connected with the notion of (first-order) social power.

Of the above facts, (a)-(f) deal with the party (A) having and exercising power, whereas (g) is concerned with the party (B) influenced. Besides (g) there are many other relevant factors that belong to the so-called motive bases of power (cf. Cartwright and Zander (1968), pp. 224-227). Thus B may want to avoid punishment or to be liked or to fulfill his obligations and so on. These aspects, important as they are, do not belong narrowly to the concept of power either but rather to the explanation of how A succeeds in influencing B.

II. OVERT SOCIAL INTERACTION

1. Given our above developments, what are we to understand by **social interaction**? To answer that question, we note that corresponding to (5) and (6) we may define two new classes, K_5 and K_6, of actions. They are the classes of actions by which A (potentially) exercises his respective control. We note that $K_6 \subset K_5$ and, furthermore,

(7) (a) $K_6 \subset K_5 \subset K_4 \subset K_1 \subset K_2$
     (b) $K_3 \subset K_4 \subset K_1 \subset K_2$
     (c) not $K_5 \subset K_3$.

Corresponding to the mentioned classes K_1-K_6 we may now define several senses of interaction (for two agents, for simplicity) as follows:

(8) A and B interact$_1$ if and only if they act in relation to each other (for some action types X_A and X_B, respectively for A and B).

(9) A and B interact$_2$ if and only if their action tokens make reference to the other agent (in the case of some action types X_A and X_B, respectively, for A and B).

(10) A and B interact$_3$ if and only if they weakly affect each other and actualize it by means of some of their action tokens.

(11) A and B interact$_4$ if and only if they indirectly and weakly affect each other and actualize it by means of some of their action tokens.

(12) A and B interact$_5$ if and only if they have control over each other and exercise their control.

(13) A and B interact$_6$ if and only if they have intentional control over each other and exercise their control.

In (10)-(13) the notions of affecting and exercising one's control (power) entail producing one or **more** action tokens. Thus fairly complicated interaction episodes are allowed to take place. On the basis of (8)-(13) we immediately get, by defining $K_i^{AB} = K_i^A \cup K_i^B$, for i=1,...,6 with K_i^A and K_i^B standing respectively for A's and B's action classes:

(14) (a) $K_6^{AB} \subset K_5^{AB} \subset K_4^{AB} \subset K_1^{AB} \subset K_2^{AB}$

(b) $K_3^{AB} \subset K_4^{AB} \subset K_1^{AB} \subset K_2^{AB}$

(c) not $K_5^{AB} \subset K_3^{AB}$.

At this point it is useful to note one thing. As our (1)(a), used to define K_1^{AB} in part, concerns the case where A and B are co-agents, we might want to consider a subclass, say K_{1a}^{AB}, of K_1^{AB} defined in terms of co-agency. More precisely, we may define K_{1a}^{AB} to consist of all tokens of (simple or complex) social actions (in the sense of our definition (5.7) of a complex social action) where A and B are agents of the action token (they need not be the only agents, i.e. the number of agents m>2). In this way we get a clear connection with our previous discussion and, more importantly, with our systematic conceptual framework.[1]) (We may note in passing that n-person interaction with $n \leq m$ may of course be defined analogously.)

I shall not here try to choose any of the above concepts of interaction$_i$ as **the** concept of interaction. Anyhow, it must be pointed out that the first four concepts are rather general and do not at least capture **face-to-face** interaction. K_5^{AB} and K_6^{AB} are narrower and presumably closely related to what social psychologists mean by face-to-face interaction (cf. Duncan and Fiske (1977)). They do not, however, quite suffice to capture this notion. First, it seems that when two agents are in face-to-face interaction, each agent must somehow causally influence the other agent's acting. Neither (12) nor (13) guarantees that, for they do not require that the interaction takes place in the same (spatiotemporally closed) social situation. Let us assume that we understand clearly enough the notion of a social situation in which mutual action-determination can take place. This determination presumes at least sufficient spatiotemporal closeness. Accordingly, my suggestion is that we strengthen (12) and (13) as follows to cover face-to-face interaction in such a situation, say C, of face-to-face contact:

(15) A and B interact$_7$ if and only if they have control over each other and there is a face-to-face contact situation C such that they exercise this control in C.

(16) A and B interact$_8$ if and only if they have intentional control over each other and there is a face-to-face contact situation C such that they exercise this intentional control in C; or, alternatively,

(16') A and B interact$_8$ if and only if they interact$_7$ and the control they exercise with respect to each other is intentional.

An agent's exercising his control entails, of course, his realizing the dispositional elements in (5), viz., his power to do X; as a consequence an action token u will occur and partially or completely determine a token z by the other agent in this spatiotemporally confined face-to-face situation C (cf. (5)). An analogous remark of course holds for intentional control. In some special cases (15) and (16) can still be considerably strengthened. Thus in many cases A's action token u produces B's token z, viz., **IG**(u,z) and z in turn produces an action token u' by A, viz., **IG**(z,u'), and so on; cf. greeting, conversing, playing tennis, and various other turn-taking activities as examples. Our (15) and (16) do not as such require that the same token z by B be both a determined and a determining action.

Corresponding to our above interaction classes K_7^{AB} and K_6^{AB} we may now define new ones. Thus we define K_7^{AB} to be the union $K_7^A \cup K_7^B$ where K_7^A and K_7^B respectively stand for A's and B's classes of actions with respect to which they interact$_7$. (We would get hold of a still stronger class of face-to-face behaviors, if we in addition would require that **all** situations in which A and B exercise their control power according to (15) be situations of type C.) Analogously with K_7^{AB} we define K_8^{AB}. Now clearly

(17) $K_7^{AB} \subset K_5^{AB}$, and

(18) $K_8^{AB} \subset K_6^{AB}$.

2. Till now we have tried to find increasingly stronger notions of interaction. In a certain sense we have now arrived at requirements which are too strong. Consider the example of A's persuading B to vote in a certain way. Regarding this as an action token, we would presumably say that A and B interacted: A persuaded B to vote so and so and B voted so and so because of this. This suggests that instead of (15) and (16) we should (or at least might) use

(19) A and B interact$_9$ if and only if (at least) one of them has control over the other one and there is a face-to-face contact situation C such that he exercises this control in situation C; and

(20) A and B interact$_{10}$ if and only if (at least) one of them has intentional control over the other one and there is a face-to-face contact situation C such that he exercises this intentional control in situation C.

(19) and (20) obviously relate to (15) and (16), respectively, in the sense that they combine A's and B's influences **disjunctively** rather than **conjunctively**. It is clear that in the case of the corresponding interaction classes K_9^{AB} and K_{10}^{AB} we have

(21) $K_7^{AB} \subset K_9^{AB}$, and

(22) $K_8^{AB} \subset K_{10}^{AB}$.

Can we use the disjunctive combination mode in other cases as well? We can obviously weaken (12) and (13) analogously as they build on the notion of an agent's controlling another agent's

action by his action. But concerning interaction$_i$, i=1,...,4, we cannot plausibly use this method of weakening for they do not deal with influence (even if interaction$_4$ anyhow is concerned with both agents' action).

It seems that the disjunctive combination mode is important when more than two agents are involved in interaction. Thus, for instance, in a group of several agents, all agents seldom have mutual control, nor do they exercise it, in the sense required by our conjunctive mode of combination. We shall not here, however, delve into further problems of n-person-interaction. Our discussions in Chapter 6 of game-theoretic interaction are relevant here even if we have emphasized its decision-making and reasoning aspects rather than its behavioral control aspects. (We shall below in Section III return to these problems when discussing covert interaction.)

3. To make our abstract discussion somewhat better digestible we shall now consider an example illustrating interaction$_{10}$ in a situation of **communicative** control. We describe what happens in a "perlocutionary" communicative act where an agent B communicates with his audience A and convinces him of his belief concerning what A ought to do, viz. in effect his intention concerning A's acting, and makes A act on his newly acquired belief. Our (partial) technical explication for this case, involving a kind of "Gricean mechanism", can be stated as follows by means of our technical concepts of Chapters 5 and 6, the principle **(PG)** of Chapters 4 and 5, and the formalism for intending and believing of Tuomela (1977), Chapter 6 (cf. also Pörn (1977), p. 76).[2]

 (23) (Ex)(Ev) (x is an action token by B and v is an action token by B such that the result episode of v (model-theoretically) satisfies the statement
(Ey)B(A,(Ez)B(B, Ought((Eu)Verbs$_i$(A,B,u) / (Et)Verbs$_j$(B,A,t)),z),y) and By(v,x)).

 (24) (Ex)(Ev) (x is an action token by B and v is an action token by B such that the result episode of x satisfies the statement
(Ey)B(A,(Ez)B(B, Ought((Eu)Verbs$_i$(A,B,u) / (Et)Verbs$_j$(B,A,t)z)),y)
and the result episode of v satisfies the statement
(Ez)I(A,(Eu)Verbs$_i$(A,B,u) /(Et)Verbs$_j$(B,A,t),z) and By(v,x)).

(25) (Ex)(Ev) (x is an action token (of Verbing$_j$) by B and v is an action token by B such that the result episode of x satisfies the statement
(Ez)I(A,(Eu)Verbs$_i$(A,B,u) / (Et)Verbs$_j$(B,A,t),z)
and the result episode of v satisfies the statement
(Ez)I(A,(Eu)Verbs$_i$(A,B,u),z) and By(v,x)).

(26) (Ex)(Ev) (x is an action token by B and v is an action token by B such that the result of x satisfies the statement
(Ez)I(A,(Eu)Verbs$_i$(A,B,u),z)
and the result of v satisfies the statement
(Eu)Verbs$_i$(A,B,u) and By(v,x)).

Informally speaking, (23) says that agent B brings it about by an action token x of his that agent A comes to believe that B believes that A ought to Verb$_i$ given that he (B) Verbs$_j$. (24) says that B by his action token induces in A the conditional commitment (intention) to do what B believes he ought to do, viz. Verb$_i$. According to (25) B convinces A that he (A) ought to Verb$_i$ categorically. Finally, (26) says that B, by x, brings it about that A carries out his commitment and Verbs$_i$.

The By-relation in the above formulas is essentially that of (6.4), but let me here redefine it for our present purposes (using the terminology of Chapter 6):

(6.4') By(x,y) if and only if
(a) x=<v,...,b,...,r$_x$> and y=<v,...,b,...,r$_y$> are action tokens by the same agent;
(b) IG(r$_y$,r$_x$) (IG defined by (6.19)).

As examples of Verbing$_i$ and Verbing$_j$ we might, in some circumstances, take greeting: A greets B (=Verbing$_i$) and B greets A (=Verbing$_j$). Formula (23) now tells us that B makes A believe that B expects A to greet B given that B has greeted A. In (24) B brings it about that this belief of A changes into A's intending to greet B given that B has greeted him. In (25) B brings it about (by greeting A) that A comes to intend to greet B. In (26), finally, B brings it about that A carries out this intention of his. What we have in our example is greeting-interaction$_{10}$ between A and B. Let us note that in the case of proper communicative actions there are several relevant mutual beliefs of A and B involved. They are usually treated as more or less implicit underlying assumptions (cf. Bach and Harnish (1979) and our comments in Chapter 10).

III. COVERT SOCIAL INTERACTION

1. In the beginning of this chapter we distinguished between the overt (or behavioral) and the covert (or mental-explanatory) aspects of social interaction. These "dimensions", while logically independent, may yet be regarded as conceptually dependent. The dependence in question is exemplified by the dependence relation between the premises and the conclusion of a social practical inference, e.g., one instantiating our (SA_i).

So far we have discussed mainly the overt aspects of social interaction. Below we shall be concerned with some structural and "semi-motivational" components of social control (or types of influence, if you prefer) **underlying** each social interaction situation. In fact, these components of social interaction can be argued to be structural or situational determinants or at least conditions of any social action (multi-agent action) in our technical sense.

To fix our ideas, we shall take up some examples. We consider some payoff matrices in the case of two acting agents. For simplicity, we assume that we are concerned with games in the technical game-theoretic sense, although the utilities in the payoff matrix are not assumed to be connected to acting via the expected utility maximization principle (see our discussion in Chapter 2 and below). Our first matrix is the following 2×2 one:

(27)

	Y_1	Y_2
X_1	3 / 3	3 / 1
X_2	3 / 1	1 / 1

Here the row player (player 1) can be assumed to prefer choosing X_1 over X_2 as the former action dominates the latter. Similarly, the column player (player 2) prefers Y_1 over Y_2. We can say that in the present situation of social interaction each player has **absolute control over his own payoffs**. Thus, for instance, the row player gets 3 units by choosing X_1 and 1 unit by choosing X_2 quite independently of what the column player does. As we are assuming that also the players' non-social environment is cooperative, we can say that each player has complete external freedom in the present case.

We also have cases where each player has **absolute control over the other players' utilities**. Thus consider the following matrix:

(28)

	Y_1	Y_2
X_1	3 \ 3	3 \ 1
X_2	1 \ 3	1 \ 1

Here the row player has absolute control over the column player's utilities, viz. over whether the column player gets 3 or 1, and vice versa.

Cases of **conditional** (or **interactive**), rather than absolute, control can be exemplified by matrices such as the following:

(29)

	Y_1	Y_2
X_1	2 \ 3	2 \ 1
X_2	2 \ 1	2 \ 3

Here the row player has conditional control over his own payoffs in the sense that he is able to determine his own payoff only given the column player's choice. The row player can always gain 2 units by matching the column player's action. For the column player again each choice is a matter of personal indifference as long as he is not interested in the row player's outcomes. But, on the other hand, the column player has conditional control over the row player's payoffs in this situation. Given the row player's choice he is able to control the former's payoff (viz. 3 or 1). Thus (29) serves to illustrate both **conditional control over one's own payoffs** and **conditional control over the other's payoff**.

Why do we speak of covert rather than overt interaction here? It is because we are dealing with the agent's attitudes towards actions rather than with the actual (overt) actions themselves. Thus, specifically, we are concerned with the agents' **mutual** beliefs concerning the utility matrix. As we saw in Chapter 7, this involves that the agents have mutual beliefs concerning the action alternatives open to each of them and the respective utilities attached to (at least the outcomes of) their (joint) action. For our present purposes we may take the utilities to reflect the strengths of the agents' action-tendencies. Or they may be taken to represent the strengths of the agents' wants or pro-attitudes concerning the actions in question. We shall here bypass the problems related to the exact definition of the utilities (but see Chapters 2 and, especially, 12). We simply assume here the availability of (fixed) utilities on an interval scale, no matter how idealized that may seem. (In any case, our basic philosophical theses and results hold for ordinal utilities as well.)

It is often assumed that it is an analytic truth that agents maximize their (personal) utilities. We shall not accept that principle below (recall our comments in Chapter 2). Thus we assume that agents need not attempt to maximize their expected personal utilities but may, for instance, try to maximize the joint utilities of all the agents (players), or, say, to minimize the differences in utilities between them, and so on. We shall return to these motivational issues in Chapter 12.

Let us now go on to characterize the above forms or components of control somewhat more generally. What is the direct object of control here is the **joint** utility distribution of the agents, we may say. Thus we are dealing with the underlying motivational structure, viz. utility structure, but not directly with actual action. Hence we are not directly concerned with action control or with the control of the agents' decisions or intention formation. We are rather concerned with factors which may be regarded as relevant for the **explanation** of how the agents come to form intentions and act in one way rather than another.

While the interacting agents then jointly control the outcomes and utilities in each cell in our above matrices, they can also be seen to control each other and their own utilities. This is what our above examples in part served to illustrate. Thus, while our starting point is the players' joint utility distribution, we yet also come to investigate their individual marginal distributions. Generally speaking, an agent's control over (his own or other's) utilities is related to his ability to perform successfully various actions or to achieve various outcomes, with certain specific utilities associated with them. The scope or range of control is the variation in the set of utility values that an agent controls (or has access to).

I will now formulate some idealized definitions of the basic types of control, viz. an agent's absolute control over his own utilities, over another agent's utilities and, thirdly, his conditional or interactive control over his own utilities (and by the same token, of the other agent's utilities in that situation). My characterizations are deliberately idealized to represent "pure" control types, to parallel our (27), (28), and (29).

Corresponding to cases such as represented by (27), let us consider the following definition of what might be called "full" absolute control over one's own utilities. Our formulation (given "non-epistemically", without reference to the agents' mutual beliefs, for simplicity) concerns a case with only two interacting agents A and B, but it is easily generalizable. We assume that A (the row player) has r action alternatives (he is capable of performing) open to him while B (the column player) has c action alternatives open to him such that the joint utility distribution has been defined and fixed for the r×c matrix as illustrated by (27). Given this, we define a notion requiring full control over all the actions:

(30) A has **full absolute control over his own utility values** if and only if by performing any X_i, $i=1,\ldots,r$, A himself can uniquely determine the utility value, say $u^A(X_i)$, he gets from his action no matter which alternative B performs, and $u^A(X_i) \neq u^A(X_j)$ for some $j=1,\ldots,r$ such that $j \neq i$.

We assume in (30) that X_i is one of the r alternatives open to A. B must perform one of his own action alternatives, it is assumed, but the definiens of (30) tells us that A will get the same utility per row no matter which actions B performs. The term 'full' in (30) accordingly refers to the fact that B has no control over A's utilities in this case.

Furthermore, A's control over his own utilities is assumed to be differential in the following sense. Consider a two-choice situation such as that of (27). There $u^A(X_1)=3 > 1=u^A(X_2)$. We may say that X_1 is differentiated from X_2 by 2 utility units. It is also appropriate to say that the larger this difference is the larger is the range of A's absolute utility control over his space of action alternatives, viz. the set $\{X_1, X_2\}$. Accordingly, we have included in (30) a requirement concerning the differential range of A's control. Thus we can hardly say that he has full control over his alternatives unless he is able to differentiate between them. Given that this idea to include range considerations is acceptable, the definiens must explicitly concern the **variation** in the utility values associated with all of A's action alternatives. In the two-choice case (that (27) concerns) we have simply required that $u^A(X_1) > u^A(X_2)$ (and that these utilities not be affected by B's acting). In the more general case with r>2 we would require that there be variation among the row sums (or, technically speaking, among the average row sums adjusted by subtracting the general utility average from them; cf. (36*)). The more such variation there is, the larger is (the range of) A's control over his own utilities.

Let me now go on to an agent's control over another's utilities. Here I refer to the illustrative example (28). I propose the following idealized characterization for the two-person case, relative to a fixed scale of utilities:

(31) A has **full absolute control over** B's **utility values** if and only if A can uniquely determine the utility value B will get from his action no matter which alternative he (B) performs. Supposing B performs Y_j, $j=1,...,c$, it is, furthermore, assumed that $u^B(Y_j/X_i) \neq u^B(Y_j/X_k)$, for some $i, k=1,...,c$ ($k \neq i$), where $u^B(Y_j/X_i)$ represents the utility value for B due to his performing Y_j, conditional to the action X_i by A.

Note that underlying (31) there is the belief that A has control over B in the sense of our (5). We recall that (31) has been formulated non-epistemically only for reasons of convenience. We are really dealing with A's and B's mutual belief to the effect that the definiens of (31) is true. Thus, only if that mutual belief is true is the truth of (5) entailed. The phrase 'full' in (31) refers to the fact that A can in the game situation in question determine the utility B gets quite irrespectively of what B does. Note that both our (30) and (31) then are concerned with situations which seldom obtain in real life. But, as our (27) and (28) indicate, they are at least conceptually possible and also quite interesting.

Analogously with (30), we can say in the case of (31) that the larger the range of outcome values through which A can "move" B, the greater is his absolute control over B's utility values. Our requirement in (31) that $u^B(Y_j/X_i) \neq u^B(Y_j/X_k)$ relates to this (see our remarks connected to (30)). These forms of control ((30) and (31)) are in operation also in impure cases, viz. in cases where the other player's actions do make a difference (contrary to what is required in the case of **full** absolute control). Thus, we may say that the greater the variation in the row sums of B's utilities that A controls the greater is A's control over B here (cf. (36*)). Or, should we like to keep our interests in A's utilities, we can say that B's control over A's utilities can by the same token be measured by the variation in the column sums of A's utilities (cf. our (37*)).

(29) represents a case of (mutual) **conditional** (or **interac-**

tive) control. We recall that **absolute** control has to do with variation in row sums or column sums. Thus, concentrating on the row player A's utilities, the more variation there is in the row sums of his utilities, the greater is his absolute control over his own utilities. Similarly, the more variation there is in the column sums of A's utilities, the greater is B's (the column player's) absolute control over A's utilities. What conditional or interactive control now amounts to in these terms is the cell-specific interactive role, which cannot be seen from either the row sums or the column sums. This type of control is thus technically closely related to the notion of interaction in the sense of analysis of variance.

As can be seen from (29), there is no variation at all in the column player's (B's) utilities. As to the row player A, there is neither row variation nor column variation. Yet there is an interaction effect, as we saw. It makes a difference of 2 utility units for A to know which action B performs. We may view cases of conditional or interactive control from the point of view of controlling either one's own utilities or from that of controlling the other's utilities. These are, as it were, the two sides of one and the same coin.

Let us start with a person's conditional control over his own utilities. We define:

(32) A has **mere conditional** (or **interactive**) **control over his own utilities** if and only if
 (a) A has no absolute control over his own utilities; and
 (b) B has no absolute control over A's utilities, but
 (c) $u^A(X_i/Y_j) \neq u^A(X_k/Y_j)$, for some i, j, and k such that $i \neq k$, where $u^A(X_i/Y_j)$, $i=1,...,r$ and $j=1,...,c$, represents the utility for A for performing X_i, given that B performs Y_j.

Clauses (a) and (b) are understood to mean that, respectively, the row sums and the column sums of A's utilities have no variation. The only variation in A's utilities thus is due to the specific cell-interaction between A and B. Notice that it follows from (a), (b), and (c) for the two-choice case that if $u^A(X_1/Y_1) = u^A(X_2/Y_1)$ then $u^A(X_1/Y_2) \neq u^A(X_2/Y_2)$. We recall that the coordination games discussed in Chapter 7 represent a case where both A and B have symmetrically conditional control over their own utilities.

How about the conditional control over the other's utilities. Let us now call the row player in (29) B and the column player A. Then it is easily seen from the definiens of (32) that the following definition is adequate:

(33) A has **mere conditional** (or **interactive**) control over B's utilities if and only if B has mere conditional control over his own utilities (in the sense of (32)).

(33) is adequate because it shows that the column player by varying his behavior can motivate the row player to vary his behavior, motivation meaning a change in the row player's utility values. This change in utility values follows from the definiens of (32). For if the row sums are the same and the column sums are the same in the case of the row player's utilities, then, given (c) of (32), there are actions Y_j and Y_1 of the column player such that his switching from Y_j to Y_1 will entail that $u_A(X_i/Y_j) \neq u_A(X_i/Y_1)$ for some i. This can be easily seen in the two-choice case where switching from Y_1 to Y_2 clearly entails change in the respective conditional utilities of X_1 and X_2.

Since conditional control over one's own utilities and over the other's utilities are equivalent (although, of course, nonidentical) notions in the sense of (33), we can measure these types of control by one and the same measure. (Our (38) below will be used for that purpose.) It also follows that it suffices to speak of three forms of control with respect to any agent's utilities and even with respect to the joint utility of agents. Thus the agents are said to (have the ability to) produce the joint utility distribution or to have control over it because of (a) the agents' absolute control over their own utilities, (b) their absolute control over each other's utilities, and (c) their interactive or conditional control over each other's utilities. Let me once more emphasize that the above **pure** forms of these controls are rarely exemplified. In the general case we have to do with different **mixtures** of them, and to be able to deal with these we will have to do some technical work.

Before going to our technical treatment I would like to emphasize one more thing. From what was said above it follows that in situations of social interaction we are typically dealing with various mixtures of types of **mutual** control. Accordingly, it is possible not only to investigate the percentages of each form of control present but also the **correlation** between these types of control. Our basic idea is to study the **joint** utility distributions and account for variation in them in terms of the percentages of various types of control exhibited and also in terms of the correlation between the (forms of control) different agents exert upon each other.

That the mentioned three general types of control can be

distinguished in situations of social interaction has been noted, with varying degrees of explicitness and exactness, in the literature, (see, e.g., Thibaut and Kelley (1959) and, especially, Kelley and Thibaut (1978), and Wilson and Bixenstine (1962)). As will be seen below, our account will reveal some new aspects related to the mentioned correlation between different agents' control components and to the general theory of control concerning m agents (m>2).

2. Given our above definitions of the basic components of social control underlying all social interaction we shall proceed to a technical elucidation yielding indicators for them. The idea is simply to analyze the joint utilities of the players in terms of the mentioned control components. We will do this by hypothesizing that the joint utilities can be **linearly** decomposed. More specifically, we shall operate with an application of the linear model that **multivariate** analysis of variance is based on. Before going on let me point out that some kind of analogy with the analysis of variance has been noticed before in the literature. Thus Thibaut and Kelley (1959), (1978) and Wilson and Bixenstine (1962) point out this. However, these authors make the connection to ordinary univariate analysis only. Thus Kelley and Thibaut (1978), p. 50, say that their analysis of the three mentioned control components in two-person games amounts to making two separate analyses of variance, one for the row player (player 1) and the other for the column player (player 2). Our account instead emphasizes that the players' utilities must be treated jointly rather than isolated, otherwise important information is left out.

Our application of the multivariate linear model analyzes the agents' joint utilities in the two-person case in terms of the following formula (cf. Morrison (1967), p. 175):

(34) $u_{ijh} = \mu_h + \alpha_{ih} + \tau_{jh} + \eta_{ijh}$

where u_{ijh} is agent h's utility at the ith row and jth column of the utility matrix. (34) is restricted to the two-person case and thus h=1,2 (abbreviating A_1 and A_2). The indices i and j represent, respectively, each agent's action alternatives. (We shall later comment on the general m-person case.) Thus we are concerned with analyzing ordered pairs of utilities, one pair for each cell of the matrix. We assume that i=1,...,r and j=1,...,c and that thus the payoff matrix is an r×c matrix. μ_h is the average of utility score for agent h:

(35) $\mu_h = 1/rc \sum_{i=1}^{r} \sum_{j=1}^{c} u_{ijh}$

α_{ih} stands for the "row effect" (in 1's terms) and is defined as

(36) $\alpha_{ih} = \sum_{j=1}^{c} u_{ijh} - \mu_h.$

Similarly, τ_{jh} stands for the "column effect" and may be defined as

(37) $\tau_{jh} = \sum_{i=1}^{r} u_{ijh} - \mu_h.$

For some purposes we may instead want to employ the following commonly used normed indices

(36*) $\alpha_{ih} = 1/c \sum_{j=1}^{c} u_{ijh} - \mu_h$

(37*) $\tau_{jh} = 1/r \sum_{i=1}^{r} u_{ijh} - \mu_h.$

The factor $1/c$ in the definition (36*) of α_{ih} and $1/r$ in the definition (37*) of τ_{jh} serve the norming function of making $\sum_{i=1}^{r} \alpha_{ih} = 0$ and $\sum_{j=1}^{c} \tau_{jh} = 0$. Such norming may be helpful for the interpretation and use of these indices.

What α_{ih} amounts to is the difference between the average row score and the total average for h. Speaking in terms of the two-choice case, the (absolute) difference between α_{11} and α_{21} reflects the amount of control of player 1 has over his own utilities. The (absolute) difference between α_{12} and α_{22} mirrors the amount of absolute control of player 1 over player 2's utilities. Using (36*), as $\sum_{i=1}^{r} \alpha_{ih} = 0$, we need only compute the value of α_{ih} for i=1 when r=2. Thus the definition of α_{ih} is able to do what was said. When r>2 we need r-1 values to measure the control components in question.

Analogously, τ_{jh} amounts to the difference between the average column score and the total average for h. τ_{j1} thus represents the absolute control that the other agent has over player 1's utilities. Again, if we use (37*) we have $\sum_{j=1}^{c} \tau_{jh} = 0$.
Then, in the two-person two-choice case the difference between τ_{11} and τ_{21} represents player 2's absolute control over player 1's utilities. The difference between τ_{12} and τ_{22} represents player 2's control over his own utilities.

It remains for us to define n_{ijh} and we may do it simply by

(38) $\quad n_{ijh} = u_{ijh} - \alpha_{ih} - \tau_{jh} - \mu_h$.

This parameter technically represents the specific interaction effect at row i and column j in the case of player h's utilities. This interaction depends on what α_{ih} and τ_{jh} represent. Thus, for instance, when h=1, we are dealing with the specific interaction effect of player 1's control over his own utilities and the other's control over them. Technically speaking, n_{ijh} is defined here simply as the difference between the utility value (u_{ijh}) and the sum of the other two control components (α_{ih} and τ_{jh}) and the general average (μ_h).

n_{ijh} represents the **conditional** (or interactive) control that the players have over h's, h=1,2, utilities at levels i and j. The general condition here is that the players end up at the intersection of the ith row and the jth column. Thus the interaction effect is concerned with individual cells rather than only row sums or column sums over cells, and the conditionality in question is concerned with restrictions specifying a cell rather than a column or row only. Viewing the matter from a certain player's, say 1's, angle we may consider, e.g., n_{i11}. It measures the interaction effect concerning 1's utility values for 1's action i given that player 2 chooses the first action alternative. Similarly, e.g., n_{1j1} measures the interaction effect concerning 1's utilities for 1's first action given that player 2 chooses the jth action alternative.

Let us note that the linear model (34) can be regarded as a "nonstatistical" two-dimensional linear model. It is nonstatistical because there are no error terms related to sampling. It is two-dimensional as there are two acting persons (h=1,2). The value of h determines not only the number of dimensions but also the number of indices i and j running over action alternatives. For as long as we associate with each agent one set of alternatives there will be equally many dimensions in the action-option space as there are agents. In the language of the analysis of variance h will stand for the dimensionality of the utility distribution and it also makes the analysis of variance h-way. As is well known, linear mathematical models can be given illuminative and informative geometric interpretations. I will not here discuss these aspects, however.

How does the linear model for the three-person case look like? It can be written out as follows, in analogy with (34):

(39) $u_{ijkh} = \mu_h + \alpha_{ih} + \tau_{jh} + \gamma_{kh} + \eta_{ijh} + \varepsilon_{jkh} + \phi_{ikh} + \rho_{ijkh}.$

In (39) μ_h represents the average utility for h (h=1,2,3) as before. α_{i1} represents the ith element in the matrix for "row effects". It represents agent 1's absolute control over his own utilities at level i (i=1,...,r). α_{i2} and α_{i3}, respectively, give agent 1's absolute control over agent 2's and agent 3's utilities at level i. Analogously, τ_{j2} represents agent 2's absolute control over his own utilities while τ_{j1} and τ_{j3} stand for his absolute control over 1 and 3 at level j. γ_{k3} represents agent 3's absolute control over his own utilities at choice k, where k=1,...,d gives agent 3's range of action alternatives. γ_{k1} and γ_{k2} represent agent 3's absolute control over 1's and 2's utilities. Analogously with (34) η_{ijh}, ε_{jkh}, and ϕ_{ikh} represent the two-person interaction effects on h's (h=1,2,3) utility score due to the specific interaction between 1 and 2, 2 and 3, as well as 1 and 3, respectively. Note especially that the variable η_{ij3} can be used to measure the **joint** control of players 1 and 2 over player 3. Analogously, ϕ_{ik2} reflects 1's and 3's joint control over 2 and ε_{jk1} reflects 2's and 3's joint control over 1. Finally, ρ_{ijkh} stands for the (conditional) interaction effect on h's score due to the specific interaction of all the three agents.

It should be easy to see how the definitions (35)-(37) can be generalized for the present case and how the new interaction parameters can be analogously defined. I shall not go into more details here (cf. Tuomela (1982) on them). Let me finally remark that the general m-person case where m is any finite number can be handled analogously. The number of terms appearing in the analogous linear equation in the m-person case is given by the expression $1 + \sum_{n=1}^{m} \binom{m}{n}$. This expression tells us that we must consider in how many ways n-agent groups can be formed from a collection of m agents without paying attention to the order of the agents. The sum of what we get for varying n (n=1,...,m) gives us what we want, given the addition of the term for the general average μ_h.

Note that we may still speak of three forms of control even here if we abstract enough. Thus we are dealing with each agent's absolute control over his own utilities, his control over other agents' utilities (or, alternatively, the other agents' absolute control over his utilities), and his interactive or conditional control over his own and others' utilities. But if we want to make a fine-grained classification, we get many more types of control. Thus, for instance, in the case of 10 interacting agents we will have in our linear model $\sum_{n=1}^{10} \binom{10}{n} = 1023$ terms designating specific types of control. We shall here opt for speaking in terms of the former abstract classification, as that terminology fits the purported underlying ontology of types of forces better.

3. Given our general definitions (30)-(33) of the components of social control and given our formulas (35)-(38) (including (36*), (37*)) for measuring averages, row effects, column effects, and interaction effects, we still need to have measures for the **range** of control in the case of each of our components of social control. Recall that the rudiments of the range factor are built into our definitions (30)-(33). Now we would like to further and technically elucidate the range of control in terms of **variation**. Accordingly, we shall operate with the parameters $\mu, \alpha, \tau,$ and η in the two-person case. Specifically, we shall below regard the variables α_{i1}, τ_{j1}, and η_{ij1} as well as α_{i2}, τ_{j2}, and η_{ij2} as our components of social control.

In the case of an r×c matrix we may decompose the original matrix into four r×c matrices corresponding to the averages and the three components of control. Let us take an example. We consider the following matrix:

(40)

	Y_1	Y_2
X_1	4 \ 0	2 \ 1
X_2	4 \ 3	0 \ 2

On the basis of (35), (36*), (37*), (38), and our earlier comments on the interpretation of parameter values as representing components of control, we may decompose the matrix (40) as the following sum:

(41)

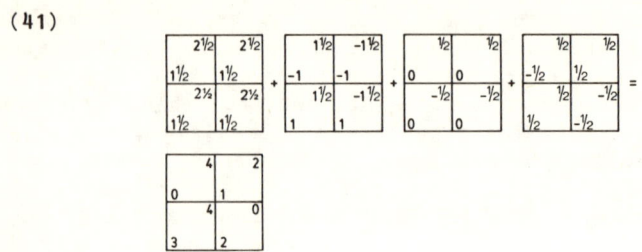

Here the first matrix in the sum is the matrix of averages, the second represents each agent's absolute control over his own utilities and the third each agent's absolute control over the other's utilities. Finally, the fourth element in the sum represents the conditional or interactive control that the other agent has over the agent whose utility component we are speaking of. We may now read from (41), considering only the row player's utilities, that his average is 1 1/2, that his absolute control over his own utilities has the range of 2 units in favor of X_2, that the column player has zero control over the row player's utilities, and that the range of the column player's conditional control over the row player is 1 unit (the range between 1/2 and -1/2) in favor of $<X_1,Y_2>$, $<X_2,Y_1>$ diagonal.

All the information our linear model (34) gives us for the present example is contained in (41). Yet, it may be claimed, to get a better overview we would profit from compressing the central pieces of information in terms of some scalar indices. My suggestion now is that we use the relevant utility variances to measure the variation and, hence, the range of the respective control components. Following out this proposal leads us to perform a non-statistical, m-dimensional (here two-dimensional), m-way (here two-way) analysis of variance. As multivariate analysis of variance is a standard technique to be found in most statistic books on multivariate methods, I will not here go much into details. I will, however, present concisely the basic formulas, as otherwise it will be hard to understand some of my later theoretical and philosophical claims.

Corresponding to the effects represented by α_{ih}, τ_{jh}, and η_{ijh} as well as to the total variation in the whole utility distribution in a given r×c matrix (we only consider the two-person two-dimensional case here) we will now have four matrices of sums. One will concern row effect variation. For that we define the following total sums (cf. Morrison (1967), p. 177):

$$(42) \quad R_{ih} = \sum_{j=1}^{c} u_{ijh}.$$

For columns we have correspondingly:

$$(43) \quad T_{jh} = \sum_{i=1}^{r} u_{ijh}.$$

We also need the following grand total sum:

$$(44) \quad G_h = \sum_{i=1}^{r} \sum_{j=1}^{c} u_{ijh}.$$

The sum of squares that our analysis needs can now be given in terms of three matrices, viz. H_1 (for row effects), H_2 (column effects), and T (total variation). The typical elements of these three matrices are, respectively, as follows, where the indices h and h' now correspond to the two agents such that h,h'=1,2, giving us four cells in each matrix:

$$(45) \quad h_{1hh'} = 1/c \sum_{i=1}^{r} R_{ih} R_{ih'} - 1/rc \, G_h G_{h'} \qquad (H_1)$$

$$(46) \quad h_{2hh'} = 1/r \sum_{j=1}^{c} T_{jh} T_{jh'} - 1/rc \, G_h G_{h'} \qquad (H_2)$$

$$(47) \quad t_{hh'} = \sum_{i=1}^{r} \sum_{j=1}^{c} u_{ijh} u_{ijh'} - 1/rc \, G_h G_{h'} \qquad (T)$$

Given the matrices H_1, H_2, and T, the matrix, say H_3, representing interactive effects (conditional control) is obtained in the obvious way by subtracting the sum of H_1 and H_2 from T:

$$(48) \quad H_3 = T - (H_1 + H_2).$$

I shall not discuss these matrices in detail here. Let us note that the degrees of freedom are r-1, c-1, and (r-1)(c-1), respectively, for H_1, H_2, and H_3. It follows that in the two-choice case these matrices amount to covariance matrices. What we need here can be seen from an example. Corresponding to the matrix (40) we get the following covariance matrices:

(49) $H_1 = \begin{bmatrix} 4 & -2 \\ -2 & 1 \end{bmatrix}$, $H_2 = \begin{bmatrix} 0 & 0 \\ 0 & 9 \end{bmatrix}$, $H_3 = \begin{bmatrix} 1 & 1 \\ 1 & 1 \end{bmatrix}$, $T = \begin{bmatrix} 5 & -1 \\ -1 & 11 \end{bmatrix}$

The figures in these matrices can be interpreted as follows. In H_1 4 and 1 represent, respectively, row variances related to row player's own and to the other's utilities. As noted before, this means that the range or strength of the row player's control over his own utilities is 4 (absolutely speaking) or 4/5 (= 80) in percentage of total variance in his utility distribution. The number 1 represents (the range of) the row player's absolute control over the column player. In percentages this amounts to 1/5 (=20). The number -2 in the remaining cells of H_1 represents the covariance between the row player's mentioned two types of control. This covariance is a measure of association between the respective components (α_{i1} and α_{i2}) of the two players' utility distributions.

In H_2, 0 and 9 mean, respectively, that the column player's control over the row player's utilities is zero (zero percent) and that it is noncorrelated (covariance zero) with his amount of absolute control over his own utilities, whose index is 9 (or 9/11 ≈ 82 in percents). Thus H_1 and H_2 represent, respectively, the total absolute control that player 1 and player 2 have at their disposal.

The upper left cell of H_3 gives the index 1 (20 percent) column player's conditional control over the row player and its lower right cell the value 1 (1/11 ≈ 9 percent) for the converse. These control forms are associated with the covariance value 1.

The total matrix T of course gives the total variances 5 and 11, respectively, for the row and the column player. The covariance -1 measures the overall correspondence between the two agents' utility distributions.[3]

4. Kelley and Thibaut (1978) have investigated at length the three basic components of control that we have been considering here. They measure these components separately for the two agents. In the two-choice case, to which they restrict themselves, their measures in our terminology amount to the suitably signed standard deviations of the distributions or row effects, column effects and of the marginal utility distribution. In terms of our above example we would have the following strengths of these components for the row player. His absolute control over his own outcomes is viewed from the point of view of the $\langle X_1, Y_1 \rangle$ cell and it thus gets a negative sign and becomes $-\sqrt{4}$ =

-2 ($= \alpha_{11} - \alpha_{21}$). His absolute control over the column player is positive from the point of view $\langle X_1, Y_1 \rangle$ and it becomes $+\sqrt{1} = +1$ ($= \alpha_{12} - \alpha_{22}$). Analogously, his conditional control becomes $+\sqrt{1} = +1$ ($= n_{111} - n_{211}$). Our analysis gives the same results no matter whether we compute the differences from our (40) or use the standard deviations signed on the basis of our (35), (36*), and (37*).

Although my above treatment has received much inspiration from Kelley's and Thibaut's excellent work, I have a couple of critical remarks against their technical implementation. First, the effects in question cannot be computed as differences in the cases where the agents have more than two action alternatives open to them. Kelley's and Thibaut's system needs modification for those more general cases, whereas our system has been designed to fit them right away. Secondly, Kelley and Thibaut treat the agents separately in the first place, while our account treats them as a unified whole right from the beginning. Later on these authors, however, in part connect the agents' utility distributions by means of an "index of correspondence" (see Kelley and Thibaut (1978), pp. 117-121). At this point an interesting connection between their and our system comes about. Let me briefly comment on it.

Kelley and Thibaut (1978) argue convincingly that the degree of overall correspondence between the agents' utility distribution is a central factor, e.g., when considering the conceptual nature of various problematic game situations and the agents' motivational aspects in them. For lack of space I cannot do better here than refer the reader to Kelley's and Thibaut's (1978) interesting analyses and discussions. Let me, however, take up their technical definition of the index of correspondence. On the basis of some criteria of adequacy they arrive at measuring correspondence in the two-person case in terms of the quotient

(50) $\quad IC = (\sigma^2_{sums} - \sigma^2_{diffs}) / (\sigma^2_{sums} + \sigma^2_{diffs})$

where σ^2_{sums} is the variance of the sums of 1's and 2's utilities in each cell and σ^2_{diffs} is, correspondingly, the variance of their differences. As Kelley and Thibaut (1978) show this index behaves as one should intuitively expect. Now it can be shown that IC is equivalent to the following index construed within our system (for the two-person case):

(51) $\quad corr_t^{12} = 2 \, cov_{t12} / (\sigma^2_{t1} + \sigma^2_{t2})$,

where $corr_t$ means total correspondence; cov_{t12} stands for the covariance between player 1's and player 2's utilities as obtained from the matrix T, and σ_{t1}^2, σ_{t2}^2 stand for the two agents' total variances as obtained from T. corr_t^{12} varies between -1 and +1. In our above example $\text{corr}_t^{12} = 2 \cdot (-1)/5+11 = -1/8$.

But our system contains handly information to account for the correspondence also with respect to the three components of control and not only for the total correspondence. Thus the index for H_1, viz. for the row player is

(52) $\text{corr}_r^{12} = 2 \text{ cov}_{r12} / (\sigma_{r1}^2 + \sigma_{r2}^2)$

where σ_{ri}^2 represents the row effect variance of player i and cov_{r12} the respective covariance. corr_r^{12} represents the degree of correspondence between the row player's control over his own utilities and over the other player's utilities. In the case of our example $\text{corr}_r^{12} = 2 \cdot (-2)/4+1 = -4/5$, which is rather close to its minimum ($-1 \leq \text{corr}_r^{12} \leq +1$).

Completely analogously we may define an index, corr_c^{12}, for the column player and an index, corr_{rc}^{12}, to account for the interactive correspondence between the two players. In the case of our example $\text{corr}_c^{12} = 2 \cdot 0/0+9 = 0$ and $\text{corr}_{rc}^{12} = 2 \cdot 1/1+1 = 1$. Note that one and the same value of corr_t^{12} is of course compatible with a great variety of value combinations of corr_r^{12}, corr_c^{12}, and corr_{rc}^{12} and that our new approach is informative particularly on this point.

There is another way of making the information on our matrices H_1, H_2, H_3, and T more conspicious. It is to compute the determinants of these matrices (or the corresponding covariance matrices, rather). Thus, for instance, the determinant of T equals the scalar $\sigma_{t1}^2 \sigma_{t2}^2 - \text{cov}_{t12}^2$, and so on. The determinant of a covariance matrix, often called a **generalized variance**, can be geometrically interpreted as the square of the area of a parallelogram (see, e.g., Green (1976), pp. 122-124). That area again may be regarded as corresponding to the range of an agent's control; thus in the case of H_1 and H_2 we are dealing, respectively, with row player's and column player's total absolute control over utility variation. The interesting point now is that, keeping the variances and thus lengths of the sides invariant, the covariance affects the area of the parallelogram. Roughly put, in the case of H_1 and H_2 we may say that the more the two components of control covary (positively or negatively), the smaller is the total control and variation exerted by the agent in question. In the case of H_3 great covariation between the agents of course means less independence. But, on the other hand, it also means more possibility for cooperation as the diagonal of the parallelogram now becomes longer. The length of the diagonal can be taken to reflect the amount of the agents' **joint** control. In general, the degree of correspondence of a game matrix can in a sense be measured also by using the notion of generalized variance, it seems. Thus, the greater the generalized variance is, the greater is the noncorrespondence.

Even the above scant remarks should suffice to indicate the importance of taking the covariation between control components into account. This has been built right into the heart of our account. Given all that, can the technical part of our system be regarded as completed in some sense? Not quite. While we wish to keep to our linear model and the accompanying measures for row effects, column effects, and interactive effects we want to compress that information into some convenient overall indices. The question we now must face is whether the matrices H_1, H_2, H_3, and T may serve to give such an overall account. The answer is negative. While these matrices account for many important factors, there is at least one general feature, which is of social psychological and conceptual interest, that they do not cover. Let me illustrate.

Consider the following matrix, which is closely related to our (40):

(53)

	5	1
1	0	
	3	1
2	3	

Completely parallel with (41) we may decompose this matrix as:

(54)

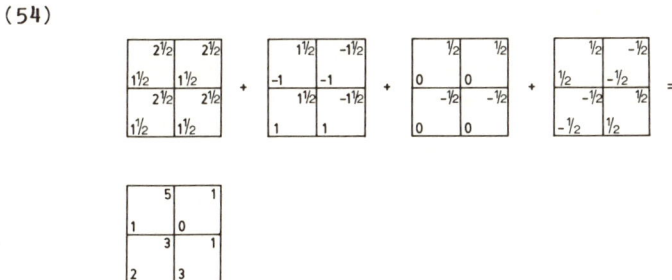

We notice that the first three matrices in this sum coincide with their counterparts in (41). The difference lies in the interaction matrices. They contain the same numbers but the diagonals have been reversed. The social psychological significance of this difference can be seen by considering the interaction matrix in relation to the second matrix in the sum concerning the agents' control over their own utilities. The row player prefers X_2 to X_1 and the column player prefers Y_1 to Y_2. But in the case of (53) these agents harmfully interfere with each other if they both choose their preferred actions. This is indicated by the interaction effect -1/2 (as contrasted with 1/2). In the case of (41) there, however, is concordance between preferred actions and selective interaction. This is indicated by the value 1/2 (as contrasted with -1/2). However, corresponding to both (41) and (54) we get exactly the same covariance matrices H_1, H_2, H_3, and T, viz. those in (49).

The importance of the above phenomenon has been emphasized by Kelley and Thibaut (1978). They speak of degrees of **concordance**. Such concordance may, secondly, be spoken of when comparing the interaction effect with the control of other's utilities, too. Thirdly, also an agent's control over his own utilities versus the other's control over his utilities may be considered in this perspective. As indicated, our linear model in itself does not, however, account for the concordance or disconcordance between the parameters α_i and η_{ij} nor between τ_j and η_{ij} (nor for any higher-order relations holding between different parameters). If such higher-order features are regarded as important they must be separately treated.

Let us now briefly consider the main types of concordance (cf. Kelley and Thibaut (1978), Chapter 3). The first type concerns the concordance between the agents' control over their own utilities and their corresponding conditional control over utilities. In the case of full concordance (in the two-person case) each prefers to perform the ("similar" or "dissimilar") action that produces coordination. (Here we technically define actions with the same subindex, e.g., X_1 and Y_1, to be "similar" if not the same.) The second type of concordance concerns the agents' control over the other's utilities and the corresponding conditional control: Each prefers the other to perform a certain action ("similar" or "dissimilar" to his action) and these corresponding actions produce coordination. Thirdly, we have the case of fully concordant control over one's own utilities and over the other's utilities: Each prefers to perform a certain action ("similar" or "dissimilar" to his) and this is the action the other prefers him to perform. (Incidentally, discordance in this situation seems to be a necessary condition for the occurrence of social exchange.) Note that the covariances in our matrices H_1 and H_2 can be regarded as measuring just this third type of concordance.

There is also a fourth type of concordance and it concerns conditional control. Thus, in the case of the agents' fully concordant conditional control there are corresponding actions ("similar" or not) which produce coordination and (typically) the other, noncorresponding actions harmfully interfere with each other (cf. coordination games). Note that, at the other extreme, a zero-sum game represents a maximally discordant case in this sense. Our matrix H_3 measures concordance or correspondence in this fourth sense by means of its covariance terms.

It is fairly easy to construe indices to account for the obtaining of the mentioned types of concordance in the two-person case. It can be done in terms of the relevant similarity or difference of the parameter values in question. I shall not here go into those details.[4] The upshot of our technical treatment now is the following, I claim. In the two-person case the matrices H_1, H_2, and H_3 together with the general average matrix and the indices for the three mentioned types of concordance in the case of both agents give us what we need in our study of the control aspects of social interaction. Let me emphasize once more that these control aspects relate to what the agents **can** do in a situation, viz. to the relevant situational limits and constraints primarily due to the presence of another actor, rather than to the effective motivational determinants of action.

The above approach can be extended to cover the case of any m>2 agents in principle. In terms of our linear model, we will be performing m-way analysis of variance on the agents' joint utility matrix. As a result we obtain $\sum_{n=1}^{m} \binom{m}{n}$ covariance matrices plus one matrix of averages. Our (39) above states the linear model in the three-person case, and some comments on it were already made above. One central new phenomenon at that level and at higher levels, as compared with the two-person case, is the possibility of some agents' **joint** control over another agent or agents.[5] Our account gives a neat explication of that. (For a discussion of the three-person case and the fully general m-person case, see Tuomela (1982).)

5. Let me now go to some related but more general comments. First, as Kelley and Thibaut (1978) have shown within their system (which formally is in fact a special restricted case or ours), the ratios of the three control components in a given matrix may greatly affect its social psychological nature. Thus, for instance, games such as the Prisoner's Dilemma game, Chicken, and so on may turn out to change motivationally when

the ratios of the different types of control and concordance relations are changed. Kelley and Thibaut also show that, for instance, social exchange, threat, turn-taking, and other relevant social psychological phenomena can be illustrated and analyzed interestingly in terms of these analysans concepts (see Chapter 12 below).

Utilities may in fact be regarded as quantified wants, and as wants in part are dispositions to act we may see a connection with the explanation of action in the context we have been discussing. More exactly, the situations of social interaction involve assumptions concerning the agents' metric wants (pro-attitudes) and their beliefs concerning how (by means of what actions) those wants can be satisfied. These assumptions are in fact mutual beliefs, resembling closely those we discussed in connection with our schemes (SA_i) and (PR_i) in Chapter 7. We may also say that we are dealing with such wants and beliefs as will appear in the social conduct plans we impute to the agents to explain their social actions. However, we should keep in mind that the control components and utilities discussed in this chapter are not yet intimately connected to intention-formation. Rather they are kinds of underlying dynamic explanatory factors (cf. Chapter 12).

Our above discussion of the components of control has given us some new ways of classifying joint action. Let us here still emphasize one more aspect, which relates to the cooperative versus competitive properties built into the interaction situation. In general, we can say that the participant agents' common interest (we-want in a cooperative sense) is represented by the sum of the agents' utilities (recall (2.2)(v), p. 49).

On the other hand, the difference between their utility scores measures the competition (and conflict, too) between them in that situation (recall (2.2)(vi) and (vii)). This difference is also closely related to an agent's threat potential (cf. the agents' threatening each other by the use of the non-cooperative strategy in Figure 7.3; also cf. Figure 12.2).

We may now ask to what extent each player controls the sum scores and the difference scores. We may thus technically put the question by asking what proportional of the variances σ^2_{sums} and σ^2_{diffs} each agent controls (recall (50)). It can be seen on the basis of our definitions (36*), (37*), and (38) that the following equations hold for the 2×2 two-agent case (cf. Kelley and Thibaut (1978), p. 126f.):

(55) $\sigma^2_{sums} = 1/4 \, [((\alpha_{11}-\alpha_{21})+(\alpha_{12}-\alpha_{22}))^2 + ((\tau_{12}-\tau_{22})+(\tau_{11}-\tau_{21}))^2 + ((\eta_{111}-\eta_{211})+(\eta_{112}-\eta_{212}))^2]$

(56) $\sigma^2_{diffs} = 1/4[((\alpha_{11}-\alpha_{21})-(\alpha_{12}-\alpha_{22}))^2 + ((\tau_{12}-\tau_{22})-(\tau_{11}-\tau_{21}))^2 + ((\eta_{111}-\eta_{211})-(\eta_{112}-\eta_{212}))^2]$.

The first component of the sums in each equation gives agent 1's control over the sum and the difference respectively. Similarly, the second component specifies agent 2's control and the third one the agents' joint control. Now we can distinguish the following four types of social action:
(a) **Differentially controlled action**: one agent controls the sum and the other one the difference.
(b) **Unilaterally controlled action**: one agent controls both the sum and the difference.
(c) **Jointly controlled action**: the two agents jointly control the sum and the difference.
(d) **Action with shared control**: each agent independently controls part of both the sum and the difference.
An example of (a) would be specified by the following utility assignment in a 2×2 matrix: $u_{111} = u_{121} = u_{212} = u_{122} = 4$, $u_{112} = u_{121} = 8$, the rest = 0. Here agent 1 may threaten to use his second action-alternative X_2 and thus force agent 2 to perform Y_2 at least sometimes. Thus the $<X_1,Y_2>$ combination may be regarded as an **imposed** joint action. An example of (b) is this: $u_{112} = u_{212} = 2$, $u_{121} = u_{221} = 4$, the rest equal 0. Next, case (c) can be illustrated by: $u_{122} = u_{222} = 3$, $u_{121} = u_{211} = 1$, the rest equal 0. (Also recall Figure 7.1.) Finally our prisoner's dilemma game in figure 7.3 exemplifies case (d). (See Kelley and Thibaut (1978), Chapter 5, for further relevant illustrations and comments.)

Let me note here that by including (d) in the above classification we make it exhaustive, or so I claim (in view of (5.5)). We may in fact formulate the idea underlying this claim directly in terms of the components of social control that we have been investigating. These components can at least sometimes be regarded as realistically representing underlying forces operating in any social acting (in our technical sense). We may think of these components along the lines of our (30)-(33) more or less irrespective of whether the linear model is strictly true of them. Given this, let us consider the following bluntly put thesis:

(C) In the case of every social action and every acting agent there are in causal operation - in varying degrees - three components of social control, viz. control over an agent's own wants (viz. utilities in our technical sense), control over other agents' wants, and conditional (or interactive) control between the agents' wants.

Is conjecture (C) acceptable? This of course depends somewhat on how the notion of social action in it is understood. We note that (C) cannot be true unless the agents are able to discriminate between various (or at least some central) action alternatives open to them and to other agents and between (at least some) resulting outcomes in a given situation. It is doubtful whether social action tokens$_1$ in the sense of (5.5), through their we-attitude components, are sufficiently rich in that respect. The same can be said of actions making reference to another agent (cf. (2) above and our class S_1 of social actions in Chapter 7). On the other hand, it is important to realize that for the mentioned control components to be causally operative, in the sense of causally disposing the agents to act in certain ways, full discrimination of the situation is by no means needed. (For instance, in a three-agent three-choice action, all the agents need not be able to discriminate between all the 27 outcomes at the moment of acting.) Thus the mutual beliefs concerning the payoff matrices we have been speaking about above need not be at least fully articulated.

But our social action tokens$_2$ in the sense of (5.8) might be conceptually and discriminatively sufficiently rich (because of relying on various notions of action type) to make it plausible to suggest that (C) holds true of them, and this is my suggestion, be the action tokens intentional or not. It is difficult to argue for or against this suggestion, as (C) seems to be partly a contingent thesis that social psychologists may empirically study (e.g., via testing the discussed linear model). On the other hand, it would seem that (C) must hold true of various classes of actions making reference to a rule that we discussed in Chapter 7. Thus, it may seem much like a conceptual truth that in the case of our S_{RU}, S_3, S_2, S_C and S_S, which classify various types of rule-referring actions, sufficiently much discrimination between action options (at least rule-conforming versus non-conforming actions) must occur.

I shall not discuss the applicability of (C) further here, as I think the notion of causal operation is rather vague and, more importantly, as I am inclined to regard (C) as a broadly factual hypothesis. Evidence for or against (C) may be obtained by means of empirical testing of the linear model (as suggested). So let me leave (C) with that and view the matter from another angle.

Notice first that, as I interpret (C), it can hold true of a social action where all the acting agents misconceive the situation in essentially the same way. But the components of control cannot causally operate if the agents make grossly incompatible errors of conception and discrimination about the situation (cf., e.g., interactive control in such a situation). Such non-systematically erroneous action can perhaps never be a social action token$_2$. Nevertheless, consider such an action. It is not true to say that while (C) is false of it, the agents could nevertheless have acted in that situation so as to make (C) true. Thus, by correcting their mistakes they would be able to acquire the appropriate wants and beliefs which suffice to make (C) true of their action. The question now becomes what 'could' here involves. Are typical human beings capable of correcting their mistakes to a sufficient extent. I shall not discuss this problem here. My point is basically just that even if (C) is not true of a given social action u, there is nevertheless "somewhere in the neighborhood" of u another (nonrealized) action token$_2$ u' of which (C) is true.

To conclude our treatment of covert interdependence patterns in terms of control components we can say that four major properties or factors in such patterns can be discerned. First, there is the factor of **mutuality of dependence**, viz. whether the dependence is mutual or unilateral. Secondly, there is the factor of the **degree of dependence** (irrespective of its kind). Thirdly, there is the aspect of the **degree of correspondence** of the utilities of the participating agents. The fourth factor is the **basis of dependence**, viz. to what degree absolute control over other utilities and to what degree conditional control over them is concerned. All of these aspects were discussed above, to varying extents.

6. In this chapter we have been discussing two different aspects or "dimensions" of interaction, viz. the overt (or behavioral) and covert (or explanatory) dimension. In section II we defined several interaction classes K_i^{AB}, i=1,...,10, which all deal with the overt aspects of interaction. After having discussed at lenght certain covert aspects of interaction, viz. the control components involved in interaction, I will make some general comments relating the present section to our earlier general discussion of social interaction.

Following our line of development in Section I, we might of course define corresponding covert notions of acting in social relation to another agent. While I will not do it explicitly here, it is still useful to consider one example. Corresponding to (1), viz. acting in relation to another agent, we thus consider the following explanatory notion:

(57) An action token u of type X by A **makes opaque reference** to B if and only if the best (social) psychological explanation of u contains non-vacuous reference to B.[6]

A social psychological explanation of an action token is (at least typically) assumed to give the agent A's **reasons** (and thus justification) for his performing u. This will often involve stating some group goal that A shares with B and/or a social belief concerning B's expectations (cf. schemas (SA_i) and (PR_i) of Chapter 7). Another, related possibility is to speak of the utility **rewards** (or profits and, perhaps, punishments, too) that A and B (or at least one of them) expect to result from their interaction. Thus, for instance, A might act on a practical reasoning according to which he should do something because it is in some sense rewarding to him; and the same goes for B. Here the explanans (explaining the agents' practical reasonings and the resulting actions) might rely on some principles of reinforcement. An example of such a theory is Homans' (1964) exchange theory.[7] There are other exchange theories which also ultimately rely on mutual profit making and, often, control in the interaction process. (This holds even when emotions, e.g., hate or love, are referred to as primary explanantia.) Not surprisingly, Kelley's and Thibaut's (1959), (1978) theory can be and has been regarded as an exchange theory, when viewed as an explanatory theory. The exchange conditions can be stated in terms of the relation between an agent's control over his utilities versus another's control over his utilities (see Kelley and Thibaut (1978), pp. 68, 104).

These remarks indicate that our lengthy discussion of control components is very pertinent here, for they are explanatory entities (whether or not one wants to build an exchange theory out of them). Thus we may think of A's performing X_1 as our explanandum action. Here no reference to B is made. But if A's performing X_1 occurs in a game-like situation, such as those we have been considering in this section, obviously a reference to B will have to be made in the best explanation of A's action (see Chapter 12).

Since we do not have to describe A's performing X_1 by reference to B before we explain it, we see that (57) neither strictly logically entails nor is entailed by (1)-(10), even if there may be otherwise intimate connections.

We may now define an explanatory concept of interaction on the basis of (57):

(58) A and B interact^1 if and only if their action tokens make opaque reference to the other agent (in the case of some action types X_A and X_B, respectively, for A and B).

The corresponding interaction class, call it K_{AB}^1, is independent (viz. it does not contain nor is contained by) any of the classes K_i^{AB}, i=1,...,10. K_{AB}^1 defines a very broad class of interactive behaviors. If our (C) is accepted as true for the class of all social action tokens$_2$ the following thesis is plausible:

(59) A and B interact if and only if A and B are co-agents of some social action token$_2$.

(59) is made plausible by (C) and by our assumption that the mentioned control components indeed are explanatory entities.

In Chapter 7 we defined several classes of actions, viz. those called S_2, S_2^*, S_3, S_3^*, S_C, S_S, S_{RE}, and S_{RU}, using the explanatory (or, rather, justificatory) dimension. Correspondingly we could define explanatory (and justificatory) concepts of interaction in terms of them analogously with (59). (The mentioned classes would all give us a stronger notion of interaction than (59).)

If we now combine (for instance, disjunctively or conjunctively) the behavioral and the explanatory "dimensions" of interaction we get more comprehensive notions of interaction. Consider, for instance, the following combination:

(60) A and B interact$_1^1$ if and only if they interact$_1$ or they interact^1.

According to (60) both interaction$_1$ and interaction^1 are sufficient, but neither is necessary, for the defined, fuller concept of interaction.

Other interaction concepts analogous to interaction$_1^1$ can be defined on the basis of our concepts of interaction$_i$, i=1,...,10, by similarly combining them with suitable explanatory interaction concepts. (Cf. especially the overt notions of interaction based on the control concepts, viz. (12), (13), (16), and (20) and covert notions of interaction definable on the basis of (30)-(33).)

What I have said in this chapter about the existence of two distinct "dimensions", viz. the behavioral and the explanatory dimension, of interaction should be taken **cum grano salis**. For this distinction is relative to the context of theorizing, especially to how explanations of interaction are given. If we, for instance, consider our earlier example about communicative control exhibiting interaction$_{10}$, we notice that it could also be analysed from the point of view of the explanatory dimension. For one may view the mental factors appearing in (23)-(26) as explanatory and perhaps even claim that this is so because all mental states and episodes are postulated to function as explanatory ones. Especially, one may regard the Gricean loop mechanism involved essentially in this example to play an important explanatory role. To be sure, our concepts of interaction$_8$ and interaction$_{10}$ involve reference to mental factors and are therefore somewhat special in comparison with the other interaction concepts dealt with above. It can still be maintained that a distinction between the behavioral and the explanatory dimensions can usefully be made, even if it is relative to pragmatic context and the purposes of inquiry (cf. our pragmatic treatment of explanation in Chapter 10).

What we have mostly been doing in this chapter has been to define various concepts of social relatedness, influence, and control which then were used to isolate various notions of social interaction in terms of explicit definitions (or, if you like, by stating sufficient and necessary conditions for interaction). This type of endeavour is somewhat limited, for it presupposes that such definientia (or analysantia) can be given. However, the "Golden Rule of Philosophizing" says: Never try to give necessary and sufficient conditions for anything (or if you do, be sure to make your analysis circular). This half-joke may contain a half-truth, even if we are not now analyzing a central philosophical concept but rather an important social concept. I will not here indulge in the self-defeating activity of trying to refute the enterprise of this chapter but leave that to my critics.

Let me, however, here mention another way of approaching the concept of interaction. This is the postulational method: Connect the concept of interaction with other central social concepts by means of some postulates regarded as constitutive for interaction! This is in fact what I recommended in Chapter 2 above (also cf. the constitutive theory about wanting constructed in Tuomela (1977), Chapter 4). What we get is a theory which has some factual import (over and above its containing more or less conceptual truths; cf. Tuomela (1977), p. 79). In fact our linear theory of the components of social control can also be regarded as a (perhaps modest) application of the postulational method.

This postulational method in fact more or less amounts to what such social theorists as Homans and Blau, for example, have been doing (cf. Homans (1950), Turner (1977)). While this method can undoubtedly be fruitfully used to complement our earlier analysis of social interaction, we must admit that at the present stage no very satisfactory specific postulational accounts exist. This, I think, is mainly due to the lack of informative substantive social theories of interaction (see, e.g., Turner (1977) for relevant discussion).

CHAPTER 10

A PRAGMATIC THEORY OF EXPLANATION

I. EXPLAINING AS COMMUNICATIVE ACTION

1. Scientific explanations can be approached from the point of view of querying and answering. Thus they can be viewed as social actions with a questioner (the explainee) and an answer-giver (the explainer) as its agents. This social action takes place in a certain scientific social context, as we shall soon see. Our aims below are twofold. First, we shall sketch a pragmatic theory of explanation which we shall later, especially in Chapter 11, use to account for the explanation of social actions, to which it seems to be well suited. Secondly, as a by-product, as it were, we obtain an account of the social action of explaining to illustrate our theory of social action and to complement our previously presented examples of actions. Thus, while a presentation of a theory of scientific explanation may be felt to be somewhat out of place here, we think that the mentioned two reasons do justify our brief excursion to the field of the theory of explanation.

What we shall do below is to sketch a **pragmatic nomological theory of scientific explanation,** which covers both deductive and inductive (or non-deductive), strict and approximate explanations, as well as the explanation of both singular events (or facts) and general laws. This theory of explanation is pragmatic in the sense that it focuses explicitly on the acts (or actions, if you like) of querying and explaining performed by scientists assumed to belong to a scientific community and to share a certain (Kuhnian) paradigm (a constellation of group commitments). We may also say that this theory embeds a deductive-nomological account of explanation in a pragmatic context.

An explanatory situation, in our analysis, will include a questioner (or explainee), and answer-giver (or explainer), a question statement, and an answer statement. The questioner queries, by means of an utterance or some other suitable linguistic token (not necessarily verbal), why (or how, when, etc.) something is (or was) the case. This token will be construed as the question sentence in our sense by translating it into its logical form. Similarly the explainer offers an explanatory answer by producing a linguistic token which we paraphrase by translating it, too, into its logical form. We therefore assume that all this can be done (although, of course, it is not unproblematic).

If we think of scientific querying and answering in general, it becomes obvious that both questions and answers depend on the paradigmatic background assumptions the explainer and the explainee share and also upon the singular pragmatic situation (context) in which these illocutionary acts of querying and explaining occur. We shall return to this problem.

Speaking in general terms, what is central to scientific (and other) explanations is that they convey **understanding** concerning why (or how, when, etc.) something is (or was) the case. Indeed, it is a conceptual truth that acts of explaining are attempts to produce such relevant understanding. Such an act, however, need not always be successful in this sense as far as the explainee is concerned. Yet we must say that an explanation **ought to** convey understanding, according to the standards of the paradigm in question, and that, indeed, it does convey understanding to some suitable (possible or actual) explainee, relative to the epistemic state in which he did not yet have that understanding. (It suffices to **pretend**, i.e., assume hypothetically, that the explainee be in such a prior state of ignorance.)

Viewed as a social action, explaining is here treated as a two-agent communicative illocutionary action of querying and answering where B's component action consists of his putting a query (to A) and A's component action consists of his producing an explanatory answer to B with the ("illocutionary") intention of making B understand why the queried matter was the case. Our later analysis can in part be viewed as an attempt to make precise what is involved in this special social action of querying and answering (see especially Subsection 7 below).

Suppose now that somebody B asks why something is the case, e.g., why water boils àt 100 C^o. We denote the logical form of that **oratio obliqua** form question by q. This logical form consists of a descriptive (declarative) sentence, say p, to which a (so-called single-example) why-question operator, say ?, may be attached to form a question, ?p (cf. Belnap and Steel (1976), p. 86). For the present purposes it is unimportant whether p is a statement in first-order or second-order predicate logic (or something else). Furthermore, we will normally assume below that q is the **complete** why-question associated with B's query (or at least that ?p is the logical form of a complete why-question related to our underlying q). We shall later clarify the notion of a complete question.

An explainer A produces a suitable linguistic statement-token u, having a certain logical form, to answer q. By producing u he intends to make B understand q (scientifically). Naturally, the producing of u should bring about B's understanding **in the intended way**, for this blocks the so-called wayward generative chains (discussed by, e.g., Goldman (1970), pp. 60-63; also cf. Tuomela (1977), pp. 255-258, and above Chapters 3 and 4). Thus the phrase 'in the intended way' (analyzed, in part, e.g., by means of the concept of purposive generation (**IG***) of Tuomela (1977)), discussed above in Chapters 4 and 6, is meant to prohibit B's understanding q, provided he lacked this understanding prior to the production of u, as resulting from some deviation from A's intention or "plan".

Accordingly, A's intention in this situation is the Gricean one that his producing u, regarded **as an answer** to q, will "naturally" generate B's coming to understand q and that it will do it so that B becomes aware of this intention. Thus also B's awareness of A's producing u becomes (part of) his reason for his coming to believe that u is a (scientific) explanatory answer to q and that A intends B to come to believe so. (Cf. Bach and Harnish (1979) and below notes 3 and 7 on this kind of "illocutionary" intentions; also recall our discussion of communication and the Gricean mechanism in Chapter 9 and of willing in Chapter 4.)

2. Let us now denote the concrete querying-explaining situation by C and let us use P to represent the fact that A and B belong to a scientific community sharing a certain paradigm (which we will also call P).[1] We then propose the following general analysis of potential (partial or complete) explaining:

(1) A **scientifically explains** q to B by producing a linguistic token u in situation C, given P, if and only if
(a) A has a belief to the effect that u is (or represents) a scientific explanatory answer to q in C, given P; and
(b) A produces u with the intention to the effect that this producing u will bring it about, in the intended way, that B, based on (a) and (b), scientifically understands q (in C, given P) and that it will do so (in part) by generating, in the intended way, B's belief, based on (a) and (b), that u is (or represents) a scientific explanatory answer to q (in C, given P).

Generally speaking, (1) accounts for all that A is doing and needs to do for his explanatory message to "get through" to

B (even if B's coming to understand q is not required). Note that the phrase 'to the effect' is used in the analysans as it is not reasonable to require that A has such technical concepts as that of a scientific explanatory answer. In (1) there are several key notions in need of further clarification and we shall indeed devote most of this chapter to that.[2] First, notice that as u may only "represent" a scientific explanatory answer, (1) reflects the possibility of having stronger and weaker (context and paradigm dependent) scientific explanatory answers (cf. our (8) and (9) and the discussion preceding them). Thus, u might, e.g., be or represent a complete (and strongest) scientific explanatory answer (cf. (8)). Secondly, sometimes even a pointing with a finger (which is something non-verbal but still broadly linguistic) may be used as a u (note 'represents'). Then, although u itself need not be a scientific explanatory answer to q, B may take it for an "abbreviation" of such an answer.

In view of (1) we may ask what explaining amounts to when viewed as a speech act in the sense of linguistic theory? While some central features have already been brought up let us now go somewhat deeper. First we note that explaining can be regarded as a communicative illocutionary act. This is true at least when explaining as approached from the point of view of querying and answering, for these undoubtedly are communicative illocutionary acts (cf. Bach and Harnish (1979), esp. p. 43).

Let us now briefly look at the components of a speech act. We let A be the speaker (explainer in our example case), B the hearer (explainee), u an expression of a language and C the context of utterance. Now the main constituents of A's speech act can be taken to be an utterance act, a locutionary act, an illocutionary act and a perlocutionary act (cf., e.g., Searle (1969) and Bach and Harnish (1979) for elucidation of this Austinian classification). The utterance act consists in A's uttering u to B in C. The locutionary act consists in A's thereby (in a literal semantic sense) saying to B in C that so-and-so. The illocutionary act has as its content A's thereby doing such-and-such. The perlocutionary act consists in A's consequently affecting B in a specific way.

Relating this to (1), with q = Why did this piece of copper expand?, we can see that A's production of u, given that it is verbal, is just the utterance act. The locutionary act consists of A's saying by means of u to B something, e.g., that this piece of copper was heated and that copper expands when heated. The illocutionary act in question is that of A's (scientifically) explaining, viz. (scientifically) answering B's question q. This answering consists in A's expressing in an intended way

(i) his belief that u is or represents an appropriate scientific explanatory answer to q and (ii) his intention that B comes to believe this because of (i) and in this sense to understand q. The intended way in question here involves A's reflexively intending that B takes A's uttering u as part of his reason for his thinking that A has the mentioned belief and does so as intended by A. The reflexivity here thus involves the loop discussed earlier: A intends that B becomes aware of his intention (and belief) in question. This "self-involving" intention by A may be called an illocutionary intention. Over and above its reflexivity it has the peculiar feature that its fulfillment consists in its recognition (by B).[3]

In the context of (1) several perlocutionary acts may be involved. For instance, A may indeed succeed in bringing about that B scientifically understands q, even if this success condition has not been built into (1), as we regard explaining merely as an illocutionary act of the explicated kind.

At this point we may notice that (1) seemingly requires nothing on B's part. But that is not at all true. For, first, there is the presumption that B has queried q. Next, there are various underlying mutual beliefs which any illocutionary act presupposes. We have not made these mutual beliefs explicit in (1). This is because they underlie **any** illocutionary act. Following Bach and Harnish (1979), pp. 5-12, we may formulate four different assumptions about them. First, there is the assumption that the speaker and hearer have mutual beliefs concerning the salient features of the situation or context C. This will help, for instance, the hearer B to disambiguate utterances by A such as 'I went to the bank' by enabling him to recognize what A intended to say. Next we have the general mutual belief that the members of the linguistic community to which A and B belong share the language, say L, to which our above token u belongs and that whenever any member of that community utters any token v to any other member, then the latter can identify what the former is saying, given that the latter knows the meaning of v in L and is aware of the appropriate background information. We also assume, thirdly, that it is a mutual belief in this speech community that whenever a member says something in L to another member he is doing so with some recognizable illocutionary intention (cf. note 3). In the context of **literal** illocutionary acts, such as we must take scientific explaining to be, we still need a further, fourth assumption. It requires that it is a mutual belief in the speech community in question that whenever a member utters any token v in L to any other member then the former is speaking literally, given that he could be speaking literally in those circumstances. We shall not here discuss these four mutual beliefs further as our treatment of explanation does not specifically hang on them, and we may, accordingly, end our brief excursion to speech act theory here.

The underlying mutual beliefs just mentioned do not yet suffice to make the notion of explanation characterized by (1) epistemic in the same sense as we have been speaking about epistemic social concepts in the previous chapters. To get such a notion we would have to add the following clause to (1):

(c) A and B have a mutual belief to the effect that (a) and (b).

But (c) seems rather strong for our purposes for we do not want to build a success condition concerning B's acquisition of the belief spoken about in (b) into our notion of explaining. To be sure (c) does not as such guarantee B's coming to believe so. Yet it comes close to it and involves B's mental states in a way we do not want to assume in general. Thus our official account will not include (c). (An analogous remark can be made concerning our notion of querying, defined by (10).)

3. Our characterization (1) involves the key notion of scientific explanatory answer (se-answer for short) which we shall next clarify.

We shall start our investigation by a characterization of the notion of a presupposition of a wh-question (why-, what-, which-, etc. question). First we characterize ordinary linguistic presuppositions (say, presuppositions$_1$) truth-conditionally following Belnap and Steel (1976), p. 5:

(2) A declarative sentence s is a **presupposition**$_1$ of a question sentence if and only if the truth of s is a logically necessary condition of the question sentence's having some true answer.

This characterization is intuitively clear, although a definition of answer based on it would of course be circular. We shall later (cf. (8)) see that (2) can be approximated in a way which does not so tightly depend on the (presystematic) concept of answer. In (2) 'logical' must be taken broadly to refer to conceptual truths over and above ordinary logical truths. As an illustration of (2), we see that presuppositions$_1$ of 'Why did Tom stop beating his wife?' are, e.g., 'Tom has a wife', 'Tom beat his wife', 'Tom beat his wife more than once', 'Tom stopped beating his wife'. Next we define:

(3)   A declarative sentence s is a **complete presupposition**$_1$ of a question sentence if and only if s entails and is entailed by the totality of all the presuppositions$_1$ of that sentence.

As earlier, we will here assume the availability of a well-defined formal language to which suitable wh-question operators (as well as epistemic operators) have been added. Otherwise our above definitions and those to be given below would lack clear meaning. Notice that a complete presupposition$_1$ of 'Why did Tom stop beating his wife?' is given by (the logical form of) 'Tom stopped beating his wife for some reason'.

Our theory of scientific explanation needs an even stronger notion of presupposition - one that goes beyond what linguistic and erotetic logic use (or have used so far). This notion is related to the underlying beliefs and values of a scientific community and is hard to characterize in exact terms. Yet this pragmatic notion of presupposition can be given a short description, viz. it covers whatever a context C and paradigm P require of the question-sentence's having a true answer. Our later treatment of the problem of emphasis gives examples of how a context C restricts the notion of answerhood by putting restrictions on the so-called relevance classes, for instance. A paradigm P may restrict, e.g., the type of "reason" allowed as answering a why-question such as 'Why did Tom stop beating his wife?'. For instance, a neo-Wittgensteinian would not admit mental causes to be cited as agent-reasons here (cf. Section III). As to the physical sciences, instrumentalistic paradigms exclude, e.g., microstructures and atomistic entities from the use in the explanation of the observable behavior of physical objects and systems. Let us thus define:

(4)   A declarative sentence s is a **presupposition**$_2$ of a question sentence relative to C and P if and only if
(a) s is a presupposition$_1$ of that sentence; and
(b) the truth of s is a necessary condition for that question sentence's having a true answer relative to the context C and to the sentences entailed (or required to be true) by the paradigm P.

The notion of a complete presupposition$_2$ is defined in strict analogy with (3).

4. We shall now proceed to a characterization of the concept of answerhood. As is seen from (2), there seems to be an inescapable conceptual dependence between the concepts of presuppo-

sition and answer, semantically understood. Yet, from a logical or formal point of view, they are clearly distinct notions. Let us consider a wh-question. We will normally assume below that it is a wh-question of the standard logical form ?p, where p is a well-formed declarative statement. We may say generally that a (single-example) question-operator introduces a variable into the complete presupposition of the question statement. For instance, if we ask 'Who is that man?', we introduce a variable ranging over persons. If we ask

(5)   Why did Tom stop beating his wife?

we introduce a variable ranging over reasons (in a broad sense not restricted to the agent's reasons).[4] We can thus write the complete presupposition of the last mentioned question in semi-formal notation as:

(6)   (Ef) Tom stopped beating his wife for the reason f; or

(7)   (Ep) Tom stopped beating his wife because p.

In (6) we have a variable f ranging over or, at least, expressing reasons in a broad sense, especially including causes. In (7) the variable p ranges over sentences (or logical forms, were we to employ a fully formalized discourse). We will regard (6) and (7) as equivalent from the point of view of querying and answering. We shall below be mainly concerned with why-questions and only with those having statements of kind (6) or (7) as their complete presuppositions.

In general, a presupposition$_i$, i=1,2, will syntactically have the form $(Ef_1)...(Ef_n) s(f_1,...,f_n)$ where s is a declarative sentence-form (matrix) containing the variables f_j, j = 1,...,n, corresponding to the factors the question admits as included in an answer. As said, we shall concentrate on questions introducing only one factor f into their complete presuppositions, which will thus have the form (Ef)s(f). Presently, it is not necessary to put any logical restrictions on the constants syntactically replacing f. They may be sentences, individual constants, predicate constants, and so on.

There is yet a broader issue that must be mentioned in connection with the logical form of presuppositions. This is that the background assumptions of a paradigm P may impose a certain form on the original question and especially on its complete presupposition$_2$. Thus changing the paradigm not only changes the set of values of f but may fundamentally change the whole nature and form of the complete presupposition. We shall at the end of the chapter discuss a psychological example relevant to this issue, but we have nothing approximating a general theory of "paradigmatic paraphrasing" of questions and presuppositions to offer. In any case, it must be kept in mind that such paraphrasing to conform to a P-pattern, as we may call it, is generally required in scientific contexts.

Let us now consider answerhood. We may answer (5) by saying 'Tom stopped beating his wife for the reason (that)__', where the blank is filled by such sentences as 'he got bored by it', 'he came to his senses', and so on. These do not need to be scientific explanatory answers, of course. For that more has to be required.

If we let f_o be a value of the variable f in $(Ef)s(f)$ then $s(f_o)$ will be an se-answer only if it is understandable to the explainee. The understanding concerned here is (scientific) understanding according to the standards of the paradigm P. As a matter of fact, any member of the scientific community sharing P could be our explainee, and therefore we will only abstractly speak of P-understandability in our characterization. Note that we need not require that an se-answer convey understanding concerning q, although an explanation (employing that answer) is **intended** to do so (cf. (1)).

While we shall say more about understanding later, a few remarks are appropriate here. Consider the following simple example concerning an object a which suddenly expands. We answer the question 'Why did a expand?' by technically answering the complete underlying question (?f) (a expanded for the reason f), that is, q. We do it by constructing the following argument: (i) a is a piece of copper, (ii) a was heated and (iii) all pieces of copper expand when heated (or, if you like, copper expands when heated); therefore (iv) a expanded. Now the statement '(iv) for the reason (that) (i) & (ii) & (iii)' (or, '(iv) for the reason f_o', for short) counts as a potential **complete** se-answer (apart from the idealizations and simplifications involved).

First, that this answer is complete can be taken to mean in part that it corresponds to the complete presupposition$_2$ of the question q in the strong sense that it entails all the presuppositions of q. Notice that we may also answer the question q by saying that a was heated, thereby assuming only implicitly the premises (i) and (iii).

What does it mean to say that this complete answer is understandable here? A full analysis of this problem is difficult to give, but at least we may say the following, illustrating the earlier mentioned linguistic mutual beliefs an illocutionary act involves (cf. Subsection 2). The members of our P-community must have at least some conceptual mastery of the answer. Since this answer is a linguistic token, they must be able to understand the type of the speech act involved and they must be able to carve it up into words and sentences in the right way. They must somehow understand the logical form of the argument, and they must have a sufficiently good conceptual grasp of the basic descriptive terms used. Thus they must know what copper is, what heating is, and what expanding is. They must of course also know (or understand) what the object a is and what it means that it instantiates the mentioned properties. Finally, they must understand that the generalization (iii) expresses a nomic causal law, here instantiated by (i), (ii), and (iv). (See Section III for remarks on the understanding of causal connections and of reason-giving connections in general.)

When we claim that our answer is a (potential) se-answer by 'explanatory' we mean that '(iv) for the reason f_o' can replace the variable u in our definition (1). An answer's being scientific means several things. What is most relevant here is its **nomological** character. That is, an se-answer must explicitly or implicitly involve some kind of laws (and a complete se-answer must explicitly contain reference to laws). It is a much debated question whether scientific explanations (even when viewed as epistemic arguments as in this chapter) should thus invariably involve laws (see, e.g., Hempel (1965), pp. 354-364 for discussion). I will here only say the following in support of my epistemic nomological view of explanation.

Science looks for general patterns (invariances or other patterns and mechanisms) in the world. It is thus also concerned with finding stable connections between universals (e.g., properties) and especially finding out the nomological propensities the studied systems have. Such connections and propensities may be, e.g., causal or developmental (genetic) or both. These connections may also concern the nomic coexistence of certain properties. Singular facts, events, etc., are not **per se** of any interest to at least pure science. All interest in them is ultimately interest in their being instantiations of some universal property or mechanism rather than another or in their instantiating a certain value of a magnitude rather than some other, for indeed there are no bare particulars. Accordingly, also singular explanations (viz. epistemic arguments going beyond citing what made these events happen) must ultimately at least in the way of justification refer to or involve laws or lawful propensities. Furthermore, to mention a particularly central case, singular causation must also, correspondingly, be understood as involving nomic processes (see the discussion in Tuomela (1976a)). This can also be seen from the fact that the truth of singular causal claims is not affected by, so to speak, small but event-type preserving changes of causes and effects (e.g., the scratching of this match which caused the fire could have occurred slightly differently without affecting the causal claim).

While I thus require explanations to involve nomic processes I am ready to admit that it may be even in principle impossible to formulate the law statements representing those processes without the use of idealized assumptions, viz. assumptions known to be false of actual systems. This connected to the view that to be able to state laws governing the behavior of an open system one may have to resort to idealizing assumptions in order to "close" the system.

Let me still emphasize that nomological explanations are reason-giving **arguments** rather than, say, descriptions. To explain something is to give epistemic reasons for (believing) its occurrence or its being the case. As in effect argued in the preceding paragraph these reasons can, and ultimately must, be nomological. An explanation's being an argument is also clearly connected to its capability of conveying understanding, for that is part of what giving (nomological) reasons involves.

5. In view of the above considerations the following analysis of a complete (potential) se-answer to a complete question q (see (17)) may now be suggested (if the question is not a complete one it may always be replaced by one):

(8) A linguistic token-statement u is a **complete scientific explanatory answer** to q in situation C, given P, if and only if
   (a) u is obtained from a complete presupposition$_2$ (relative to C and P), say $(Ef)s(f)$, corresponding to q (formalized by $(?f)s(f)$ in its **oratio recta** form) by dropping the existential quantifier and by substituting a constant, say f_0, for f in it;
   (b) u is P-understandable in the context C; and
   (c) u constitutes an E-argument for q such that this argument has f_0 as its conjunction of premises.

We need not here explain (a) and (b) further. It should be pointed out that clause (a) by itself, using 'a presupposition$_1$' instead of 'a complete presupposition$_2$' in it, may be regarded as an explicate of the presystematic notion of an answer that occurs, e.g., in our (2), (4), and (24). Clause (c) employs the technical notion of an E-argument, viz. a potential **explanatory argument**, for q.[5] What is an E-argument then? I have elsewhere (see Tuomela (1977), Chapters 9 and 11) technically explicated it as an ε-argument in the case of deductive explanation and as a p-argument in the case of non-deductive (inductive) explanation (see the Appendix for a summary account). In both cases we are dealing with **nomological** arguments, viz., an E-argument always contains at least one lawlike statement among its premises. Let me especially emphasize that explanations by reference to the propensities of objects (and, generally, systems) to behave in certain ways are typically, or at least often, probabilistic (involve general probabilistic propensity statements). Thus the E-argument involved in them will be inductive.

An E-argument **for** q means the following. Let $(?f)s(f)$ be the **oratio recta** form of the why-question q (cf. clause (a)). Let s_e be the declarative statement obtained from the matrix $s(f)$ by omitting the phrase 'for the reason f' or whatever paraphrase of it occurs in $s(f)$. Now we say that an E-argument is **for** $(?f)s(f)$, or **for** q, just in the case this E-argument has the statement s_e as its conclusion. Thus, in our semiformal notation, the complete question $(?f)$ (a expanded for the reason f), i.e., the **explanandum**, has as its counterpart, viz. s_e, the **explanandum-content** 'a expanded' in the relevant E-argument. (Thus declarative statements are objects of explanation only in this derivative sense.)

For many purposes, e.g., for giving singular explanations without explicit reference to specific laws, the following wider notion of answer, to explicate partial explanation, will be useful:

(9) A linguistic token-statement v is a **scientific explanatory answer** to q in situation C, given P, if and only if there is a statement u such that
 (a) u is a complete scientific explanatory answer to q in C, given P; and
 (b) v is identical with one of the statemental components occurring in the premises of the E-argument that u constitutes, or v consists of the conclusion of the E-argument in question flanked by 'for the reason that__' or 'because__' or any alternative paraphrase, where the blank is occupied by one or more of the premises of the E-argument.

Possessing scientific explanatory answers in the sense (9) makes it possible to give explanations v which explicitly contain, e.g., only a premise mentioning a singular causal factor, although the corresponding complete se-answer u, postulated only to exist, does contain a law statement. A stronger notion of a scientific explanatory answer is obtained by requiring, in addition:

(c) Any explainee (in P) can (at least ideally) construct a complete se-answer (in C, given P) on the basis of v.

We shall below not require (c) as it seems too restrictive. Yet it can be regarded as a kind of desideratum, for the ability entailed by (c) is clearly one closely connected to the explainee's understanding q.

6. The acts of querying and explaining are illocutionary acts with a certain propositional content. For instance, the linguistic token u in (1) represents part of the propositional content of the explanatory act. When u is a complete se-answer it entails all the presuppositions$_2$ of the question q. Such a u must be taken to represent the complete propositional content of the answering act in question, it seems natural to think. But since we have in effect identified explanatory acts with suitable acts of answering, it is almost compelling to think that a complete se-answer u (related to an act of explaining as specified in (1)) gives the complete propositional content of that act of scientific explaining. Accordingly, we may also say that an se-answer v (in the sense of (9)), related to such a complete se-answer u, is an answer statement associated with that explanatory act.

We may analyze acts of querying as analogous to acts of explaining. Let us consider a questioner B who belongs to a scientific community which has internalized a paradigm P, i.e., a P-community. Then consider the following suggestion:

(10) B **scientifically queries** (or performs an act of scientific querying with the content) q by producing a linguistic token r in situation C, given P, if and only if
(a) B produces r with the intention (or aim) to the effect that his producing r will bring about, in the intended way, the outcome wanted by B that some member A of the P-community scientifically explains q to B (by producing a linguistic token u) in situation C, given P;
(b) q is a complete question associated with the query in question; and
(c) q entails r.

Clause (a) of (10) should be clear enough on the basis of our discussion related to (1). In clause (b) we in effect require that q represents the total propositional content of the query in question. We shall clarify the notion of a complete question in more detail below.

Clause (c) requires a notion of entailment for questions. We must assume that q and r at least share their mode, that is, both are, e.g., why-questions. Consider now the following two questions:

(11) Why did Tom open the window at midnight?

(12) Why did Tom open the window?

Next consider the following two respective presuppositions of (11) and (12), rendered in our semiformal notation:

(13) (Ef) Tom opened the window at midnight for the reason f.

(14) Tom opened the window for the reason f.

In this notation the questions (11) and (12) become:

(11') (?f) Tom opened the window at midnight for the reason f.

(12') (?f) Tom opened the window for the reason f.

Let us now assume that (11') gives the complete propositional content of a query. Assume, furthermore, that (12') (rather than (11')) gives the logical form of r, viz., the (question) statement B uses to "put" his query. Then we may suggest that, analyzing adverbs conjunctively in a Davidsonian fashion, (11') (corresponding to q) entails (12'). This (somewhat problematic) elucidation of entailment as entailment between the contained matrices (of questions) will have to suffice for our present purposes. (Note that if the token related to a query is non-verbal, e.g., a pointing with a finger, we will assume it has the linguistic logical form which r represents.)

What is a complete question? In the above example, the complete question associated with the query in question is (11'), which was in effect obtained from (13), assumed to be a complete presupposition$_2$. Let us say that a (question) statement r **puts** a query, say Q, just in case r is the kind of statement (10) characterizes. Then we may elucidate the notion of a complete question as follows:

(15) q is a **complete question** (in **oratio recta** form) associated with a scientific query Q in C, given P, if and only if there is a linguistic token r such that
(a) r puts the query Q (in situation C, given P); and
(b) q has the form $(?f)s(f)$ such that $(Ef)s(f)$ is a complete presupposition$_2$ of r, relative to C and P.

We are now in a position to define exactly what a scientifc explanation is. An (actual) explanation is simply a se-answer to a question q given in connection with appropriate explaining act (cf. (1)) brought about as an adequate response to a (scientific) query Q in C, given P. More explicitly, we may express this as follows:

(16) u is a **scientific explanation** if and only if there exist a question statement q, persons A and B, a singular context C, a paradigm P, and acts E and Q such that
(a) u is a linguistic token which is (or represents) a scientific explanatory answer to q in C, given P;
(b) q is a complete question associated with Q in C, given P;
(c) Q is a scientific query by which B, a member of the P-community, scientifically queries q by producing some appropriate linguistic token (such as r in (10)) in C, given P; and
(d) E is an act of explaining in which A, a member of the P-community, scientifically explains q to B (in response to the latter's query Q) by producing u in situation C, given P.[6]

The above clauses use only previously defined notions, except that (d) requires E to be a "response" to Q. This of course entails that E must satisfy clause (a) of (10). Let us recall here that our analysis of explanation is made in terms of querying and answering but that we do not propose to reduce away the latter notions. Querying and answering are, in a sense, interdefinable but at least they surely cannot **both** be analyzed away. A notion of potential scientific explanation can be obtained from (16) by requiring in its analysans potential rather than actual existence (and using, e.g., 'might exist' instead of 'exist' in it). Note finally that as u constitutes an E-argument (16) also comes to define indirectly what is involved in saying that an E-argument is a scientific explanation.

7. Before going into some special topics of our theory of explanation let us pause briefly to consider asking and answer-

ing quite generally as a communicative illocutionary action from the point of view of our theory of social action. Let me therefore give a somewhat simplified analysis of the following situation. We assume that agent B utters a linguistic expression, say v, asking by it why p, viz. ?p, quite analogously with the situation (1) above is meant to analyze. By so uttering v B wants A to tell him why p. In view of our discussion related to (1) and assuming that the four assumptions concerning underlying mutual linguistic beliefs of Subsection 2 hold true I propose the following simplified analysis of the action of asking:

(17) B's uttering a linguistic expression v was an action of **asking** A why p if and only if B uttered v because (due to the reason that)
(a) he wanted A to tell him why p; and
(b) by uttering v he intended to bring about, in the intended way, that A come to believe that (a) and that A tell him why p (in part) because of his (A's) belief that (a).[7]

Notice that (17) does not speak of any "preparatory" conditions (such as B's not knowing why p, etc.); clause (a) is a kind of "sincerity" condition, independent of (b). I shall not here discuss whether they are strictly speaking needed in a full blown analysis (and if needed whether they can be understood to have been packed in the notion of wanting in clause (a)). Clause (a) gives a central element distinguishing asking from other communicative illocutionary actions, and (b) just states the relevant reflexive illocutionary intention of the kind we have been discussing (see notes 3 and 7). The phrase 'because' in (b) is meant to express reason-giving. (It seems plausible that a causal process of reasoning stands at the back here; cf. the SAS-schema of Bach and Harnish (1979) and our analysis of reasons in Chapter 11 below. But we shall not here go deeper into that.) Anyway, B's uttering v qualifies as a token of asking because it was performed due to his reason as expressed by clauses (a) and (b). To spell out 'due to his reasons', B's underlying practical reasoning, related to our schema (PR_i) or something similar, presumably is needed.

Analogously with (17), and simplifying and modifying our (1) slightly, we may analyze answering in general as follows:

(18) A's uttering a linguistic expression w was an action of **answering** B why p if and only if A uttered w because (due to the reason that)
(a) he believed that w is an answer to why p, and
(b) by uttering w he intended to bring about, in the intended way, that B come to believe that w is (or represents) an answer to why p and to believe it (in part) because of his (B's) belief that (a).

In our present context of trying to find out the special conceptual elements of communicative illocutionary actions as social actions, (18) needs no further explicatory comments. Let me yet emphasize that due to its clause (b) (18) is centrally connected with understanding (recall the formulation in (1)).

Given (17) and (18) we may now claim that the action sequence of B's uttering v followed by, and partly generating, A's uttering w now constitutes a two-agent social action $token_2$ in the sense of (5.8) and, indeed, an intentional social action token in the sense of (5.10), given of course that (17) and (18) hold true here. Why is this so? First, both B's uttering v (say u_1) and A's uttering w (say u_2) can rather obviously, in view of (17) and (18), be regarded as single-agent action tokens (in the sense of (4.5)). As claimed in our discussion related to serial generation (in the sense of (6.16)) it should be acceptable that the result event (r) of the two-agent action token (say u) of asking-answering can be taken to be the sequence r_1r_2, viz. $r = r_1r_2$, where r_1 is the result of B's uttering v and r_2 is the result of A's uttering w. Given this, obviously we have $IG(u_1,u_2,u)$ in the sense of (6.19). Is u now a social action $token_1$ in the sense of (5.5)? This depends essentially on whether a social attitude is involved here; and that is certainly the case in view of clauses (b) of (17) and (18). Indeed it is plausible to assume that a we-intention to perform an action of asking and answering is involved such that clauses (a) and (b) of (17) can be taken to entail that B intended to ask, viz. to perform his part of the social action of asking and answering, and analogously for A. Thus (**WI**) of Chapter 2 can plausibly be regarded as satisfied.

Accordingly, given all this, not only can we take u to be a social action $token_1$ but a social action $token_2$ (in the sense of (5.8), in view of what we said of generation above). It is, furthermore, clear from (17) and (18), due to our explication of 'in the intended way', that u was **purposively** generated by u_1 and u_2. Thus also (5.10) can be taken to be satisfied, and we have completed our task of indicating, indeed showing, that u is an intentional social action $token_2$ in the sense of our theory and that, hence, our theory is able to account for such important social actions as communicative illocutionary actions.[8] Interestingly enough, some linguists have recently claimed that standard speech act theory is not capable of dealing with joint actions such as "collective directives". Given that, a theory of social action can be used to genuinely enrich speech act theory; see Clark and Carlson (1982).

Speech acts relying on the Gricean mechanism represent a strong type of communication, which, however, may be regarded as conceptually fundamental; other, weaker forms of human communication should be judged, evaluated, and criticized with respect to this kind of full blown communication. But note that as our theory of social action bases on we-attitudes rather than anything like Gricean intentions it is in principle easy to incorporate weaker types, even non-linguistic communicative behavior into its scope (cf. Bennett's (1976) sub-Gricean "Plain-Talk" as a case in point). Also such interesting cases of distorted and contradictory communication as double-bind communication can in my view be analyzed from the point of view of speech act theory, suitably weakened. In double-bind communication a person, e.g., a child, receives contradictory messages from another person, e.g., the mother (cf. Swensen (1973)). The words of the latter may contradict some of her (unintentionally performed) bodily actions. The resulting confused communication has to do with the uncertainty the participants, especially the receiver, have concerning the holding of the presuppositions of communication (e.g., the veracity presumption).

II. EMPHASIS

1. The conceptual framework of explanatory concepts created above relies on some notions, such as presuppositions$_2$ and scientific understanding, which would require further analysis. We shall below briefly discuss them. Before that, however, the topic of emphasized explananda must be briefly considered.

Let us consider the following two sentences:

(19) Tom opened the window **at midnight**.

(20) Tom opened **the window** at midnight.

In these sentences the boldfaced phrases are emphasized. Here they are understood to express **contrast**. (Emphasis need not always signal contrast; cf. Achinstein (1975), (1977a).) Accordingly, (19) may be paraphrased either as

(19') It was at midnight that Tom opened the window;

or (perhaps)

(19") Tom opened the window at midnight, rather than some other time (considered relevant in the present context).

By contrast, (20) makes the point that Tom opened the window rather than, e.g., the door at midnight:

(20') It was the window that Tom opened at midnight;

or (perhaps)

(20") Tom opened the window rather than something else (considered relevant in the present context) at midnight.

In spite of the fact that (19) and (20) differ with respect to emphasis, they may be considered to have the **same meaning** (cf. Dretske (1972), pp. 421-425, for discussion). Or better, (19) and (20) may be taken to have the same **representational** meaning (and hence the same truth conditions). Yet I claim that they differ with respect to their **speech-act** meaning: (19) and (20) are simply used to make different points as, e.g., the explicates (19') versus (20') indicate, and when embedded in why-questions they are used to ask for different reasons.

We shall below call (declarative and erotetic) sentences with one or more boldfaced (or otherwise emphasized) contained phrases **emphasis-sentences**. We will now require that our earlier characterizations of the central question-theoretic and explanation-theoretic concepts be allowed to encompass emphasis-sentences. (Sometimes we will, accordingly, speak of emphasized answers, presuppositions, etc.) Thus our analyses (1)-(4), (8)-(10), and (17)-(18) can and should be understood to cover emphasis-sentences as well. (Definition (8) will require yet another change to be explained below on p. 333.)

Continuing with the above example, we assume that the complete questions corresponding to (19) and (20) are:

(21) (?f) Tom opened the window **at midnight** for the reason f.

(22) (?f) Tom opened **the window** at midnight for the reason f.

We might now take (21) and (22) to express our (full) **explananda**. When the emphases are spelled out as above it is seen that (21) and (22) are different questions as they require different answers. (21) requires an explanation (answer) in which especially the time of Tom's action is determined or given a reason for. In (22), on the contrary, we have to determine especially what Tom opened, by giving an explanation of that. Thus, (21) and (22) are different as explananda, and so are their related explanandum-contents (as we call (19) and (20) when regarded as conclusions of explanatory arguments).

2. In our analysis, contrastive emphasis is a factor related to such pragmatic factors as the situation C and the paradigm P. These factors serve to determine which aspects of the explanandum-content require explanation and which are taken for granted in a given context. They also serve to indicate what kind(s) of explanatory factor(s) to look for. For example, when we explain (19), we are primarily interested in the time of the action. In our explanation, we take it for granted that Tom opened the window, even though we do not have to formally include this information as an initial condition (or anything like that) in our explanans (see Tuomela (1977), pp. 272-274, on this).

We notice that the explication (19'') of (19) quite explicitly refers to a class of relevant alternative times. In general, we may think that the pragmatic context C, together with the paradigm P, "determines" a partition class, say R, of alternatives (of the right ontic type), relevant to the aspect to be explained. In the case of explaining (19), i.e., in answering (21), we might have, e.g., R = {evening, midnight, morning}, in some suitable context. Accordingly, we are dealing with the midnight-aspect (say m) and R in the case of (21). We might write this out explicitly as

(21) (?f(m,R)) Tom opened the window at midnight for the reason f.

Here we have packed the emphasis aspect into the question-quantifier, so to speak. The variable f is made to depend on m and R in the sense that only such values of f are asked for (and accepted in our answers) as determine the m-aspect of Tom's action relative to R.

The important thing about explanandum emphasis is that it forces us to simultaneously consider **several** (actual or potential) explanations instead of only one, at least as long as there is epistemic uncertainty concerning the truth value of the explanandum-content description (which is frequently the case; cf. especially **corrective** explanation). This is because we are in a sense **comparing** (or taking responsibility for) all the explanations given to the items (e.g., properties) in R. What the quantifier $(?f(m,R))$ invites us to do is to consider the following explanations simultaneously. We go through the elements in R and look for their "reasons" (e.g., causes); or better, we look for their **best** explanations (the best reasons or best E-arguments for them). Thus, if $R = \{m_1,\ldots,m_n\}$, we may, for simplicity, want to assume a one-to-one correspondence between such (best) explanations and the ordered couples $<f_1,m_1>,\ldots,<f_n,m_n>$, where the f_is are the (best) partial or full determinants of their respective m_is. We then look for the best explanation among these (best) explanations. If that best explanation is represented by, say, $<f_k,m_k>$, and if m_k is the emphasized item (in our example $m_k=m$), then we have found an acceptable explanation, at least as far as the emphasis-problem is concerned. Note that the explaining factors (reasons) $f_1,\ldots,f_n$ may or may not differ. It should be emphasized, however, that in many contexts, such as when dealing with mutually exclusive causes, it is only the best explanation for m_k that really matters.

I have required above that each f_i gives a **best** explanation (best E-argument) for the respective m_i-aspect of the explanandum-content. This is because the m_i-aspect may be explainable by several different f_js $(j=1,\ldots,n)$, and thus it seems we should restrict ourselves to the best one. How do we then find that best explanation and how do we compare such different best explanations? These are difficult questions which we shall not here attempt to solve in general. As to the first question, citing the actual cause of m_k is one way of answering it. As to the second, perhaps we may say that 'best' means best taken relative to the goodness of the alternative explanations $<f_i,m_i>$ **on the average.** That is, $<f_k,m_k>$ should be better than all the other explanations on the average. Alternatively, we might require that $<f_k,m_k>$ be better (or at least not worse) than every $<f_i,m_i>$ for $i \neq k$. (See, e.g., Niiniluoto and Tuomela (1973), Chapter 7, for relevant probabilistic explicates of the notion of explanatory power relied on here.)

Let us emphasize, however, that often or, perhaps, typically only the pair $<f_k,m_k>$ qualifies as a best explanation (or even as explanation at all). For instance, it is quite clear that if the m_is are mutually exclusive, m_k is realized, and f_k gives the only actual cause of the m_k-aspect, then $<f_k,m_k>$ qualifies both as the best explanation of m_k and as the best of the best explanations, given that the question quantifier is $(?f(m_k,R))$. Typical deductive-nomological explanations clearly fit this situation.

Notice that quantifiers of the type $(?f(m_k,R))$ are merely shorthands. They can be spelled out in a rather obvious way along the above lines so that in fact we only need ordinary question quantifiers (?f). We have not dealt explicitly with cases employing **several** emphasized items here. They can also be handled along the above lines, although their treatment, of course, is more complex.

Let us finally note that our account of explanandum-emphasis forces us to make a small change in our definition (8) of a complete scientific explanatory answer. The change is that in its clause (c) we now have to require u to constitute a **best-explaining** E-argument for q instead of the previous requirement of its merely constituting an E-argument for q. Here 'best explaining' means best among the best-explaining explanations relative to R in the sense explicated above. (See Tuomela (1980a) for some further developments and illustrations of the theory of explanation presented above.)

III. UNDERSTANDING AND PRESUPPOSITIONS

1. In this subsection we shall briefly discuss the difficult notion of understanding, which this account of explanation largely depends on. **In medias res,** we propose that the following conditions be satisfied in the case of (actual) scientific understanding within a paradigm P:

(23) A person B (**scientifically**) **understands** q in situation C, given P, only if
  (a) q is a sound question and B believes it is;
  (b) B has at least some acquaintance with and some (conceptual) mastery of the items mentioned in, or presupposed by, q;
  (c) B knows an answer u to q that is correct in C, given P;
  (d) B has some acquaintance with and some (conceptual) mastery of the items mentioned in, or presupposed by, the answer u (or, if u is not a complete answer, in the complete answer u* which corresponds to u).

Note that contrary to our definitions of, e.g., se-answer, explanation, etc., (23) has, for change, been phrased to deal with **actual** rather than only **potential** understanding, whence the requirement of a correct (or true) answer in (c). Clause (c) clearly shows that more is at stake here than merely understanding what the question **means:** B's knowledge of a correct value (relative to C and P) of the question-variable is required. As to condition (a), I will not further clarify it here beyond recalling our earlier definition (**17**) of a complete question.

What we earlier said about the (hermeneutic) understanding of an answer applies, mutatis mutandis, to understanding a question as well. Thus I will not here further elucidate (b) either.

Clauses (c) and (d) concern understanding an answer to a question, viz., the reason factor (when q is a why-question) and its connection to the declarative content of Q. In (c) 'answer' means answer in the presystematic sense elucidated by means of a modification of (8) (a) as indicated. In (d) we use the analogous presystematic notion of complete answer.

Let us briefly consider the "(conceptual) mastery of items" spoken about in (d). First there is the problem whether such mastery can be elucidated without relying on the notion of understanding. To this my answer is that some such circularity is unavoidable. In fact, I will below unabashedly use the term 'understanding' when elucidating clause (d). Yet I believe my elucidation is informative and far from viciously circular. (In Tuomela (1977), pp. 48-62 a naturalistic analysis in terms of behavioral uniformities of the concept of conceptual acticity is discussed. If that approach is tenable, it will work in the case of the concept of understanding, too.) Given this prolegomenon, we may proceed to discuss the patterns of understanding that (23) is about.

When we are dealing with why-questions, we are dealing mainly with the **reason pattern** of understanding. Of course, there is also the **hermeneutic pattern** of understanding (and thus also the hermeneutic sense of "having the concepts" u deals with) involved when interpreting, say, a linguistic utterance as a sequence of meaningful words and sentences of a language. Interpreting an item of behavior as a certain kind of action (viz. classifying the behavior as such and such action) also represents hermeneutic understanding in this sense. But given all that, it is the logical space of reasons, especially nomological scientific reasons, which we are dealing with here. Giving a nomological scientific reason for an explanandum-content means rationally fitting it into a broader nomological network of laws and facts. Thus some degree of **unification** and some degree of **systemicity** are always involved in the nomological reason pattern of understanding.

In many typical cases, citing a cause gives the reason we are seeking. Let us consider an example. Flipping a switch causes the light to come on, we assume. We understand why the light came on only if we **know** (or justifiedly believe) that it was caused by the switch being flipped. Our knowledge of the causal connection involved or, almost equivalently, our knowing the reason (here: the cause) for the light coming on gives the understanding requested. On our analysis, this is explicated by requiring there to be an E-argument (using the relevant factor mentioned) for the light coming on.

Understanding why something is so-and-so is not primarily connected to some kind of "purely" intellectual knowing that-some-proposition-is-true or what-an-entity-is but rather to one's related **powers**, viz., to one's capacity to **reason** in various appropriate ways and to perform different linguistic and nonlinguistic **actions**. For instance, if I understand why the light came on in the above example, I can reason about what happens when I flip the switch, about what happens when there is a blackout, and so on. Furthermore, I can also **produce** and **prevent** the light's coming on by appropriately operating with the switch itself. Similar points can be made about, e.g., wants and beliefs resulting in relevant actions (with wants and beliefs playing a role similar to the flipping of the switch and the actions roles similar to the light coming on). (For further elucidation of the notion of understanding see Tuomela (1980a) and Chapter 11, Section VI, below.)

2. In defining our key notions, such as explanation, presupposition$_2$, se-answer, and so on we have systematically relativized them to a concrete pragmatic situation, called C, and to a paradigm, say P. I believe that, no matter how hard it is to explicate these latter notions, they are quite central to the theory of explanation. Explanations **are** relative to accepted and internalized (partially normative) constellations of group commitments or disciplinary matrices, to use Kuhn's (1969) terms, and to concrete situations conceptualized and described in light of them. (As to relativity to C recall, e.g., choosing the relevant class. We shall, however, concentrate on P-relativity below.)

Our view of the role of explanation seems to be almost the opposite to, e.g., Bromberger's: "The search for and discovery of scientific **explanations**, we think, is essentially the search for and discovery of answers to questions that are unanswerable relative to prevailing beliefs and concepts. It is not, therefore, merely a quest for evidence to settle which available answer is correct, it is a quest for the unthought-of." (Bromberger (1966), p. 91).

To be sure, we allow the "non-paradigmatic" kind of explanations Bromberger has in mind. They typically amount to creating something like new paradigmatic beliefs, it seems. Yet these explanations are borderline cases for us, whereas Bromberger seems to regard them as typical. Explanatory answers can be evaluated as to goodness by such familiar criteria as the degree of relevance, correctness, depth, completeness and nomic unification they give or exhibit (see, e.g., Achinstein (1971) for an analysis). I think that Bromberger may have to accept some such view, too. But these criteria cannot be applied except relative to some or other paradigmatic beliefs and assumptions, no matter how many or how few adhere to them at the time of giving the explanation - and no matter whether they were in some sense thought-of or unthought-of (or unthinkable) before the invention of the explanatory theory and argument. Thus even in the case of previously unthought-of possible answers there are some - perhaps poorly articulated - paradigmatic background assumptions which serve to determine the presuppositions$_2$ of answers.[9]

When making claims about P-relativity as above, one should of course try to be clear regarding what one is talking about, but unfortunately strict identity criteria for paradigms (disciplinary matrices, constellations of group commitments) are hard to come by. Especially in areas where exactly formulated scientific theories are scarce (cf. the social sciences), talk about paradigms almost necessarily remains rather vague. Kuhn (1969) distinguishes between the following four components of a paradigm (or disciplinary matrix):

(1) "symbolic generalizations" which have been "immunized" from falsification by scientists; e.g., Newton's law f=ma;
(2) metaphysical elements; e.g., 'all events have deterministic cause', 'all perceptible phenomena are due to the interaction of qualitatively neutral atoms in the void', 'no intentional actions are caused';
(3) values; e.g., theories should be simple, compatible, plausible;
(4) shared examples; e.g., the Newtonian analysis of freely falling bodies, planets, pendulums, tides, etc.

Recent explications by Sneed and Stegmüller (among others) have helped somewhat to clarify the first and fourth of these elements (see Stegmüller (1976)). But what is still lacking is a clear systematic account of these components (especially (2) and (3)), their interdependence and their function in an independently characterized scientific community. In the case of scientific explanation, as discussed above, it appears that the first and second components are especially central, viz., in the determining the nature of presuppositions$_2$, questions and answers. We are in need of a general account of how what might be called P-patterns serve to determine these key notions. Lacking that, I will here only illustrate the situation by means of an example related to the explanation of (single-agent) intentional actions.

Let us consider the earlier example of Tom's opening a window **at midnight** (cf. (19) and (21)). Suppose first that the following singular "common sense" explanation is offered:

(24) Tom opened the window **at midnight** for the reason that he wanted to listen to a nightingale.

Against a suitable background story (containing, e.g., the claim that nightingales sing around midnight, etc.) (24) may seem plausible. However, (24) is not yet an E-argument. It can be reconstrued to become one by relying on a suitable theory of action. Let us first consider the purposive-causal theory of action. Given it, the explanation will have to involve (explicitly or implicitly) the agent's relevant intending, which purposively causes his overt action. (Purposive causation is a technical concept here.) If we construe the wanting in (24) to contain episodic elements and assume it plays the role intendings play (viz., that the wanting "develops" into an effective intending to listen to a nightingale at midnight), we arrive at roughly the following singular explanation:

(25) Tom's opening the window **at midnight** was purposively caused by his wanting to listen to a nightingale.

(We may assume that the emphasis is taken care of, so to speak, by the "involved" causal determination along the lines sketched earlier and do not explicitly consider rival explanations here.) The answer (25) is an se-answer, which, accordingly, may be claimed to implicitly contain an E-argument. I will not argue for this here (see Tuomela (1977), Chapter 9).

The complete emphasized presupposition corresponding to (24) can be taken to be

(26) (Ef) Tom's opening the window **at midnight** was purposively caused by f.

Thus we see that whatever specific psychological theory of action is relied upon it must be able to make sense of (purposive) action-causation (as a species of event-causation) by somehow assuming such causation to be present in the case of all intentional actions. This may be regarded as a "broadly factual" assumption, and thus it has an aposteriori character. Yet it may be included in the second component of a paradigm, I think. Notice also that our causal theory of action requires actions to be events brought about by an agent's willings (effective intendings). Thus the explanandum-contents and their explananda (why-questions, transformed into what-cause-questions) are highly laden with the general assumptions of our action theory.

Other (competing) action theories interpret the original explanation statement (24) differently. For instance, von Wright (1971) presumably would handle the above situation as follows (cf. Chapter 3 above). Tom's wanting must be construed as an intending to begin with. The following practical syllogism will then give (roughly) the required explanation:

(27) Tom intended to listen to a nightingale. Tom considered that unless he opens the window **at midnight** he cannot listen to a nightingale. Therefore, Tom opened the window **at midnight**.

Although I will not write out explicitly the presuppositions entailed by von Wright's intentionalist theory, it is easy to see how radically different this theory is from the one first considered. Here it is presupposed that the action to be explained can be "hermeneutically" explained by means of a suitable practical syllogism (such as the one above). No action-causation is involved and intendings are construed in a Rylean fashion (without any inner episodic elements).

There is several other rival accounts of action-explanation. Chisholm, for instance, would explain an action by reference to non-episodic agent-causation. Skinner would explain actions by somehow referring to external events and to the agent's conditioning history, and so on. All the different resulting accounts of action-explanation are in any case seen to be strongly affected by the paradigm (or P-pattern) underlying them. It should go without saying that what has above been said about single-agent action theories equally well applies to multi-agent action theories.

Our above treatment illustrates how context and paradigm guide explaining and how, accordingly, types and levels of scientific understanding may be generated by these factors. Thus, the more articulated and specific they are, the more fine-grained will presuppositions$_2$ be and the more informative (at least relative to some "common-sense" stance and to presuppositions$_1$) will the ensuing explanations be.

APPENDIX

We have frequently spoken about E-arguments in this chapter. It is the purpose of this appendix to characterize them briefly. In doing so we shall primarily rely on Tuomela (1977). In that work, E-arguments are divided into ε-arguments and ρ-

arguments. ε-arguments represent **deductive** nomological explanatory arguments and ρ-arguments **inductive** or non-deductive ones. The properties of an ε-argument are formulated by means of the so-called DE-model and those of a ρ-argument by the so-called IE-model. ε-arguments may - for the obvious reason - be called **conclusive** and ρ-arguments **inconclusive** (see Tuomela (1977), Chapters 9 and 11). Before turning to them, I would like to point out that the developments in the present book only presuppose **some** viable account of deductive and inductive explanatory arguments. What follows is my specific proposal for such an account.

We shall start by giving a brief summary of the DE-model for (potential) deductive scientific explanation. (This model was first published in Tuomela (1972), expanded in (1973), and revised in (1976b); also see (1977).) Here only the logical aspects of the model will be summarized (for other aspects see the above mentioned works).

To begin, we need some technical concepts. Let us say that two components or statements P and Q are **noncomparable** exactly when both not $\vdash P \to Q$ and not $\vdash Q \to P$. To refine the notion of component, we define two additional concepts.

A sequence of statemental well formed formulas, $<W_1, W_2, \ldots, W_n>$, of a scientific language L is a **sequence of truth functional components** of an explanans (here: theory cum initial conditions) T if and only if T may be built up from the sequence by the formation rules of L, such that each member of the sequence is used exactly once in the application of the rules in question. The W_is are thus to be construed as tokens. The formation rules of L naturally have to be specified in order to see the exact meaning of the notion of a sequence of truth functional components of a theory finitely axiomatized by a sentence T. A **set of ultimate sentential conjuncts** Tc of a sentence T is any set whose members are the well formed formulas of a longest sequence $<W_1, W_2, \ldots, W_n>$ of truth functional components of T such that T and $W_1 \& W_2 \& \ldots \& W_n$ are logically equivalent. (If T is a set of sentences, then the set Tc of ultimate conjuncts of T is the union of the sets of ultimate sentential conjunct of each member of T.) We will below associate with T a Tc-set and define a relation of explanation ε(E,Tc) (or ε(E,T), if you like) to represent the (minimal) reason-giving deductive explanation of the singular or general declarative explanandum statement (or explanandum content) E by the explanans T. T will be in a language L($\lambda \cup \mu$), and it may thus contain "new" or explanatory or μ-predicates. E is assumed to contain only λ-predicates, i.e., "old" or "observational" predicates.

We say that the relation ε(E,Tc) satisfies the logicoinferential conditions of adequacy for (potential) **deductive reason-giving explanation** if and only if

(1)   {E,Tc} is consistent;
(2)   Tc ⊢ E;
(3)   Tc contains at least one universal lawlike statement (and no non-lawlike general statements);
(4)   for any Tc_i in the largest set of truth functional components of T, Tc_i is noncomparable with E;
(5)   it is not possible, without contradicting some of the previous conditions (1) through (4), to find sentences $S_i,\ldots,S_r$ ($r \geq 1$) at least some of which are essentially universal such that for some $Tc_j,\ldots,Tc_n$ ($n \geq 1$):
$Tc_j \& \ldots \& Tc_n \vdash_{\overline{p}} S_i \& \ldots \& S_r$
not $S_i \& \ldots \& S_r \vdash Tc_j \& \ldots \& Tc_n$
$Tc_s \vdash E$,
where Tc_s is the result of the replacement of $Tc_j,\ldots,Tc_n$ by $S_i,\ldots,S_r$ in Tc, and '$\vdash_{\overline{p}}$' means 'deducible, without increase in quantificational depth, by means of predicate logic but not by means of universal or existential instantiation only'.

Condition (5) is not quite unambiguous as it stands. The reader is referred to Tuomela (1976b) for clarification (note especially conditions (V) and (Q) discussed in that paper) and for an alternative interpretation of '$\vdash_{\overline{p}}$'. See Tuomela (1972) for a detailed discussion of the formal properties of this model (especially of the structure of the explanatory hierarchies it generates).

In the case of explaining laws (generalizations), the following conditions may still be imposed on ε(E,Tc):

(6)   If Cn(Tc)=H(μ)∪O(λ)∪C(λ∪μ), then there is a E'≠E (E∈O(λ), E'∈O'(λ)) such that not ⊢E→E' and such that ε(E',Tc') for some Tc' (of a T') for which Cn(Tc')=H'(μ)∪O'(λ)∪C'(λ∪μ) and H⊆H'; in addition, not {E}∪(H'-H)∪(O'-O)∪(C'-C)⊢H.

(7)   If H(μ) is an established core theory, and if, for some E, ε(E,Tc) with Cn(Tc)=H_r(μ)∪O(λ)∪C(λ∪μ), then the difference H-H_r=∅. (H_r is the Craigian μ-reduct of Cn(Tc)).

These conditions, corresponding to (7.6) and (7.7) of Tuomela (1973), require some comments. 'Cn' means the consequence operation. The sets H(μ), O(λ), and C(λ∪μ) represent, respectively the core theory ("pure theory"), the empirical (or observational) content, and the correspondence rules connecting λ and μ which Craig's elimination theorem gives us. It is assumed here that μ-predicates are so-called (purely) theoretical ones and that λ-predicates are broadly observational.

Condition (6) requires, roughly, that the explanans together with some auxiliary assumptions is capable of explaining other laws than E and that the theory should not be explainable by E and the auxiliary assumptions.

Condition (7) prevents **ad hoc**-expansions of the core theory in the context of the explanation of λ-laws.

What our DE-model is supposed to explicate is **minimal** and **direct** deductive explanatory arguments. Roughly, 'direct' means explanation by means of a direct covering under the explanans law. 'Minimal' refers mainly to the fact that the covering law is to be minimal in the sense of not containing more general information about the world than the phenomena being explained need to be covered. It may be debated, of course, whether every deductive explanatory argument should be given in such a piecemeal fashion in terms of minimal explanation. I shall not further discuss this problem here (cf. Tuomela (1972), (1976b)). Let me just point out that minimality comes from condition (5). Therefore, the omission of (5) leaves us with a partial characterization of a broader notion of ε-argument. Let it be noted in connection with this minimality condition that it is closely related to the question-theoretic requirement that an answer should provide a proper but minimal amount of information: a (direct) answer is a piece of language that completely, **but just completely,** answers a question (see Belnap and Steel (1976), p. 3).

As the connections between E-arguments and explanatory questions, answers, etc., were already discussed earlier in this chapter, we need not review them here. One closing remark on ε-arguments, however, is yet needed. Whereas we have dealt only with **strict** deductive explanation above one may also want to consider **approximate** deductive explanation. As shown in Tuomela (1979), such approximate explanation may be taken to mean this: T approximately ε-explains E if and only if T strictly ε-explains some E* such that the distance (dissimilarity) between E and E* is (regarded as) small. For an account of sentence-distance (for first-order statements), see Tuomela (1978).

2. Next we shall give a concise summary of our so-called IE-model, which defines the logical aspects of the notion of a ρ-argument, viz., a (minimal and direct) nomological inductive argument. As in the case of DE-model, the present IE-model also relies strongly on the notion of lawhood and (hence) on the

notion of nomological predicate. As the summary to be given below is concise and even inadequate the reader is strongly advised to consult Tuomela (1977), Chapter 11, and (1981) from which the following has been condensed.

A central feature of the IE-model is that it connects deductive and inductive explanation in certain formal respects. Many of the conditions of the DE-model of deductive explanation carry over intact. Some modifications are naturally needed and one entirely new kind of condition - a special language-relative requirement of maximal specificity - is added. Notice especially that inductive explanation on the IE-model does not necessarily require any **probabilistic** laws at all.

Suppose that we are given a putative declarative explanandum statement E and a putative explanans T. As above, we form a set of ultimate sentential conjuncts Tc and T. A probability statement $p(G/F) = r$ ("semantically" defined for predicates G and F on the basis of Loś's representation theorem as shown in Chapter 11 of Tuomela (1977)) occur either directly as a member of Tc, or as a member of the largest set of truth functional components of T (if, e.g., a disjunction, $(p(G/F)=r) \vee S$ for any S, is a member of Tc).

We shall be concerned here only with **direct** and **single-aspect** inductive explanations of **singular** statements. In the case of inductive-probabilistic explanations, this means that only one covering law of probabilistic form $p(G/F)=r$ will occur in the explanans as a member of Tc. We restrict ourselves here to this kind of probabilistic laws for reasons of simplicity. In principle, it seems possible to extend this approach to cover probabilistic laws, e.g., of the kinds $p(G/F) \geq r$ and $r_1 \leq p(G/F) \leq r_2$ as well. As before, G and F will be atomic or compound nomological predicates.

If the original explanans T contains several probabilistic laws relevant to the explanandum, it may be possible to "combine" them into one law - and thus into a **single-aspect** explanation - by means of the probability calculus; the resulting law may then be used in Tc. (If the probability laws are not all connected with respect to their vocabulary, of course this is problematic.)

Let E be a singular non-probabilistic statement and let Tc be a set of ultimate sentential conjuncts. In the probabilistic case we let E be $G(a_1,...,a_m)$, i.e., a singular statement with m singular names. ($G(a_1,...,a_m)$ may (but need not necessarily) represent an atomic statement corresponding to an n-place predicate G.) We now define a relation $\rho(E,Tc)$ which may be read 'Tc (potentially) inductively explains E'. (Here "explaining" must be understood widely enough to cover "contributes to explaining".)

The probabilistic case is relativized to a set λ of nomological predicates "generating" what is called a nomic field $\mathbf{F}_\lambda$; this is necessary for our version (v) of the requirement of maximal specifity to operate. We define our IE-model as follows: $\rho(E,Tc)$ satisfies the logical requirements for (direct and single-aspect) potential singular **inductive explanation** if and only if

(i) $\{Tc,E\}$ is consistent.
(ii) $I(Tc,E)$ but not $Tc \vdash E$.
(iii) Tc contains among its elements at least one lawlike statement and at most one lawlike probability statement. (Tc is not allowed to contain any generalizations which are not lawlike.)
(iv) For any Tc_i in the largest set of truth functional components of T, Tc_i is noncomparable with E.
(v)   If Tc contains a lawlike probabilistic statement, it must be of the form $p(G/F) = r$, where F and G may be complex predicates, and Tc must contain a singular statement of the form $F(a_1,...,a_n)$ such that the following requirement is satisfied:
For any predicate F_1 in λ such that $F_1(a_1,...,a_n)$ and F_1 is stronger than F and entails neither G nor $\sim$G if $p(G/F_1) = r_1$ is a lawlike statement then $r_1=r=p(G/F)$.
(vi) It is not possible, without contradicting any of the previous conditions, to find sentences $S_i,...,S_r$ ($r \geq 1$) at least some which are lawlike such that for some $Tc_j,...,Tc_n$ ($n \geq 1$):
$Tc_j\&...\&Tc_n \vdash_p S_i\&...\&S_r$
not $S_i\&...\&S_r \vdash Tc_j\&...\&Tc_n$
$I(Tc_s,E)$,
where Tc_s is the result of replacing $Tc_j,...,Tc_n$ by $S_i,...,S_r$ in Tc and '$\vdash_p$' means 'deducible, without increase in quantificational depth, by means of predicate logic but not by means of universal or existential instantiation only'.

In this definition we primarily think of the following interpretation for the relation of **inducibility** $I(Tc,E)$, i.e., 'Tc inductively supports E':

(ii') $I(Tc,E) =_{df} P(E/Tc) > P(E)$ and $P(E/Tc) > 1/2$.

In other words, I is taken to stand for the positive probabilistic relevance requirement together with the so called Leibniz-condition. In (ii') the **inductive** (or epistemic) probability measure P is defined for sentences, which we can do for ordinary first-order statements. How to define it for probability statements is more problematic. In any case, even a qualitative or comparative characterization of P will do for our purposes. In Tuomela (1977), pp, 365-366, the qualitative counterpart of (ii') is studied and its consequences for the properties of ρ are briefly investigated. It is to be noted, however, that for some inductive explanations (ii') is inappropriate. For instance, probabilistic causation based on low-probability laws require dropping at least the Leibniz-condition. (Cf. Tuomela (1977), Chapter 12.) Also note that (vi) here is the minimality condition corresponding to (5) in the DE-model.

For lack of space we shall not discuss here the logical properties of ρ-arguments. Notice finally that ρ-arguments may be pragmatically backed and "explained" in a certain sense (as shown in Tuomela (1977)). Roughly speaking, if a scientist strives for the maximization of his expected epistemic utilities, here taken to be information and truth, he will be led to **accept** a singular statement when a ρ-argument for it can be given. This is closely connected to our definition (**1**) of explaining (or to a pragmatic explanation of such an act of explaining actually), but I shall not here present the details in a precise fashion. (The connections are quite obvious and easily construable; see especially Tuomela (1977), pp. 370-373.)

CHAPTER 11

PROXIMATE EXPLANATION OF SOCIAL ACTION

I. EXPLANATION AND SOCIAL ACTION

1. In this and the next chapter we shall outline a theory of the explanation of social (i.e., multi-agent) action and discuss some specific issues related to this broad topic. Our account will in part connect with the purposive-causal theory of social action developed in this book and hence emphasize the agents' causal action propensities. In addition, we shall also emphasize that the explanation of social action can be handled within the pragmatic nomological account of scientific explanation presented above in Chapter 10. A third key aspect of our theory of the explanation of (intentional) social action is that such explanation should in part consist in laying bare the participating agents' conduct plans and relevant practical reasonings leading to their joint action.

In this chapter we shall concentrate on the explanation of intentional actions in terms of proximate mental factors such as intentions and beliefs. We wish to arrive at an account of explanation which in principle covers the explanation of various social actions such as two or more agents' carrying jointly a heavy piano, greeting each other, asking questions and answering, ordering the other to do something, and so on. We would also like to account for such broader collective phenomena as a wedding ceremony, an orchestra's playing a musical piece, a political demonstration, etc., when conceived as social actions.

Let us start by considering a simple example of an intentional social action. Suppose that A_1 and A_2 are agents intending to move a piano to the next room. They consider that in that particular context it is necessary for them to jointly carry it there. (It is too heavy for either one to carry alone.) We may now suppose that each agent undergoes a process of practical reasoning which leads to this concluding in favor of doing his part of the complete social action. Interpreting the relevant intentions as conditional ones, the following simplified practical reasoning can now be attributed to agent A_1 (cf. (PR_i) of Chapter 7):

(PR_1) ($P1_1$) A_1 intends to move the piano (to the next room), given that (he believes that) A_2 will move it.
($P2_1$) A_1 believes that unless he and A_2 jointly carry the piano (to the next room), it cannot become jointly moved there by them.
($P3_1$) A_1 believes that A_2 will move the piano.
($P4_1$) A_1 believes that A_2 will carry the piano (to the next room).
(C_1) A_1 intends to carry the piano (to the next room).
(C_1') A_1 carries (with A_2) the piano (to the next room).

In (PR_1) the conclusion (C_1) follows "logically" (analytically) from the premise-conjunction ($P1_1$)&($P2_1$)&($P3_1$)&($P4_1$), given that normal conditions obtain. We may look at the inference from the premises to the conclusion in two steps. First we infer that A_1 intends to move the piano (or do "his part" of the moving in the group $\{A_1, A_2\}$, if you prefer) from ($P1_1$) and ($P3_1$). This inference relies on the validity of an inference of the form: 'A intends p, given that (A believes that) q' and 'A believes that q' entail 'A intends p'. I think that, at least if **akrasia** is barred, this is a sound principle. Next we infer from the just obtained unconditional intention-statement and ($P2_1$) the statement 'A_1 intends to carry the piano (to the next room), given that (he believes that) A_2 will carry it'. (Again, we could use the phrase 'A intends to do his part of carrying...' instead of 'A intends to carry...' if the latter formulation looks misleading.) This inference is made plausible by the validity of the (ordinary) practical syllogism (see Tuomela (1977), Chapter 7 on that). Finally, the deconditionalization of the just obtained intention-statement by means of ($P4_1$) gives us (C_1).

The statement (C_1') can even be taken to follow analytically from (C_1), given normal conditions for the realization of intentions (see Chapter 7). Furthermore, within the purposive-causal theory of action we can say that A_1's **intentional** action token of carrying the piano in a sense contains as its element his willing or effective intending to carry the piano.

We may symmetrically write out a completely analogous schema of practical inference for agent A_2 by replacing 'A_1' by 'A_2' and 'A_2' by 'A_1' throughout. Let us call this schema (PR_2). What is interesting and important here is that (PR_1) and (PR_2) are **interconnected** (recall our discussion in Chapter 7). This is seen already from the premises of these schemas, but it is better highlighted by considering the justification of the third and fourth premises, ($P3_1$) and ($P4_1$). The truth of these premises can be justified on the basis of A_1's belief that A_2 reasons analogously with him. For the fact that A_1 believes that the premise conjunction $(P1_2)\&(P2_2)\&(P3_2)\&(P4_2)$ is true (and that it entails (C_2)) entails both $(P3_1)$ and $(P4_1)$. Consider thus the deductive justification of $(P3_1)$. It is, in fact, seen to follow, by deconditionalization, even from the following two statements corresponding to 'A_1 believes that $(P1_2)$ and that $(P3_2)$' (cf. our discussion of belief-deconditionalization in Chapter 7):

(α) A_1 believes that A_2 intends to move the piano, given that A_2 believes that A_1 will move the piano.
(β) A_1 believes that A_2 believes that A_1 will move the piano.

The deductive justification of $(P4_1)$ is obtained by noticing that A_1's belief that (PR_2) is valid entails A_1's belief in its conclusion: A_1 believes that A_2 will carry the piano (to the next room). This statement is just $(P4_1)$.

Even if the above observations may seem rather obvious and trivial they are important, for they show that in the case of social (i.e., multi-agent) action the agents' processes of reasoning which causally lead them to act must be strongly interconnected. In other words, we may plausibly assume that the acting agents have such relevant mutual knowledge (or beliefs) about each other's conative and doxastic attitudes and processes of practical reasoning that without such mutual knowledge (of beliefs) joint social acting is not possible. (Note, however, that our above schemas (PR_1) and (PR_2) do not fully incorporate the mutual beliefs unless the justifications of these interconnected schemas are also taken into account; see Chapter 7, Figure 7.2.)

Let us generalize our above example. We are then dealing with m agents $A_1,...,A_m$ performing a social action X, which is analyzable as the conjunction $X_1\&...\&X_m$. We will now add a premise stating in effect that normal conditions for performing X obtain and that it is a mutual belief of the agents that they do. Normal conditions for the successful carrying out of intentions are assumed to be included, and so we may use an action-statement as the conclusion of our schema. As was mentioned in connection with our schema (SA_i) of Chapter 7, the extra mutual belief requirement is not needed for the logical validity of the schema. It is rather an underlying justificatory assumption and it is, therefore, put in brackets. What we now get is our schema (PR_i) of Chapter 7. We reproduce it here for the purposes of our subsequent discussion, for i=1,...,m:

(PR$_i$) (P1$_i$) A_i intends to do (his part of) X, given that (he believes that), for all j=1,...,m with j≠i, A_j will do (his part of) X.
 (P2$_i$) A_i believes that unless A_1,...,A_m, respectively, do X_1,...,X_m they cannot jointly do X.
 (P3$_i$) A_i believes that, for all j=1,...,m with j≠i, A_j will do (his part of) X.
 (P4$_i$) A_i believes that, for all j=1,...,m with j≠i, A_j will do X_j (as his part of X).
 (P5$_i$) Normal conditions for doing X obtain, and A_i believes they obtain.
 [(P6$_i$) It is mutually believed by A_1,...,A_m that, for all j=1,...,m, that ((P1$_j$)&(P2$_j$)&(P3$_j$)&(P4$_j$)&(P5$_j$), and that hence (C$_i$)).]
 (C$_i$) A_i does X_i.

Our generalized schema (PR$_i$) can be considered valid essentially on the grounds presented above to justify the validity of (PR$_1$), mutatis mutandis.

The scope of the schema (PR$_i$) is quite broad. As indicated in Chapter 7, when (P6$_i$) is regarded as belonging to it, (PR$_i$) corresponds to the schema of Figure 7.2 when it is generalized to the case of m agents and applied to social actions. Given this (PR$_i$), together with the justification of its belief-premises, amounts to Lewis' so-called (rearranged) replication schema (see Lewis (1969), pp. 113-116). Viewed in game-theoretic terms, it, as well as (SA$_i$), actually fits any game with a proper equilibrium strategy which the intention in (P1$_i$) can be taken to concern. As any m-person game is known to have an equilibrium (although not necessarily a proper one and one in unmixed strategies or actions) this indicates the large scope of (PR$_i$). As indicated in Chapter 7 schemas like our (SA$_i$) and, hence, (PR$_i$) can be modified to account not only for rule-obeying action but also for rule-violating action.

(PR$_i$) can be weakened in various ways analogously with its closely related counterpart (SA$_i$) (see Chapter 7). Here we may mention its probabilistic weakenings. We could, for instance, use 'believes it is probable' instead of 'believes' in the premises (or use some more specific "probabilification" method). We shall not here discuss the resulting schemas for practical reasoning except for noting the following. While (PR$_i$) - being logically conclusive - may be regarded as giving A_i a **conclusive reason** (or conclusive reasons) for doing X_i, we then only get a logically inconclusive, but yet (perhaps) inductively satisfactory, schema giving A_i an **inductive reason** for doing X_i.

2. Our schemas (PR_i) and (SA_i) can be used either as schemas for practical reasoning or - with proper tensing - as schemas for explaining a singular social action (assuming its occurrence). Our present interest is in its latter function. Let us thus consider in what sense (PR_i) can be of help in explaining the occurrence of a token u of a social action X. First, it should be acceptable that (PR_i) can be taken to explain the exemplification of the component action X_i (of X) by A_i. Calling this action token u_i, within the purposive-causal theory of action we get, for instance, a causal explanation of u_i by stating that it was purposively caused by the mental episode (effective intending cum believing) realizing the premises of (PR_i). Other theories of action may treat the situation differently, but it can nevertheless be accepted, I think, that (PR_i) has proper explanatory uses. (Not all instantiations of this schema need to be explanatory, though, for there are idle intentions and beliefs.)

Suppose that we get an explanation of every u_i, i=1,...,m, tokening a component X_i of X (=X_1&...&X_m). Have we thereby explained u (a token of X)? No, it seems that we have not. For u is in general not merely a sum of the u_is, even if these subtokens serve to generate u (cf. our definitions of notions of complex social action in Chapter 5). What we thus seem to need is an explanation of each u_i and an account stating that, and how, the u_is generated u. However, the situation can also be viewed differently. For we may assume, to begin with, that our explanandum u indeed is, in the technical sense, a token of a complex social action X having the u_is as its parts. Then the formation that the u_is generated u has already been built into our explanandum. Thus citing the premise conjunction ($P1_1$)&... ...&($P6_1$)&($P1_2$)&... ...&($P6_m$) will indeed suffice to give a kind of explanation of u, provided it gives satisfactory explanations of the subtokens u_i. Our cited explanans - the long premise conjunction - can be regarded as a **social conduct plan** (cf. Chapters 5 and 6 on this). Notice that a social conduct plan requires reference to a relevant we-intention by each A_i in the present case. But we may regard the intention in premise ($P1_i$) to be a we-intention, for we have in ($P6_i$) the mutual beliefs that (**WI**) presupposes. (Normally the schemas (**W1**) and (**W2**) of Chapter 2 will also be satisfied in this case, and we will below assume they are.)

While the above sketch of explanation is just a rather preliminary and incomplete one, we can already here point out that it fits our general pragmatic account of scientific explanation. Let us thus consider our earlier example of A_1 and A_2 jointly moving a piano to the next room (action token u). We assume that u is a social action token which was generated by (here: consists in) A_1's and A_2's carrying the piano (the subtokens u_1 and u_2). Let us now go to an explanatory context with B as our explainee and A as our explainer. Suppose B puts his explanatory query (Q) as follows: "Why did A_1 and A_2 perform u (intentionally)?" The **oratio obliqua** form of this question will be our q. Then A states his explanatory answer (v): "A_1 and A_2 performed u intentionally because $(P1_1)\&...\&(P6_1)\&(P1_2)\&...\&\&(P6_2)$". This v qualifies for a scientific explanatory answer, given that it can be suitably backed by a complete scientific explanatory answer. Let us for the sake of argument assume that it is so backable. Then, disregarding context and paradigm, we have a case of scientific explanation, roughly, if A intended to make B understand q by producing v and if he believed that v is a scientific explanatory answer to q via coming to have a belief that v is a scientific explanatory answer to q. The context C, disregarded above, is just constituted by our singular explanatory situation. There is no need to discuss here its details (such as A's and B's relevant aims and beliefs). The paradigm P could be taken to amount, more or less, to the purposive-causal theory of action and hence the interpretation of 'because' in v to purposive causation (or generation).

The above is a rough sketch of how a rudimentary example of explaining social actions can be fitted into our general theory of explanation. A final comment on it to be made here relates to our assumption that v indeed can be backed by a complete explanatory answer. This essentially amounts to showing the possibility of constructing a nomological argument (an E-argument) to back the singular explanans v. The pressing problem here is the problem about the existence of an appropriate backing law. If it could be somehow proved that such a law cannot exist, then it would follow that action-explanations do not fit our account of scientific explanation. As the backing law in question need not be couched in the same vocabulary as v, it is indeed a difficult task to produce such a proof, be it an a priori one or not.

I am actually willing to defend the possibility of **social laws**, viz., laws in the same (type of) vocabulary as v with the possible addition of some theoretical predicates. In Tuomela (1977) I have discussed the possibility in principle of psychological laws and argued for that. It seems that the problem of the existence of social laws is quite similar to the corresponding problem in psychology. Thus, for instance, if it would be a nomic regularity that single agents in such and such appropriate conditions act or at least are disposed to act on the basis of their practical reasonings (and thus exercise their relevant causal powers) then we may surely have a social psychological law of an analogous kind, e.g., "Whenever some agents $A_1,\ldots,A_m$, in a certain type of situation C, reason according to (PR_i), $i=1,\ldots,m$, then they will do or at least strongly tend to what they take to be X". It is arguable that in view of the difficulty of specifying the conditions C and thus forming "closed systems", in actual research practice the best to be hoped for might be only idealized nomic tendency statements (or, speaking quantitatively, propensity statements in the form of probabilities well below maximal). However, we shall not here discuss the possibility nor the exact form of social laws further but just go on and assume that it is quite possible a priori that the social realm (individualistically conceived) is lawful not only in the single-agent case but indeed in the multi-agent case (cf. our further remarks in Chapter 12).

3. Let us now consider in some more detail the explanation of social action. As earlier we will focus on fully **intentional** social actions. By a **proximate** action-explanation we mean one in which the explanatory factors are such mental factors as the agents' intentions and beliefs from which the action more or less directly flows. For instance, the practical reasoning on which an action is performed represents such a proximate mental explanans. We contrast proximate explanations with explanations in terms of more **distant** motivational factors such as deeper underlying wants, policies, wishes, emotions, mood, character, or norms, roles, social status, and so on. Within the purposive-causal theory of action such factors will play a dynamic, causal role. We therefore call action-explanations in terms of such distant factors **dynamic** explanations. Such dynamic explanations, in a suitably qualified sense will be the topic of the next chapter.

I will distinguish between three central types of explanatory queries that can be made when explaining an action (a single-agent or a multi-agent one). They can be stated as follows:

(1) What was done?
(2) What was it done for? (For what sake was it done?)
(3) Why was it done?

The first question asks for a **classification** or **interpretation** or **redescription**: What are those people in the street doing? They are demonstrating against the use of nuclear energy. We shall not be much interested in this first type of query below, and we shall normally assume that a satisfactory classification of the action has been given. Let me here just say that answering a what-question takes place by suitably classifying the action. Thus if we classify a social action token$_1$ u as an action token$_2$ of type X we have classified it in a certain way (cf. Chapter 5). We may also go on and further classify it in terms of, e.g., the actors' underlying wants and beliefs. Attributing suitable wants and beliefs to indicate what the action "expresses" then gives further interpretation and redescription to the action often in terms of something more stable and durable than the action token itself.

Question (2) represents a **teleological** query: For what sake are you pupils rehearsing that song? **In order to** present it at our school at the Independence Day celebration. Teleological queries and explanations are quite typical, and we shall below explicate their form and nature in the case of social actions.

Question (3) asks for either a **reason** (a teleological notion) or a **cause**. The preceding example can in fact be regarded as implicitly giving the agents' reason: They intended to sing that song at the celebration and thought that to be able to do that properly they had to rehearse it. It can also be claimed that (3) can be answered by a directly teleological locution such as by means of the in order to -locution (cf. the preceding paragraph). Anyhow, we get a causal explanation of the social action in question when we say that the agents acted **on** that reason, entailing that their mentioned intendings and believings causally led them to do (their part of) the social action.

There is still a fourth type of query that can be regarded as important. We represent it by:

(4)   How was it done?

Question (4) asks for the manner (or style) or process of the action or for the way in which it came about. We shall come back to this problem area at the end of this chapter.

In Tuomela (1977), I have presented a purposive-causal account of the explanation of single-agent action. Although that account might be refined in some respects, I will below accept it as tenable for the explanation of single-agent action. But multi-agent actions, the topic of this work, provide additional problems, and it is these problems that we shall now encounter.

Concentrating on teleological explanations, reason-explanations and (intentional) causal explanations, my basic view is the following. An intentional social action performed by some agents $A_1,...,A_m$ can be proximately explained by, ideally and ultimately, laying bare the (joint) social conduct plan on which these agents performed the action to be explained. (Recall here our distinction between complete and mere scientific explanatory answers; the latter need not require laying bare the conduct plan while the former do.) A conduct plan deals with the agents' practical reasoning (at least some rudimentary reasoning). Practical reasoning gives reasons for acting. Practical reasoning is also teleological as it mentions the agents' joint goal(s), typically by reference to their relevant intendings. Causal considerations enter at least when it is required that the agents act **on** their social conduct plan. For this involves each agent A_i's acting on his personal conduct plan (cf. the premises of (PR_i)), and such acting may be argued to involve purposive causation and generation and hence act-relational intentions (see Tuomela (1977), Chapter 8 and cf. Chapter 4 above).

Let us now go into some details. We consider the proximate explanation of a token u of a social action type X. The underlying explanatory question may be taken to be either (2) or (3) from our above list.

1.A. Our first type of explanation of u assumes that it is known to the explainee (and to the actors) that u is fully intentional and indeed that it is intentional when conceived to exemplify a social action type X. In our explanation we now specify that u is a complex social action of the type X, analyzed as $X=X_1 \& \ldots \& X_m$ in our theory. As we can see from the definition of a complex social action type in Chapter 5, this entails that it is known that u is generated by **some** (so far at least partly unspecified) subtokens u_i (respectively exemplifying an X_i). Our explanation specifies in detail these u_is and how they produced u. In our present type of explanation we next "micro-explain" u in part by explaining each of the subtokens u_i (i=1,...,m) via the agent A_i's intendings. Here we may use (PR_i) (or some weaker version of this schema), and, as claimed, thus the A_i's we-intendings to do X get involved, too. We also have to specify how the result events of the u_is generated that of u. One way of doing it would be to say that the agents' social conduct plan was indeed realized by the u_is and u. Another way would be to simply state: $IG^*(u_1,\ldots,u_m,u)$; see (9') of Chapter 6 for this notion of indirect purposive generation IG^*, meant to apply to all types of social action, including actions "by representation". (Also probabilistic generation should be allowed here and below.)

Our first type 1.A gives rather little information. But in any case it gives a (partial) specification of the exact inner structure of the social action involved and specifies how u in fact came about, and it often states that the agents intended to do X (cf. (PR_i)). (As argued in Chapter 7, this intention can plausibly be regarded as a we-intention.) As will be seen from our explication below, explanatory intendings are directed towards goals. Therefore we may call this explanation of X a minimal teleological (or intentional-teleological, because of its involving act-relational **intendings**) explanation. Note that it is also a reason-explanation as it specifies the agents' joint reason for doing X. Furthermore, it is arguably causal (or, more specifically, purposive-causal), for the explanations of the u_is involved here are also explanations of single-agent actions and accordingly causal, given the tenability of the purposive-causal account of Tuomela (1977).

1.B. In this subcase of explanation we assume that the m-agent social action u to be explained is not known (to the explainee) to be a social action of a certain (presystematic) type. (It need not either be known (to him) that u was intentionally performed by $A_1,\ldots,A_m$.) Thus the "microstructure" of u, viz. the u_is and even the general mechanism generating u out of them, is not known (to him). Then we can give an explanation of u by saying that it is of type X, where X is a (complex) social action type. But when giving that classification in detail we also get a "microexplanation" of u by specifying the subtokens u_i and the patterns by which they generated u. (We shall later in the context of so-called invisible hand explanations discuss this microexplanation in some more detail.)

In the case at hand, viz. the **intentional** social action u, we need purposive generation: $IG^*(u_1,\ldots,u_m,u)$. But the purposiveness in question entails reference to the agents' social conduct plan. This means that we (implicitly, at least) use the social conduct plan of $A_1,\ldots,A_m$ to explain u. Thus at least in terms of our **complete** explanatory answers, which in cases like this will have to specify the social conduct plan, the structure of this subtype of explanation is similar to the first subtype. It is therefore also teleological. The only essential difference is **epistemic**. In the first case 1.A it is known to the explainee that u is an intentional action token of type X, in the second case this bit of information must be given in the explanans. Our second type of explanation is more informative that the first one as it gives more information relative to its explanandum-content that does the first relative to its explanandum-content.

2.A. Assume first that the agents $A_1,\ldots,A_m$ intentionally performed a social action token u of type X. Then we may rather shallowly and minimally explain u by stating that these agents we-intended to do X. This "holistic" explanation directly in terms of a we-intention - their reason for acting - need not specify the microstructure of u at all nor need it speak of I-intentions (and I-beliefs) at all. On the other hand, if it would employ (PR_i) then this case would be reduced to 1.A. I am willing to accept an account which ultimately builds we-intentions out of I-intentions in this way, as clarified in Chapters 2 and 7. Given this, our explanatory case 2.A ultimately is reducible to 1.A. Nevertheless, as it stands, 2.A gives us a minimal holistic teleological explanation of u.

2.B. Let us make case 2.A epistemically imperfect exactly analogously with 1.B. Then, as compared with 2.A, we also get a classification of u as an X intentionally performed by $A_1,\ldots,A_m$ and, hence, a somewhat more informative explanation.

3.A. We may next in a sense combine 1.A and 2.A. Thus we start with we-intentions from them according to the following idealized schema (recall (**W1**) and (**WI**) of Chapter 2) assumed applicable to all the agents A_i; i=1,...,m:

(S)   We will do X.
      I am one of us (viz. $\{A_1,\ldots,A_m\}$).
      I will do (my part of) X.

In other words, (S) shows how A_i derives from his we-intention and I-intention. This I-intention is the one that we then use in our (PR_i) to give an explanation of the type 1.A. In this type of explanation we may leave it open whether we-intentions can strictly be reduced to I-intentions and I-beliefs. (Note that while each intentional social action is required by our (**5.10**) to involve a we-intention that we-intention need not be the we-intention **to do** X, which intention we are here concerned with.)

3.B. This type of explanation is the epistemically reduced counterpart of 3.A. Thus it combines 1.B and 2.B in the obvious way.

4.A. Assume again u to be an intentional social action of type X. Now we give a proper holistic teleological explanation as follows. We assume, perhaps idealizing somewhat, that all of our agents reasoned according to a schema of the following type:

(T)   We will do Y.
      We consider that unless we do X we cannot do Y.
      We will do X.

(T) is a somewhat simplified, conceptually conclusive schema of we-intention transfer. A more realistic version would be obtained by letting X be considered only in some way, perhaps probabilistically, conducive to Y. In any case, this schema gives us a we-intention to do X and then we may continue our explanation as in case 2.A.[1]) What we get is a proper teleological explanation of u referring to a further joint goal (Y) of the agents $A_1,\ldots,A_m$. As all the other cases of explanation considered so far, this explanation is at bottom also a purposive-causal explanation (see below).

4.B. This case is the epistemically reduced counterpart of 4.A analogously with the preceding B-cases.

5.A. We start as in 4.A and use (T). Then we continue with 3.A. This gives us a proper teleological explanation of u, which gives the full "microcontent" in terms of the single agents' intentions and beliefs (as specified by (PR_i)).

5.B. This is the epistemically reduced counterpart of 5.A.

6.A. Given an intentional social action u of type X we may give it a proper teleological explanation in individualistic terms and even by means of different further goals. Thus we start with the following schema (simplified analogously with (T)), applicable to A_i, i=1,...,m:

> (IT) I will do Y_i.
> <u>I consider</u> that unless I do X I cannot do Y_i.
> I will do X.

This schema for the transference of intentions is individualistic and when all the Y_is coincide it gives us an individualistic counterpart of (T). Otherwise we have a situation where $A_1,\ldots,A_m$ perform a social action on the basis of different further reasons (viz., intentions to do Y_i). The conclusion of (IT) is an expression of A_is intention to do X. Given this conclusion we may continue our explanation with 1.A.

6.B. This case gives the epistemically reduced counterpart to 6.A and concludes our list of the types of explanation.

There are several issues that may be taken up in connection with the above analysis of the types of explanation of social action. First, I would like to recall that all of the types of action-explanation we are discussing in this chapter are assumed to fit the pragmatic nomological account of explanation of Chapter 10.

I will not here try to prove it in detail except that I refer to the illustration given above in subsection 1 concerning a simple explanation in terms of (PR_i).

Our above accounts of six types of explanation are simplified and idealized, and these types are not claimed to exhaust all the possibilities for giving proximate explanations of intentional actions. But I want to maintain that these explanations, all involving relevant intendings, provide us with some important conceptual "dimensions" of such explanation worth further study and worth connecting with explanations in terms of "deeper" underlying, intention-generating, factors (see Chapter 12). The discussed types of explanation have some philosophically central features which we shall discuss in some more detail below. These features are, as mentioned above, that they are (at least minimally) **teleological** (or, better, **intentional-teleological**), they involve **purposive causation**; and they are at least usually **reason-explanations**. They are also often closely related to explanation in terms of rules or, as is often said, **"normative" explanations**. Let us now turn to these issues.

II. TELEOLOGICAL EXPLANATION

1. What is a teleological explanation of action? Such an explanation must at least be taken to involve a **goal** or an **end** the agent actively has and in order to achieve which (or for the purpose of achieving which) the agent acted. Let us say in a preliminary way that an end is either an action of the agent or an event (or state) which is a result (or consequence) of such an action. An end which is an action type we call a goal. Thus an agent's having a goal entails the agent's having a certain proattitude with the goal as its object (or at least somehow contained in it). A teleological action-explanation typically also says something about the agent's belief concerning a means-action for achieving that goal. This means-action must be taken to be at least (e.g., probabilistically) conducive towards the agent's achieving his goal. As is well known from the literature of the topic (cf. Woodfield (1976)), it can be granted that the means-action need be neither necessary nor sufficient for the goal.

As we are concerned with the explanation of intentional action we will actually be involved with **intentional-teleological** explanations. They are teleological explanations "involving" the agents' relevant intendings, indeed act-relative intendings (cf. Chapters 3 and 4). They do not necessarily involve their intentions to do the action X to be explained but often some broader intentions from which nevertheless the agents' intentions to do X (or their parts of X) are conceptually obtainable by a suitable intention-transference schema (cf. our (IT)), even if ontically these latter intendings may be non-existent. Such a broader intention has as its object the achieving of the (or a) goal, say G. The sense in which intentional-teleological explanations **involve** relevant intendings is that a **complete** explanatory answer will either directly or opaquely (viz., under some other, e.g., a non-psychological, or a purely functional description) refer to relevant explanatory intendings (cf. Tuomela (1977), Chapters 8 and 9 on this).

Before discussing goal-directedness in more detail let me first propose a characterization of the notion of intentional-teleological explanation of a single-agent or social action in terms of the notion of scientific explanatory answer. This answer is an answer to a teleological for what -question, say q (= For what was the intentional action token u performed by the agent(s)?). Omitting reference to context and paradigm, my characterization is:

(ITE) v_t is an **intentional-teleological** scientific explanatory answer to q if and only if
 (1) v_t is a scientific explanatory answer to q;
 (2) the complete scientific explanatory answer c_t corresponding to v_t satisfies the following clauses (or, if there are several such complete answers, all of them satisfy):
  (a) c_t contains a statement to the effect that the agent(s) had a certain goal G such that he (they) believe(s) that doing X (or their part of X), of which type u is, is conducive towards G;
  (b) c_t involves a statement about the agent's (or agents') explanatory relevant intending (or, respectively, we-intending), related to achieving G;
 (3) the agent(s) acted on his (their) relevant intending(s) and beliefs in order to achieve G (clause (2)(b)) and the accompanying belief (clause (2)(a)).

The intention in (2)(b) can be an intention to achieve G or a related, usually more general intention (cf. (5.10)). Accordingly, (2)(b) can be taken to entail that the agents have G as their goal, yet it does not entail the whole (2)(a). Requirement (3) I find rather important. Unless the agent(s) had acted on his (their) goal (viz. goal-attitude), and his (their) belief concerning the means in order to achieve G we do not obtain an explanation. Idle attitudes do not determine behavior and therefore cannot serve to explain it. In some cases clause (3) may perhaps be taken to be implied by the clauses (1) and (2). But I have stated it to cover the cases where it is not so implied by (1) and (2). We shall, anyhow, below explicate the phrase 'acting on' in terms of purposive causation: an agent acted on an intending and believing just in case, roughly speaking, they purposively caused (or probabilistically so caused) his action. In the social case we respectively speak of acting on a we-intending and a we-believing.

Our above six patterns for explaining social actions are obviously compatible with (ITE). Taken in the context of the purposive-causal theory, it is of course assumed that the "relevance" in clauses (2)(b) and (3) of (ITE) is determined relative to the conduct plan with the respect to which u is intentional and on which the agent in question is in effect assumed to act in clause (3).

Note that the intentional-teleological explanatory answer v_t might simply be 'A did u (of the kind X) in order to achieve G', which is perhaps the most familiar explanatory teleological statement we encounter in this kind of context. The effective intending lying at the back of v_t in the sense required by clause (2)(b) is an act-relative one when realized as a willing: A willed, by X-ing, to achieve G (cf. our discussion in Chapter 4).

I am willing to claim that all proximate mental explanations of intentional social action can be reformulated and complemented to ultimately become intentional-teleological action-explanations. Let us call this broad thesis (ST1). By an explanation we here technically mean an explanans, viz. a scientific explanatory answer, irrespective of what it is an answer to.

We can easily see that our thesis (ST1) holds true of the above six types of proximate social action-explanations and that the 'in order to' locution properly applies to them. I shall not here try to give further arguments for it. Let me, however, point out that the thesis (ST1) is the analogue of the single-agent thesis called (T1) in Tuomela (1977), p. 215. There some arguments for the latter thesis were presented. As at least all individualistic explanations of social actions seem to involve as their elements explanations of single-agent actions, we have here support for (ST1). I would say then that it is the presence of intendings in proximate mental explanations which guarantees (ST1), for these intendings, when spelled out as act-relational, make purpose-talk and in order to -talk appropriate. Thus if A_i intended, by X_i-ing, to contribute to achieving G (or intended of his X-ing that it contribute to achieving G), then achieving G is his purpose and the goal in order to achieve which he acted.

Thus irreducible act-relational intendings are important both in describing and in explaining action. We recall from Chapters 3, 4 and 5 that our notion of willing is act-relational (for otherwise the mental realm and the physical realm - behavior - do not properly meet) and therefore action descriptions on our account involve act-relational intendings. Now I argue that similarly proper teleological explanations involve act-relational intendings, for otherwise accidental causal behavioral consequences of intentions (cf. wayward causal chains) and behavior by means of which the agent genuinely intends to achieve a goal cannot be conceptually separated.

It is close at hand to suggest that (ST1) is at bottom a conceptual truth about proximate mental explanations of intentional social actions. Due to the vagueness of the concept of proximate mental explanation I would not really have to object to this suggestion, although I do. As (ST1) is not central for our present purposes I will not, anyhow, pursue the matter further here.

2. Let us next discuss in some more detail the notion of goal-directedness relevant to our (**ITE**). Goal-directed behavior can be regarded as behavior which is appropriately systematically directed towards a goal. That such behavior is **appropriate** for a goal can be taken to entail that it is **conducive** to (or promotive of) the goal. Furthermore, and this may be taken to add to conduciveness, goal-directed behavior should be **persistent** as well as **plastic** with respect to the goal. The properties of conduciveness, persistence, and plasticity have been widely discussed in the literature (for a survey, see Woodfield (1976)), and I shall not here try to analyze these notions in general.

I would like to emphasize that within intentional acting, as conceived by the purposive-causal theory, these aspects of goal-directedness are certainly present. This is due to the notion of **acting on a conduct plan**. First we note that within the purposive-causal theory it is true to say that (concentrating on the single-agent case, for simplicity) an agent performed an action intentionally just in case he **acted on** some conduct plan or other (or, performed the action purposively **because of** some conduct plan or other); see (**PC**) and (**PCS**) of Chapter 4 (as well as Chapter 10 of Tuomela (1977)). A conduct plan typically involves, first, a goal action of an agent and, secondly, some action believed by him to be conducive for bringing about that goal (cf. (**PC**)). Thirdly, acting intentionally on a conduct plan involves the agent's "act-relationally" having that goal (and willing it) and his belief purposive-causally generating his behavior cum the result involved in the action. But, acting on a conduct plan also involves the agent's interacting with his environment in an appropriate way (see Tuomela (1977), Chapter 9). His conduct plan may involve "information gaps" which he must fill in when acting. This typically involves acquiring new perceptual beliefs and , accordingly, the creation and implementation of new "subplans" of action. This is connected to, and involves, **plastic** adaptive acting. Furthermore, the operative conduct plan is supposed to **control** the agent's behavior, and this normally involves his being aware of what he is doing or at least of the basic action part of what he is doing (cf. the notion of "satisfaction$_2$" of Tuomela (1977), Chapter 9, explicating this). It normally also involves the agent's **persistently** pursuing his goal, even in the face of great obstacles.

In view of our above remarks and our discussion in Chapter 4 we may characterize intentional goal-directed (or teleological) actions as follows (for single agents):

(IGA) An action token u (of type X) was performed **intentionally** by A **in order to achieve a goal** (or u was **intentionally goal-directed**) if and only if there was a conduct plan K of A such that
(1) according to K, there was a goal G of A that A intended, by Xing, to achieve and X was believed by A to be conducive towards G; and
(2) A acted on K.

Suppose G* is a specific goal making the analysans of (IGA) true. Then we say that A performed u intentionally in order to do G*. Note that, as indicated, the appropriateness of u for a goal G is in part accounted for by its conduciveness towards G (clause (1)) and in part by the persistence and plasticity involved in the agent's acting on K.

(IGA) is related to, for instance, Charles Taylor's and Wright's views. According to Wright (1976), an agent (or organism) does something X in order to achieve something G just in case (i) X tends to bring about (or is appropriate for) G and (ii) X is performed because it tends to bring about G (Wright (1976), p. 39). In the analysans, G must be a goal, I have gathered from Wright's discussion. In view of what I said above, the satisfaction of (1) of (IGA) entails (i) above and (2) goes some way towards meeting (ii). If A's belief that X is conducive to G is correct, then indeed (2) entails (ii), and (IGA) can be regarded as a special case of Wright's schema, given a specific goal (except that my analysis of goals is different from

Wright's, as will be seen). The converse does not hold even in the case of true belief, for Wright's analysis does not require act-relational pro-attitudes or intendings (and it allows for non-intentional actions as well). In (2) of (**IGA**) purposive causation is involved to the effect that (2) deals with **intentional** acting on K.

Given that (**IGA**) is an adequate explication of teleology for intentional single-agent actions, two consequences immediately follow. First, we get an equivalence between intentional action and intentional teleology. For acting on K can be taken to entail the truth of (1) and (3) of (**PC**) (and conversely) while (1) of (**IGA**) can be regarded as equivalent to (2) of (**PC**), as 'end' in the latter just refers to a goal. This result is not very informative perhaps, for we operate with a very broad notion of goal (end); see (G) below. To make (**IGA**) equivalent with (**PC**) it should be taken broadly enough to cover such expressive intentional acting as applauding by clapping one's hands of jumping for joy (as they may be regarded as ends in themselves: G coincides with X). What our observation shows is that the purposive-causal theory analyzes intentional acting teleologically, for we arrived at (**IGA**) in part on the basis of considerations other than (**PC**). That is, we did not strictly take (**PC**) as our basis for construing and understanding the concept of intentional acting that (**IGA**) is concerned with.

The second obvious consequence that follows is that if an action token u is explained in terms of (**ITE**) then u is an intentional goal-directed action performed in order to do G in the sense of (**IGA**). Note that while (**IGA**) existentially quantifies over goals (as does (**PC**)), (**ITE**) does not. In contrast (**ITE**) explains u in terms of a specified goal.

What happens in the case of a social (or multi-agent) action? The generalization of (**IGA**) to this case is quite obvious. We just substitute '$A_1,...,A_m$' for 'A' in (**IGA**) and insert the word 'social' in front of 'conduct plan' in clause (1) of (**IGA**). Then obviously we make $K = K_1 \& ... \& K_m$. Given this, we have an analysis for the social case and analogous comparisons with (**PCS**) can be made. (No separate mutual belief requirement covering the agents' awareness of social action is needed.)

We have not so far presented any analysis of goalhood except from indicating that goals are action types "occurring in" some proattitudes an agent actively has. This is an **internalist** view of goals. An **externalist** view would define goals somehow in terms of overt behavior and behavior-dispositions (see Woodfield (1976) for a relevant discussion). We shall later in Chapter 13, Subsection I.4, discuss end and goals in some more detail. Here I will just state generally what I take to be characteristic of goals. First, an agent (or a collective of agents in the social case) must either (a) intrinsically want the action G which is to be called a goal or (b) he (or they) must extrinsically want G such that this want conceptually presupposes he (they) believe(s) it is his (or their) duty of obligation to act so that that action tends to generate the goal-action G. Secondly, that want or that belief must be capable of motivating the agent(s) to perform appropriate means-actions with respect to G.

Put more explicitly, we have for an action type or, more generally, want-content G (cf. (5.16)):

(G) G is a **goal** of S (where S is a single agent or a group of agents) if and only if
(1) (a) S intrinsically wants to do G, or
(b) S extrinsically wants to do G, where this extrinsic want is conceptually based on S's believing that doing G is his (or S's operative members') duty or at least that he (they) ought to do G; and
(2) S's (intrinsically or extrinsically) wanting to do G can motivate (and typically or at least ideally does motivate) S (in the single-agent case) or the operative members of S (in the group case) to perform actions believed by him (them) to be appropriate for G.

What kind of want-contents, and thus goals, can there be? At least ordinary action-types (in our sense) and disjunctions of them qualify. One may also want to omit to do something. In addition, there are conditional want-contents (e.g. to do X, given C) and variable goals which are functions of time and circumstances, for instance, but we shall not discuss them specifically here. In any case, goal-directed action in the sense of (**IGA**) need not then be unconditionally directed towards the performance of a single specific action type.

As we want to include unconscious goals in our account (**G**) does not involve a relevant mutual belief-requirement - which in the case of conscious goals surely must be satisfied.

As to the condition (1) in (**G**), its (a) is concerned with desires and the like **intrinsic** pro-attitudes. Its clause (b) again is concerned with so-called **extrinsic** wants or pro-attitudes, viz. duties and obligations recognized by the agent(s) to be such. In the case of (**IGA**) and (**ITE**) intendings, indeed act-relational ones, are involved. But as indicated in Chapter 4, they still involve the presence of either intrinsic or extrinsic wants (pro-attitudes) here playing a special **conative** role in the production of action (as well as carrying on and controlling it). The second condition of goalhood is concerned with potential motivation. Note that clause (2) of (**IGA**) requires that the goal also actually motivates in that the agent's (or agents') having a goal purposive-causally produces action.

Surprisingly or not, in social psychological literature there are very few analyses of the notion of goal available. Let me here just mention one. Shaw, after considering some previous attempts and rejecting them as inadequate, proposes this: a group goal is an end state desired by a majority of the group members (Shaw (1981), p. 350). This agrees with our (**G**) as far as clause (1) goes. But Shaw's analysis is inadequate for there may be completely idle wants, and surely ends corresponding to such wants cannot plausibly be called goals. Clause (2) of (**G**) is supposed to handle this problem.

Both (**G**) and (**IGA**) incorporate the externalist idea of goal-directed behavior being **appropriate** for the goal, and this should typically include the aspects of conduciveness, persistence and plasticity. But (**G**) and (**IGA**) also embody an internalist notion of a goal, thus unifying in part externalism and internalism. (As to the problem of how to analyze goals in the case of goal-directed organism to which propositional attitudes cannot plausibly be ascribed, I think the right way to go about would be to find out the dispositional **bases** of the goal-attitudes and try to see what specific features in the case of lower goal-directed animals somehow analogically correspond to them in the sense of motivating behavior.)

We may here pause to notice that within the conceptual framework of the purposive-causal theory of action it is possible to define weaker notions of goal-directed behavior that that defined by (**IGA**). Thus looking at our definitions (4.5) of an action token$_1$ and (5.5) of a social action token$_1$ we can see some teleological elements. Any action token$_1$ is goal-directed in the sense that the behavior in it has been causally produced by an episodic action token of a propositional attitude. However, the propositional attitude in question need not strictly be taken to be directed towards a goal-action, as characterized above. This is because an action token$_1$ need not be **appropriate** for the goal it is directed towards. Accordingly, it need not be conducive towards it nor show relevant persistence or plasticity. A completely analogous point can be made about the goal-directedness of arbitrary social action tokens$_1$.

A much more adequate notion of goal-directedness is obtained by requiring in addition that the action token$_1$ be appropriate for the goal-action (which indeed becomes a goal-action in our above technical sense). Thus we may define:

(GB) A piece of behavior u by A is **goal-directed**$_g$ if and only if
(1) that item of behavior u is an action token$_1$, say u = <v,...,b,...,r>,
(2) v is an event realizing a pro-attitude with the content V such that V is a goal, and
(3) u is appropriate (at least in the sense of conduciveness) for V.

This definition gives a general but adequate notion of goal-directedness applying to, e.g., non-intentional action. It can be considered to be a special case of Wright's above analysis. (Note that (3) requires objective rather than believed appropriateness.) Our definition, especially clause (3), can be explicated to involve that by doing u A aimed at V (cf. act-relational intending in (IGA)). As is to be expected, a completely analogous definition of goal-directedness can be formulated for social action tokens$_1$ in the obvious way. Explanation of goal-directed$_g$ action can of course be treated analogously with the relation between (ITE) and (IGA).

III. PURPOSIVE-CAUSAL EXPLANATION

1. Let us next consider purposive-causal action-explanations. The notion of purposive causation was introduced in Tuomela (1977) as a functionally characterized notion basically to account for the notion of **acting on a conduct plan**. To recapitulate, the following two aspects are involved here. First, acting on a conduct plan is a causal notion in the sense that the event (or state) of the agent's actively holding or entertaining a conduct plan, such as the premises of a practical syllogism, purposive causally produces and controls his relevant action in cases where the agent actually carries out (or tries to carry out) his conduct plan. Secondly, the produced action must be in accordance (in a strong **de re** aboutness sense) with the conduct plan. It is by his action that the agent aims at or intends achieving his ends. In other words, the agent's intentions are act-relational in that he intends of his behavior that it realize the conduct plan. The presence of act-relational intending, and especially willing, secures the conceptual tightness needed between the conduct plan and what realizes it, so to speak.

Purposive causation means ordinary event-causation taking place according to and due to a conduct plan (and thus the agent's act-relational attitudes and intentions) - and so "preserving" the agent's purpose (whence the name) and, we claim, blocking wayward causal chains (cf. Chapters 3 and 6). Purposive causation is a teleological notion, not reducible to mere causation in the conceptual realm. By what ontological mechanism purposive causation operates is a different matter - something to be decided by scientific research rather than by philosophical speculation.

What interests us in the present context is that wayward causal chains can be constructed also in the case of social actions. To take simple example, assume that two agents A and B are duelling with revolvers. Duelling is a social action, we may assume. Each participant intends to kill the other one by shooting him - and to do all this in the normal, intended way. But suppose things go wrong. A's bullet first misses B but it suitably ricochets (perhaps in a very complicated manner) finally hitting B and killing him. Yet we would not like to say that A killed B by shooting, in the normal way, fully intentionally. This is because the causal chain leading from A's trigger pulling to B's dying was wayward (because unintended and against the implicit or explicit content of A's operative conduct plan). Suppose then that B tried to shoot A simultaneously and the analogous thing happened here, too. B came to kill A via a wayward causal chain. We thus have here a social action where the total end result of A's killing B cum B's killing A came about non-intentionally and not in conformity with the agents' social conduct plan or with what they we-willed to do by their behaviors.

There are many other ways wayward causal chains can arise, but we shall not here consider them. To repeat, our claim is that our notion of **acting on a conduct plan** - as explicated in terms of act-relational purposive causation and generation - will block them. That this will be the case we cannot argue for here generally (but cf. Tuomela (1977), Chapter 9). Let me, however, emphasize that the basic underlying idea here is that intendings and willings are act-relational in the sense of the agent's intending and willing something always **by his bodily behavior** (or **of it** that so and so), discussed in Chapters 3 (Note 4) and 4 of this book. The act-relationality of willings (effective intendings) conceptually ties together (1) the willings, (2) the relevant bodily behaviors (actions) needed for satisfying these willings as intended and (3) the satisfying ends themselves. That a theory of action indeed needs such causally active and act-controlling willings needs argumentation beyond that, of course, but that is provided by the overall adequacy of our theory of action.

The concept of a social action as characterized in Chapter 5 is a causal (or causal-generational) concept. It is no wonder then that the explanations of social action within this theory of action become causal. Consider thus an intentional m-agent social action token u = <t,...,b,...,r> = <t,t_1,...,t_m,...,b_1, ...,b_m,...,r_1,...,r_m> such that u tokens a social action type X (= X_1&...&X_m). Here t = t_{we}^1+...+t_{we}^m, and b = b_1+...+b_m. Each t_i, i=1,...,m, represents agent A_i's willing, by his bodily behavior, to do X_i and the b_is just the total behaviors involved in doing X_i. Each t_i has been generated by the we-intention t_{we}^i, indeed according to schema (S) of Section I. The r_is represent the results of the subtokens u_i exemplifying X_i, and r is the total result of u, and it is generated by the r_is. We have above been claiming that the explanation of an intentional social action token, such as u, takes place by laying bare the social conduct plan on which the agents A_1,...,A_m acted when producing u. Now this entails that the mental episodes activating the social conduct plan are mental episodes taking place in the agents A_1,...,A_m and that they involve at least t_{we}^i and t_i in the case of each A_i. It is essentially these episodes, characterized in the terminology of the social conduct plan as intendings cum believings (or, slightly better, the temporal "end slices" of these episodes), which, when ultimately describable as willings, cause the behaviors b_i. Each b_i generates the corresponding r_i, and finally the r_is jointly generate, causally and/or conceptually, r. (See Chapter 6 for a precise statement of this.)

As we can see from the above succinct description, the production of a social action token u by A_1,...,A_m ontologically reduces to some individual causal event chains (corresponding to each A_i) and to the interaction effects of these causal chains (to produce the full result r). The explanation of u lays bare at least some of the involved causal links (see our earlier description of the six types of the proximate explanation of social action). This strongly indicates that explanations of social actions require the specification of some causal links. And, as argued above, the causal (and other generational) processes in question have to be **purposive** to involve the idea that the agents by their behaviors intend to perform X.

2. We may now try to formulate a little more explicitly what can be meant by the notion of purposive-causal action-explanation. Corresponding to our (ITE) I thus propose, in the case of an explanatory question q = Why was the intentional action token u performed by A_1,...,A_m, the following analysis:

(PCE) v_{pc} is a **purposive-causal** scientific explanatory answer to q if and only if
(1) v_{pc} is a scientific explanatory answer to q;

(2) the complete scientific explanatory answer c_{pc} corresponding to v_{cp} (or every such complete answer, if there are several) involves strict or probable purposive generation comprising some causal generational link.

The requirement of purposive generation in clause (2) concerns the use of **IG***(t,r) or its probabilistic version (or at least the use of some suitable strict or probabilistic near-equivalent) such that $t = t_{we}^1 + \ldots + t_{we}^m$. (See (9') of Chapter 6 for an exact characterization of **IG*** and Note 4 of that chapter for the probabilistic version.) The causal links required in clause (2) are typically concerned with the causal generation of a t_i by t_{we}^i, b_i by t_i, r_i by b_i, and r by the r_is. (**PCE**) can be satisfied by making use of any of the six kinds of explanation of social action discussed earlier in this chapter. Some of these kinds give better purposive-causal explanations than others; much also depends on the content of the social conduct plan underlying **IG***.

Now I am ready to state my second broad philosophical thesis about the explanations of social action: All intentional-teleological explanations of intentional social actions can be recast as purposive-causal explanations (**ST2**). (This thesis corresponds to an analogy entailed by the conjunction of (**T3**) and (**T4**) in the single-agent case; see Tuomela (1977), p. 215.) In effect (**ST2**) amounts to the partial translatability of teleological explanations into purposive-causal ones (yet not to mere causal ones because of the presence of act-relational intentions). Accordingly, it does not reduce away the central teleological notions our (**ITE**) employs, as also purposive causation is a teleological notion. (The converse of (**ST2**) may conceivably fail because of clause (2)(a) of (**ITE**).)

(**ST2**) is true basically because of clause (3) of (**ITE**), for I have already argued for the entailment of the presence of purposive generation by the notion of acting on a conduct plan, involving act-relational intentions (see also the arguments in Tuomela (1977), Chapter 8).

IV. REASON-EXPLANATION

1. Let us next consider reason-explanations as well as explanations connected to the agents' practical reasoning. We shall consider the common sense idea that one's reason for acting is his wanting or believing something to which the action is suitably conducive. I will first reproduce my earlier characteriz-

ations of a single agent's acting for (direct) reason from Tuomela (1977), p. 230, but using mainly nontechnical terminology:

(R) p was agent A's (direct) **reason** for performing u (an action token) if and only if
    (1) (a) 'p' is a statement to the effect that A wanted that q, where q is an action description; or
       (b) 'p' is a statement to the effect that A believed that q', where q' is an action (or action-end) description or a statement directly or indirectly about action (or action-end) generation (or probable generation);
    (2) A had a belief to the effect that there is a singular action y which u indirectly or directly purposively generates or probably so generates, and y satisfies q (in the case of (1)(a)) or q' (in the case of (1)(b));
    (3) A acted on p (viz. on that he wanted that q or believed that q').

In (R) the notions of wanting and believing should be taken in their broader senses; thus, for instance, extrinsic wants such as duties are involved. (R) is only concerned with **direct** reasons as opposed to **indirect** ones. To see what this distinction involves consider the following example. We sometimes say that an agent's reason for his taking his umbrella with him is his belief that it will rain. This belief I call his **indirect** reason while, e.g., his belief to the effect that he will stay dry if he takes his umbrella with him (cf. q' in clause (1)(b)) I call his direct reason, in accordance with (R). Roughly put, indirect reasons serve to activate wants and beliefs which are direct reasons and in this sense underlie the latter. We shall here only consider direct reasons. There is also a distinction between **guiding** and **explanatory** reasons which cuts across our distinction between direct and indirect reasons (see, e.g., Raz (1979) on this one). Thus the fact that it will rain or the fact that one's taking his umbrella with him will generate his staying dry may be guiding reasons for an agent to take his umbrella with him while his **belief** that it will rain may be an indirect explanatory reason and his belief that his taking his umbrella will generate his staying dry is a direct explanatory reason for his taking it with him (cf. Tuomela (1977), Chapter 8 on the explanatory power of reasons). In this chapter we are explicitly concerned only with direct explanatory reasons.

    One further thing that may be noted about (R) is that in

(3) 'acting on' is meant to be explicated in terms of (strict or probabilistic) purposive generation (**IG***). As we have in effect seen earlier, this entails that the agent is intentionally acting on a conduct plan involving ρ and that he accordingly is at least in a minimal sense aware of what he is doing. Especially, he is required to be so aware of his acting on ρ, viz. his want or belief in question. But even more must be required in the fullest case of acting for a reason. Put in terms of our example, the belief that it will rain must occur in the agent's relevant, often very rudimentary, practical reasoning which is contained or involved in his acting on his operative conduct plan (involved in acting on ρ and in (**IG***) in (3)). Thus, the reasoning might here simply be to the effect that the agent intends to avoid getting wet and believes that taking his umbrella with him is necessary and (probably) sufficient for achieving that end and that, therefore, he should take his umbrella with him. I shall assume that however it is explicated in the general case, acting on ρ will, in the context of (**R**), involve A's practical reasoning, concluding in favor of his performing the action (type) that u exemplifies. The practical reasoning in question may be quite rudimentary and often it may hardly deserve to be so called; thus even so-called "mutilated" practical syllogisms lacking a belief premise may qualify in the present context. As I have elsewhere (in Tuomela (1977)), pp. 228-232) discussed (direct) single-agent reasons in detail I will not here further comment on (**R**) nor is that perhaps required for our present purposes.

2. I would next like to give a characterization of what it is for some agents $A_1,\ldots,A_m$ to act for a (complete or partial) joint reason when performing a social action token u (cf. explanatory questions of type (3) in Section I). This notion seems to involve at least that each A_i acted for a reason (in the sense of (**R**)) in producing his subtoken u_i. But we of course need more if we want to get hold of the idea that our agents acted on a joint reason, and even the agents' merely acting for the same reason does not suffice (for that might be accidental). My suggestion is that, to capture this, the agents must share a suitable common reason or "we-reason" of which they are mutually aware. Let me propose the following characterization of (explanatory) joint reasons, in the case of a social action token u of type X such that $X = X_1 \& \ldots \& X_m$:

(SR) ρ_{we} was a **joint** (direct) **reason** for which $A_1,\ldots,A_m$ performed u (a social action token) if and only if
(1) (a) 'ρ_{we}' is a statement to the effect that $A_1,\ldots,A_m$ we-wanted that q, where q is a statement describing some social action; or
  (b) 'ρ_{we}' is a statement to the effect that $A_1,\ldots,A_m$ we-believed that q', where q' is either a statement describing some social action (or action-end) or a statement directly or indirectly about social action (or action-end) generation (or probable generation);
(2) $A_1,\ldots,A_m$ we-believed a statement to the effect that there is a social action token y which u directly or indirectly purposively generates or probably so generates such that y satisfies q (in the case of (1)(a)) or q' (in the case of (1)(b));
(3) $A_1,\ldots,A_m$ acted on ρ_{we}; and
(4) $A_1,\ldots,A_m$ had a mutual belief to the effect that (1), (2), and (3).

A few comments are in order here concerning the aspects in which (SR) goes beyond (R). First, we use the notions of we-want and we-belief in (1). Whatever else a we-attitude of either kind may involve it at least entails - in the present context where u has been performed intentionally - that each A_i has that we-attitude and that it is a mutual belief among the agents $A_1,\ldots,A_m$ that this we-attitude is shared in this group (cf. our discussion of these matters in Chapter 2). Let me emphasize that u must be intentional, for one cannot, strictly speaking, non-intentionally act on a reason, I will assume. If so, then the wanting in (1) will often play a role of a we-intending. Note that ρ_{we} need not always be (or play the role of) a we-intending, for the intentionality of u may be due to some other we-intending (we-willing), as our (5.10) allows. Yet it is true to say here that the agents by performing u, as an X, intended to satisfy 'ρ_{we}', for we regard reasons as act-relational (as well as all the other attitudes and intentions involved in operative conduct plans).

As to the clarification of clause (3), let me suggest that it can be taken to entail the following two statements:

(i) there were reasons ρ_i, i=1,...,m, such that ρ_i was A_i's reason for doing u_i (an action token of type X_i such that it is a subtoken of u, if the latter is of type X);
(ii) ρ_i, i=1,...,m, was purposively generated by ρ_{we}.

If 'ρ_{we}' is a we-intention statement such as 'We will do X' then our earlier inference schema (S) explicates the generation in (ii) giving as its conclusion the individual reasons ρ_i. In general, the purposive generation required in (ii) may be non-deductive as well, but it should always be "justification-preserving". We shall in Chapter 12 discuss the motivational problem of which joint reasons really make actors move when faced with a multitude of reasons. This is a rather intriguing problem. To see that one need only think of a prisoner's dilemma situation (cf. littering, tax-paying). The agents have a good joint reason to cooperatively (for that yields a Pareto-optimal outcome), but the individually most rational and tempting action is the non-cooperative one. (Note, however, that typically there is no ρ_{we}, we-want, concerning the non-cooperative social action and thus clause (ii) would fail in those cases.)

Let us next consider our clause (4). This mutual belief clause is quite analogous to the one in (5.1) in our definition of a basic social action (see our comments there). As we argued in Chapter 4, single-agent basic actions, as analyzed by our (4.1), do not explicitly require an awareness clause. Similarly our single-agent reasons as analyzed by (R) do not either require it. Yet in the social case we need it, for, as we argued, a collection of agents cannot be taken to be aware of their reasons for acting in the same obvious and immediate sense as single agents. The role of (4) now is to require that $A_1,\ldots,A_m$ in a sense be aware of their acting for a reason when they indeed are acting for a reason. To act for a reason is to act in the light of the reason, we may say. We may also put it in a somewhat circular way by saying that these agents must, at least typically, believe or be aware that they are acting for a reason. This belief may be regarded as a **de re** one and therefore as one which does not presuppose that the agents have the concept of that reason (cf. a group of children acting for a we-reason).

To take an example of we-reasons, consider our earlier case of two agents' carrying the piano. Their reasons for doing it is given (in a somewhat minimal sense) by (PR_1) and (PR_2) as formulated in Subsection I.1. Roughly put, the agents' common want (in fact, intention) to move the piano to the next room together with the appropriate belief concerning the means (carrying) constitute the (or, at least, a) joint reason for which A_1 and A_2 carried the piano. Had they not been at least minimally aware of each other's reasonings they clearly need not have performed their action even if we assume that they share the intention and the relevant beliefs. (Recall, however, that $A_1,\ldots,A_m$ need not have the concept of reason even if they act in the light of or for the reason.)

The above indicates the need for a mutual awareness (at least shared awareness) requirement. It is easy to find other resembling examples where the agents indeed do their component actions (and where the token u comes about as a result) but, from a social interdependence point of view, somewhat "accidentally", viz. without their being aware of the other agents' reasons (if they so do). In such cases $A_1,\ldots,A_m$ cannot be said to act for a joint reason even if all the agents happened to act for the same reason.

The we-attitudes in (1) and (2) of (SR) may indeed plausibly be explicated to involve mutual awareness, as we just said above. But, in any case, we still need mutual belief concerning clause (3). While our mutual belief requirement in (4) concerning (1) and (2) thus may be superfluous, it is yet harmless in that case (see our discussion concerning such repetition of mutual belief in Section II of Chapter 7).

Let us now consider acting for a reason and practical reasoning. In view of our comments on (R) and (SR), recall especially (i) and (ii), there is a good ground for claiming that acting for a joint reason is connected with (at least rudimentary) practical reasoning. We may perhaps thus consider the following general claim:

(RPR) ρ_{we} was a joint reason for which $A_1,\ldots,A_m$ performed u (a social action token of type X) if and only if $A_1,\ldots$ $\ldots,A_m$ did u due to their concluding their (social) practical reasonings, involving ρ_{we} essentially, in favor of performing X.

If we could accept (RPR) we might hope to get a broader concept of practical reasoning than that defined by (PR_i) and (SA_i) (and their weakened variants). As it stands, (RPR) is rather vague and without further elucidation of its right hand side much definite cannot perhaps be said about its truth. Let us yet try to say something and consider the central and problematic implication from left to right.

Whether or not acting from a reason entails the presence of practical reasoning depends on one's notion of practical reasoning, as said. I am inclined to characterize practical reasoning functionally on a par with a functionalist construal of mental episodes and processes in general (cf. Chapter 2 and Tuomela (1977), Chapters 3 and 4). Thus a person's entertaining the premises of a practical inference and his infering a conclusion from them is to be conceptually characterized on the basis of overt "stimuli" or "inputs" affecting him, his relevant actions and, especially, dispositions to act, as well as various interrelations between his mental states and episodes. Furthermore, inner mental practical reasoning is to be construed analogically with overt reasoning, viz. reasoning-out-loud. How to do all this is quite problematic, But I shall not try to accomplish it here.

One thing that yet follows from my above functionalist remarks is that there are no special mental qualities (qualia) that are part of practical reasoning. For instance, given that I construe him right, Audi (1982a) argues that such features of consciousness are present in practical reasoning. Accordingly, he arrives at a narrower notion of practical reasoning than the above one. He also argues that acting from a reason does not entail more than **potential** (not actual) practical reasoning. I shall not here enter a deeper discussion of the differences between functionalist and non-functionalist accounts of practical reasoning. Let me just say that a functionalist construal together with our earlier remarks make the implication from left to right in (**RPR**) rather plausible. For we just argued that (**SR**) involves some, perhaps weak kind of social practical reasoning involving ρ_{we} and concluding in favor of the agents' performing X.

How about the implication from right to left? It seems that it fails only if clause (2) of (**SR**) fails to come out true, given that any social practical reasoning must be taken to contain a mutual belief requirement. If we can accept that practical reasoning must always be teleological roughly in the sense of (2), we seem to be through. More exactly, if it is true that whenever $A_1,\ldots,A_m$ conclude their practical reasoning in favor of doing X, then there is a y (of type Y) such that Y is referred to in the premises of the reasonings and Y is a goal-action somehow generatable by means of X, then (**SR**) will be satisfied. I do find this suggestion at least somewhat plausible. It seems that at least our social practical reasoning schemas (**SA$_i$**) and (**PR$_i$**) and their close analogues can be taken to normally satisfy this. I will not here pursue the matter further but leave the truth of the implication from right to left in (**RPR**) as an open conjecture. (See Audi (1982a) for arguments to the effect that acting on practical reasoning involves acting for a reason.)

3. There is a special class of reasons which is central in the case of normative actions. This is the class of **normative** reasons or, more broadly, the class of **rule**-reasons, where (part of) the reason consists essentially in an intention to obey a rule. The norms or rules in question may be moral or legal ones

or they may, in fact, be any kind of community rules (recall our discussion in Chapter 8). For instance, when drivers stop at red light their actions may, presumably, be explained by saying that they do so because "that's the rule", viz., because they intend to obey and do obey (at least something like) the rule 'Every driver must stop at red light'. To be sure, often drivers are not directly aware of having such an intention (even if they retrospectively would accept having one) nor do they of course consciously rehearse the traffic code book in their minds. But an explanation does not require that. Another example is provided by the social action of greeting by shaking hands. In many societies it is a rule of etiquette that friends greet each other by shaking hands; they do it because "that's the rule".

Role behavior is an important case of acting because of rules (cf. Chapters 7 and 8). One need only think of a priest, a policeman, or a teacher performing his duties to realize this. In our account role-actions will accordingly be explained by reference to the agents' intentions to obey the rules characteristic of the role positions they occupy.

In general, both in the single-agent case and in the multi-agent case we may make a rough distinction between actions which are performed for an (internal) end only and those which are performed as a kind of responses to symbolic or semi-symbolic challenges (cf. the above examples and see von Wright (1980) for an illuminating discussion). This corresponds to an internal-external dichotomy of reasons falling within the scope of (R) and (SR). An action performed for the sake of an end is an action performed because the agents have some end they want or intend to achieve. The action in question is considered by the agents somehow conducive to the end. This end serves as an internal "guiding" reason for the action (see above).

Responses to symbolic (and semi-symbolic) challenges are social in the important sense of being centrally grounded in social rules. We may divide the challenges in question into the following two classes (cf. von Wright (1980)): (1) challenges presented in communicative action patterns, and (2) prescriptive rules and norms and analogous things (such as customs, manners, fashions and traditions). The first class is characterized by von Wright by reference to (allegedly) Habermas' notion of a communicative action. A communicative action consists of the occurrence of a challenge followed by a response to it (cf, Chapter 10). For instance, asking a question and answering it represents a two-person communicative action. Another type of example is provided by orders and requests followed by appropriate responses to them. An example of a semi-symbolic challenge would be a red traffic light, which together with a driver's response of stopping at it would constitute a communicative action, although here of course only a rudimentary notion of communicative action is involved. As in effect said, it is central in any case that responses to both types of challenges (1) and (2) involve rules (of some sort) and obeying these rules.

I shall here consider only one topic related to symbolic and semi-symbolic challenges, viz. their role in the explanation of action. It is von Wright's claim that challenges function as **external** reasons as contrasted with intrinsic wants and intentions based on them which function as **internal** reasons. Thus, if an agent passes the salt as a response to the request 'Will you, please, pass the salt' or if he stops his car at red light, no intention to obey the request (in the first case) or the traffic rule (in the second case) is present in the typical case. The agent simply acts, and he acts because of the external reason (the request or the traffic light). Here we have a reason-explanation of an intentional action without reference to an intention. It is required by von Wright that the external reason not only be "instituted" (belong to an institutionalized practice) but that the agent also **acknowledge** (and "internalize") this reason.

While I, too, emphasize the importance of external reasons and actions due to challenges I yet require the presence of an intention (willing) in the case of intentional action. The intention need not, though, be an intention to respond to the challenge (cf. our definition of intentional action in Chapter 4). Neither need the intention be an intention based on an **intrinsic** want. Indeed, typically (viz. when the agent has properly internalized the external reason and thus does not act from "normative pressure") it is not so based. But it is rather based on an **extrinsic** want. We recall that duties, obligations, and so on function as extrinsic wants. In general it is just external reasons in the above sense that are extrinsic wants.

Now the question may arise whether my dispute with von Wright is only verbal. Is it just that I call his external reasons extrinsic wants and that this is all there is to it? That is not the case, it seems. The basic problem seems to be the need for conation in intentional action and in the explanation of intentional action. Here my view is that when an agent intentionally acts on an acknowledged (or believed) ought-rule (challenge) there must be a conation, viz. intention, involved. Thus there is no intentional acting on mere (acknowledged) challenge. This I take to be a fundamental principle of action. I simply cannot make sense of **intentional** action without it. (But cf. my discussion of action token$_1$ and social action token$_1$

and of non-intentional actions generally in Chapters 4 and 5.)

Perhaps it should be emphasized that there are also mixtures of actions performed for the sake of an internal end and actions performed due to an external challenge. Thus if a person visits his sick aunt he may simultaneously act **both** on his intrinsic desire to please his aunt **and** on his thinking he ought to do so (or because it is a custom). In real life such mixtures of reasons are perhaps the most typical cases.

4. My view of the explanation of action also surely differs from that of von Wright but there is no need to discuss that here (cf. Tuomela (1977), Chapters 7 and 8). Instead we shall pursue our own approach and turn to the technicalities of reason-explanation. Following our previous schemas (**ITE**) and (**PCE**) I now propose for an explanatory question q = Why (for what reason) was u done by $A_1,\ldots,A_m$:

(**RE**) v_r is a scientific explanatory answer to q in the case of **reason-explanation** if and only if
(1) v_r is a scientific explanatory answer to q;
(2) the complete scientific explanatory answer c_r corresponding to v_r contains (or all such complete scientific explanatory answers, if there are several, contain) a statement expressing or playing the role of a joint (direct) reason for which $A_1,\ldots,A_m$ did u.

A simple example of a reason-explanation fitting (**RE**) would be the following (involving a single agent). Let our explanandum-content be 'A stopped his car'. It can be explained simply by 'A stopped his car because he believed there was a red traffic light in front of him' (v_r). This explanation does not (explicitly) refer to any intention of A but it is yet clearly compatible with our above analyses. Note that in the social case wa may of course employ the patterns of explanation sketched in Subsection 3.

Our concept of acting on a reason is a purposive-causal notion because of clause (3) of (**SR**). Thus every reason-explanans in the sense of (**RE**) also satisfies (**PCE**), disregarding q. Hence all reason-explanations of social actions are purposive-causal explanations (**ST3**).

Next, because, in view of our discussion of (**ST1**), all proximate mental explanations, partly due to stipulation, can be taken to involve act-relational intendings and because of (2) of (**SR**) we can see that a reason-explanans satisfies the central clauses (2)(a) and (2)(b) of (**ITE**). ((1) and (3) of (**ITE**) obviously cause no trouble.) Then we are in the position to state that all reason-explanations of social actions are intentional-teleological explanations (ST4).

Let us finally summarize our above general philosophical theses, with their stated qualifications, on the explanation of intentional social action:

(ST1) All proximate mental explanations of intentional social actions can be reformulated so as to become intentional-teleological explanations.
(ST2) All intentional-teleological explanations of intentional social actions can be reformulated so as to become purposive-causal explanations.
(ST3) All reason-explanations of intentional social actions can be reformulated so as to become purposive-causal explanations, but not conversely.
(ST4) All reason-explanations of intentional social actions can be reformulated so as to become intentional-teleological explanations, but not conversely.

The central role of intentional teleology (especially of act-relational intentions) and purposive causation in the explanation of social action becomes apparent from the examination of these theses. As suggested earlier, also acting on practical reasoning is closely connected with reason-explanation and, if (RPR) really were acceptable, through (ST4) also with teleology. Its close connection with purposive causation should in any case be at least plausible on the basis of our discussion.

V. EXPLAINING THE STYLE OF ACTION

1. Every social institution, organization and other similar collective is defined and characterized in terms of **rules** (norms, more specifically). It follows that rule-following action, such as acting for the reason 'That's the rule', is of central importance in social life. In the context of reason-explanation above we briefly discussed this kind of explanation. We also mentioned that our approach can be extended to cover the explanation of rule-violating behavior. Thus we can handle all rule-referring action, it seems.

Not all acting (nor every aspect of acting) is governed by social norms, however. Also other behavior - perhaps rule-following in a wider sense - must be considered in a theory of action-explanation. We can see this even from a consideration of "institutionalized" action such as role behavior. For instance, to act as a teacher does not (typically) entail anything about the amount of kind of gesticulation accompanying teaching behavior. The role norms for a teacher do not either say much about the specific kinds of interaction with his pupils and his fellow teachers that he should engage in. Role norms thus leave room for much unspecified and "uninstitutionalized" interaction. The same can be said of conventions and social rules in general.

What interests us especially here is not so much the fact that social rules leave room for many kinds of social interaction not governed by rules but rather that any kind of action, rule governed or not, can be performed in different **ways**. That is, we are here interested in the **manner** and, more broadly, **style** of performance. Following Goffman (1959) we may speak of manner and style as **dramaturgical** or script-following aspects of acting.

To get a good example of the dramaturgical aspects of action let me quote Birdwhistell on the military salute:

"During World War II, I became at first bemused, and later intrigued, by the repertoire of meanings which could be drawn upon by an experienced United States Army private and transmitted in accompaniment to a hand salute. The salute, a conventional movement of the right hand to the vicinity of the anterior portion of the cap or hat, could, without occasioning a court martial, be performed in a manner which could satisfy, please, or enrage the most demanding officer. By shifts in stance, facial expression, velocity or duration of the movement of salutation, and even in the selection of inappropriate contexts for the act, the soldier could dignify, ridicule, demean, seduce, insult, or promote the recipient of the salute. By often imperceptible variations in the performance of the act, he could comment upon the bravery or covardice of his enemy or ally, could signal his attitude toward army life..." (Birdwhistell (1970), pp. 79-80).

For instance, Goffman (1959) and, following him, Harré and Secord (1972) have gone far in their emphasis of the dramaturgical aspects of action. The basic idea is to compare real life with a theater play and real life acting with acting in a play. In acting people can monitor their performance (especially its stylistic aspects), and even monitor their control of the performance, and they often do so. The utilization of this power is called by Harré and Secord 'taking the dramaturgical standpoint'.

Given that people have the above dramaturgical power (the power to take 'role distance" in Goffman's terminology) Harré and Secord, following Goffman, formulate the following principle for **explaining** social activities:

(SE) "In order to understand, that is to provide a plausible account for the details of what people are doing, one must see their activities in terms of deliberate followings out of one or more rules or conventions of style. In fact what people are doing is rarely properly described as **just** eating, or **just** working, but has stylistic features which have certain conventional meanings associated with recognized types of personae." (Harré and Secord (1972), p. 216)

I agree with (SE) in so far it is not regarded as exhausting all there is to the explanation of social action. For instance, (SE) does not really directly help us in explaining why a social action **came about,** it seems, and that is certainly an important explanandum. It seems to me that Harré and Secord think that (SE) suffices to cover all of interest in the context of action-explanation. If that is so, I strongly disagree (cf. Chapter 3 above and Tuomela (1977), Chapter 8). Anyhow, the stylistic aspects of action are certainly important both for the description and the explanation of action.

2. Let me now go on to sketch how the stylistic (and expressive) aspects of action might be explained within the pragmatic theory of explanation presented in Chapter 10. My approach is quite different from Harré's and Secord's dramaturgical approach and is meant to cover only a part of the general and complex problem of style.

It seems that linguistically we may describe the stylistic aspects of action by means of suitable adverbs (especially the adverbs of manner). For instance, 'A opened the door angrily' is an action-describing statement where the manner of the opening is expressed by the adverb 'angrily'. Given this, we may ask what the class of such manner adverbs is and, indeed, how the stylistic aspects of an action really should be systematically classified. To these questions I do not presently have answers. I shall, accordingly, rely on our presystematic understanding of these notions.

In general, when describing the stylistic aspects of actions we can use the following kind of (single-agent) action statements:

(1) A did X α-ly.

Here 'α' expresses an adjective, e.g., 'angry', accounting for manner, and 'α-ly' the derived adverb. Now if we want to have an explanation of the manner of the action we may stress or emphasize this adverb:

(2)   A did X α-ly.

The emphasis in (2) is denoted by underlining the adverb. This emphasis may be taken to express **contrast** here. Thus, in (2) we implicitly compare 'α-ly' with other manner-adverbs such as 'β-ly', 'γ-ly', and so on. In terms of our example we may compare 'angrily' with 'calmly', 'carefully', and so on in

(2*)   A opened the door **angrily**.

With which other manner aspects we indeed do compare the original manner of (2) in general depends on the pragmatic context and the relevant background assumptions (expressed by C and P in Chapter 10). In our example case we could have a class R = {angrily, calmly, carefully, cheerfully, gloomily,...} of manner-features implicitly assumed. In the terminology of Chapter 10 we may call this class the **relevance class** (of alternatives) corresponding to the emphasized item in (2*). Now our explanandum corresponding to (2*) can be put as follows:

(3)   Why did A open the door angrily, rather than in the R-manner?

In (3) 'R-manner' refers to the list of manner-features of R (minus 'angrily').
   To put the explanandum corresponding to (2) in full generality we use the terminology of Chapter 10 and get as our complete explanandum

(4)   (?f(m_α,R)) A did X α-ly for the reason f.

Here '?' is the why-operator. $f(m_\alpha,R)$ is the question variable ranging over "reasons" which are concerned with the manner features in the relevant class R = {$m_\alpha, m_\beta,...$}, where m_α corresponds to 'α-ly', and so on.
   How do we answer the explanatory questions (3) and (4)? We do it along the lines described in Chapter 10. Let me briefly summarize that account. Let us, for simplicity, concentrate on (3). This question cannot be answered without a consideration of several rival explanations. To see this we consider the following potential (scientific explanatory) answer to (3): 'A opened the door angrily because his boss had just yelled at him',

implying that the boss's yell had made A angry. This explanation takes for granted that A opened the door. It provides information concerning the manner aspect of the action. The explanans is supposed to make it reasonable for one to expect that A performed his action angrily, rather than, e.g., calmly, if one had not known the manner beforehand.

There are actually two different problems involved here. First, we are looking for the best explanation (account) of the anger aspect. Is the above explanans better than, for instance, 'A opened the door in an angry manner because his boss had yelled at him and, although that did not make him angry, he thought that it was reasonable to exhibit anger behavior'? (It is not necessary here to answer this question nor even give exact criteria for evaluating explanations.) We note, incidentally, that manners such as the anger manner may or may not be due to an emotional state. An actor in a theater play may, I think, be taken to genuinely exhibit an emotional manner without really being in that emotional state. But this is in fact not a necessary presupposition above, and our discussion could as well be conducted in terms of non-emotional adverbs like 'skillfully'.

The second problem we are or may be dealing with in explaining (3) is how to exclude the explanatory accounts according to which A's opening the door should in fact have exhibited some different manner such as calmness. In bringing up this problem I really rely on the theory-ladenness (or, better, explanans-ladenness) of all description and argue that, depending on what our best explanation says, A might actually have been acting in a different manner than what our original describing of this action claims. So I am saying, in effect, that even in so-called actual explanation supposedly dealing with a **true** explanandum-content statement (such as (2*)) its asserted truth value is only putative and the additional "evidence" given by finding the best explanans may change this truth value; and in any case rivalling accounts of the explanandum are relevant to the adequacy of explanation even if the assumption of the truth of the explanandum-content were only counterfactually lifted. (Compare the present situation with prediction where the predicted event or state is epistemically completely uncertain. Corrective explanation is also a case in point.)

By 'best explanans' above I mean the best among the best explanantia for the different manner-aspects in R, supposing, for the sake of the argument that there is only one best explanation of each sort. I will not discuss here how to generally characterize the notion of a best manner-explanans for each manner in R nor, when that is needed, what we should take the best of these best explanations to be (but cf. the relevant remarks in Chapter 10). Normally in practice, however, we only need to find the best explanans for the manner actually exhibited, if we are reasonably sure of the explanandum-content description such as (2). For instance, if we have found something like the full determinant (cause) of the manner in (2) then it seems that the other manner-aspects become excluded: our determinant fully accounts for the 'rather than β-ly, etc.' phrase.

What kind of contentual features do the explanatory factors of the stylistic aspects of action possess? Without attempting to go very deep into this question, let me make a couple of suggestions. One typical explanatory factor surely is emotion. If A does something angrily, normally this manner of action arises from his anger via an "anger-determined" intention and some relevant beliefs guiding and directing the action, we may say. (I am here assuming a presystematic "overt" use of 'angrily' allowing for its applicability to, e.g., pretended anger-behavior.) In addition to the resulting kind of **emotive** style we may also speak of **cognitive** style. For instance, people may solve problems in different cognitive style. They may value goals differently, select means for achieving those goals in a different way, and so on. (Think of different styles in writing a philosophical paper on some given problem, for example.) To cognitive style also belong an agent's intention to **communicate** something by the style of his action. Consider here our earlier example of the military salute as used by an agent to, say, dignify or to demean somebody, or to comment on the bravery of his enemy, or to signal his attitude towards army life. Or think of Berne's (1964) "games" played either in an adultish, parentish or childish way to communicate the corresponding "ego states" (to use Berne's term). Differences in emotive and cognitive style are often explainable in terms of such temporary factors as moods and/or such permanent factors as temperament and character, but we shall not here go into details.

What can we say about the stylistic aspects of social actions? In most respects the situation here seems to be quite analogous with the single-agent case. Thus, corresponding to the explanandum-content (2) we now get either

(5) $A_1,\ldots,A_m$ did X α-ly.

or, perhaps,

(6) $A_1,\ldots,A_m$ did X α-ly such that A_i, $i=1,\ldots,m$, did, respectively X_i α_i-ly.

In (5) we use the emphasized manner-adverb 'α-ly' to characterize the manner in which $A_1,\ldots,A_m$ did X. In (6) we have in addition specified the individual styles by the adverbs 'α_i-ly' and implicitly claimed that each agent's doing his component action X_i α_i-ly amounts to their jointly doing the social action X α-ly.

If we use (5) then what we have above said about the explanation come across the problem of, so to speak, composing styles. Suppose some A_i does X_i hilariously (or skillfully) while the other agents perform their component actions sadly (or clumsily, respectively). What is the manner of the social action in this case? It seems hard to find anything general to say about such composition except that when every A_i does his X_i α-ly then $A_1,\ldots,A_m$ do X α-ly. (At least I cannot think of counterexamples to this principle; cf. our related remarks in Chapter 5.)

Suppose now that $A_1,\ldots,A_m$ do a social action X **cooperatively** and with the **same** style or at least with a **"cooperative" style**. For instance, a theatrical group of actors is supposed to operate not only cooperatively (viz., cooperate with respect to the **kinds** of actions they perform) but also to adapt their styles cooperatively. Thus when playing a sad and gloomy tragedy nobody in the group should act comically, and so on. (Incidentally, Goffman's (1959) notion of team seems to amount to that of cooperative group sharing a certain style.)

This ends our brief treatment of the stylistic aspects of (social) action. What it has at least brought forth is that often, when given an action token u of the kind X, we want and need to explain not only why (or what for, etc.) u, or an action of the kind X, was performed but also how (in what style or manner) it was performed and why (or what for, etc.) it was performed in a certain style, say α-ly (given that it indeed was performed α-ly).

VI. UNDERSTANDING ACTION

1. We started our discussion of action-explanation with the general idea that to explain a social action is to lay bare, in an appropriate sense, the operative social conduct plan of the actors. We showed how this idea could be developed within our pragmatic question-theoretic framework to account for, e.g., teleological, purposive-causal and reason-explanations and the style of actions. As a kind of result we ended up with appropriate types of scientific explanatory answers.

We recall from (8) of Chapter 10 that a scientific explanatory answer v is supposed to be "P-understandable in context C". We discussed such understandability in general terms in Chapter 10. Let me now make some more remarks specifically geared to understanding actions. First note that the nature of P and C will in part be impregnated and determined by one's underlying view of action. The general account advocated in this book is of course the purposive-causal theory of action (recall our relevant discussion in Chapter 10). I shall not here go more deeply into that but rather connect our account with rather similar views recently developed within the framework of artificial intelligence by Schank and Abelson (1977). (Their account also resembles in some ways the dramaturgical point of view discussed in Section V.)

Corresponding to our notion of a conduct plan Schank and Abelson speak of **scripts, plans,** and **themes.** Perhaps the best way would be to say in general, and overlooking technical differences, that their scripts are specific and routinized conduct plans while their plans are more general and nonroutinized conduct plans.[2] Their themes again might be regarded as very general knowledge structures underlying conduct plans.

To be a little more specific, a script might be generally regarded as a knowledge structure describing appropriate sequences of events in familiar situations. A script stands for a complex routine typically involving several actors. Let us briefly consider the coffee shop variation ("track") of their restaurant script (cf. Schank and Abelson (1977), p. 42ff.). Here the props are tables, a menu, food, and money. The characters or role players are the customers, the waiter, cook, cashier and owner. A script is always viewed from some role player's point of view, here from the customer's point of view. Thus we are in our terminology dealing with the customer's conduct plan which is part of the total social conduct plan of all the active participants.

Now, the script begins when the customer is hungry and has money, and it ends when the customer has less money and is not hungry and the owner has gained money. The first scene involves the customer entering the restaurant. His actions consist of the sequence of his walking into the restaurant, looking at the tables, making up his mind as to where to sit, walking to a table, and sitting down. Here each action is a causal precondition of the next one and could be described in terms of our account of generation (see Chapter 6 and cf. especially the formal grammars in its Section III).

The second scene concerns ordering. There are several alternative ways here. One is that the customer picks up the menu on the table, considers the choices, chooses one item of food, and signals the waiter. The waiter walks to the table; the customer orders the food from the waiter; the waiter walks to the chef, places the order with the chef, who then prepares the food. In this sense there are three actors, the customer, the waiter, and the chef, and there is clearly a generative connection between these agents' actions. The third scene concerns eating and the fourth exiting, but I will not describe them here.

Scripts can then be regarded as conduct plans dealing with more or less routinized, often habitual, sequences of (typically intentional) actions without paying attention to such details as particular bodily movements or sayings, etc. Often a person need not even specifically intend the sequence of actions the script is concerned with even if these actions are intentional. A great part of human activity seems to be script-based, and often habitual, intentional action, and our account can well acknowledge and account for this.

Plans are in many ways similar to scripts but they are less specific (cf. Schank and Abelson (1977), p. 72). A plan is made up of general information about how actors achieve goals. (See Schank and Abelson (1977), pp. 83-88, for a classification of goals relevant to plans and thus to social action.) In a sense scripts can be said to come from plans. For a poor beggar or for a Papuan eating in a restaurant would probably take place on the basis of a plan rather than a script. He would have to plan almost every action in advance and make inferences (cf. the practical syllogism); and he might not be able to foresee the relevant consequences of these actions.

Even if plans and scripts deal with complex social activities they are still limited in scope and duration. They are accordingly organized under general knowledge structures called themes. Corresponding to themes there are general dispositions of agents to act in certain ways. They can be said to generate conditions under which scripts and plans are followed. Schank and Abelson divide themes (or theme-dispositions) into three types, viz. role themes (e.g., being a waiter), interpersonal themes (e.g., being an employee), and life themes (being an industrious person).

2. I shall not here further describe the details of Schank's and Abelson's theory. The above account should suffice to indicate the relevancy of their developments to our theory of social action (even if their technical account is very much different from ours). Let me instead take up their view of action-understanding. They approach the understanding of actions via the understanding of stories of complex human activity. It

is characteristic of stories that information about intermediate steps and about goals of the agents is left unstated. It must be inferred. Understanding a story consists in one's being able to provide an account of these missing steps and goals (cf. our relevant remarks in Chapter 10). A good test of understanding is whether the understander is able to answer questions about these missing items. The understanding of stories is achieved by comparing the present case with suitable background information containing all the details. Typically the understanding of stories is achieved by assimilating the stories to stored past ones. This past information has been put in terms of scripts, plans or themes. As very much behavior is (or can be regarded as) script-based also script-based understanding is very central.

Schank's and Abelson's account can, I think, be taken to apply not only to stories about human activity but indeed directly to any human activity. One can indeed claim that an agent's action is understandable if it can be part of a script, plan or theme of that agent. I would conjecture that the class of such actions more or less amounts to the class of action tokens$_1$ in our sense (and analogously for social actions). All actions, viz. action tokens$_1$ of an agent can then be regarded as understandable; and the analogous statement holds for social actions.

Applied to our question-theoretic framework of explanation we can put the matter about understanding as follows. An explainee queries by putting a suitably explanatory question to the explainer. The explainer gives a relevant scientific explanatory answer which, as we saw, relies on the agent's (or agents') operative conduct plan. Such conduct plans can, if wanted, be explicated in terms of scripts, plans or themes, as just argued. But what is central here is that scientific explanatory answers, as contrasted with complete ones, may be very sketchy. And even complete scientific explanatory answers contain lots of gaps. Now, when a scientific explanatory answer is required to be "P-understandable in context C" this may just be taken to refer to the explainee's (potential or actual) understanding in something like Schank's and Abelson's sense. Given this, what understanding comes to involve is the explainee's comparing the information given by the explainer with his stored information (especially, scripts, plans, and themes). What the explanation is supposed to do is that it (actually or at least potentially) brings about in the explainee the ability to fill in the missing details and goals in a coherent (but perhaps not necessarily in a unique) way.

CHAPTER 12

DYNAMIC EXPLANATION OF SOCIAL ACTION

I. EXPLANATION AND OTHER-REGARDING UTILITIES

1. In Chapter 11 we distinguished between two general kinds of action-explanation, viz. (a) proximate mental explanation and (b) motive-explanation or dynamic explanation. In the case of proximate explanation the agent's (or agents') **intentions** were referred to as an important factor (cf. thesis (**ST1**) of Section I in Chapter 11). Here we will be more interested in motive-explanations or dynamic explanations by which we mean explanations in terms of deeper underlying mental factors leading to, and generating, intentions and (sometimes directly) action.

Let us say a little more about such dynamic explanations in terms of underlying motives and start by saying what relevant underlying factors we will **not** directly include among those to be investigated below. One group of factors is that of broad sociological and demographic ones. Thus, e.g., the socio-economic type of the agent's society will not be our direct concern, even if it may become indirectly involved. Similarly, such social-demographic factors as age, sex, occupation, wealth, social status, religion, or education will not be explicitly discussed. Nor will we say much about such clearly relevant factors as personality features (e.g., introversion - extraversion, authoritarianism, submissiveness). In addition to the above features, one might propose that the motivational profile and the general policies and strategies of actors are important explanatory factors. Indeed they are, and they are at least not far from our concerns below. Finally, one may propose that the immediate physical and social circumstances in which actions are undertaken are important determinants. We need not deny that. Yet we shall not do much situational analysis below.

What do we then mean by the underlying motivational factors meant to explain intention-formation and action? We mean, roughly speaking, the agents' wants, beliefs (and other similar affective and doxastic attitudes) as well as emotions that play the relevant kind of motivational role. As the explaining force of emotions and feelings (cf. love, fear) seems to be accountable in terms of the wants and beliefs they generate we shall really concentrate on the (extrinsic and intrinsic) wants and beliefs, both notions understood in a wide sense, underlying the agent's intendings and actings (cf. Chapter 4). Such wants and beliefs can be hypothesized to have been themselves generated by the general kinds of factors mentioned in the previous paragraph.

We will thus take for granted the existence of such wants and beliefs. Following our treatment in Chapters 2 and 9 we shall indeed assume, somewhat idealizingly, that we are given **utilities,** understood as want-intensities, and subjective **probabilities,** understood as degrees of belief. (As earlier, we shall also be dealing with mutual beliefs or awarenesses concerning especially the agents' utility matrices.) Let us then say that these utilities (and probabilities) are the **given** ones or the original ones. We shall below investigate some conceptually central features of the process by which the given utilities change, as a function of the social interaction between the agents, into what we will call the effective or **operative** ones. There are the ones **on** which the agents act (and on which they evaluate their actions). Speaking in terms of **conduct plans,** we will thus investigate some aspects of the process leading from pre-interaction conduct plans to operative ones. We shall below concentrate on utility-change and leave probability-kinematics out of our discussion. Given the operative utilities and probabilities, we shall later on in the chapter analyze how they are relevant to answering why agents act as they do and, especially, why they form intentions to act as they do.

Our treatment of the complex and sophisticated problems of motivation will be idealized but yet hopefully conceptually illuminating. First, we shall view agents as (at least moderately) rational in several aspects. Thus we shall take them to have at least momentarily consistent utilities and probabilities and to be free from short-term emotional disturbances, fatigue, and so on. But we shall not require our agents to be utility-maximizers (even if we in a sense come close to that). Secondly, as earlier, we shall concentrate on epistemically somewhat idealized situations. Thus we shall in general assume that the agents are mutually aware (or at least have reliable mutual probabilistic beliefs) of each other's action-alternatives and utilities (and usually also of the relevant outcome-probabilities conditional on action). We accordingly assume that our agents have gone through a (usually communicative) process of scrutinizing the available action-alternatives and come to accept a certain set of action alternatives as the one from which to make their choices, one at a time. These actions are valued by them in a certain way and probabilities to their leading to various anticipated goals or goal-relevant outcomes are assigned by them, too. As we in general assume that the agents are mutually aware of all this, we can say that they are assumed to "play the same game", be this a game in a strict game-theoretic sense or not.

To be sure, many real life situations take place in epistemically less pure and less idealized situations. While we cannot really below offer an explicit treatment, it can be hoped that a good account of them can nevertheless be provided by regarding them as a kind of deviations from the epistemically perfect cases.

It has frequently been argued in the literature that in interpreting behavior as action we somehow necessarily assume that behavior to be to some extent rational (cf. Davidson (1980), p. 267, Tuomela (1977), Chapter 9). Without really arguing for that here let me just say that indeed the application of the conceptual framework of agency to human beings does entail imputing some rationality to them, otherwise we could not make sense of their behavior nor of their cognitive capacities and states nor of their use of language either (cf. Davidson (1980), esp. Essay 14). Nevertheless while some general kind of rationality is presupposed, this presupposition may be only hypothetical and non-specific. It is at least in part an empirically testable matter in what **specific** sense people are rational (cf. the conflicting rationality criteria, such as maximin and maximax, etc., within decision and game theory).

We shall below devote relatively much space to discussing single agents' utilities and motivation. However, this is intimately connected to our main topic of social action because we shall concentrate on **other-regarding** utilities (and probabilities) and thus all the time be concerned with interpersonal interaction. But we shall also directly discuss group-utilities and group-probabilities and ask what makes social groups act, viz. collectives of interconnected agents perform social actions. Accordingly, we will end up with an admittedly somewhat sketchy account of what the dynamic explanation of social action conceptually amounts to.

2. Let us now go to the main topic of the present section, to give an account of operative utilities starting from given utilities. The given utilities can often be regarded as selfish or at least to a less degree other-regarding (not necessarily altruistic) than the operative ones. It is very central, however, that the operative utilities can be construed as other-regarding (see our comments below). Our account is going to be psychologically rather idealized mainly because of the complexity of the matter, but we hope it will capture, in an approximate sense, the conceptually important aspects of the situation.

We shall below rely on our relevant discussions in Chapter 2 and, especially, 9. We assume in the manner of Chapter 9 that utilities can be linearly decomposed into control components. To avoid unnecessary technical complications, we shall below restrict our formal treatment to the case with two agents, A_1 and A_2 or 1 and 2, for short. Accordingly, our basic assumption, formula (34) in Chapter 9, is, for $i=1,\ldots,r$, $j=1,\ldots,c$, and $h = 1,2$:

(1) $\quad u_{ijh} = \mu_h + \alpha_{ih} + \tau_{jh} + \eta_{ijh}$

where u_{ijh} is agent h's utility at the ith row and the jth column in the matrix of given utilities (assumed as our prerequisite on the basis of our earlier discussion). I will not here discuss the interpretation of (1) except for one comment. I want to recall that in the case of agent 1 the square of $\alpha_{11}-\alpha_{21}$ is our global measure of the scope of 1's control over his own utilities and the square of $\tau_{11}-\tau_{21}$ is that of his control over 2's utilities; the square of $\eta_{111}-\eta_{211}$ measures the scope of his conditional control over 2's utilities. In the case of agent 2 we have analogous measures except that α_{i2} and τ_{j2} switch interpretations. The reader may want to look up further relevant comments in Section III of Chapter 9.

Let us now consider the possibility that, when the agents ponder on the given utilities and on how to proceed to action in view of them, their evaluations change. Take the prisoner's dilemma situation of Figure 12.1, as an example. An agent may come to think that something good happening to his partner would, after all, be desirable also to himself. Maybe he then comes to think that he ought to act so as to maximize the **joint** utilities rather. Given that both agents think so, we get the transformation shown in Figure 12.1.

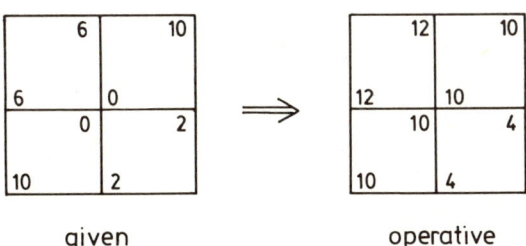

given   operative

Fig. 12.1

The operative matrix in Figure 12.1 has of course been obtained by simple summation over the agents' utilities in the given matrix. Acting on the basis of the effective matrix clearly leads to the choice of the first alternative (cooperative action), given that both agents maximize their expected utilities and do not assign quite unreasonable conditional outcome-probabilities to each other. Notice that our decision to leave probability-changes unaccounted is justified at least as long as the utilities are "prior to" (indeed, partly "determine") the probabilities rather than vice versa. The probabilities of outcomes are relative to the actions of the other players, the latter including, perhaps, the "chance-player" (when the probabilistic contribution of nature is included).

In any case, we shall assume that the players may transform the utilities of the results and consequences of their actions merely upon considering the other agents' utilities, without direct consideration of the relevant conditional outcome probabilities. There are both experimental evidence and theoretical psychological reasons for expecting such utility transformation to take place (see, e.g., Kelley and Thibaut (1978), Chapter 7 and McClintock (1972); also cf. Eibl-Eibesfeldt). As to the theoretical psychological reasons, a utility transformation may, first, provide a basis for action when no basis existed in the given matrix. A case in point is just our above example in Figure 12.1 where the effective matrix (as contrasted with the given one) gives a dominant action to both players. Secondly, a person may so attain better outcomes (utilities) than without such a transformation. Our example of Figure 12.1 is again pertinent here. Thirdly, a person may have more general reasons, such as **moral** ones, for being responsive to others and for making transformations which are strongly other-regarding.

Let us put the transformation problem generally as follows. We first assume as in (1) that

(2) $\quad u_{ijh} = f(\mu_h, \alpha_{ih}, \tau_{jh}, \eta_{ijh})$; f linear.

Thus, f might be just the function (1). Next, we consider the probability that the u_{ijh}s are functionally transformed into effective utilities, say u'_{ijh}. Let us write this as

(3) $\quad u'_{ijh} = g(u_{ijh}, u_{ijh'})$

where g is some suitable function and h,h'=1,2. Then

(4) $\quad u'_{ijh} = g(f(\mu_h, \alpha_{ih}, \tau_{jh}, \eta_{ijh}, \mu_{h'}, \alpha_{ih'}, \tau_{jh'}, \eta_{ijh'})$

is what we are looking for, given our assumptions. To know g, if there is an empirically and conceptually adequate one, would be to know much about want-dynamics and, in fact, intention-generation as well. Now g might be at least approximately linear. There seems to be at least some interesting empirical situations or types of cases where a linear g would seem approximately appropriate (see, e.g., McClintock (1972), p. 447 and the references to experimental literature given there).

Considering the two-person situation, there are in particular four linear transformations suggested by experimental evidence. They are as follows, using agent 1 as our reference individual:

(5) $\quad u'_{ij1} = u_{ij1}$ $\quad\quad$ (own gain)

(6) $\quad u'_{ij1} = u_{ij2}$ $\quad\quad$ (other's gain)

(7) $\quad u'_{ij1} = u_{ij1} + u_{ij2}$ $\quad\quad$ (joint gain)

(8) $\quad u'_{ij1} = u_{ij1} - u_{ij2}$ $\quad\quad$ (relative gain)

Formula (5) indicates that player 1 will make no utility transformation (g is the identity function) but will operate on the basis of his given utilities, be they egoistic or not. Transformation (6) involves a person's identification with his partner as to his utilities in the way a caring mother might be thought to identify herself with the child. The joint utility approach defined by (7) is the one discussed in our above example. (8) defines a particularly competitive kind of utility transformation: what matters is how much you are ahead.

The above transformation functions have been presented in a pure form corresponding to (1) of Chapter 2. A more realistic formulation would give the arguments suitable weights (values of a and b different from 0 and ±1 in (2.1)). Note that the agents of course need not "use" the **same** transformation function. Thus the first agent might use joint gain transformation against the second agent's relative gain transformation, say.

We may now ask what the composite functions f∘g corresponding to (1) and (6) - (8) give us. The main results are easibly obtainable. In fact, we can even state the new parameters occurring in the effective utility function

(9) $\quad u'_{ijh} = \mu'_h + \alpha'_{ih} + \tau'_{jh} + \eta'_{ijh}$

in terms of the old ones. Thus, corresponding to (6) we immediately get:

(10) $\mu_1^* = \mu_2$; $\alpha_{i1}^* = \alpha_{i2}$; $\tau_{j1}^* = \tau_{j2}$; $n_{ij1}^* = n_{ij2}$.

For the case (7) we get:

(11) $\mu_1^* = \mu_1 + \mu_2$; $\alpha_{i1}^* = \alpha_{i1} + \alpha_{i2}$; $\tau_{j1}^* = \tau_{j1} + \tau_{j2}$; $n_{ij1}^* = n_{ij1} + n_{ij2}$.

Finally, corresponding to (8) we have:

(12) $\mu_1^* = \mu_1 - \mu_2$; $\alpha_{i1}^* = \alpha_{i1} - \alpha_{i2}$; $\tau_{j1}^* = \tau_{j1} - \tau_{j2}$; $n_{ij1}^* = n_{ij1} - n_{ij2}$.

As (10)-(12) are, technically viewed, rather obvious - the control components behave as expected - I will not comment on them except for a couple of remarks. First, mutual other's gain transformation (6) reverses the roles of the two players. One interesting thing about it is that it goes no way towards resolving problematic situations like the prisoner's dilemma. Thus if it is prudential or wise for the agents to make the non-cooperative choice prior to the transformation it is equally prudential to do so after the transformation. Thus in the two-person case extreme personal altruism does not socially lead to what it is meant to lead. (However, this conclusion does not hold for many-person cases equally dramatically - but depends on how altruism is defined in those cases.)

Our second remark concerns the "macro-description" of the control components in terms of variances and covariances. Concerning the covariance matrices H_1, H_2, H_3, and T in Section III of Chapter 9 we may ask what happens to them in the above transformations. We recall that the variances are quite directly connected to the parameter values (e.g., row effect variance is $(\alpha_{11} - \alpha_{21})^2$, and so on). But what happens to the covariances? In the general case it is not easy to answer this, even if only linear transformations of utilities are concerned. However, it is obvious that **mutual** other's gain transformation leaves covariances the same. Mutual joint gain transformation again makes them grow to their maximum, while mutual relative gain transformation drives them to their minimum. But the intermediate cases must be investigated **in casu**, it seems, and simple results may not be forthcoming.

Before proceeding to further developments let me still emphasize the general significance of the utilities u_{ijh}^* as **other-regarding**. This is conceptually and theoretically quite important. It is a central feature of interpersonal situations that other persons' (thoughts and) actions as perceived and evaluated by an actor affect his way of thinking and acting. In this sense they become a **new utility source** for him. Considering the two-person case, we see that, for instance, the expression $\alpha_{12} - \alpha_{22}$ (or its square, if you like) measures 2's preference concerning 1's actions. Thus, as $\Sigma\alpha_{i2}=0$, α_{12} is a measure of 2's preference of X_1 over X_2. In all, 1's actions can be said to be a utility source for 2 (and vice versa).

But there is even more involved here. For the fact that 1's actions have certain utility for 2 can and will also be evaluated by 1 in a certain way (when the utilities u_{ijh}^1 are at stake). In other words, we have a kind of **social utility-loop** here. Formally, we might put this by:

(13) $u_1^1(\alpha_{12} = v) = v'$, for some v, v'.

That is, in our example the fact that agent 2 values agent 1's action X_1 to the degree v has the operative value v' to $1(u_1^1$ meaning utility for 1 generally). To this we can add that our general mutual awareness requirement ensures that not only is agent 2 aware of the fact that $\alpha_{12} = v$ but agent 1 is aware of the whole content of (13).

Formula (13) is a **second-degree** utility expression. While we do not quite operate with this type of formulas in this book, we are dealing with the second-order information it contains. For our g-function of (3) is a utility function containing utilities as its arguments. Thus we have incorporated the mentioned important kind of **social utility loop** into our system, as an adequate account should. So, in all, we have come to emphasize the importance of not only social loop beliefs but of socially looped utilities as well.

How about the three-person case? Formulas corresponding to (5)-(8) can be constructed but not unambiguously. However, (5) and (7) generalize in an obvious way (perhaps some averaging might be used in (7)). As to the counterpart of the other's gain transformation there are two conceptually different ideas. The first is to act on some particular other person's gain (e.g., agent 1 might decide to act on 2's rather than 3's utilities). The second is to act on the sum or average of the other two persons' utilities. In the case of relative gain transformation corresponding to (8) one may operate either with pairwise differences (e.g. 1 against 2 and 1 against 3) or compare a person's gain with the average gain the others get (e.g., 1's gain compared against 2's and 3's average gain). Given exact criteria for the three-person case, formulas corresponding to (10)-(12) can be computed. We shall not here go into that nor shall we discuss the m-person case ($m \geq 3$).

3. As we said earlier, the transformation function g might be non-linear. Indeed, in realistic cases it generally is. For instance, one might employ non-linear utility transformations generated on the basis of one's **aspiration level** (roughly, desired level of "reasonably" obtainable gains). Thus a person might compare his gain with the other person's gains and aspire for the same level of gains. Thus, when behind he would act selfishly and when ahead he would act altruistically, and all this might entail using a non-linear transformation function. (In this kind of cases the covariances might also change drastically.) Another case in point might be the situations that cognitive dissonance theorists have investigated. The retrieval of consonance would typically seem to require non-linear utility transformations (in addition to the changes in beliefs).

Kelley and Thibaut (1978) have discussed utility transformations using a set-up fairly similar to ours. They make interesting comments on two-person non-linear transformations. I refer the reader to their stimulating discussion of examples concerning not only non-linear but also other complicated transformations. Recall that the control components we have been discussing in Chapter 9 and above are essentially the same that Kelley and Thibaut use as the basis of their treatment. The main technical difference between their approach and ours is our employment of **joint** utility distributions as contrasted with their use of separate ones, we recall. The main philosophical difference again is our use of an explicit action theory (viz. the purposive-causal theory). But, in any case, their discussion of utility transformations is easily and immediately applicable to our treatment. Because of this and the fact that I do not really have new results to add to their treatment of those more complex cases, I shall not here survey their discussion but only make some sketchy remarks.

Let us consider Figure 12.2 to begin with.

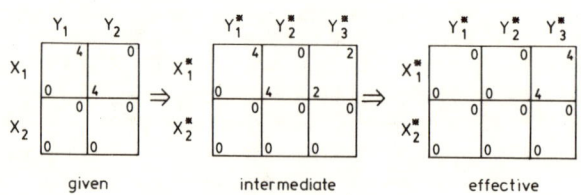

Fig. 12.2.

This figure is meant to exemplify a possible case of reconceptualization of the original, deadlocked given matrix. We assume

DYNAMIC EXPLANATION OF SOCIAL ACTION   397

that the given matrix represents interaction which is meant to occur repeatedly. Then we suppose the original sets of choice alternatives are redefined as follows: $X_1^* $ = choose X_1 always, X_2^* = choose X_2 always, Y_1^* = choose Y_1 always, Y_2^* = choose Y_2 always, and Y_3^* = alternate between Y_1 and Y_2 (with equal probability). The result is the intermediate matrix. Here $<X_1^*, Y_3^*>$ clearly provides a possible solution to the given deadlocked situation. Yet there is a temptation for player 2 to choose Y_1^*; and player 1 would prefer 4 utility units to 2 and may threaten by X_2^*. The result of the communication between the agents might be that they make a **joint gain** transformation while at the same time deciding to avoid cases where the outcomes have different utility value to them separately; and the effective matrix would be the result. And clearly it is rather compelling that normal rational agents then form an intention to choose $<X_1^*, Y_3^*>$.

The above strongly idealized case exemplifies at the same time both a reconceptualization of the original situation and shift in the evaluative criteria adopted. There are lots of interesting interaction situations in which a suitable reconceptualization of the choice alternatives may help the agents to find solutions to problematic cases. Let me just mention a couple of such here. In cases where the agents act in temporal sequence, knowledge of the choice by the first agent may lead the second agent to view the situation in terms of **matching** versus **non-matching** the first choice (see Kelley and Thibaut (1978), pp. 151-155, on this).

Next, we have the broad spectrum of cases of **repeated** play where some clear patterns can be discerned in the agents' choices (e.g., always choose a certain alternative or alternate or play "tit-tor-tat"). It is clear that normally one's **learning** concerning the other person's strategies and reconceptualizations as well as re-evaluations may play quite a central role here. (Cf. Kelley and Thibaut (1978), pp. 155-166 on interesting analyzes even if they do not focus on learning.)

Kelley and Thibaut also discuss such (two-person) situations as **exchange, bargaining** and **coordination** games and show that the same control components we have been discussing can be put to interesting work when combined with suitable utility transformations (see Kelley and Thibaut (1978), Chapter 7). To take just one example, a **sequential shifting** between the joint gain transformation and the egalitarian transformation of minimizing the absolute difference between utilities can be shown to lead to good solutions for both agents in the case of, e.g., turn-taking games, Hero, Battle of the Sexes, and several others. Consider thus as our final example the **turn-taking** game shown in Figure 12.3. By shifting suitably between $<X_1,Y_2>$ and

$\langle X_2, Y_1 \rangle$ the agents can divide up 8 units in corresponding proportion. Without any transformation players 1 and 2 get nothing by merely following their preferences (over their own utilities). When the joint gain transformation is introduced both players have a basis for coordinating on $\langle X_1, Y_2 \rangle$ and $\langle X_2, Y_1 \rangle$ in **some** way or other. If they, in addition, decide to be egalitarian and minimize their absolute differences, **strict** alternation or turn-taking will occur.

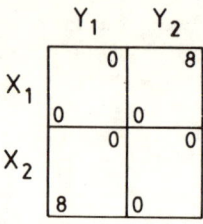

Fig.12.3.

There is rather much experimental evidence concerning the occurrence of utility transformations, as said earlier. There are also many data on the various conditions under which a certain type of transformation is likely to take place. However, as the evidence is not very conclusive and as its chief interest is clearly social psychological rather than philosophical I shall not review it here (but see, e.g., Kelley and Thibaut (1978), pp. 181-206). It should yet be recalled that as we take our linear theory of utility decomposition to be at least indirectly empirically relevant (even if it approaches a conceptual truth), the mentioned experimental data have a bearing on what we have been claiming in Chapter 9 and above. Let me emphasize that this empirical material is directly philosophically relevant in that, by allowing all kinds of reconceptualizations and re-evaluations, it strongly raises the question **what** game the agents really are playing and, if complicated transformations occur, to what extent can the agents have mutual knowledge about each other's operative matrices (and conduct plans). (There are many good examples of cases of conflict, e.g., the "Gruesome Twosome" situations, where distorted communication prevents such mutual knowledge and the participants thus are playing a different game than they think; cf. Swensen (1973).)

While there is not yet very much empirical knowledge of what transformation functions g (of (3)) agents tend to use in situations of interaction, I would still like to make some general concluding remarks on this. The transformation an individual uses may, first, be one relating to the tactics of the situation, so to speak, without more general significance. Thus an agent may in a certain situation use a competitive transformation function even if in general he is not competitive. But, secondly, the transformation function may be one used repetitively by a certain person so that he can be said to have the disposition to use it typically. Indeed, it can be taken as defining a trait or motive such as competitiveness that a competitive person is disposed to use (or act as if using) a competitive transformation function. In this kind of case the effective utility matrices in part reflect general underlying traits and motives (e.g., competition, love, aggression) of the agents, and these traits then clearly become highly relevant for explanation. But remember that the same effective utilities may be due to different underlying motives; thus a transformation function g may reflect different traits, depending on the case.

There is still the third possibility that the agents can, as it were, choose at will the general underlying dispositional motive or trait. At the end of Chapter 7 we discussed norm-violation from this perspective in terms of player-types (confirmer vs. non-confirmer). But we may now put the matter more generally and say that in cases of interpersonal dependency there often, or perhaps typically, is interdependence on the level of the underlying general traits or motives - in particular when the players can choose which motive to exhibit in a situation. Thus in our example of conforming versus non-conforming we can set up a 2×2 utility matrix for the combinations of these general traits (in Chapter 7 only relevant probabilities were discussed). In this utility matrix the same control components can of course be discussed as in the utility matrices on the level of the actions which such a second-level utility matrix leads to. A general theory of explanation of social action would ultimately have to clarify the interplay between the second level utility matrices and the corresponding first level ones (cf. the highly analogous and directly relevant problem in the single-agent case concerning the relationship between second-order and first-order wants or utilities; see Tuomela (1977), pp. 150-154). Of course, there are even more general utility matrices (or conduct plans, if you like) than the mentioned second-order ones, and they too should be brought into play (cf. the analogous distinction between scripts, plans, and themes of Schank and Abelson (1977)).

II. EXPECTED UTILITIES, MOTIVES, AND THE EXPLANATION OF SOCIAL ACTION

1.   Explanation of action is a very complicated affair as we all know. In the previous chapter we concentrated on explanations which more or less directly involved the agents' intendings. In this chapter we are concerned with the complex variety of features that are dynamically (causally) and also conceptually relevant to people's forming intentions in certain ways. Thus we are concerned with evolving conduct plans, with deliberation and reasoning, and also with causal processes less connected with explicit reasoning. One **Leitmotif** in the present chapter is that it is important to distinguish between the given utilities (often straightforwardly connected to objective payoffs) and the operative or effective utilities on the basis of which people form action intentions and act. In this section we shall investigate in some detail what more is needed besides operative utilities to learn what makes people act. Especially we shall be concerned with motivational problems related to **risky situations**, viz. to situations where the agents are confronted with a number of action-alternatives each of which leads to a certain goal or to certain goals with certain specifiable probabilities.

Another theme needing emphasis is that explanation is **idealized**. Even in physics idealization plays an important role. If we want to account for, say, the behavior of a system of particles we must, in an idealizational way, assume it is **closed**, viz. suitably dynamically isolated. In the case of a group of agents analogous idealization necessarily must take place. We thus theoretically assume that the agents are confronted with a fixed set of action-alternatives (of which they are normally assumed to be mutually aware to at least some degree) and we attribute certain wants (or utilities) and beliefs (or probabilities) to the agents. We also assume that these wants and beliefs are suitably consistent and stable and we take people to act more or less rationally (in some sense of rationality) on these wants and beliefs. All this involves idealization: we 'idealizingly' close an open psychological system. This idealization seems necessary. If we think of examples of such closed systems it seems that we can always find some restrictions which are clearly untenable. This is at least in part because, to present a truism, our mental life is rather holistic and creative and because it is moulded by our individual history and our interaction with an open environment.

Consider thus somebody's wanting food and believing he must go to the refrigerator to get it. This may causally lead him to go there in one case but not in another case. What he will do depends on, say, whether he knows what a refrigerator is, whether he is on a diet or not, whether he wants to save food for tomorrow morning. But it may also depend on such less usual factors as whether he thinks it is socially appropriate at that time of night, whether he thinks there is a poisonous snake in front of the refrigerator, whether he thinks Zeus' thunderbolts will strike him if he acts, and so on.

In all, there seems to be no a priori guarantee that we can realistically (i.e. without idealization) close the system and, equally well, there seems to be no a priori guarantee that we cannot do it. This I take to be at least compatible with saying that it is possible that human agents act in a lawful (perhaps individually parametrized) way and that there can be a nomological psychology and social psychology.

Quite irrespective of the idealizations we have to make when explaining, it is, accordingly, possible to think that agents' actions may be explained (in part at least) by reference to their active **action propensities** or **tendencies**. Such propensities are or may often be probabilistic (or indeterministic at least), for either **epistemic** or, perhaps, **ontic** reasons. This is how we shall think below (cf. Tuomela (1977), Chapter 12 for pertinent discussion).

Metaphysically speaking, the competing nomic action propensities (wants cum beliefs or, briefly, reasons) can jointly operate in either a **compensatory** or in a **non-compensatory** fashion. The compensation view, advocated by, e.g., Lewin, argues that the competing action tendencies can be regarded as forces so that the **resultant force** directly leads to the agent's relevant intending (or decision or willing). On the non-compensational model again the momentarily strongest want-belief or reason complex (propensity) wins and yields the action (or its final determinant).

I take it to be ultimately a factual question which of these two metaphysical views will give us better explanatory motivation theories. Following the current trend in psychology we shall adopt the compensation model as the basis for our discussion. In particular, we shall adopt a decision-theoretic approach operating with expected utilities for explicating this view. Thus, roughly at least, the action with the maximal (or at least in some sense optimal) expected overall utility would be the action with the maximal resultant propensity or force. We shall elaborate on this later in the present section.

When going to our detailed treatment of the motivational and dynamic explanation of social action we shall accordingly start with considering the agents' expected utilities. This is of course consistent with what we have been doing earlier, and, indeed, we shall normally use as our utilities (or as parts of them) just the operative utilities (u') discussed in the previous section. As we shall see, it is indeed a kind of (relative) conceptual truth that a kind of maximal expected utilities (wants) underly intentions to act (if not action). In addition to this kind of philosophical reason there is also strong empirical evidence coming from psychological motivation research in favor of using some sort of maximal expected utility (or valence) element in accounting for the motivation of intentional action (see, e.g., Atkinson and Birch (1970), Atkinson and Raynor (1974), Heckhausen (1980)).

2. To develop our necessary conceptual machinery we need to consider four kinds of technical concepts. First, we will naturally use our previously developed action concepts. Thus, our canonical formulation for an intentional action token v will be <t,...b,...r> - a complex event sequence - both in the case of single-agent and multi-agent action (see Chapters 4 and 5). Viewing this from another angle, v is normally an exemplification of some action type, say X_i. We can almost say that v is what X_i "amounts to" in a particular situation or circumstance, say S_j. We may sometimes assume that X_i has only v as its exemplification in S_j. This can also be put linguistically by saying that we have nominalization with the referent v such that in this nominalization a relevant action predicate and a situation predicate are used. Accordingly, when the uniqueness assumption holds we can also here use a complex predicate, which we may here write simply as '$X_i \& S_j$'.

The notion of action-situation is our second needed technical concept. A situation S_j is often a social-physical situation in that it may in part consist of other agents' actions and in part of certain physical events; or it may sometimes be interpreted so as not to include others' actions. The physical events may be accounted for in terms of a chance player's actions in a game-theoretic setting.

Thirdly, we need our previously defined notion **IG*** of purposive generation (see (9) of Chapter 6). In fact we will use a **probabilistic** version of it (see Chapter 6, esp. Note 4, and Tuomela (1977), p. 396). Thus $IG^*_r(v, o^k_l)$ means 'action token v purposively generated event o^k_l with probability r'. Here we take v to be of a certain type, say X_i, and o^k_l to be of the type O_k. Thus o^k_l can be regarded as the l-th exemplification of the outcome type O_k. Purposive generation means, we recall, generation in accordance with an operative conduct plan. Accordingly, the generated events o^k_l can be called **anticipated outcomes** or **consequences** of the action token v or, assuming unique exemplification, of X_i in situation S_j. The so defined notion of anticipated consequences will then be the fourth basic concept in our set-up below.

Let us now consider an actor (a single-agent or a collective of agents) who has a certain number of action options, say $X_1,\ldots,X_c$, available to him in a risky social situation. By a risky social situation we mean here that with each action X_i, $i=1,\ldots,c$, there is a finite set of outcomes O_k^i to which X_i leads, in the associated social situation S_j^i, with some specifiable reasonable subjective probabilities. These generation probabilities will, depending on the case at hand, be of the form $p(O_k^i/X_i)$ or $p(O_k^i/X_i\&S_j^i)$, or to be more exact, they will in the most general case be probabilities of the corresponding generation conditionals roughly of the type "If X_i would occur then so would O_k^i" or "If X_i and S_j^i would occur then so would O_k^i", to be discussed below. For our present purposes O_k^i, X_i and S_j^i can be regarded as sets, but as argued in Tuomela (1977), Chapter 11, they can also be construed as property-predicates or event-predicates. When we will be dealing with game-theoretic situations (or something similar), then of course the other agents' actions will contribute to the generation of an outcome. We should then in principle use subjective probabilities of the form $p(O_k^i/X_i\&S_j^i)$ (or probabilities of the corresponding conditionals) and include in the S_j^is the other agents' actions and the other relevant circumstances, and j might be taken to vary across all the possible **total** circumstances the actors consider relevant. Even under this broadest interpretation these probabilities might differ from zero and one (at least if indeterminism is tenable). We might also in some interpretations take j to vary across all the player's actions including the chance player and get the same conclusion (given that all the random external factors can be accounted for by the chance moves).

However, normally we can in our "actual practice" get along just by assuming the availability of the subjective generation probabilities $p(O_k^i/X_i)$ (or the probabilities of the corresponding conditionals) and assuming that the effect of the situations S_j^i has been amalgamated into these probabilities. Indeed, supposing that the S_j^is have been carved up so as to be disjoint we have, using conditional probabilities:

(14) $\quad p(O_k^i/X_i) = \sum_j p(S_j^i/X_i)\, p(O_k^i/S_j^i)$

(Try this for j=1,2; you can imagine that (14) is concerned with two alternative chains, one via S_1 and the other via S_2, from X_i to O_k^i.) I am not suggesting that the right hand side probabilities should be known to the agent when he knows the left hand side (even if he may be required to be disposed to have them). Yet (14) gives a kind of partial justification for our normally leaving out the explicit treatment of the S_j^is.

Let us now consider the probabilities of the corresponding generation conditionals. Corresponding to our relation IG_r^* we may define a probabilistic generation conditional $\looparrowright_r$ or $p(D_1 \looparrowright_r D_2)=r$ as pointed out in Note 4 of Chapter 6 but interpreting p now as a **subjective** probability (also see Tuomela (1977), p. 396). In words, $D_1 \looparrowright_r D_2$ becomes roughly 'if D_1 would have been exemplified by an event then it would (indirectly) purposively have generated an event exemplifying D_2 with probability r'. (Here D_1 and D_2 should be either proper singular event-descriptions or open formulas with event-predicates; e.g., $D_1=X_i(x)$ and $D_2=O_j^i(y)$, when using a linguistic way of describing actions and outcomes.[1]) As indicated in Chapter 6 this probabilistic conditional may be defined in two alternative ways, either on the basis of the ρ-relation or the ε-relation (see the Appendix of Chapter 10). When defined in the latter way it may in some cases fail to equal the corresponding purposive conditional generation probability ($p(O_k^i/X_i)$ above). As argued, e.g., by Gibbard and Harper (1978), in those cases where probabilities of conditionals differ in value from the corresponding conditional probabilities one should deal with probabilities of conditionals, for, e.g., maximization of expected utilities by using them gives more natural situations to various problematic cases, such as Newcomb's problem. Below when using probability statements of the form '$p(X_i \looparrowright O_k^i)=r$' it, however, seems inessential which way they are defined and we need not make a definite choice for our limited purposes in the present chapter. In any case the use of conditionals as arguments in the probability statements guarantees that causal generational connections become adequately represented.

3. As said earlier, our approach will be in part Lewinian. According to him the central determinant of motivation is the **valence** of the relevant goal(s). If G is the goal its valence (**va(G)**) is:

(15) $va(G) = f(t,G)$,

where f is a suitable function representing a psychological force; t represents a personal tension (or need) and G the goal as perceived (and evaluated) by the person. Now the operative **motivational force** (F(G)) towards G for the person will be

(16) $F(G) = va(G) \times po(G)/d(G)$,

where po(G) represents the "potency" or, as we might say, the degree of expected reachability of G; d(G) represents the psychological distance between the acting person and the goal G. Now potency can be called an expectancy, and its quantitative counterpart is subjective probability. What we have here is clearly related to expected value or utility in modern terminology. We shall below partly explicate (16) or at least arrive at a suggestion resembling it.

People are disposed to act to get what they want provided they expect their wants to become so satisfied and provided they do not have stronger incompatible wants expected to be satisfied equally or more likely. This statement expresses a conceptual truth (or at least nearly so), it can be and it has been argued (cf., e.g., Tuomela (1977), pp. 78-79 and Audi (1973a,b) and below). It seems to contain the core of truth in the sure-thing principle (see Chapter 2, Section III). This seems to account in part for the plausibility of expected value accounts of motivation. (It also may partly account for the good empirical support some such accounts, e.g., Atkinson's (1964), have received!)

But there are many things that can be valued in action contexts and there are many ways of carving up the world into alternatives whose expected values will be motivationally central. Let us consider this. We shall first define in detail what we mean by the anticipated consequences of an action, for they obviously may have an important influence on the agent's acting. We can here proceed in terms of the probabilistic conditional $\models\!\!\!\rightarrow_r$ for indirect purposive generation. (Note also the possibility of using as our basis the corresponding might-conditional, viz. $\sim(X_i \models\!\!\!\rightarrow \sim O^i_k)$, instead of $\models\!\!\!\rightarrow$, even if we shall not pursue this possibility below.) We apply it to open formulas obtained from action predicates (e.g., X_i) and outcome predicates (e.g., O^i_k). Let us propose the following definition for the class of anticipated consequences (AC) of an action type X_i:

(17) $AC(X_i) =_{df} \{O^i_k | p(X_i \models\!\!\!\rightarrow O^i_k) > 0\}$

In words, $AC(X_i)$ is the set of all outcome types O^i_k which X_i-ings purposively generate with a probability >0. Note that that class of X_i-ings is thought to vary across the situations S_j we spoke about earlier. Each exemplification of X_i takes place in a certain situation S_j (and sometimes S_j may serve to determine a unique exemplification), but (14) (or its analogue, say (14'), for probabilities of conditionals) justifies our ignoring them here.

Our just defined notion of anticipated consequence class will contain lots of consequences which are unrelated to the actor's goals. Therefore it may seem more adequate for some purposes to consider the following narrower class:

(18) $AC'(X_i) =_{df} \{O_k^i \mid p(X_i \mapsto O_k^i) > 0,$ and O_k^i is goal-related$\}$

By saying that O_k^i is goal-related we mean roughly the following. We assume that our actor's operative conduct plan (serving as a basis for $\mapsto$) refers to one or more goals, say $G_1, \ldots, G_g$, of the actor. An outcome is goal-related if it either is a goal or if it increases or decreases the actor's psychological distance from his goal (or his goals in the average). I shall not here attempt to explicate the Lewinian notion of psychological distance. Let me just add for further reference that the utility of an outcome can normally be taken to be the higher the closer to the actor's goal(s) it is. Consequences distant from his goals are a kind of cost-factors in relation to his action.

Let us now consider the conjunction of the O_k^is in AC (or AC' if you prefer). I assume it is normally a finite one. (If it isn't, some technical complications will arise, but I shall here ignore them as unessential for our present purposes.) Let us call this conjunction O^i. Given this, we are ready to consider what kind of elements an actor can regard as value-relevant for his acting. In principle almost anything can be so relevant. But if we try to hypothesize what kind of items as a matter of fact do have motivational value for the agent, we may perhaps come up with something nontrivial.

It seems plausible to think that at least a rational actor will be able to assign a utility value to O^i. Also various components (conjuncts) of O^i, perhaps all of them, will probably be valued by the actor. (It is not necessary here to propose any principles according to which, e.g., utilities of wholes can be obtained from utilities of their components, or vice versa.)

But also other items may be value-relevant here. Most importantly, the very process by which a given outcome is reached may have value in itself, as has frequently been pointed out. Thus there may be a great difference between, say, the ways a song is getting sung or a sentence being said. In fact all parts of the process leading to an outcome may be value-relevant. Thus anything in the sequence from an agent's willings (t) to his behaving (b), to the result (r) and to the final outcome (exemplification of O_k^i) should be theoretically accounted for. Furthermore, as we know from decision theory the utility of gambling itself (and the utility of risk taking) may be central.

(This may perhaps be taken to entail the untenability of the Postulate of probabilistic equivalence discussed in Section III of Chapter 2.) It would seem that phenomena like risk-taking may be taken into account by letting utilities and beliefs be interdependent and by then taking beliefs about gambles or prospects themselves into account when characterizing the utility of the process (with all its believed characteristics) leading to an outcome.

On the whole it is a matter of a motivation psychologist to find out in detail which elements really are motivationally central and which are not. But in any case it seems at least plausible to take into account not only the utility of an outcome but also the whole process leading to the outcome. Somewhat roughly put, we then have to deal at least with (1) the utility of O_k^i, say $u(O_k^i)$ (and thus with $u(O^i)$), with (2) the utility of the action X_i in itself, say $u(X_i)$, as well as with (3) the utility of the process leading from the performance of X_i in a situation to the realization of O_k^i. Let us call that process $pr(O_k^i)$ and the corresponding utility $u(pr(O_k^i))$.

The utility $u(X_i)$ will be concerned with all the "internal" aspects of a token $<t,...b,...r>$ of X_i. If needed each of these internal elements (t, b, and r) might themselves be separately valued. Let me here emphasize that we here, as earlier, make a distinction between the result and the consequences of an action token. When we below speak of the success of actions that may mean either their results having come about or some relevant goals (consequences) having been achieved, depending on the case (and analogously for failure). This will have to be accounted for when specifying what the actions involved really are and when assigning relevant utility values.

In all, then, I will assume that utilities, understood as want-intensities can feasibly, but perhaps somewhat idealizingly, be defined for the items O_k^i (and O^i), $pr(O_k^i)$ (and $pr(O^i)$), and X_i. I will not discuss how to do it technically. (See, e.g., the Fishburn (1981) for a variety of present-day candidates, none of them perhaps quite adequate for our purposes.) Furthermore, I will assume that the utilities u to be dealt with are **other-regarding** utilities in the sense of the utilities u' discussed in Section I. Our present utilities may be taken to be just those utilities, or they may be regarded as those utilities suitably **reinterpreted**. Or, if needed, some new utility sources may be introduced, e.g., additively. Thus we obtain our present utilities $u(G)$, where $u(G) = u'(G)$ or $u(G) = u'(G)+u''(G)$, for some additional utility u". Here G is a variable which can take as its values anything valued in the present context. Thus we let G range over actions (e.g., X_i), components of actions (e.g., behaviors and results), outcomes (O_k^i), outcome processes ($pr(O_k^i)$), total consequences (O^i) and finally $pr(O^i)$. The largest entity that our utility function u may be applied to is action (X_i) together with $pr(O^i)$. We may denote this argument by $X_i \& pr(O^i)$, viz. by a predicate or type conjunction. Note that there is of course no contradiction between saying that our utility function u represents, say, the utility of an action together with its consequences and saying that u is decomposable into control components, as we have done.

4. How do we now compute expected utilities? We have our utility function schema u(G) and what we need is the relevant generation probabilities $p(X_i \mapsto G_j^i)$. We let the index of our utility source j run over all the possible episodes which our actor considers relevant or which he, consciously or not, operate with. Unless otherwise specified the reader may take G_j^i to range over the $X_i \& pr(O^i)$-episodes (possible exemplifications of $X_i \& pr(O^i)$ for the agent). We are simply going to assume below the availability of the relevant subjective probabilities all along. Recall that our actors can be single agents or collective agents such as groups as long as the relevant utilities and probabilities can be defined and regarded as meaningful. (We shall later return to the group case.)

All expected utilities are relativized to **prospects** (gambles, lotteries, whatever they are called). We recall from Chapter 2 that a prospect P^i associated with X_i is a sequence of the form $P^i = <G_1^i, p_1^i, \ldots, G_k^i, p_k^i>$ where the G_j^is (the goal-like situations or episodes relevant to X_i) are outcomes, goals or whatever relevant, as just characterized, and $\sum_{j=1}^{k} p_j^i = 1$ (where $p_j^i = p(X_i \mapsto G_j^i)$). Now we define the expected utility (EU) of action X_i relative to prospect p^i as follows:

(19) $\quad EU(X_i) = \sum_{j=1}^{k} p(X_i \mapsto G_j^i) u(G_j^i)$

It should be emphasized that expected utilities are **prospect-relative** and so are action-explanations in so far as they involve expected utilities. In (19) all the k "valences" (probability utility products) receive the same weight. We also want to consider what we call the generalized expected utility

$$(20) \quad GEU(X_i) = \sum_{j=1}^{k} W_j p(X_i \mapsto G_j^i) u(G_j^i)$$

Here the weights W_j sum up to one, viz. $\sum_{j=1}^{k} W_j = 1$. We propose that W_j could be interpreted as representing a general **"motive"**, e.g. a personality characteristic, operative in situation G_j. Note that our discussion below does not trade on the differences between the mentioned two interpretations of the probabilities $p(X_i \mapsto G_j^i)$, and, for our immediate purposes below, we might use conditional generation probabilities $p(G_j^i / X_i)$ alternatively in (19) and (20).

5. Atkinson's (1964) theory of **achievement motivation** is a Lewinian type of theory meant to apply to situations where agents are confronted with tasks of varying difficulty. Atkinson considers, for each action, whether it succeeds (the goal, whatever it is, is achieved) or fails (the goal is not achieved). The total resultant force or action tendency, say T, is taken to be the sum of the tendency to succeed (T_s) and the tendency to avoid failure (T_f). Omitting mention of X_i and the index i,

$$(21) \quad T = T_s + T_f.$$

T_s and T_f are defined by:

$$(22) \quad T_s = M_s P_s I_s$$

$$(23) \quad T_f = M_f P_f I_f.$$

Here M_s represents the actor's general motive for success or achievement and M_f that for avoiding failure. I_s stands for the situation-specific incentive value of success and I_f for that of avoiding failure. The product $M_s I_s$ represents the valence of success and $M_f I_f$ that of failure (cf. our (15)). Finally, P_s represents the probability of success (of the action X_i) and P_f its probability of failure. Next Atkinson measures the incentive value in terms of the difficulty of the task (of reaching the goal) and this difficulty is taken to be the inverse of probability, whence $I_s = 1-P_s$. The incentive value of failure is taken to be $-P_s$. Now making $P_f = 1-P_s$ we get

$$(24) \quad T = M_s P_s (1-P_s) + M_f (1-P_s)(-P_s) = M_s P_s (1-P_s) - M_f (1-P_s) P_s.$$

Atkinson's formula (24) can be seen to be a special case of (20) as follows. Let $P^i = \langle G_s, P_s; G_f, P_f \rangle$ with G_s = success, G_f = failure. Here obviously $P_s = p(G_s^i/X_i)$ and $P_f = 1-p(G_s^i/X_i)$. Then make $u(G_s)=I_s$, $u(G_f)=I_f$, and let $W_s=M_s$ and $W_f=M_f$. Thus, neglecting the possible difference between conditional probabilities of conditionals, Atkinson's formula fits GEU relative to a success-failure prospect and with a rather special assignment of utilities. Note that in this case, with a success-failure prospect, it is appropriate to deal with questions like "Why did the actor perform X_i rather than omit performing it?'. This indicates the **prospect-relativity of explanations**.

It may be noted here that Atkinson's theory has received strong empirical support in several experiments related to situations of achievement, with tasks varying in difficulty (see, e.g., Atkinson (1964); Atkinson and Raynor (1974) also cf. Zander (1971) for the group case). However, it seems to me rather obvious that Atkinson's utility function cannot work well in cases of interpersonal interaction, for it lacks **other-regarding** utilities (known to be needed; cf. above). A second criticism that I have is that there seem to be several other general motives known to affect people's acting. In addition to achievement motivation, for instance the **social power** motive and the motive of **social affiliation**. Our weight W_j can in principle represent any of them or perhaps even some suitable conglomeration of them. Note, too, that by using Lewin's formula (**16**) we get a product in our (**20**) by putting $G=G_j$ and $va(G)=W_j u(G_j)$, and $d(G)=1$ (also cf. (**15**)).

In fact Atkinson has recently, jointly with Birch, developed a more general dynamic theory of motivation which is not geared to achievement motivation only (see Atkinson and Birch (1970), Atkinson and Raynor (1974), and, e.g., Heckhausen (1980) for its evaluation). The new theory postulates basically that the rate of change in the strength of an action tendency (T) at any moment of time (t) is equal to the **instigating** force (F) minus the **consummatory** force (C), i.e.

(25) $dT/dt = F-C$.

Now Atkinson and Birch postulate that $C=cT$, where c is a special constant related to consummation. Given this, (**25**) yields the explicit solution

(26) $T = T_I e^{-ct} + F/c(1-e^{-ct})$,

where T_I represents the **initial** action tendency. We shall not here discuss Atkinson's and Birch's elegant theory in detail but only mention it as an example of an empirical theory fitting together with our Lewinian thoughts in this chapter.

It is, however, still worth pointing out that Atkinson and Birch (1970) postulate, for a static situation, and ignoring the role of the consummatory force, that a **single** instating force is equivalent to, using our terminology, a particular product $p(G_j^i/X_i)u(G_j^i)$ or $p(X_i \triangleright G_j^i)u(G_j^i)$ while the total instigating force will essentially equal our **(19)**, viz. $EU(X_i)$ (see Atkinson and Birch (1970), p. 176). A general motive is, in these authors' view, in a sense dispositionally or functionally characterized (using my phrase) via the different products in the EU-formula. This is quite compatible with what we have been doing. We have, however, introduced specific weights, in addition, to catch better the Lewinian idea of personal motive ("tension"). Atkinson and Birch also argue that statements about individual differences in the strength of various general motives (motives for achievement, affiliation, etc.) are equivalent to statements about the relative strengths of different families of instigating forces. This also dovetails with our above account, for a family of instigating forces may be made correspond to a prospect, and different prospects may be made correspond to different general motives (recall also our remarks at the end of Section II).

Considering our formula **(20)** for GEU, we can now see that it is a rather wide schema that can incorporate a variety of motivational factors. Let us still summarize these factors. First, we have both **intrinsic** and **extrinsic** wants accounted for (recall this distinction from Chapter 4). Extrinsic wants are often connected to social factors like duties, obligations and "normative pressure", we remember, while intrinsic wants relate to personal, often selfish needs. Note that we allowed that not only the total consequences, viz. $pr(O^1)$, of an action X_i be valued but also the action itself (possibly together with some beliefs intimately related to it). The utility function used was supposed to be an other-regarding, effective one. The weights W_j may vary from one situation to another (cf. M_s and M_f in (24)); the symbol W in itself was taken as a place-holder for general motives (such as achievement, power, affiliation, curiosity, etc.) and thus of stable personality characteristics.

My suggestion is that some kind of conditional maximization of GEU (or at least "expected wants") is central for any motivational account of intentional action (see Section III for details). This suggestion was earlier given some conceptual and intuitive backing. We also noted that the presence of some sort of value × expectancy component is strongly suggested by current empirical evidence (cf., e.g., Heckhausen (1980)). However, I do not mean to suggest that maximization of GEU in itself would suffice. The idea is rather that **conditional** on a suitable background of other factors maximization of GEU would lead the agent to form an intention to perform the action (given there is one) maximizing GEU. The conditional factors relevant here I will not try to spell out in detail. In any case, they involve some degree (and a certain type) of rationality on the part of the actor as we have in fact pointed out. Thus we may have to take into account such other factors as initial action tendency, consummatory force, and aspiration level, not to speak of memory or of more usual "normal" and "facilitating" conditions such as suitable physiological arousal, and of broader societal factors, etc. All such factors, which surely may be very relevant, have here been taken as part of a relatively stable background, silently assumed to cooperate.

6. Let us still consider GEU and its maximization. In applying it to the case of achievement motivation we employed a kind of success-failure framework related to social **exchange theory** and **equity theory**. Suppose that in a two-choice situation an actor attempts to do something (X_1) which either succeeds (G_s^1 occurs) or fails (G_f^1 occurs) such that if it fails a certain other action X_2 succeeds. If X_1 succeeds the actor gains $u(G_s^1)$ but if it fails he looses $u(G_s^2)$, viz. what he would have gained had he chosen to perform X_2. Thus we make $u(G_f^1) = -u(G_s^2)$ and obtain from (20):

(27) $\quad GEU(X_1) = W_1 p(X_1 \triangleright G_s^1) u(G_s^1) - W_2 (1 - p(X_1 \triangleright G_s^1) u(G_s^2))$.

This is a kind of a **gain-loss** or, if you like, **reward-cost** expression (as in fact is (24)). It may serve to express within our framework part of what exchange and equity theorists have had in mind (to the extent that they have had a clear technical proposal in mind). Let me here point out that Homans' "rationality proposition" is that "every man, in choosing between alternative actions, is likely to take that one for which, as perceived by him at the time, the value (v) of the result, multiplied by the probability (p) of getting the result, is the greater; and the larger the excess of pxv for the one action over the alternative, the more likely he is to take the former action" (Homans (1970), p. 318). As is seen, Homans is here operating with success of action only and does not perhaps strictly propose maximization of expected utility or even reward minus cost. Yet, putting $W_1=W_2=1$, what Homans says at the end of the quotation is quite compatible with, and almost amounts to, requiring the maximization of (27). (If you like, we may also say technically that he urges us to consider (27) with $W_1=1$ and

$W_2=0$ and compare it with its analogue for X_2.)

However, exchange and equity theorists often think that rewards and costs should be accounted for in the primary utilities themselves (see, e.g., Berkowitz and Walster (1976), p. 2). Thus we would have $u(G_j^i) = u_r(G_j^i) - u_c(G_j^i)$, with u_r = reward utility (due to X_i and G_j^i) and u_c = utility of cost (due to X_i and G_j^i). This is in fact compatible with how we have above thought the utilities u may come about. Let me now mention two suggestions related to maximizing expected net gain. They are (I have especially in mind the case $G_j^i = X_i \& pr(O^i)$):

$$(28) \quad GEU^{rc}(X_i) = \sum_{j=1}^{k} W_j p(X_i \looparrowright G_j^i)(u_r(G_j^i) - u_c(G_j^i))$$

$$(29) \quad GEU_{rc}(X_i) = \sum_{j=1}^{k} W_j p(X_i \looparrowright G_j^i) u_r(G_j^i) - \sum_{j=1}^{k} W_j p(X_i \looparrowright G_j^i) u_c(G_j^i).$$

Obviously (28), defining expected reward minus cost, is a special case of (20) and compatible with our above suggestion for how to get u. (29) defines expected reward minus expected cost. (28) and (29) are generally non-equivalent, as is easily seen, but I shall not here discuss their technical differences.

7. As said, I propose that our formula (20) for GEU also be applicable to the case of a group or collective of agents performing a social action (in our technical sense). Then we need to be able to make sense of **group** (or **social**) **goals, group utilities** and **group probabilities**. First, our variable G_j will now range over group goals, processes leading to such goals, as well as social actions. Group goals are supposed to be joint ends capable of motivating (and normally doing so) the agents to act. Let me here refer the reader to our analysis (G) of goals discussed in Chapters 11 and 13. Zander (1971) also discusses group goals but without saying much detailed and specific about them. He regards group goals as goals that the group has somehow come to agree on and to accept. While I do not strictly require that much, it is useful to have this view in mind.

We have discussed social or group utilities in Chapter 2, primarily in the two-person case. There we concentrated on linear social utilities u_{12} (= $a \cdot u_1 + b \cdot u_2$); also see Section I of the present chapter. I shall not here discuss them further. How about group or social probabilities? I have rather little to say about them over and above requiring them to be individualistically construed in congruence with our (CI) of Chapter 2. In the quantitative case a we-belief that q in a group can be taken to amount (at least ideally) to everyone's believing that q and to there being a mutual belief (awareness) concerning this. In the qualitative case at hand, we might ideally have a situation where the group has, through discussion and negotation, come to agree on the relevant group probabilities and thus to share them and have mutual awareness on them. In less ideal cases we may assume that group probabilities be obtained by **aggregation**, e.g., by suitable **weighted averages** from the members' individual probabilities. However, even in these cases mutual awareness of the group probabilities will have to be required in the case of intentional social action. (Perhaps probabilistically liberalized mutual belief might do here; cf. Chapter 7.) I shall not here say more about social utilities and probabilities, partly because I suspect that there are no further central conceptually necessary requirements to impose. As to the application of (20) to the group case let me still point out that the weights W_j now will represent group motives, and such motives are likely to be much less stable and enduring than individual motives (and personality characteristics).

As said earlier, Zander (1971) and his co-workers have successfully applied Atkinson's theory (24) to the group case. However, I think that as compared with the individual case there has so far been too little research to say warrantedly that (24) really applies to group tasks. However, there are good reasons to think that our idea about conditional GEU-maximization is on the right track even in the case of social actions and social groups.

Zander (1971) and others have also investigated, in various ways, the interrelationship between group motivation (on the level of a member) and personal motivation in the case of group members and found that, in the sense of (24), there are clear differences (cf. Chapter 2, Section III). For instance, depending on, e.g., a member's status in the group his group achievement motivation tendency is stronger or weaker than his personal achievement motivation tendency (cf. Shaw (1981), too).

Given our idea that the maximization of GEU is motivationally important we may ask how a group's maximizing GEU is related to the group's members' GEU-values or at least to their effective utilities and probabilities. Let us thus consider a two-choice case with two agents. Agent 1 (or A_1) has X_1 and X_2 and agent 2 (or A_2) has Y_1 and Y_2 as his options. Next assume that the situation is such that all the four combinations $Z_1 = X_1 \& Y_1$, $Z_2 = X_1 \& Y_2$, $Z_3 = X_2 \& Y_1$, and $Z_4 = X_2 \& Y_2$ qualify as social action types. Now we let the consequences to be valued be G_{11}, G_{12}, G_{21}, and G_{22}, respectively. Then we consider the expected utility of one of the above social actions, say Z_1. Let our prospect be the following success-failure one: $P(Z_1) = <G_{11},p_{11};G_{11},1-p_{11}>$. Then

(30) $\quad GEU(Z_1) = W_1 p(Z_1 \mapsto G_{11}) u(G_{11}) + W_2(1-p(Z_1 \mapsto G_{11})) u(G_{11})$

Now consider the corresponding individual expected utilities for X_1 and Y_1 relative to the obvious prospects $P(X_1) = <G_{11},p_{11}^1; G_{12},1-p_{11}^1>$ and $P(Y_1) = <G_{11},p_{11}^2;G_{21},1-p_{11}^2>$ to answer why X_1 (or Y_1) rather than X_2 (or Y_2) was performed by A_1 (or A_2). We get the following formulas

(31) $\quad GEU(X_1) = W_1^1 p^1(X_1 \mapsto G_{11}) u_1(G_{11}) + W_2^1 (1-p^1(X_1 \mapsto G_{11})) u_1(G_{12})$

(32) $\quad GEU(Y_1) = W_1^1 p^2(Y_1 \mapsto G_{11}) u_2(G_{11}) + W_2^2 (1-p^2(Y_1 \mapsto G_{11})) u_2(G_{21})$

Let us now consider a very simple case in which the given utilities are $u_1(G_{11})=u(G_{22})=1$, $u_2(G_{11})=3$, $u_2(G_{22})=1$, and the other utilities are zeros. Then assume that the effective group utility function is simply $u_{12}=u_1'+u_2'$ and that both agents transform their given utilities according to the function $u_1' = u_2' = 1/2(u_1+u_2)$. As usual in this kind of set-up, we assume that the choices of X_1 and Y_1 determine Z_1: $p(G_{11}/Z_1)=1$. Thus (30) (with $W_1=1$) gives us $GEU(Z_1)=4$, $GEU(Z_2)=GEU(Z_3)=0$, $GEU(Z_4)=2$. We may also plausibly assume that $p^1(X_1 \mapsto G_{11}) = 1 = p^2(Y_1 \mapsto G_{11})$. Then (31) and (32) analogously give us $GEU(X_1)=GEU(Y_1)=2$ and $GEU(X_2)=GEU(Y_2)=1$. Thus, Z_1, X_1, and Y_1 get the maximal expected utility values. This trivial example illustrates that at least in some cases the maximization of (30) may depend on the simultaneous maximization of (31) and (32).

But the example is easily changed to show that sometimes maximization of (30) leads to a different result than what the maxima of (31) and (32) give. Thus suppose that the agents instead want to maximize their relative gains. Then $u_1(G_{11})=-2$ and $u_2(G_{11})=2$ and all the other personal utilities are zeros. Then it is not implausible to think that agent 1 would more likely choose X_2 than X_1 and agent 2 again Y_1 more likely than Y_2. Thus Z_3 would result. However, if 1 and 2 instead operated jointly they might come to agree that, e.g., $u_{12}=u_1+u_2=4$ (perhaps to be divided to make $u_1'=1$ and $u_2'=3$), then Z_1 would clearly get the maximal GEU-value. Another well known example of this kind is provided by the prisoner's dilemma game, not to speak of several other mixed motive games.

We shall not here systematically investigate under what circumstances maximization of (30) depends on the joint maximization of (31) and (32) in the above sense. Let me finally point out that maximization of (30) of course is going to depend on the personal utilities and probabilities, given our above individualistic assumptions. Thus we may assume that group utilities depend on operative individual utilities according to some function g (linear or not), and this may even be taken to follow from our principle of Conceptual Individualism. Analogously, we may assume that a group probability depends, according to some function, say f, on the relevant individual probabilities concerning the same goal but relative to the respective individual actions as above. If, for instance, the agents happened to have independent subjective beliefs, say p_1 and p_2, then the relevant group probability would of course be $p_{12}=p_1 \cdot p_2$. But in the case of social action these probabilities are presumably often inductively dependent and f cannot just be simple multiplication.

To end, we suggest as a near-conceptual truth (given (**CI**)) for game-like situations in the case of m agents and k goal-like items the following general connection (p and u represent group probability and utility):

$$(33) \quad EU(Z_i) =_{df} \sum_{j=1}^{k} p(Z_i \mapsto G_j) u(G_j)$$

$$= \sum_{j=1}^{k} f(p_1(X_1 \mapsto G_j)), \ldots, p_m(X_m \mapsto G_j)) g(u_1(G_j), \ldots, u_m(G_j)),$$

for some f and g.

Here $Z_i = X_1 \& \ldots \& X_m$ and the goals G_j have been valued independently of the actions supposed to lead to them.

III. THE NATURE OF DYNAMIC ACTION EXPLANATIONS

1. Our last topic in this chapter is the problem of how the maximization of expected utility relates to intention formation and especially how the explanatory arguments (and answers) are going to look like in the case of dynamic, motivational explanation. In order to be able to consider properly these questions and to connect our present discussion to what was done in the previous chapter we shall first take up some examples related to game-theoretic situations and so to the explanation of rational single-agent and multi-agent action.

We recall that games, in the sense of "classical" game theory (cf. Luce & Raiffa (1957)), can be divided into games where the players have strictly identical interests, games where the players have strictly opposite interests (so-called zero-sum games), and games where the players have mixed interests, i.e., where their interests are partly similar and partly dissimilar (cf. Chapter 6). We shall next briefly comment on these types of games by means of some illustrative examples. We assume that the reader is familiar with the standard game-theoretic analyses of these types of games (see, e.g., Luce & Raiffa (1957) and Chapter 7) and we may thus concentrate on some relevant philosophical issues.

Let us start by considering a coordination game as illustrating a game with identical interests. We recall from Chapter 7 our telephone calling example requiring coordination to restore the broken connection (see especially Figure 7.1). In that example X_1 and Y_2 represent calling back and X_2 and Y_1 waiting. The combinations $<X_1,Y_1>$ and $<X_2,Y_2>$ give a utility unit of 1 to both A_1 and A_2 while the other two combinations give only zero units to both. In this case obviously $<X_1,Y_1>$ and $<X_2,Y_2>$ are equally good action-pairs. A convention (or rule) to act **coordinatively** has to be established between A_1 and A_2 in this game of coordination. In this case we might say that the original caller is the one who should call back. Thus if A_1 called first, $<X_1,Y_1>$ will be the cell determined by this rule.

In general, a coordination norm picks out one cell, which technically will be a so-called coordination equilibrium, in the case of coordination games. This may be taken to change the given utilities so that the distinguished cell gets higher operative utility value in the case of both agents than the $<X_2,Y_2>$ combination. Then we get a situation which closely resembles the first one discussed in the previous section when comparing (30) with (31) and (32). We may in fact plausibly assume that the operative matrices in these two cases coincide. Thus the maximization of both agents' personal utilities and of social utility leads to the cell $<X_1,Y_1>$. Now it is very plausible, of course, to assume that A_1 and A_2 come to think that the original caller is the one to call back and form their intentions to secure the combination $<X_1,Y_1>$. If the agents expect each other to choose the first rather than the second alternative then the first alternative comes to have a higher expected value than the second. Then, we shall argue later, neither agent can, nearly for conceptual reasons, properly form the intention to choose the second alternative, given the above utilities (cf. below our amended (34) with the clause (3')). Given the agents' intentions to perform X_1 and Y_1 respectively we can use, e.g., our schemas (SA_i) or (PR_i) of Chapters 7 and 11 to handle the explanations of their actions (recall from Chapter 7 the connection of (SA_i) and (PR_i) to the justification of the kind of conventional action we are discussing here).

The total social action A_1 and A_2 are performing here may be taken to be $Z_1 = X_1 \& Y_1$. In (PR_i), $i=1,2$, we now substitute 'Z_1' for 'X' and let the agents' respective component actions of course be X_1 and Y_1. As to the agents' intentional total social action Z_1 resulting in the restoration of the connection, any of the detailed six types of explanation presented in Section I of Chapter 11 may be used for explaining it. Not all of those explanations require that there be a we-intention to do specifically Z_1. But it is very plausible to assume that in the present case the agents formed a we-intention to do Z_1, in view of its maximizing GEU, analogously with the above single-agent case.

Let us next consider games with opposite interests, and, in particular, let us consider the two-agent game shown in Figure 12.4.

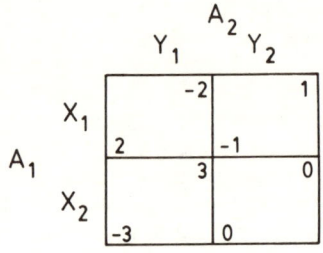

Fig. 12.4.

Here $<X_1, Y_2>$ is an equilibrium point (and a maximin-point). How about GEU (cf. (31) and (32))? Even if $<X_1, Y_2>$ is an equilibrium point maximizing each player's security level it is not reasonable for them to assign probability one to the cell $<X_1, Y_2>$ (or G_{12}). For the underlying assumption is that each player could exploit the other one if he knew the latter's choice for sure. Therefore players rational in the sense of game theory (see Luce and Raiffa (1957), pp. 49-50) must assign their probabilities so that X_1 and Y_2 will maximize their GEUs. It also seems likely that less rational agents would in the long run come to assign their probabilities in this way. Of course there is even here the possibility that the players fundamentally change the given name and perhaps reduce its conflict character. I shall not here try to investigate the specific mechanisms for doing that.

Contrary to the coordination situation we do not here need to assume the presence of interdependent intentions and choices. If fully rational (in the game-theoretic sense), A_1 chooses X_1 and A_2 chooses Y_2 "come what may". But does A_1's performing X_1 and A_2's performing Y_2 constitute a social action after all? In view of our (5.10) Z_2 must then have social action tokens$_2$ brought about partly by relevant we-intending. (With A_1 and A_2 representing two superpowers Z_2 might stand for engaging in nuclear arms race, for example.) The only problematic matter here is whether a relevant we-intention, indeed typically a we-intention to perform Z_2, can exist. The answer provided by our characterization (WI) of Chapter 2, and our account of personal intention (see note 1) of Chapter 4, is that there can in principle be such we-intentions without formal contradiction (as far as only intentions to perform a specific action rather than, e.g., to win are concerned). But they need not satisfy the schema (W2) of Chapter 2, as emphasized earlier.

Note that in the context of zero-sum games we-intentions are based on self-interest and "aggression" (even if the acceptance of the rules of the game is a kind of other-regarding feature). It is clear that we-intentions to do something which is known to be mutually harmful to the members of the group certainly are odd. (Note too that if $u_{12}=u_1+u_2$ then always $u_{12}=0$; or, more generally, if we have a constant sum game we can always have $u_{12}=0$ through rescaling.) There is then an intuitive difference between such we-intentions and non-aggressive or "proper" ones, to be sure. In accordance with the discussion in Chapter 2, I have chosen not to take directly into account this in the very definition of a we-intention. Thus, I will technically accept non-altruistic we-intentions as a kind of borderline case in the case of zero-sum games, but nothing important should be read into this stipulation.

On our account maximization of expected utility can be taken to justify and perhaps to explain the personal intendings to do X_1 and Y_2 (and the resulting actions themselves). Whether an explanation is obtained will depend on factual matters; justification (reasonableness) again depends on the above kind of conceptual grounds. Note that the social action Z_2 will get zero as its GEU-value, along with Z_1, Z_3, and Z_4, if we assume $u_{12}=u_1+u_2$. So there is a tie, and this also indicates the slight oddity of calling Z_i, i=1,2,3,4, a proper social action. As classical game theory gives a solution to every zero-sum game in terms of pure or mixed equilibriums strategies the above remarks related to maximization of GEU are widely expendable.

Let us now go to games with mixed interests, which perhaps come closest to representing ordinary real life games. Of these games we have earlier in Chapter 7 discussed the prisoner's dilemma game. We recall that it is a game with the features shown in Figure 12.5 (when played as a two-agent game):

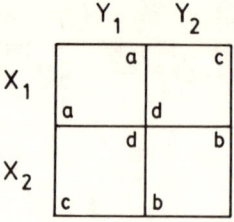

Fig. 12.5.

with d<b<a<c and c+d<2a. To be concrete, let us here exemplify this game type by the so-called mortarmen's dilemma (cf. Ullmann-Margalit (1976) for an extensive discussion of it). Consider thus the given utility matrix shown in Figure 12.6.

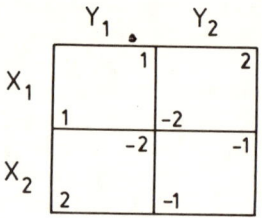

Fig. 12.6.

Here A_1 and A_2 are mortarmen in isolated outposts, facing enemy attack. Each of them thinks that he can either remain at his post and fight (X_1, Y_1) or desert (X_2, Y_2). If both remain at their posts ($<X_1, Y_1>$), they will repel the enemy's attack. If one deserts and the other remains at his post, the former will be helped to reach safety by the latter's fire but the latter will eventually be killed ($<X_1, Y_2>$ and $<X_2, Y_1>$). If both desert, the enemy will succeed in taking them as prisoners.

How can the mortarmen's dilemma be resolved? As we saw in Chapter 7, the pair $<X_2, Y_2>$ is an equilibrium point, but it is clearly unsatisfactory to both players. The best A_1 and A_2 can jointly get is represented by $<X_1, Y_1>$ (even if this does not give them their individually best utility, viz., 2 units). But the trouble with $<X_1, Y_1>$ again is that it is not an equilibrium point and that it, accordingly, is unstable. Only a fully **binding** agreement or norm excluding A_1's choice X_2 and A_2's choice Y_2 could guarantee $<X_1, Y_1>$. Indeed, for instance, Harsanyi's (1977) theory of solutions gives $<X_1, Y_1>$ as the solution of this game when it is played with binding agreements. Otherwise $<X_2,Y_2>$, maximizing the player's security level, is the solution in his theory.

But how do we establish the binding agreement or norm ensuring $<X_1,Y_1>$? We may either impose some strong and idealized rationality postulates about the players, as, e.g., Harsanyi (1977) does, or, more realistically, we may think along the lines of Section I of the present chapter that the very establishment of this norm changes the utilities of the original game. In the case of our mortarmen we may try to educate them to think that it is a great **honor** for them to remain at their posts fighting and to educate them to respect that honor. Then we might be able to enforce a norm of the form 'A soldier ought never to desert in a battle'. Suppose we succeed in all this. (There may be many alternative ways of achieving this; e.g., hardened discipline or chaining the mortarmen to their posts might do the job.)

Imposing the above norm might imply that the original utility matrix changes into the operative matrix shown in Figure 12.7, with utilities obtained by a non-linear transformation from the original ones.

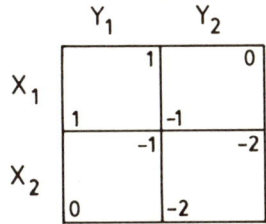

Fig. 12.7.

In this new game the cooperative cell or outcome $<X_1,Y_1>$ is an equilibrium and, by any available rationality criteria, it represents the only sensible action combination.[2] As the reader can easily see, our GEU-formulas (30), (31), and (32), applied analogously with the earlier cases, also lead to this result under minimally rational probability assignments. Accordingly, using our previous terminology, we may claim that the establishment of a "honor-norm", and enforcing it, is very likely to lead the agents A_1 and A_2 to obey it and to form an intention to fight and remain fighting in battle. This, if acceptable, gives us a dynamic explanation of their intention to continue fighting at their posts; it can also be taken to dynamically explain their fighting at their posts. As before we shall not here bother to specify the precise structure of the proximate action-explanation involved here (see Chapter 11); nor shall we discuss the difference between explaining fighting and remaining to fight.

Prisoner's dilemma type games far from exhaust games with mixed interests. For instance, so-called games of inequality (or partiality) represent another interesting type of game where the situation is inherently unstable and where, therefore, some external physical or, rather, social and/or psychological factors, which are not directly "built into" the original utility matrix, can be brought to play.

Perhaps it is proper here to emphasize that we have used game-theoretic examples mainly for the purpose of illustration and that we of course do by no means commit our account to the highly rationalistic assumptions of utility theory and game theory. As should be obvious, a theory of dynamic explanation cannot rest merely on game theory and strong rationality assumptions. Note, too, that we have been discussing only two-person games with perfect and complete information. The assumption of **perfect** information means that the players always know their place in the game tree (of the extensive form of the game). The assumption of **complete** information means that the players know the rules of the game and that hence they have full knowledge of their own and the other players' utility functions and action alternatives (cf. our discussion in Chapter 7 of this assumption). However, in real life it is quite often the case that agents do not know exactly which action (or strategy) alternatives are open to them nor what consequences the known alternatives have; and even if they know all that, they often fail to know exactly each other's payoffs and "rationality" or "motivation" types (cf. self-regarding and other-regarding attitudes in prisoner's dilemma games).

Furthermore, the restriction to two-person games again has meant the neglect of **coalition formation** processes and their effect on the coming about of social action. A full blown theory of dynamic explanation of social action must, of course, be able to relax all the above rationality assumptions. Detailed criticisms of them are familiar from the literature and it is not necessary here to discuss that topic further. (See, e.g., Tversky (1975) and Elster (1979) for informative discussion and sharp criticisms.)

2. Our above game-theoretic examples suggest that there may be a close connection between the maximization of expected utility and at least intention to act if not action. Let us now consider the matter a little more clearly and start with the following

partial account (necessary condition) of (complex) intending (given in Chapter 6 of Tuomela (1977), p. 133, and summarized above in Note 1 of Chapter 4; also cf. Audi (1973b)):

(34) An agent A **intends to perform** X **by performing** Y only if
   (1) A believes (and has not temporarily forgotten that he believes) that he, at least with some non-negligible probability, can perform X by performing Y (or at least can learn so to perform X);
   (2) A wants (and has not temporarily forgotten that he wants) to perform X by performing Y;
   (3) A either has no stronger incompatible want (or set of incompatible wants whose combined strength is at least as great), or if A does have such a want or set of wants, he has temporarily forgotten that he wants the object(s) in question, or does not believe he wants the object(s), or has temporarily forgotten his belief that he cannot both realize the object(s) and perform X by performing Y.

(34) is meant to apply to single agents in the first place. Recall that group-level intending reduces to the members' we-intendings and we-intendings in turn rely on personal single-agent intendings (cf. Chapter 2).[4] I believe that a finer formulation of personal intending would have to relativize (34) explicitly to some suitable normal conditions - over and above those clause (3) is concerned with. Note, too, that as (34) only gives a necessary condition for intending (and cannot be regarded as sufficient, as I have argued), there is room for, e.g., irreducible deciding and other intention-formation.

I will here accept (34) as at least roughly adequate except for criticizing an obscurity in it which turns out to be crucial for our present concerns. This obscurity is that (34) does not make clear what intending in risky situations with several incompatible wants and beliefs presupposes. For we may raise the question whether (34) entails a kind of comparative version of the maximization of expected utility hypothesis. Here that would amount to the assumption that A's want in clause (2) and belief in (1) override all the other rivalling (intrinsic and extrinsic) wants of (3) cum the relevant beliefs. The trouble with (34) now is that its (3) says nothing about such accompanying beliefs.

I would like to say that A can have the intention in (34) even in a case where there are rivalling wants which in some sense are stronger than the want in clause (2) and without the forgetting and not-believing the second disjunct of clause (3) speaks about taking place. This would be the case when such rivalling wants would have a low probability of satisfaction. Thus, for instance, moderately strong but easily satisfiable wants may be preferred to wish-like wants with a low chance of satisfaction. Thus a scientist may want to have his research paper published in a leading international journal (acceptance with a low probability in this case) rather than in a local journal (acceptance with a high probability) and end up intending to send - and sending - his paper to the local journal.

Accordingly, I am claiming that, ceteris paribus, we should be comparing want-belief combinations in (34). Now if strength in clause (3) is taken to mean expected strength or resultant strength we could take that to give us what we need. But even in that case it would be better to have a clearer formulation of the idea (3) then is about. Let us consider the following suggestion in which we call the action (Y above) by which the goal action (X) is supposedly probabilistically reachable a **means-action**:

(3')   A either has no rivalling incompatible want to do something X' accompanied by a relevant belief about a means-action Y' such that this want-belief constellation is equally strong or stronger than the want-belief constellation determined by clauses (1) and (2) (nor does he have a set of incompatible wants cum relevant beliefs about appropriate means-actions whose combined strength is at least as great) or if A does have such a want or set of wants cum the relevant means-beliefs he has temporarily forgotten that he wants the object(s) in question (cum the belief in question), or does not believe he wants the object(s) (and has the relevant belief), or has temporarily forgotten his belief that he cannot both realize the object(s) and bring about X by doing Y.

My proposal is that we now use (3') instead of (3) and take it in conjunction with the other clauses to explicate (intrinsic or extrinsic) wanting **on balance** (viz. A's taking into account all relevant things) in an objective sense. There is however the trouble that it is not perhaps sufficiently clear how to compare want-belief constellations as to their strength. Notice, however, that many versions of utility theory proceed just by assuming an analogous sort of comparability, for a **prospect** is essentially just a want-belief constellation and the comparability of prospects is assumed by utility theory (cf. Chapter 2 above). What such a utility account ends up with is numerical degrees of belief and want. Then it would instead use expected values p(X'/Y')u(X') (or p(Y'|⊳ X')u(X')) in (3') and make the comparison in terms of them. But, if we could disregard the second main disjunct in (3'), that would amount to accepting the maximal expected utility assumption here. That is, A could intend to do only something which has maximal expected utility for him.

Yet we need not accept what utility theory so gives us as anything like an unrevisable common sense truth (or analytic truth relative to the common sense framework). But our present (3'), as it stands, seems to me defensible as a kind of common sense framework conceptual truth (to the extent there are any). Given this, intending becomes (in cases where the second disjunct of clause (3') fails) related to a kind of maximization of the strength of want-belief constellations, but this strength need only be a comparative notion. I also suggest that not all of the axioms for such comparative strength that utility theory imposes need to be regarded as conceptual truths in a similar sense as (3'). For instance, the Probabilistic Equivalence postulate mentioned in Chapter 2 is one such axiom; indeed almost any axioms using the mathematically explicated notion of probability are ones common sense is unsure about.

Our conclusion then is that intending to do something X does **not** conceptually entail that X has maximal EU or GEU in our sense, but it does conceptually entail a kind of weak comparative version of the maximal expected want-strength idea given, however, that normal conditions obtain at least in the sense of the second disjunct of clause (3') failing to be true. Notice, too, that as our account of intentional action entails the presence of a relevant intention it follows that if an actor performed something intentionally under normal conditions, he was maximizing expected want-strength in the above sense. However, note that this maximization need not necessarily be **directly** related to X (but rather to the content-action of that relevant intention). Note, furthermore, that our agent may merely be acting **as if** he were consciously maximizing his expected utilities, for he need not consciously have deliberated his want-belief constellations.

But even with these relaxations, this notion of intentional action may seem a strong one and it is important to keep in mind that, as emphasized in Chapter 4, there are plenty of nonintentional and unintentional actions (for which nothing comparable needs to hold). Habitual actions, or some of them, might be cited as relevant here and, in general, actions with less than a full degree of intentionality. Also notice that there are lexicographic (and other non-Archimedean) preferences which might satisfy our (3') but would fail to be metrically representable.

Intentional actions out of love, honor, or pride might be cited as examples (recall our remarks in Section III of Chapter 2).

My conclusion concerning the epistemic status of the maximization of expected utility assumption accordingly is that it is not a purely conceptual truth; it has some empirically testable content. Thus explanations making reference to the maximization of expected utility have empirical content beyond that contained in the attribution of specific wants and beliefs to people. The other side of the coin is that some weaker notions such as Simon's **satisficing** (taken to mean, e.g., the choice of X_i if $GEU(X_i) \geq s$, for some suitable value of s) may find room here even in the case of fully intentional actions.

If those broadly factual claims we earlier in Section II made about the motivation of (single-agent and multi-agent) action are on the right track it follows that, in normal circumstances, the final motivation of action generally does not only depend on expected utility (cf. the case with several actions simultaneously maximizing GEU) but on other factors as well, starting perhaps from the variation in the utilities (or the variance of prospects, often used to measure risk-taking). (Note that expected utilities, or wants at least, yet seem to have to be an important component of the final motivating constellation.) In any case, when actions are dynamically explained one does not merely - explicitly or implicitly - refer to expected utilities but to several other factors as well.

3. Let us finally consider what kind of explanatory answers the kind of dynamic explanations we have been considering give us. In so far as only intentional actions are concerned it is always **possible** to give an intentional-teleological explanation in terms of dynamic factors, for the explanatory elements (intendings, goals and relevant beliefs) of our schema (**ITE**) of Section II of Chapter 11 will always be there (under our wide interpretation of the term 'goal'). In other words, I am here imposing the constraint on dynamic or motivational explanations answering questions of the type 'For what was the intentional action token v performed by the agent(s)?' that they fit our schema (**ITE**).

Now, if our thesis (**ST1**) saying that all proximate explanations are rephrasable as intentional-teleological explanations is acceptable, it seems easy to extend it to cover dynamic explanations. So let us here rely on our discussion in Chapter 11 and accept (**ST1**). Then it suffices to notice that what we mean by a dynamic or motivational explanation of an intentional action is just an explanatory account of how the proximate explanatory factors referred to by (**ITE**) came about. Thus it seems quite plausible if not almost tautological (relative to (ST1)) to put forth this claim: All dynamic mental explanations (answering a why-question or a what for -question) of intentional (single-agent or multi-agent) actions can be turned into intentional-teleological explanations (ST1*). The phrase 'turn into' in (ST1*) involves that once you have given a dynamic explanation (a suitable scientific-explanatory answer) you can enrich it and spell out the underlying intending to get an intentional-teleological explanation in the sense of (ITE). Given (ST1*) we can connect dynamic explanations with purposive-causal explanations and reason explanations as specified by the theses (ST2), (ST3), and (ST4) of Section II of Chapter 11.

However, what interests us more presently is that one can give dynamic explanations which are sound even without one's actually turning them into intentional-teleological explanations and without the complete scientific-explanatory answers underlying these dynamic explanatory answers being directly intentional-teleological ones. Let me give an example which dovetails with what we have been doing earlier in this chapter. We consider an actor A, an individual or a group, who has performed a certain action X_i by producing a token v of it. We may ask: Why did A perform X_i? Or we may ask: For what did A perform X_i? Now assume that A acts according to what a certain motivation theory specifies. For simplicity, assume that it might just say that agents of some relevant kind K, of which kind A is, have a certain (resultant) propensity r (where r is a specific value or an interval) to be, normally or in certain circumstances S, maximizers of GEU in the sense of our (20), suitably factually interpreted.

This explanation can be formulated as an inductive-probabilistic explanation in the sense of Chapter 10 (Appendix) and Tuomela (1981) informally and roughly as follows:

(35) (L) All agents of the kind K are intentional GEU-maximizers with (resultant) propensity r under circumstances S.
     (S1) Action X_i maximized GEU in a circumstance of the kind S.
[r] (S2) Agent A is of the kind K.
     (E) Agent A intentionally performed u (of the kind X_i).

What we have in brackets is an **inductive** or **epistemic** probability expressing the epistemic strength of the connection between the premises (L), (S1), (S2), and the conclusion (E) of the above inductive argument. We have here, in the brackets, made the value of this **epistemic** probability equal the value of the

objective propensity-probability in the law (L). Note that as our (20) for GEU contains **subjective** probabilities, (L) and our present explanation also involves them; and so we are dealing with three kinds of probabilities here. I shall not here discuss the premises (S1) or (S2) nor the more technical aspects of explanations of the kind (35) but refer the reader to Tuomela (1981). Let me just say that (35) can be embedded into a complete scientific answer involving a ρ-argument in the sense of the Appendix of Chapter 10 (and specifically of (17) of Tuomela (1981)). To spell this out in detail one has to keep in mind the **prospect-relativity** of GEU. This is indeed a pragmatic factor very closely related to our **relevance-classes** of Chapter 10 and thus to the specification of the context C in (**10.8**). Note that the paradigm conditions P may contain the relevant explanatory motivation theory to the extent (L) does not exhaust it.

(35) can also be spelled out as a reason-explanation: A's reason for X_i was that it maximized GEU in S and so excluded the reasons for the competing actions or for omitting X_i, depending on the prospect used. The maximization of GEU helps A to pick out one of several reasons (viz. expected utilities) on which to act. It goes without saying that the law schema (L) may fail to be true for many interpretations of K and S. Yet in situations of achievement, when giving (20) an interpretation somewhat along the lines of Atkinson's theory (perhaps with other-regarding utilities), (L) seems at least somewhat plausible both in the case of single agents and groups (cf. Heckhausen (1980) and Zander (1971)).

More generally, the law used in our inductive explanations might concern the final resultant action tendency (cf. T in (26)) and specify the exact propensity-degree with which agents of different kinds will perform the action in question. As remarked in Section I, even such laws will be idealized. Yet, given their existence, a nomic explanatory science of psychology and social psychology will be possible. (This does not yet necessarily give us a good predictive science because, for instance, the situations S may be difficult to specify in advance of the occurrence of X_i; but that is a different story.)

The occurrence of a social action X can be explained dynamically, for instance, by reference to the group's resultant action tendency as just discussed or it can be explained by reference to the participating agents' individual resultant action tendencies together with an account of what connects these action tendencies (e.g., by reference to suitable group attitudes); and, depending on the case, it may not be necessary to assume that the agents be mutually fully aware of each other's choice-probabilities and views concerning their acting.

The six patterns of proximate explanation of Section I of Chapter 11 are very relevant in the present connection, for they can rather easily be modified, viz. backed and enriched, to become dynamic explanations in the sense of the present chapter. It is not necessary here to go into details, for the matter really would become doing what we have basically done above - viz. showing how individual and group intentions and intention-formation (and, indeed, operative conduct plans) can be explained in terms of underlying mental factors.

To end, let me note that I have not above said much about such less idealized cases as explaining nonintentional and habitual social action and social action with incomplete and distorted knowledge about the other agents' possibilities and views. Yet I believe the above Lewinian ideas related to the specification of resultant action tendencies can be made work in these cases as well, but I must leave the complex details for another occasion.

CHAPTER 13

FUNCTIONAL AND INVISIBLE HAND EXPLANATION OF SOCIAL ACTION

I. ACTION-FUNCTIONS AND FUNCTIONAL EXPLANATIONS

1. A functional explanation of the presence of an item (e.g., behavior) is typically an explanation telling us that it is there because it has such and such a function in some suitable system. Before we can try to spell out this kind of functional explanation we obviously must say something about what it is for an item to have a function in a system.

Function-talk abounds in biology, as we all know. From there it was borrowed to the social sciences especially by those social scientists who compared social systems to biological organisms. Our claim below will be to study social functions or, rather, action-functions in the case of collectives of agents (such as social groups) and social institutions.

There have been several attempts to characterize functions in recent philosophical literature. It seems that at least the following types of characterization can plausibly be distinguished (cf. Achinstein (1977b)): (1) the **good-consequence** doctrine, (2) the **goal** doctrine, and (3) the **explanation** doctrine. The Aristotelian good-consequence doctrine, advocated recently by, e.g., Hempel (1965) and Woodfield (1976), can be taken to basically assert the following. The (or a) function of an item A (in a system S) is to do something X if and only if A does X (in S) and doing X (in S) confers some good (upon S, or perhaps upon something associated with S, e.g., its user in the case of artifacts). According to the goal doctrine, the (or a) function of A (in S) is to do X if and only if A does X (in S) and doing X (in S) is or contributes to some goal which A (or S) has (or which the user, owner or designer of A (or S) has). A well known representative of this goal-view is Nagel ((1961) and (1977)). One of the leading advocates of the explanation doctrine is Wright (1976). His version of it can be summarized as follows. The function of A is to do X if and only if A is there because it does X, and X is a consequence of A's being there.

Achinstein (1977b) has discussed the above doctrines in a comprehensive and penetrating way. He has provided criticisms of each of them to the effect that, at least without some modification, none of them can be regarded as tenable. Because of the availability of Achinstein's lucid discussion I shall not here go deeply into these doctrines. Let me just briefly present some examples which serve to indicate the faultiness of the above formulations of these views. Consider thus a sewing machine which contains a special button designed by its designer to activate a mechanism which will blow up the machine. This button can be said to serve a function even if activating the mechanism will not have any good consequences for the machine, its user, or its designer. Here we seem to have a counterexample against the necessary condition-part of the good-consequence doctrine. This example may seem, not unproblematically, to work analogously against the goal doctrine if we assume that neither the designer nor the user of the sewing machine has the activation of the exploding mechanism as a goal and that doing this contributes to no goal of the designer or the user.

A counterexample against the sufficient condition-part of the good-consequence and goal doctrines is provided by Wright's (1976) watch example. Suppose that the second hand in a watch happens to work in such a way that it sweeps the dust from the watch and makes the watch work more accurately. The last mentioned consequence confers good upon the watch and its owner and it contributes to the owner's goal to have an accurate timekeeper. Yet the function of the second hand is not to sweep dust.

Counterexamples against the explanation doctrine of Wright can also be provided. One is the following one, directed against the necessary condition-part. We are told that the function of a divining rod is to detect the presence of water. Let us assume now, for the sake of argument, that such a rod is incapable of detecting water. The rod can yet be said to have that function. But obviously the divining rod cannot be there because its detecting (or capability of detecting) water. Counterexamples against the sufficiency-part of the explanation doctrine can also be provided; see, e.g., Achinstein (1977b), p. 348.

I do not want to say that the above simple examples really destroy the discussed doctrines but at least they seem to call forth some further discussion and reformulation. We shall not here stop to consider these doctrines in a deeper way but will proceed to develop our own view (which will have some similarity to the goal account).

While the discussion of functions in the social sciences is very common I do not know of many recent **philosophical** treatments which specifically discuss social action functions - our main concern. Nagel (1961) and Hempel (1965) do discuss social functions but they are not specifically concerned with action-functions and, furthermore, they represent views we have come to regard as objectionable above.

2. There is one important explanatory view on functions which I have not seen criticized in the literature. It is the view of Cummins (1975), whose main idea is the following. To ascribe a function to something in a system is to ascribe a capacity to it which is singled out by its role in accounting for or explaining a capacity of the system. Thus it is the function capacity which is taken to (partially) explain the system's capacity. Recall that in Wright's (1976) analysis it is the consequence which explains the presence of the item to which that consequence-function is ascribed. Although Cummins' and Wright's set-ups are different and cannot be strictly compared, still it can be said that the direction of explanation is opposite, as it were, in their views.

As I find some features of Cummins' approach attractive and worth further development let me here reproduce his view, as applied to behavior-functions:

(F) The function of O in S is to do X relative to an analytical account T of S's capacity to do Y if and only if
(1) O is capable of doing X in S;
(2) T appropriately and adequately accounts for S's capacity to do Y by, in part, appealing to the capacity of O to do X in S.

Here O stands for an object or agent, S for a system, and X and Y for activities or actions. It is to be noted that the action-function X of O is relativized to another action-capacity Y and to an "analytical account" T. By an analytical account Cummins here means, roughly, an explanatory story of how the broader capacity to do Y by S comes about as a product of some component capacities, such as O's capacity to do X, such that "programmed" manifestations of the component capacities result in a manifestation of S's capacity to do Y.

I find Cummins' idea of the explanation of the system's capacity to do Y in terms of O's capacity to do X to be important even if he does not clarify in detail what such an explanatory account amounts to and even if he gives us very little clarification of what an "appropriate and adequate" explanatory account really is. We shall in fact below not speak of capacity-explanation at all nor shall we employ the unclear requirement of "appropriate and adequate" explanation. Consequently, I will not discuss further these issues in the present context.

The basic idea in Cummins' analysis of functions is that the functional parts of a system are such parts as contribute in an explanatory way to the total system (clause (2)); what is a function must, furthermore, belong to the part's repertoire (clause (1)). As said, I find these ideas important but I will not here attempt to give a general philosophical defense of them (see Cummins (1975)). We shall below see that the two mentioned ideas are not in fact sufficient at least for an analysis of social action-functions. But before going to that let us pretend for a while that (F) gives a viable account of functions and let us consider social functions from its perspective.

3. How can we apply (F) to our conceptual framework? First, we may interpret O to be a certain agent (or, perhaps, role position) A_i in a collective J with the agents $A_1,...,A_i,...,A_m$ such that J=S and X to be A_i's action type to be realized when J (or S) does Y. In our second interpretation we make O=J and let S be a suitable broader social system, e.g., an institutional collection of role positions, which $A_1,...,A_m$, among others, hold (cf. (5.16)). It is only under this second interpretation that we get a **social** action (viz. the m-agent action X) properly as our explanandum, as will be seen. We shall concentrate on it below and only later comment briefly on the first interpretation. In the place of Cummins' analytical account we shall speak of the (indirect or direct) generation of a social action token by another, and we shall assume without further discussion that our IG (possibly together with conceptual generation R_2) can be used to give an "appropriate and adequate" explanatory account of social action token generation (cf. (6.13) and (6.19)).

But why do I speak of action token generation when clause (2) of (F) speaks about the explanation of action **capacities** in terms of other action capacities? This poses no difficult problem as long as generation is defined (in part) by reference to (strict or probabilistic) type-type action laws (cf. (6.13) and (6.19)). Such a law might, assuming determinism, ideally say this: If, given conditions C_x, $A_1,...,A_m$ (jointly) do X, then, given conditions C_y, they will (jointly) do Y. Let us now accept, for our present purposes, a simplified conditional analysis of capacities (powers, abilities) according to which $A_1,...,A_m$ have the capacity (or power) to do X (jointly) just in case, given some suitable (external and internal) releasing conditions C_x, each A_i will do X_i and this will generate their (jointly) doing X (for a technically detailed account of action-powers see (5.9); also cf. Chapter 9). We may now reformulate (2) of (F) by putting the releasing conditions $C =_{df} C_x \& C_y$ in front of it (even if C_y may depend on C_x) and then speak about the social action type X generating Y, given C. The the following analysis of functions in the case of social actions is obtained for our consideration (we omit the phrase 'jointly', for convenience):

(F_s) A **function** of $A_1,\ldots,A_m$ in S is to do X relative to an action-generational account of S's capacity to do Y if and only if
   (1) $A_1,\ldots,A_m$ have the capacity to do X in S.
   (2) Given the releasing conditions C, the agents' $A_1,\ldots,A_m$ doing X partially generates S's doing Y.

As said earlier, the agents $A_1,\ldots,A_m$ need not be concrete agents but they may, depending on the characterization of S, be regarded as role-holders in the social system S. S will consist of a number of agents (or role-holders) $A_1,\ldots,A_m,A_{m+1},\ldots,A_p$, and, perhaps, some either normative or factual relations specified to hold between A_i, $i=1,\ldots,p$. S may be an institution, for instance. Then we take the A_is, $i=1,\ldots,p$, to be role-holders and take the roles to be normatively specified (e.g., 'Given conditions C_i, A_i ought to do X_i', and so on). As "ought implies can", corresponding to such oughts there will be some powers or capacities bestowed upon A_i (or otherwise presupposed A_i to have) by these oughts (recall our discussion in Chapter 8). It is these capacities - the factual counterpart properties of the norms of S - and the exercise of them that (F_s) is concerned with. (F_s) speaks of **a** rather than **the** function of $A_1,\ldots,A_m$ for the reason that these agents obviously can have several functions in S (none of which need be **the** function).

The action-generational account of (F_s) means the (conjectured) fact that all (complex) social actions are (or can be) built up from some more primitive actions by means of action-generation. (See Chapters 5 and 6 for the system of social action types and the generational mechanisms.) Note especially that all conjunctions such as X&Y, where X and Y are compound social action types, are themselves compound social action types if merely the action-generational aspects of a compound social action type are taken into consideration.

In (2) of (F_s) the notion of partial generation is used. We take it to entail that while subtokens u_i, $i=1,\ldots,m$, of X_i in $X=X_1\&\ldots\&X_m$ do not as such suffice to generate the agents' $A_1,\ldots,A_m,A_{m+1},\ldots,A_p$ doing Y, the u_is together with whatever "functional" actions $A_{m+1},\ldots,A_p$ here are performing do generate S's doing Y. I shall not here attempt to give a more precise account of this but in view of (**6.19**) and (**CON***) of Chapter 6 it can be seen how to do it technically, and thus we finally can come to explicate action token generation in terms of IG (and if needed R_2, too) as before. Note that sometimes all the agents of

S will be the agents of both X and Y, and then we may speak of partial generation in a fuller sense in clause (2). To account for all cases of action-generation we seem to need **probabilistic** generation. Here it is most convenient, however, to operate as if determinism were true. But probabilistic generation will have to be included in clause (2) of (F_s) in the general case.

Let us now ask the crucial question: Is (F_s) an adequate schema for expressing action-functions ascribed to agents? I will argue that it is not but that it can be modified to give a viable account. What, then, are the difficulties that (F_s) faces?

One minor drawback with (F_s) is that it is relativized to an "analytic account" (given in terms of (indirect) generation) and to an action capacity. The first relativization is removed simply by assuming that the action-generational account is objectively true and that it contains all the information that a best (proximate) explanation of S's doing Y in terms of the agents' $A_1,...,A_m$ actions can and need utilize (cf. our definitions (6.15) and (6.19)). Thus we simply omit (from the analysandum) the relativity of functions to a certain action-generational account. We shall also omit the relativity to the action Y and instead require in the analysans that such an action type or, more broadly, a state or episode exists and that this state be an end of S. The motivation for the last requirement will soon become apparent.

A graver difficulty connected with (F_s) is illustrated by the following example. We are told that among the Navaho some members (say $A_1,...,A_m$) of the tribe hunt (and kill) witches and that the function of their witch hunting is to ward off evil spirits. Let us first put this in terms of the agents' $A_1,...,A_m$ action-function, rather, and say that it is their function in S to hunt witches. (We shall later discuss what the talk about the function of witch hunting being warding off evil spirits amounts to.) The point about the example we are concerned to make is that it seems difficult if not impossible to analyze it in terms of (F_s). This is because, we assume, there are no evil spirits and hence there is no warding off evil spirits (but let us assume that there is **witch** hunting, under a suitable description at least). Yet the Navaho **believe** that there are evil spirits and that witch hunting does ward off evil spirits (cf. our earlier example of the divining rod).

In this example we are dealing with what I would like to call a **subjective** function, viz. an action-function (witch hunting) which is someone's function in virtue of a certain **believed** consequence of it (viz. warding off evil spirits) in the sense that the generational relationship in question is believed by the system S to obtain (while in fact it does not, or at least we as scientists have strong reasons to believe it does not). If we now grant that it is correct function-talk to say that the function of $A_1,...,A_m$ is to hunt witches in order to ward off evil spirits or relative to warding off evil spirits, we have here a notion of function which (F_s) does not capture. What (F_s) deals with is **objective** functions. We may continue our above example and assume that in fact witch hunting lowers intra-group hostility (even if the Navaho most likely don't believe or at least think of that). According to (F_s) it is then an objective function of $A_1,...,A_m$ to hunt witches relative to lowering intra-group hostility, even if they do not themselves recognize that relativization. There is some oddity about this and we shall later account for it.

One way to handle subjective functions in terms of (F_s) might be to say simply that whenever S believes that the conjunctions of the clauses (or perhaps only clause (2)) of (F_s) is true, while in fact it is not or at least need not be, we are dealing with a subjective function. As we shall in any case modify (F_s) in other respects we prefer below to operate in a somewhat different fashion and will not pursue the present suggestion.

We shall now consider an objection against (F_s) which states that its clauses (1) and (2) are not sufficient even in the case of objective functions. Think of a team of basket ball players $(A_1,...,A_m)$. We assume that by means of certain skillful and complicated bodily movements (amounting to, e.g., as passing the ball to each other and throwing it towards the basket) they are able to score. Let us assume that their passing-throwing action-sequence amounts to a social action, say X, in our technical sense. Call the team's scoring-action Y. Now clauses (1) and (2) can be regarded as satisfied, and it correctly follows from (F_s) that it is the function of $A_1,...,A_m$ to do X (jointly) relative to Y (and the action-generational pattern involved). But let us now consider another consequence of X. By means of X the players disturb air molecules around their bodies. Now, relative to the players' disturbing air molecules (say Y*) clauses (1) and (2) become true; yet it is not the function of the players to do X relative to Y*. They have as their function to do X only relative to some **ends** of the team, such as Y. Thus I think we have found a counter-example here against (F_s) and against Cummins' (F), too, as (F_s) can be regarded merely an application of (F) to the social case. In the social case at least the agents' natural ends must be involved, it seems (cf. the sewing machine example of Subsection 1).

If we add that Y must be an end, do we get an adequate

analysis then? It seems that we do not quite. This is because underlying any function talk in the social sciences there seems to be an assumption of division of labor, activities and tasks among the members (agents) of the social system, community or group S under discussion.[1] The agents in general occupy asymmetric positions, so to speak. Functions are often assigned to positions (rather than to concrete holders of positions) and to activities associated with them, it seems. Considering the above basket ball team, or, better, a soccer team, assume that one of the players, say A_i, has been assigned the task of launching the penalty shoots and free shoots. Then it is only his function to free-shoot or penalty-shoot (relative to the team's scoring) even if all the players have that capacity and could equally well contribute to the team's goal (end) of scoring. Analogously we may think that in the witch hunting case not any collection of m agents will have the function to witch hunt. It is only the Witch Hunters which have that function, and, let us assume, they have that function because it has been bestowed upon them by the eldest of the tribe (or by tradition, if you prefer). Examples closer to home are, e.g., christening a baby by a priest or dubbing someone a knight by the Queen.

The point I am trying to make is that there are clear cases where function ascriptions are affected by the division of labor and tasks in the social system in question and that no analysis of social functions can ignore that. That is, no analysis is sufficient without giving that information. The division of activities in question may be biologically evolved, due to historical tradition or prescribed by some norms or by some authority, and so on. Here it is not essential from where that division comes, so to speak, but only that it is there and affects the functioning of the social community.

It may be argued that any social system (S) by definition involves some kind of division of labor, activities and tasks. If so, then no extra clause would be necessary. But it seems that this holds only when the social system concerns role-positions rather than specific role-holders. But as I want to include cases where S is merely a social collective consisting of specific agents, a clause about the division of activities seems necessary.

At this point we seem ready to suggest an improved analysis of what is involved in saying that it is the (joint) function of some agents $A_1,...,A_m$ to do something X (jointly) in a system. Our new attempt omits the relativization to the consequence action Y and to an action-generational account. It requires the existentially given Y to be an end of S. It covers, and makes a distinction between, subjective and objective functions. Furthermore, it respects the division of activities in S. Finally, analogously with our analyses of other social constructs earlier in this book we have added an optional mutual belief requirement. Its function is to create an epistemic concept out of a non-epistemic one. We thus propose:

(F_S^*)   A **function** of $A_1,...,A_m$ in S is to do X if and only if there is a state or episode Y such that
(1)(a) $A_1,...,A_m$ have the capacity to do X in S, or
    (b) it is believed in S that, in effect, clause (1)(a) is true;
(2) (a) given the releasing conditions C, the agents' $A_1,...,A_m$ doing X partially generates S's achieving Y, or
    (b) it is believed in S that, in effect, clause (2)(a) is true;
(3) (a) Y is an end of S relative to X (in the case of (2)(a)), or
    (b) it is believed in S that, in effect, clause (3)(a) is true (in the case of (2)(b)); and
(4) (a) $A_1,...,A_m$ do X in appropriate circumstances (in part) because of the natural (or natural-historical) and/or normative division of labor, activities, and tasks in S; or
    (b) it is believed in S that, in effect, clause (4)(a) is true.

The optional mutual belief requirement that may be considered in connection with (F_S^*) is:

(5) The members of S have a mutual belief to the effect that (1)(a), (2)(a), (3)(a), and (4)(a) are true.

In (F_S^*) the conjunction (1)(a)&(2)(a)&(3)(a)&(4)(a) analyzes **objective** functions while (1)(b)&(2)(b)&(3)(b)&(4)(b) covers **subjective** functions. Note that a function may of course be both objective and subjective in this sense. Indeed, in the case of epistemic functions if it is objective, it must, because of (5), be subjective as well. By the phrase 'it is believed in S' we mean in (F_S^*) only weakly that some members, not necessarily most, of S have the belief in question. In addition, it is taken to involve that at least some of $A_1,...,A_m$ do have the belief in question.

Let us go through the elements of (F_S^*). Y is now required to be a state of S which (3) requires to be an (objective or subjective) end. In the objective case, Y is a consequence of doing X and of some other required circumstances' obtaining. Thus, given those auxiliary circumstances, $A_1,...,A_m$ perform an action with the end Y as its result **by** doing X (cf. our earlier analysis (6.4) of the by-relation). Note that in many cases, but not always, $A_1,...,A_m$ can be said also to have the function to do that consequence action (which is either a social action in the strict sense of Chapter 5 or at least in the liberalized sense of making reference to another agent discussed in Chapter 9). For instance, if it is the function of $A_1,...,A_m$ to pass the ball in a certain way (contributing to their scoring) in a basket ball game it is also (normally) their function to score; and it is the function of witch hunters to ward off evil spirits although not to lower intra-group hostility (as clause (4) is not fulfilled). If one would like to include such "latent" objective and non-subjective functions (cf. Merton (1957)) as lowering intra-group hostility one can simply omit clause (4)(a); if latent functions come to do something more than the conjunction (1)(a)&(2)(a)&(3)(a) and the denial of (3)(b) it is up to the proponents of the latent function doctrine to spell that out.

Consider the following objection to clause (1). Assume that it is the function of the Finnish army to ward off evil aggressors (or to guarantee the country's independence). Yet, we assume, it seems not to have that capacity nor is it even generally believed to have it. So is (1) too strong? First, I think at best a subjective function is concerned here and it is not clear that (1)(b) is false. If it is false, then I submit that we simply should not even say that a subjective function is spoken about here.

Clause (2)(a) does not require further comments here except that, for generality probabilistic (or indeterministic) generation must be used in its technical explication (at least if indeterminism is true). In (2)(b) (and, analogously, in (3)(b)) we require that at least some agents believe, in effect, that the generation specified in (2)(a) holds for **some** end Y (perhaps often the end could even be required to be specified). Otherwise the agents' acting would not be goal-directed (or end-directed) and it would lack (further) motivation (cf. here our analysis of ends below).

Clause (3) of (F_s^*) makes all functional acting end-directed, and thus our account moves towards the goal theory of functions. For goals are, for me at least, ends which are results (in the technical sense) of social action types. To be sure, we accepted earlier that the goal theory is too strict. But I think that in the case of social functions ends are needed, as argued, and we shall below briefly analyze them. We may here recall the sewing machine example purporting to criticize the necessity of a goal. I would say that it nevertheless was (or might be) an end, if not a goal in a strict sense, of the designer (or the user) of the machine to activate the exploding mechanism. That end need not be considered favorable or desirable by the designer (or user). At least in the case of acting towards an end, the end may be (in some sense) bad for the involved agent(s). (See our below analysis of endhood, clause (1)(b).)

In clause (4) the division of activities is assumed to be grounded either on natural (natural-historical) factors such as biological evolution, biological properties, historical tradition, etc., or on normative factors such as on institutions, organizations, etc., with their normatively characterized positions.

As in the case of other social constructs the mutual belief requirement (clause (5)) partly accounts for "social reality". Thus, it cannot be the function of Witch Hunters to hunt witches unless they themselves have a belief essentially to that effect, one may say. That is fine, but it shows that the speaker has in mind an epistemic notion of function. This speaker would probably also abhor saying that the Witch Hunters have the (objective) function of lowering intra-group hostility, and his ground would be just that the Navahos lack the relevant (mutual) belief to this effect. But yet it must be admitted that one can speak of functions also in a non-epistemic sense, and this is what our (F_S^*) (less (5)) does.

Note that, clearly, our objective versus subjective dichotomy is different from the epistemic versus non-epistemic dichotomy. Thus, for instance, there may in principle be cases of purely subjective functions in the non-epistemic case, for instance, as the belief-requirement does not amount to a requirement of mutual belief. A suitable religious activity in a primitive, unreflective society might qualify here, perhaps even the above hunting example (although I have above treated it differently, perhaps distorting the anthropological facts).

A technical detail about clause (5) is that it does not concern the b-clauses of (F_S^*). This is just because of the occurrence of 'or' in (1), (2), (3) and (4) between (a) and (b). If (1)(a), (2)(a), (3)(a) and (4)(a) in fact are false that does not, of course, affect our analysis for (1)(b), (2)(b), (3)(b) and (4)(b) will yet be satisfied as long as (5) is.

I shall not here further discuss the adequacy of (F_S^*) against our earlier, or other, examples. My preceding discussion will have to serve as my defence of (F_S^*) except that I still have to say something about end states and episodes.

4. I will now present an account of ends in an internalist fashion - in terms of S's attitudes (see Woodfield (1976) for a cogent criticism of externalism). My analysis concerns the state or episode Y or (F_S^*) relative to the action-function X. Recalling (5.16) and our relevant discussion in Chapter 11, I now propose this:

(E) A state or episode Y is an **end** of S relative to an action-function X if and only if
(1) (a) S intrinsically wants Y, or
(b) S extrinsically wants Y such that this extrinsic want is based on S's believing that it is its duty to bring about Y or that it at least ought to bring about Y;
(2) S's (intrinsically or extrinsically) wanting Y can motivate (and typically or at least ideally does motivate) the appropriate operative members of S (viz., $A_1,...,A_m$ in the case of (F_S^*)) to do X; and
(3) doing X is a (naturally evolved or normatively specified) means of bringing about Y (or a means contributing to the bringing about of Y).

(E) speaks of a social system's (e.g., group's) attitudes and thus of holistic attitudes. Clause (1)(b) specifically allows for the cases where (E) is not intrinsically desired by S. In it the extrinsic want is said to be based on the belief that it is S's duty or obligation to bring about Y. It is thus assumed that such a belief can motivate or dispose S to act, and this motivational factor related to it is called an extrinsic want. Note that (1) can be satisfied by the we-intentions of S. But it covers a broader notion. Indeed, S's wants (and beliefs) must now be understood almost in a metaphorically broad sense as some kind of behavioral proto-wants (and proto-beliefs) in order to cover non-epistemic cases of latent functions involving, say the Navaho having as their end the lowering of intra-group hostility. Even if I intend the individualistic programme of concept formation sketched in Chapter 2 to be applicaple to all the we-attitudes of collectives, I shall not try to work out the details (but recall our remarks in Chapters 2 and 12). Let me just say that what would be involved in such an analysis of wants (or proto-wants, if you prefer) would be (all or most of) the individual agents' persistent and plastic actions and action-dispositions directed towards Y rather than, e.g., their explicitly avowed wants (cf. our remarks on a group's we-intending vs. its members' we-intendings in Chapters 5 and 7).

Clause (2) is meant to account for the motivational power (for individual agents) of a communal end and in that sense it explicates the "internalization" (by the agents $A_1,...,A_m$) of the holistic social end. In a sense it also accounts for the persistence of the members of S in their attempts to realize X and for their relative immunity to disturbances operating against their attempts to do X. While (2) would obviously benefit from a more detailed analysis of the phrase 'can motivate' and 'ideally' we shall not here do more than refer to our earlier relevant remarks in Chapter 8, Section I. One more remark related to (2) that may be made here is that in the case of **believed** ends (cf. clause (3)(b) of (F_S^*)) the same motivational force must obviously be there.

Clause (3) requires that X be a (full or partial) means of Y. Given (F_S^*), this is no news as (3) of (E) can normally be regarded as following from (2)(a) of (F_S^*). (A finer analysis of the concept of means would presumably spell out 'normally' in terms of some extra qualifications.)

We may speak of **intended** functions (or **purposive** functions) in the fullest sense in the case of (F_S^*) when the function in question is both objective and subjective as well as epistemic and when in (1) of (E) we-intentions (and we-beliefs) are employed and when, accordingly, (2) of (E) becomes satisfied via a mechanism of practical inference from we-attitudes to I-attitudes (cf. Chapter 11). Several additional combinations are possible. Thus we recall that in the non-epistemic case (F_S^*) allows that generational connection between X and Y either (i) is or (ii) is not there. The first possibility (i) can be combined both with the case where the agents believe it is there and with the case where they have no such belief. The second possibility (ii) can be combined only with the agents' (false) generational belief. All of these possibilities related to generation can still be combined with S's having an end and a believed end or only the latter. What interests us especially in this context is that in all of the above cases the end (or believed end) may be either intended or unintended, for we deliberately construed clause (1) of (E) broadly enough to cover unintended ends.

Our analysis (E) is geared to our analysis of functions because of its relativity to an action-function X. But this relativity can easily be removed or at least relaxed. For instead of the analysandum of (E) we may employ 'State Y is an **end** of S relative to a means-action X of Y'. Then we only need the clauses (1) and (2) of (E) in the analysans and may omit (3). Call this more general analysis of endhood (E*). This broader notion of end gives what is needed in an analysis of instrumental goal-directed action, for an end relative to a means-action X is just a goal whenever Y is an action type (for the agents in S).

A still broader notion of an end than that provided by (E*) is obtained as follows. We define that a state Y is an **end** of S if and only if **there is** a means-action X of S such that Y is an end of S relative to X. In this non-relative definition of endhood, which we may call (E**), the means-action X can perhaps be taken to satisfy clause (3) of (E). If so there must be a contributory means-action to every end. If, however, that is felt to be too strong it may at least be allowed that the action X satisfying the mentioned clause (3) need not be one that S (or the agents of S) has the power to do (a mere attempt to do X would suffice). Still weaker requirements concerning the means would be that X be conducive towards Y or, more generally, that it be "appropriate" for it. Then in fact X need not and perhaps cannot any more be called a means.

At this point we may take a brief new look at goals and goal-directed behavior, discussed earlier in Chapter 11. Let us thus consider goalhood and the appropriateness of actions performed for the sake of (or in order to achieve) a goal. When an action X is **appropriate** for a goal it must be somehow systematically organized and directed to bring about the goal. The requirements of **persistence** and **plasticity,** imposed by such theorists as Braithwaite (1953) and Nagel (1961), are, in addition to **conduciveness** or generation, a central part of this notion of appropriateness. Woodfield (1976) discusses the notions of persistence and plasticity in an informative way, and I will not here go into that. (His criticisms on pp. 100-102 of the plasticity requirement seem weak to me - they have no force against potential or dispositional plasticity; but I shall not here pause to argue.)

Now, relying on (E**), I propose the following general analysis of goals (where S is a single agent or a collective), where we let G be an action type or more generally a want-content (cf. Section II of Chapter 11):

(G)   G is a **goal** of S if and only if
       (1) (a) S intrinsically wants G, or
            (b) S extrinsically wants G such that this extrinsic want is based on S's believing that doing G is its duty or that at least it ought to do G; and
       (2) S's (intrinsically or extrinsically) wanting G can motivate (and typically or at least ideally does motivate) the appropriate operative agent or agents (members of S) to perform actions believed by him

(them) to be appropriate for G (in the sense of these actions being believed by him (them) to exhibit persistence and plasticity and to be conducive with respect to G).

(G) is essentially just the account of goalhood given earlier in Section II of Chapter 11. Note that (G) can be used to give a general analysis of teleology, viz. goal-directed behavior. For we may propose the following analysis:

(OT) S does X **in order to** bring about Y if and only if
(1) Y is an action type (or, more generally, want-content) which is a goal of S;
(2) X is believed by S to be appropriate (typically in the sense of conduciveness, persistence and plasticity) for Y; and
(3) S does X because of (1) and (2).

Let us first note that the informative clause (1) does not entail (2) nor (3). For these two clauses are needed to spell out, respectively, that X indeed is the kind of (subjectively) appropriate action clause (2) of (G) speaks about and that Y indeed is a motivating goal for S (viz. a goal because of which S acts). (Recall here our remarks in Chapter 11 concerning expressive actions as goal-directed.) It is obvious on the basis of our comments in Chapter 11 that if u is an action token (of type X) **intentionally** performed by S in order to achieve the goal Y (in the sense of (IGA) of Chapter 11), then S performed this action in order to do Y (in the sense os (OT)). If the belief in (2) of (OT) is true, then X can be said to be objectively appropriate for Y.

Let us compare (OT) with Wright's (1976), p. 39, analysis which builds on Taylor's (1964) account. According to Wright, S does X for the sake of Y if and only if (i) X tends to bring about Y and (ii) X occurs because (i.e., is brought about by the fact that) it tends to bring about Y. It seems that Wright would like to understand Y as a goal. If so, our (OT) is related to his analysis, for Wright seems to treat his (i) as almost a synonym for our (1). There is one central thing to notice here, however. It is that Wright treats goals, although he does not explicitly analyze them, in an external fashion, without reference to the actor's attitudes. Our analysis again builds on an **internalist** account of goalhood. Similarly, (OT) treats subjectively (in terms of beliefs) such traditional external features of goal-directed behavior as conduciveness, persistence, and plasticity with respect to the goal, while Wright's analysis is objective and externalist.

5. Returning to functions, till now we have been dealing exclusively with some agents' $A_1,...,A_m$ function to jointly perform an action X. What can we say of the function of the action X, then? Let us assume that a surgeon's function is to operate on (suitable) patients with the goal of making them healthy. Then the function of his operating is to make the patients healthy. Schematically, and more precisely, we get the following rather obvious result. A function of an action X (performed by $A_1,...,A_m$) in S is to achieve end Y if and only if it is a function of $A_1,...,A_m$ in S to do X relative to the end Y (as characterized by (F^*_S)). Our equivalence statement need not be regarded as a definition of the function of X, for we could in the obvious way define its function (viz. Y) in terms of a further end, say Y', to which Y contributes. Thus we could continue till we get to some ultimate ends, if there be any.

Analogously we could also characterize the functions of any elements, structures, or activities (and processes) in social systems in general along the lines of (F^*_S) and its non-epistemic counterpart as well as their above extension to functions of actions. While such a task is central for a study of society it goes beyond the scope of this book. (See, e.g., Sztompka (1974) for a relevant discussion.)

When we started our discussion of functions we pointed out that in the original schema (F) we might alternatively let O stand for a single agent A_i (or role-position) in a collective J consisting of $A_1,...,A_m$ (such that J may contain some specification of the social bonds holding between the agents). We then make S=J and let X be A_i's action type to be realized when J (or S) does Y. Here we may, following our earlier terminology in Chapter 5, take the conjunction $X_1\&...\&X_m$ to be a (complex) social action type. Let us call it Y, to use the notation of (F^*_S). (To cover a slightly more general case we could call $X_1\&...\&X_m$ X and require Y to be an action generated by X.) Then we may define what A_i's function amounts to in this case, and we do it by the following modification of (F^*_S):

(F^{**}_S) A **function** of A_i, i=1,...,m, in S is to do X if and only if there is a social action type Y such that
(0) $Y=X_1\&...\&X_m$;
(1) (a) A_i has the capacity to do X_i in S, or
(b) it is believed in S that, in effect, clause (1)(a) is true;
(2) (a) given the releasing conditions C', the agents' A_i doing their component actions X_i generates S's doing Y, or
(b) it is believed in S that, in effect, clause

(2)(a) is true;
(3) (a) Y is an end (social goal-action) of S relative to X (in the case of (2)(a)), or
(b) it is believed in S that, in effect, clause (3)(a) is true (in the case of (2)(b)).

The optional mutual belief requirement now becomes:

(4) The members of S have a mutual belief to the effect that (1)(a), (2)(a), and (3)(a) are true.

In (F_S^{**}) the new clause (0) requires Y to be a social action type consisting of the X_is. Clauses (1), (2), and (3) are in effect the same as their counterparts in (F_S^*) (in (2) C' of course corresponds to C in its counterpart). (F_S^{**}) contains no counterpart to clause (4) of (F_S^*). This is because the relevant information is incorporated in (F_S^{**}), as the division of activities is already assumed in the specification that Y is a social action which consists of the (single agent) component action types X_i, corresponding to A_i, i=1,...,m.

6. Let us next consider singular functional explanations (as to the explanation of laws, see Chapter 14). As explanations are to be regarded as relative to explanatory questions, we may start with the latter. Thus we may ask, related to (F_S^*), why $A_1,...,A_m$ performed a token u of X. We may also ask why Y was achieved (if it was), or by what means Y was achieved, and so on. Let us here concentrate on the question 'Why was u (of type X) done by $A_1,...,A_m$?'. This question, which we call q, is ambiguous. It may ask for an efficient cause of (the occurrence of) u or for a "final" cause of it. It may also be answered by stating the function the agents $A_1,...,A_m$ performed in this situation or by stating the function that the token u had in this situation. There are several possibilities here. We shall not investigate all of them but only concentrate on the one corresponding to (F_S^*) just to illustrate how function-talk can be connected with functional explanation.

We shall thus consider the above why-question q. We are now interested in a functionalist answer which can be roughly stated as follows: It was the function of $A_1,...,A_m$ to do X (in S), and they exercised this function. An example would be to explain a church choir's singing a certain hymn by saying that it occurred because it is the function of the choir to do so with respect to the church officials and the church goers performing the liturgy. More exactly, the answer refers to a function as stated in the analysandum of (F_S^*). Now we see that as doing X in part serves to explain doing Y, according to (F_S^*), we, in giving a functional explanation, in a sense take doing Y to teleologically explain doing X.

Technically we may explicate singular functional action-explanation by means of an explanatory answer as follows:

(FE) v_f is a scientific explanatory answer to q in the case of **functional explanation** if and only if
 (1) v_f is a scientific explanatory answer to q;
 (2) the complete scientific explanatory answer c_f corresponding to v_f (or every such complete scientific explanatory answer, if there are several) contains a statement to the effect that a function of $A_1,...,A_m$ (in S) was to do X relative to the end Y (in the sense of (F_S^*)), and that $A_1,...,A_m$ exercised this function and did X (or, equivalently, that $A_1,...,A_m$ did X because it was their function to do it).

Functional explanations in the sense of (FE) are related to teleological explanations mainly due to the end state or episode Y. For in (FE) Y can be said to be a (not always **intended**) goal action (or a result of such a goal action) of S and also of $\{A_1,...,A_m\}$, X (partially) generates Y, and $A_1,...,A_m$ believe so (assume (2)(b) of (F_S^{**}) to be true); and $A_1,...,A_m$ did X because it was their function to do X. In view of our (T) I take these conditions to entail the truth of the statements '$A_1,...,A_m$ did X for the sake of Y', and '$A_1,...,A_m$ did X in order to contribute to S's doing Y'. In this sense, all functional explanations with subjective functions can be regarded as (subjectively) teleological (although of course not necessarily as intentional-teleological; cf. our (ITE)). Perhaps I should finally add that what in my view ultimately makes teleological explanations work (when they do so) in the long run is that the agents' actions are correctly believed by them to reach their goals and that there is some positive feedback (want-satisfaction) from that to the agents. But this feedback really becomes pertinent only when explaining action patterns and regularities rather than singular actions as above.

(FE) can be used to give "micro-explanations" of a system's actions (such as Y in (F_S^*)) in terms of its component actions (such as the X_is in (F_S^*)). This micro-explanation can be regarded the better (a) the more complex Y is relative to the X_is and (b) the more different Y is from the X_is, and (c) the more complex the generational process between the X_is and Y is.

Let us finally consider our (F_S^{**}) and its connection to functional explanation. Corresponding to the explanatory schema

(FE) we obtain a new schema (FE') by substituting, respectively, '$X_1,...,X_m$' for 'X' and 'the goal-action Y (in the sense of (F_S^{**}))' for 'the end Y (in the sense of (F_S^*))' in clause (2) of (FE). (I will not write out (FE') explicitly.) The new schema now serves to give functional explanations of each A_i's doing X_i (viz. his producing u_i), and thus of single-agent actions. But if we add that the u_is generated u (tokening Y) we get a **kind** of "functional" explanation also of u: S, with the operative agents $A_1,...,A_m$, did u because it was the function of each A_i, i=1,...,m, to do X_i, each A_i did X_i because it was his function to do X_i, and the resulting action tokens u_i generated u (recall (5.16)). But this kind of "functional" explanation, which corresponds to type (1.A.) in the case of explaining intentional social action in Chapter 11, Section I and to the "micro-explanation" related to (FE) and mentioned above, is of course not a proper functional explanation of u at all. This is because u (tokening Y) is not explained in terms of the agents' function to do Y nor of Y's function in S.

II. INVISIBLE HAND EXPLANATIONS OF SOCIAL ACTION

1. As we saw in the preceding section, functional explanations may quite well be concerned with non-intentional explanandum-action. We shall in this section concentrate on so-called **invisible hand** explanations which can be said to deal only with non-intentional explananda. Before going to them it is appropriate to make some remarks on non-intentional actions and their explanation quite generally.

It has sometimes been claimed that all actions are intentional under some description or some conceptualization. But, as I have argued in Tuomela (1977), Chapter 10, and above in Chapter 4, that is not true. For instance, when writing this, let us suppose, I non-intentionally scratch my ear. This latter action is not intentional under any description. Technically speaking, this is because there is no operative conduct plan of mine in which I intend it or in which it is somehow intimately related to what I intend. As our discussion in Chapter 5 shows (cf. (5.10)), the (full) intentionality of social actions seems to be reducible to the intentionality of the single-agent actions it has as its components (note: these subactions still involve we-attitudes). Thus I am willing to claim that a social action u is **fully** intentional just in case all its component actions u_i, i=1,...,m, are intentional with respect to the we-intention they are related to (recall again definition (5.10)). We can also speak of degrees of intentionality, when some but not all agents act intentionally (see Chapter 5 on this). Especially interesting are those cases of social action where the leader (or the leading "clique") does something intentionally while the underdogs do not participate in doing that intentionally.

Let us now go into some of the issues involved in the explanation of partly intentional social actions controlled by a leader acting fully intentionally. We consider a military unit consisting of the collective S with $A_1,...,A_m$ as its operative members (cf. (5.16)). Let us suppose A_1 is its leader. Assume that A_1 intends to deceive the enemy (Y) by making his unit overtake a certain enemy post (X). The deception might consist in getting the enemy to believe that the main attack is going to take place there while, in fact, this is only a camouflage attack to be soon followed by the real one elsewhere. For obvious motivational reasons A_1 does not tell his men his real purpose. Suppose now that $A_1,...,A_m$ do X intentionally due to A_1's command. They also do Y (for their doing Y is generated by their doing X) albeit only partly intentionally; only A_1 does his part of Y intentionally.

How do we explain the social action u (tokening X) and y (tokening Y)? Consider u first. As it is an intentional social action we may employ any of the ways described in Section I of Chapter 11 to give a proximate explanation of it. For instance, we may assume that $A_2,...,A_m$ formed an intention to obey A_1's command to do X and then use (PR_i) (see Chapter 11) to give an explanation of the subtokens u_i, i=1,...,m and the generation of u. A dynamic explanation of u may be given by referring to the leader's command (and, perhaps, his power to command) and perhaps the men's maximizing their utilities by obeying this command (cf. Chapter 12).

But our problem here is rather the (proximate) explanation of y. It seems that if we just say that y was partially purposively generated by u, or, perhaps, the u_is, we do not get a satisfactory explanation of, say, why y was done partly intentionally or for what was it so done. I suggest that we rather give our proximate explanation in terms of the leader's intention and his power to get his men to move. Thus we first state that A_1 intended that S do Y (partly non-intentionally), which we may take to entail that A_1 intends to do whatever in his action repertoire he regards as necessary to make S do Y. Next, A_1 considered (a) that unless S does X, S will not do Y and (b) that if and only if he commands S to do X, S will do (or at least attempt to do) X. So A_1 commanded S to do X, but did not tell $A_2,...,A_m$ that S's doing X would generate S's doing Y. As a consequence of A_1's command S did X, and X generated Y. So S did Y, and it did it only partly intentionally. In this explanation we may assume that A_1's intention and his relevant beliefs purposively generated his commanding the company S to do X. This command had as its purposive-causal consequence that $A_2,\ldots,A_m$ came to believe that they should obey A_1's command, in view of A_1's power over them, and that they accordingly formed a we-intention to do X. This we-intention led purposive-causally, through the men's I-intentions, to their doing their u_is (tokens of X_i), which (with u_1) purposively generated u (tokening X). Finally, u non-purposively (or, better, only partly purposively) generated y (tokening Y). We have assumed that $A_2,\ldots,A_m$ were not aware of u's generating y, and that hence they did their subtokens u_i non-intentionally.

2. There are interesting connections between the explanations of non-intentional actions, on the one hand, and both the so-called invisible hand explanations and the functional explanations of such actions (discussed in Section I). Let us now consider invisible hand explanations, which are so called after Adam Smith: "Every individual intends only his own gain, and he is in this, as in so many other cases, led by an invisible hand to promote an end which was no part of his intention". Invisible hand explanations do not, however, literally refer to any invisible hand but, rather, deny that any hand, visible or not, was present at all. They explain what **looks** to be the product of someone's intentional design as not being brought about by anyone's intentions (cf. Nozick (1974), p. 19). Invisible hand explanations are concerned with unintended and unanticipated consequences of human action, but with the restriction that initially an explanation of them in terms of intentional design seems plausible, too. Thus not every unintended and unanticipated consequence of human action qualifies as an explanandum of an invisible hand explanation. As examples of hidden hand explanation, e.g., the following have been mentioned (cf. Nozick (1974), pp. 20-21, Ullmann-Margalit (1978), pp. 264-265): (a) the process of how public goods are supplied not solely by individual action; (b) the continuous creation of money within the banking system; (c) the development of media of exchange; (d) the rise of the so-called ultra-minimal-state.

Ullmann-Margalit (1978) provides a rather extensive discussion of the nature of invisible hand explanation. She seems to restrict the scope of invisible hand explanations to the explanation of social patterns and institutions. I shall below, on the contrary, mostly be concerned with singular action-explanations (but see Chapter 14). The difference here is, roughly, that when explaining social patterns and institutions we are explaining social laws and regularities by means of an "invisible-hand theory" but that when explaining singular social actions we do it, in part, by relying on the social laws and regularities - the explananda - of the first case.

Although I cannot completely accept Ullmann-Margalit's view of invisible hand explanations I fully agree with her on the general features such explanations - be they explanations of social institutions, social action regularities, etc., or singular social actions. What an invisible hand explanation typically does is the following. It replaces an easily forthcoming and initially plausible explanation according to which the explanandum is the product of **intentional design** with a rival account according to which it is brought about via a process involving the separate actions of many individuals who are supposed to be minding (only) their own business unaware of and hence not intending to bring about the ultimate overall outcome (cf. Ullmann-Margalit (1978), p. 267).

Real life examples of invisible hand explanations are rather complex to spell out in a few sentences. Let us therefore continue with our earlier imagined case of the military unit S overtaking a certain enemy post (i.e., doing X). This example can be used to make the points I want to by changing it a little. We assume that A_1 simply commands S to do X without having the intention that S do Y. Next we suppose that S did X and that that generated its doing Y. Suppose further that, to make the example more dramatic, that S's doing Y generated, through some complex process, the defeat of the enemy. Let us call S's bringing about the enemy's defeat Z. Then, instead of having a partly intentional (and partly invisible hand) explanation of the unit's deceiving the enemy (S's doing Y) we get a fully non-intentional (and a fully invisible hand) explanation of a token z of type Z.

Our invisible hand explanation now takes as its explanandum-content the token z of type Z. The result event r_z of z is or represents the collapse of the enemy. The invisible hand explanans now is taken to comprise a statement to the effect that u (of the type X) non-purposively generated z, or if you like, that the u_is, i=1,...,m, non-purposively generated z. Our explanans must also state that z was not purposively generated by S even if initially that might have looked plausible. (Let us, furthermore, assume that when we say that S brought about z then S's doing something or other was necessary for the occurrence of the enemy's defeat.)

Let me thus propose an explication for invisible hand explanations of social actions. We may assume in our example that q = Why was the enemy defeated (r_z)? and more generally that q = Why was r_z produced? We then get (cf. our (**ITE**), (**PCE**), and (**RE**) of Chapter 11):

(IHE) v_{ih} is a scientific explanatory answer to q in the sense of **invisible hand explanation** if and only if
(1) v_{ih} is a scientific explanatory answer to q;
(2) the complete scientific explanatory answer c_i corresponding to v_{ih} contains (or all such complete scientific explanatory answers, if there are several, contain) statements to the effect that for some action tokens u_i (i=1,...,m), z, and social action types X_i, X, and Z by some agents $A_1,...,A_m$:
(a) $IG(u_1,...,u_m,z)$, where u_i tokens X_i (with X = X_1&...&X_m) and z tokens Z and r_z is the result event of z;
(b) not $IG*(u_1,...,u_m,z)$, regardless of how $u_1,......,u_m$, and z are conceptualized; although
(c) it is initially plausible that, for some social action token y (by some agents $A_1,...,A_k$) with the subtokens $y_1,...,y_k$ and for some social action type Y such that y tokens Y: $IG*(y_1,...,y_k,z)$.

The real hidden hand explanation of r_z by $u_1,...,u_m$, which (**IHE**) deals with, is basically given by (2)(a), of course. (2)(c) compares it with an explanation in terms of some intentional design, which looks "initially plausible" but ultimately fails to be and look so. The explication of the notion of initial plausibility is bound to be a complicated affair, hanging on various culture laden background assumption. I will not here attempt to give such an explication. In (2)(b) of (**IHE**) the notion of conceptualization of an action token entails that it is meaningful to speak of different conceptualizations of a token. If that conclusion is not granted a suitable different phrasing should be used. Let me say here that often (or sometimes) the putative initial explanation in terms of intentional design (viz. IG*) precedes and guides the search for an invisible hand explanation in terms of IG in the sense that the (generational) structure of the latter is the same as that of the former and obtained, as it were, by redescription from it, and thus Y=X and perhaps even the agents in clauses (a) and (c) are the same.

As earlier in this chapter, instead of IG (and IG*) we may want to use the corresponding probabilistic notions in some cases. That should certainly be allowed, although I will not here go into the details of such "probabilification" (but see Chapter 6).

We may now say on rather obvious grounds that an invisible

hand explanans is the better (a) the more **complex** the type Z as compared with the (component) types X_i, (b) the more different Z is in **kind** as compared with the X_is, (c) the more **complicated** the generational process represented by $IG(u_1,...,u_m,z)$ is, and (d) the more unexpected relative to its intentional rivals the given invisible hand explanation is. As to (a) and (c), which are interrelated I refer to the discussion of the structure of social actions in Chapter 5. As to (b) and (d) I will not here try to explicate them except for one remark on (d). Even if the invisible hand process may be unexpected, it must be emphasized that, as I have explicated IG in Chapter 6, it must yet be a **nomic** (and non-accidental) one.

In some cases we can give a social action token u both an invisible hand explanation (satisfying (**IHE**)) and a functional explanation (satisfying (**FE**)). This may happen when u (tokening X) is generated from some tokens of some action types generating X according to (**IHE**) (so that they correspond to the X_is and X to the Z of (**IHE**)) and when at the same time u is said to be due to the agents $A_1,...,A_m$ producing u because it is their function to do X with respect to the goal action (or end) Y. In this case we may say that the invisible hand explanation explains the **origin** (coming about) of u while the functional explanation gives the **raison d'etre** of this social action token. (But note that we may obviously have invisible hand explanation also in the case of actions which are not functional in our technical sense.) Of course, sometimes also the global action (or end) Y of ($\mathbf{F_S^*}$) might perhaps be given an invisible hand explanation in terms of the X_is, components of X, in ($\mathbf{F_S^*}$).

In the case of the explanation of non-intentional action it is sometimes, such as in the context of invisible hand explanations, pertinent to ask whether the action token z to be explained by reference to IG really **can** be a social action token. For, as defined by (5.5), a social action token must involve a **social** propositional attitude. It would seem that often in the case of invisible hand explanations it cannot at least be derived from a we-attitude in the sense of Chapter 5. I now suggest that a weaker notion of a social attitude may be employed here. Specifically, I suggest that the notions of an action **making reference to an agent,** defined by (9.2) could be employed here. We may say quite generally that invisible hand situations are epistemically "poor", as clause (b) of (**IHE**) indicates. Thus it is not surprising if they fail to satisfy strict criteria, at least epistemic ones, for social action. It also follows that a standard game-theoretic perspective does not quite well fit them. Let me comment briefly on that.

Elster (1978), p. 108, claims that we may characterize

invisible hand situations by saying that in them (1) each actor has a dominant strategy (in the standard game-theoretic sense) and (2) the outcome that results when all actors use their dominant strategies dominates all the other outcomes. Now I think it is an advantage rather than a drawback that our (**IHE**) does not presuppose the applicability of the game-theoretic framework. Thus (**IHE**) does not require (1) and (2) nor even their common sense analogues to hold. But I do not want to deny that Elster may have a good point to make here that many invisible hand situations perhaps satisfy his (1) and (2). In fact I am quite willing to think that our earlier examples satisfy at least (1) and maybe (2) as well.

But yet I would like to emphasize that (**IHE**) clearly allows for cases where nothing like (2) holds. Indeed, (**IHE**) is meant to allow cases where dominated and suboptimal outcomes become created. Thus I allow that the invisible hand situation may operate benevolently as well as malevolently. For instance, a prisoner's dilemma situation where the actors use their dominant strategies (actions) and where a suboptimal (Pareto-inferior) social action (outcome) is created count as an invisible hand situation in the sense of (**IHE**). It may here be emphasized, too, that we may consider Elster's (1) and (2) in the case of epistemically more perfect cases (e.g., in the standard game-theoretic cases) and make completely analogous comments. It is only that then we speak of intended (normally) and anticipated outcomes (social actions) rather than of unintended and unanticipated ones in the case of invisible hand situations.

CHAPTER 14

EXPLANATORY INDIVIDUALISM AND EXPLANATION OF SOCIAL LAWS

I. EXPLANATORY INDIVIDUALISM

1.   Earlier in this book we have mentioned in passing that there are several types of individualism in the context of the philosophy of the social sciences. The following three are the most central: (1) conceptual individualism, (2) ontological individualism, and (3) explanatory individualism. In Chapter 2 we discussed conceptual individualism at some length. Ontological individualism is not really discussed in this book, except for some remarks, mainly because we take questions of ontology to be settled not a priori but a posteriori by the best explanatory scientific theories in the spirit of scientific realism.

Below we shall discuss some aspects of explanatory individualism. Explanatory individualism can tentatively be taken to be the doctrine that it is conceptually and epistemically possible that all social phenomena and patterns be explained by individualistic explanantia. To state this more precisely, we shall employ our developments and terminology in Chapters 2 and 10. Let λ_i be the set of all (primitive) individualistic predicates and η_s the set of all (primitive) social predicates in the sense defined in Chapter 2 (and with an explicit individualistic definition of we-attitudes). Then recall from our relevant definitions and characterizations in Chapter 10 that an explanandum is a (suitable) question statement and that an explanans is a scientific explanatory answer. Then we can reformulate explanatory individualism as follows, taking an adequate question to mean a question with a true presupposition:

(EI) For every social phenomenon or pattern which is the object of a scientific query there is an adequate (complete) explanatory question statement about that social phenomenon (or pattern) such that this question statement can in principle (viz. as far as conceptual and epistemic constraints are concerned) be answered by a correct scientific explanatory answer containing only λ_i-predicates or, more generally, individualistically acceptable predicates as its extralogical predicates.

(**EI**) claims essentially that all singular social phenomena (events, facts, etc.) and all social patterns (regularities, invariances, etc.) that are scientifically studied can be objects of explanation-seeking questions such that those questions have individualistic explanatory answers. We are assuming in (**EI**) that all social phenomena and patterns studied can be linguistically described. What makes a phenomenon or pattern social is a problematic issue, it should be noted. Let us say that the social realm (phenomena, patterns, etc.) is characterized by the applicability of **social predicates** to its elements and features. In other words, a social phenomenon (pattern) is something conceptualizable in terms of social predicates. While this characterization is not perhaps too helpful for the purposes of ontology it seems to suffice for our present purposes.

The main reason for adopting an individualistic doctrine such as (**EI**) is due to the following intuition. If a holistic social entity such as an institution, organization or a group is to have causal impact on the world, so to speak, surely that impact must be exerted and come about due to some concrete individual persons (and their actions). (**EI**) sharpens this intuition and in effect implicitly claims, among other things, that all actions by social collectives are in some way generated and explained by some relevant participating individuals' actions (recall (**CON***) of Chapter 6).

Our emphasis below will be on the explanation of social laws (social patterns) rather than on singular social statements (social phenomena). Recall, however, that in our view every singular explanation is at least implicitly nomological as every complete scientific explanatory answer is nomological. Therefore our discussion below also touches the topic of singular explanation since if the law backing the explanation of a singular explanandum is individualistically explainable then surely we must at least be close to having an individualistic explanation of the singular social explanandum content subsumable under that backing law.

Before going to discuss the explanation of laws a problem connected with (**EI**) should be considered. They can at best be commented by reference to singular explanations. Let us consider a singular explanation of a social event e given in terms of a scientific explanatory answer (cf. (**10.9**)). Such an answer is an answer to a certain question, say q, and that question normally conceptualizes the event e in a certain propositional way. Thus we may assume that e consists of an object a's F-ing, say. Then we are dealing with the explanandum content 'a F's' (or 'a is F'), where F is a social predicate. Now a case may be made for the claim that that explanandum content can properly be explained only in terms of a law having the predicate F, or at least a synonym of F or some other closely related predicate, in its consequent. Or, we may also argue that if F is a nomic predicate then 'a is F' requires F to occur in the explanans law. Requirements of this kind rely on the idea that we cannot explain a singular event of a certain type F unless we nomically guarantee the occurrence of an event of type F. If we only give an explanation of e as a G-event, say, and state that, as a matter of fact, e also is an F-event we do not get an explanation of e as an F-event.

The above idea of singular explanation is not as such (quite) entailed by our pragmatic theory of explanation of Chapter 10. However, at least if we concentrate on deductive explanation and explicate it in terms of ε-arguments (and hence "minimal" deductive explanation) in the sense of the Appendix of Chapter 10 we do have that as a consequence, given the availability of laws with the required event types in their consequents. (What holds for inductive ρ-arguments depends on the specific properties of the inducibility relation I.) Given this, it can be understood why our (**EI**) has been formulated in terms of the explanation of social phenomena and patterns for which there exist question statements "about" these social phenomena and patterns (rather than by speaking of explananda described by means of social predicates). The idea here is of course that the question statements can be taken to be in a relevant sense "about" social phenomena without themselves containing social predicates. In other words, we allow that the question statement in (**EI**) about such social phenomena need not necessarily concern social phenomena and patterns as social (viz. in terms of social predicates), and we allow, in (**EI**), for a **reinterpretation** of the phenomena (and patterns) in question.

This hangs together with our scientific realism and our associated rejection of the myth of the given, briefly discussed in Chapter 1. Applied to this situation, our scientific realism entails that there are no "given" social (and holistic) phenomena which cannot in principle be reconceptualized in terms of another conceptual framework, such as our individualistic framework employing λ_i-predicates. This does not yet mean the reducibility of social phenomena but only reinterpretation. Such reinterpretation may be taken to underlie and give reasons for attempts to eliminate social phenomena, which we shall comment on below. Thus, allowing for such reinterpretation to be reflected in the interests of inquiry and specifically in the formulation of the question statement q, we need not regard (**EI**) as unacceptable.

As to the individualistic (and reductive) explanation of

social laws the basic issue has often been claimed to be the problem about the existence of correspondence or bridge laws connecting social predicates with individualistic predicates. If the social domain is nomically closed there cannot be such correspondence rules, we may claim. This claim can be regarded as true by virtue of the very concept of nomic closure, which may be taken to exclude the possibility of either any correspondence laws or at least of correspondence laws needed for reduction (viz., roughly, correspondence laws with social predicates in the consequents).

Can there be, and are there, such correspondence rules or laws claimed to be needed for reduction? I am inclined to argue that this matter cannot, fully at least, be settled a priori but that science will ultimately tell us whether there are such laws. The only a priori argument against the possibility of correspondence laws and reduction I consider to have any force is the following. The complete reduction of a social theory to a social psychological theory requires that the correspondence rules in question be general **identity** statements. But at least not all social predicates are strictly identical with definientia containing only λ_i-predicates (or individualistic predicates). Thus, the argument concludes, we cannot have required correspondence rules nor, consequently, reduction (cf. Nickles (1976)).

I am indeed inclined to accept that social predicates need not have individualistic **synonyms**. The meanings of social predicates are determined by means of their roles in social theories (and other social discourse) and those roles need not be identical with the roles of any conglomerations of individualistic predicates. I shall not argue for this here as my basic point against the above argument is not this but simply that we do not need full identities for reduction. What we need is **at most** extensional identities, viz. social predicates should have suitable extensionally identical individualistic counterparts, and I don't know of any forceful a priori argument against this. In fact, I am not even inclined to accept that extensional identities are necessary for reduction. For reduction extensionally **replaces** one nomological network (theory or framework) by another and this does not require correspondence rules of the form of identities (cf. Tuomela (1973)). Furthermore, given such reduction in terms of correspondence rules weaker than identity statements, there are often good **grounds for eliminating** the reduced framework or theory. What I am claiming here is that science may and will come to give us the best reasons we can possible have for making ontological claims about the world such as the following: The reduced framework or theory only speaks about appearances, so let us eliminate it in favor of the reducing theory or framework which putatively correctly says what there is and isn't.

What is more, we shall claim below that there is another route to elimination as well. As in the case of singular statements, that route goes via reinterpretation and does not have to assume any correspondence rules at all. Before going to that let me summarize part of the above discussion by saying that we have not so far found any strong a priori obstacles for the acceptability of our thesis (**EI**).

2. Let us note that by 'social predicate' two things can be meant. Under the stronger interpretation a social predicate is a presystematic or "original" holistic and/or explanatory social predicate in the sense discussed in Chapter 2. These original social predicates, whose set may be called n_s^o, have as their **counterparts** the n_s-predicates of $L(\lambda_i \cup n_s)$. The latter predicates are individualistically constructed, according to (**CI**), from the λ_i-predicates as explicated in Chapter 2. Accordingly, the weaker interpretation of the phrase 'social predicate' is just 'n_s-predicate'. This issue will turn out to have significance.

We will now proceed to a more detailed discussion of the explanation of social laws and theories by means of individualistic theories, viz. (actual or possible) theories of social psychology (or psychology). (**EI**) involves that for every explanatory social theory S employing social predicates there is a true (or truthlike) individualistic theory, say T, employing λ_i-predicates and, possibly, μ_p-predicates (viz. theoretical psychological predicates) plus perhaps some other relevant non-social predicates such that T explains S. According to the above weak and strong interpretations of 'social predicate' we may distinguish between two different senses of explanation. We shall call them the (mere) **correspondence rule** and the **reinterpretation** account. Let us see what is involved herein.

It has been pointed out and emphasized by several authors that in the context of the growth of science successor theories should somehow improve on their predecessor theories. More precisely, a successor theory should (1) account for the success of its predecessor theory and it should, in addition, (2) account for at least some of the anomalies facing the predecessor theory (cf. Popper (1963), Sellars (1963)). An explanatory individualist may now plausibly consider a social theory, S, as a predecessor theory and look for an individualistic successor theory, T, to explain it and, perhaps, to replace it. Indeed this will be our starting point. We assume that any talk about a successor's giving an account of a predecessor means giving an **explanatory** account (see Tuomela (1973), (1979) on this). We shall then say that what a successor does is that it in a sense **correctively explains** the predecessor theory, viz. it gives an explanatory account of both what is right about the predecessor and what is wrong about it (cf. Sellars (1963), Tuomela (1979), (1984), Rosenberg (1980b)). In other words, the successor theory accounts for the predecessor theory's anomalies and it also accounts for its successes.

We may make a rough distinction between revolutionary and non-revolutionary theory-succession. The first type corresponds to our reinterpretation approach and the latter to our mere correspondence rule approach. Roughly speaking, the (mere) correspondence rule approach assumes that there are correspondence rules (indeed laws) connecting social predicates with individualistic ones. The reducing (complete) individualistic theory, say T, (directly) explains not quite the (complete) social theory, say S, but a related theory, say S*, containing what is true in S.

I am here idealizingly speaking about complete theories in the hypothetical sense that we could at any particular time think of formulating such theories covering, respectively, the whole social realm and the whole individualistic social psychology and psychology. Let me here emphasize that I am not advocating the reduction of current social science to psychology. Even if I accept ultimate reduction in the sense of (**EI**) I am quite willing to encourage the formulation of holistic social theories. Indeed, there are many methodological reasons for employing holistic social predicates (e.g., most arguments for the methodological desirability of theoretical concepts of Tuomela (1973) seem applicable here).

Our correspondence rule approach clearly goes well together with evolutionary cases of theory change just because of the assumption of the existence of correspondence rules. How about the more revolutionary kind of cases of theory change? If we think that no correspondence rules between social predicates and individualistic predicates can exist we are likely to speak about the semantic incommensurability (even if not incomparability) of these predicates. Then the set-up plausibly also becomes one of **reinterpretation** of the predecessor in terms of the successor framework as well as the **replacement** and elimination of the predecessor theory by the successor theory. More specifically, the predecessor theory S is assumed to be reinterpretable by means of counterpart concepts and general statements in the framework of T in such a way that the counterpart images of the assumptions of S within the framework of T are correctively explained by T or at least by T together with suitable auxiliary hypotheses. (Corrective explanation means, roughly, the explanation of a suitable approximation of the image of S.)

But also within the correspondence rule approach we may, and often will, have good reason for eliminating the reduced theory (or framework). For we may be able to say that the reduced framework only speaks of appearances. So why not eliminate it in favor of the reducing theory which putatively correctly says what there is and isn't.

While theory change and corrective explanation can be discussed without making specific ontological commitments, at bottom we, accordingly, have here an ontological doctrine as well. What is at stake then is a "seeming-being" dialectic in the sense of scientific realism (cf. Rosenberg (1980)). The successor theory T is then assumed to be at least approximately correct and thus to at least putatively and approximately say what there is. In replacing S it shows that S applies to nothing - it is only about appearances, viz. what there **seems** to be. In our present case it is indeed not necessary to enter deeper this seeming-being dialectic. Yet we can say about it that the successor theory T is taken to be closer to the truth than S. But it is so only relative to the manifest image. What there really is and what there is not in the world is to be determined by the best-explaining scientific theory (in the scientific image), and our T is not such a theory. We shall not here explicate nor defend this realist view, which we adopt (but see, e.g., Sellars (1963), (1968), Tuomela (1984) for such a defense).

II. EXPLANATION OF SOCIAL LAWS

1. After the above general motivating discussion we can go into the details. Our proposals for corrective explanation (explanation in the sense of an E-argument; cf. (**10.8**) and thus, in part, for the successor relation, in the case of the correspondence rule view (I) and the reinterpretation view (II) are the following (cf. Tuomela (1979) for a previous formulation of the idea underlying (I)):

(I) T **correctively explains**$_1$ S if and only if
   (a) there exist a correspondence rule C and a theory S* such that
      (i) T&C adequately explains S*, and
      (ii) S is an approximation of S*;
   (b) T has greater explanatory power than S has.

(II) T **correctively explains$_2$** S if and only if
   (a) there exist a translation τ of the conceptual system of S, CS_S, into CS_T, the conceptual system of T, an auxiliary assumption C and a theory S* in CS_T such that
      (i) T&C adequately explains S*, and
      (ii) $\tau(S)$ is an approximation of S*, where $\tau(S)$ is the translation, under τ, of S into CS_T;
   (b) T has greater explanatory power than S has.

Our (I) and (II) require several explicatory comments. Let us start with the more specific account (I) which explicates the traditional (mere) correspondence rule approach. In (I) there is no need for our present purposes to distinguish between "original" and "reconstructed" social predicates, for the non-revolutionary view under discussion assumes the existence of correspondence rules no matter how the social predicates are interpreted. Accordingly, we may here call the set of social predicates η_s. We note that if the conceptual system or language of S has η_s as its vocabulary and T, correspondingly, $\lambda_i \cup \mu_p$, then C must be stated in the vocabulary $\lambda_i \cup \mu_p \cup \eta_s$. This follows from clause (a) where we simplifying mean by explanation **deductive** explanation. (If indeterminism were true for the social realm, then we might have to speak of indeterministic, e.g., probabilistic, explanation instead; cf. Tuomela (1981) on that.) The theory S* can be taken to have η_s (viz. S's vocabulary) as its extralogical vocabulary. We are assuming, for simplicity, in (I) that S, S*, T, and C are finitely axiomatizable so that we can regard them as complex axiom-conjunctions, as is usual; but nothing central hangs on this simplifying assumption.

The correspondence rule C can be either a bridge law or a definition (or an analytic statement); cf. our (**CI**) and discussion in Chapter 2. At least in some evolutionary cases of theory change we may take C to be an identity statement effecting a redescription of a holistic predicate in individualistic terms (cf. Causey (1977) for a discussion of such a view). We shall not here discuss when C should be given the status of a law and when the status of a definition or an identity. The basic idea of (I) is, in any case, quite simple. T, when taken in conjunction with C, corrects S by giving an adequate explanation of a theory S* which S approximates. (For some purposes we might complicate (I) by requiring that it is not T but an approximation, say T', of T that explains S*.)

There are three main notions in (I) which are in need of explication, namely adequate explanation, explanatory power, and approximation. As to approximation, I will not say much about it here. Suppose that we are able to measure the conceptual distance (d) between two theories, S and S*, in the same language. Then we may say that S is an approximation of S* just in case $d(S,S^*) < \delta$ (δ is a small number $<<1$). Here d can be taken to be the measure of distance defined in Tuomela (1978) for theories formalizable within first-order predicate logic; see Chapter 8. (The above definition of approximation has been discussed from a methodological point of view in Tuomela (1979) to which work the reader is referred.)

As to adequate explanation, I will require, following the account of Chapter 10, roughly this. It is assumed that to any explanatory question 'Why S*?' a correct scientific explanatory answer is obtainable such that in the complete explanatory answer corresponding to it, T&C (or, sometimes, some suitable equivalent statement) constitutes the premise of the required nomological E-argument (cf. (8) and (9) of Chapter 10). An adequate E-argument will have to satisfy complicated formal requirements in order to become a ε-argument, we recall. I shall not here further discuss these requirements except for the remarks below in connection with the notion of explanatory power.

Note, next, that if T gives an adequate deductive explanation of S* then, in a sense, T accounts for the success of S, given that S is "close to" S*. In other words, adequate deductive explanation of what is correct in S accounts for the success of S, and we now assume that the approximation between S and S* is of the right sort to guarantee this. For instance, the famous "correspondence principle", discussed by, e.g., Krajewski (1977), seems to state the intended kind of approximate relationship, suitable at least for some physical sciences. For it requires, roughly, the successor theory to imply, given some counterfactual limiting conditions, that the predecessor theory accords with the facts.

Requirement (b) of (I) is meant to involve that T has broader explanatory scope than S in a stronger sense than merely that T entails S* but S* doesn't entail T. Thus, T should give an explanatory account of at least some facts anomalous for S. It should do this, in part, by entailing new lawful statements about these anomalous phenomena and do it in a non-ad hoc way. Therefore, conditions (6) and (7) of the Appendix of Chapter 10 should be imposed on this connection to give a partial explication of the concept of greater explanatory power. Another requirement that we may also take to be entailed by clause (b) of (I) is that the verisimilitude of T be greater than that of S, assuming such comparability of verisimilitude. (See Tuomela (1978), (1979), (1984) on verisimilitude and on this requirement; the verisimilitude of a theory within a conceptual system can roughly be defined as the closeness of that theory to "the truth" in that system - given by a singled-out constituent in the sense of the theory of distributive normal forms; cf. Chapter 8.) In a sense, we can say that were T not more true than S there would not be much point in the reductive explanation of S by T, for greater verisimilitude must also be taken to entail greater "correctness" of ontology (viz. the theory's account of what there is and isn't), even if we are in the social case explicitly concerned with the manifest image only.

Let us now go to the reinterpretative view (II). Corrective explanation in this sense of reinterpretation is much trickier than in the previous "classical" sense. This is because it involves the difficult notion of translation, which is just the technical explicate of reinterpretation. Why do we then have to involve such a difficult notion of translation or reinterpretation? This follows from the set-up used here. For to bring out all the philosophically central aspects of the situation we must now deal with social predicates under the strong interpretation (viz. in their presystematic senses). Each such holistic or explanatory predicate in η_s^o occurs in some social theory (or other similar relevant piece of discourse) and it gets its meaning or sense in part from that context, we assume here. When we create the social predicates in η_s on the basis of our individualistic principle (**CI**) what we get is only explicatory **counterparts** of the original presystematic social predicates. The meanings of these counterpart predicates (η_s-predicates) are determined by their constitutive theory in the sense of (**CI**), we assume. Thus the original social predicates and their counterpart predicates have (or may have) different meanings (or senses). In this sense we have "incommensurability" and "meaning-variance" here. We may also say that, in addition, the perceptual or observational epistemic roles of the original social predicates and their η_s-counterparts are likely to be different.

On the other hand, the original social predicates (members of η_s^o) might perhaps be taken to have the same (putative) references as their counterparts in η_s. But even that is very problematic. For if something like the ontological principle (**R**) of Chapter 2 is true, then the original social predicates simply lack references while the η_s-predicates do have references. The latter references are individualistic, though; and what the (ultimate) correct description of them is, need not, and probably will not, be statable in terms of the $\lambda_i \cup \mu_p$-predicates nor any "manifest" predicates at all (but that is a different story; cf. Chapter 1). It follows that we cannot even have translation principles stating the coreference of any original social predicate and its η_s-counterpart, if the present view is accepted in its strictest sense. (Our technical treatment of Subsection 2 below can be ontically interpreted to comply with this.)

The best and perhaps only way out may now seem to be the reinterpretation or translation (τ) of the original social discourse (CS_S) into the η_s-discourse or, more broadly, into the conceptual framework CS_T.

Let us say in a preliminary way that, technically speaking, τ is a translation function mapping the language L_S of the social theory S into the language L_T of the individualistic theory T; and from hereon we shall speak of languages rather than conceptual systems in order to be precise. We assume that the extralogical vocabulary of S (and L_S) is η_s^o. The extralogical vocabulary of T may be taken to be either λ_i or $\lambda_i \cup \eta_s$ or $\lambda_i \cup \mu_p \cup \eta_s$, as the case may be. Here the set η_s of social predicates is assumed to be construed individualistically on the basis of (**CI**) and the set μ_p of theoretical (social) psychological predicates on the basis of (**CF**) - (recall the discussion in Chapter 2). The extralogical vocabulary of L_T will be $\lambda_i \cup \mu_p \cup \eta_s$.

Why it is possible to be so liberal as to the extralogical vocabulary of T is due to the auxiliary assumption C of (II). The extralogical vocabulary of C is $\lambda_i \cup \mu_p \cup \eta_s$. Now the idea of (II) is that T conjoined with C correctively explains S* and indirectly the translation or image, $\tau(S)$, of S. It may be asked why the assumption C is needed here. Why can't we, at least technically, require the individualistic theory to be comprehensive enough to alone correctively explain (S)? From a purely technical point of view we could indeed do that, for such a comprehensive theory in the vocabulary $\lambda_i \cup \mu_p \cup \eta_s$ would surely satisfy our individualistic vocabulary restrictions. The general point here is, however, that in cases such as the attempted reduction of macrophysics to microphysics, chemistry to physics, psychology to physiology, and sociology to psychology there is an ontic and conceptual macro-micro-relation between the science to be reduced and the reducing science, and it cannot be a priori assumed that the reducing micro-science contains among its basic axioms all the relevant **organizational** principles needed to construe the behavior of the macrothings out of the microthings, so to speak. Thus if neurophysiology is going to reduce in the reinterpretative fashion (some central parts of) psychology it is to be expected that some new assumptions must be introduced over and above the basic principles of neurophysiology to account for the new organizational features of psychological phenomena (viewed neurophysiologically).

Or consider a case from social science - Marx's explanation of economic phenomena. In his theory of capitalism Marx discusses how, under certain conditions, human production can lead to the institution of exchange, and how such exchange then leads to a new form of production, production of commodities. He discusses how production of commodities for exchange can lead to production of commodities for profit, to wage labor and capital. Now the relevant organizational product here is (something like) people being able to modify appropriately both the forces of production and the relations of production to guarantee the satisfaction of basic human needs in changing macrocircumstances. There is no guarantee that the basic axioms of even complete psychology and social psychology alone can account for such organizational macrofacts which are strongly dependent on cultural, historical, political, etc. factors. Thus, it seems that auxiliary assumptions will be needed here.

The above reasons should suffice to account for employment of individualistically acceptable extra assumptions or correspondence principles (in a broader sense than in (I)) over and above T. Let us now go on to discuss the crucial and difficult problem of how to define or characterize the translation function τ, for this amounts to at least partially solving the problem of how to compare two incommensurable conceptual frameworks.

Obviously τ should at least correlate the original social predicates (members of η_S^o) and the η_S-predicates and find a translation of S. The simplest situation would be that where η_S^o and η_S contain homonymically corresponding predicates, and this may be a realistic case, too. Thus, e.g., for 'state' $\in \eta_S^o$ we might have, correspondingly, 'state' $\in \eta_S$, and so on, such that, typically, whenever a predicate of η_S^o is applicable to a singular situation, then its counterpart in η_S is also applicable, and conversely. If in this tentative homonymic translation indeed the counterpart predicates would play an **approximately similar role** (involving, e.g., similarity in singular applications in the above sense) in the respective languages L_S and L_T, we would have an acceptable translation in the case of predicates. The (general) statements of L_S, such as just S, can then be mapped into those of L_T (see the discussion preceding and leading to formula (11) of Chapter 8 for an exact account). Thus we have for the present case found a function τ translating both the predicates and the statements of L_S into L_T, and clause (a) of (II) becomes meaningful.

Note that the present situation parallels that within the physical sciences as exemplified by the "identification" of temperature with mean kinetic energy. In this example 'temperature' in its original sense belongs to the phenomenological theory. When reducing this theory to the kinetic theory of gases we redefine temperature as mean kinetic energy within the reducing theory. So we are dealing both with temperature in a presystematic sense and with its counterpart as constructed within the kinetic theory.

It may, however, be that often it is not that easy to find a translation function τ even when η_S^o and η_S are equipotent sets. If, furthermore, η_S enriches and refines η_S^o and thus is a bigger set, the task becomes still more difficult. Earlier in Section II of Chapter 8, when discussing problems of similarity, we technically defined a counterpart relation and, on its basis, a concept of analogy-linkage. That machinery applies to translation also in those cases where η_S^o and η_S are not equipotent. (But we have to reverse the direction of the translation defined there.) Thus in principle we have available one possible technical solution also for the general first-order case.

We recall, however, that the general method sketched in Chapter 8 has the (potential) drawback that it makes translation independent of the excess content of the richer theory, say T, over and above its reduct r(T). In the general case such a restriction must be removed.

2. I shall now go on to discuss a very general, yet powerful, solution to the problem of translation which seems applicable to our cases of interest, even if it will not exhaust the content of our (II) due to a couple of restrictive assumptions. This solution comes from the modern branch of logic called **general** or **abstract** logic. I will make use of a result by Feferman (1974) for languages which satisfy an algebraic, generalized version of Craig's well known interpolation theorem. Before going into technicalities let me point out in a preliminary way what the outcome will be. Given that the two languages L_S and L_T, differing in their purported ontology, to be compared can be model-theoretically connected in terms of a suitable, so-called projectively definable relation, L_S becomes translatable into L_T in a certain well defined sense (not far from our earlier expressed intuitive idea of translation). Furthermore, given such translation, the (approximate) reductive explanation of S by means of T can be rather directly explicated.

My exposition of general logic and Feferman's result will be very brief and it may not be sufficiently self-contained for most readers. Yet, as good expositions exist elsewhere, I will not do more here than sketch the barest skeleton (see, e.g., Feferman (1974) and Pearce (1979) and (1981) for more details).

A general logic, say L, can be regarded as a quadruple L = $<Typ_L, Sent_L, Str_L, \vDash_L>$. Here Typ_L is a class of similarity types for L. Roughly speaking, a similarity type, s, consists of a set of symbols standing for or representing "sorts" (kinds of domains), relations, operations, and individual constants. (L is typically a many-sorted logic.) Sent_L and Str_L are operations on Typ_L such that $\text{Sent}_L(s)$ and $\text{Str}_L(s)$ stand for the classes of sentences and structures (possible models, say M, of type $s \in \text{Typ}_L$), respectively, of L. (Notice that we may conceptually **start** with a class of structures and then associate a logic with it: the structures that we are dealing with might be merely conceptual, lacking ontic import, as is the case when they deal with holistic social entities.) Finally, $\models_L$ is an operation on Typ_L such that $\models_L(s)$ stands for the satisfaction relation of L related to s. (We will omit s and write $M \models_L$ for $<M,\phi> \in \models_L(s)$.) We shall not discuss L in more detail here except for requiring that it be regular in the sense of Feferman (1974) and pointing out that ordinary first-order logic and its usual extensions are included among such general logics.

Let us now consider our case of reducing the social theory S into the individualistic social psychological theory T. We assume that CS_S and CS_T can be discussed from the point of view of a general logic L which admits both models of S and of T as its structures and which, of course, admits S and T as its sentences. If CS_S and CS_T are technically explicated to be the languages (sets of statements) associated with S and T then L may here be regarded as a logic which has among its class of sentences both L_S (explicating CS_S) and L_T (explicating CS_T). We may indeed make $L_S = \text{Sent}_L(s)$ and $L_T = \text{Sent}_L(t)$, with the similarity types s, representing the social domain, and t, representing the individualistic domain. Now we let M_t be a model of L_T, with t as its similarity type. Correspondingly, we let M_s be a structure of L_S, with the similarity type s. In general M_t and M_s may be completely different. Thus, for example, if we take them to be single-sorted, the domain of M_t could consist of elements representing people while the domain of M_s could consist of elements purportedly representing groups (or other organized collectivities), and the relations and functions in M_t and M_s would accordingly be quite different.

Let us now assume that L_S and L_T are comparable not only in the weak sense of being based on the same general logic but that they are extensionally comparable also in the following sense. The models of L_S and L_T can be correlated by a relation, say R, such that the domain of R belongs to the models of L_T while its range is the class of models of L_S. Thus every model M_S of L_S is assumed to have a counterpart model M_t of L_T. Technically, we let $R \subseteq \text{Str}_L(t) \times \text{Str}_L(s)$, and let $\text{Str}_L(t)$ be just the class of individualistic possible models and $\text{Str}_L(s)$ to be the class of possible social models. Intuitively, the counterpart relation R will in our application correlate with each social structure an individualistic structure, but there is no requirement, so far, to the effect that anything general be (linguistically) said or sayable of the social realm versus the individual realm, so to speak. The following definition of translation connects the counterpart relation **R** with a language and with claims relating the social and the individual realm. We propose:

(**TR**) Let L be a general logic and let $s, t \in Typ_L$ and $L_S = Sent_L(s)$, $L_T = Sent_L(t)$, $R \subseteq Str_L(t) \times Str_L(s)$ such that R is defined onto $Str_L(s)$. Then L effects a **translation** of L_S into L_T relative to R if and only if for all $\phi \in L_S$ there is a $\psi \in L_T$ such that for all **M**, **N** $R(M,N) \Rightarrow [M \models_L \psi \Leftrightarrow N \models_L \phi]$.

The notion of translation defined by (**TR**) is a weak one. First, it deals only with the preservation of truth but it says nothing about meanings. Secondly, it does not in any way define the primitive concepts of L_S in terms of those of L_T nor does it require each atomic formula of L_S to have an **R**-correlate in L_T. Strengthening (**TR**) is somewhat complicated since if ψ is to be a formula translating ϕ we need to guarantee either that ψ and ϕ have the same free variables or, which is the more realistic case, that some means is available for transforming the free variables over which formulas of type s range into free variables over which formulas of type t range. We cannot go into those problems here (cf. Pearce (1979) for a discussion).

Our present (**TR**) gives a general solution to the translation problem for statements sharing an underlying general logic, for it claims that for each general sentence ϕ (e.g., the whole theory S) there exists an **R**-counterpart ψ (e.g., T) and it puts no conditions on the vocabularies in question (any more than **R** does). This means that, if (**TR**) is satisfied, we can translate each sentence (e.g., theory) of L_S into L_T, and we may then go ahead and compare theories stated in L_T as to their mutual distances, for instance. When L is a first-order logic the measures of Tuomela (1978) become applicable.

Note that whenever S and T are both assumed "given" prior to, and independently of, the translation, our (**TR**) need not translate (or reduce, we may even say) S into T even if it does translate L_S into L_T. This is because **R** has been defined only generally for models of L_S and L_T, and it need not correlate each model of S with a model of T in cases when T is not a translation of S by definition. If that is regarded as a problem the remedy is obvious: require that **R** always correlates models of S with models of T only (such that **R** is a relation onto the class of models of S). I shall not explicitly spell this out here, but this modification in the definition of **R** is important to keep in mind (cf. our (II) above). However, we shall here retain (**TR**) as it stands and in the first place regard translation as a relation holding between languages rather than theories. (The stronger notion of correlation discussed in this paragraph rather serves to characterize **reduction** - a notion stronger than translation.)

Under what conditions do we obtain translations in the sense of (**TR**)? One interesting answer to this is provided by Feferman's (1974) "Uniform Reduction Theorem". To state this theorem we need the concept of a projectively definable relation (see Feferman (1974), p. 157). We say that, assuming $s \cap t = \emptyset$, a relation **R** is projectively definable (in **L**) if it in a relevant sense determines an **L**-projective class of models of type $s \cup t$. Roughly speaking, a class of models of type s is **L**-projective if there is an extension s' of s and a sentence ξ of **L** of type s' such that this class coincides with the class of models of ξ restricted to s. Notice that typically projective definability in **L** entails connecting the structures of type s and t via some new relations appearing only in structures of some extended type (for concrete examples, see Pearce (1979)).

Now we state a version (actually a corollary) of Feferman's theorem suitable for our purposes, assuming $s \cap t = \emptyset$.

(**URT**) Assume that **L** is a general logic with $L_S = \text{Sent}_L(s)$ and $L_T = \text{Sent}_L(t)$ and with the interpolation property (viz. with a form of Craig's interpolation theorem holding for **L**) and that **R** is, in the above sense, a projectively definable relation in **L**. Then, if
$(\forall M)(\forall N)(\forall N')[R(M,N) \& R(M,N') \Rightarrow (N \equiv_L N')]$
holds, it also holds that for all $\phi \in \text{Sent}_L(s)$ there is a $\psi \in \text{Sent}_L(t)$ such that for all **M,N**
$R(M,N) \Rightarrow [M \models_L \psi \Leftrightarrow N \models_L \phi]$,
and thus **L** effects a translation of L_S into L_T relative to **R** (in the sense of (**TR**)).

Here $\equiv_L$ means elementary equivalence with respect to **L**, and the antecedent of the theorem assumes that the translation or correlation defined by **R** is unique up to elementary equivalence.

As Pearce (1981) has shown, various structuralist notions of scientific reduction, such as a counterpart of Sneed's (1971) notion, satisfy the antecedent of (**URT**). Thus, for such notions, it is true that reduction entails translatability in the sense of (**TR**) (or its simile) but yet the converse fails to hold. Note thus that translatability in the sense of (**TR**) (or the satisfaction of the antecedent of (**URT**)) does not entail reduction, for the relation R may fail to connect each model of S with some model of T. We recall that the notion of translatability employed here is compatible with semantic (as well as ontic) incommensurability. Thus one can have reduction while incommensurability obtains between the reducing and the reduced conceptual framework.

As projective definability is a rather general and weak notion we are left with the possibility of strengthening the antecedent of (**URT**) in various ways. Thus we might require model-theoretic definability in Beth's sense or we might require some sort of partial definability or identifiability of the relations occurring in $Str_L(S)$ and hence of the predicates in L_S (see, e.g., Tuomela (1973) on such notions). Alternatively (or at the same time) we might also strengthen our notion of translatability by analogously qualifying **R** (but so that in the consequent of (**URT**) R is not made stronger than in the antecedent). One such strengthening qualification would be to require that R at least approximately preserves the meanings (or conceptual roles) of the predicates in L_S. How to exactly characterize conceptual roles we shall not, however, try to clarify here (but recall our earlier discussion of this in the present chapter).

As to the general problem of translation let me finally say that it is good to have a general notion of translation, such as (**TR**), which can flexibly be applied to different cases. We may think that the concept of translation is in part a scientifically specifiable concept. Thus actual examples from science may indicate, for instance, how the relation R really should be specified in detail. This remark is especially pertinent in the case of translating holistic social talk into individualistic talk, for the future development of both sociology and (social) psychology may greatly affect the relevant conceptual frameworks and their interrelations. Note here, too, that our notion of translation is compatible with Quinean indeterminacy of translation, for our notion is relative to a particular relation R. As there may be several such acceptable relations, indeterminacy may result. It is not, however, important for our present discussion whether or not indeterminacy will always or typically arise in the context of theory change, and we shall not hence discuss this problem here.

3. A few remarks connecting the above treatment of translation to our schema (II) may still be made. First, as we indicated, the sentence ϕ of (**TR**) and (**URT**) may be just our social theory S. The translation $\tau(S)$ will accordingly be the sentence ψ of L_T that (**TR**) requires and (**URT**) gives us. Our translation function τ may then just be regarded the syntactic counterpart of the

model theoretic relation R. Formally we may make τ a function $\tau_L: L_S \to L_T$, viz. τ is a function relative to L mapping L_S into L_T. Relating this to the definiendum of (TR) we may say that τ is a translation function relative to L mapping L_S into L_T if and only if there is a relation R such that L effects a translation of L_S into L_T relative to R (in the sense of (TR)).

Note that $\tau(S)$ may be taken to be a sentence in the vocabulary η_s if the - individualistically acceptable - vocabulary of L_T is $\lambda_i \cup \eta_s$ or $\lambda_i \cup \mu_p \cup \eta_s$. Of course, a strict individualist might want to make L_T have only λ_i as its extralogical predicates, and then $\tau(S)$ would have to be in that vocabulary. (But we do not require that.) If we then assume that $\tau(S)$ is in the vocabulary η_s and T in λ_i then the auxiliary assumptions C need to be couched in $\lambda_i \cup \eta_s$.

Applying clauses (i) and (ii) of (II)(a) to this situation now amounts to the following. We assume that there is a "corrected" counterpart theory S* which is an approximation and correction of $\tau(S)$. According to (i), T&C is then taken to adequately explain S*. Here we are dealing with exactly the situation that our (I) speaks about. Thus what we earlier said about approximation and adequate explanation can be directly applied here.

How about (b) of (II)? It amounts to the requirement that T has greater explanatory power than S, and hence $\tau(S)$, has, and that notion was clarified in connection with (I). The fact that we must speak of the translation of S in (II) involves that the explanatory power of S is being judged from the point of view of T, we may say. And this is the best we can do here, for the successor theory is posited at the putatively correct theory that we have accepted at the time of making the judgement. We do not have any completely "trans-theoretic" or "trans-contextual" standard of comparison. To assume that would be to accept a version of the myth of the given and so-called metaphysical (as contrasted with internal) realism - if one wants to be a realist (see Chapter 1 and Tuomela (1980), (1984) on this connection).

(II) gives our most general account of the reductive explanation of social laws and theories in terms of individualistic ones. As we indicated, (II) could easily be reformulated in terms of our pragmatic theory of explanation (of Chapter 10) and thus also partly in terms of (correct) scientific explanatory answers in analogy with our classification of various types of action explanation in Chapter 11.

As indicated earlier, at least interpretative corrective explanation in the sense of (II) may be used as a method of eliminating non-acceptable holistic discourse. It is obvious that the above method of translation is in this context superior to such much debated methods of replacement as Craigian and Ramseyan elimination. (See, e.g., Tuomela (1973) for an extensive discussion of them and of the famous theoretician's dilemma argument.) This is simply because they assume commensurability (connectability in terms of suitable correspondence rules) of the framework to be replaced and the replacing framework. We do not need such an assumption when using our above method of translation as a method of replacement and elimination.

4. Given the above account of corrective reductive explanation we may discuss various special topics that involve the explanation (both corrective and other explanation) of social laws. Thus we may discuss invisible hand explanations and functional explanations of social patterns and structures, for social patterns and structures conceptually involve dispositional laws of actions (see Chapters 8 and 12). Let us here briefly consider these two types of explanations and end with a comment on Olson's theory of provision of goods that we discussed in Chapter 5.

What takes place in the invisible hand explanation of social structures and patterns can be sketched as follows. If we consider examples of invisible hand explanations of, e.g., the continuous creation of money within the banking system, or the development of media of exchange, or the rise of the so-called ultraminimal state (in Nozick's theory) what we are dealing with is just the explanation of social laws and regularities in terms of some suitable individualistic "invisible hand" theory (see Ullmann-Margalit (1978) and Nozick (1974) for discussion of, e.g., the above examples).

As I basically accept Ullmann-Margalit's (1978) illuminating account of the invisible hand explanation of social patterns I shall not here go into a philosophical discussion of the matter. What I will do is to indicate the technical changes to be made in our schema (**IHE**) of invisible hand explanation for this case. The basic idea now is the following. The action type Z of (**IHE**) should be taken to have as its result the state or pattern to be explained. This could be, for instance, the lawful process of the creation of money within the banking system. At least this example can be taken to involve a lawful generality of the type 'In environmental circumstances E, a social collective S has property P (or is in state P)'. Let us call a law of this type (or roughly this type) L. Now we take L (or some more complex but related law) to be the regularity to be explained. Thus, we may have q = Why does L obtain? L is to be explained by means of some operative agents' $A_1,...,A_m$ actions X_i by saying, roughly, that whenever these agents perform their component actions X_i (and when, as consequence, X becomes performed by them) it is generated that, under E, S has P (cf. (5.16)). Then it is added that these agents continuously perform X and thus S continues to have P. Now, if we call this (general) individualistic story about the creation of S's having P in E the theory T, we may modify our (**IHE**) of Chapter 13 as follows.

In (2) of (**IHE**) we now require that the complete scientific explanatory answer c_i satisfies the following conditions. In the place of (a) we require that there is an individualistic theory T such that T (possibly together with some further "initial condition" statements) gives an E-argument (in the sense of the Appendix of Chapter 10) for L. T has the content specified above. In the place of (b) we now have the requirement that $A_1,...,A_m$ do not at least normally or typically perform X with the intention of generating S's having (or continuing to have) P. As to (c), we now instead require that there is no (individualistic) theory T* such that (i) according to T some agents $A_1,...,A_k$ recurrently (or "continuously") perform some action Y in E with the intention of making S have (or continue to have) P, and (ii) T serves to give an E-argument for L.

I shall not here formulate more exactly the new version of (**IHE**) for the explanation of laws nor shall I examine what other patterns or versions of invisible hand explanations of laws there might possibly be in the case of more complex explanandum-contents that our L.

Let us finally briefly touch on the topic of action-functions and functional explanation. Considering our ($\mathbf{F^*_S}$) and (**FE**) of Chapter 13, the following obvious comments may be made in the case of the explanation of laws. (**FE**) would now be replaced by a new condition speaking about the explanation of a "function-law". This law would say, roughly, that in normal circumstances the agents' $A_1,...,A_m$ doing X generates the end Y to come about or, if Y is a state, to continue to obtain. How can this type of law, say L*, be explained? If sociological functionalism is to have any truth in it at all, L* could be explained by a functionalistic theory, say T, saying something like the following at least. In the social system S (cf. ($\mathbf{F^*_S}$)) the end Y somehow contributes to the well-being (or survival or something of the kind) of S and the obtaining or attainment of Y specifically through X may have some intrinsic importance (cf. clause (4) of ($\mathbf{F^*_S}$)). Note that while we have earlier characterized endhood internalistically, here T does it externalistically and objectively gives grounds for the X-Y regularity to be functional for S, but for functional explanations to work in the long run there must be objective feedback from Y back to X, it seems. The specific details of functional theories cannot be discussed here and the clarification of their nature belongs to sociology proper (cf., e.g., Sztompka (1974) and Turner (1977) for such sociological discussions).

Let us end by a brief reconsideration of Olson's theory of the provision of collective goods by social groups that we discussed in Chapter 5. This theory gives an individualistic explanation of how social groups provide, or fail to provide collective goods. While Olson's theory essentially amounts to stating what Figure 5.2 involves, it suffices here to consider only one consequence of the full theory. This consequence is what we called Olson's general thesis. Informally put it says that unless the number of individuals in a group is quite small, or unless there is coercion or some other special device to make individuals act in their common interest, rational self-interested individuals will not act to achieve their common or group interests (concerned with the provision of collective goods). Olson assumes that what a group does depends on what the individuals in that group do and that what the individuals do depends on the relative advantages to them of alternative courses of action. In other words, individualistic utility theory is being applied here to explain a holistic theory. While it is not necessary to go over the details once more, it may be recalled that the collective concepts, such as V_g, are individualistically defined. Thus the holistic theory can be taken to be of the type $S(\eta_s)$ and the individualistic theory of the type $T(\lambda_i \cup \mu_p)$, where the predicates of η_s have been explicitly defined in terms of the predicates in $\lambda_i \cup \mu_p$ relative to $T(\lambda_i \cup \mu_p)$. This clearly fits our pattern (I) (even if no corrective element is present) and thus exemplifies and supports our general thesis of explanatory individualism (EI).

NOTES

CHAPTER 1

1) The main assumptions of our **Causal Internal Realism** that we are discussing here can be stated concisely as follows:
(A1) There are mind-independent real entities (objects, etc.).
(A2) These entities causally interact with human beings (in a way making, e.g., learning possible).
(A3) There is no ontically given "ready-made" world.
(A4) There is no concept-free, yet epistemic commerce with the world.
(A5) There are no conceptual frameworks which are a priori privileged and irreplaceable (in the order of conceiving).
(A6) As to describing and explaining the world, science is the measure of what there is.
(Cf. Tuomela (1980) and (1984) for a discussion of these assumptions.)

2) As a decision maker, social reformer, etc., a social scientist naturally employs prescriptive and axiological discourse in a prescriptive sense. Some interesting situations of this kind can be reconstructed in terms of the practical syllogism with a value judgement in its first premise and a normative prescription as its conclusion. Very roughly put, such a practical syllogism might have the following form: (1) Agent A regards end E as (e.g., morally) good; (2) A considers that his performing action X is necessary for his achieving E; so, (3) A thinks he (morally) ought to do X.
    Let me still emphasize that I may grant more generally that all key social concepts have central value-laden uses. Yet my point is that **qua** scientist a social scientist needs to be concerned only with the descriptive uses of social concepts (or, if you like better, with the descriptive aspects of the uses of social concepts).

3) Habermas (1981) strongly emphasizes the importance of the concept of communicative action for social theory. What he calls communicative actions are illocutionary speech acts that involve reflexive illocutionary intentions. As the two-volume book by

Habermas came to my hands only after this book had gone into print I cannot here really comment on his account (but see Chapter 10 below). My theoretical emphasis in this book is different and so are the most discussed examples of social action. Let me note that in my account the notions of **factual** vs. **conceptual** action generation (cum the relevant semantical mutual beliefs) play roles resembling somewhat the roles played by the notions of "result-directed" (**Erfolgs-orientiert**) and "understanding-directed" (**Verständigungs-orientiert**) action.

CHAPTER 2

1) To speak of a theory in this context is admittedly to idealize the situation considerably, for it is indeed hard to produce one explicitly (but see the attempt in Tuomela (1977), pp. 77-80). It would be more realistic to speak more vaguely in terms of an explanatory scheme or framework, I suppose, but then the claim-making character of this theory would become obscured.

2) Lukes (1973) distinguishes four different kinds of predicates that can be applied to individuals: (i) physiological predicates, e.g., predicates about certain brain states, genetic make up; (ii) psychological predicates that presuppose no social context in their application, e.g., predicates about stimulus-response, gratification; (iii) predicates that presuppose a certain social context for their application but that nevertheless do not presuppose any particular type of group institution, e.g., predicates about power, cooperation; (iv) predicates that do presuppose some particular type of social institution or group, e.g., predicates about cashing checks, voting. Our set λ_i is assumed to consist of predicates of the first three types (primarily of type (iii), of course).

Lukes and others have considered individualistic programmes that leave out predicates of type (iv) implausible and those including (iv) empty or question-begging. Accordingly, our approach should at least not be regarded as uninformative. Note, however, that we do not claim that social science can do with only λ_i-predicates. Rather we should say that λ_i is our basis set which will serve to generate, in a sense to be specified, all the needed social predicates.

3) The present formalization is too simple, for it pretends that the predicates in η_s and in λ_i apply to the same entities. This cannot be assumed generally or at least without further argument. The reader is referred to Chapter 14 for tools to take this into account properly. There, a translation function con-

necting the holistic and individualistic realms is defined, and it can be applied to the present case as well. Then also the fact that the Qs in λ_i corresponding to holistic Ps in n_s will generally be relational and complex can be made explicit.

4) In the technical terminology Sellars uses we, accordingly, get the necessary equivalence of the following two statements (a) and (b) (see Sellars (1968), p. 219):

(a) It shall$_w$ be the case that each of us does A_i in C_i;
(b) If any of us is in C_i he ought to do A_i.

Of these (a) is an expression of a we-intention and (b) states a norm.

Castaneda and Aune have presented closely similar analysis of normative statements in terms of practical reasoning and intentions. (See, e.g., Aune (1977), Chapter IV for a lucid discussion.)

5) It is not easy to specify on purely conceptual grounds what kind of condition in the intention of (i) would prove motivationally sufficient. I use above the phrase 'sufficient number', where 'number' need not be understood in a distributive sense and where the substantive content of 'sufficient' may well vary from agent to agent and from situation to situation.

Clauses (i) and (ii) might still be relaxed, perhaps. Thus instead of 'believes that...' we might consider 'believes that probably...', but I shall leave such further tinkering till another occasion.

6) In this connection we may note an interesting parallel between semantical and normative discourse. Sellars, for one, bases semantical discourse on Rylean facts. (Still he regards semantical discourse as irreducible and sui generis; cf. Sellars (1974), pp. 274-275.) We may now ask what this factual basis of semantical discourse really amounts to. Does λ_i suffice or do we, in addition, need λ_h? And, especially, do we need holistic we-intentions? These questions are appropriate also in the case of normative discourse, and we have, in fact, just above been discussing the factual basis of norms. I shall not here try to answer the above questions in the case of semantical discourse but only suggest that the proper answers are closely parallel with the normative case.

7) At this point it may be proper to point out that not all preference structures can be represented by metric or even

ordinal utilities. The so-called non-Archimedean preferences are a case in point. Of these the so-called **lexicographic preferences** can be used to illustrate the point. We say that a vector $<p_1,...,p_m>$ of items is lexicographically preferred to another vector $<q_1,...,q_m>$ if and only if for some i, $p_i > q_i$ (p_i is strictly preferred to q_i) and for all $j<i$, $p_j = q_j$. Here the situation with respect to the ith item is decisive. Differences in preference concerning p_j and q_j with $j>i$ do not matter at all: the ith item is incomparably more important than the i+kth item, for every k>0. It is a well known result in utility theory that lexicographic (and other non-Archimedean) preferences cannot be represented by utilities.

It may be suggested that, for instance, life, love, dignity, honor, etc. are items which behave like non-Archimedean preferences. (Thus they would stand for items in the ith place in the above vectors.) I believe that it is ultimately up to empirical research to find out which preferences are Archimedean (or nearly so), and I will leave the matter at that. Our purposes in this book are not essentially affected by this problem.

8) While our emphasis in this book is on social motivation and other-regarding utilities (also cf. Chapter 12) it should be obvious that all of the just mentioned motivational tendencies are deep-rooted in human beings. What is more, it seems that they are also **innate**, as recent ethological studies indicate (see, e.g., Eibl-Eibesfeldt (1974)).

CHAPTER 3

1) It may, however, be pointed our that while game theory (including decision theory) certainly makes very important contributions to the study of rational strategic behavior it does not give much elucidation of overt action. Thus, for instance, Savage treats actions as functions from the set of situations to a set of outcomes. While this need not be objected to as such, it gives little philosophical clarification if nothing substantive is said about the functions in question and if situations and outcomes are left unanalyzed (and the intentional elements of action are omitted). Analogous remarks may be made about other decision and game-theoretic accounts (see, e.g., Fishburn (1981) for a recent review).

2) When we speak of some agents' $A_1,...,A_m$ performing a social action actually several interpretations of the agent-collective are possible. First, we may indeed speak of a holistic collective comprising $A_1,..,A_m$ as its elements (in some sense). Sec-

ondly, we may mean by the collective a mereological sum of the agents, viz. $A_1+\ldots+A_m$ (cf. Massey (1976)). Thirdly, we may consider the collective individualistically and mean simply the singular agents $A_1,\ldots,A_m$ and their interactions.

Our purposive-causal theory of social action to be developed can be said to rely on the third interpretation and in the final analysis to reject both the first, holistic interpretation (cf. Chapter 2 but also (5.16)) and the second interpretation. (I find the notion of agent sum somewhat obscure and almost devoid of philosophical explanatory power. In contrast, sums of spatio-temporal objects (e.g., human bodies) and events make good sense to me.)

3) Davis (1979), p. 67, presents the following analysis of 'aiming at':

"An agent x aimed at doing an A if and only if:
(i) x willed to do an A; or
(ii) for some B, x aimed at doing a B because he believed his doing a B would generate his doing an A; or
(iii) for some B and some C, x aimed at doing a B because he believed his doing a B would generate his doing a C; and x believed at the time that if his doing a B indeed generated his doing a C, his doing a C would have been generated by his doing an A. (But x did not aim at doing a B because of this latter belief.)"

I shall not here discuss Davis' reasons for arriving at this definition. One fault with the definition itself may be noted here, however. It is that it is clearly **circular** as the notion of aiming at occurs in (ii) and (iii). Let me now suggest the following remedy to make Davis' analysis fit our purposes. Replace 'aimed at doing' in (ii) and (iii) by 'intended to do' and 'aim at doing' in (iii) by 'intend to do'. As to 'willed' in (i), it can remain there. (As Davis himself points out, there is, furthermore, some reason for using the weaker 'might' instead of 'would' in (ii).) It seems that the resulting analysis complies with Davis' discussion of several examples and that it also seems to serve our present purposes to be used in (**A**). A more general and better account of aiming, in the act-relational sense (see Note 4 below), seems to be obtainable in terms of the notion of conduct plan, to be discussed in Chapter 4, for if an agent performs an action X acting **on** a conduct plan, he can be said to have aimed at or intended doing X.

Incidentally, Davis (1979) presents a volitional account of action resembling our purposive-causal theory. I do not comment on Davis' theory in this chapter, which was written before the appearance of Davis' book.

4) According to Wilson (1980), p. 108, the canonical act-relational intention locution is of the form 'A intends of b that it ψ', where the term 'b', occurring in **de re** position, refers to a singular item of behavior and 'ψ' stands for an action type of "doing". He argues that this kind of act-relational notions are crucial for a viable theory of action and that they irreducibly contain reference to behavior (see Chapters V, VII, and VIII of Wilson (1980) for insightful argumentation). I agree with Wilson on the importance of such irreducible act-relational intentions (and especially willings) but argue, seemingly contrary to him, for the centrality of purposive causation in accounting for human action. (I think that the purposive-causal theory is nevertheless logically compatible with Wilson's account.)

By claiming that an act-relational notion is irreducible one claims that, for instance, the following simple thesis, which seems to be one that mental cause theorists are inclined to accept, is false: A intended (or wanted) of b that it ψ if and only if A intended (wanted) to ψ & his having that intention was a cause of b. The right hand side of this claim clearly allows for wayward causal chains, and this fact is one of the main reasons for employing irreducible act-relational intentions. Another reason is that A's intending of b that it ψ entails that A must have the intention to ψ, on this simple analysis, and that is too strong (cf. Wilson (1980) for related discussion). I do not mean to suggest that mental cause theorists accept just the above simple claim. Rather they would accept something more complex (involving beliefs and a more general action ψ', say) which yet breaks the internal connection between the intention and the behavior. A still stronger argument against the above simple analysis and also against these more complex analyses is that the intention statement (whatever it is exactly) intrinsically involves an act-relational intention (see Wilson (1980), Chapter VIII). This, if true, makes the mental cause theorist's analysis viciously circular, of course.

CHAPTER 4

1) In Tuomela (1977) a partial analysis of intending is given. It may be summarized (with two slight changes) as follows for so-called complex intending (cf. Tuomela (1977), p. 133; also cf. Audi (1973)):

An agent A **intends to perform X by performing** Y only if
(1) A believes that he, at least with some nonnegligible probability, can perform X by performing Y (or at least can learn so to perform X by performing Y);
(2) A wants (and has not temporarily forgotten that he wants) to perform X by performing Y;
(3) A has no equally strong or stronger incompatible want (or set of incompatible wants whose combined strength is at least as great), or, if A does have such a want or set of wants, he has temporarily forgotten that he wants the object(s) in question, or does not believe he wants the object(s), or has temporarily forgotten his belief that he cannot both realize the object(s) and perform X by performing Y.

(Also see Chapter 12, Section III, below.) Note that our notion of willing (effective intending now) can best be construed as relying on complex intentions (involving the by-locution) rather than simple ones (see the text below). I refer the reader to Wilson (1980) for a clear and plausible account of the logical form of intention sentences.

2) From a metaphysical point of view my account of willing and of action resembles O'Shaughnessy's (1980) recent account, viz. his theory Z (see O'Shaughnessy (1980), especially pp. 261-270). However, my account also resembles (but does not coincide with) the volitionist theory Y O'Shaughnessy discusses in this context. Especially, it seems to me that his proof of one of the basic differences between theory Y and theory Z is not sound. O'Shaughnessy claims that in his Z a willing or volition (V, striving in his terminology) cannot cause bodily events such as an arm raising (ϕ). Let now Φ be a bodily action, e.g., arm raising. Then: "if V = strive Φ, and strive-Φ-that-succeeds = Φ, and Φ does not cause ϕ, it follows that V cannot cause ϕ" (O'Shaughnessy (1980), p. 269). But here our action token u (= <t,...,b,...,r>) could be a Φ:ing and yet it seems we could have: a striving-Φ = t, a striving-Φ-that succeeds = <t,...,b,...,r>; and this would invalidate O'Shaughnessy's proof. Thus O'Shaughnessy wants to drive too much of a wedge between the theories Z and Y. (Let me remark that putting a striving-Φ = t above is an oversimplification as t is rather a complex event serving in part to make true a statement about an agent's striving to Φ.)

As a matter of fact, O'Shaughnessy concedes that "nonautonomous" part-events of strivings can be causes of ϕ's (see, e.g., p. 287). Thus we might after all regard t as such a part-event (which is also plausible on the ground that t is in our theory functionally characterized partly in terms of ϕ). This would bring our theory very close to O'Shaughnessy's account.

3) Brand (1979a) presents a classification of action theories which clearly differs from the one we have been discussing in this chapter. He divides action theories into the following four kinds: (1) Causal Theory, (2) Mental Action Theory, (3) Oldtime Volitional Theory, and (4) Double Action Theory. In his review of Tuomela (1977) he classifies the purposive-causal theory as an oldtime volitional theory (see Brand (1979b), p. 464). I shall not go into details, but it seems to me that this is true only in the order of being, so to speak, but **not** in the order of conceiving (which is at stake here). This is because the purposive-causal theory does not conceptually reduce away the concept of action although it, in a sense, does so in the causal order. Thus my theory is not reductive in the sense Brand thinks it is.

4) Here the question may be raised how the purposive-causal theory may account for omissions. Basically the answer is that they are not actions at all - contrary to what many authors think (cf. von Wright (1968)). Roughly speaking, we may say that an agent A omits to do something X just in case he does not do X while he yet has the ability and opportunity to do X. An intentional omission to do X is, roughly, an omission to do X such that either A specifically intends not to do X or that he intends to do something else Y (on that occasion) such that he is aware that his doing Y generates his omission to do X (on that occasion). (This attempt of course needs an account of what it is to intend not do X which does not presuppose the concept of intentional omission.)

Let me, however, point out that the purposive-causal theory is compatible also with a view according to which omissions are actions - albeit actions of a different type than ordinary "positive" actions.

5) It may seem that the present definition (analysis) as well as many of those to be presented below suffer from the possibility of vacuous satisfaction on the antecedent of the definiens. This is not true, however, for we accept an "inferential" analysis of 'if ... then ...' conditional statements. According to this analysis the falsity of such a conditional does not give us a sound argument for the consequent on the basis of the antecedent.

6) Note that '&' here does not mean ordinary linguistic conjunction. It could perhaps be called ontic conjunction, defined for quasi-universals. However, we do not here want to commit ourselves to any particular ontological doctrine (such as a version of ontic realism or nominalism).

It is important to notice that, e.g., the causal powers of X may be different from the "sum" of the causal powers of the X_is. This is because of the "interaction" effect of (the tokens of) the X_is (cf. our definitions (11) and (12), in particular).

Were we, after all, to construe our types linguistically as predicates we would have to say analogously that 'u is an X' is not analytically equivalent to 'u_1 is an X_1 &...& u_m is an X_m' for the joint effect of the u_is (making X exemplified by u) need not yet be there.

The identity in the expression $X = X_1 \& ... \& X_m$ is to be regarded as a **relative** one. It is relative to the circumstances in A is at T in that the action X (e.g., playing a piece of music) may in one circumstance amount to a conjunction $X_1 \& ... \& X_m$ while in another circumstance it amounts to, say, the conjunction $Y_1 \& ... \& Y_k$. Thus we should read into '=' an implicit index referring to circumstances although there is no need to make it explicit below.

7) After finishing the manuscript of this book I came upon the recent paper by John Searle (1981). In this paper and in some other papers going back to 1979 (see the references in Searle (1981)) he speaks of **intentional causation** and develops some of its features. This notion of intentional causation by Searle is conceptually quite similar to my notion of purposive causation, yet Searle does not refer to my work. I would like to emphasize that I originally developed my account of willing and purposive causation in 1974 and have since then several times discussed it in print, most notably in Tuomela (1977).

CHAPTER 5

1) Social actions in our sense can be connected to social processes and process laws in terms of systems theory. See Tuomela (1983), where a systems theoretic approach is connected to the present framework; also cf. Aulin (1982).

2) It seems to me that Olson does not always separate marginal costs and total costs sharply enough (cf., e.g., Olson (1965), pp. 22, 32).

3) It has been claimed by Riker and Ordeshook (1973), pp. 73-74, that Olson's analysis cannot be connected to group size in the way indicated in the case of **pure** collective goods. They assume that in the case of such pure collective goods (a) $V_i=V_j$ for all i and j and (b) $V_i=T$. Given this $dV_i/dT = 1$, in which case the condition for what the individual, acting alone, will by becomes $1-(dC/dT) = 0$; and this condition has nothing to do with S_g. I think that Riker's and Ordeshook's criticism is a valid one and that, e.g., public peace and order, freedom of speech, etc. indeed qualify as such pure collective goods. Thus, in the case of pure collective goods Olson's above conclusions must be taken to follow from assumptions about C (and efficacy of action), to the extent any such empirically true conclusions follow, rather than assumptions about F_i (which here is the constant $1/S_g$).

4) Hardin (1971) argues that Olson's thesis is false even for (continuous) collective goods. This is because in any m-person prisoner's dilemma game of social action concerned with continuously varying goods there is a so-called Condorcet choice (outcome) which corresponds to the alternative of paying and which guarantees a ratio of benefits to costs exceeding one to each paying player. Roughly speaking, a Condorcet choice is simply a choice (outcome) preferred by most players. However, it is a rather problematic point to what extent it yet is rational for the players to expect the other players to reason in favor of the Condorcet choice. Note that in the case of stepwise varying collective goods there is no such Condorcet choice for every situation.

5) See Note 4 of Chapter 7 for altruistic behavior in prisoner's dilemma situations.

CHAPTER 6

1) Hornsby (1980), pp. 7-9, argues that the by-relation cannot hold between two actions. Consider the sentence 'He replenished the water supply by operating the pump'. According to Hornsby this sentence does not contain any mention of an action of operating the pump or a relation between such an action and another one. The sentence simply tells us that there was an action of replenishing-the-water-supply-by-operating-the-pump.

To this argument my reply is the following. The above sentence can be formalized in a Davidsonian way and seen to have a logical form quite analogous to (2). In accordance with this, I argue that there are two non-identical singular actions involved, viz. replenishing the water and operating the pump. This is shown by the fact that they differ with respect to their results. As just argued in the present paragraph the by-relation can be taken to represent a factual relation in this type of case.

2) As is well known, Davidson's programme for formalizing action sentences (cf. (2) above) faces several difficulties which we, however, bypass here (cf. Thomson (1977), Tuomela (1977), Horsnby (1980), Wilson (1980)). An interesting reformulation of Davidson's approach is due to Wilson (1980). He takes an action statement 'A X-d' to be equivalent to

 (a) A performed an act which X-d.

In the case of so-called direct Agent-to-Event reducible predicates such as 'buttering the toast' we have as our explicate of (a) for this example

 (b) (Ex)(A performed x & x buttered the toast).

For so-called indirect Agent-to-Event reducible predicates such as 'smiling' we have

 (c) (Ex)(A performed x & x was an act of smiling).

In the case of causatives such as 'killing' and 'shooting', we need a more complicated analysis. To give an example, our (1) becomes

 (d) (Ez)(A performed z & (Ex)(x was a shooting of John by Lee & MH(z,x)) & (Ey)(y was a killing of John by Lee & MH(x,y))).

Here 'MH(x,y)' reads 'x made y happen', and this locution is a counterpart for our 'By(x,y)' in (2). (Note that 'z' in (d) can in our analysis be taken to represent the bodily action <v,... ...,b>.) We shall in this chapter be concerned with analyzing action generation, and, therefore, with analyzing the content and inner structure of the By-predicate and the MH-predicate equally well. I take it that what will be said below of generation is more or less independent of particular versions and reformulations of the Davidsonian programme (compare, e.g., (d) with (3)).

3) Although we shall not be much concerned with this, b could also be an action token performed by some other agent (see Subsection 5). This is central in the study of social interaction. (Principle (**PG**) must be reinterpreted accordingly to cover this.)

4) Let me here present a technical result which is relevant for our later developments (see esp. Chapter 12) and which generalizes the account given in Chapter 12 of Tuomela (1977). We consider the conditional $\models$ defined above by (10)(ii) for indirect purposive generation. The corresponding probabilistic conditional, denoted by $\models_r$ (introduced in Tuomela (1977), p. 396) can be analyzed as follows. A probabilistic conditional statement of the form $D_1 \models_r D_2$ ("if a occurred then it would indirectly purposively generate b with probability r", D_1 and D_2 describing a and b, respectively) can be taken to equal $p(D_1 \models D_2) = r$, where p is a suitable probability measure defined over formulas as defined in Chapter 11 of Tuomela (1977).

Perhaps it is appropriate to indicate here how the definition of '$p(D_1 \models D_2) = r$' goes. Let me simplify the situation by assuming that our (13) gives an adequate definition of IG(a,b). Given that, we change (13) by substituting '$\rho(D_2^i, D_1^i \& L)$' for '$\epsilon(D_2^i, D_1^i \& L)$' in it. (Let D_1 and D_2 be the descriptions used in the particular chain that occurred when a generated b, assuming an **ex post facto** situation.) The resulting formula (call it (13')) gives a definition of $IG_r(a,b)$, viz. (indirect) probabilistic generation of b by a of degree r. The relation ρ is a relation expressing an inductive argument, indeed an explanatory one. Thus '$\rho(D_2^i, D_1^i \& L)$' can be read '$D_1^i \& L$ inductively explains D_2^i'. The definition of ρ is given in a summary way in the Appendix of Chapter 10 below. L is now supposed to be a suitable probabilistic law, here of the form $p^*(G/F) = r$, with D_1^i and D_2^i containing suitable F and G, respectively. The objective probability measure p^* and the measure p are assumed to coincide in value, and p may be regarded either as an epistemic or as a subjective measure. Given the relation $IG_r(a,b)$ we define $IG_r^*(a,b)$ by using '$IG_r(a,b)$' for 'IG(t,r)' (and of course 'a' for 't' and 'b' for 'r' in (9). Then the substitution of '$IG_r^*(a,b)$' for 'IG*(a,b)' and '$p(D_1 \models D_2) = r$' for '$D_1 \models D_2$' in clause (ii) of (10) gives us what we want.

When $\models_r$ is defined as above on the basis of the ρ-relation it is (in part) directly based on a conditional probability, viz. $p^*(G/F)$. However, we may alternatively define $\models_r$ directly on the basis of $\models$ (and thus the ϵ-relation). How the probabilities $p(D_1 \models D_2)$ are then obtained I will not consider here (they might be just subjective probabilities, rational or not). When this second approach is used, it may be noted that in general, probability statements of the form $p(D_1 \square\!\!\rightarrow D_2)=r$ are stronger than the corresponding conditional probability statements, viz. $p(D_2/D_1)=r$. It remains for future research to investigate the exact connections involved here.

However, it is illuminating to consider the following result due to Gibbard and Harper (1978). They show that any conditional, say $\square\!\!\rightarrow$, which satisfies the following conditions

(1) $(D_1 \,\&\, (D_1 \square\!\!\rightarrow D_2)) \supset D_2$

(2) $D_1 \supset [(D_1 \square\!\!\rightarrow D_2) \equiv D_2]$

(3) $p(D_1 \square\!\!\rightarrow D_2/D_1) = p(D_1 \square\!\!\rightarrow D_2)$

also satisfies

(4) $p(D_1 \square\!\!\rightarrow D_2) = p(D_2/D_1)$.

Our conditional $\diamond\!\!\rightarrow$ trivially satisfies (1) but it fails to satisfy (2). Thus even if the deconditionalization property (3) would be true we do not have (4) for $\diamond\!\!\rightarrow$.

Let me finally note that in addition to the would-conditional we may in some cases want to use the corresponding might-conditional defined as $\sim(D_1 \diamond\!\!\rightarrow \sim D_2)$ and consider its probability.

5) Kim (1974) discusses action generation and conjectures that the project of giving a general account of it involves finding a certain relation: "A central problem in carrying out such a project would be to characterize a relation R for events and states such that if an agent brings about p, then, for any q, p is related by R to q if and only if the agent brings about q by bringing about p" (Kim (1974), p. 46). Although we have not above formulated our problem in exactly these terms we could have done so. Our automata theoretic explication of action-generation and the by-relation can thus be regarded as giving a technical explication of the relation R (cf. (4) and (5)).

6) Let me here note that the "cause maps" that some organization theorists have employed resemble very much what we have called social conduct plans. A cause map, used this way, is a graph which is shared (or shared to a great extent) by the members of the group and represents perceived or believed causal relationship between suitable variables such as means and goals. (See, e.g., Bougon, Weick, and Binkhorst (1977) for the use of cause maps as a kind of social conduct plans in our sense.)

CHAPTER 7

1) Raz (1979) presents an interesting analysis of reasons for acting in terms of first-order and second-order reasons. According to his analysis, an agent follows an ought-norm (or mandatory norm) if and only if he believes that the norm is a valid (viz. justified) reason for him to do the norm-act when the conditions for application obtain and that it is a valid reason for disregarding conflicting reasons, and he acts on those beliefs. Thus these norms are regarded by those who follow them both as first-order reasons for performing the norm-acts and as undefeated second-order reasons for not acting on conflicting reasons. Our above schema of practical reasoning can be taken to justify an ought-rule in the required sense. The overridingness we attribute to intentions can indeed be explicated in terms of the above kind of second-order reason as Raz does.

2) I will below make the simplifying assumption that each agent is aware of each other agent and the corresponding conforming action under a certain description or name. Accordingly, we may use the symbols $A_1,\ldots,A_m$ and X_k^i to make our exposition more perspicuous. But the present simplification can easily be removed - the agents need not in principle be known to each other by means of fixed names or descriptions.

3) The above claim and a few related ones can easily be formally proved correct. To do that we use our sentential operators B_E and B_M as introduced by (1) and (2). Let us assume that we have available an infinitary logic in which (1) and (2) make sense. It is easy to see that the following is true:

(a) (2) $\vdash B_M B_M p \equiv (B_E B_E p \ \& \ B_E B_E B_E p \ \& \ \ldots$ (ad infinitum)).

Thus we have

(b) (2) $\vdash B_M p \supset B_M B_M p$, and

(c) (2) $\vdash B_M p \equiv (B_M B_M p \ \& \ B_E p)$;

and these two claims were just discussed above in the text.

Let us now consider n-fold iterations of the operators B_M and B_E, writing B_M^n and B_E^n for them, respectively. We can now immediately see the truth of the following claims for every finite n:

(d) (2) $\vdash B_M^n p \supset B_M^{n+1} p$

(e)   (2) ⊢ $B_M^n p \equiv (B_M^{n+1} p \ \& \ B_E^n p)$.

Of course, (d) and (e) are direct generalizations of (b) and (c).

4) Pruitt and Kimmel (1977), p. 384, summarize the research findings relevant to altruistic behavior in prisoner's dilemma situations. According to them, the **goal** of achieving mutual cooperation is
"more likely to the extent that: (a) one has had experience with the situation over time, especially if this experience has involved mutual noncooperation; (b) one has had time to think or has otherwise been stimulated into examining his experience; (c) the PD (prisoner's dilemma game) is decomposed such that one must look to the other for his best outcomes; (d) high outcomes are associated with mutual cooperation; (e) low outcomes are associated with exploitation and mutual noncooperation; (f) mutual cooperation yields equitable outcomes; (g) decisions can be reversed so long as either party is dissatisfied with his outcomes; (h) the other party employs a tit-for-tat strategy, especially if it involves slow reciprocation of newly cooperative behavior; (i) the parties communicate with each other; (j) one sees oneself as weaker than the other party; (k) one anticipates continued interaction with the other; and (l) one's aspirations are so high that the other's cooperation is apparently needed to achieve them."
The **expectation** of (future) cooperation from the other is "stronger to the extent that (a) the other has recently cooperated with oneself or another party; (b) the other has consistently cooperated; (c) one has sent a message requesting cooperation or received one assuring cooperation; (d) one knows that the other's incentives or instructions favor cooperation; (e) the other is seen as dependent on oneself; (f) the other employs a tit-for-tat strategy involving slow retaliation when one fails to cooperate; and, assuming that one has adopted a goal of mutual cooperation, (g) the other is seen as similar to oneself or as a friend."

The maximal rate of cooperative action is to be found when both the goal and the expectation of cooperation are present; it is minimal when neither is present.

5) It may be pointed out here that there are several ways of extending two-person prisoner's dilemma games to the m-person case (m>2). Hamburger (1973) presents two such extensions, one for **contribution** situations and another for **conservation** situ-

ations, and shows that they are incompatible.

A central class of contribution situations (such as some people contributing to keep their joint yard clean) can be elucidated by a **deterministic give-some game**. In it each player (simultaneously) picks up one number from a set of positive numbers. The sum, S, of the numbers picked determines a value, V(S). This function V(S) is strictly monotonically increasing and is known to the players in advance. Each player's payoff is equal to V(S) minus the number he picked. Conservation situations (such as conserving electricity to avoid blackout) again correspond to **probabilistic take-some games**. In such a game each player (simultaneously) picks one number from a set of positive numbers. The sum, S, of the numbers picked is compared to a number L determined by the outcome of a random event independent of the players' choices. Players know the distribution of L but not the outcome. If $S \leq L$, each player's payoff is the number he picked. Otherwise (cf. blackout) everyone gets payoff 0. Corresponding to such contribution and conservation situations we can naturally speak of m-agent contribution actions and conservation actions.

6) What Habermas has called communicative action patterns such as orders, requests, question-askings and answerings, and so on clearly rely on social rules, and these "institutionalized practices" cannot be participated in without knowing the relevant rules (and, indeed, without the participating agents having mutual knowledge of them) and having the ability to follow these rules. Communicative actions obviously form a subclass of (at least) our class S_{RU} of rule-referring actions. We shall not, however, in this book study communicative actions very much (see Chapter 10 and Habermas (1981) on them).

CHAPTER 9

1) In his short note Brooks (1981) discusses joint action and asks under which conditions an n-place predicate can be regarded as an n-place action predicate, viz. as a predicate designating n-person social (or joint) action. Thus he claims that "an n-place predicate is an n-place action predicate if it is true of n agents in virtue of (i) each of those n agents acting (ii) the descriptions under which the actions of each of those agents are intentional mentioning the other agents under some description" (Brooks (1981), p. 118). This sufficient condition (which perhaps should be regarded as necessary, too) is closely related to what our (8) and (9), generalized to n agents, give us. (I shall not speculate which one it comes closest.) But as a criterion of

proper social action or joint action Brooks' condition is clearly too weak. Consider thus the case with two agents A and B where A intentionally walks on B's land and B intentionally walks on A's land. Brooks' condition may be taken as satisfied, but clearly no joint action need to be involved here. (However, at another place on the same page Brooks claims that for two agents to be involved in a joint action they must intend to be involved in a joint action under some description even though that description may not be a description which applies to them. This resembles our idea of intentional social action as expressed by (5.10).)

2) In this formalism we translate 'A believes that p' by '(Ex)B(A,p,x)', where 'x' refers to a state or episode of believing. 'A intends to do X' is assumed to be paraphrasable by 'A intends that p(X)', where p(X) is a suitable propositional clause (the exact form of which cannot be discussed here). Analogously with statements about believing we then formalize the last mentioned paraphrases by '(Ex)I(A,p,x)'. Action statements can at least in cases where no adverbs are present be formalized in the Davidsonian way. Thus, e.g., 'A opens the window' becomes '(Ex)Opens(A,the window,x)'. More complex cases require predicate-modification and possible other additional devices.

3) It may be noted here that while our above treatment gives the covariances between the variables α_{i1} and α_{i2} on the one hand and between τ_{j1} and τ_{j2} on the other hand, it does not give the analogous covariances between α_{i1} and τ_{j2} (the players' controls over their own utilities) or between α_{i2} and τ_{j2} (the players' controls over each other's utilities). That can, however, easily be done, if wanted. For then we simply switch the meaning of 'row' in the case of the column player and take it to refer to his columns. (Technically, in our above terminology we then use the cross products $R_{ih}T_{jh'}$ and $T_{jh}R_{ih'}$, respectively, in (45) and (46), i and j having the same number of values.) Our subsequent comments are easily extendable to these new measures of association.

4) Let me, however, briefly indicate how to measure concordance in those two cases (the first and the second) when our covariance matrices fail to do that. We let $\alpha_{\cdot 1} =_{df} \max(\alpha_{11}, \alpha_{21})$, $\alpha_{+2} =_{df} \max(\alpha_{12}, \alpha_{22})$, $\tau_{\cdot 2} =_{df} \max(\tau_{12}, \tau_{22})$, and $\tau_{+1} =_{df} \max(\tau_{11}, \tau_{21})$. Then we may define for obtaining of the first type of concordance, say C_1, and the second type of concordance, say C_2, the following expressions:

(1) Given $\alpha_{.1} > 0$, $\tau_{.2} > 0$,
  C_1 if and only if $\eta_{..1}$ & $\eta_{..2} \geq 0$.

(2) Given $\alpha_{+2} > 0$, $\tau_{+1} > 0$,
  C_2 if and only if η_{++1} 0 & $\eta_{++2} \geq 0$.

In (1) the dots in $\eta_{..1}$ and $\eta_{..2}$ correspond to the dots in $\alpha_{.1}$ and $\tau_{.2}$ in that order, and analogously for the pluses in (2).

5) Speaking more generally, in the case of three or more agents the most central phenomenon, but one closely related to joint control, is **coalition formation**. It can plausibly be claimed that, in the case of three agents A_1, A_2, and A_3, the following situations, for instance, are promotive of coalition formation between two agents, say A_1 and A_2: (a) cases of high degree of correspondence between A_1's and A_2's utilities in the joint utility matrix of all agents, (b) cases where A_3 has some control over A_1's and A_2's utilities but A_1 and A_2 can by their joint action exercise greater power counter to A_3's control than by acting alone. In Thibaut and Kelley (1959), Chapter 11, and Kelley and Thibaut (1978), Chapters 9 and 10, there is a pertinent informative discussion of coalition formation within a framework very close to ours. Their treatment complements our discussion in this book and the interested reader is referred to their work concerning this topic.

6) This idea of social action seems close to what Max Weber meant: "Action is social in so far as, by virtue of the subjective meaning attached to it by the acting individual (or individuals), it takes account of the behavior of others and is thereby oriented in its course." (Weber (1947), p. 88.) However, also our (1) is relevant and covers a part of what Weber is saying.

7) Homans (1964), p. 35, states as a sufficient condition (which perhaps also is meant to be a necessary condition) for interaction: "when as activity (or sentiment) emitted by one man is rewarded (or punished) by an activity emitted by another man, regardless of the kinds of activity each emits, we say that the two have interacted".

CHAPTER 10

1) We will thus assume here and in the sequel that all scientific explanations are going to be dependent on some such C and P. As we shall see in Section III, paradigms are not easy to

characterize in exact terms. In any case, understanding them in the sense of Kuhn's constellations of group commitments (broadly understood) would seem to make it a nearly conceptual truth that all **scientific** explanations are paradigm-dependent (see Section III for illustrations). Paradigms and contexts can be taken to operate as constraints on explanations. (If needed, they may be analyzed or elucidated in terms of suitable may do- and ought to do -rules, which are then required to be satisfied in our definitions.)

Notice that a certain scientist is allowed **de facto** to be a member of several scientific communities sharing different paradigms. Our analysis only claims that the correctness of an explanation depends on one such context-paradigm pair.

2) In fact, we cannot below discuss all the problems relevant to (1). One such problem is how exactly to account for nonintentional explanation given that (1) clarifies intentional (or, better, intended) explanation (cf., however, the weakened analysis (18)). Another problem is how broadly the term 'intention' can be understood in (1). It seems that here and below, e.g., the broader term 'aim' (but not, e.g., 'want') could be used in its place. A further relevant problem is how to analyze the notion of belief in (1). For instance, there is the problem whether the belief that a certain u is a scientific explanatory answer should be taken to entail belief in clauses (a) and (b) in our definition (9) of scientific explanatory answer.

3) In the present kind of situation (cf. (1), (17), and (18)) a reflexive illocutionary intention by A is directed towards B's becoming aware of something, say p (e.g. that A has a certain intention). If we let I_A represent A's intending and B_B B's awareness or belief we are dealing with statements of the type $I_A(B_B(p))$. The reflexivity here involves the rationalizing iterability of the loop expressed by $I_A(B_B(p))$ (yielding statements such as, e.g., $I_A(B_B(I_A(B_B(p))))$). Such resulting loop-hierarchies, required to be **mutually believed** true by A and B, can be interpreted, as similar iterated mutual beliefs were interpreted in Section II of Chapter 7, not only as involving dispositional intentions but in the finitary sense of involving only the agents' dispositions to come to acquire such dispositional intentions. These additional loops can be taken to justify or rationalize lower level loops; yet we need not require their existence in typical communicative situations (cf. Note 7).

A weaker possibility for explicating rationalizing reflexivity, suggested by Bennett (1976), p. 127, would be to require only A's not intending B not to believe so and so at each stage.

Thus we would have $I_A B_B$-loops up to some level and from thereon add $\sim I_A \sim B_B$-loops, thus creating an infinite set $\{I_A(B_B(p)), \sim I_A(\sim B_B(I_A(B_B(p)))), \sim I_A(\sim B_B(I_A(B_B(I_A(B_B(p)))))), \ldots\}$, whose elements are required to be true. But this solution - while it is almost correct - still requires some modifications to get the rationalizations right (see Kemmerling (1980) for them). As said above, we need not require the psychological existence of further $I_A B_B$-loops or $\sim I_A \sim B_B$-loops beyond the lowest level loop (cf. Kemmerling (1983)).

4) In a finer analysis we would have to worry about quantifying over such queer entities as reasons (in the mentioned broad sense). Our analysis, however, makes explanatory reasons equal to premise-conjunctions of suitable (nomological) arguments, which we must be able to make sense of and identify anyhow (cf. Tuomela (1973), Chapter VII and (1976)).

5) We call an explanatory argument **actual** only when it is a potential one and its premises and conclusions are true or approximately true. (Approximate truth may be what one has to settle for when "closing" an open real system requires the use of idealizing assumptions.) There are further requirements which one need to impose on actual explanations. One is that the laws occurring in the premises be "laws of working", viz., the laws be really operating in the explanatory situation at hand. As to our (1), in an actual act of explaining A's and B's beliefs referred to in the definiens must be **correct**.

6) Note that (16) allows that there could be two logically contradictory scientific explanations u and u'. If this is considered a drawback it can be remedied by relativizing a scientific explanation (the definiendum) to q, A, B, C, P, E, and Q instead of existentially quantifying over them in the definiens.

7) We may try to formalize (17) by means of the modification of the Davidsonian approach employed in Tuomela (1977), esp. Chapter 6, and above in Chapters 6 and esp. 9 (pp. 282-283). As we emphasized, several mutual beliefs are presumed by (17). Let us here still emphasize that we shall below take it for granted that, among other mutual background beliefs, A and B mutually know (or have correct mutual **de re** beliefs about) who they are and that they have a mutual belief about what B's singular action is, viz. an uttering of v. Thus letting B's action token be u we define $u =_{df} (\imath x) \text{Utters}(B,v,x)$ in the Davidsonian fashion (but omit considerations of tense and use present tense

below). Thus we assume below, without incorporating this in our formalism: (Ex)(Ey) (x = A & y = B & Mutually believe (A,B, x = A & y = B)), (Ey) (y = u & Mutually believe (A,B, y = u)).

Our formalization, employing rather self-explanatory symbolism, now becomes as follows:

(17') B's uttering a linguistic expression v (= singular action u) is an action of **asking** why p if and only if
(a) (Ey) Wants (B, (Ez) Tells-why (A,B,p,z), y) &
(b) (Et) Intends (B, (Ey) (Brings-about (B, (Ew) (Tells-why (A,B,p,w) & (Er) (Believes (A, (Eq) Wants (B, (Ez) Tells-why (A,B,pz), q) & (Es) Intends (B, (Em) Brings-about (B, (En) Tells-why (A,B,p,n), m) & By$_B$ (m,u),s),r) & IG*$_A$(r,w))), y) & By$_B$ (y,u)), t)

Here 'Wants', 'Believes' and 'Intends' are three-place predicates for persons, propositional contents, and realization-states (or episodes), 'Tells-why' is a four-place predicate for two persons, a propositional content, and an episode and 'Brings-about' analogously a three-place predicate. Note that IG* explicates the because-relation (cf. (R) of Chapter 11). The By-relation is defined by (6.4).

Note that the intending presented by t is a reflexive intention (although it was not necessary to formalize it in full above, making (b) completely circular). Using the terminology of Note 3 above (with 'A' and 'B' switching places), it has the form $I_B(B_A(I_B(q)))$, where $I_B(q)$ (q here representing A's action) corresponds to p and where A is supposed to act on $B_A(I_B(q))$, viz. his belief that $I_B(q)$. We may call the intending of clause (b) a simple Gricean loop intention. My thesis now is that in the very analysis of a speech act we do not need more than this (cf. Kemmerling (1983)). However, that the intending in clause (b) yet is a reflexive one - which we assume - involves that it is in principle (partially) justifiable by means of iterating the $I_B B_A$-loops and $I_B B_A$-loops (and thus obtaining formulas like $I_B(B_A(I_B(B_A(p))))$ in Note 3). A and B are assumed to be mutually aware of this possibility of iteration. Thus, what was said in Note 3 on the whole becomes applicable here.

8) Habermas (1981), p. 384ff., 439, divides social actions (viz., roughly, actions involving several interacting agents) into strategic and communicative. The former are primarily connected to achieving ends and the latter to processes of understanding. Concentrating on linguistic actions, we have among strategic actions perlocutionary speech acts and imperatives. The class of communicative linguistic actions includes (1) con-

versation ("constantives"), (2) normative actions ("regulatives"), and (3) dramaturgical actions ("expressives").

As the focus of this book has been on strategic action it has not been possible to discuss communicative linguistic actions to a great length. Yet, as the above example indicates, there are good reasons for thinking that our theory can be fruitfully extended to cover all communicative actions in Habermas' sense (even if I do not accept his sharp dichotomy between **Erfolgsorientiert** and **Verständigungsorientiert** actions). (Generally speaking, when in a communicative context two agents understand each other there need not necessarily be an intention on the part of any agent to the effect that he brings it about that the other comes to understand (and consent to) what he says or does; yet such understanding - an "ability-state" - is something necessarily brought about by the other agent in a successful communicative act such as asking.)

9) It is another, but central, matter that revolutionary situations arise when it becomes increasingly hard to believe that a question q could have a true answer related to some given context C and paradigm P and when, as a consequence, a "paradigm-shift" (to some C' and P') occurs and an answer is given relative to C' and P'.

CHAPTER 11

1) Note that we must be able to bar **akrasia** when applying our above schemas of inference. When a social action X fails to be performed this may be due to only one agent's weakness of will. In this sense the group will can be said to be rather vulnerable.

2) As to the technical aspects of Schank's and Abelson's framework there are several criticizable features. For one thing, the primitive concepts of their formalization seem to me arbitrary. Secondly, formalizing natural language sentences within that framework entails loss of information. Thus, e.g., the statements 'John walked to the restaurant' and 'John ran to the restaurant' are quasi-formalized by one and the same statement 'John PTRANS John to restaurant'. Furthermore, their framework does not seem to be able to handle, e.g., adverbial and sentential transformation or even logical quantification. The modification of Davidsonian formalization sketched in Chapters 2, 6, and 9 of Tuomela (1977) for representing psychological statements (including conduct plans) fares much better in the above respects.

CHAPTER 12

1) In Chapter 6 and in Tuomela (1977) $\models_r^+$ was strictly speaking defined only for singular descriptions such as, say, $A(a) \models_r^+ B(b)$. However, it is easy to generalize this for open formulas such as $A(x)$ and $B(y)$. We may do it as follows: $A(x) \models_r^+ B(y)$ if and only if, letting a and b be any respective values of x and y, $A(a) \models_r^+ B(b)$.

We shall below use the open formula definition when comparing probability conditionals with conditional probabilities.

2) We may say that a goal (or outcome) G is a **cooperative** one just in case (1) it is in the **intrinsic** interest of the participating agents that G be achieved (cf. (2.2)); (2) G cannot (or at least cannot without great difficulty) be achieved by any agent alone (without the positive help or lack of harmful interference by others); (3) G can be (or is at least likely to be) achieved by all the agents together, by their performing their parts of a social action. (If an action X has G as its generic result, then this characterization immediately defines what it is for such an action to be cooperative; cf. loading a ship or keeping the air clean as examples.) If a cooperative goal G is the object of a we-intention, then we can speak of cooperative we-intentions. What kind of game-theoretic outcomes can be objects of cooperative we-intentions? The requirement of **intrinsic** interest in (1) presupposes an absolute interest-disinterest distinction, perhaps one made by reference to the agents' aspiration level such that it is not changeable by any suitable rescaling of utilities. The term 'intrinsic' is taken to entail clear **positive** interest (utility) in this absolute sense. Given this, we at least exclude equilibrium points of games of opposite interests from the permissible objects of cooperative we-intentions. Outcomes in games of identical interests always qualify and those in games of mixed interests often do, depending on the case (cf. $<X_1, Y_1>$ as a positive example in the prisoner's dilemma).

3) The criticism against utility theory have to do with the unacceptability of several postulates, e.g., the probabilistic equivalence and sure thing postulates, of this theory in the case of ordinary people. Furthermore, experiments seem to indicate that on some occasions agents' preferences are non-transitive (and inconsistent) and their subjective probabilities inconsistent.

There are also criticisms of game theory that we have not so far mentioned. Thus, e.g., Elster (1979) argues that there are games which have intuitively no solution even if game theory gives them one, that there are games with incompatible solutions, and so on.

4) Perhaps it is worth pointing out here that, given (WI) of Chapter 2, if a person we-intends to do X and so I-intends to do his part of X he must, in accordance with (34), also want to do his part of X. But at least when the person in question is aware of his want to do his part of X he must also, at least in the case of cooperative actions X, want (in a broad sense) that X be performed by the group. This can be regarded as a conceptual truth relating we-wanting to I-wanting.

CHAPTER 13

1) It might be asked whether the social division of activities requirement could be used to replace the end-serving requirement. Perhaps ends should be brought in only when explaining the division of activities?

BIBLIOGRAPHY

Abelson, R.: 1976, **Persons: A Study in Philosophical Psychology**, Macmillan, London.
Achinstein, P.: 1971, **Law and Explanation**, Oxford University Press, Oxford.
Achinstein, P.: 1975, 'Causation, Transparency, and Emphasis', **Canadian Journal of Philosophy 5**, 1-23.
Achinstein, P.: 1977a, 'What is an Explanation', **American Philosophical Quarterly 14**, 1-15.
Achinstein, P.: 1977b, 'Function statements', **Philosophy of Science 44**, 341-367.
Alston, W.: 1967, 'Wants, Actions, and Causal Explanation', in Castañeda, H. (ed.), **Intentionality, Minds, and Perception**, Wayne State University Press, Detroit.
Alston, W.: 1974, 'Conceptual Prolegomena to a Psychological Theory of Intentional Action', in Brown, S.C. (ed.), **Philosophy of Psychology**, Macmillan, London and Basingstoke.
Apostel, L.: 1978, 'The Elementary Theory of Collective Action', **Philosophica 21**, 129-157.
Arbib, M.: 1968, **Theories of Abstract Automata**, Prentice-Hall, Englewood Cliffs.
Atkinson, J.: 1964, **An Introduction to Motivation**, Van Nostrand, Princeton.
Atkinson, J. and Birch, D.: 1970, **The Dynamics of Action**, Wiley, New York.
Atkinson, J. and Raynor, J. (eds.): 1974, **Motivation and Achievement**, Winston, Washington, D.C.
Audi, R.: 1973a, 'The Concept of Wanting', **Philosophical Studies 24**, 1-21.
Audi, R.: 1973b, 'Intending', **The Journal of Philosophy 70**, 387-403.
Audi, R.: 1980a, 'Tuomela on the Explanation of Human Action', **Synthese 44**, 285-306.
Audi, R.: 1982a, 'Acting for Reasons', **American Philosophical Quarterly 19**, 25-39.
Audi, R.: 1982b, 'Believing and Affirming', **Mind 91**, 115-120.
Aulin, A.: 1982, **The Cybernetic Laws of Social Progress**, Pergamon Press, Oxford.
Aune, B.: 1977, **Reason and Action**, Reidel, Dordrecht and Boston.

Bach, K. and Harnish, R.M.: 1979, **Linguistic Communication and Speech Acts**, The MIT Press, Cambridge, Mass. and London.
Baier, A.: 1971, 'Ways and Means', **Canadian Journal of Philosophy 1**, 275-293.
Bates, F. and Harvey, C.: 1975, **The Structure of Social Systems**, Gardner Press, New York, N.Y.
Beckermann, A.: 1977, **Gründe und Ursachen**, Scriptor, Kronberg.
Belnap, N. and Steel, T.: 1976, **The Logic of Questions and Answers**, Yale University Press, New Haven.
Bennett, J.: 1976, **Linguistic Behavior**, Cambridge University Press, Cambridge.
Berkowitz, L. and Walster, E. (eds.): 1976, **Equity Theory: Toward a General Theory of Social Interaction, Advances in Experimental Social Psychology**, Vol. 9, Academic Press, New York.
Berne, E.: 1964, **Games People Play**, Penguin Books, London (Penguin-edition 1970).
Biddle, B.: 1979, **Role Theory: Expectations, Identities, and Behaviors**, Academic Press, New York, San Francisco, and London.
Birdwhistell, R.: 1970, **Kinesics and Context**, University of Pennsylvania Press, Philadelphia.
Bougon, M., Weick, K., and Binkhorst, D.: 1977, 'Cognition in Organizations: An Analysis of the Utrecht Jazz Orchestra', **Administrative Science Quarterly 22**, 606-639.
Braithwaite, R.: 1953, **Scientific Explanation: A Study of the Function of Theory, Probability and Law in Science**, Cambridge University Press, Cambridge.
Brand, M.: 1979a, 'The Fundamental Question in Action Theory', **Noûs 13**, 131-151.
Brand, M.: 1979b, 'Review of Tuomela, R. (1977), **Human Action and Its Explanation**, Reidel, Dordrecht', **The Philosophical Review 88**, 464-467.
Brandt, R., and Kim, J.: 1963, 'Wants as Explanations of Action', **The Journal of Philosophy 60**, 425-435.
Bromberger, S.: 1966, 'Why-Questions', in Colodny, R. (ed.), **Mind and Cosmos**, Pittsburgh University Press, Pittsburgh, 86-111.
Brooks, D.H.M.: 1981, 'Joint Action', **Mind 90**, 113-119.
Care, N. and Landesman, C. (eds.): 1968, **Readings in the Theory of Action**, Indiana University Press, Bloomington and London.
Cartwright, D. and Zander, A.: 1968, **Group Dynamics Research and Theory**, Harper and Row, New York.
Castañeda, H.-N.: 1975, **Thinking and Doing**, Reidel, Dordrecht and Boston.

Causey, R.: 1977, **The Unity of Science**, Reidel, Dordrecht and Boston.
Chisholm, R.: 1966, 'Freedom and Action', in Lehrer, K. (ed.), **Freedom and Determinism**, Random House, New York.
Chisholm, R.: 1970, 'The Structure of Intention', **The Journal of Philosophy 67**, 633-647.
Chisholm, R.: 1976, **Person and Object: A Metaphysical Study**, Allen and Unwin, London.
Churchland, P.: 1970, 'The Logical Character of Action-Explanations', **The Philosophical Review 79**, 214-236.
Clark, H. and Carlson, R.: 1982, 'Speech Acts and Hearers' Beliefs', in Smith, N. (ed.), **Mutual Knowledge**, Academic Press, London, 1-36.
Copp, D.: 1979, 'Collective Actions and Secondary Actions', **American Philosophical Quarterly 16**, 177-186.
Cummins, R.: 1975, 'Functional Analysis', **The Journal of Philosophy 72**, 741-765.
Dahl, R.A.: 1957, 'The Concept of Power', **Behavioral Science 2**, 201-215.
Danto, A.: 1973, **Analytical Philosophy of Action**, Cambridge University Press, Cambridge.
Davidson, D.: 1963, 'Actions, Reasons, and Causes', **The Journal of Philosophy 60**, 685-700.
Davidson, D.: 1967, 'Causal Relations', **The Journal of Philosophy 64**, 691-703.
Davidson, D.: 1970, 'Mental Events', in Foster, L. and Swanson, J. (eds.), **Experience and Theory**, University of Massachusetts Press, Amherst.
Davidson, D.: 1973, 'Freedom to Act', in Honderich, T. (ed.), **Essays in Freedom of Action**, Routledge and Kegan Paul, London.
Davidson, D.: 1974, 'Psychology as Philosophy', in Brown, S.C. (ed.), **Philosophy of Psychology**, Macmillan, London and Basingstoke.
Davidson, D.: 1980, **Essays on Actions and Events**, Oxford University Press, Oxford.
Davis, L.H.: 1979, **Theory of Action**, Prentice-Hall, Englewood Cliffs.
Dray, W.: 1957, **Laws and Explanation in History**, Oxford University Press, Oxford.
Dray, W.: 1963, 'The Historical Explanation of Actions Reconsidered', in Hook, S. (ed.), **Philosophy and History: A Symposium**, New York University Press, New York.
Dretske, F.: 1972, 'Contrastive Statements', **The Philosophical Review 81**, 411-437.

Duncan, S. and Fiske, D.: 1977, **Face-to-face Interaction: Research, Methods, and Theory**, Lawrence Erlbaum Associates, Hillsdale, N.J.
Eibl-Eibesfeldt, I.: 1974, **Love and Hate: The Natural History of Behavior Patterns**, Schocken Books, New York.
Elster, J.: 1978, **Logic and Society**, Wiley, London.
Elster, J.: 1979, **Ulysses and the Sirens**, Cambridge University Press, Cambridge.
Feferman, S.: 1974, 'Two Notes on Abstract Model Theory: I. Properties Invariant on the Range of Definable Relations Between Structures', **Fundamenta Mathematicae** 82, 153-165.
Fishburn, P.: 1981, 'Subjective Expected Utility: A Review of Normative Theories', **Theory and Decision** 13, 139-199.
Fodor, J.: 1968, **Psychological Explanation: An Introduction to the Philosophy of Psychology**, Random House, New York.
Fodor, J.: 1975, **The Language of Thought**, Crowell, New York.
Gean, W.D.: 1965, 'Reasons and Causes', **Review of Metaphysics** 19, 667-688.
Gean, W.D.: 1975, 'The Logical Connection Argument and De Re Necessity', **American Philosophical Quarterly** 12, 349-354.
Gibbard, A. and Harper, W.L.: 1978, 'Counterfactuals and Two Kinds of Expected Utility', in Hooker, C.A., Leach, J.J., and McClennen, E.F. (eds.), **Foundations and Applications of Decision Theory**, Vol. I, Reidel, Dordrecht and Boston, 125-162.
Gilbert, M.: 1981, 'Game Theory and Convention', **Synthese** 46, 41-93.
Goffman, E.: 1959, **The Presentation of Self in Everyday Life**, Anchor Books, New York.
Goldman, A.: 1970, **A Theory of Human Action**, Prentice-Hall, Englewood Cliffs.
Goldman, A.: 1972, 'Toward a Theory of Social Power', **Philosophical Studies** 23, 221-268.
Goodman, N.: 1966, **The Structure of Appearance**, Bobbs-Merrill, Indianapolis.
Green, P.E.: 1976, **Mathematical Tools for Applied Multivariate Analysis**, Academic Press, New York.
Grice, H.P.: 1957, 'Meaning', **The Philosophical Review** 66, 377-388.
Griesinger, D.W. and Livingston, J.W.: 1973, 'Toward a Model of Interpersonal Motivation in Experimental Games', **Behavioral Science** 18, 173-188.
Habermas, J.: 1981, **Theorie des kommunikativen Handelns**, Band 1, Suhrkamp, Frankfurt.
Hamburger, H.: 1973, 'N-person Prisoner's Dilemma', **Journal of Mathematical Sociology** 3, 27-48.

Hardin, R.: 1971, 'Collective Action as an Agreeable n-Prisoner's Dilemma', **Behavioral Science 16**, 472-481.
Harré, R. and Secord, P.: 1972, **The Explanation of Social Behavior**, Blackwell, Oxford.
Harsanyi, J.C.: 1962, 'Measurement of Social Power, Opportunity Costs and the Theory of Two-Person Bargaining Games', **Behavioral Science 7**, 67-80.
Harsanyi, J.C.: 1967-68, 'Games with Incomplete Information Played by "Bayesian" Players', **Management Science 14**, 159-182, 320-334, 486-502.
Harsanyi, J.C.: 1976, 'Advances in Understanding Rational Behavior', in Harsanyi, J.C., **Essays on Ethics, Social Behavior, and Scientific Explanation**, Reidel, Dordrecht and Boston, 89-117.
Harsanyi, J.C.: 1977, **Rational Behavior and Bargaining Equilibrium in Games and Social Situations**, Cambridge University Press, Cambridge.
Harsanyi, J.C.: 1979, 'Bayesian Decision Theory, Rule Utilitarianism, and Arrow's impossibility Theorem', **Erkenntnis 11**, 289-317.
Hart, H.L.A.: 1961, **The Concept of Law**, Oxford University Press, Oxford.
Heckhausen, H.: 1980, **Motivation und Handeln**, Springer, Berlin, Heidelberg, and New York.
Heider, F.: 1958, **The Psychology of Interpersonal Relations**, Wiley, New York.
Hempel, C.: 1965, **Aspects of Scientific Explanation**, The Free Press, New York.
Hintikka, J. and Tuomela, R.: 1970, 'Toward a General Theory of Auxiliary Concepts and Definability in First-Order Theories', in Hintikka, J. and Suppes, P. (eds.), **Information and Inference**, Reidel, Dordrecht.
Homans, G.C.: 1950, **The Human Group**, Routledge and Kegan Paul, London.
Homans, G.C.: 1964, **Social Behavior: Its Elementary Forms**, Routledge and Kegan Paul, London.
Homans, G.C.: 1970, 'The Relevance of Psychology to the Explanation of Social Phenomena', in Borger, R. and Cioffi, F. (eds.), **Explanation in the Behavioral Sciences**, Cambridge University Press, Cambridge.
Hornsby, J.: 1980, **Actions**, Routledge and Kegan Paul, London.
Kelley, H.H. and Thibaut, J.W.: 1978, **Interpersonal Relations: A Theory of Interdependence**, Wiley, New York.
Kemmerling, A.: 1980, 'How Many Things Must a Speaker Intend (Before He is Said to Have Meant)?', **Erkenntnis 15**, 333-341.

Kemmerling, A.: 1983, 'Utterer's Meaning Revisited', in Grandy, R. and Warner, R. (eds.), **Philosophical Grounds of Rationality: Intentions, Categories, Ends**, Oxford University Press, Oxford.
Kim, J.: 1976, 'Intention and Practical Inference', in Manninen, J. and Tuomela, R. (eds.), **Essays on Explanation and Understanding**, Reidel, Dordrecht, 249-269.
Kim, J.: 1974, 'Noncausal Connections', **Noûs 8**, 41-52.
Krajewski, W.: 1977, **Correspondence Principle and Growth of Science**, Reidel, Dordrecht and Boston.
Kuhn, T.: 1969, **The Structure of Scientific Revolutions**, Second Edition, University of Chicago Press, Chicago.
Landis, J.R.: 1971, **Sociology: Concepts and Characteristics**, Wadsworth, Belmont.
Lewis, D.: 1969, **Convention: A Philosophical Study**, Harvard University Press, Cambridge, Mass.
Lipsey, P.E.: 1979, **Introduction to Positive Economics**, Harper and Row, New York.
Luce, D. and Raiffa, H.: 1957, **Games and Decisions**, Wiley, New York.
Lukes, S.: 1973, 'Methodological Individualism Reconsidered', in Ryan, A. (ed.), **The Philosophy of Social Explanation**, Oxford University Press, 119-129.
MacCrimmon, K.R. and Messick, D.M.: 1976, 'A Framework for Social Motives', **Behavioral Science 21**, 86-100.
Madsen, K.B.: 1961, **Theories of Motivation**, Munksgaard, Copenhagen.
Madsen, K.B.: 1974, **Modern Theories of Motivation**, Munksgaard, Copenhagen.
Malcolm, N.: 1968, 'The Conceivability of Mechanism', **The Philosophical Review 77**, 45-72.
Martin, R.: 1977, **Historical Explanation: Re-enactment and Practical Inference**, Cornell University Press, Ithaca.
Maslow, A.H.: 1970, **Motivation and Personality**, Harper, New York.
Massey, G.: 1976, 'Tom, Dick, Harry and All The King's Men', **American Philosophical Quarterly 13**, 89-107.
McClintock, C.G.: 1972, 'Social Motivation - A Set of Propositions', **Behavioral Science 17**, 438-454.
Melden, A.: 1963, **Free Action**, Routledge and Kegan Paul, London.
Merton, R.K.: 1957, **Social Theory and Social Structure**, The Free Press, New York.
Morrison, D.: 1967, **Multivariate Statistical Methods**, McGraw-Hill, New York.
Nagel, E.: 1961, **The Structure of Science**, Harcourt, Brace, and World, New York.

Nagel, E.: 1977, 'Functional Explanations in Biology', **The Journal of Philosophy 74**, 280-301.

Nickles, T.: 1976, 'On Autonomy Arguments in Social Science', in Suppe, F. and Asquith, P.D. (eds.), **PSA 1976**, Vol. I, Philosophy of Science Association, East Lansing, pp. 12-24.

Niiniluoto, I. and Tuomela, R.: 1973, **Theoretical Concepts and Hypothetico-Inductive Inference**, Reidel, Dordrecht and Boston.

Nordenfelt, L.: 1974, **Explanation of Human Actions**, Philosophical Studies published by the Philosophical Society and the Department of Philosophy, University of Uppsala, No. 20.

Nozick, R.: 1974, **Anarchy, State, and Utopia**, Basic Books, New York.

Olson, M.: 1965, **The Logic of Collective Action**, Schocken Books, New York.

O'Shaughnessy, B.: 1980, **The Will: A Dual Aspect Theory**, Vols. I-II, Cambridge University Press, Cambridge.

Parsons, T. and Shils, E.A. (eds.): 1951, **Toward a General Theory of Action**, Harvard University Press, Cambridge, Mass.

Pearce, D.A.: 1979, **Translation, Reduction, and Equivalence: Some Topics in Intertheory Relations**, Doctoral Dissertation, University of Sussex.

Pearce, D.A.: 1981, 'Is There Any Theoretical Justification for a Nonstatement View of Theories?', **Synthese 46**, 1-39.

Pears, D.: 1975, **Questions in the Philosophy of Mind**, Barnes and Noble, New York.

Peters, R.: 1958, **The Concept of Motivation**, Routledge and Kegan Paul, London.

Popper, K.R.: 1963, **Conjectures and Refutations: The Growth of Scientific Knowledge**, Routledge and Kegan Paul, London.

Pruitt, D.G. and Kimmel. M.S.: 1977, 'Twenty Years of Experimental Gaming: Critique, Synthesis, and Suggestions for the Future', **Annual Review of Psychology 28**, 363-392.

Pörn, I.: 1977, **Action Theory and Social Science: Some Formal Models**, Reidel, Dordrecht and Boston.

Rawls, J.: 1971, **A Theory of Justice**, Harvard University Press, Cambridge, Mass.

Raz, J. (ed.): 1978, **Practical Reasoning**, Oxford University Press, Oxford.

Riker, W.H. and Ordeshook, P.C.: 1973, **An Introduction to Positive Political Theory**, Prentice-Hall, Englewood Cliffs.

Rosenberg, J.: 1980a, **One World and Our Knowledge of It**, Reidel, Dordrecht, Boston, and London.

Rosenberg, J.: 1980b, 'Coupling, Retheoretization, and the Correspondence Principle', **Synthese 45**, 351-462.

Rozeboom, W.: 1963, 'The Factual Content of Theoretical Concepts', in Feigl, H. and Maxwell, G. (eds.), **Minnesota Studies in the Philosophy of Science III**, University of Minnesota Press, Minneapolis, 273-357.
Ryle, G.: 1949, **The Concept of Mind**, Hutchinson, London.
Salomaa, A.: 1973, **Formal Languages**, Academic Press, New York.
Schank, R. and Abelson, R.: 1977, **Scripts, Plans, Goals, and Understanding**, Lawrence Erlbaum Associates, Hillsdale, N.J.
Scheff, R.: 1967, 'Toward a Sociological Model of Consensus', **American Sociological Review 32**, 32-46.
Schelling, R.: 1960, **The Strategy of Conflict**, Harvard University Press, Cambridge, Mass.
Schiffer, S.: 1972, **Meaning**, Oxford University Press, Oxford.
Searle, J.: 1981, 'Intentionality and Method', **The Journal of Philosophy 78**, 720-733.
Secord, P. and Backman, C.: 1974, **Social Psychology**, 2nd ed., McGraw-Hill, New York.
Sellars, W.: 1956, 'Empiricism and the Philosophy of Mind', in Feigl, H. and Scriven, M. (eds.), **Minnesota Studies in the Philosophy of Science I**, University of Minnesota Press, Minneapolis, 253-329.
Sellars, W.: 1963, **Science, Perception, and Reality**, Routledge and Kegan Paul, London.
Sellars, W.: 1966, 'Fatalism and Determinism', in Lehrer, K. (ed.), **Freedom and Determinism**, Random House, New York, 141-202.
Sellars, W.: 1968, **Science and Metaphysics**, Routledge and Kegan Paul, London.
Sellars, W.: 1973, 'Actions and Events', **Noûs 7**, 179-202.
Sellars, W.: 1974, **Essays in Philosophy and Its History**, Reidel, Dordrecht and Boston.
Sen, A.: 1977, 'Non-Linear Social Welfare Functions: A Reply to Professor Harsanyi', in Butts, R.E. and Hintikka, J. (eds.), **Foundational Problems in the Special Sciences**, Reidel, Dordrect and Boston, 297-302.
Shaffer, J.: 1968, **Philosophy of Mind**, Prentice-Hall, Englewood Cliffs.
Shaw, M.E.: 1981, **Group Dynamics: The Psychology of Small Group Behavior**, 3rd ed., McGraw-Hill, New York.
Sherwood, M.: 1969, **The Logic of Explanation in Psychoanalysis**, Academic Press, New York.
Shwayder, D.: 1965, **The Stratification of Behaviour**, Routledge and Kegan Paul, London.
Sneed, J.D.: 1971, **The Logical Structure of Mathematical Physics**, Reidel, Dordrecht.

Stegmüller, W.: 1969, **Wissenschaftliche Erklärung und Begründung: Probleme und Resultate der Wissenschaftstheorie und Analytischen Philosophie**, Band I, Springer, Berlin, Heidelberg, and New York.
Stegmüller, W.: 1976, **The Structure and Dynamics of Scientific Theories**, Springer, Berlin, Heidelberg, and New York.
Stenius, E.: 1972, **Critical Essays, Acta Philosophica Fennica 25**, North-Holland, Amsterdam.
Stoutland, F.: 1975, 'von Wright's Theory of Action', in Schilpp, P. (ed.), **The Philosophy of Georg Henrik von Wright**, The Library of Living Philosophers, Open Court, LaSalle.
Stoutland, F.: 1976a, 'The Causal Theory of Action', in Manninen, J. and Tuomela, R. (eds.), **Essays on Explanation and Understanding**, Reidel, Dordrecht and Boston.
Stoutland, F.: 1976b, 'The Causation of Behavior', in Hintikka, J. (ed.), **Essays on Wittgenstein in Honour of G.H. von Wright, Acta Philosophica Fennica 28**, North-Holland, Amsterdam, 286-325.
Swensen, C.: 1973, **Introduction to Interpersonal Relations**, Scott, Foresman and Company, Glenview, Ill.
Sztompka, P.: 1974, **System and Function: Toward a Theory of Society**, Academic Press, New York.
Taylor, C.: 1964, **The Explanation of Behaviour**, Routledge and Kegan Paul, London.
Taylor, C.: 1970a, 'Explaining Actions', **Inquiry 13**, 54-89.
Taylor, C.: 1970b, 'The Explanation of Purposive Behaviour', in Borger, R. and Cioffi, F. (eds.), **Explanation in the Behavioural Sciences**, Cambridge University Press, Cambridge, 49-79.
Taylor, R.: 1966, **Action and Purpose**, Prentice-Hall, Englewood Cliffs.
Thalberg, I.: 1976, 'How Does Agent Causality Work', in Brand, M. and Walton, D. (eds.), **Action Theory**, Reidel, Dordrecht and Boston, 213-238.
Thibaut, J.W. and Kelley, H.H.: 1959, **The Social Psychology of Groups**, Wiley, New York.
Thomson, J.: 1977, **Acts and Other Events**, Cornell University Press, Ithaca.
Tichy, P.: 1976, 'Verisimilitude Redefined', **British Journal for the Philosophy of Science 27**, 25-42.
Tuomela, R.: 1972, 'Deductive Explanation of Scientific Laws', **Journal of Philosophical Logic 1**, 369-392.
Tuomela, R.: 1973, **Theoretical Concepts**, Springer, Vienna and New York.

Tuomela, R.: 1976a, 'Causes and Deductive Explanation', in Michalos, A.C. and Cohen, R.S. (eds.), **PSA 1974**, Boston Studies in the Philosophy of Science, Vol. 32, Reidel, Dordrecht and Boston, 325-360.
Tuomela, R.: 1976b, 'Morgan on Deductive Explanation: A Rejoinder', **Journal of Philosophical Logic 5**, 527-543.
Tuomela, R.: 1977, **Human Action and Its Explanation: A Study on the Philosophical Foundations of Psychology**, Reidel, Dordrecht and Boston.
Tuomela, R.: 1978, 'Theory-Distance and Verisimilitude', **Synthese 38**, 213-246.
Tuomela, R.: 1979, 'Scientific Change and Approximation', in Niiniluoto, I. and Tuomela, R. (eds.), **The Logic and Epistemology of Scientific Change**, Acta Philosophica Fennica 30, North-Holland, Amsterdam, 265-297.
Tuomela, R.: 1980a, 'Explaining Explaining', Erkenntnis 15, 211-243.
Tuomela, R.: 1980b, **Metaphysical versus Internal Realism**, Reports from the Department of Philosophy, University of Helsinki, No. 8.
Tuomela, R.: 1980c, 'Analogy and Distance', **Zeitschrift für Allgemeine Wissenschaftstheorie 11**, 276-291.
Tuomela, R.: 1981, 'Inductive Explanation', **Synthese 48**, 257-294.
Tuomela, R.: 1982, **Social Control and Its Components**, Research Reports, Department of Social Psychology, University of Helsinki, No. 1.
Tuomela, R.: 1983, 'Social Action, Systems Theory, and Scientific Progress', paper presented at the VII International Congress for Logic, Methodology and Philosophy of Science (Salzburg, 1983); forthcoming in its proceedings.
Tuomela, R.: 1984, **Science, Action, and Reality: The Philosophical Foundations of the Scientific World-View**, Reidel, forthcoming.
Turner, J.H.: 1978, **The Structure of Sociological Theory**, The Dorsey Press, Homewood, Ill.
Turner, M.: 1971, **Realism and the Explanation of Behavior**, Appleton-Century-Crofts, New York.
Tversky, A.: 1975, 'A Critique of Expected Utility Theory: Descriptive and Normative Considerations', **Erkenntnis 9**, 163-174.
Ullmann-Margalit, E.: 1976, **The Emergence of Norms**, Oxford University Press, Oxford.
Ullmann-Margalit, E.: 1978, 'Invisible-Hand Explanations', **Synthese 39**, 263-291.

Weber, M.: 1947, **The Theory of Social and Economic Organization,** Oxford University Press, New York.
Wilson, G.M: 1980, **The Intentionality of Human Action,** **Acta Philosophica Fennica 31,** Nos. 2-3, North-Holland, Amsterdam.
Wilson, K.V. and Bixenstine, V.E.: 1962, 'Forms of Social Control in Two-Person, Two-Choice Games', **Behavioral Science 7,** 92-102.
Woodfield, A.: 1976, **Teleology,** Cambridge University Press, Cambridge.
von Wright, G.H.: 1968, **An Essay in Deontic Logic and the General Theory of Action,** Acta Philophica Fennica 21, North-Holland, Amsterdam.
von Wright, G.H: 1971, **Explanation and Understanding,** Cornell University Press, Ithaca.
von Wright, G.H.: 1974, **Causality and Determinism,** Columbia University Press, New York and London.
von Wright, G.H.: 1976, 'Replies', in Manninen, J. and Tuomela, R. (eds.), **Essays on Explanation and Understanding,** Reidel, Dordrecht and Boston, 371-413.
von Wright, G.H.: 1980, **Freedom and Determinism,** Acta Philosophica Fennica 31, No. 1, North-Holland, Amsterdam.
Wright, L.: 1976, **Teleological Explanations,** University of California Press, Berkeley.
Zander, A.: 1971, **Motives and Goals in Groups,** Academic Press, New York.

NAME INDEX

Abelson, R. 57, 69-70, 74-75, 86, 385-387, 399, 497
Achinstein, P. 329, 336, 430-431
Allport, G. 58
Alston, W. 56-57, 59, 62
Apostel, L.117
Arbib, M. 178-181
Atkinson, J. 402, 405, 409-411, 414
Audi, R. 56, 76, 211, 374, 405, 423, 481
Aulin, A. 484
Aune, B. 71, 203, 478
Austin, J. 56
Bach, K. 250, 263, 283, 314-316, 327
Backman, C. 250
Baier, A. 162
Bandura, A. 57
Bates, F. 266
Beckermann, A. 77
Belnap, N. 317, 341
Bennett, J. 197, 329, 494
Berkowitz, L. 413
Berne, E. 383
Beth, E. 471
Biddle, B. 250
Binkhorst, D. 488
Birch, D. 402, 410-411
Birdwhistell, R. 83, 379
Bixenstine, V. 291
Blaw, P. 311
Bougon, M. 488
Braithwaite, R. 443
Brand, M. 91, 483
Brandt, R. 56, 73
Bromberger, S. 335-336
Brooks, D.H.M. 115, 491-492
Carlson, R. 329
Cartwright, D. 262-265, 273, 278
Castañeda, H.-N. 203, 478
Causey, R. 462

Chisholm, R. 57, 61, 64, 75-76, 338
Churchland, P. 56, 77
Clark, H. 329
Copp, D. 184, 186-188
Craig, W. 341, 467
Cummins, R. 432-433
Dahl, R.A. 276-277
Danto, A. 56, 77
Davidson, D. 45, 56, 59, 71, 73-75, 77-79, 89, 93, 390, 486
Davis, L.H. 85, 107, 480-481
Dewey, J. 207
Dray, W. 58, 69, 74, 77
Duncan, S. 190, 280
Eibl-Eibesfeldt, I. 392, 479
Elster, J. 422, 453-454, 498
Feferman, S. 467-468, 470
Fishburn, P. 479
Fiske, D. 190, 280
Fodor, J. 56-57
Freud, S. 57
Gean, W.D. 73-75, 77, 93
Gibbard, A. 404, 488
Gilbert, M. 199
Goffman, E. 379, 384
Goldman, A. 56, 59, 61, 65, 75, 77, 95, 99, 106, 109, 159-164, 167, 314
Goodman, N. 142
Green, P.E. 300
Grice, H.P. 197, 282, 314
Griesinger, D.W. 46
Habermas, J. 13, 375, 476-477, 491, 496-497
Hamburger, H. 490
Hardin, R. 485
Harnish, R.M. 250, 263, 283, 314-316, 327
Harper, W.L. 404, 488
Harré, R. 379-380
Harsanyi, J.C. 40-43, 50, 223, 225-227, 234-235, 239, 277-278, 420-421
Hart, H.L.A. 237, 239
Harvey, C. 266
Heckhausen, H. 402, 410-411, 428
Heider, F. 57
Hempel, C. 73, 77, 321, 430-431
Hintikka, J. 258
Homans, G.C. 311, 412, 493
Hornsby, J. 485

Kant, I. 2
Kelley, H.H. 143, 291, 298-299, 302-305, 308, 392, 396-398, 493
Kemmerling, A. 495-496
Kim, J. 56, 69, 73, 82, 488
Kimmel, M.S. 490
Krajewski, W. 463
Kuhn, T. 335-336, 494
Landis, J.R. 263
Lewin, K. 57, 410
Lewis, D. 197-199, 205, 208-209, 212-213, 225, 230-231, 233, 348
Lipsey, P.E. 151
Livingston, J.W. 46
Luce, D. 204, 221, 225, 227-228, 416-418
Lukes, S. 477
MacCrimmon, K.R. 46, 51
Madsen, K.B. 57-58
Malcolm, N. 57
Martin, R. 58, 68
Marx, K. 465
Maslow, A.H. 58, 267
Massey, G. 115, 480
McClintock, C.G. 392-393
Mead, G.H. 207
Melden, A. 57, 69, 71-72, 75, 84
Merton, R. 114, 439
Messick, D.M. 46, 51
Moore, G.E. 58, 106
Morrison, D. 296
Nagel, E. 430-431, 443
Nickles, T. 458
Niiniluoto, I. 258, 332
Nordenfelt, L. 68
Nozick, R. 450, 473
Olson, M. 14, 150-158, 473, 475, 484-485
Ordeshook, P.C. 485
O'Shaughnessy, B. 482-483
Parsons, T. 57
Pearce, D.A. 467, 469-470
Pears, D. 77
Peters, R. 69
Popper, K.R. 459
Pruitt, D.G. 490
Pörn, I. 55, 170-171, 175-176, 193, 197, 270, 276, 282
Raiffa, H. 204, 221, 225, 227-228, 416-418
Rawls, J. 42
Raynor, J. 402, 410

Raz, J. 203, 243, 369, 489
Riker, W.H. 485
Rosenberg, J. 25, 33, 460-461
Rozeboom, W. 20
Ryle, G. 71-72, 74
Salomaa, A. 192, 194
Schank, R. 86, 385-387, 399, 497
Scheff, T. 197, 207, 212
Schelling, T. 197, 208
Schiffer, S. 197, 205
Searle, J. 315, 484
Secord, P. 250, 379-380
Sellars, W. 2-5, 9, 17-19, 23, 28, 30-35, 37-39, 43-44, 56, 71, 74-75, 195, 243, 245, 459-461, 478
Sen, A. 41
Shaffer, J. 56
Shaw, M.E. 364, 414
Sherwood, M. 57
Shwayder, D. 197, 230-231, 233
Simon, H. 426
Skinner, B. 338
Sneed, J.D. 336, 470
Steel, T. 317, 341
Stegmüller, W. 73, 336
Stenius, E. 247
Stoutland, F. 57-58, 60-61, 74-76, 78, 89
Swensen, C. 83, 329, 398
Sztompka, P. 445, 475
Taylor, C. 58, 74, 361, 444
Taylor, R. 57, 64, 72, 75, 77, 84
Thalberg, I. 65
Thibaut, J.W. 143, 291, 298-299, 302-305, 308, 392, 396-398, 493
Thomson, J. 164, 166
Tichy, P. 257
Tolman, E. 57
Tuomela, R. 2-3, 13, 19-21, 24, 26-27, 30, 33, 45, 56-58, 62, 67, 69, 71-77, 79-80, 82-85, 87, 89-106, 108-109, 124, 139-140, 159, 164-168, 170, 175-176, 192, 195, 200-202, 218, 250-251, 253, 255-256, 258, 274, 282, 303, 310, 314, 321-322, 331-335, 337-341, 344, 350, 352-354, 358-361, 365-366, 368-370, 373, 377, 380, 390, 399, 401-405, 423, 427, 448, 458, 460-463, 469, 471-473, 476-477, 481, 483-484, 487, 495, 497-498
Turner, J.H. 57, 311, 475
Tversky, A. 41, 422
Ullmann-Margalit, E. 238-240, 243, 420, 450-451, 473

Walster, E. 413
Weber, M. 133, 493
Weick, K. 488
Wilson, G.M. 73, 76, 89, 481-482
Wilson, K.V. 291
Woodfield, A. 75-76, 357, 430, 441, 443
von Wright, G.H. 57-58, 66-70, 74-75, 77, 82, 89, 172, 338, 375-377, 483
Wright, L. 361-362, 365, 430-432, 444
Zander, A. 262-265, 273, 278, 410, 413-414, 428

SUBJECT INDEX

achievement motivation 409-412
acting on a conduct plan 76, 140, 168, 360, 365ff.
action
    as achievement 58
    as an event sequence 84
    consequence of 58
    goal directed ((**IGA**), goal directed$_g$, (**OT**)) 361, 444
    habitual 86
    intentional 59ff.
    logical opportunity of 58
    multi-agent 55, 94
    result of 58
    single-agent 55, 94
    social 111ff.
    see action token, action type, action theory, action-explanation, action generation, social action
action-explanation
    see explanation
action-function 430ff.
action generation 94-110, 159-196
    A-model of 175
    B1-model of 175
    B2-model of 176
    by-relation (By) 159, 164ff., 283
    causal (C,$\triangleright\!\!\rightarrow$) 98, 112
    conceptual (R_2,$\triangleright_2$) 112, 167, 177
        conventional 160
        simple 160
    conceptual purposive ($\triangleright_2$) 97ff., 169
    constitution-relation (**CON***) 188
    direct factual (R_1) 167
    generated vs. non-generated action 101
    indirect factual (IG) 168, 172ff., 182, 184-185
    indirect purposive (IG*, $\triangleright\!\!\rightarrow$) 166, 168-169, 184-185
    indirect purposive causal ($\triangleright\!\!\rightarrow$) 97ff., 169
    indirect purposive probabilistic ($\triangleright_r$) 487
    principle (PG) 104
    probabilistic 176

action propensity 401
action repertoire 105ff.
    see power
action theory 10, 55-110
    agency theory 56-58, 64-66
    hermeneutic theory 56-58, 66-71
    factual 55
    mental cause theory 56-63, 71-78
    normative 55
    philosophical 55
    purposive-causal theory 79-110
action token, u, v 59, 84
    action token$_1$ 102-103
    action token in relation to another person 270
    action token making reference to another person 270
    action token making opaque reference to another person 308
    generation 104, 167-168, 177, 182
    goal-directed$_g$ 365
    intentionally goal-directed 361
    performed intentionally in order to achieve a goal 361
    social action token$_1$ 130
    social action token$_2$ 136
    u = <v,...,b,...,r> 84
action type, X, X_i 59, 94-105, 122ff.
    basic single-agent 97
    basic social 123
    bodily single-agent 102
    bodily social 129
    complex single-agent 105
    complex social 136
    compound basic single-agent 98
    compound basic social 128
    compound bodily single-agent 102
    compound bodily social 129
    compound single-agent 104
    compound social 134
    epistemic vs. non-epistemic 95
    simple vs. compound 94
advantage, A_i 151
affecting 271ff.
    weak 271
    indirect and weak 272
agency (framework of) 2
agency theory, (A), (AS) 64-66
aggression 48ff.
aiming at 64, 67, 480

akrasia 43, 203, 212
altruism 48ff.
analogy 255ff.
    between λ_1 and λ_2 255
    between e_1 and e_2 255
    between CS_1 and CS_2 256
answering (why p) 328
anticipated consequence of action 405ff.
appropriateness of action 443ff.
    conduciveness 443-444
    persistence 443-444
    plasticity 443-444
approximation 466
asking (why p) 327
aspiration level 396
average, μ_h 291-292
automaton 170ff.
    see finite automaton
belief, B 90, 205ff.
    detachment rule for beliefs 213
bodily behavior involved in action, (b) 60ff.
cascade connection of automata (the cascade of M_1 and M_2 with connection K) 180ff.
    repeated 180-181
cause
    causal conditional 98ff.
    causal generation 133
    causal verb 165-167
    causation $C(e_1,e_2)$ 167
    purposive causation 79ff.
    see action generation, causal generation
causal generation 112, 133, 162, 164
circumstances, C 145-146
closed vs. open systems 400-401
coalition formation 422
collective (social collective) 114, 116ff., 144ff.
collective good 191
collective's action 114, 144-150
column-effect parameter, τ_{jh} 292
communicative control 282
competition 48ff., 191
conation 90, 103
conceptual functionalism 19ff.
conceptual individualism 25ff.
concordance (four types of) 302-303
conditional probability 403-404

conduct plan 85ff., 139ff.
    social 139-140, 195-196
conflict 191
conforming action 230, 233
consensus 207
consummatory force 410
context, C 333
control 190
    see social control
convention 199ff.
conventional action 230, 233
conventional (or conceptual) generation 112, 160, 162, 166
cooperation 48ff., 136, 191
cooperative goal 498
coordination 136, 190
coordination problem 199
corrected social theory, S* 460
corrective explanation 461ff.
    corrective explanation$_1$, (I) 461
    corrective explanation$_2$, (II) 462
correspondence rule 457ff.
    identity as correspondence rule 458
    correspondence rule, C 461
correspondence rule account of explanation 459
cost, C 151
counterpart predicate 459
counterpart relation 255ff.
covert interdependence patterns 307
    basis of dependence 307
    degree of correspondence 307
    degree of dependence 307
    mutuality of dependence 307
crowd 263
deductive reason-giving explanation, $\varepsilon(E, Tc)$ 340
degree of intentionality of action X, I(X) 147-150
descriptive-prescriptive dichotomy 1, 7
destruction 48ff.
disposition 250-253
    factual basis of 251
distance 149, 253ff.
    measures of, d, d, δ 254ff.
division of tasks and activities 190
egalitarian group 149
egalitarianism 51
eliminative explanation 458-459

emphasis 329-333
    emphasis sentence 330
end 357, 441
    schema (E) 441
epistemic concept 269
equilibrium 199
    proper 199
    coordination equilibrium 199
equity theory 412
evolutionary theory-succession 460
exchange 191, 412
expected utility, EU, GEU 41, 400, 408-409
explanandum 323
explanandum-content 323
explanation
    deductive reason-giving, ε 322, 340
    dynamic 351, 388ff.
    explanandum 323
    explanandum content 323
    explanatory argument (E-argument) 322-323, 338ff.
    explanatory individualism 455ff.
    explanatory question 313, 324ff.
    explanatory reason 369
    functional 446ff.
    inductive, ρ 323, 339, 343
    inductive-probabilistic 343, 427ff.
    intentional-teleological 357ff.
    invisible hand 448-454
    of social action 345ff., theses (ST1), (ST2), (ST3), (ST4) 378
    of social laws 461ff.
    prospect relativity of 410
    purposive-causal 365-368
    reason 368-378
    scientific explaining 314
    scientific explanation 326
    teleological 357ff.
    see corrective explanation, correspondence rule account, scientific explanatory answer
explanatory answer 314
    see scientific explanatory answer
explanatory individualism 455-461
    thesis (EI) 455
explanatory power 460, 472
explanatory question 313
    complete 326

explanatory reason, f 330ff.
extrinsic aim 59
face-to-face group 263
finite automaton (machine), M 170ff.
    deterministic generalized sequential 170
    without outputs 171
    Mealy automaton 170-171
    sequential Moore machine 171
formal grammar 192ff.
formal organization 192
fraction for A_i of total group gain, F_i 151
frame of reference 220
function 430ff.
    explanation doctrine 430-432
    goal doctrine 430-432
    good-consequence doctrine 430-432
    schemas (**F**) 432, (**F_s**) 434, (**F_s^***) 438, (**F_s^{**}**) 445
functional explanation 446ff.
    schemas (**FE**) and (**FE'**) 447-448
    of social structures and patterns 474
gain 393ff., 412
    joint 393
    one's own 393
    other's 393
    relative 393
gain of A_i, V_i 151
game-theoretic explanation of social action 416ff.
game theory 221-229
    and practical inference 221ff.
    games with complete information 228-229
    games with identical interests 221ff.
    games with incomplete information 229, 234
    games with mixed interests 222ff.
    games with opposite interests 221ff.
    games with perfect information 228
general logic 467
general motive 409
generalized belief 130-131
given (or original) utility 389
goal 119, 362-365
    schema (**G**) 363
    externalist view 362
    internalist view 362
goal-directed$_g$ behavior 365
Gricean mechanism 282

group interest 150
    see we-intention
group motivation 413ff.
    see we-intention
group pressure 220
group probability 389ff.
group utility 389ff.
Harsanyi's rationality criterion 225-227
hermeneutic theory (**H**), (**HS**) 66-71
hermeneutic pattern of understanding 334
holistic social concept 17ff.
illocutionary intention 494
incentive value, I_s 409
indices of correspondence, IC, corr_t^{12}, corr_r^{12}, corr_c^{12} 299ff.
individualistic theory, T 459ff.
inductive explanation, ρ 343
inductive-probabilistic explanation 427
initial action tendency 410
input alphabet (set), I 170
instigating force 410
intended function 442
intention (intending), (to perform X), I 80ff., 106ff., 423, 482
    act-relational 76, 83, 481
    conditional 212ff., 222
    deconditionalization of 212, 347
    illocutionary 494-496
    reflexive 494-496
intentional social action 138ff.
    fully 139
    partially 139
intentional social action token$_2$ 139
intentional goal-directed action 361
    see (**IGA**)
intentional-teleological explanation 358-360
    intentional-teleological scientific explanatory answer v_t,
    schema (**ITE**) 358
interaction 269ff.
    see social interaction
interaction-effect parameter, μ_{ijh} 293
intrinsic aim 59
invisible hand explanation 448-454
    schema (**IHE**) 452
    of social structures and patterns 473
joint social action 113ff.
    principles (a)-(d) 113-116
latent function 440

level of achieving collective good, T 151
lexicographic preferences 479
Lindenmayer grammar 193-194
linguistic token-statement, u, v 323
manner of action 127, 190
maximization of expected utility 199ff., 411ff.
    conditional sense 411-412
mental cause theory (**MC**), (**MCS**) 58-63, 71-78
mob action 130-131
motivational force 404-405
mutual belief 17, 35, 111, 120-121, 126-127, 205-212
    idealized version (**MB**) 206
    mutual wh-belief 126
    mutual beliefs underlying communication 329
    weakened versions 208ff.
natural-normative description 6
necessary connection 74-75
    de dicto 75
non-Archimedean preferences 478-479
non-conforming action 231ff.
non-epistemic concept 269
normal condition 203
normative explanation 374ff.
normative organization 195
norm of obligation 237
norm-violating action 231ff.
objective function 436, 438
occurrence, occ 143
OL-system 194-195
Olson's argument 150ff.
ontological individualism, principles (**PE**), (**R**) 23-24
operative (or effective) utility 389
operative member of a collective 145-146
original social predicate set, η_s^o 459
output alphabet (set), O 170
output function, ϕ 170
paradigm, P 314ff.
parallel connection of automata 179
Pareto optimality 152
performance 58ff., 80
personal motivation 414
    see utility
PD-norm (prisoner's dilemma) 238-240
potency 405
power 276ff.
    amount 277

base 276
extension 277
means 276-277
scope 277
power (ability) 96-97, 105-110
    to do a simple action 105ff.
    to do a compound action 105ff.
    joint 138
practical inference 197ff.
    social 197
practical syllogism, (PS) 68-69
presupposition$_1$ 317
    complete 318
presupposition$_2$ 318
    complete 318
prisoner's dilemma (PD) situation (game) 152, 221ff.
    2-person PD 224-225, 490-491
    m-person PD 224-225, 490-491
probability of a conditional 403-404
prospect (lottery), L 40, 408
prospect-relativity of explanation 410
proximate explanation 345ff.
    types of proximate explanation 351ff.
proxying (representing) 112-113, 164, 191
purposive-causal explanation 365-368
    purposive-causal scientific explanatory answer 367-368
purposive-causal theory of action (PC), (PCS) 79-110
purposive causation 87, 97ff.
purposive generation 87, 97ff., 183
    relation, S* 122
    (indirect) purposive generation, IG*, $\triangleright\!\!\!\rightarrow$, $\triangleright\!\!\!\rightarrow$ 97ff., 166, 168-169, 184-185
    (indirect) probabilistic, $\triangleright\!\!\!\rightarrow_r$ 487
    conceptual, $\triangleright\!\!\!\rightarrow_2$ 97ff., 169
    see action generation
range of influence 275
rationality postulate 389
reason for acting 368ff.
    direct 369
    external 191, 376
    guiding 369
    indirect 369
    internal 191, 379
    joint 371
reason-explanation 368-378
reinterpretation 457, 459

relevance class, R 331-333, 381
replicative justification of beliefs 212ff.
restriction class (role-category) 247
resultant force 401
revolutionary theory-succession 460
rewriting rule (production rule) 193ff.
risky situation 400
ritual 191
role of predicates 466
row effect parameter, α_{ih} 292
Rylean language 18ff.
scientia mensura 2, 5
scientific explaining 314
    see explanation
scientific explanation 326
    see explanation
scientific explanatory (se) answer 320, 323
    complete 322
    in the case of functional explanation 447
    in the case of invisible hand explanation 452
    in the case of reason-explanation 377
    intentional-teleological 358
    purposive-causal 367-368
scientific querying 324
scientific realism 1ff.
scientific understanding 333
    see understanding
self-interest 48ff.
self-sacrifice 48ff.
series connection of automata 179
set of internal states, S 170
size of group, S_g 151
similarity of social roles 252ff.
situation, C 314ff.
skill 127, 189-190
social action
    action in relation to another person 270
    action (indirectly and weakly) affecting another person 272
    ceremonial 191
    classification of social action types 122ff.
        basic 123
        bodily 129
        complex 136
        compound 134
        compound basic 128
        compound bodily 129

communicative 12, 375, 496-497
conformative (class S_S) 233
conjunctive 143
controlled 305
    differentially controlled 305
    jointly controlled 305
    unilaterally controlled 305
    with shared control 305
conventional (class S_C) 233
disjunctive 143
epistemic vs. non-epistemic 95
functional 430ff.
goal-directed 362, 365
intentional (in the full blown sense) 119ff.
intentionally controlled 276
interaction 278ff.
joint action 113ff., 141
making reference to another agent (class S_1) 229
maximizing expected utility 199ff.
mereology and social action 141ff.
multi-agent action 1, 12, 55, 62, 111
partly intentional 148-149
probabilistically controlled 274
rationalizable by means of replication (class S_{RE}) 233
rationalizable by means of (SA_1) (class S_2) 229
rationalizable by means of (SA_1^*) (class S_2^*) 230
rationalizable by means of (SA_1') (class S_3) 233
rationalizable by means of ($SA_1'^*$) (class S_3^*) 233
rule referring (class S_{RU}) 233
scope of social action 229ff.
social exchange 308, 412
social action token$_1$ (class $S_1^\dagger$) 130, 229
social action token$_2$ (class $S_1^{\dagger*}$) 136, 229
social practical reasoning and social action 212ff.
speech act 326-329
strategic interaction 55, 221ff., 416ff.
strict sense (multi-agent action) 1
turn taking 190
wide sense 1
social affiliation 410
social community 266
social control 190, 273ff.
    covert 191
    overt 269, 284
    over another person 273, 276
    probabilistic control over another person 274

    full absolute control over one's own utilities 287
    full absolute control over the other person's utilities 288
    mere conditional control over a) one's own or b) the other
        one's utilities 289, 290
    linear components of control 291ff.
        2-person case 293
        3-person case 294
        m-person case 294-295
social group 262ff.
social interaction 269ff.
    classes of interaction behaviors, K_i^A, K_i^B, K_i^{AB}, $i=1,\ldots,10$
        278-282
    covert social interaction 284ff.
    $interaction_i$, $i=1,\ldots,10$ 279-281
    overt social interaction 278-283
    explanatory concepts of 308ff.
    see social action
social law 350-351
social loop belief 197
social norm 231, 236-246
    prescriptiveness 236ff.
    pressure 236ff.
    uniformity of relevant action 236ff.
social organization 266
social pattern governed behavior 137
social position 266
social power motive 410
social (propositional) attitude 132-133
social role 246ff.
    factual basis of 259
social rule 229ff.
social status 267
social structure 262-268
social theory, S 459
social utility loop 395
social wayward causal chain 366
social welfare 42ff.
socialese (S1) 29-30
socialese* (S2) 29-30
society 266
style 378ff.
    emotive 383
    cognitive 383
subjective function 435, 438
teleological explanation 357ff.
tendency to avoid failure, T_f 409

tendency to succeed, T_s 409
total group gain, V_g 151
total resultant force (action tendency), T 409
transformation function for utilities 392ff.
transition function, f 170
translation, 462ff.
    general notion of translation (TR) 469
turn taking 190, 397-398
understanding 333-338
    scientific understanding 333
    P-understandable scientific explanatory answer in C 333, 385
    understanding action 335, 384-387
    reason pattern 334
    hermeneutic pattern 334
Uniform Reduction Theorem (**URT**) 470
utility 40ff.
    given (or original) 389
    operative (or effective) 389
    personal 41ff.
    social ("moral"), w 41ff.
    other-regarding 390
utility for A from doing X, $u^A(x)$ 287ff.
utility for A from his doing X_i when B does Y_j, $u^A(X_i/Y_j)$ 289ff.
valence 404
want (wanting) 60-63, 81-82, 411
wayward causal chain 61, 75-76, 93, 366
we-attitude 111
we-belief (we-expectation) 132
we-intention 31ff., 111ff.
    and conceptual individualism 34ff., 265-266
    and game theory 416ff.
    and intentional social action 139
    and morality 38-39
    and mutual belief 36, 126
    and social practical reasoning 31, 215ff.
    as internalization of a group 31
    as satisfying schemas (**W1**) and (**W2**) 33-34
    defined (schema (**WI**)) 35
    proper (one based on same combination) 54
    of self-interest, altruism and cooperation 54, 419
    vs. (mere) I-intention 33
    vs. shared intention 32
    vs. social utility 43ff., 52ff.
    vs. underlying wants 52-54
we-want (we-proattitude) 131-132

we-willing 91-92
willing (trying) 82-85
ε-argument 338ff.
ρ-argument 338ff.

INDEX OF SYMBOLS, DEFINITIONS, AND THESES

(A)	agency theory (of intentional single-agent action) 64
(AS)	agency theory (of intentional multi-agent action) 65
(C)	conjecture on social, viz. multi-agent action and the components of social control 306
(C1)	conjecture on the scope of social action 136
(C2)	conjecture on the scope of social action 137
(C3)	conjecture on the scope of joint action power 141
(C4)	conjecture on the scope of joint action power 141
(CF)	Conceptual Functionalism 20
(CI)	Conceptual Individualism 25
(CON)	constitution relation 186-187
(CON*)	constitution relation (automata-theoretic version) 188
(E)	end (of collective S) 441
(EI)	explanatory individualism 455
(EU)	expected utility 41
(F)	function (Cummins' analysis) 432
(F_s)	function (of agents to do X) 434
(F_s^*)	function (of agents to do X) 438
(F_s^{**})	function (of A_i to do X_i) 445
(FE)	scientific explanatory answer within functional explanation, v_f
(G)	goal (of S) 363, 443
(GB)	goal-directed$_g$ behavior 365
(GSA_i)	game-theoretic generalization of SA_i 227
(H)	hermeneutic theory (of intentional single-agent action) 67
(HS)	hermeneutic theory (of intentional multi-agent action) 70
(I)	corrective explanation$_1$ 461
(II)	corrective explanation$_2$ 462
(IGA)	action token performed intentionally to achieve a goal 361
(IHE)	scientific explanatory answer within invisible hand explanation, v_{ih} 452
(IP)	indirect power 272
(IT)	I-intention transferral schema 356
(ITE)	intentional-teleological scientific explanatory answer, v_t 358

(MB)	mutual belief 206	
(MC)	mental cause theory (of intentional single-agent action) 60	
(MCS)	mental cause theory (of intentional multi-agent action) 63	
(OT)	S does X in order to bring about Y 444	
(PC)	purposive-causal theory (of intentional single-agent action) 86	
(PCE)	purposive-causal scientific explanatory answer, v_{pc} 367	
(PCS)	purposive-causal theory (of intentional multi-agent action) 91	
(PE)	Principle of Expression 24	
(PG)	action generation principle 104	
(PR_i)	practical inference schema for social action 217	
(PR_1)	practical inference schema for social action 346	
(PS)	single practical syllogism 68	
(R)	ontological reduction principle 23	
(R)	(direct) reason, ρ 369	
(RE)	scientific explanatory answer in reason-explanation, v_r 377	
(RPR)	joint reason, ρ_{we} 373	
(S)	schema of practical inference for we-intention (cf.(W1)) 121	
(S)	schema of practical inference relating we-intention and I-intention (cf.(W1)) 355	
(SA_1)	schema of practical inference for a coordination game 200	
(SA_2)	schema of practical inference for a coordination game 201	
(SA_i)	schema of practical inference for a coordination game for m agents 204	
(SA_i')	liberalized version of (SA_i) 233	
(SA_i^*)	liberalized version of (SA_i) 229	
($SA_i'^*$)	liberalized version of (SA_i) 233	
(SI)	range of influence 275	
(SR)	joint (direct) reason, ρ_{we} 371	
(SSA)	thesis on the scope of social action 233	
(ST1)	thesis on the explanation of social action 378	
(ST2)	thesis on the explanation of social action 378	
(ST3)	thesis on the explanation of social action 378	
(ST4)	thesis on the explanation of social action 378	
(S1)	socialese (language) 29	
(S22)	socialese* (language) 29	
(T)	we-intention transference schema 355	
(TR)	translation 469	
(URT)	uniform reduction theorem 470	

532   DEFINITIONS AND THESES

(WI)   we-intention 35
(W1)   schema of practical inference for we-intention 33
(W2)   schema of practical inference for we-intention 34

NUMBERED DEFINITIONS

(4.1)   basic action type 97
(4.2)   compound basic action type 98
(4.3)   simple bodily action type 102
(4.4)   compound bodily action type 102
(4.5)   action token$_1$ 102-103
(4.6)   compound action type 104
(4.7)   complex action type 105
(4.8)   power (to do X) 105-106
(4.9)   power (to do X); generalization of def. (4.8) 108
(5.1)   basic social action type 123
(5.2)   compound basic social action type 128
(5.3)   simple bodily social action type 129
(5.4)   compound bodily social action type 129
(5.5)   social action token$_1$ 130
(5.6)   compound social action type 134
(5.7)   complex social action type 136
(5.8)   social action token$_2$ 136
(5.9)   joint action power 138
(5.10)   (full) intentionality of social action token$_2$ 139
(5.16)   collective intentional action 145-146
(6.4)   by-relation 165
(6.5)   social by-relation 166
(6.6)   (direct) factual generation, $R_1(e_1,e_2)$ 167
(6.7)   conceptual generation, $R_2(e_1,D_1,D_2)$ 167
(6.8)   (indirect) factual generation, $IG(e_1,e_n)$ 168
(6.9)   (indirect) purposive factual generation, $IG^*(t,r)$ 168
(6.10(i)) conditional for (indirect) purposive causal generation, $D_1 \triangleright\!\!\!\rightarrow D_2$ 169
(6.10(ii)) conditional representing (indirect) purposive factual generation, $D_1 \triangleright\!\!\!\rightarrow D_2$ 169
(6.10(iii)) conditional for purposive conceptual generation, $D' \triangleright\!\!\!\rightarrow_2 D$ 169
(6.11)   deterministic generalized sequential automaton, M 170
(6.13)   (indirect) factual generation (first automata-theoretic analysis), $IG(a,b)$ 174
(6.14)   (indirect) factual generation (second automata-theoretic analysis), $IG(a,b)$ 174
(6.15) $R_2(a,D_1,D_2)$ 177
(6.16)   series connection of automata 179

DEFINITIONS AND THESES

(6.17) parallel connection of automata 179
(6.18) the cascade of automata (with a certain connection K) 180
(6.19) (indirect) factual generation (final automata-theoretic analysis), $IG(u_1,\ldots,u_m,u)$ 182
(7.1) it is believed that p, $B_E p$ 208
(7.2) it is mutually believed that p (strong sense), $B_M p$ 208
(7.3) it is not disbelieved that p, $B_E^* p$ 209
(7.4) it is mutually believed that p (weak sense), $B_M^* p$ 209
(7.5) general schema for mutual belief-disbelief, MBD_p 211
(8.1) social norm 242
(8.1') social norm (qualified) 249
(8.4) social role 249
(8.5) A_i has the disposition D, $D(A_i)$ 251
(8.11') (full) similarity of roles, $a^*(R_1,R_2)$ 259
(8.19) (full) similarity of groups, $a^*(G_1,G_2)$ 261
(8.20) social group 264
(9.1) A's action in relation to B 270
(9.2) A's action making reference to B 270
(9.3) A's weakly affecting B 271
(9.4) A's indirectly and weakly affecting B 272
(9.5) A's control over B 273
(9.5') A's probabilistic control over B 274
(9.6) A's intentional control over B 276
(9.7) theses on classes of actions 278
(9.14) 279
(9.17) 281
(9.18) 281
(9.21) 281
(9.22) 281
(9.8)-(9.13) $interaction_i$, $i = 1,\ldots,10$ 279
(9.15)-(9.16') 280
(9.19) 281
(9.20) 281
(9.6.4') redefinition of the by-relation 283
(9.30) A's full absolute control over his own utility values 287
(9.31) A's full absolute control over B's utility values 288
(9.32) A's mere conditional control over his own utilities 289
(9.33) A's mere conditional control over B's utilities 290
(9.57) A's action making opaque reference to B 308
(9.58) $interaction^1$ 309
(9.59) $interaction_1$ (redefinition) 309
(9.60) $interaction_1^1$ 309
(10) relation of deductive reason-giving explanation, $\varepsilon(E,Tc)$ 340

(10)	relation of inductive explanation, $\rho(E,Tc)$ 343
(10.1)	A's scientifically explaining q to B 314
(10.2)	presupposition$_1$ 317
(10.3)	complete presupposition$_1$ 318
(10.4)	presupposition$_2$ 318
(10.8)	complete scientific explanatory answer 322
(10.9)	scientific explanatory answer 323
(10.10)	scientific querying 324
(10.15)	complete question 326
(10.16)	scientific explanation 326
(10.17)	asking why p 327
(10.18)	answering why p 328
(10.23)	(scientific) understanding 333
(12.17)	the class of anticipated consequences of X_i, (AC) 405
(12.18)	the class of anticipated goal-related consequences of X_i, (AC') 406
(12.19)	expected utility, (**EU**) 408
(12.20)	generalized expected utility, (**GEU**) 409
(12.34)	A's intending to perform X by doing Y 423